Adventurism and Empire

Adventurism and Empire

The Struggle for Mastery in the Louisiana-Florida Borderlands, 1762–1803

DAVID NARRETT

Published in association with The William P. Clements Center for Southwest Studies, Southern Methodist University, by The University of North Carolina Press, Chapel Hill

© 2015 The University of North Carolina Press
All rights reserved
Designed and set in Adobe Caslon by Rebecca Evans
Manufactured in the United States of America

The paper in this book meets the guidelines for permanence
and durability of the Committee on Production Guidelines for
Book Longevity of the Council on Library Resources.
The University of North Carolina Press has been a member
of the Green Press Initiative since 2003.

Jacket illustration: William Augustus Bowles (RC06489).
Courtesy of the State Archives of Florida.

Library of Congress Cataloging-in-Publication Data
Narrett, David E., 1951–
Adventurism and empire : the struggle for mastery in the
Louisiana-Florida borderlands, 1762–1803 / David Narrett.
pages cm
Includes bibliographical references and index.
ISBN 978-1-4696-1833-3 (cloth : alk. paper)
ISBN 978-1-4696-3603-0 (pbk. : alk. paper)
ISBN 978-1-4696-1834-0 (ebook)
1. West Florida—History. 2. Borderlands—United States—History—
18th century. 3. Louisiana—History—To 1803. 4. Florida—History—To 1821.
5. Gulf States—History—To 1803. 6. United States—Foreign relations—Spain.
7. Spain—Foreign relations—United States. I. Title.
F301.N37 2014   973.27—dc23
2014039230

TO MY BRIGHT STAR
ISAAC SOLOMON NARRETT

CONTENTS

Acknowledgments xi

Introduction
1

PART I
Struggles for Empire in Peace and War,
1762–1787

PROLOGUE
The Open and Hidden Features of Peace
*Louisiana, Florida, and the Imperial
Settlement of 1762–1763*
11

CHAPTER 1
Maritime and Interior Colony
Beginnings of British West Florida, 1763–1766
21

CHAPTER 2
The Conundrum of "Spanish-French" Louisiana
*British Imperialism and the Mississippi-Gulf
Frontier, 1766–1775*
45

CHAPTER 3
Opening Salvos in a Revolutionary War,
1776–1779
69

CHAPTER 4
Multiple Conflicts
Warfare and a Disputed Peace, 1779–1783
91

CHAPTER 5
Bidding and Conspiring for Access to the Realm,
1783–1787
115

PART II
New Empires, New Republics,
1787–1803

PROLOGUE
Wilkinson and the Imperial Self
137

CHAPTER 6
License to Venture
Colonization and Commercial Adventurism
141

CHAPTER 7
Frontier Separatism and Integration
164

CHAPTER 8
Conspiracies and International Turmoil
187

CHAPTER 9
Intrigues across Creek Country and Beyond
209

CHAPTER 10
The Imperial Question at Century's End
233

CONCLUSION
The Impermanence of Boundaries
257

Notes 267
Bibliography 337
Index 365

ILLUSTRATIONS

Bellin, *Carte reduite des costes de la Louisiane et de la Floride* 14

Bellin, *Cours du Fleuve Saint Louis* 17

Captain George Johnstone 22

Plan of the Bay and Island of Mobile 29

Plan of Point Ibberville [sic] 38

A Map of Part of West Florida 59

Bernardo de Gálvez 102

Coat of Arms and Patent of Nobility awarded to Gálvez 102

Brion de la Tour, *Suite du Théatre de la Guerre* 112

James Wilkinson 138

Esteban Miró 168

Manuel Luis Gayoso de Lemos 168

Hutchins, *A New Map of the Western Parts of Virginia*... 180

William Augustus Bowles 216

Flag of William Augustus Bowles—First Ensign 219

Flag of William Augustus Bowles—Second Ensign 219

Town and Fort of Natchez 236

Plan of Nogales 237

ILLUSTRATIONS

Bellin, *Carte reduite des costes de la Louisiane et de la Floride* 14

Bellin, *Cours du Fleuve Saint Louis* 17

Captain George Johnstone 22

Plan of the Bay and Island of Mobile 29

Plan of Point Ibberville [sic] 38

A Map of Part of West Florida 59

Bernardo de Gálvez 102

Coat of Arms and Patent of Nobility awarded to Gálvez 102

Brion de la Tour, *Suite du Théatre de la Guerre* 112

James Wilkinson 138

Esteban Miró 168

Manuel Luis Gayoso de Lemos 168

Hutchins, *A New Map of the Western Parts of Virginia*... 180

William Augustus Bowles 216

Flag of William Augustus Bowles—First Ensign 219

Flag of William Augustus Bowles—Second Ensign 219

Town and Fort of Natchez 236

Plan of Nogales 237

ACKNOWLEDGMENTS

I have many wonderful people to thank who have shared insights and lent encouragement over the years in which this book came to fruition. Robert May has been an extraordinary and unstinting supporter, reading numerous draft chapters, tendering sage counsel, and boosting this project from its early days onward. I cannot thank him sufficiently for everything. I am grateful to friends and colleagues at the William P. Clements Center for Southwest Studies at Southern Methodist University, where I was a research fellow in 2008–09. The late David Weber was a remarkably generous friend and mentor who continually encouraged me to attempt a broad study of the borderlands. Andrew Graybill has graciously supported the book's progress to publication. Edward Countryman helped by reading chapters during a crucial period in the project's genesis. I am thankful to Andrea Boardman, former Clements Center executive director, and to Ruth Ann Elmore, her successor, for their cheerful guidance. I also appreciate the assistance of Russell Martin, head of the DeGolyer Library, and of librarian Pamalla Anderson.

I have benefited greatly from the generosity of fellow scholars in borderlands history and related fields. Here I thank Light Cummins, Gene Smith, and Eliga Gould. Cameron Strang read the entire manuscript in its final stages and provided most helpful comments. I thank David Floyd of the LSU Rural Life Museum for bringing me to Baton Rouge on several occasions and educating me through a lively tour of historic sites. Greg Cusick of the P. K. Yonge Library at the University of Florida was a gracious and helpful host during my stay in Gainesville. The staff of The Historic New Orleans Collection has been very helpful—and I also appreciate the assistance of librarians at all archives visited during my research.

My friends and colleagues at The University of Texas at Arlington merit special thanks. Richard Francaviglia, former director of UTA's Center for Greater Southwestern Studies and the History of Cartography, helped me greatly as this book took shape by reading chapters and sharing insights in historical geography. Sam Haynes has also provided generous assistance through the Center. I am thankful to Dean Beth Wight and UTA's College of Liberal Arts for supporting my archival research through travel grants. Marvin Dulaney and Robert Fairbanks, as heads of UTA's Department of History, lent valued encouragement as this book approached completion.

There are dear friends and treasured family members who are vital in the deepest sense. The late Michael Kammen, my mentor and a masterful historian, has lighted my path since our old Cornell days, and I am grateful for his guidance in countless ways. Stephen Maizlish has been a friend and colleague for three decades. His support was extraordinary in reading my entire book manuscript. Alex Weiss and Juli Hobdy have been wonderful friends since we all arrived in Texas in 1984. My brothers—Zach, Seth, and Matthew—have always been in my corner. Their love is reciprocated. My elder brother Eugene, who died tragically in the last year, was a scholar-artist of remarkable learning and passion. His spirit lives in us, along with the memory of my late parents. Marcy Paul has given a great deal beyond words. I dedicate this book to my son, Isaac, star of the rising generation.

Adventurism and Empire

Introduction

The imperial map of North America changed dramatically and frequently from the end of the Seven Years War in 1763 to the Louisiana Purchase in 1803. Whether by choice or compulsion, European powers transferred vast continental expanses among themselves with scant regard for colonials, let alone for the Indian peoples whose land was at stake. International gyrations pushed the Mississippi Valley and southeastern North America into new political orbits. France secretly gave Louisiana to Spain in 1762, while Madrid returned the favor to Paris by another *sub rosa* compact in 1800. Florida changed colonial masters and carried variable geographic definitions over decades. In 1763, Spain ceded Florida to Great Britain, which concurrently acquired eastern portions of French Louisiana. From these gains, England created two new colonies—West and East Florida—along the continent's southern rim. Spain subsequently snared the Floridas from Britain in warfare from 1779 to 1781 and the resulting peace settlement of 1783. The war's end brought new controversy as the United States and Spain contended over West Florida's boundary and the use of the Mississippi. Given these permutations, historians are challenged to explain how imperial rivalries interfaced with colonialism, slavery, and evolving Indian societies across southeastern North America during the late eighteenth century.[1]

Imperialism and *colonialism* are often taken as synonyms, though they signify distinct if related historical processes. Imperial rule presumes a system of political-military-economic dominance by a polity reaching beyond strictly national bounds to incorporate multiple ethnicities and territories. Empires, which have historically assumed a myriad of political forms, are typically characterized by the exercise of power over vast physical space and the practice of distinguishing between various subject peoples or territories. Colonialism implies the transplanting of individuals and groups to regions outside their national homelands—and the consequent development of new settler societies whose character frequently evolved through relationships with indigenous peoples and with others outside the dominant settler community. Colonials and their descendants furthered imperial power in many cases, but they also developed interests and identities distinct from their ancestral countries. This process was a commonality among diverse empires in the Americas.[2]

Imperial and colonial manifestations of power certainly diverged within the territories that lie at the core of this book. Spain had imperial dominion over Louisiana during the years 1763–1803, but it was only minimally a colonizing nation in the region. Although France abandoned its imperial title to Louisiana in 1762, French colonials remained a vital force from Mobile and New Orleans to the Illinois country. Colonial allegiances did not simply coincide with ethnic ancestry. By the early 1770s, for example, some Anglo merchants preferred to live and do business under the Spanish flag in New Orleans rather than under the Union Jack in Pensacola. Collaboration across ethnic lines often hinged on racial hierarchy. Whites of various nationalities shared a commitment to African slavery—the linchpin of economic growth in the Lower Mississippi Valley and elsewhere in the Gulf region. By the 1780s, Choctaw, Chickasaw, and Creek allegiances were complicated by the rise of an Indian mestizo elite that adopted black slaveowning as a means of wealth and power. Intrigue was at a premium when various individuals—red, white, and black—hedged their bets on whether they could find protection or profit across ethnic and national lines.

The term "borderlands" connotes territories in which boundaries are fluid, uncertain, and commonly subject to dispute between nationalities and empires. In eighteenth-century North America, borderland rivalries had interrelated local, regional, and transoceanic dimensions. For example, British-Spanish tensions in disparate global settings—from the Falkland Islands in the South Atlantic to Nootka Sound in the Pacific Northwest—periodically threatened clashes between those powers in Europe and North America. The Seven Years War marked a turning point in European imperial competition since the sparks of conflict flared in North America even before France and Britain formally went to war against one another. The American Revolutionary War signified a still greater change in continental and global affairs. Civil conflict within the British Empire expanded into a major international conflagration in which France and then Spain exploited English vulnerabilities. In the process, the Lower Mississippi Valley and Gulf Coast became a war zone in which Indian peoples, free persons and slaves, and contending empires were all engaged. Frontiers were the cutting edge of borderlands where ethnicities overlapped, variously clashing and collaborating among one another. The motif of multiple "entangled" histories is therefore a dominant theme in borderlands-frontier history.[3]

There are three central propositions in this book. First, Louisiana and Florida were borderland regions characterized by a high degree of geopolitical instability, personal adventurism, and intrigue from the denouement of the Seven Years War through the Louisiana Purchase. Second, British-Spanish rivalry, both before and during the American Revolution, had a profound impact on subsequent U.S.-Spanish competition. Third, diverse nationalities vied over the control of rivers and pathways linking coastal to interior zones. Southern Indians sought trade goods through Pensacola and Mobile no less avidly than U.S. frontier folk clamored for free navigation on the Mississippi and access to the New Orleans market. Power struggles emerged in which commerce and immigration were as important determinants as war and violence.

Colonial adventurism came to the fore when individuals acting in a private capacity attempted to exploit uncertain borderland conditions to their own emolument and power. During the late eighteenth century, adventurism attested to the weakness of imperial or national authority over large portions of North America—and the latitude that private individuals and groups possessed in infiltrating Indian lands and shaping frontier environments with or without state license. The emergence of the United States brought this phenomenon to the foreground because of the federal government's immense territorial claims and its limited control over citizens, some of whom plotted to wage their own battles against bordering Spanish territories.[4] U.S. Manifest Destiny was barely in view during the 1790s when private adventurers vied for mastery in shaping colonization, commerce, and political allegiance in the Louisiana-Florida borderlands.

There are two main parts to this book. The first, "Struggles for Empire in Peace and War," traces imperial rivalries in the Mississippi-Gulf region from the close of the Seven Years War through the American War of Independence and the Anglo-Spanish conflict of 1779–1783. Throughout this era, Britain and Spain contended against each other for French colonial allegiance and Indian support. During the American Revolutionary War, the United States and Spain developed a sometimes collaborative but also competitive relationship over control of the Mississippi-Gulf theater. Part I culminates with a major, if often neglected watershed in

North American history—Spanish wartime triumph in the Gulf region, British imperial withdrawal from the Floridas, and the consequences for colonials and native peoples.

The book's second part, "New Empires, New Republics," considers transformations in the Louisiana and Florida borderlands from the mid-1780s to the Louisiana Purchase. In this period, the Mississippi-Gulf region witnessed an unstable mix of transnational collaboration and contention. Spanish authorities wrestled with the challenge of shoring up Louisiana's defenses by allowing foreign nationals, including U.S. settlers, to settle in crown territories. Madrid's colonial officers moved boldly on the political front by concurrently encouraging southern Indian confederation and western American secession from the United States. These endeavors were ultimately futile given metropolitan Spain's mercurial policies that moved from a failed war against republican France in 1793–1795 to an even more disastrous conflict with Britain from 1796 to 1802. A slew of adventurers preyed on international confusion by conspiring for British or French support to take hold of Louisiana and the Floridas—and in the process to create new republican or imperial governments serving their interests.

English competition against Spanish America, born in the Elizabethan era, had a profound impact on British and Anglo-American rivalry with Spain across centuries. "Adventurism"—a modern rendering of "adventure"—lies at the core of this historical phenomenon. The ranks of Elizabethan adventurers who challenged the Spanish Empire famously included John Hawkins, Francis Drake, Walter Raleigh, and others. Their exploits were inspired by the quest for personal glory and wealth as much as by the advancement of national power.[5]

During the Elizabethan era, merchants as well as privateers were essential players in the panorama of overseas enterprise. An English "adventurer" was then any person who ventured or risked his money in a commercial endeavor. Richard Hakluyt, the famed chronicler of English "voyages" and "discoveries," recounted how gentlemen "adventurers" of London funded John Hawkins's slave-trading mission from West Africa to Hispaniola in 1562–1563. More than two decades later Francis Drake reaped "three score thousand pounds" through attacks on Santo Domingo, Cartagena, and St. Augustine. This immense sum was divided into two portions—twenty thousand for the actual voyagers and forty thousand for "the adventurers" financing the enterprise. In his *Generall Historie of Virginia*, John Smith distinguished between ordinary colonists and the more privileged who were on a par with the Adventurers in London because they owned stock in the Virginia Company.[6]

Lacking sufficient state resources, English rulers relied on private adventurism to extend national power through privateering against the Spanish realm, the subduing of Ireland, and the financing of Virginia colonization. English empire-building was not unique in its resort to private interests, but rather distinguished by the degree to which individual profit-seeking permeated colonizing ventures amidst the growth of state power.[7] In 1642, for example, Parliament passed an Act for Adventurers that designated 2.5 million acres in Ireland for sale to Protestant investors who in turn raised funds and equipped military forces to protect their interest. The objectives of private individuals thereby shaped the exercise of English power over conquered Irish land.[8]

The aggressively individualistic side of overseas adventuring was captured in eighteenth-century British speech. In his *History of England*, David Hume described early English intrusions into the Spanish Indies to be the work of "many adventurers" who "met with severe punishment when caught; as they . . . often stole, and, when superior in power, forced a trade with the [Spanish] inhabitants, and resisted, nay sometimes plundered, the Spanish governors."[9] John Campbell, a prolific Scottish author on Spanish colonialism, commented on Castilian royal edicts, which "compelled the adventurers and planters to treat the Indians as subjects, and not as slaves." The mandates of imperial law were hereby differentiated from unrestrained power grabbing by "turbulent adventurers, who endeavoured to render themselves independent of the crown of Spain."[10]

Both Campbell and Hume characterized adventurers in various ways— as enterprising colonists, military conquerors, or as overseas roustabouts behaving in a cavalier or ruthless manner. This rhetorical suppleness is historically apt. Adventurism encompassed a range of behaviors, in which individual risk-taking and journeying across national boundaries were common elements. In fact, Anglo-Americans of the mid- to late eighteenth century still applied the language of mercantile and colonial adventurism to their own undertakings. Benjamin Franklin, himself a colonial promoter, expressed this idea while a lobbyist in London in 1767. Bemoaning British political misunderstanding, he shared his historical sense with an eminent Scottish friend:

> It is a common but mistaken Notion here, that the Colonies were planted at the expence [*sic*] of Parliament, and that therefore the Parliament has a Right to tax them, &c. The Truth is they were planted at the Expence of private Adventurers, who went over there to settle with Leave of the King given by Charter. On receiving this Leave and these Charters, the Adventurers voluntarily engag'd to remain the King's subjects, though in a foreign Country, a Country which had not been conquer'd by either King or Parliament, but was possess'd by a free People.[11]

Colonial adventurism had an important visionary character aimed at transforming particular social and physical environments into new arenas for mastery or domination. While this process often worked to the detriment and even decimation of native peoples, that was not always the case. Several colonization projects conceived for Louisiana and the Floridas in the late eighteenth century were predicated on colonial-native coexistence. The most remarkable adventurer in this regard was William Augustus Bowles, a Tory Marylander who cast himself as head of the Creek nation from 1789 to 1803—and successively roiled Florida in the process.[12]

Whether colonial adventurers were perceived as noble or villainous in the past had much to do with the national outlook of those rendering judgment. One anonymous author, styling himself a "British Sailor" in 1739, deplored Spanish expeditions launched from the Caribbean during the early 1500s that made a habit of "*murdering* and *pillaging*" Indians "on the *Islands* and Continent." The writer summoned numerous historic episodes to denounce Madrid's claims of supreme dominion in the Americas—and above all to justify the current British movement to war against Spain. English chauvinists had no doubt that Spaniards were upholders of an outmoded and oppressive empire.[13] Ironically, the Spanish imperium of the mid-eighteenth century was characterized by modernizing trends that historians broadly describe as the Bourbon reforms. Administrative efficiency and economic progress occupied a central place in this movement, which extolled the advancement of national power relative to Britain and France.[14]

English prejudice against Spain had its roots in intense national and religious struggles of the mid- to late sixteenth century. Hispanophobia fed into "the Black Legend"—the idea that Spaniards were uniquely cruel, despotic, and treacherous among European nations. Such attitudes certainly passed from the British to their Anglo-American progeny. Unfortunately, one of the most commonly cited books on this subject—Philip Wayne Powell's *Tree of Hate*—is highly misleading because of its own blatant ethnic and religious prejudice.[15]

Rather than viewing cultural biases as the root of international conflict, this book explores the phenomenon of "intrigue" as an expression of competing imperial, colonial, and Indian agendas in the borderlands. Intrigue connotes policy based on stratagem, covert maneuver, rumor or conspiracy, and ruse or deception. These elements are arguably the common stuff of politics—and therefore may be too easily taken for granted without being closely analyzed in historical perspective. During the colonial era, Europeans of various nationality generally cited "intrigue" as a characteristic of rival countries and not their own. When attributed to a foreign nation or people, intrigue connoted deliberate trickery and insidious manipulation. The same word did not necessarily carry a pejorative meaning if applied to political leaders as individuals. To be adept at intrigue was the diplomat's challenge—and doubtless often an element of personal pride.[16]

Intrigue is a useful point of reference in this book because it captures basic features of transnational competition and collaboration in borderlands remote in distance and time from metropolitan centers of government. Four aspects of intrigue recur in my analysis. First, there was the tendency of colonial officers, magnates, and settlers to manipulate imperial authorities toward policies serving individual self-interest and not simply national need. Second, numerous parties in frontier zones furthered their interests by rumor or deception in the absence of coercive power to achieve their ends. Third, individuals or groups commonly shifted national allegiance or professed loyalty to contending governments at the same time. Lastly, transnational commerce frequently assumed the character of contraband traffic in violation of imperial or national laws proscribing such conduct. Intrigues affecting the Louisiana-Florida borderlands originated in various locales—frontier environs, more distant continental areas, and in European capitals. The sheer distance between frontiers and metropolitan centers contributed to the flow of rumors about military operations and political currents. Intrigue flourished where the distinction between fact and fiction—and between aspirations and fears—were jumbled.

Adventurism and Empire has a broad geographic scope in keeping with the shifting configuration of power across Louisiana and the Floridas. Multiple vantage points come into view—for example, ties between New

Orleans and the Upper Mississippi Valley and linkages between the Florida Gulf Coast and the Bahamas. In this way, I heed D. W. Meinig's dictum that most geographic regions are "abstractions and approximations" of the physical environment where people live. Particular regions evolve in relationship to others, so that "it is necessary to give attention to their diverse character" while examining "the interests and networks that bind them into larger associations."[17] "Louisiana" and "Florida" were assuredly abstractions or approximations if we consider their imprecise and changing bounds from 1762 through 1803. Successive boundary changes attest not only to continual imperial jousting, but also to the human struggle of colonizing and living within regions posing formidable environmental and disease hazards.[18]

While drawing on a rich secondary literature, this book explores borderlands adventurism and intrigue by culling Spanish, British, and U.S. archives, as well as other manuscript sources. This method is vital not only to convey diverse national perspectives but also to bring Louisiana, Florida, and bordering Indian spheres to the foreground of North American history. *Adventurism and Empire* is oriented toward political and diplomatic events as informed by economic, social, and cultural influences. Elites—those in leadership positions in imperial and frontier contexts—occupy a major place in our story. Such individuals did not simply control events, and their failures were as common as their successes. Indeed, unrealized ambitions are critical to understanding historical alternatives and outcomes. Our story begins in 1762—a climactic year of warfare and imperial intrigue recasting American bounds.

PART I

Struggles for Empire in Peace and War, 1762–1787

PROLOGUE

The Open and Hidden Features of Peace
*Louisiana, Florida, and the Imperial
Settlement of 1762–1763*

On January 13, 1762, Charles Wyndham, second Earl of Egremont, sent momentous instructions from his majesty's privy council to General Jeffrey Amherst, commander-in-chief of British forces in North America. The long war against France had just entered a new stage. Great Britain was now in conflict with Spain, too, and therefore intending to strike at Madrid's overseas possessions. The English decision for war answered King Carlos III's renewal of the Bourbon Family Compact—the dynastic alliance between the Spanish and French monarchs aimed at humbling their common British enemy.[1]

Amherst's orders were to dispatch 4,000 British regulars and American provincials from New York City to support an amphibious assault on Havana. Once that key to the Antilles had fallen, Sir Jeffrey was to embark from New York with another 8,000 men in a maritime invasion of French Louisiana—a province considered by Egremont to be "both a desirable and a practicable Object of Attack."[2] Commanding the Cuban expedition, George Keppel, Earl of Albemarle, had license to continue his offensive beyond Havana, and to proceed against St. Augustine in Florida, Santiago de Cuba, "or any other part of the Spanish Colonies" he thought could be taken.[3]

Albemarle achieved Havana's capture on August 14, 1762, but at such a heavy cost that additional conquests were unthinkable. Besides casualties through fighting, British forces lost 4,700 soldiers and sailors to yellow fever and other illnesses within six weeks of Havana's capitulation.[4] As English transports staggered from Cuba to Manhattan's dockside in September, ship crews had too few healthy men to drop anchor by themselves. A disappointed but realistic Amherst had no choice except to call off a Louisiana campaign.[5] Had tropical diseases not had such a lethal impact, it is possible that British arms could have brought New Orleans into the empire in the fall of 1762. The city's defenses were weak since soldiers were few, and munitions and foodstuffs in short supply. The Choctaws and Alibamons, usually French allies, chafed at the lack of customary royal gifts. Metropolitan France could scarcely satisfy Louisiana's needs amidst far greater wartime struggles.[6]

Because Amherst never set sail for Louisiana, it is easy to overlook the British government's conception of bringing the Gulf Coast within the imperial orbit of the Caribbean and Atlantic. As in many wars, victories achieved in a central theater—in this case the West Indies—created an impetus to extend conquests to more peripheral zones. Amherst's projected Mississippi offensive was precisely the type of far-flung military campaign that Spanish officials had dreaded for years. To anxious Bourbon statesmen, English naval and mercantile power appeared boundless, capable of dominating seas from the tropics to the poles.[7]

Fortunately for Madrid, the British government was not perpetually bellicose. As the siege of Havana was underway, English diplomats negotiated peace terms with French and Spanish representatives in Paris. George III and his first minister, the Earl of Bute, desired an end to an exhausting war. Bute especially feared that a prolonged conflict would restore William Pitt, his dreaded political foe, to power on a platform of belligerent nationalism.[8]

There was nothing unusual about the dual pursuit of war and peace in eighteenth-century imperial conflicts waged simultaneously in Europe and the Americas. While battles raged, rulers in London, Paris, and Madrid carefully assessed their respective strengths and weaknesses in various geographic spheres. Total victory over enemy states was not to be expected. Territories won by arms might be restored to a foe upon the conclusion of peace, particularly if some commensurate or superior benefit could be extracted. Similarly, defeat in a particular military theater did not preclude regaining lost ground, especially by proffering peace to antagonists whose victories drained national resources. Peace talks commonly stirred as much political contention among allied powers as between hostile nations. This was certainly true in 1762, when France and Spain had borne the brunt of war to such unequal degrees. The duc de Choiseul, Louis XV's foreign minister, sought to salvage what he could from a long and disastrous conflict. Madrid was far more reluctant to quit the battlefield short of achieving its major national objective—the wresting of Gibraltar from Britain.⁹

Choiseul, a gifted diplomatist, had no doubt that the West Indies counted far more than North America in the competition for wealth and power. During the summer of 1762, France prepared to cede extensive American territories to Britain in order to recoup captured Caribbean isles, especially Guadeloupe and Martinique. Choiseul was resigned to the loss of Canada. He was also willing to surrender all continental claims *east* of the Mississippi, apart from New Orleans and vicinity. The lands in question stretched from the Illinois country to Mobile Bay—all part of Louisiana in theory, though in reality largely an Indian country under French influence rather than possession.¹⁰

The marqués de Grimaldi, Spain's foremost negotiator at Paris, felt the sting of French self-interest and British ambition during the movement toward a peace settlement. He could do little, however, to prevent a diplomatic downslide after Havana's fall. The only question was what price the English would demand in return for evacuating Cuba.¹¹ While some British government ministers aimed for Puerto Rico and Florida, George III finally accepted Florida alone. Spain thereby parted with a financially burdensome colony, which had served in recent decades to halt British incursions from the Carolinas and Georgia.¹² The cession was limited but still pregnant of change. For two hundred years, the Spanish presence in Florida shielded the Bahama Channel (the "Florida Straits" on current maps)—a prime corridor for ships sailing with Mexican silver via Veracruz and Havana for Spain. That passage was scarcely secure in the wake of British gains that included Spanish St. Augustine and Pensacola, along with French Mobile. There seemed little left of Spain's traditional conception of the Gulf (*el Seno Mexicano*) as an imperial lake foreclosed to foreigners.¹³

Considering the Bourbon powers' woes, Choiseul could do no better than to mollify Madrid's bitterness over a failed war. Prodding Spain to peace, the French minister tendered a royal gift in the name of Louis XV to his younger cousin, Carlos III. On the table was the secret French cession to Spain of New Orleans, the delta lands lying below that city, and all Louisiana west of the Mississippi. Choiseul and Grimaldi concurred on this proposal at Fontainebleau Palace on November 3, 1762, just hours after the two men had agreed to preliminary peace articles with Britain at the same venue. Ten days later, Carlos III formally accepted Louis XV's tender of Louisiana.¹⁴

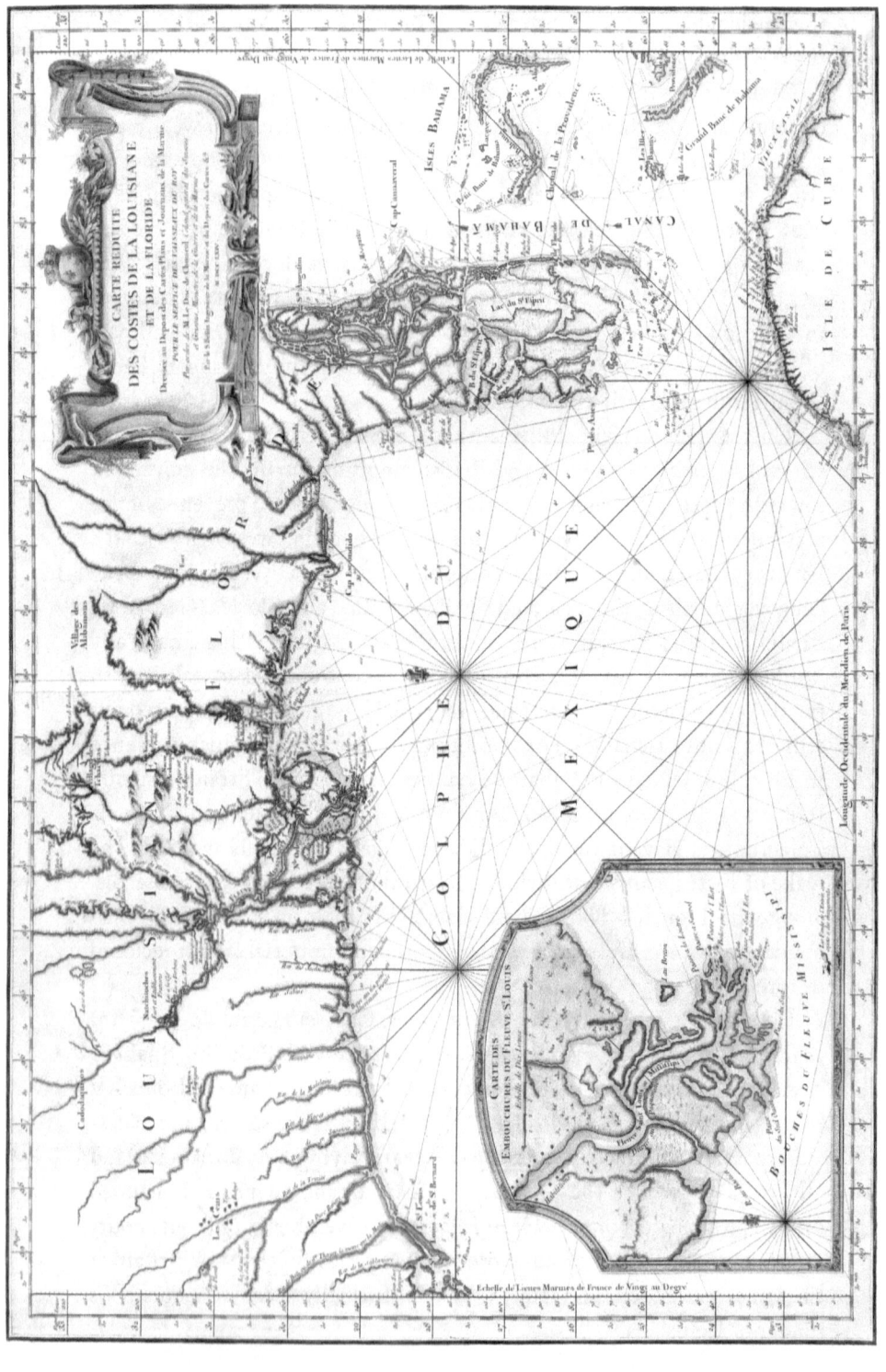

Spanish military defeat had economic consequences that were as significant as North American territorial adjustments. By the definitive peace settlement of 1763, Madrid confirmed previous Anglo-Spanish commercial treaties, including an accord of 1750 granting Britain most-favored nation status in trade with peninsular Spain. Carlos III had entered the war seeking to abrogate these existing obligations, which hampered domestic industry, encouraged smuggling, and enabled British merchants to siphon profits from Spain's commerce with its American dominions. The English ranked supreme among foreigners who flouted the law of the Indies by trading with his Catholic Majesty's overseas colonies. Silver was the great prize, whether gained by consensual transactions or extracted by force in war.[15]

The European peace settlement of 1762–63 was notable for both its hidden and open features. Indian peoples had no say over imperial decision-making affecting their lives. There was only one point in the Paris peace negotiations when their situation directly entered discussions. As the Spanish court struggled to stanch British expansion, it suggested the creation of a vast trans-Appalachian Indian reserve that would be foreclosed to European settlement. This proposal was summarily dismissed by English foes.[16]

Native peoples suspected being betrayed by the French king—their supposed "father"—well before official news of European treaty-making came to the Mississippi. In July 1763, the chiefs of several nations—the Biloxis, Chitimatchas, Houmas, Choctaws, Quapaws, and Natchez—arrived at New Orleans to meet Jean-Jacques Blaise d'Abbadie, Louisiana's director-general. The headmen aired disquieting fears that France had surrendered parts of Louisiana to both Britain and Spain. Abbadie's journal refers to this meeting, though without noting his response to the visitors. A Cherokee, Choctaw, and Alibamon delegation had already voiced anger over pending French cessions to Britain east of the Mississippi. In early May 1763, Louis de Kerlérec, then director-general, reported the headmen saying openly "that they are not yet all dead; that the French

(opposite) Jacques Nicolas Bellin, *Carte reduite des costes de la Louisiane et de la Floride* (Paris, 1764). This map shows limited geographic understanding of peninsular Florida, whose land mass is broken by numerous rivers and lakes between the Atlantic and Gulf Coast. The map clearly depicts the *"Canal de Bahama"*—a prime maritime corridor between Florida's eastern coast and the Bahamas. Courtesy of The Historic New Orleans Collection, acc. no. 1977.66 i,ii.

have no right to give them away." Far to the east Creek spokesmen voiced similar trepidation of pending Spanish departure.[17] The rumors circulating in Indian country were quite on the mark. Imperial powers had acted as if they were "lords of all the world," altering boundaries and transferring native territories with "the scratch of a pen"—to employ phrases aptly used by recent historians.[18]

While Choiseul made no secret of French territorial concessions to England, he catered to Spanish sensitivities by delaying public notice of Louisiana's transfer. Madrid was thankful for the respite because it required time to take a new and quite unfamiliar colony under its wing. On April 21, 1764, Choiseul finally dispatched a proclamation to Louisiana announcing the province's total cession. The notice reached New Orleans that September, arousing colonial shock and despair. Choiseul had long since informed the British government that his king relinquished all interest in Louisiana whatsoever.[19]

Prior to 1763, French Louisiana extended in theory from Carolina's western rim to New Mexico's borderlands, and from the Gulf Coast to Canada. Antoine-Simon Le Page du Pratz, a French observer who resided in Louisiana from 1718 to 1734, wrote that the Mississippi "divides this Colony from North to South into two parts almost equal." This conception died with the Treaty of Paris, which defined the river for the first time as an international boundary between imperial states.[20]

To gain a clearer understanding of the Mississippi issue, we may consult a map drafted in 1763 by Jacques Nicolas Bellin, an accomplished French cartographer. (Bellin labeled the Mississippi by both its Indian name and its formal French title, the River *Saint Louis*.) Quite strikingly, the map pinpoints New Orleans by a red dot on the river's east bank just a few miles below bulging Lake Pontchartrain, an oval-shaped waterway with a narrow eastern channel leading to the Gulf of Mexico. The town, then home to some 3,000 residents, occupied a small place within a lengthy expanse of land frequently though not continually encircled by

(opposite) Jacques Nicolas Bellin, *Cours du Fleuve Saint Louis depuis ses Embouchures jusqu'a la Riviere Iberville et Costes Voisines* (Paris, 1763). This map depicts New Orleans, and the position of the Iberville River and Lakes Maurepas and Pontchartrain, whose midstream course formed part of the new international boundary established by the Treaty of Paris of 1763. Courtesy of The Historic New Orleans Collection, acc. no. 1975.24.

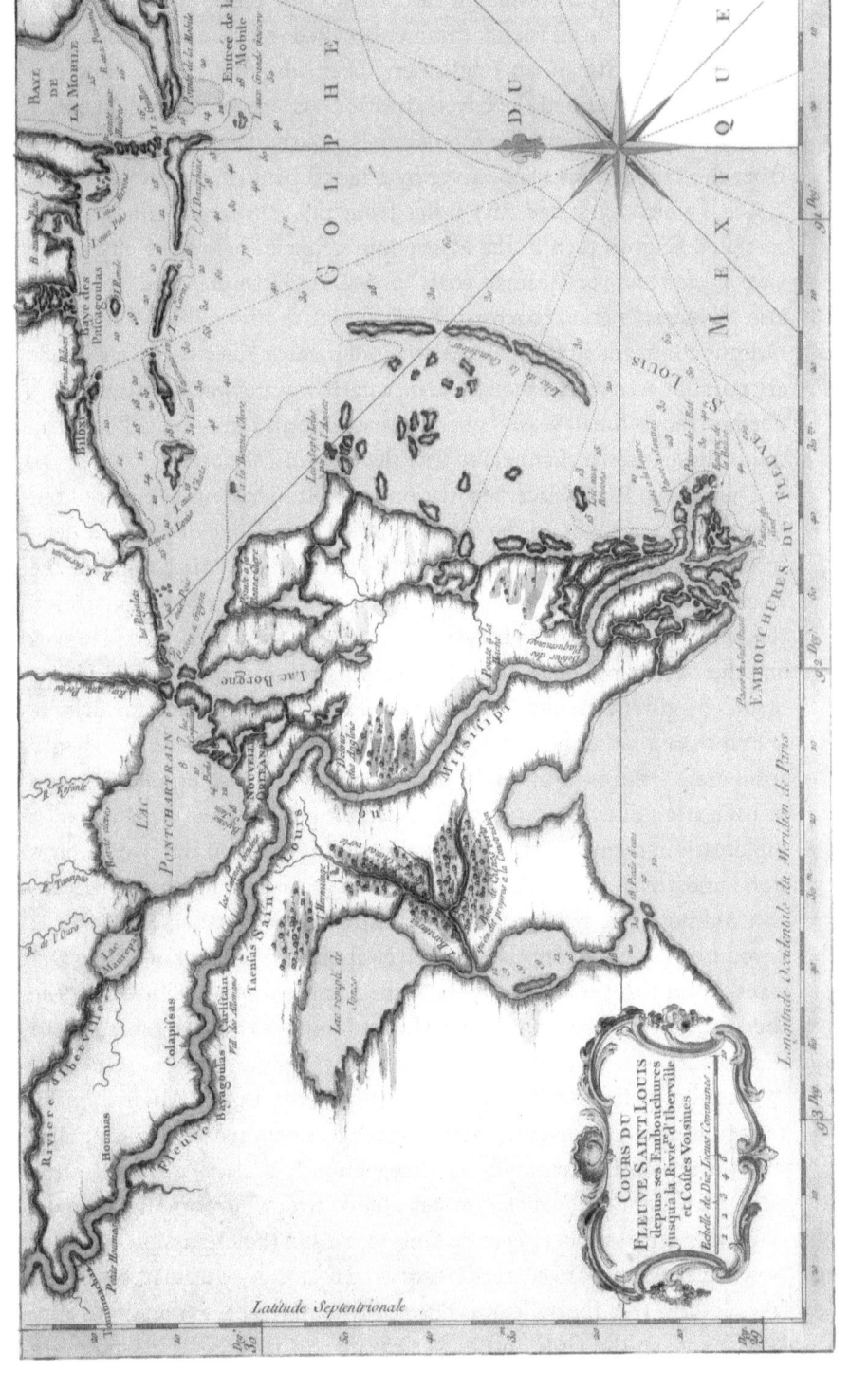

water. Bellin's map expressed the rather simplistic European view of New Orleans as a city on an island, commonly called the "Isle of Orleans."[21]

Lt. Phillip Pittman, an English engineer who first visited New Orleans in 1763, described the city's "situation" as "extremely well chosen." Located 105 miles above the Mississippi's mouth, the town was "secured from the inundations of the river by a raised bank, generally called the Levée," which extended fifty miles from the "*Detour des Anglois*" (the so-called English turn in the Mississippi's course) below the city to the *Cote d'Allemands* (or German coast) above. As Pittman noted, the *Levée* also served as "a good coach-road" of more than fifty miles. While New Orleans commanded the main Mississippi passage, the city had a secondary point of access via Bayou St. Jean, a narrow waterway near the town's northern edge. Small vessels plied the bayou to and from Lake Pontchartrain whose eastern channel fed into the Gulf of Mexico.[22]

During the Paris peace negotiations of 1762, Choiseul hammered out a tentative agreement on the Mississippi with the Duke of Bedford, who insisted that England have navigational rights on the Mississippi for the river's entire length. Choiseul acquiesced on this point but maneuvered the new international boundary so that France retained New Orleans and the Mississippi delta entirely within its colonial sphere—soon to be Spain's by gift.[23] This circumstance raised a potential problem for Britain. If France or another hostile power had control of the Mississippi's banks from New Orleans to the Gulf, how would the English uphold freedom of navigation during a future war? According to the final Anglo-French diplomatic agreement, the new dividing point between the two empires stood midstream in the Mississippi from the river's far northern source—still unknown to Europeans—far southward to the Iberville River, a bayou flowing east from the great river about 100 miles above New Orleans. From that point the border shifted to the southeast, bisecting the Iberville and then cutting through Lakes Maurepas and Pontchartrain to the Gulf.[24]

Choiseul deflected British concerns over the Lower Mississippi by geographic sleight-of-hand and soothing reassurances. Avoiding any show of diplomatic triumph, he disingenuously acclaimed the new English boundary on Louisiana's eastern flank, which purportedly offered a viable water passage between the Gulf Coast and the Mississippi north of New Orleans. Bedford correctly suspected that this route, via Louisiana's lakes and the tiny Iberville, was not nearly so navigable as the Mississippi itself between the Gulf and New Orleans. Still, he could do no more than obtain the right of undisturbed navigation on the river and an international boundary hovering over New Orleans but stopping just short of that city.[25] The Choiseul-Bedford agreement had important consequences for decades to come. While defining the Mississippi as a shared imperial waterway for France and Britain, it restrained English territorial control in the river's southerly and most strategic portion. By the Treaty of Paris, British and French subjects were to have "equally free" navigational rights for the river's "whole breadth and length." Vessels belonging to persons of either nation were not to be "stopped, visited, or subjected to the payment of any duty whatsoever."[26] This clause literally prohibited the levying of duties for moving up or down the river, while leaving quite open the exaction of customs for trade.

Choiseul's decision to offer Louisiana to Spain was clearly driven by strategic and fiscal considerations—above all, the necessity of releasing a costly and remote colony that could scarcely be defended against Britain in war. Louisiana lay far to the west-northwest of Saint-Domingue (Haiti)—the nearest French-ruled Caribbean colony. Ships sailing the Gulf's northern rim faced the danger of storms and hurricanes besides shoals and shallow water. Few ship captains rested easy when entering the Mississippi, moving up its winding course against swirling currents, and escaping the perils of driftwood and sandbars. The journey from La Balize, the French outpost at the Mississippi's mouth, to New Orleans could take six weeks—as long as a favorable voyage from France to the Caribbean.[27]

Louisiana's marginal value at Versailles did not mean that private French interests were unwilling to invest in the region. After the peace of Paris, one French firm petitioned Madrid to administer and defend Louisiana in Spain's interest—in return for a monopoly on the colony's overseas commerce and its Indian trade for twenty years. Though this project failed to win Madrid's approval, it is significant for displaying a capitalistic intent of frontier colonial development through the massive importation of African slaves and European Catholic settlers. Over the next four decades, Spanish Louisiana officials and foreign entrepreneurs developed a slew of ambitious immigration schemes for the Mississippi Valley.[28]

Imperial Spain was less than enthusiastic about Louisiana, which was to be kept out of English hands but scarcely required immediate and substantial outlays. Madrid busily upgraded defense in Cuba and Mexico while tolerating a caretaker French administration in New Orleans for months. Beset by logistical difficulties, the first Spanish governor and his tiny military contingent did not arrive in New Orleans until March 5, 1766—more than three years after his Catholic Majesty had acquired title to Louisiana.[29]

Unlike Spain's tardiness in occupying New Orleans, the British movement to Florida's shores was rapid. English troops put into Pensacola from Havana on August 6, 1763. Another detachment reached St. Augustine from New York in early September. Two British regiments from the Cuba expedition made their way into Mobile Bay the following month.[30] These entries denoted colonial enclaves along a maritime perimeter with little hint of imperial dominance. It had yet to be seen how Britons would manage their new southern domain, whose Gulf ports and rivers reached inland to the Mississippi Valley and outward toward the Caribbean and Atlantic.

CHAPTER 1

Maritime and Interior Colony
Beginnings of British West Florida, 1763–1766

George Johnstone was a lobbyist about London with a clear mission in early 1763. As a naval captain just out of wartime service, he desired an honorable station in Britain's triumphant empire. Eyeing a Florida governor's post, he made his case in an unsigned brief to the Board of Trade, advisory committee to the Privy Council on colonial affairs. Though Johnstone had not yet set eyes on Florida's shores, he had learned from books and maps to imagine what was most desirable. He fixed his gaze on Pensacola Bay, which he believed "a good Port . . . for Commerce as well as Command."[1] In his judgment, Spanish Caribbean colonials would unquestionably prefer to buy English goods carried from Florida than to pay higher prices for taxed commodities brought from Cádiz. Spain's laws of the Indies prohibited foreign entry into colonial ports, but that scarcely seemed a drawback when the contraband trade was commonplace for well over a century.[2]

A stout and balding man of thirty-two years, Johnstone was a Scotsman whose patriotism was wholeheartedly British. As a young naval officer, he absorbed lessons from the War of Jenkins' Ear (1739–1743)—a conflict incited by English smuggling in the Caribbean and Spanish retaliatory measures.[3] British contraband had a systemic cause: Spain's inability to provide its American colonies with a steady flow of marketable goods at reasonable prices. English commercial mastery was in full display after Havana's capture in 1762. In the eleven months that the city was under foreign occupation, British and Anglo-American merchants earned buckets of specie from the sale of manufactures, dry goods, and slaves to Cuba's residents.[4]

Britons were drawn by an almost magnetic force to Spanish silver dollars and bullion. John Campbell, a Scottish authority on Spain's overseas

Captain George Johnstone, ca. 1768–1774, copy from an original portrait by Henry Raeburn. Courtesy of National Maritime Museum Picture Library, Greenwich, London, image BHC2808. This portrait captures Johnstone in naval uniform and suggests his pensive side rather than his tempestuous character.

dominions, enthused over lucre culled in the Caribbean trade, and more generally in South America: "The Spanish Americans consider gold and silver as very valuable commodities, yet they are extremely willing to barter them for other commodities, which they have not, and which would be more useful to them than large heaps of either of these metals."[5] Tales of Spanish profligacy fed English appetites for commerce in which Britons held the upper hand.

Lured by the Gulf Coast, Johnstone was relieved to learn in July 1763 that he had obtained the governorship of the new British colony of West Florida at Pensacola—and not a post at St. Augustine in East Florida. In the captain's judgment, the portion of Florida "bordering on the Mississippi" and "along the Bay of Mexico" was "infinitely more advantageous" than its eastern counterpart. Johnstone won his prize through timely lobbying by his patron, the Earl of Bute—fellow Scotsman, former first minister, and the king's friend.[6]

Johnstone's blueprint for Florida assumed private and imperial aggrandizement to be strictly congruent, though matters were not so simple. The king's government was financially strapped. However superior in naval and commercial might, England faced great challenges in extending royal authority within interior North America and mediating between settlers and Indian peoples. Johnstone rather naively assumed that little imperial assistance would be necessary at the onset of Florida colonization. By his reckoning, a bevy of venturesome colonists with but "the smallest encouragement from Government" was sufficient for success.[7] The reality proved far different during British West Florida's beginnings as a Gulf Coast and Mississippi colony with maritime and inland dimensions.

The Floridas: Projections of Empire

When Johnstone lobbied for a governor's post, Florida was a target of ridicule among British political satirists, especially the notorious John Wilkes, who castigated the Bute ministry for gaining so little for the restoration of Havana to Spain. "Florida Turf"—the satirist's label for swamp ground—had no value except to afford "*comfortable fires* to our cold, frozen *West-Indian* islands."[8] An extreme English chauvinist, Wilkes derided the appointment of two Scotsmen—George Johnstone and James Grant—for governors' posts in West and East Florida. Ethnic put-downs scarcely altered the course of empire. Scots officeholders, merchants, and traders assumed a major role in North American affairs, not least in southern frontier zones.[9]

While Wilkes derided the peace treaty, the administration's friends found much to embrace. Florida's harbors could assuredly serve as bases for future strikes against Spanish galleons plying the Gulf, Caribbean, and the Bahama Channel to Iberia.[10] For all this braggadocio, few British commentators in 1763 had more than simplistic notions of coastal Florida, let alone the relationship between the littoral and interior zones. The distinction between what constituted "Florida" as compared to "Louisiana" was another subject portrayed in broad strokes, especially since neither colony had definite boundaries when respectively under Spanish and French jurisdiction.

The initial British debate regarding Florida was a rhetorical fight among duelists shooting in the dark toward a distant North America. Since the disputants did not know of Louis XV's transfer of Louisiana to Spain, they generally assumed that France would remain a vigorous rival in New Orleans and the trans-Mississippi West. Some British critics took this point further by arguing that Florida would be of little value without control of Louisiana. These writers focused on the Gulf-Mississippi region as the key to mastering the Indian trade of the interior. One author put the matter bluntly: "We have Canada ceded to us, and the French are left on the Mississippi to enjoy the profit." The same commentator belittled Florida, which he termed "a country of little use to the Spaniards and . . . as little to us."[11]

British publicists frequently conjured fears of French-Indian collaboration undermining recent English territorial gains. As one penman observed, the French in Louisiana would employ "sly intrigues" to excite Indian attacks against British settlements from the Great Lakes, the Wabash, and the Ohio.[12] The North American interior was seen as a perilous zone even before Englishmen learned of Pontiac's War, the great Indian uprising that broke out in the Great Lakes and Ohio regions in the spring of 1763.

British reckonings of Florida acquired specificity when the Board of Trade drew boundaries for former Spanish and French territories in the aftermath of war. In a report of June 8, 1763, the "Lords Commissioners" (Board members) recommended the establishment of two new colonies—East and West Florida—along the continent's southern littoral. Both jurisdictions were to receive "a due proportion of natural Advantages and Conveniences of Commerce and Navigation." A maritime perspective came naturally to men who conceived of commerce as the fount of empire. As a dividing point between the Floridas, the Board chose the Chattahoochee River, whose waters flow southward into the Apalachicola River, itself feeding into Apalachicola Bay and the Gulf of Mexico. East Florida was designed with an Atlantic orientation with some extension along the Gulf. West Florida took in the entire coastal region from Apalachicola Bay westward to the new Louisiana treaty line of 1763, thereby bringing Pensacola and Mobile within the same provincial jurisdiction. These outposts, just sixty miles apart, were the scene of Spanish-French clashes of the early 1720s, but now jointly slated for British imperial purposes.[13]

The Board of Trade's stipulations for the Floridas were incorporated, with minor modification, into the Royal Proclamation of October 7, 1763, the British Empire's charter for postwar North America. The proclamation prohibited white settlement west of the Appalachians—a zone officially recognized as Indian "Hunting Grounds."[14] Significantly, the proclamation exempted the Floridas and Quebec—new imperial acquisitions—from this ban. But the British crown was in no mood for unrestrained Florida colonization in interior regions above the Gulf. West Florida's northern boundary was set along the 31st parallel and extended about 380 miles due east from the Mississippi to the Chattahoochee. This line generally ran within fifty miles of the Gulf Coast, with somewhat greater breadth along the Apalachicola River in the east and above Lake Pontchartrain in the west. The Board of Trade confessed caution in moving no deeper into the interior: "the 31st Degree of North Latitude . . . We humbly apprehend, is as far North as the Settlements can be carried, without interfering with Lands claimed or occupied by the Indians."[15] An imperial modus vivendi was sought with native peoples who were themselves considered worthy of royal protection.

Though both Floridas had a very small European population, the Board believed the region afforded potential for the production of "Indigo, Silk, Cotton, and many of the Commodities now found in the West Indies only."[16] The use of slave labor was clearly intended for this purpose. The British government's first regulations for the Floridas allowed each white male immigrant to claim one hundred acres for himself and an additional fifty acres for each white or black man, woman, or child brought with him.[17]

Britons believed their nation would "improve" previously undeveloped regions that Spaniards had apparently done little to change. The first notice of East Florida's land regulations stated that "all the Fruits and Productions of the West-Indies may be raised here; tho' either from the want of Industry in the late [Spanish] Inhabitants, or the frequent Interruptions they met with from their Neighbours the Indian[s], no Improvement of that Kind was ever attempted." Lt. Col. Augustine Prevost, one of the first English officers to land at Pensacola in 1763, perceived the country "still uncultivated" because of "the insuperable Laziness of the Spaniards."[18] Assumptions of English moral superiority had a decidedly anti-Spanish tone.

British governance of North American frontiers implied an imperial order transcending particular colonial interests. In reality, self-seeking provincial officeholders jostled over cartographic ink as soon as Florida's fledgling bounds were set on paper. James Grant, East Florida's first governor, successfully lobbied the Board of Trade to expand his colony's jurisdiction northward so that it encompassed lands between the St. Johns and St. Marys Rivers that had previously been allocated to Georgia. In this zero-sum gain, one colony's gain was another's loss. Georgia had itself just emerged victorious before the Board of Trade in a boundary dispute with South Carolina.[19]

George Johnstone entered the boundary game with a flourish in the months following his appointment as West Florida's governor. Remaining in London, he petitioned the Board of Trade to extend his colony's interior border by more than two hundred miles northward so that it took in more of the Mississippi Valley and also the Alabama and Tombigbee Rivers above Mobile Bay. Had he achieved his full demand, West Florida would have encompassed most of what later became the states of Mississippi and Alabama rather than their southerly portions. Two Scottish noblemen, who happened to be Johnstone's allies, supported his intrigue, and acquired West Florida land grants of 20,000 acres in the process.[20]

On March 23, 1764, the Board of Trade gave Johnstone much though not all of what he requested. The Lords Commissioners recommended that West Florida's northern boundary be moved to the confluence of the Yazoo and Mississippi Rivers—about one hundred miles above the 31st parallel—and run eastward from there to the Chattahoochee. This decision, soon confirmed by the Privy Council, brought Indian villages and hunting lands amounting to nearly 38,000 square miles within West Florida's nominal jurisdiction. Most important, the new territory included some of the richest soil in the Lower Mississippi Valley, notably the former French post of Natchez and vicinity.[21] West Florida had suddenly become an interior as well as a maritime colony—at least by official reckoning.

West Florida's enlargement was a quiet piece of imperial business—important to Governor Johnstone and a few privileged allies—but hardly gaining widespread public attention. The measure did not signal a sea change in British policy, since the primary colonial-Indian boundary line remained intact along the Appalachians. Still, the decision marked the first royal reduction of the native reserve established by royal proclamation. The West Florida boundary adjustment legitimated geopolitical linkages that ambitious colonizers wished to create between the Mississippi Valley and the Gulf Coast.

While Johnstone envisioned Florida as a naval base in war against Spain, he had no desire to displace current Spanish colonials. For wholly pragmatic reasons, he wished those inhabitants to be treated fairly and guaranteed religious freedom so that they might facilitate commerce with the Spanish Empire. His sentiments expressed a broad interpretation of the Treaty of Paris, which granted "liberty of the Catholick religion" to inhabitants of ceded Spanish and French territories, "as far as the laws of Great Britain permit."[22]

Johnstone's views were generous, if naïve. Madrid had no intention of allowing its subjects to live under British rule and to serve enemy interests. And some inhabitants dared not stay. Florida's black refugees from Georgia and the Carolinas feared that the English might reenslave them. By early 1763, Spanish authorities had already begun the process by which nearly all Florida colonials and their dependents—more than 3,000 persons—were evacuated to Havana or Veracruz. Since very few remained behind, Spanish Florida came to an abrupt end after nearly two centuries of settlement.[23] St. Augustine's evacuation dumfounded one British officer, who observed Spanish ships carrying away "all the living," and also "the Bones of the late governor and a number of Saints" to Havana.[24]

French colonials of Mobile and vicinity responded in varied ways to changing imperial governance in 1763. Perhaps half of the region's 300 to 350 white residents, along with enslaved blacks in their households, departed for French Louisiana within several months of the English arrival that autumn. Some émigrés returned a year later upon learning that Spanish rule was to displace French governance at New Orleans. By October 2, 1764, Major Robert Farmar, British commander at Mobile, recorded the names of 112 Frenchmen who had taken oaths of allegiance under his administration. Other French colonists held their ground in English territory along Lake Pontchartrain and eastward to the Pascagoula.[25]

Britons might enthuse over Pensacola and Mobile at an ocean's distance, but it was another matter to view the ports firsthand. Both towns had dilapidated forts without decent or healthful quarters for troops. Pensacola had a fine bay for sizeable ships, but it lacked any navigable river offering passage to interior lands beyond the sandy coastal plain and bordering pine barrens. An incoming British naval officer believed it "a great unhappiness, that Pensacola harbour, should be placed in such a deplorable, barren situation." Though Mobile was well situated for Indian trade, it had the disadvantage of lying on an estuary fifty miles above the Gulf. Large vessels could not traverse a bar impeding entry to Mobile Bay, requiring incoming cargoes to be conveyed by small craft and boats to port.[26]

No sooner did Britons arrive in the Floridas than they avidly sought ownership of Spanish properties in St. Augustine and Pensacola, and French lands in Mobile and vicinity. From December 1763 through November 1764, Mobile's French residents sold a slew of city houses and outlying plantations to Anglo purchasers paying mostly in hard Spanish currency.[27] Major Robert Farmar set a daunting example, acquiring sizeable acreage from Dauphin Island at the head of Mobile Bay to the Tensaw River north of town. He also negotiated a personal land purchase from the Creeks, though the crown later annulled this legally dubious transaction. Army and navy officers pursued their self-interest as diligently as merchants in Britain's empire of fortune.[28] Farmar's entrepreneurial bent mirrored far larger schemes of American colonization and land speculation then underway in Britain and its Atlantic colonies.

British victory in the Seven Years War not only stirred new visions of Mississippi colonization, but it also revived plans devised decades before. In late 1762, an anonymous pamphlet appeared in London promoting the English claim to "Carolana," a royal patent bestowed by Charles I entitling the beneficiary—in this case one Robert Heath—to all lands in North America between the 30th and 36th parallels. The patent lay dormant until the 1690s when it was acquired by Dr. Daniel Coxe of London. A man of vast ambition, Coxe sponsored an English reconnaissance voyage to the Mississippi in 1699, only to have his exploratory ship turned back by French competitors. In addition to adventurist projects of continental scope, the doctor became a substantial absentee proprietor in New Jersey, where his heirs settled.[29]

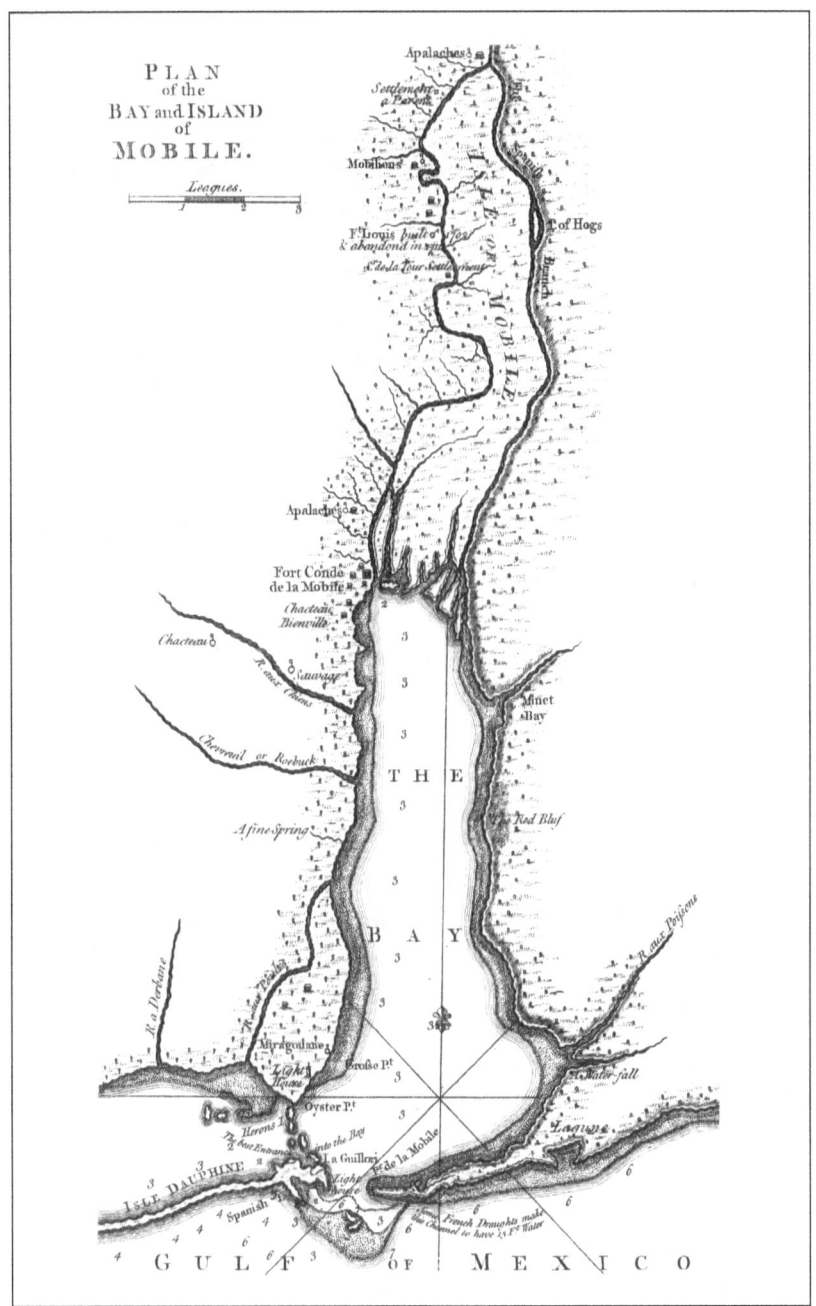

[Thomas Jefferys], *Plan of the Bay and Island of Mobile* (London, 1763). Courtesy of The Huntington Library, no. 295806. This map shows the narrow and shallow passages from the Gulf of Mexico into Mobile Bay. It also depicts widespread marshes, including the lowlands between the Mobile and Tensaw Rivers above the bay.

It was not coincidental that the Coxe family renewed its claim to "Carolana" in 1762 as soon as Britain obtained imperial title to the Mississippi's east bank by the preliminary Paris peace settlement. According to the London publicist touting Carolana, the late Dr. Coxe's title was still valid. France had no business remaining in New Orleans or the trans-Mississippi West, which should rightfully be English possessions.[30] Personal family ambition happened to coincide with unbridled patriotism. As the Coxe publicist pronounced, "That *Great Britain* should be possessed of the whole *North American* Continent, seems to be a favourite, and, indeed, necessary Maxim of modern Policy."[31] The author of this declamation was not entirely boastful, since he feared the French would still be formidable foes controlling the fur trade, fashioning Indian alliances, and obstructing British commerce with the Spanish in New Mexico and along the Gulf of Mexico.[32]

The Coxe publicist's geographic knowledge was badly flawed, but his errors are less significant than his broad endorsement of Mississippi settlement as a crucial nexus of territorial and commercial expansion. Most strikingly, Benjamin Franklin and his son, William, exhibited a keen interest in advancing the Coxe patent once war gave way to peace. Benjamin left England for Philadelphia in the late summer of 1762 while William followed by the year's end. The younger Franklin was just about to begin his tenure as New Jersey's royal governor.[33]

The Franklins promoted the Carolana patent in collaboration with William and Daniel Coxe, two of the presumptive claimants living in Pennsylvania and New Jersey. Their scheme presaged northern colonial involvement in the settlement and commercial development of the Mississippi Valley. By the time of the Revolution, Philadelphia and New York City had growing mercantile connections with the British Gulf Coast and New Orleans. Northern whites, some of whom were slaveholders, joined a diverse array of Anglo-Americans and Britons as landowners in the Lower Mississippi Valley.[34]

Benjamin Franklin promoted the Coxe scheme through correspondence with Richard Jackson, his personal friend and Member of Parliament. Strategic considerations coincided with personal interest in this quest. As Franklin summarized the postwar environment, Mississippi colonization was a logical measure to "secure our Territory and extend our Commerce; and to separate the Indians on this side [of the river] from those on the other, by intervening Settlements of English." He was keenly interested in opening north-south river passages: "I am convinc'd that a new Colony, that should be plac'd within Coxe's Bounds, on the Rivers that discharge themselves into the Bay of Mexico, between Cape Florida and the Missisipi [sic] would have a more rapid Progress in Population than any heretofore planted."[35] This assessment was written when imperial policy appeared open-ended. The crown had still to define Florida's colonial bounds, and had not yet proscribed trans-Appalachian colonization.

Jackson had disappointing news for Franklin after investigating the Carolana patent. Combing through heaps of dusty records at several government venues, he reported in November 1763 that he could find no trace of William III's purported confirmation of title to Dr. Coxe. By the next April, he still had no luck and took a dim view of current ministerial thinking, which he described as prejudiced "against Settlements on the Mississippi and in what is called the back Country."[36] Pontiac's War made interior colonization seem a pipedream for the time being, though that conflict hardly quieted Anglo-American quests for royal land grants in Trans-Appalachia or on the Mississippi. In 1763, General Phineas Lyman of Connecticut, colonial commander at the siege of Havana, formed the Company of Military Adventurers—a group of veteran officers seeking to found a new British colony in the mid- to upper Mississippi Valley. Three years later, Lyman turned his attention to the Natchez district and, after years of lobbying, finally brought some Yankee settlers to the Lower Mississippi Valley before the Revolutionary War.[37]

Colonial-Indian Relations on the Gulf

The arrival of British forces by sea to St. Augustine, Pensacola, and Mobile in 1763 was an important though limited assertion of sovereignty within the full compass of territories ceded by Spain and France. European maps might show that England held sway over peninsular Florida and extensive portions of the Gulf Coast and Lower Mississippi Valley. The reality was far different. Beyond a few coastal outposts, Great Britain's new territories were dominated by native peoples—the Creeks and closely related Seminoles in eastern zones, the Choctaws in central to western portions, and the Chickasaws to the northwest. In addition to these substantial groups, there were many smaller native bands throughout the region.

Long before West Florida was conceived, European rivalries had introduced great changes to North America's southeastern regions. By the dawn of the eighteenth century, both England and France had made inroads at Spanish expense while challenging one another for primacy. During the ensuing half-century, the Indian world was transformed by expanding European trade, colonial competition for native allies, and the increased destructiveness of warfare. Native groups suffered deep internal divisions over the choice of European allies and resulting contention between civil and war chiefs. Many indigenous peoples migrated under the weight of new pressures, while some sought safety through absorption into more powerful groups.[38]

Few alliances held steady amidst imperial contention and shifting Indian loyalties. The British relationship with the Chickasaws was a striking exception to this rule. The Chickasaws, whose heartland was close by the upper Tombigbee and Yazoo Rivers, welcomed English traders during the early 1700s and became stalwart suppliers of Indian war captives for the Carolina slave market. The Choctaws, meanwhile, built their strongest ties to French Louisiana, but were susceptible to English commercial influence that rent their villages into warring factions by the late 1730s. The French later restored their prestige among the Choctaws, only to lose ground during the Seven Years War when they were unable to supply their native friends with sufficient goods or presents. Alliances could not hold without reciprocal ties of allegiance and protection.[39]

British observers were struck by the dense population of southern Indian groups compared to native peoples above the Ohio. In 1764, John Stuart, superintendent for Indian affairs in the southern department, identified forty-one Creek towns capable of fielding 3,600 fighting men. Similar to other British observers, he differentiated between the "Upper" and "Lower" Creeks—a geographic distinction that by no means captured the complex linguistic, ethnic, and familial bonds of native identity. (The Creeks called themselves the Muscogulge or Muskogee, though not all persons or clans among them were of that linguistic or ethnic background.) Stuart, meanwhile, estimated Choctaw villages as capable of raising 5,000 warriors. The less populous Chickasaws included some 450 gun men. The Cherokees, whose lands abutted the Creeks to the north, resided in some forty towns numbering about 10,000 to 12,000 persons.[40]

In contrast to Indian power, the first British forces at Pensacola and Mobile together had perhaps 1,000 men—but were less than half that effective number because of death and rampant illness suffered since the siege of Havana. By February 1765, West Florida's non-Indian inhabitants amounted to only 1,473 whites and 842 blacks in addition to military personnel.[41]

Major Robert Farmar, senior British officer at Mobile, had a large task before him during the fall of 1763. Even while securing the town, he was expected to mount an expeditionary force to occupy ceded French posts in the Illinois country. On November 9, he received orders from General Jeffrey Amherst, outgoing commander-in-chief at New York, to hasten his movement upriver. British forces were badly needed at midcontinent as Pontiac's uprising gathered strength among numerous Indian peoples.[42] There was a central irony to Famar's pending mission. Though British authorities suspected French agents of covertly stoking Indian resistance, they had no choice except to call on France's remaining officials in Louisiana to facilitate their own upriver passage via New Orleans. Anglo-French cooperation initially appeared unlikely since distrust permeated both sides along the Gulf Coast. Jean-Jacques Blaise d'Abbadie, Louisiana's director-general, had the irksome duty of personally overseeing Mobile's cession to British foes. Upset by Farmar's demands, he vented his displeasure to a fellow officer: "What a commission to have to deal with people intoxicated with their success who regard themselves as the masters of the world!"[43]

Notwithstanding petty contention, Abbadie and Farmar discovered a common interest in securing Indian acquiescence in the new imperial peace settlement. French officials wanted to stabilize affairs after losing prestige through wartime defeat and territorial cession. The British, meanwhile, needed French services, not least for colonial interpreters in talks with native peoples. On November 14, 1763, Abbadie and Farmar jointly conferred with Choctaw and Alibamon headmen at Mobile, where a few thousand Indian men, women, and children gathered close by to witness events. Commonplace diplomatic gestures were subject to varying interpretation among the parties. One British officer surmised that the French offered their customary presents to chiefs "rather with a view to divert the Choctaws resentment from themselves than to turn it against us."[44]

Farmar and Abbadie justified the new imperial boundary along the Mississippi as a peace-making necessity that Indians had an interest in preserving. The Choctaws and Alibamons were henceforth said to be living "on the side of the English," east of the great river and therefore within British jurisdiction.[45] This formula brushed aside actual complexities. From an Indian perspective, the British acquired the use of previously occupied French outposts rather than command of native territories. Some Choctaws decried their abandonment by the French and expressed distrust of English intentions. Farmar eased native concerns for the moment by distributing presents and pledging trade and fair treatment.[46]

The Mobile peace accord of 1763 was a makeshift arrangement omitting one rumored but scarcely known imperial fact—France's secret transfer of Louisiana to Spain. Abbadie did his best to allay Indian fears of British control by offering protection to native groups desiring to live within the French colonial sphere west of the Mississippi. Some Alibamons from the Mobile region migrated to Bayou Lafourche in Louisiana. Other tribal bands—Apalaches, Taensas, Pacanas, Mobilians, Biloxis, Chatos, and Pascagoulas—relocated in 1763-64 from the Gulf Coast's northern rim to the Mississippi's lower banks. This exodus actually brought Indians into Spain's imperial bounds, though the migrants had no idea of that point.[47]

Vulnerable before native peoples, the British encountered extreme environmental hazards along the Gulf. Troops stationed in Mobile and Pensacola suffered gravely from malaria, dysentery, typhoid, and other ailments. The situation was particularly bad at Mobile, which George Johnstone once called the "the most unhealthy place on the face of the earth." Elias Durnford, West Florida officeholder, dreaded the town's sickly summer season when prevailing southeasterly winds blew "Thick Foggs and Stinking Exhalations from the Marshes" along the bay. In 1775, James Adair labeled Mobile "that grave-yard for Britons."[48]

Geographic limits, and not expansive power, marked the initial British presence by the Gulf. As one junior officer explained in late 1763, there was no prospect of holding a former French post on the Tombigbee River above Mobile should a conflict erupt with the Choctaws, who had a large village within "Musquet Shot of the Fort." Though the British kept a token force of fewer than twenty men on the Tombigbee, they declined to approach more distant Fort Toulouse situated on the Coosa River in Creek territory. The Wolf King of the Muscogulge bluntly warned a British major at Pensacola not to dare colonize his people's territories. Robert Farmar advised against any movement that way, worrying that the Creeks might join the "Northern Indians" arrayed against the English above the Ohio.[49]

The first British military movement from the Gulf toward the Illinois country failed to come remotely close to its goal. On March 20, 1764, Major Arthur Loftus's expedition of 340 men was attacked by Tunica warriors along the Mississippi's shoreline about two hundred miles north of New Orleans. Trapped in their boats, the soldiers had no choice but to flee downriver from an enemy that could scarcely be seen behind trees covering both banks. The defeat was sobering to royal officials, partly because the Tunicas were among the Lower Mississippi Valley's "small nations" presumed to be far less threatening than the more powerful Choctaws. Moreover, both Loftus and Farmar believed that French Louisianans had secretly incited the Tunicas to launch their deadly attack.[50] Loftus's men endured the humiliation of retreating through New Orleans—the same foreign city that was their base of operations.

Mysterious and unproven French intrigues stoked English suspicion and anger. Loftus was particularly outraged that "savage Chiefs," who had led the attack against his men, freely entered New Orleans while he was in the city overseeing the retreat.[51] Stung by English accusations, director-general Abbadie denied collusion and insisted that he was discouraging Indian hostilities. By his account, the Tunicas admitted their assault on the British expedition but maintained that they had respected Abbadie's authority by striking north of French territory.[52] Mississippi Valley natives had their own sense of territoriality that had yet been little affected by European imperial claims.

Johnstone's Maritime and Interior Perspective

Seven months passed between the Tunica attack and George Johnstone's delayed arrival at Pensacola in late October 1764. Finally taking post as West Florida's chief magistrate, Johnstone was alarmed by the colony's precarious state and longed for the day when British forces would dictate terms to native peoples rather than defer to "powerful Tribes." While holding fast to his plan of encouraging Caribbean commerce, he also coveted the Mississippi Valley's deerskin and fur trade. Maritime and interior spheres simultaneously commanded his attention.[53]

Johnstone was greatly cheered by favorable news from London during his first days in Pensacola. France had unequivocally ceded Louisiana to Spain. French withdrawal appeared a British gateway to dominance of the Indian trade and commercial access to the Spanish Caribbean. Johnstone was so struck by Louisiana's cession that he wrote a propagandistic notice to the South Carolina *Gazette*. The governor predicted an end to Indian conflict and invited colonial migration to West Florida, where fertile interior lands were *"capable of producing wine, oil, silk, indigo, tobacco, rice, and all the fruits of southern climates."* Above all, commercial opportunities abounded through Pensacola's proximity to New Orleans: *"And now*

New-Orleans is ceded to the Spaniards, it must serve as a means to introduce our commodities to the Spanish dominions without a rival, and in a manner deliver to us the key of the wealth of Mexico." West Florida was poised to become the shining *"EMPORIUM"* of the Gulf Coast—and *"the most pleasant part of the new world."*[54]

Johnstone moved quickly to realize his heady predictions. In February 1765, he informed London that he had received numerous letters from Cuban and Yucatán officials eager to receive British textiles in exchange for dyewoods and silver.[55] The governor was of the same mind as an anonymous English pamphleteer who wrote in 1764 of crafty shippers using West Florida ports to funnel Spanish silver to Britain's Atlantic colonies. According to this formula, skill and cunning were the route to riches: "A thorough knowledge of the coast, and navigation of the gulph is indeed necessary for this trade; but a little practice will soon enable an industrious adventurer to surmount all difficulties, and enrich himself by means equally just and laudable, though prohibited by the Spaniards to every nation but their own."[56]

Eager to promote Spanish commerce, Johnstone appealed to London for a relaxation of the Navigation Acts, which prohibited foreign ships from entering British colonial ports. The governor wanted similar allowance for West Florida that the empire accorded Jamaica—permission for Spanish ships to bring in specie even if prohibited from importing merchandise. Leaping past daily woes to future grandeur, Johnstone predicted that "we should have Dollars as plenty as halfpence in London" if the Spanish trade were opened. His bleak alternative was British flight from West Florida altogether. Johnstone's all-or-nothing pleading failed to persuade London. The Board of Trade withheld license for Spanish vessels entering Pensacola, but without insisting on stringent enforcement of the Navigation Acts. Spanish ships carried specie into Pensacola with some frequency, if in more modest quantities than the town's merchants wished.[57]

Johnstone's projections for the Mississippi Valley were acquired through second-hand information. Despite his great interest in that region, he was so caught up in political wrangling in Pensacola that he never had the time to make a tour westward of Mobile. Relying on military officers for scouting, he quickly identified "Point Iberville," a spit of marshland at the confluence of the tiny Iberville and great Mississippi, as the key to projecting British power at mid-continent.[58]

Otherwise known as Bayou Manchac, the Iberville comprised part of the boundary between the Isle of Orleans—an area under titular Spanish sovereignty—and British West Florida. To Johnstone, this small waterway had great potential as a route connecting the Gulf and Lakes Pontchartrain and Maurepas with the Mississippi above New Orleans. If the bed of the brush-choked Iberville could be dredged, the British could use it to navigate from the Gulf to the Mississippi without passing through foreign territory from the great river's mouth to New Orleans and points north. Above the Iberville—though not below it—England had sovereignty over the Mississippi's east bank. In sum, Johnstone viewed the placement of a fort on the bayou as a means of "keeping so material a passage open . . . & rendering New Orleans dependant [sic] on us for all things instead of our being dependant on New Orleans."[59] Though not originating the idea of the canal, the governor vigorously pushed it to the forefront of his imperial agenda.

In late 1764, British engineers prepared to clear the Iberville, hiring more than fifty slaves in New Orleans for the task, to be supervised by a French overseer. Slave laborers were in this case, and in so much else, the underpinnings of colonial endeavors along the Mississippi. Work on the Iberville seemed promising to British officers after a few months. Johnstone quickly proclaimed success and won royal authorization the following year to establish a garrison at Manchac—to be named Fort Bute in honor of his patron. But triumph was illusory. Trees were felled and brush cleared, but the Mississippi's next seasonal upsurge poured "a barricado" of logs and other "rubbish" into the bayou that eviscerated signs of progress.[60]

Surveying Point Iberville in early 1765, Lt. Philip Pittman labored to reach the site when moving west by bateau from Lake Maurepas. As his small party of soldiers and two slaves went up the Amit (Amite) River toward the Iberville, they found their path blocked by floating logs. Accompanied by an Indian guide and two soldiers, Pittman took three days to paddle the bayou's jammed channel to the Mississippi, no more than ten to fifteen miles distant. By February 21, the lieutenant had completed his survey, which was soon made into a "plan" or map. Pittman's map is fascinating for juxtaposing the great Mississippi, colored light green, with the minuscule Iberville, appearing as a narrow watercourse on the river's east bank. A storehouse and nearby "Negroe hutts [sic]" are depicted as small rectangles, colored red, close by the bayou's confluence with the Mississippi. The drawing has a raw quality matching the landscape, marked by crude lines indicating trees and tall canes. Pittman noted the

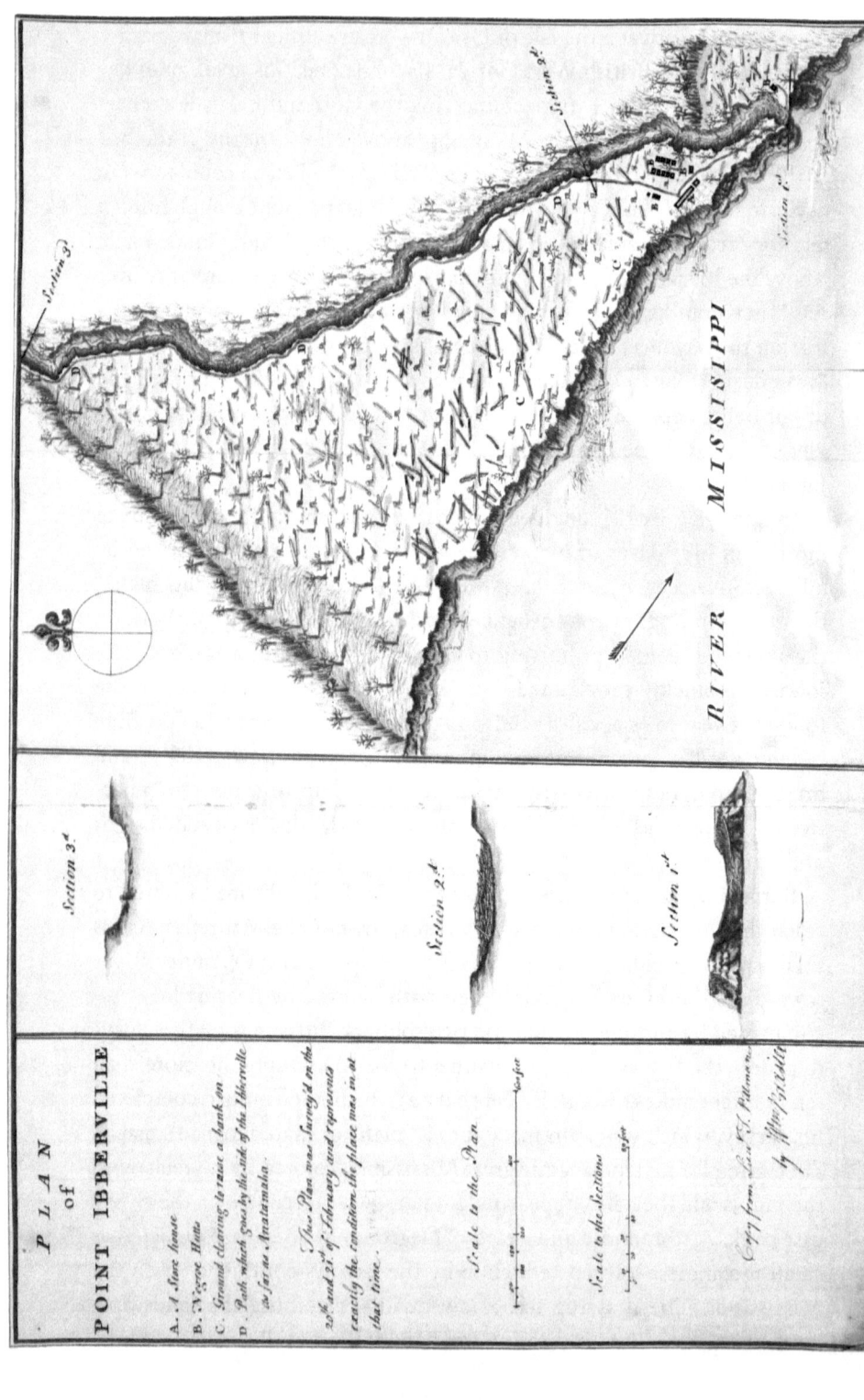

Iberville's path toward the "Anatamaha," a rivulet he described as an Indian fishing ground with a "vast number of crocodiles" (actually alligators). Another British officer discovered mosquitoes even more ferocious and bothersome than the reptiles.[61]

Fort Bute by the Iberville was a miserable place for troops. Built in the summer of 1765, Johnstone conceived of it as a stronghold, but it never approached that standing. Alibamon and Houma Indian raiders soon plundered the post, forcing a skeletal guard of ten soldiers to flee for safety to New Orleans. Another detachment occupied the site the following year, only to suffer from illness, fevers, and flooding. The British withdrew the entire garrison in 1768, and would not restore it for ten years. Rather than command the Mississippi, Fort Bute was overwhelmed by the river.[62]

British designs to construct an Iberville-Mississippi canal were far more daunting than maintaining a marshland fort. West Florida officials remained interested in the project, however, well after the military halted dredging in 1768. The king's surrogates at Pensacola could no more forswear the idea of a British-controlled Gulf-Mississippi route than English navigators could surrender the vision of the Northwest Passage two centuries before. The economic and military benefits of bypassing New Orleans were too powerful to be quickly laid aside.

While British officials contemplated changing the natural environment, they repeatedly raised the issue of new colonial allegiances with Indian peoples. Meeting with Choctaw and Chickasaw spokesmen at Mobile in late March 1765, Johnstone and superintendent John Stuart explained Louisiana's pending cession to Spain. As Stuart declared, "all the Frenchmen" in New Orleans and west of the Mississippi were henceforth to be considered "Spaniards"; those dwelling or lawfully migrating to the east, "you must look upon as Brittish [sic] Subjects [and] your Brothers & Children of the Great King."[63] This message neatly assigned French colonials either to British or Spanish jurisdictions even though settler allegiances were scarcely so clear-cut.

British Indian diplomacy at Mobile hinged on French mediation through the Chevalier Montault de Monberaut, a leading resident, who

(opposite) Philip Pittman, *Plan of Point Ibberville* [sic], 1765, copied by Wm. Brasier. Courtesy of William L. Clements Library, University of Michigan, Maps 8-L-14. This map shows British plans to construct a fort at the confluence of the Mississippi with the Iberville River (Bayou Manchac)—a point perceived as crucial to linking the British Mississippi to the Gulf of Mexico via Lakes Maurepas and Pontchartrain.

furthered English talks with the Choctaws and Chickasaws just as he had previously assisted with the Creeks at Pensacola. The chevalier provided services in return for British guarantees of his personal freedom, including the option of living in Louisiana while drawing an English salary. This mutually satisfactory arrangement lasted a few months, but it was undone by British suspicions of French "intrigue" and Montault's frustrated pleas for money and respect.[64]

Johnstone's diplomacy could not have been easy for a Frenchman to swallow. "The English," the governor admonished the Choctaws and Chickasaws, "took almost all the Ships which belonged to the French" in the recent war, while the British "were Sailing unmolested thro' the whole World." Indians could expect no relief from the Spanish, "who hardly make any Manufactures of their own." Johnstone emphasized that royal favor was not a free gift. If native peoples desired beneficial commerce, they should willingly cede fertile interior lands to the English. The governor declared that the British required territory for cultivating corn and rice as food crops—a less invasive demand than his actual goal of developing plantation staples such as tobacco, cotton, and indigo for export.[65]

Choctaw negotiators yielded as little as possible for maximum gain. While ceding coastal territory largely south of their homeland, they also established boundary limits. Tomatly Mingo, a principal chief, obtained a British pledge that no whites were to settle above a certain creek by the Tombigbee River—though that site lay well within West Florida's official boundaries. He also let Johnstone and Stuart know that they should respect customary ways of bargaining: "We hope you will be as generous as the French were, & send us all home contented [with gifts] to our Nation." Alibamo Mingo, an old chief who confessed to be toothless and nearly blind, recalled using French guns "these Eighty Winters Back," and wished he were young so that he could try English weaponry and powder. But his openness to British weaponry came with concern about English traders who by reputation "caused disturbances" and "lived under no government." Choctaw headmen repeatedly raised their old French alliance as a standard for new British relationships in both gift-giving and trade. They insisted on respect for their customary social hierarchy rather than permitting Stuart to distribute medals to his choice of chiefs.[66]

Through reasonably successful talks with the Choctaws and Chickasaws, Johnstone and Stuart opened the way for some two hundred British troops under Robert Farmar to ascend the Mississippi River to Illinois in 1765 without encountering native opposition. Franchimastabé, a

Choctaw headman, led a warrior escort that guided the soldiers upriver. The Chickasaws supplied bear meat and other game as the weary troops approached their destination. The mission's success also depended on French compliance at New Orleans, where the army procured provisions at no small expense.[67]

On December 2, 1765, Farmar's expedition at last reached Fort Chartres, a former French post in Illinois. By British reckoning, the troops were then 963 and one-half miles above New Orleans. Five months had passed since they had left that city and seven months from their initial departure from Mobile. At Fort Chartres, the West Florida contingent greeted fellow soldiers who had arrived a few months previously from Fort Pitt. Royal troops from distant quarters—the Gulf Coast and the source of the Ohio—jointly raised the Union Jack along the Mississippi. All was possible because the British had recently reached diplomatic understandings with Pontiac and chiefs of the Wabash. An uneasy peace came to the mid-Mississippi Valley, with English soldiers occupying garrisons but a mere thimble of the vast land itself. British officers had no sooner arrived in Illinois than they observed French *habitants* moving across the Mississippi, where the western bank was still under France's purview. Some Indian peoples took a similar path, much to English chagrin.[68]

French colonial aptitude in Indian trade continually troubled British newcomers from the Gulf Coast to Illinois. In February 1764, Mobile's Anglo settlers expressed concern that "the French people, after taking the oath of allegiance, will be permitted to trade among the savages." British imperial administration adopted a liberal course by not discriminating against bona fide subjects of French ancestry.[69] Johnstone was meanwhile frustrated by his inability to confine West Florida's Indian trade to resident subjects alone. In the fall of 1766, he complained of his "Evil disposed Countrymen" selling rum to New Orleans merchants who then marketed liquor to natives living under British territorial jurisdiction. The governor even aired the idea of deporting French Louisiana traders to Europe if the latter were caught operating in his province. The deerskin and rum trades freely traversed the Mississippi, notwithstanding Johnstone's wishes.[70]

Indians living east of the Mississippi evaded British strictures about trading exclusively with Mobile and Pensacola, and instead continued to sell deerskins to French Louisianans. Charles Stuart, deputy Indian superintendent, raised this issue in talks with the Coosadas, a small Creek group, and the Choctaws in 1766. Topoye, a Coosada headman, took a conciliatory tone by acknowledging the need for British goods, which kept his people from living "like Deer" and "Wild Beasts." Stuart welcomed this outwardly submissive talk, but still followed with a threat. The Coosadas would have "repented it very much," he told Topoye, if they kept old commercial attachments. The French "are going Away, & would have left you under the Spaniards, whom all Indians say they cannot love." In other words, Indians must satisfy the English or else be left without European goods and consigned to poverty.[71] British officials strived to deny Indians the type of free market in New Orleans that their own venturesome merchants attained.

Charles Stuart's warnings to Shouloushamastabé, "Red Shoes" of the Choctaws, disclose a tug of war between British commercial control and native assertiveness. If Indians lacked ammunition, it was "their own fault," since they trafficked with the French rather than procured "Powder & Ball" from English traders. Answering similar accusations, Tomatly Mingo confessed that he could not prevent his "young People" from going to New Orleans, but that he still valued English goods and friendship. The Choctaws were themselves divided by their growing dependence on British traders. In the southerly Choctaw heartland of the Six Towns, a pro-French faction killed a medal chief for his English connections in 1766.[72]

The British presence in Pensacola had a variable economic impact on Creek villagers depending on their geographic orientation. The Upper Creeks, especially those living in northerly towns by the Coosa and Tallapoosa Rivers, wished to maintain their primary trading routes to Augusta and Charles Town (Charleston). The Muscogulge dwelling just southward—even among the Upper Towns—put increasing stock in supplies furnished through the Gulf ports.[73]

Muscogulge-English relations revolved about a paradox. Though the Creeks desired British commerce, they bristled at unscrupulous traders who made a killing through inordinate rum sales, abused native women, and committed other wanton acts on Indian ground. The floodtide of traders arriving via both the Gulf and the Georgia frontier reduced the price of British goods, but still had damaging consequences. In 1767, Georgia's well-established merchants complained of colonial "adventurers" pouring into the Creek country, selling goods at cut-rate prices, and violating licensing regulations. British Chickasaw traders operating out of Mobile meanwhile refused to comply with a price schedule that disadvantaged them relative to Charleston. George Johnstone repeatedly scorned the rum trade as "the Primary Cause of all Mischief" with Indians, but he finally balked at ordering West Florida's traffickers to restrict liquor sales until the Carolinas and Georgia complied with imperial recommendations on that head. British licensing by provincial authority—and not under a unitary imperial standard—was an invitation to commercial adventurism at native expense.[74]

While the Creeks battled intrusive roustabouts and settlers on their eastern flank, they warred with the Choctaws in order to prevent their rivals from gaining access to English weaponry. In one episode of 1766, Creek warriors killed two British traders for attempting to supply munitions to the Choctaws. The perpetrators deliberately shaped their victims' scalps to portray the slain men as Indians rather than whites. Creek fear of British retaliation quite possibly motivated deliberate disfigurement of the dead.[75]

Johnstone's Failure

George Johnstone shared the common British view that the Creeks were the greatest threat to West Florida's security and prosperity. Unlike most royal officials, however, he demanded unquestioning Muscogulge subordination. Though sharply critical of renegade white traders, the governor would not tolerate Indian retaliatory violence. In June 1766, he fumed that the Creeks had killed five whites in the last thirteen months, besides commonly stealing cattle and harboring fugitive slaves.[76] His fundamental concern was imperial mastery—whether Great Britain could even "pretend to Dominion" if it failed to punish "the Murder of her Subjects." He was meanwhile careful not to stir general Indian enmity. In the fall of 1766 he saw to the trial and execution of an English colonist who murdered a Choctaw man.[77]

Impatient to destroy the Creeks, Johnstone frenetically dispatched war plans to New York City and London. Imagining West Florida to be an imperial priority, he proposed a massive offensive launched simultaneously from Augusta and Pensacola. The size of the allied forces—as Johnstone envisioned matters—would have far surpassed any previous colonial campaign in the region. His presumed attacking force, gathered in two wings, would combine 2,100 regulars and marines, 1,000 provincials, 200 West Florida colonial rangers, 500 Choctaws, 300 Cherokees, and an unspecified number of Chickasaws. The naval squadron at Jamaica, aided by other ships, would transport troops to Pensacola.[78]

On paper, Johnstone's scheme had the imaginary brilliance of projecting power from the Atlantic seaboard and Gulf Coast. In practical terms, however, the governor was wildly off target, not least in assuming Indian peoples to be willing auxiliaries in his scheme. Thomas Gage, commander-in-chief at New York, fumed against the notion that Johnstone had any prerogative over war and peace. Writing to Brigadier General William Tayler at Pensacola, Gage vented his disgust: "If Governor Johnstone is determined to bring on a war at all Events, let him answer the Consequences."[79]

At the time Johnstone conceived his offensive, he had just received royal permission for a six-month leave to attend to his private affairs in England. The governor's mercurial conduct did not please London. In February 1767, the imperial ministry relieved Johnstone of office. In a sharp rebuke, the Earl of Shelburne, secretary of state for the colonies, upbraided him for "rashly rekindling" Indian war following the end of Pontiac's uprising. Imperial authorities had no taste for Johnstone's bloodthirsty urge to lay waste Upper and Lower Creek towns—with "the destroying" of "Men, Women, and Children" in the southerly villages. Shelburne would not, moreover, abide an adventurist governor who quarreled incessantly with military officers and who moved aggressively without London's prior approval. The imperial government—and not Pensacola—had power over war and peace.[80]

Johnstone departed Pensacola for England by early 1767 and never returned. West Florida's riches still beckoned from afar. In 1768, the former governor secured a royal grant of 10,000 acres bordering the Mississippi at Baton Rouge.[81] At the time, Britain had a stake in the region but only a handful of settlers from the Iberville to Natchez. Johnstone's choice of land was carefully made even if he had never seen the immediate locale, let alone the great river itself. In his view, the Lower Mississippi Valley was the fertile corridor linking the Gulf Coast to the North American interior. Seeking to enhance Britain's regional prowess, he intended to lure prosperous Louisiana colonials to migrate to West Florida's Mississippi frontier. Though unable to execute this idea during his brief stay in Pensacola, his project would be furthered by his immediate successors. The geographic boundaries between West Florida and Louisiana might be clear, but there was great uncertainty in the political, economic, and social relationships across those lines.

CHAPTER 2

The Conundrum of "Spanish-French" Louisiana
British Imperialism and the Mississippi-Gulf Frontier, 1766–1775

On December 12, 1771, Lt. John Thomas, British Indian agent at Manchac, expressed contempt for those he called the "Spanish French"—French commandants in the Mississippi Valley who now served the Spanish crown in Louisiana. Thomas's disdainful words exemplify the English difficulty of deciphering and controlling political allegiances in the Gulf region. His opponents' national identity was itself ambiguous.[1]

The lieutenant's confusion is not surprising given fluctuating circumstances along the Mississippi. In late October 1768, French colonial rebels ousted Antonio de Ulloa, Madrid's first governor at New Orleans, and sent him packing to Havana. Responding vigorously to this affront, Carlos III dispatched General Alejandro O'Reilly, one of his ablest commanders, to quell the uprising. Sailing from Cuba with more than 2,000 troops, O'Reilly quickly took hold of New Orleans during the summer of 1769. His military success did not, however, resolve the issue of how Spain might integrate Louisiana into its empire and stave off English encroachments.[2]

Sensing Spanish vulnerability, British West Florida's governors believed they could master the Mississippi borderlands by forming a de facto alliance with French Louisianans. Secret diplomatic channels sprung to life between Pensacola and New Orleans in which intrigue and ambition went hand in hand. Louisiana merchants and planters valued an open trade with the English and considered colonizing the Mississippi's east bank under British auspices. It seemed for a time that Anglo-French frontier amity might overturn customary European rivalries.

Multiple uncertainties hovered in the Louisiana-Florida borderlands in the decade prior to the American Revolutionary War. French

Louisiana loyalties hung in the balance while the possibility of a new British-Spanish war remained alive. Imperial rivalry in the Lower Mississippi Valley revolved around overlapping issues—immigration and trade, population growth, and competition for Indian alliances. Though the British possessed great advantages over Spain on the colonization and commercial fronts, they were hamstrung by differences between Pensacola and London on borderlands development and expansion. A divergence between British imperial and colonialist objectives played to Spanish advantage over time.

Population, Migration, and Imperial Rivalry

Governor George Johnstone and his successors at Pensacola thought of West Florida in grandiose terms beyond present weakness. Their province might be minuscule in population, but it was part of a mighty empire—and would surely partake of national greatness. By the early 1770s, West Florida magistrates took heart from a burst of settlement activity, which, if small in absolute terms, seemed to hold great promise. The center of colonial expansion was along the Mississippi—within a ribbon of alluvial land between Manchac and the Natchez district some 140 miles to the north. White settlers arrived in the region from the southern colonial backcountry, the mid-Atlantic region, and New England, along with smaller numbers from Britain and the Caribbean. The more affluent colonists brought enslaved blacks with them or purchased newly imported Africans, who were themselves of diverse backgrounds. Elias Durnford, provincial lieutenant governor, estimated in 1774 that 2,500 whites and 600 slaves resided along the great river or its immediate tributaries in British West Florida. He put the entire colonial population elsewhere in the province, including Pensacola and Mobile, at 1,200 whites and 600 blacks.[3]

Besides the Mississippi Valley and the Gulf Coast enclaves, West Florida was still an overwhelmingly Indian country, especially in interior zones. Small groups of French settlers could be found on the Pearl, Biloxi, and Pascagoula Rivers, while scarcely any colonials lived in the sandy terrain and pine barrens east of Pensacola Bay to the Apalachicola. Elias Durnford saw colonial dispersion as a weakness: "The Various Settlements in West Florida are so unconnected that The Settlers in case of Attacks from Indians, can give no Assistance to each other."[4]

Just as "Florida" carried a new meaning in 1763, so too did Louisiana by European reckoning. Shorn of nearly all territories east of the Mississippi, the latter province was still remarkably vast. Apart from white traders, very few Europeans could be found among Indian peoples living amidst prairies and woodlands from the Missouri southward to the Red River—all nominally part of Louisiana. After France's cession of the Mississippi's eastern watershed to Britain, some *habitants* of the Illinois country migrated to the river's west bank in order to stay under their native flag. White families and their slaves clustered at newly established St. Louis and at Ste. Genevieve, a village founded by the French in the 1750s.[5]

In 1763, the 3,000 inhabitants of New Orleans accounted for about one of every three persons of European and African ancestry residing in what may be termed "Lower Louisiana." This region, bounded by the Gulf marshlands on the south, had its northern apex at Pointe Coupée, a village 130 miles above New Orleans on the Mississippi's west bank. While New Orleans had more white than black inhabitants, the opposite was true of plantation districts below the town. According to Daniel H. Usner's careful estimate, Lower Louisiana in 1763 had approximately 4,000 whites, 5,000 enslaved blacks, 200 mulatto slaves, 100 Indian slaves, and 100 free persons of color.[6]

A Spanish census of 1777 shows a notable increase in the provincial population. Lower Louisiana's non-Indian inhabitants then amounted to more than 16,000—a roughly 70 percent leap in fourteen years. A region of striking contrasts, Louisiana had colonial districts oriented around subsistence, along with cattle raising or timber harvesting, and slave-based plantations producing indigo, tobacco, and sugar for commercial export. Rice was the staple food crop, though some was shipped for sale to the Caribbean. Black inhabitants continued to outnumber whites in the province as a whole.[7]

Lower Louisiana exceeded West Florida in population, but that was scarce comfort to Governor Ulloa in the spring of 1766. Entering New Orleans with only ninety Spanish soldiers at his call, he felt as if he had entered a foreign province. Ulloa cautiously deferred the declaration of Spain's full sovereignty at New Orleans and provisionally shared authority with Charles-Philippe Aubry, resident French governor, who commanded soldiers of his own nation and all colonial militia. One historian has likened this arrangement to a "government with two heads"—a weak régime of uncertain legitimacy.[8]

Louisiana affairs seemed strange from a British perspective in Pensacola. Unsure of who was in charge in New Orleans, George Johnstone exchanged outwardly courteous letters with Ulloa, himself a scientist renowned for Andean exploration. But Johnstone had no fear of his Spanish counterpart—as his vulgar remarks to London attest: "Mr. Ulloua [sic] has been Examining every part of the Province, as *narrowly as a Jew does his Bride*, & still seems in doubt; He is undoubtedly a man of Indefatigable Genius & Industry, tho' there is something Piddling in the Mechanical Part."[9]

Ulloa was keenly alert to the English threat from West Florida. After visiting the country above New Orleans in May 1766, he commented on the new British fort at Manchac, where the Iberville River formed a narrow channel between West Florida and Louisiana. English-armed vessels routinely cruised Lakes Maurepas and Pontchartrain. In August, Ulloa received a French trader's report of British designs to establish a large garrison on the Texas Gulf Coast. Responding to similar rumors, Spanish authorities in Mexico conducted a thorough reconnaissance but found no wayward Britons.[10]

Britain and Spain placed tiny and ineffectual military garrisons along their common Mississippi border. Ulloa struggled to quarter troops by the Missouri, while his fort at the Balize by the Mississippi's mouth sank into the morass within a year.[11] British forces in West Florida faced similar hazards. Mired at Fort Bute on the Iberville, some English soldiers decamped to New Orleans, where they found employment and some freedom. General Frederick Haldimand, British commander along the Gulf, published a proclamation in that town in January 1768 offering amnesty to deserters reporting to Pensacola. Commandant Aubry and Governor Ulloa jointly approved the proclamation in "the Sovereign Right of [their] two Kings."[12] Cooperation was a trilateral affair in this case!

Royal magistrates in Spanish Louisiana and British West Florida competed against one another within certain limits. Metropolitan authorities expected their provincial officers to be prepared for hostilities, but not to provoke conflict. Decision making for war and peace resided in Madrid and London and not along the Gulf. Paris, too, had a say through the Bourbon Family Compact. The West Florida–Louisiana frontier was a warmly contested region, but without one potentially combustible element. Neither Britain nor Spain disputed the international boundary drawn by the treaty of 1763. Madrid generally respected the right of English ships to navigate the Mississippi and acted only intermittently against an expansive and illicit river commerce involving British traders and Louisiana residents.[13]

Since Louisiana had no lure for Spanish immigrants, Ulloa put considerable stock in Acadian refugees who were already entering the colony before his arrival. The newcomers, who had suffered deportation at British hands, appeared ideal candidates to defend the Mississippi frontier against the English. Ulloa responded with paternalistic care by providing funds, livestock, and munitions to grateful settlers. All turned sour, however, when newly arriving refugees were ordered to colonize unhealthful and isolated Mississippi posts opposite British Natchez and Manchac. Acadian settlers had no stronger wish than to live by their compatriots in well-established districts. Proudly defiant, they refused to be pawns pushed about to serve Spanish imperial needs.[14]

Though disturbed by Acadian disaffection, Ulloa kept to his policy of encouraging Catholic immigration whenever possible. In early 1768, he arranged a hospitable tour of Lower Louisiana for James (or Jacob) Walker, agent for Dr. Henry Jerningham, a Maryland Catholic who proposed bringing his co-religionists as "adventurers" to the Gulf region.[15] The doctor assured Ulloa that his project was wholly lawful, since "a British subject is free, that he may emigrate Where he pleases, in time of peace, nothing Can Stop him but his Creditors." Jerningham's eloquence was unavailing, however, since the Marylanders failed to follow through on their initial colonizing plan.[16]

British West Florida's governors promoted immigration through favorable newspaper and magazine articles published from South Carolina, New England, and Scotland. They also maneuvered to attract French and Acadian settlers from Louisiana, thereby strengthening their Mississippi frontier and undermining the Spanish hold in New Orleans. In the fall of 1764, George Johnstone sounded out Swiss, German, and French Louisiana men on the prospect of moving to British territory. Curiosity traversed both sides of the international divide. In 1765, François Caminade, a native Swiss Protestant and New Orleans merchant, secured an appointment on West Florida's provincial council after expressing pro-English views.[17]

When Johnstone quit West Florida in early 1767, Lt. Governor Montfort Browne succeeded him as first magistrate though without being elevated in rank. A former army subaltern, he was an unscrupulous profiteer who showed no regard whatsoever for poor Irish colonists who ventured with him to West Florida. One Pensacola critic found the lieutenant governor to be "avaricious, ignorant, and notorious for saying what he should not say, and for denying what he doth say." However unsavory to rivals,

Browne was no slouch at gaining local support. In December 1767, he secured the provincial council's permission to locate 17,400 acres of "vacant" land for himself wherever he thought suitable in the colony.[18] His next step was to tour the Mississippi frontier to size up land for personal enrichment and to win Indian and colonial allies in the process.

Eager for London's backing, Browne described his Gulf Coast–Mississippi journey in glowing detail to the Earl of Hillsborough, his patron and secretary of state. Sailing from Mobile on March 1, 1768, with just a few companions and slave porters, Browne visited tiny coastal isles where more cattle dwelt than people. Further west, the scouting party passed through the Rigolets, a narrow channel linking the Gulf of Mexico to Lake Pontchartrain. Navigating in a schooner suited to shallow waters, Browne came to Tangipahoa, a French settlement on the lake's marshy northern shoreline within West Florida's jurisdiction. Impressed by the colonists' slaveholdings and cattle, he hastened to bring French settlers into the British fold by administering oaths of allegiance. He also imagined attracting new subjects from nearby Spanish territory. The lieutenant governor's report was all rosy, bypassing any political uneasiness that local residents might experience by swearing loyalty to Great Britain if they owned land in Louisiana, too.[19]

As Browne traversed the region from the Gulf to the Mississippi, he cultivated good relations with the region's small Indian nations. He was most pleased when feted by the Tunicas, who had formerly attacked British soldiers but now wanted English friendship. As Browne headed further upriver toward Natchez, he entered what he declared to be "one of the finest countrys [sic] in the British American Dominions, The Soil is Exceedingly fertile Consisting of black Mould, three feet deep on the hills, and much deeper in the bottoms, & with little trouble will produce Wine, Oyls, Wheat, Barley, Rice, R[y]e, Buckwheat Oates, Hemp, flax, Cotton, Indigo, Hopps, Tobacco (Equal to the best Nackitosh) & Saffron." "Nackitosh" was a reference to Natchitoches, a French settlement on the Red River, well known for tobacco production. Browne's journey pleased his friends in Pensacola, but also stirred envy among rivals who suspected him of cornering "all the good land round the Fort of Natchez"—as one British lieutenant put matters.[20]

Browne's description of "the Natchez"—a region rather than a town—had an ecstatic tone of discovery meant to awaken interest in London. Similar to other British newcomers, the lieutenant governor marveled at verdant uplands at variance with the Mississippi's alluvial plain. A few years after Browne's upriver tour, another English gentleman described the Natchez as "a fine undulating Country which even the celebrated Campania of Rome cannot exceed in Beauty." Browne was intrigued by regional history, explaining that "the Natchez" was named after "a Nation of Indians . . . who were Extirpated . . . by ye french." In actuality, the French achieved their victory only through alliance with the Choctaws.[21] That bloody conflict of the 1730s opened areas for British settlement that would have otherwise been foreclosed.

The subtext of Browne's message was clear. With sufficient imperial support, the Mississippi could thrive as an area of British endeavor. Louisiana's Acadians were seemingly poised to leave Spanish territory for West Florida. Browne needed but a trifling salary for a French priest at Mobile who would minister to the immigrants. In a cynical way, he dubbed the Acadians "a Bigotted people" whose only tie to Spain was their Catholic faith.[22]

Browne's intrigues seemed on the verge of fulfillment in the fall of 1768. On October 29, French colonials arrested Governor Ulloa in New Orleans, charged him with malfeasance, and proclaimed their wholehearted fealty to "Louis the Beloved," king of France. Given three days to quit the colony, Ulloa embarked with fellow Spaniards for Havana on November 1. New Orleans merchants masterminded the revolt with support from rural French, German, and Acadian settlers. Jubilant supporters hailed these events by toasting "the good wine of Bordeaux" and scorning "the poison of Catalonia."[23]

Three months prior to the revolt, the conspirators sent two emissaries to Pensacola for secret talks with Brigadier General Haldimand. In July 1768, the general hosted the chevalier Jean-Baptiste de Noyan, a prestigious New Orleans resident, and Balthasar Masan, a former infantry captain. There was no language barrier to overcome; Haldimand was a native Swiss Protestant more fluent in French than English.[24] Customary French antagonism to England turned to friendship with the hope of overthrowing Spanish rule. Once back in New Orleans, Noyan wrote Haldimand of his desire for "an indissoluble union between the two nations" (the French and English). The Spanish, he added, would never possess "the shrewdness" (*sagacité*) for achievements in the arts and sciences. The chevalier hoped that Haldimand would himself visit New Orleans in the next few months.[25] Other Louisiana colonists sent similar encouragement. François Caminade, then in New Orleans, assured Haldimand of popular support for the English, and his own desire to settle along the British Mississippi: "At Natchez one finds the true terrestrial paradise [*le véritable paradis terrestre*]. And there are not under Heaven any more excellent Lands for Tobacco."[26]

Louisiana rebels put so much stock in British support that they renewed contact with Pensacola just a few days after ousting Ulloa. On November 2, 1768, Masan wrote triumphantly to Haldimand that "the event has arrived which the ch[evalier] de Noyan and I have had the honor of discussing with you several times." Masan penned a follow-up message five days later, relaying news that New Orleans residents had chosen Monsieur Saintelette as deputy to Versailles.[27] No time could be lost, as months would elapse before Louisiana colonials learned whether they would gain France's approval. They were clearly anxious for British assistance in case Spain attempted to retake Louisiana by force.[28] A careful officer, Haldimand distanced himself from the revolt rather than assisting the rebels as the latter had imagined. The general evidently played a confidence game all along, sounding out creole opinion but withholding any commitment.[29]

In formal appeals to France, the New Orleans insurgents were intensely critical of Spanish governance but rather soft toward their English neighbors. One declaration frankly stated that peace with Britain had stimulated Louisiana's trade, though Spanish rule "makes every free-born man shake with fear."[30] Being formerly accustomed to loose governmental control, New Orleans merchants bridled at Ulloa's attempts to reduce contraband and to monitor the price of imported goods. Most galling was a shift in Spanish commercial policy from liberality to strictness. Though initially tolerating Louisiana's customary trade with France and the French West Indies, Madrid drastically curtailed these privileges in March 1768 by a royal order directing provincial commerce to Spanish peninsular ports. Nicolas Chauvin de Lafrénière, a fiery champion of revolt, described that measure as "the last fatal stroke" to decades of hard-won colonial progress. There was no time in his view to see whether the order would be enforced or rather circumvented with Ulloa's tacit consent.[31]

Louisiana traders were angered by shortages of specie and slaves; they also felt hampered because Spain scarcely required their tobacco, indigo, sugar, cotton, lumber, and peltry—and could not furnish manufactures. As the complainants explained to French authorities, their new imperial master was an economic "tributary" of other nations, compelled to purchase foreign wares at high prices with the precious metals of the Indies.

This same declaration lambasted Ulloa for abusing colonists as if they were "the savages of Peru and Mexico." Anti-Spanish prejudice was not exclusively English or Dutch by any means.[32]

Montfort Browne appreciated Louisiana's insurgents for their pluck and ambition. He eagerly read their published declarations, which touted "liberty and competition," denounced monopoly, and espoused commerce and population growth.[33] Continuing his campaign for creole migration to Natchez, Browne now urged that the British Mississippi be erected into a new royal province apart from the rest of West Florida. In fact, he coveted a governor's post by the great river bordering Louisiana. His plea to Hillsborough was unmistakable: "My Lord, I hope I shall not be forgot."[34]

Browne could only go so far in his Louisiana intrigue without imperial support. However much he promoted Natchez settlement, he was unlikely to attract Louisiana planters to the district without royal military protection against potential Indian foes, especially the Choctaws. Moreover, his scheme for the Lower Mississippi Valley went precisely against current British retrenchment in the North American interior. On June 27, 1768, Major General Gage in New York City sent word to Haldimand that his Majesty's government had decided to evacuate all interior continental posts, and those in "settled Parts," "unless necessary for the facilitating of Commerce, or the publick Safety."[35] This order marked an imperial step-back from the Mississippi. All soldiers were now to be withdrawn from the two small English garrisons on the Lower Louisiana frontier: Fort Bute by the Iberville and Fort Panmure at Natchez. Only three companies of troops were to remain at Pensacola and Mobile. Gage earmarked most of the departing redcoats for St. Augustine, where the incidence of disease and death was not as great as along the Gulf.[36]

From Pensacola's perspective, British troops were the backbone of economic growth. As Browne explained to Haldimand, soldiers would safeguard supply routes along the Mississippi vital to "the Indian and Spanish Trades." Troops would also maintain security at an uncertain time, "especially while the Government of New Orleans remains unsettled and divided, between the Spaniards and French."[37] West Florida's legislature bemoaned troop departures that would deliver the Indian trade to the French in New Orleans, who were "remarkably assiduous in alienating the affections of the Chacktaws [sic] from our Interest." If left unaided, British traders simply could not vie with seasoned French officers and interpreters whose "method of managing the Savages is much superior to ours." Another colonial petition warned that military withdrawal meant "the entire Ruin of every British Settler on the River Mississippi—the immediate Reduction of the Value of Private Property and in short an end to every Degree of Credit in the Country."[38] Unlike Atlantic colonies recoiling from tighter imperial control, West Floridians demanded immediate British protection.

Colonial Upheaval, Spanish Invasion, and British War Plans

Louisiana's insurgents were personally contemptuous of Spanish colonialism, but they took a more politic stand in their public pleas to France. In fact, they argued that they could effectively defend Spanish interests in the province under the French flag, thereby saving Madrid the costs of colonial administration. The New Orleans revolutionaries touted their longstanding Indian alliances as proof that they could safeguard Mexico against British advances from the east. Spain should defer to their experience in native affairs as a matter of self-interest alone.[39]

Creole diplomacy was a plea to France to reverse the Bourbon accord of 1762 that had handed Louisiana to a foreign power without the inhabitants' knowledge or consent. Mobile and Illinois residents were a case in point. They had acted loyally by departing British territory for neighboring French soil in 1763, only to discover months later that they were Madrid's subjects. Surely, Louis XV and his ministers would amend the past, honor colonial patriotism, and mollify Spanish security concerns.[40] But these heartfelt appeals were unavailing. Choiseul, still the king's first minister in 1769, was not the least inclined to jeopardize the Bourbon Family Compact on account of impetuous colonials. He had rejected a Louisiana petition to reverse the province's cession five years earlier—and he remained steadfast in that decision. His evolving war plans depended on full Spanish commitment against Britain. France would not dissuade Madrid from reoccupying Louisiana if it so chose.[41]

Carlos III's ministers decided on suppressing the New Orleans rebels after a careful policy review in March 1769. Madrid dreaded a renewed French Louisiana that would be a sieve for contraband in the Gulf, and an outlet for spreading arms to Indians besetting New Spain's northern frontier settlements. France was not to be trusted, despite the formalities of Bourbon alliance. The conde de Aranda, presiding officer of the Council of Castile, emphasized the Mississippi's importance as a "natural barrier" and "indelible cordon" between British territory and Mexico. Unless retaken, New Orleans might even become a free port and the capital of a republic that would be a dangerous example to New Spain. With the monarchy's honor at stake, Carlos III chose Irish-born General Alejandro O'Reilly to lead an expedition from Cuba that would set matters aright.[42]

Lest France decide at the last moment to intercede on its former colonists' behalf, the Spanish court kept O'Reilly's punitive expedition a secret for as long as possible. Choiseul requested Spanish moderation after learning that Madrid was in the process of mounting a substantial invasion. This plea rang hollow since Louis XV's government had already acquiesced in Spanish reoccupation. Choiseul's expectations of invasion were curiously similar to English assessments of Louisiana affairs. If Spain acted too harshly, the minister warned that a majority of French colonials would migrate to British territory.[43]

Montfort Browne had no way of anticipating European decision making that determined Louisiana's fate. Writing to Hillsborough in February 1769, he observed vaingloriously that he could capture New Orleans with only five hundred men. This feat could be performed "without the loss of a Man" since the colony's "opulent" residents had no stronger wish than "becoming English Subjects" if allowed "the Free Enjoyment of their Religion." Browne admitted that Whitehall might find military intervention impractical. In any case, he still urged the establishment of a new provincial government along the British Mississippi, with its capital town built either by the Iberville or further north opposite Pointe Coupée.[44] A profiteering windfall beckoned. Browne glowingly recited a Louisiana encomium on the Mississippi Valley's peltry trade: "*C'est une mine abondante dont l'ouverture présente des richesses.*"[45]

Whitehall countenanced Browne's subterfuges if executed with proper discretion. In July 1769, Hillsborough instructed the lieutenant governor to "avoid all Appearance whatever" of instigating French colonial migration, but also advised him "not to refuse reasonable Protection to such persons, as may voluntarily and without Invitation come from New Orleans to West Florida."[46] Like other assertive provincial governors, Browne nudged Whitehall to approve steps he had already undertaken. Had he waited for explicit instructions to initiate Louisiana diplomacy, he would have lost the opportunity to shape the Mississippi frontier. His challenge was to move a step ahead of London without being rashly adventurist.

Headquartered in Pensacola, Browne relied on agents to carry out his designs toward Louisiana. John Campbell, a Pensacola merchant, journeyed up the Mississippi in the fall of 1769, conversing with numerous French residents who vowed hatred of Spain. While near Lake Pontchartrain, he administered British oaths of allegiance to eight men and one woman who collectively owned 1,140 cattle. He had no doubt that many Louisiana slaveholders—including individual planters with 130 to 150 blacks—would migrate to West Florida if British troops provided security upriver. In the competition for immigrants, officers of rival empires greatly valued the affluent, especially if the latter brought bond laborers with them. Campbell imagined the wealth of Louisiana—rice, indigo, cotton, tobacco, naval stores—falling into English hands. Besides, "we could easily secure to ourselves the whole Peltry and Fur Trades and those in my Opinion, are advantages infinitely Superior to the Spanish Mines. What a Barrier might we form Here, not only to protect and Secure North America, but on a proper Occasion, to Allarum [sic] and Annoy South America."[47]

On August 14, 1769, Browne was dumbstruck by news of a Spanish fleet's passage up the Mississippi River to New Orleans—a movement that had actually begun three weeks earlier. Relying on mistaken intelligence, he dashed off an alarming letter to General Gage. O'Reilly's force was said to number 4,500 regular troops, besides "600 free Negroes and Milattoes [sic]." This last point was grossly exaggerated. O'Reilly's 2,000 soldiers consisted mainly of Spanish regulars, along with Havana militia who indeed included whites, mulattos, and blacks. Browne appears intentionally to have raised the specter of a hostile black soldiery to provoke Gage to military countermeasures. He still expected a mass colonial migration of Acadians and German Louisianans to the British Mississippi.[48]

Browne was wrong. Rather than stirring a French exodus, O'Reilly strengthened Spanish authority through a mixture of fist and glove. While overseeing the trial of prominent rebels—five of whom were executed by firing squad—he offered royal clemency to the general colonial population on condition of absolute fealty.[49] The people, he proclaimed, had been "seduced by the intrigues of Ambitious, Fanatical, and badly intentioned men." Acadian and German settlers largely fell into line by taking a loyalty oath to Spain.[50] Learning of these events, Gage sent O'Reilly a message promising amicable Anglo-Spanish relations on the Mississippi. London alone would decide when wartime measures were in order.[51]

Some French colonials were indeed planning to move to British territory, but were unprepared for O'Reilly's rapid takeover and unbending resolve.⁵² James Jones, an English merchant in New Orleans, affirmed that insurgent leaders Lafrénière, Jean-Baptiste de Noyan, and several others intended to flee eastward, but were finally unable to escape: "The difficulties attending the enterprize on the one hand, and the hopes they were flattered with of a less rigorous fate on the other, kept them in a State of Suspence 'till it was too late!"⁵³

Besides the absence of British troops at upriver posts, other factors obstructed Browne's plan. The issue of Catholic rights under English rule remained uncertain despite the lieutenant governor's talk of religious toleration. In 1770, the Privy Council annulled a West Florida Assembly act of the previous year that would have allowed religious freedom and local self-governance to "all persons"—implicitly including Catholics—settling along the colony's Mississippi and western frontier.⁵⁴ The weight of British Protestant nationalism undermined this limited concession to potential Louisiana Catholic immigrants.

Under scrutiny for corruption, Montfort Browne was relieved of office and returned to England in 1770. Not one to halt, he continued to lobby for a new Mississippi colony, to promote immigration projects, and to amass West Florida landholdings, which he claimed amounted to 150,000 acres in 1775. All his gamesmanship proved idle adventurism in the absence of imperial support.⁵⁵

Although neither Britain nor Spain assumed an offensive military posture on the Louisiana-West Florida frontier, the possibility still existed that an international crisis could ignite regional hostilities. In late 1770, a genuine war scare erupted over the Spanish seizure of Port Egmont in the Falkland Islands (*Islas Malvinas*). On London's orders, Gage planned an invasion of Louisiana within a few months, but the operation was called off when the Spanish government acceded to British demands in the South Atlantic.⁵⁶ Though no military action resulted, the crisis is still revealing about English imperial thinking. A competent if risk-averse commander, Gage proposed a seaborne operation from New York City, supported by the Jamaica naval squadron and aimed at the Mississippi's main channel from the lower delta to New Orleans. He nixed the idea of a campaign launched from Fort Pitt down the Ohio and Mississippi because of possible Indian resistance along the way—a journey he calculated at 2,800 miles and three months in duration.⁵⁷ The continent's interior appeared foreclosed to English movement irrespective of naval supremacy.

Gage retained his interest in Louisiana well after the Falklands war scare had passed. In 1772, he appointed Lt. Thomas Hutchins, an engineer who had first surveyed the Mississippi six years before, to spy on the defenses of New Orleans. The lieutenant gathered a wealth of information through extensive conversations with hospitable Louisiana residents. From these discussions, he learned of creole dissatisfaction with Spanish commercial regulations, despite widespread respect for Governor Luis de Unzaga y Amezaga as a lenient and moderate man. Hutchins implied that Louisiana inhabitants would put up little opposition to a British wartime offensive, especially if executed in rapid fashion down the Mississippi.[58] His ideas of creole cooperativeness in an Anglo-Spanish clash proved a poor prediction of events during the American Revolutionary War, when Spain would be allied with France against Britain.

Indian Relations and Anglo-Spanish Competition

Hutchins gathered information not only from French colonials but also from Indian nations living in the Lower Mississippi Valley. He was not the first British officer to seek Indian geographic knowledge in the quest for imperial mastery.[59] Elias Durnford, West Florida lieutenant governor and a skilled military engineer, did so when he devised a new plan for a Mississippi-Gulf waterway via the small Iberville River and Lakes Maurepas and Pontchartrain. In 1770, he proposed digging a "cut" or trench in the Mississippi's east bank just above the Iberville, unleashing the great river's torrent into the bayou, and opening a reliable passage to the Gulf. In one sketch of the route, he interlined an historical note: "The Indians say that the course of the Mississippi towards the sea was formerly to the westward of the present Channel." Durnford took this to be good news because he believed the river was naturally shifting eastward toward Lakes Maurepas and Pontchartrain—thereby easing the British quest for their own Gulf-Mississippi passage.[60] This rather ingenious plan fell by the wayside since it failed to gain British military backing. Gage was skeptical of Durnford's motives as a provincial officeholder who could

(opposite) *A Map of Part of West Florida, from Pensacola to Mouth of the Iberville River, with a View to shew the proper Spot for a Settlement on the Mississipi* [sic], engraved by J. Lodge (*Gentleman's Magazine*, London, 1772). Courtesy of The Huntington Library, 105:394 S. This map is based on the plan of Elias Durnford, West Florida's lieutenant governor, who envisioned a colonial settlement above the Iberville that would overlook the strategic corridor between the Mississippi and the Gulf of Mexico.

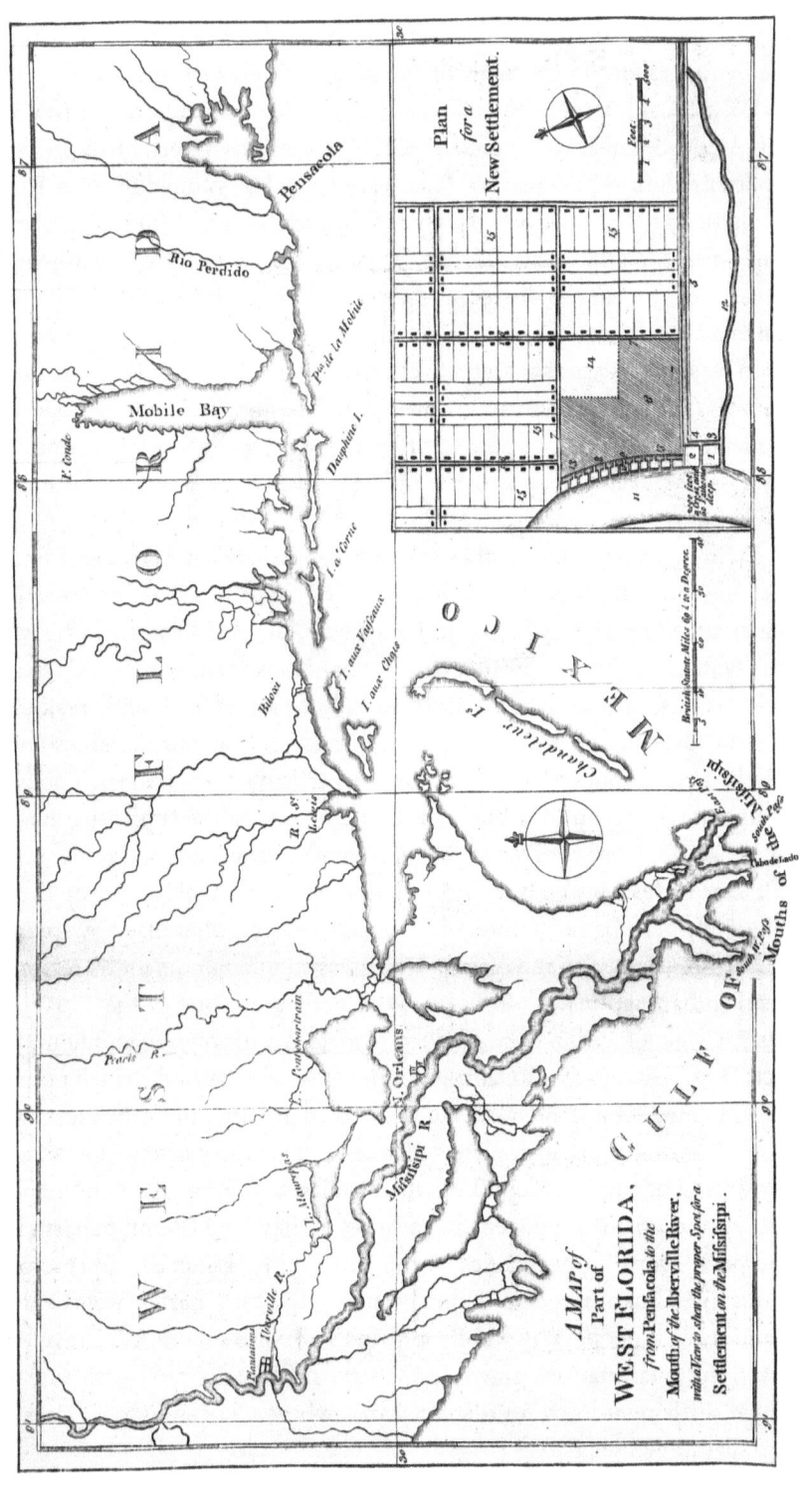

personally benefit from the canal project. He also nixed the proposal as ineffectual as long as the Spanish commanded New Orleans.[61]

West Florida's royal officers, who regarded Indian support as vital in any Anglo-Spanish war, bemoaned their incapacity to establish orderly frontier conditions. Governor Peter Chester, who assumed office at Pensacola in 1770, complained of white "vagabonds" and "Licentious Persons" intruding onto native lands for hunting and "building Houses and Huts."[62] Abuses in the deerskin trade were a major impediment to winning native friendship. Choctaw spokesmen resented traders who cheated them by selling flaps that scarcely covered their nakedness. Uncontrolled liquor sales were a continuous problem. One headman complained of the rum "that pours in upon our nation Like a great Sea from Mobile [sic]." Given such grievances, the Choctaws were scarcely committed to the British.[63]

Lt. John Thomas, tempestuous British Indian agent at Manchac, fumed that he could not restrain rum sellers, whose unbridled profiteering undercut his efforts to secure native allies. A diehard Protestant, he was hardly pleased that the profiteers in his bailiwick included John Fitzpatrick, an Irish Catholic, and Jacob Monsanto, a former Jewish resident of New Orleans. Thomas complained bitterly of "Roman Catholics Jews Hirelings &c.," but he ultimately lost his battle with the traders. Though killing one merchant in a brawl, he could not arrest the traffic that made Manchac a byword for freewheeling commerce and smuggling.[64]

Charles Descoudreaux, commandant at Spanish Manchac on the Iberville's southern bank, countered Thomas's frenetic diplomacy by spying on British maneuvers and distributing presents and honors to the region's small Indian nations. Thomas labeled his adversary one of the "Spanish French"—an officer in cahoots with Madrid for his own emolument. In fact, Descoudreaux was an adroit commander who battled British political influence even as he purchased gunpowder, guns, and other supplies from Manchac's Anglo traders.[65] Borderlands comity often superseded any notion of rigid borders. The small Indian nations were open to both British and Spanish inducements as long as they could hunt, fish, trade, and plant crops on both sides of the Mississippi. Latanash, a principal Tunica headman, rejected deputy superintendent Charles Stuart's demand that his people stay wholly within the British sphere. Within a few years, the small nations gravitated toward the Mississippi's west side as Anglo settlement grew on the east bank, where Choctaw-Creek clashes also threatened security.[66]

Intrigue assumed a major role in Indian-colonial relations when various sides had strong reasons to conceal their aims. In early 1772, John Stuart chided Choctaw chiefs for a recent visit paid to the Spanish at New Orleans. The headmen answered that they had gone to the city only at the urging of three Frenchmen whom they had known for years. In fact, two of the French interlocutors were now Spanish officers. Native leaders denied any double-dealing even as they cleverly leveraged New Orleans against Pensacola. Stuart himself played a divide-and-conquer strategy by declining to mediate a Choctaw-Creek peace, though Choctaw spokesmen wished him to do so. Hundreds were killed on each side of this fierce conflict from 1766 to 1777.[67]

Stuart rightly regarded the Creeks as the most powerful native group in the southern borderlands. Though not a single unified nation, the Creeks cooperated sufficiently amongst one another to stanch West Florida's movement up the Alabama and Coosa Rivers—the southern gateway to Upper Creek towns. Emistesguo, a principal Upper Creek leader, ceded little land to the British during negotiations at Pensacola in the fall of 1771. Escochabey of the Lower Creeks exasperated English officials by countenancing talks between his people and the Spanish at Havana. Stuart suspected conspiracy from commonplace contacts between the Lower Creeks and Cuban fishermen along the Florida coast.[68]

The continental balance of power evolving from the Seven Years War appeared so fragile that British agents as well as natives believed it vulnerable to sudden and violent eruptions. John Stuart's greatest fear was of a pan-Indian confederacy unifying the Shawnees, Cherokees, Creeks, and others against all English. Communications along these lines did develop, if not producing interregional union. Rumors and "talks" swirled from one Indian nation to another, taking wing across mountains and rivers until coming into earshot of crown officers and settlers. In September 1772, John McIntosh, commissary to the Chickasaws, reported Indian talk of an impending Cherokee war against the English, which would supposedly spark a Creek assault on Pensacola. The British, Spanish, and French would then war on each other—and "all the Red People is to be at Peace."[69]

Visions of native freedom ran against the reality of growing Indian dependence on British mercantile power across southeastern continental zones. For example, the Creeks suffered in late 1773 when Georgia's Anglo traders withdrew from their territory because of settler-Indian clashes. Lacking weaponry and munitions to fight the Choctaws, a Creek war party then headed to New Orleans to obtain desperately needed supplies. Choctaw fighters ambushed the Creeks, killing the Mortar, an old pro-French chief. Emisteseguo was himself wounded in this clash. John Stuart was glad the latter survived since he was a reliable if tough negotiator.[70] Governor Chester at Pensacola had a more cynical view. A peace between the Creeks and Choctaws would be "fatal to our back settlements." The conflict instead worked "to our great safety."[71]

Colonization and Commercial Inroads

In early 1770, there were so few settlers in the Natchez district that a small band of Choctaw warriors drove off nearly all whites and their slaves. In this instance, Indian hostility was little more than banditry aimed at seizing rum from a storehouse. Beleaguered whites took up arms for a few days, but then fled downriver and received General O'Reilly's succor in New Orleans.[72] Within four years of this episode, the British colonial presence in the Natchez-Manchac corridor was secure and rapidly growing. A turning point came in the summer of 1770 when a group of frontier folk reached Natchez from the Pennsylvania and Virginia backcountry by passage down the Ohio and Mississippi. These settlers included seventy-nine white men, women and children, and eighteen enslaved blacks. They came with farming tools, equipment for erecting mills, and seeds for planting wheat, corn, hemp, and flax. The pilot who guided the group downriver was so enthusiastic about their choice of land that he vowed to return to North Carolina and bring his family to the Mississippi.[73]

By 1772, Spanish authorities in Louisiana were so concerned about British Mississippi colonization that their reports triggered a policy review in Madrid. Alejandro O'Reilly, then in Spain, downplayed the threat since he regarded the settlement upsurge as impelled by private economic gain and not British imperial design. In fact, the issuance of Mississippi Valley land grants in Pensacola far outpaced actual settlement, which lagged behind speculative ambition. From August 1770 to November 1773 West Florida's provincial council issued grants totaling 957,567 acres, with nearly all acreage (99.8 percent) located along the Mississippi and nearby tributaries. Colonists obtained far more land by purchase than by "family right" allotted by household size. There was nothing comparable to the scope of Mississippi land purchases in any other region of the Floridas. An East Florida land boom flourished among the British aristocracy during the late 1760s, but diminished rapidly thereafter as it came to be realized that there was no sudden wealth to be gained from nominal holdings of swamplands.[74]

Thomas Gage was annoyed by news of the backcountry movement to the Mississippi Valley, which he sensed could hasten calls to reoccupy unhealthful and costly river garrisons. As he bluntly wrote Haldimand: "It is Somewhat Surprizing how the Avidity for Lands in a Country where there is so much, has tempted so many Familys to scramble thro' the Desart, to seek for Lands at the Natchés. I am determined not to take Post on the Mississippi under any Pretence, without the King's orders, tho' double the number of people should get down to the Natchés."[75] Gage made this declaration several months before the Falklands war scare, which did nothing to alter his opinion against fortifying the Mississippi in peacetime. Whitehall concurred on the garrison issue, but it was more open to Natchez settlement. In February 1771, Hillsborough authorized Chester to use certain funds to assist "those who become Adventurers in that Country."[76]

As colonial adventurers put in their stake for Mississippi lands, British and Anglo-American traders gained an increasing hold on the import-export trade of New Orleans. O'Reilly had intended quite otherwise when taking command of the city in 1769 and expelling virtually all British merchants, and a few suspected Jewish and French smugglers.[77] Foreigners had no lawful residency rights in the Indies, but they alas proved too vital to Louisiana's commerce to be kept out for long. When O'Reilly had to supply New Orleans, he turned to Oliver Pollock, native Irishman and former Pennsylvanian, who had just come to the Mississippi from Baltimore with a shipment of flour. Pollock had previously met O'Reilly in Cuba, and he sensed profit in serving Spanish military needs. Besides, he understood transnational commerce since he had engaged in the contraband trade for years with Havana as a factor for the Philadelphia firm of Willing and Morris. Pollock now shifted his business to New Orleans, and remained there even when other Anglo merchants were temporarily forced out. Within a few years, he was a slaveholder and trader in both Louisiana and West Florida. Besides owning land by the British Mississippi, he also managed plantations there for his Philadelphia associates. These activities presaged Pollock's role as foremost U.S. agent in the region during the Revolutionary War.[78]

British merchants flourished in New Orleans under Unzaga's generally permissive administration (1770–1776). When Bernard Romans, the noted geographer, was visiting the city in 1772, he took pride in hearing a French gentleman wryly admit that English traders were Louisiana's "little masters." Creole merchants competed in numerous ways, importing sugar and tafia, a low-grade rum, from Havana and underselling Anglos whenever possible. New Orleans shipowners persistently maneuvered to evade Spanish regulations prohibiting trade with the French West Indies and other foreign ports. The British reaped handsome profits in illicit traffic through their rapidly developing Atlantic and Caribbean connections to the Gulf Coast.[79] In 1773, one anonymous Briton, styling himself "R," felt so comfortable living and trading in New Orleans that he forwarded three lengthy articles to the New York *Gazette* boasting of commercial opportunities along the Gulf. The author was very probably Robert Ross, a Scottish migrant to West Florida, who typified that colony's elite merchants by owning a substantial tract along the British Mississippi while shifting business headquarters from Pensacola to New Orleans. Similar to others, he purchased Louisiana tobacco and indigo, and in turn sold slaves, British dry goods, and rum in Spanish territory.[80] "R" mused that New Orleans trade was so profitable that it was doubtful whether an English takeover of the city "would be of any real service, especially as in that Case the Spaniards would not in all Probability keep so many troops in Louisiana, nor send so many Dollars there."[81] Private adventurism in commerce could be a more lucrative business than conquest.

Not all British newcomers to Louisiana fared so well. Athanase de Mézières, commandant in Natchitoches, was a native Frenchman and a stalwart Spanish officer who demanded that four English residents convert to Catholicism or be expelled from the community. Two of the four men abjured their faith on this condition.[82]

British enterprise grew in the Gulf region, notwithstanding parliamentary restrictions prescribed in the Navigation Acts. For example, West Florida naval stores found a market in New Orleans even though they were supposed to be exported to England alone. Official attitudes toward contraband depended on where profit was directed. Elias Durnford deplored the shipment of furs from the British Mississippi to New Orleans, but personally concocted an abortive scheme to spy on Veracruz and to open trade with "the Spanish Main."[83]

Madrid was adamant about stopping the flow of contraband into Mexico by land or sea. Spanish imperial regulations prohibited commerce between the crown's subjects in Louisiana and those in neighboring Texas or elsewhere in New Spain. Only a licensed Indian trade met royal approval across the sparsely colonized Louisiana-Texas frontier.[84] Spanish-speaking settlers in Texas were considered corruptible if living too close to French Louisianans, especially Natchitoches traders selling guns and goods to westerly Indians in exchange for cattle and horses. Texas colonists customarily joined illicit trading networks with the Caddos, Wichitas, and other Indian peoples. In 1772, Madrid attempted to cut the chain of contraband by ordering East Texas settlers to remove far from their frontier homeland to San Antonio. The evacuees lobbied crown officials for redress; many of the dispossessed made their way homeward by the decade's end.[85] Spanish borderlands policy had its rigors but also a humane side, as shown by O'Reilly's prohibition of Louisiana's Indian slave trade. This measure certainly reduced that traffic but without stopping it.[86]

West Florida on the Eve of the American Revolution

Interest in Mississippi colonization germinated from New England to the Carolinas in the early 1770s, reflecting tendencies evident since the end of the Seven Years War. After withstanding imperial indifference for years in London, General Phineas Lyman of Connecticut finally received a West Florida royal grant of 20,000 acres in 1770. Still, this achievement was but a partial victory, since the general gained far less acreage than he desired—and without any express rights for shareholders in the Company of Military Adventurers he represented.[87] With his eye on the main chance, Lyman continually lobbied crown officials to heed his project's practicality and its imperial importance. In one heady projection of 1766, he claimed that journeying up the Mississippi from the Gulf to Natchez should prove no more difficult than moving up the Hudson from New York City to Albany! Such booster talk was intended to convince the British ministry that Natchez would be a ready market for British manufactures as well as a strategic locale for countering French and Spanish influence.[88] Though wary of "Hot Climates" from his wartime experience in Cuba, Lyman persuaded himself that Natchez was quite healthful after the Illinois country was foreclosed to settlement by the proclamation of 1763. In the process he accepted the idea of colonizing the Lower Mississippi Valley where settlers would be both slaveholders and sentinels of empire. In 1770, he wrote the Board of Trade that his family was worthy of special favor because of "the insults & Losses the settlers will be exposed to suffer from . . . the Spaniards at New Orleans either by their influence on the Indians, by the breaking out of war, or by encouraging the slaves to desert."[89]

After Lyman returned to New England in 1772, several of his closest associates voyaged to Pensacola to request provincial township grants and to scout the Mississippi for themselves. The adventurers included Colonel Israel Putnam—later of Revolutionary War fame—cousin Rufus Putnam, and Thaddeus Lyman, the general's trusted son. Peter Chester cheerfully welcomed the group in March 1773. The New Englanders were precisely the kind of respectable folk that the governor favored as colonists.[90] The adventurers next set out for the Mississippi, where they marveled at all that was new to them. They paid particular regard to the countenances of French colonists, simply to assure themselves that the latter looked healthy. The upriver journey reached a northern point at the Yazoo, where a Choctaw warrior warned the visitors to stay to the south. The New Englanders pledged compliance. The following year, a group of Yankee adventurers and family members (absent the Putnams) settled by the Big Black River and Bayou Pierre.[91]

Besides hosting New Englanders, Chester was pleased by other gentlemen arriving at Pensacola as a prelude to Mississippi settlement. In April 1773, Reverend Samuel Swayze, of New Jersey, secured a provincial grant of 25,000 acres in the Natchez district on his pledge of bringing "a great Number of Families from the Northward." The Swayze grant, though unconfirmed by the crown, provided the foundation for the Natchez's "Jersey settlement," initially consisting of a several white families and their slaves.[92] Several southern slaveholders meanwhile made their way to the Mississippi, evidently coming via the Ohio River rather than by sea. One Virginia newcomer had over eighty slaves.[93] George Washington seriously considered acquiring West Florida lands in 1773, telling his scout to look for Mississippi acreage that was sufficiently high up the river to be temperate in climate and still within navigable reach of the Gulf. He begged off after his agent found that such choice lands were "already engaged" by emigrants.[94]

The prospect of steady Mississippi colonization was suddenly eclipsed by Whitehall's movement to a more restrictive North American colonial policy. On April 7, 1773, his Britannic Majesty ordered several provincial governors, including West Florida's, to cease making land grants until further notice. The Privy Council also suspended gubernatorial licenses to individual persons for purchasing Indian lands. The Earl of Dartmouth, a leading figure behind these measures, took an unequivocal stance against the "dangerous spirit of unlicensed emigration into the interior parts of America." Unchecked colonization posed a host of problems from an imperial perspective—troubled Indian relations, excessive transatlantic migration by British and Irish laboring folk, and the movement of colonials beyond the reach of law and the mother country's manufactures. Imperial policy not only crimped West Florida, but also turned aside major trans-Appalachian colonizing projects initiated by Anglo-American land companies.[95]

Although Thomas Gage had criticized colonial expansionism for years, he was taken aback by the restrictive measures applied to West Florida. Most significantly, he questioned stanching the British Mississippi's growth, since numerous settlers in that quarter would help seize New Orleans in a war. Sensing a loss of control on the Atlantic seaboard, Gage briefly adopted a provincial perspective—as if he were speaking for Montfort Browne, Elias Durnford, Peter Chester, and others. These second thoughts came too late to change the drift of affairs.[96]

A tightened imperial policy cut short the West Florida government's plan to dispense immense land grants to petitioners pledging to bring colonists to the Mississippi. The order especially disconcerted individuals who had already received provisional permission at Pensacola, but were now unable to bring their claims to fruition. Lt. Thomas Hutchins had no opportunity to test his scheme of settling Pennsylvania farm families on a pending 25,000-acre grant in the Natchez district. Connecticut's Company of Military Adventurers sent only small groups of settlers to the Mississippi rather than the great numbers Phineas Lyman and others envisioned. The general himself established a plantation at Bayou Pierre, but caught a fever during his first summer and died there on September 10, 1774. The dreaded hot clime claimed him at age fifty-nine. The Mississippi exacted a heavy toll on New Englanders, young and full-grown, in the next few years.[97] There was no guarantee that colonial sponsors would be able to realize their settlement plans in a remote and disease-prone environment even if blessed with the king's imprimatur.

West Florida leaders wanted orderly settlement, and not an uncontrolled influx of lawless frontier folk. During the summer of 1773, Chester was shocked by the murder of three French Louisiana peltry traders and their two slaves by Anglo renegades crossing the river from British to Spanish territory. Putting aside any element of imperial rivalry, he pledged his cooperation to Governor Unzaga in apprehending the malefactors. Without British troops on the Mississippi, Chester relied on Natchez's leading men to hunt down the criminals and dispatch them to Pensacola for justice.[98] George Urquhart, a wealthy Mississippi planter, linked the murders to the chaos unleashed by North Carolina's Regulator movement in 1771. "Since the late Chastisement" suffered by the "Banditti" of Carolina, "they have poured themselves down this River like the Stream which carries them; it is to awe such [men] Sir, that some Military force is now become Absolutely Necessary."[99]

West Florida authorities vied to gain imperial attention as political tensions escalated in Britain's Atlantic colonies. Lobbying Whitehall in 1774, Chester forwarded a lieutenant's report urging that the British Mississippi be an outlet for loyal settlers from disaffected provinces. In case of war with Spain, "Our whole Force in North America might, thro' this Channel, most opportunely be let loose on South or Spanish America, whilst our Ships of War in Pensacola Harbour would be most advantageously Situated to intercept their Galleons." In the fall of 1775, Chester vainly advocated a massive imperial effort to transport loyal subjects by sea to his colony. He had already shown his personal contempt for American rebels by refusing to publish a friendly letter from the First Continental Congress to West Florida inhabitants.[100]

West Florida stirred the ambitions of Britons and Anglo-Americans of diverse social ranks—from ordinary men who obtained a few hundred acres of land to grand projectors with schemes of introducing hundreds of colonists from New England, Pennsylvania and New Jersey, or Protestant Europe. Prior to the Revolution, the colony's leading magistrates ardently pushed the cause of population growth and economic development—and avidly obtained their own personal stake in Mississippi lands during their tenure, and even thereafter. For more than a decade, they persistently pleaded with London to invest in the colony for strategic purposes, initially to counteract any resurgence of French power and thereafter to strengthen Britain's position in a future war with Spain.

Ultimately, Whitehall attached less importance to the colony's growth than restraining expenditures by withdrawing Mississippi garrisons, and later declining to reoccupy those sites even when settlement grew substantially in the region. The crown halted work on the Iberville canal project and rejected the idea of establishing a new provincial jurisdiction on the Mississippi. The imperial government's most obvious inconsistency was to tolerate a permissive and loosely controlled land grant system for years before imposing restrictions in 1773–1774. In effect, Great Britain limited its own stake in the West Florida frontier, thereby unwittingly giving Spain some room to exploit English vulnerability during the War of American Independence.

CHAPTER 3

Opening Salvos in a Revolutionary War, 1776–1779

The conde de Aranda, Spanish ambassador at Paris from 1773 to 1787, was a brilliant observer of international affairs. While viewing the outbreak of the American Revolutionary War as a boon to the Bourbon powers, he also looked at events with sober realism. On July 24, 1775, he informed his government that Spain could take little comfort no matter which side prevailed in the conflict. If Britain restored its rule, it would employ Florida as a base to conquer Louisiana and open the portals to Mexico. If the Americans succeeded, they would expand toward the same region, "by a communication via lakes and rivers that they already hold and annex, by the advantages of soil and climate, [and] by . . . the ease of continental commerce that could not possibly be hidden from their future attention."[1]

Aranda did not arrive at a sudden answer to the North American crisis, but he became convinced that Spain could not be a bystander to events. By 1777 he argued that Madrid should forswear neutrality, accede to French entreaties for war against Britain, and enter an alliance with the United States that would restrain future Anglo-American expansionism.[2] The Spanish court rejected, however, any precipitous movement into a war exposing its own American dominions to British maritime assault. Madrid instead lent material aid to the rebellious English colonies, but without any binding political commitment. When Spain at last joined the war in 1779, it did so as an ally of France. No treaty with the American confederation was forthcoming.[3]

The Spanish approach to the United States was a recipe for intrigue since it licensed aid outside any formal diplomatic accord. Americans in turn assumed the guise of supplicants and schemers—men hungering for Spanish assistance while coveting the same British Gulf ports and Mississippi corridor over which Madrid desired exclusive control. The seeds of competition were not far below the surface even when Spain's officers collaborated with American revolutionaries against British colonialism.[4]

Absent a clear U.S. national agenda, individual citizens and states vied to shape American policy toward the region. Among the key players were George Morgan and James Willing of Philadelphia, Patrick Henry of Virginia, and Oliver Pollock of New Orleans. All had forged connections to the Mississippi or West Florida before the Revolution. These men broke with the British realm politically while building on an adventurist spirit that galvanized both American Whigs and Loyalists.

From the Ohio to New Orleans

During the summer of 1776, Captain George Gibson and about twenty fellow Virginian militiamen made a river passage of nearly 2,000 miles from Fort Pitt to New Orleans. The soldiers hoisted "Rebel Colours" as they passed Natchez and cheered American liberty before startled Anglo settlers.[5] After a friendly stay in New Orleans, most of the American party returned upriver with 10,000 pounds of Spanish gunpowder for Virginia's frontier defense. Oliver Pollock, British subject turned U.S. agent, financed this transaction with Governor Unzaga's tacit consent. He also provided a ship for Captain Gibson to send news, along with a supply of gunpowder, to Robert Morris, his Philadelphia associate and a powerhouse in Congress.[6] Pollock's choice of allegiance was a calculated risk, strengthening his New Orleans and Philadelphia connections, but jeopardizing his business with Pensacola and his West Florida landholdings. Personal pride was also at stake. During the summer of 1776, a British warship seized one of Pollock's ships on the Mississippi for carrying goods allegedly bound for American armies. Finding no satisfaction at Pensacola, Pollock heralded "the glorious Cause" and scorned the British Loyalists of New Orleans who damned him as a traitor.[7]

Virginia's first gambit to Louisiana was itself audacious since it originated in May 1776, weeks before the Declaration of Independence was issued. The Old Dominion's Committee of Safety dispatched Captain Gibson with the aim of conquest, and not simply supply routes in mind. While in New Orleans, the captain presented Unzaga with Virginia's proposal for an American invasion of British West Florida in the spring of 1777. According to plan, the expeditionary force would descend the Mississippi, dislodge the English from Manchac, and then move against Mobile and Pensacola. Gibson subsequently put two crucial questions in writing for Unzaga. First, he asked if Spain would approve the American capture of Pensacola—and second if his Catholic Majesty would "receive possession" of that town and harbor from the conquering force.⁸

Virginia's Committee of Safety did not disclose its full hand when sketching the outline of a Gulf Coast offensive. Pensacola was a prize that might be transferred to Spain for unstated concessions—perhaps the American right to navigate the Mississippi and commercial access to Gulf ports.⁹ The notion of transfer was not necessarily a gift, but more likely a quid pro quo. Even if American forces captured Pensacola, they could certainly not hold it without Spanish assistance against British naval power. Virginia's leaders were as keen on commerce as conquest. As they plotted the Gibson mission, they enlisted General Charles Lee, former English political radical and now second-in-command of the Continental Army, to write Louisiana's governor of the American desire for trade with Spanish dominions. This request came with cautionary advice. If the colonies were vanquished, Britain would invariably employ Anglo-American manpower for the invasion of Cuba and Mexico.¹⁰

Unzaga sorted out Lee's message, handed him by Gibson, just as he weighed Virginia's overtures about attacking British West Florida. Communicating this whirlwind of news to Havana and Madrid, the governor was disturbed by the idea of a sudden American military descent from the Mississippi to the Gulf. He had no way of knowing the peculiarities of "the United American States" (*Estados Unidos Americanos*), a newfangled country with a fledgling government. In fact, Congress held no formal discussion of Virginia's proposals to Louisiana. Washington's correspondence gives no hint of a projected Mississippi offensive when his small army was struggling to survive the fall of New York City. Captain Gibson, far removed from the epicenter of war, told Unzaga with no small exaggeration of 80,000 continental troops, with an additional 130,000 provincial soldiers in support.¹¹

Unzaga replied courteously to General Lee while indicating that decisions regarding Spanish commercial policy lay beyond his authority. He similarly awaited royal instructions on Virginia's projections of a Mississippi-Gulf offensive.¹² On December 24, 1776, José de Gálvez, minister of the Indies, sent word that arms, munitions, clothing, and quinine were to be shipped from Havana to New Orleans for American use. Private traders were to fulfill this mission in order to conceal the crown's involvement. (The Spanish government had already pledged one million *livres* to the French operation of transporting war materiel to the

United States.) In principle, Gálvez favored the American capture of the British Mississippi and Pensacola, though he indicated that Spain should stay at arm's length from any such business until the colonies achieved independence. Madrid was desirous of weakening Britain but dared not prematurely enter the war.[13]

José de Gálvez regarded Louisiana as sufficiently important to appoint his beloved and trusted nephew Bernardo to replace Unzaga. The younger Gálvez, a spirited man of thirty years, enthusiastically embraced the policy of abetting the American rebellion after arriving in Louisiana in late 1776. By the next spring, Oliver Pollock wrote Robert Morris that Gálvez was ready to open commerce with American vessels and even to permit New Orleans to become a venue for the sale of British prizes by U.S. privateers and cruisers. Pollock eagerly anticipated Spanish cooperation in American intrigues. As he told Morris: "The more Mischief the better Sport." Pleased by this report, Morris's commerce committee formally confirmed Pollock's role as U.S. agent.[14]

British military weakness on the Mississippi was the essential precondition to Spanish-U.S. regional cooperation. No English soldiers had garrisoned the river since 1768. Ensconced in Pensacola, Governor Peter Chester protested in vain to Unzaga against the upriver shipment of supplies to American forces. In September 1776, royal troops at Pensacola and Mobile numbered fewer than 500—including soldiers too sick for duty. Moreover, Whitehall instructed Chester to avoid any conflict with the Spanish that might broaden the war.[15]

Indian Allegiance, the Gulf Ports, and American Designs

George Germain, royal war minister, was little troubled by the irritant of American-Spanish collusion on the peripheral Louisiana-Florida frontier. A rebel invasion down the Mississippi seemed improbable. Germain reassured Pensacola that Britain's Indian allies were alone a sufficient guard against the enemy. The natives, in his view, were "in solemn League to oppose any encroachments upon their hunting Grounds and, and in support of His Majesty's Government." The Choctaws would "watch over the Navigation of the Mississippi. . . . The Chickasaws were always faithful . . . and the Cherokees have given full proof of their Enmity to the Rebels, nor will the Creeks be less disposed to attack them."[16] These words, tossed off rather cavalierly, assumed a depth of native support for the crown beyond what then existed.

Superintendent John Stuart formed ambitious plans of British-Indian military operations in the war's early stages. While proposing Mobile as a site for a joint offensive into the Georgia and Carolina backcountry, he had even greater hopes for Pensacola because of its deep-water bay. As early as October 1775, he envisioned West Florida's capital as a primary supply post, diplomatic center, and military depot for British-Indian alliances from the Gulf to the southern Appalachians and westward to the Mississippi. His strategy of 1776 was linked to a new negotiating posture aimed at building "a coalition of all the Indian tribes" throughout the region. This policy discarded the longstanding British stance of either stoking or tolerating Creek-Choctaw rivalry. Old habits had to be cast aside to defeat the American rebellion.[17]

Though Stuart imagined a broad British-Indian alliance, his plan fell victim to events beyond his control. Arriving at Pensacola in late July 1776, he soon received disturbing reports from the north. Frontier militia of Virginia and the Carolinas were devastating the Cherokee country. By early 1777, two hundred Cherokee refugees had fled all the way to Pensacola for safety. Stuart glumly shelved the idea of a grand offensive.[18]

Southern Indian peoples had a growing dread of American military advances during the summer of 1776. Charles Stuart, agent to the Choctaws, relayed that "the Virginians"—a name southern Indians generally used for Anglo colonists—"have sent a Talk into the Chickasaw Nation that they are coming so thick that they are like the Trees in the Woods and their Intention is to take Mobile." Emisteseguo of the Upper Creeks heard from a Georgia Indian agent that 7,000 American militia—an exaggerated figure—were at war with the Cherokees. If the Creeks sided with the Cherokees, it was said that "the Carolinians and Georgians will send an Army under General [Charles] Lee to Cut of[f] their Nations and march against West Florida to take Pensacola." Emisteseguo pleaded his people's need for British ammunition, presents, and advice.[19] Indians cared deeply about control of the Gulf ports, where they had perhaps even more at stake than imperial contestants.

In mid-November 1776, Emisteseguo directly addressed the issue of maritime-interior supply in talks with British agents. He urged an open path between "the Great king" George and the Creeks: "I know that St. Augustine, Pensacola, and Mobile are the places from which we may expect assistance, and should the Virginians get possession of these places we are ruined." Emisteseguo was a shrewd geopolitical analyst whose words were echoed by British Indian agents eager for an aggressive imperial stance.[20] Though the Creeks often complained of abusive British traders, they shuddered at the idea that a hostile power might seize the places where so many necessary articles arrived from across the sea. A more immediate problem arose from uncontrolled liquor sales in Indian country. Stuart informed London that 30,000 gallons of rum shipped to Pensacola had been totally consumed in just three months. As a result, the Indians "are poor, wretched, naked, and discontented."[21]

The American Congress outlined an ambitious agenda when pressing for a French alliance in the last days of 1776. Meeting in Baltimore at some distance from the battlefront, the delegates offered to assist Louis XVI in the conquest of the British West Indies—the islands to become the sole property of "his most Christian Majesty." Other ventures with France were contemplated against Nova Scotia, Cape Breton Island, and Newfoundland.[22] Outlining instructions for its European envoys, Congress concurrently made its first serious bid for a Spanish alliance. Should his Catholic Majesty Carlos III join the war against Britain, American troops would fight to bring Pensacola under Spanish possession, "*provided the citizens and inhabitants of the United States shall have the free and uninterrupted navigation of the Mississippi and use of the harbour of Pensacola.*" In a gesture of good will, Congress stated its willingness to declare war on Portugal, then in conflict with Spain over the Brazilian–Río de la Plata frontier.[23]

The terms for a Spanish treaty were similar to Virginia's previous propositions in New Orleans. Some congressional delegates clearly knew of the Gibson mission through Robert Morris—and the latter's communications with Pollock. U.S. diplomacy directly linked commercial access to the Florida Gulf Coast to the use of the Mississippi. Pensacola might be suitably transferred to Spain—as long as its harbor remained open to American shipping. While struggling to keep a small army in the field, Congress still imagined a future in which the United States absorbed Britain's maritime gains from the peace of 1763. To most delegates, these expectations included free navigation of the Mississippi.[24]

The revival of American military fortunes by the spring of 1777 brought a new plan for a Gulf Coast offensive mounted from the Ohio country. The author was Colonel George Morgan, Philadelphia merchant and U.S. Indian agent at Fort Pitt, who had great interest in the trans-Appalachian West. He had first journeyed to the Mississippi in 1766 as a partner in the Illinois Company, in which Benjamin and William Franklin were leading lights. Within a few years he was a major shareholder in the Indiana Company, a speculative firm claiming a vast area on Virginia's western perimeter below the Ohio.[25] When joining the revolutionary cause, Morgan worked under continental and not state auspices. Indeed, he was embroiled in a heated legal battle with Virginia over his Indiana Company claims, which that state staunchly opposed.[26]

Morgan was a gifted and versatile man who moved freely between Philadelphia's Philosophical Society, his ample farm near Princeton, New Jersey, and the Ohio country's native villages. As a biographer has observed, he had "a supreme confidence in his own opinions" and did not flinch from opposing frontiersmen who clamored for a more bellicose Indian policy than he thought politic.[27] His grand aim was to develop American trade routes supplanting the British from the Great Lakes to the Gulf. Morgan's plans had an adventurist core as much as Pollock's endeavors at New Orleans. Private mercantile pursuits and profiteering overlapped with nationalistic military strategy.

Acting in advance of congressional authorization, Colonel Morgan made his case by letter to Louisiana's governor, an officer he did not address by name. Introducing himself as "Representative" of "the United American States" in "this Quarter," he extolled recent victories at Trenton and Princeton: "America cannot be conquered even by 50,000 Troops. By Caution & delays we shall overcome & establish our Empire. This & the Treaties of Friendship & Commerce between Spain, France, & America will overthrow Great Britain—for a Reconciliation is out of the Question."[28] Empire—and not mere nationhood—was the goal.

Morgan's observations led to his main inquiry. Would the Spanish governor permit an American army, estimated at 1,000 men, to descend the Mississippi and to procure vessels and cannon at New Orleans for an assault on Mobile and Pensacola? Morgan offered to pay well for intelligence on British Gulf Coast fortifications and naval strength. He adroitly made his case for U.S.-Spanish commercial cooperation even if Louisiana's governor would not permit an American army passing through his province. "But if this liberty [for supplying a campaign] cannot be obtained, we flatter ourselves we shall be indulged in a free trade from hence [Fort Pitt] to New Orleans."[29]

Although Morgan requested Louisiana's governor to contact him by express, Bernardo de Gálvez chose not to reply until August 1777—nearly four months after Morgan wrote, and weeks after the latter's entreaty arrived. Though outwardly welcoming an American expedition, Gálvez explained that his government could not lend direct aid. He instead encouraged Morgan to advance his campaign through an unnamed agent—Oliver Pollock by inference. Gálvez kept his options open given the unforeseen consequences of a foreign army, however friendly in theory, descending the Mississippi for an attack on British territory. He meanwhile surreptitiously channeled supplies to U.S. forces in the Ohio Valley.[30] His aim was to enhance Spanish influence rather than to enter a binding alliance.

Morgan's project itself smacked of intrigue because it was sold quite differently to New Orleans than to Philadelphia. By letter to Gálvez, Morgan stated the limited objective of assailing Pensacola and Mobile, but not occupying either port. His principal aim was pillage—to "bring off the Stores" from enemy forts and to "destroy their Works." Addressing the Board of War in late June 1777, Morgan clearly stated his preference to keep Pensacola, Mobile, and nearby territory—and *not* to give the ports to the Spaniards "as an Equivalent for Services" rendered the United States. Gálvez would have been most upset by this opinion, since he had no desire to see American interlopers ensconced in Pensacola and Mobile in any permanent sense.[31]

Morgan aspired to line his pockets as military supply agent for the Gulf campaign, in which American soldiers were to receive Mississippi land bounties as "an irresistible Inducement" for military service. In the process, the rank and file could lay claim to the soil granted as "Manors" to "Nobles and Gentlemen in England."[32] Of middling class birth, Morgan infused his scheme with revolutionary fervor even as he hungered after a fortune.

Morgan's plan had its mercenary aspects but it was not mere opportunism. The Revolutionary War could not be won by patriotic appeals without harnessing self-interest to the cause. The Continental Army's transatlantic supply functioned through high-risk dealing between American seaboard merchants and Caribbean and European traders of diverse nationalities. U.S.-Spanish commercial ties depended on collaborative diplomacy and mutual self-interest. Arthur Lee, emissary to Spain, scored a breakthrough in 1777 when the marqués de Grimaldi introduced him to Diego María de Gardoqui y Arriquibar, a Bilbao merchant whose firm became his country's foremost supplier of war materiel and provisions to the United States.[33]

On July 10, 1777, the Board of War recommended a Mississippi River expedition for the capture of Pensacola and Mobile. Interestingly, General Benedict Arnold, himself a New Haven merchant, wrote in favor of a West Florida campaign, predicting that capturing the Gulf ports "will open a door for a very considerable & lucrative Trade, with the Spaniard[s] & Indians." The Board authorized Morgan, pending congressional approval, to journey to New Orleans "with Power to negotiate with the Governor of that Place, and endeavour to gain his Interest and assistance in the Business."[34] This charge was open-ended and suggestive of large purposes.

Philadelphia merchants and their associates backed the proposal in Congress. So did the Old Dominion's representatives with their keen interest in the Mississippi, territorial expansion, and the export of backcountry produce. Benjamin Harrison of Virginia, who was Robert Morris's partner in the tobacco trade, supported Morgan's venture. James Wilson of Pennsylvania contended that opening the Mississippi trade would be worthwhile even if Pensacola and Mobile were not captured.[35] Remarkably, some delegates had an eye on the distant Gulf Coast even as Burgoyne's army was yet advancing toward Albany and General Howe was embarking 14,000 men from New York harbor to the Chesapeake.

Congressional skepticism finally undid the idea of a Mississippi campaign. Henry Laurens of South Carolina led the charge against Morgan's plan, which he believed militarily unfeasible and unwarranted in light of Georgia's defensive needs. Self-interest doubtless swayed these remarks. Since Laurens had invested heavily in East Florida before the war, he set his sights on the capture of St. Augustine rather than Pensacola. Moreover, he scoffed at the idea of U.S.-Spanish coordination at Havana. Confiding his suspicions to fellow Carolinian John Rutledge, he remarked that "the vulgar Spaniard for a little Gold would convey intelligence in a very few hours" to the British navy at Jamaica.[36] These jaundiced remarks not only expressed personal prejudice but also more widespread doubts about the compatibility of U.S. and Spanish interests. For example, Thomas Burke of North Carolina argued against Gulf Coast conquests that would fall into Spanish hands.[37] The prospect of a Mississippi offensive raised international issues that Congress had not yet clearly resolved.

Bernardo de Gálvez—Reversing the Treaty of 1763

Congress would not have seriously considered a Gulf Coast campaign without favorable reports from New Orleans. There was good cause for optimism. On April 17, 1777, Bernardo de Gálvez ended business as usual on the Mississippi by ordering the seizure of eleven British merchant vessels involved in customary illicit trade with Louisiana. Having arrested the ships' officers and crewmen, he issued a proclamation giving British subjects fifteen days to depart the colony, and ordering inhabitants not to receive foreign visitors without permission. Being careful to justify his actions, he cited the need to curtail smuggling and to retaliate against the recent British naval seizure of a Louisiana schooner and two canoes on Lake Pontchartrain.[38]

Having but modest military force, Gálvez relied on subterfuge and bluff, parrying British protests with rhetorical outrage, sharp aphorisms, and legalistic rejoinders. He was not averse to gross denial, either. He claimed to be neutral between English royalists and rebels, though he allowed two shipmasters of American allegiance to recoup confiscated vessels, apparently after a payment. Both men subsequently became privateers on the Mississippi in league with Oliver Pollock.[39] When English naval captain Thomas Lloyd accused Gálvez of conspiring with Pollock, the governor admitted knowing the latter, "but in no other Character than an honest Merchant a Native of Ireland."[40] Was this reference to Pollock's Irish ancestry a jibe at the British Empire? Quite likely, it would seem. Captain Lloyd bristled at news that a rebel vessel had recently saluted the Spanish garrison at New Orleans while flying "an American Jack at her mizzen Topmast head."[41]

Gálvez's seizure of British merchantmen deliberately redefined the Treaty of Paris of 1763 in Spain's favor. For more than a decade, Anglo ship captains had evaded Madrid's fiat by exploiting the Mississippi as a trading artery with Louisiana. The British right of "free navigation" on the great river was a boon to foreign domination of the New Orleans market. Spanish imperial sovereignty seemed a shadow—barely visible to venturous British and Anglo-American importers who placed their ships as floating warehouses open to business. Gálvez's sudden shattering of the norm brought a storm of protest from Pensacola. The Spanish governor held fast. Contraband was not legitimate no matter if previously practiced. As Gálvez replied to British critics, "Custom has the Force of Law, but abuse does not" (*La costumbre tiene fuerza de Ley, pero no el abuso*).[42]

Besides international law, physical and geographic circumstances had a place in British-Spanish contention. Because of the Mississippi's varying currents and winds buffeting the area, ships could seldom take a straightforward passage northward. As one Englishman commented, vessels necessarily used ropes to "make fast to the trees on the banks, and haul close" as they navigated, being unable to anchor because of the river's muddy bottom. Because pilots had to beware of logs and other debris obstructing their path, their success often required warping between opposite banks. The river trade that flourished in this manner could be easily arrested if Spanish officers boarded vessels "hauling close" to shorelines. The most critical area for British ships was the zone where the river passed entirely between Spanish territory: 105 miles from the Balize near the river's mouth to New Orleans and then another 100 miles to the Iberville, where the east bank at last was under English control.[43]

Gálvez struck at British traffic at a time when his government was moving closer to France. Soon after assuming office, he published a royal edict allowing the export of Louisiana produce and lumber to the French Caribbean. Moreover, Gálvez liberally interpreted his instructions by permitting French merchants to make purchases in Louisiana with slaves and goods, which were supposed to be imported by Spanish subjects alone. He cooperated fully with Captain Favre Daunnoy, authorized by Versailles to facilitate Louisiana-Caribbean commerce in New Orleans.[44] Governor Chester and his council vainly protested that international treaties entitled British merchants to privileges bestowed on the French.[45]

The British insistence on treaty rights irked Gálvez, who upheld Spanish national honor with a simple acclamation: Carlos III was responsible to God alone in deciding what commercial privileges he extended to foreigners in his overseas dominions.[46] Gálvez was fortunate in his timing. His seizure of British merchantmen occurred ten days before an English war sloop sailed up the Mississippi and hovered about New Orleans. Within a few months, the governor released imprisoned British crewmen, but not until confiscating most of the owners' ships, cargo, and slaves for the benefit of the Spanish crown. English merchants resumed business in New Orleans, though their peace would not go undisturbed for long.[47]

Willing's Mississippi Raid

When an American military foray finally went ahead against British West Florida in early 1778, it came about through Robert Morris's commerce committee rather than Congress as a whole. In fact, the committee entrusted the task to Captain James Willing, the younger brother of Morris's business partner. This episode again reveals the link between the prewar era and the Revolution. James Willing had first journeyed to Natchez in late 1771 as a young agent for his brother's firm. Collaborating with Oliver Pollock, he applied for a contract to supply Pennsylvania flour to British troops in West Florida. The newcomer was no rebel at this point, but rather an ambitious colonist bemoaning the lack of royal military protection on the Mississippi.[48]

Just a few years later, James Willing's politics were of an entirely different character. Departing West Florida for Philadelphia in 1777, he carried grievances against Mississippi Tories and other personal rivals. When he next set foot in Natchez on February 19, 1778, he came as a revolutionary marauder plundering Loyalists and all others who stood in his way.[49] Though sanctioned by Congress, Willing's enterprise blurred any recognizable line between lawful warfare, profiteering, and downright rapacity.

American adventurism toward the Gulf and Mississippi combined commercial goals of opening markets with predatory wartime blows at enemy resources. In early 1777, Robert Morris outlined a Caribbean and Gulf Coast offensive to John Paul Jones, then an impetuous junior-ranking naval captain. According to plan, Jones and a small flotilla would prey on British Caribbean ports, harass Pensacola, and then move westward. Morris advised that American ships "Wear English Colours" when entering the Mississippi—so as to deceive the enemy. Prizes were aplenty if all went right: "There is at this time not less than £100,000 Sterlg. Value in goods up that River . . . in Indi[g]o, Rice, Tob[acco], Skins & Furs." Pillage had a political value. Morris wished to humble the British by "disturbing their Settlements & spreading alarms, Shewing & keeping up a Spirit of Enterprize, that will oblige them to defend their extensive possessions at all points [which] is of infinitely more Consequence to the United States of America than all the Plunder that can be taken." Though Morris could not direct Jones toward the Caribbean and Gulf, his prospective Mississippi offensive later culminated in Willing's raid.[50]

Besides Morris's influence, Willing owed something to George Morgan, who lent assistance at Fort Pitt by ordering provisions for the downriver journey, advising on Spanish cooperation, and supervising boat-building at congressional expense. Plans were made for shipping military stores and other supplies back upriver. Recruiting was not an easy business. Captain Willing finally headed down the Ohio on January 11, 1778, with only twenty-nine soldiers—whose numbers would later swell to one hundred with hunters and other volunteers. His boat, *The Rattletrap*, had a name appropriate to its commander's acerbic persona.[51]

Like a viper startling its prey, Captain Willing terrorized Anglo inhabitants of the fertile Natchez-Manchac corridor as the gentle southern winter gave way to spring in 1778. His raiders ravaged the landscape with abandon, slaughtering hogs and cattle, destroying crops, burning a few houses, and relentlessly plundering farms and estates. They tore slaves from their dwellings as prizes appropriated to themselves or sold for the coffers of the United States. Willing was not entirely rapacious. He ordered his men to spare the estate of William Dunbar, a Scots planter of literary and scientific talents whom he evidently admired.[52] But his marauders took matters into their own hands by stripping Dunbar's plantation after the owner had fled with his slaves into Spanish territory. Recounting events a few months later, Dunbar was still aghast that Willing, whom he mockingly labeled "the Heroick Captain," lined his pockets by pillaging "Old Friends" who had hosted him before the war.[53] William Wilton, an English Mississippi settler, imagined the raiders "the greatest Banditti's that was ever Seen"—"they were now ... searching all the Plantations for Negroes &c."[54] With no British troops by the river, inhabitants were virtually defenseless. A year before, Germain had dismissed any idea of reoccupying Manchac, whose situation would "expose many brave Men to the fatal effects of an intemperate Climate."[55]

Willing's exploits were premised on Gálvez's tacit support for Mississippi privateering and the sale of plunder in New Orleans. By early March 1778, the American raiders had prizes aplenty, including several boats carrying peltry, indigo, and slaves, and a merchantman laden with lumber for Jamaica. The lure of booty enticed some local residents to cast their lot with the rebels. Peter Chester described Willing's Mississippi recruits as a few Natchez residents and "a Number of French & Spanish Batteau Men, Hunters, & other Banditti."[56] Joseph Calvert, an Anglo ship captain under Pollock's wing, seized a British schooner carrying fifty slaves near the Mississippi's mouth—and then shipped his human cargo via a channel in Spanish territory from Barataria Bay to the vicinity of New Orleans. Some blacks were evidently held in irons during this passage. Francisco Bouligny, Louisiana's lieutenant governor, assisted the captives' movement from his plantation to American guerillas in New Orleans. In April 1778, Pollock reported to Congress that he had obtained about one hundred seized blacks—fifty of whom he had already sold for the United States. In the process, he boosted his own standing as a government creditor.[57] Willing took perhaps two hundred slaves in all. Liberty was as directly bound to slavery in New Orleans as in any locale in North America.

There was nothing in Bernardo de Gálvez's official instructions that ordered him to confiscate English merchant vessels, let alone to shelter and supply American raiders. Why did he risk provoking British naval power that might pound his government seat? For one, Gálvez sensed weakness in Pensacola, where British officials were under orders not to ignite hostilities with Spain. For another, the governor knew through Willing's dispatches that the American raid proceeded with congressional backing—and with Morris's pledges of shipping flour to New Orleans in exchange for Spanish military supplies.[58] Moreover, Gálvez viewed the Mississippi frontier as a region outside certain European diplomatic and political strictures. American rebel privateering was not permissible at Spanish peninsular ports, but the Louisiana scene allowed greater scope for anti-British activities.[59]

Gálvez adroitly upheld the veneer of Spanish neutrality by proclaiming the same rule of hospitality to Anglo-Americans (*ingleses Americanos*) descending the Mississippi as to visiting British subjects. While definitely favoring American raiders, he maintained the guise of impartiality by allowing harassed British Loyalists to seek refuge in his province. He played magnanimous host to the distressed even as he sheltered Willing and his pillagers.[60]

Stung by Willing, British Mississippi settlers were grateful for succor received to the west. Henry Alexander, a planter fleeing West Florida for Pointe Coupée in Louisiana, lavished praise on Gálvez, whose officers "Opened the Doors of a Safe wheal and received under your protection all His Britan[n]ick Majesty's Subjects who applied for it." While the Spanish governor gave "every comfort of Hospitality and Civility," British colonials had been "most cruelly treated by a Set of people [Willing's men] who ought to have thought us the same with themselves; nay even as to our political principles they neither ask'd a Question nor gave us a choice." Alexander acted wisely. One report had the rebels swearing to cut him "into a hundred pieces."[61]

The movement of British West Floridians into Louisiana reversed the direction of colonial migration that Pensacola's chief magistrates had labored so strenuously to induce before the war. George Johnstone and

Montfort Browne assumed that French creoles could be swayed to depart Spanish territory for British soil. All was now altered. In the spring of 1778, thirty-six leading Anglo residents of Manchac publicly thanked Gálvez for offering asylum and permitting them to raise crops with their slaves in Louisiana. Anglo refugees were allowed to lease land on a provisional basis as long as they obeyed the law and refrained from anti-Spanish acts.[62] One anonymous English correspondent at Pointe Coupée hoped that Governor Chester would permit him and other Britons "to Settle with our Negroes here for a Season. I believe we Shall Save the greatest part of them. We have received much friendship and Hospitality from the People here."[63]

Planters on both sides of the Mississippi expected government support for slavery. Although there was no major black uprising in West Florida, white residents felt far from secure. In July 1776, Anglo inhabitants summarily executed four blacks for allegedly plotting rebellion near Baton Rouge. On the eve of the Willing's incursion, Manchac colonists decried their exposed situation, "not only . . . from the Savages who surround us, but from the great number of Slaves daily increasing [and] being without a Militia, or Troops to protect us." A "dangerous Conspiracy" had recently formed among blacks, but was "discovered" before it could be executed. Willing's raid increased the number of slave runaways, described by one colonist as "scattered about in the Country." In 1779, West Florida planters complained to London that they had still not recovered blacks that American raiders carried to Louisiana, even though Governor Chester and his provincial secretary had regained their own slaves by a private understanding with Gálvez.[64]

British officers had little sympathy for the Mississippi's Anglo residents who decamped for Spanish territory during the Willing affair. On March 23, 1778, Captain John Fergusson, commanding H.M.S. *Sylph* on the Mississippi, ordered all loyal subjects to depart Louisiana—and to depend on their own government for the restoration of their property. British residents in Louisiana were unmoved, vowing to stay put as long as necessary to recoup possessions and slaves lost during Willing's raid. These defiant Britons, some of whom had lived in New Orleans for years, were highly protective of all they had gained in a precarious borderland. While vowing allegiance to George III, they expressed great disappointment in the king's government for not having any troops safeguarding the Mississippi. The Loyalist manifesto stated that eighty or one hundred soldiers, "properly Stationed upon the River," would have been enough to stop Willing's "Banditti." The complainants had risked their fortunes along the great river, and would not hear of removing to Pensacola whose "Inhospitable Barren sands . . . present us with a prospect little better than Starving."[65]

Captain Fergusson used persuasive and coercive measures to call Britons in Louisiana to their duty. In April 1778, he received Loyalist claims to fugitive slaves taken aboard his ship. Gálvez meanwhile asserted that some of the blacks actually belonged to Spanish subjects. Fergusson therefore urged British masters to act soon. If slaves went unclaimed, they would simply be put ashore in Spanish territory. The African desire for freedom from masters of all kinds was as constant as colonial commandeering of slave labor.[66]

Pensacola's provincial authorities were highly displeased with British self-seeking along the Mississippi. On April 27, 1778, the West Florida council urged defensive measures for Manchac, but recommended that any troops stationed there be transferred upriver unless the outpost's inhabitants returned from Spanish territory within two months. Governor Chester approved this measure, explaining to Whitehall that placing regular troops by the Iberville was essential not only to prevent the loss of all "western parts of the Province" but also to dissuade Britons in Louisiana from becoming Spanish vassals.[67]

Pensacola's mixed signals—the dangling of carrot and stick—failed to satisfy some British traders along the Iberville, the rivulet that was still officially a boundary between English and Spanish territory. For much of 1778, John Fitzpatrick resided by the Spanish garrison on the bayou's southern side even while British troops were constructing a new fort near his former residence on the northern bank. Writing to a Pensacola associate, he complained of being shortchanged by a British captain who rented housing and bought provisions from him. Fitzpatrick wanted to continue business with Pensacola, but he admitted to being fed up with the captain's "arbitrary Government" and grateful for being under Gálvez's protective banner.[68]

Gálvez was not one to let go of an advantage arising from dissension within British ranks. On April 15, 1778, he summoned all English subjects in New Orleans to appear at his government house the next day to swear a provisional loyalty oath to the Spanish monarchy for the period they enjoyed his Catholic Majesty's protection. Britons could be discharged from the oath once they settled their affairs and left the province, provided they pledged not to take up arms against Spain for a period equal to the time they had enjoyed royal favor.⁶⁹ Englishmen had little choice but to acknowledge Carlos III as having a claim on their good behavior.

As Captain Fergusson's warnings escalated, Gálvez offered signs of meeting British demands in order to avoid open hostilities. For example, on March 16, 1778, he privately requested that Willing return a ship and two river boats, along with several slaves that American partisans had seized from British subjects in Spanish territory. This directive, however, was more political cover than an enforceable order. One of the English boat owners, who sustained a loss of £8,000 in deerskins and indigo and other goods, received no satisfaction when he applied to Pollock for restitution of his confiscated property.⁷⁰

Gálvez weighed U.S. ambitions along the Mississippi at the same time he dealt with British refugees in his province. He ordered Juan de la Villebeuvre, Spanish commandant at Manchac, to proceed cautiously if Willing offered to cede any English territory to his Catholic Majesty. The American captain remained mum on this subject, however. U.S.-Spanish regional collaboration operated through informal understandings rather than by binding compacts.⁷¹ Gálvez meanwhile tailored his correspondence to Madrid so as to minimize the security risks entailed by English residency in Louisiana. In April 1778, he even described most British refugees in the province as Catholics! This assertion seems dubious since fleeing Anglo Protestants were not required to make any religious conversion. In Gálvez's view, Louisiana's Anglo settlers were especially valuable as "great enemies" of the Americans, whose "ambition" would invariably lead to aggression "against our Dominions."⁷² The idea that wartime exigencies would produce any lasting U.S.-Spanish friendship was foreign to Gálvez's thinking.

To deceive an enemy is a commonplace aspect of statecraft. Gálvez was unusually skillful in this way. In February 1778, he sent Captain Jacinto Panis on a diplomatic mission to Pensacola for the purpose of spying on British fortifications.⁷³ Gálvez worked closely with New Orleans allies among the creole elite in secretly conveying cloth, weaponry, and other items to Pollock and onward to Willing and northward to U.S. frontier posts on the Ohio. Crates with provisions for the Americans were stored in warehouses, while the Spanish sentinels who guarded them were kept ignorant of their contents. Slaves were then employed to carry the boxed supplies to places where Pollock could take charge of them. None of these maneuvers averted British knowledge of Spanish complicity, but they lessened embarrassing mistakes and, perhaps most important, demonstrated Gálvez's carefulness to Madrid.[74] The governor even patrolled New Orleans's streets on horseback for several nights to prevent any collusion between Anglo town residents and British naval personnel on the Mississippi that might threaten Willing's men. The governor was most thankful when two hundred Spanish troops arrived as reinforcements from Havana in early June 1778 along with two naval ships.[75]

James Willing found himself at once helped and constrained by Spanish authority. Gálvez aided American rebels as he saw fit, and without conceding royal sovereignty. After giving free quarter for several weeks, he began to tighten the reins. Willing bridled at being cooped up in New Orleans, and he felt cheated when Gálvez returned some seized vessels and slaves to Britons. In late May 1778, the American captain was unable to execute a plan to destroy the Iberville levee, "drown the Country," and burn British Manchac. Gálvez subsequently rejected Willing's appeal to force his way up the Mississippi after the English garrisoned Manchac and Natchez.[76] In this instance, the governor quite probably saved his American guests from destruction.

Willing had furiously launched his initial assault, but his men's departure from Louisiana by early September 1778 was a tame business. The American captain remained at New Orleans to settle affairs while two subordinates, Lieutenants Robert George and Richard Harrison, took command of sixty soldiers and volunteers for the long northward journey to Illinois. Pollock mediated between Gálvez and Willing's band by arranging a safe exit route. U.S. officers pledged that their men would not disturb any British subjects on their trek. Pollock took no chances with soldiers he regarded as having "but little Order or Discipline." Lt. George was to "take the greatest Care" to prevent his men's "Committing any Riot anywhere on the Spanish dominions."[77]

New Orleans was a place of great intrigue where secrets sometimes came into view when passing across political lines. One obscure man, Little Page Robertson, a former overseer on Robert Morris's Mississippi plantation, served as Willing's aide and stood sentinel for Pollock, but later he told the British at Pensacola about the American supply line from New Orleans to the Spanish at Arkansas. Robertson also disclosed the roundabout route of Willing's men west from New Orleans before their northern turn up the Mississippi. The raiders were by then safely underway and reached Illinois without major incident. They were most fortunate compared to Captain Willing, who left Louisiana by sea only to be captured by a British war vessel in the Atlantic.[78]

From the beginning of Willing's adventure, American marauders spread rumors to magnify their strength and to intimidate foes. Landing at Walnut Hills above Natchez on February 18, 1778, the raiders seized a few frightened white men in the British Indian service. The captors announced that they were the advance party for two thousand American soldiers. Willing put a scare in the enemy by falsely boasting that "General Morgan would be down the River in the Spring to take possession of this Country."[79]

Willing feared the Choctaws might deal his band a fatal blow if they took Britain's side—and he used intimidation and diplomacy to prevent Indian intervention. His soldiers appeared menacing in hunters' frocks, with each man reportedly armed with a rifle, cutlass, and a pair of pistols. At Walnut Hills, one of Willing's lieutenants instructed an old Choctaw man in American ways: "We are come down to take possession of these Lands, and We must look upon each other as Children from the same Breast, for we alike Till the Earth." This soft message was followed by a threat: "Tell them [the Choctaws] that if they lift the Hatchet against us Rifle men of America, We never will bury it." Indian neutrality, not alliance, was expected. The Choctaws were warned "by no means to kill a White Brother . . . whether English, French, Spanish or American."[80] This harangue aired a widespread colonial assumption that all whites had a common interest in keeping Indians in order. Taking no chances when first moving downriver, Willing imposed a neutrality oath on Natchez's remaining Anglo settlers, who pledged to withhold "Warlike Stores" from the Choctaws that might be used by "the Savages" against the United States.[81]

Willing's threats had a startling counterpoint in a message of Franchimastabé, a foremost Choctaw headman, to Natchez's white inhabitants in June 1778. Ready to fight alongside the British, he warned that his people would look on Anglo settlers as "Virginians" and "enemies" if they took the Americans "by the hand" or entered into any treaty with them. The Choctaws did not trust a settler population in a frontier world where friends might suddenly become foes. Some Indian warriors exploited regional unrest by turning to banditry outside any paramount chief's purview. During the Willing raid, Gálvez reported that Choctaw raiders were burning houses and plundering the British Mississippi even though there was no general Indian-colonial warfare in the area. The governor told commandant Villebeuvre at Manchac to distribute gifts to Choctaw chiefs in order to sate what he called their "thirst" for "pillage."[82]

While Gálvez cultivated Indian allies, his frontier commandants feared that Britain had the upper hand over native peoples along the Mississippi. In July 1778, both Villebeuvre and Carlos de Grand Pré at Punta Cortada (Pointe Coupée) feared that hundreds of Choctaws, incited by English agents, were about to pillage their outposts.[83] In reality, the English hold was not nearly so strong as Spanish officers imagined. Insecurity abounded on all sides. Gálvez fed the gristmill of rumor for his own purposes. According to an Indian source, the governor told the Choctaws that American rebels "Killed all before them—Men Women and Children, both white and Red." This message had a practical purpose. If the Choctaws worried about the American threat, they would be more apt to seek Spanish alliance and protection.[84]

Interregional and Transatlantic Currents

Oliver Pollock, busy on several fronts during the Willing raid, was a supplier to George Rogers Clark as the latter led Virginia's campaign into the Illinois country in June 1778. Gálvez's loans to Pollock were crucial in this respect—as was assistance lent by Spanish frontier commandants. Baltazar de Villiers, a former French officer, gained Willing's gratitude at Arkansas by offering "every Service . . . in his power" to ward off pro-British Chickasaws.[85] When Clark approached Kaskaskia in the first days of July 1778, he brought news of the French-American alliance to mid-continent. Announcing this grand event was good politics; it helped the Virginia colonel win support from French *habitants* in his campaign against the British. Clark also sent word to Pollock, who in turn forwarded encouraging messages northward by Willing's comrades.[86]

U.S. connections between New Orleans and Illinois indicate an unmistakable competition with Spain. Pollock badly wanted Clark to move southward and secure U.S. control of the British Mississippi before Spain entered the war and launched its own Gulf offensive. If Madrid gained the prize, he remarked, "we will lose a Valuable Conquest Which might now be Easily Obtained."[87] Pollock assiduously courted Gálvez, but he was still a U.S. agent who knew where his bread was buttered. Having ventured his fortune for "the glorious cause," he could not afford an American retreat from the Lower Mississippi Valley. Months before, he lobbied Congress to ship flour downriver for his account so that he could honor debts to Gálvez and make remittances to French shippers in Cap Français (in Saint-Domingue) who were major suppliers to New Orleans.

Unfortunately for Pollock, neither the flour nor the troops materialized as he hoped. And he was badly stung by the American confederation's fragmented politics. Congress declined responsibility for Spanish loans to Virginia, for which Pollock was liable as a broker in transnational exchanges.[88]

Willing was as eager as Pollock for U.S. mastery of the Louisiana market for flour and provisions. In that case, "the produce of Fort Pitt and the back Country will sell here very high, and Goods may be got in return." Though Willing admitted that his own expedition had been thwarted, he took pride in having "distressed the Enemy very considerably." He cared little that British soldiers presently occupied Natchez and Manchac. As he saw matters, both sites "will be of great utility to the States, in a future day as this Country of course must fall to Us."[89] Americans, and not the Spanish, would subsume the British Mississippi.

Willing's prediction was far from being realized when his mission ended. U.S. regional influence was episodic and not sustained. Gálvez put off two successive Virginia governors—Patrick Henry and Thomas Jefferson—in their requests for large loans and formal commercial ties. He courteously brushed by Henry's proposal of annexing West Florida to the United States.[90] Gálvez's political sense was again on target. In late October 1778, Congress ruled out a full-fledged Mississippi campaign after receiving unfavorable reports of Willing's raid. Individual volunteers in that mission still received Continental pay for their services.[91] Willing eventually returned to the Mississippi Valley in 1782, scouting for new opportunities. His visit left one ironic twist. In November 1783, Betty, a free black woman, sued in Natchez court for ten *piastres* that Willing owed her for washing and mending his clothes. She won judgment under Spanish authority, but it is unclear whether she received her due since the former marauder had already left the district.[92]

Because Madrid did not recognize U.S. independence, its first emissary to Congress had the status of an observer rather than a diplomat with full-fledged authority. Juan de Miralles, a Havana merchant, fulfilled this position quite ably from his arrival in Charleston in early 1778 to his death in Philadelphia two years later. Amiable by nature and fluent in English, he was on friendly terms with many delegates—and especially close to Robert Morris, with whom he collaborated in shipping flour to Cuba. Miralles had conducted business with British North American ports since the 1750s while supplying provisions to Spanish Florida.[93]

Cooperation in the economic sphere did not, however, translate into political accord. Miralles had high expectations for his U.S. diplomatic mission, but was taken aback by the American insistence on open Mississippi navigation and commercial access to Florida ports. In August 1779, he became quite edgy when dining with Henry Laurens and the Marquis de Brétigny, a French soldier of fortune who presented a plan for capturing St. Augustine by U.S. troops and his own volunteers.[94] Miralles glumly reported this affair to Madrid since he believed that Spain would be best served by conquering East Florida without foreign assistance. The same rule of thumb applied to Pensacola, Mobile, and the Mississippi River, which must of course be foreclosed to U.S. navigation.[95] Laurens was no more at ease than Miralles about U.S.-Spanish relations. He worried over one report, which proved false, that had Spanish troops occupying the abandoned English post of St. Marks by Florida's Gulf Coast.[96] The South Carolina statesman warned "that the Spaniard had his Eye upon the Florida's [sic] and Providence [in the Bahamas], in order to secure the streights [straits] of the Gulph."[97]

Though Laurens anticipated U.S.-Spanish competition over East Florida, the war's course precluded any such contest. Congress resolved to capture St. Augustine in the fall of 1778, but American forces were unable to launch an offensive below the St. Marys River. By the year's end, British troops moved into Georgia, capturing Savannah and threatening South Carolina. Laurens, who had imagined American soldiers taking Florida lands as a war prize, felt the sting of the enemy's success. He calculated British gains not simply in territory, but above all in agricultural wealth and slaves.[98]

As long as Spain remained officially neutral in the war, Miralles favored a U.S. takeover of East Florida under strict limitations. During his first year at Congress, he persistently lobbied that the United States should transfer to Spain any territorial acquisitions made at British expense in the Floridas or by the Mississippi. In May 1779, Miralles suggested to José de Gálvez that the crown might compensate Congress for relinquishing wartime gains in the region.[99] This idea does not appear to have been seriously entertained at Madrid. Before Miralles's message reached his native country, Spain was at war with England and putting the Gulf Coast and Mississippi to the forefront of its American agenda.

CHAPTER 4

Multiple Conflicts

Warfare and a Disputed Peace, 1779–1783

A hawk by temperament, Bernardo de Gálvez was already readying an offensive against British West Florida when definite news of war reached him in early August 1779. Not even a hurricane, which struck New Orleans on the 18th, stayed his resolve. A few days later, he warned the public that the British were about to strike because "Spain has declared in favor of the independence of the Americans ... just as France has done."[1]

Galvez's words were actually a "pretext" or ruse—as he explained to the Spanish court. The governor knew quite well that Spain had entered the war without acknowledging American independence. His speech was calculated to galvanize French colonial support by giving the appearance of marching step-in-step with Versailles. Gálvez's stratagem worked. Many Louisiana settlers embraced Spain's cause as their own. Finding the British unprepared, the governor's army captured Manchac and Baton Rouge—and obtained the surrender of Natchez—all within a few weeks in September 1779. Success on the Mississippi was a prelude to greater triumphs—the capture of Mobile in 1780 and Pensacola the following year.[2]

Gálvez's declaration in favor of American independence was a brilliant tactical move, though it did not signal a shift in Spanish imperial policy. By 1781, Spain and the United States locked diplomatic horns in Europe over the navigation of the Mississippi and related boundary issues. It would be misleading, however, to see Gulf warfare as leading ineluctably toward a simple binary imperial competition. The course of military conflict, and the peace that followed, hinged greatly on Indian peoples—especially the Choctaws, Chickasaws, and Creeks. Diverse colonial groups also shaped events—from Mobile's French settlers to Natchez's Anglo residents who did not accept Spanish victory without resistance. Peace negotiations in Europe coincided with intricate maneuvering for advantage on the local and regional scene.

Conquest of the British Mississippi

General John Campbell, commanding his Majesty's forces at Pensacola, was shocked by the speed and skill with which Gálvez took Manchac on September 7, 1779, and forced the surrender of British troops at Baton Rouge two weeks later. In fact, Campbell did not even receive word of hostilities to his west until September 14. The British position on the Mississippi was undone by a dearth of naval support and inadequate communication with Pensacola, some of whose residents hardly expected any wartime interruption in their customary Louisiana trade.[3]

In a post-mortem of defeat, Campbell raised the issue of misleading intelligence with war minister George Germain, who had previously assured him that French Louisiana was "indisposed to the Spanish government"—and that a British victory could be readily achieved by a Mississippi offensive.[4] If not quite scolding Germain, Campbell let him know that Britain could find no friends in Louisiana "when France and Spain are united in the same Cause." Germain's preconception of easy triumph was a hangover from the prewar era, and a result of outdated information recently furnished by Captain Thomas Hutchins, a Mississippi Valley landholder and cartographer who was then staying in London.[5]

As Campbell accurately reported, Gálvez had attacked "with the United Strength of the whole Province of Louisiana." The Spanish force of 1,400 men included not only regular troops but also colonial militia, Indians, and armed blacks.[6] In preparation for the campaign, Captain Pedro Favrot, a Louisiana native, urged the enlistment of youthful creoles for their skills as hunters and riflemen. Gálvez led his army on a grueling eleven-day march in sweltering heat through the wooded and swampy terrain between New Orleans and Manchac. This trek depleted his force by a third without arresting its progress.[7]

Spanish clarity of purpose stood in contrast to British inefficiency along the Mississippi where military and civilian interests did not easily coalesce. When Lt. Colonel Alexander Dickson assessed the situation about Manchac in early 1779, he bemoaned the paucity of labor, and the lack of stone, brick, and lime for building fortifications. Anglo planters would lend their slaves only "at a dear rate nor will they hire them otherwise."[8] Distressed by Manchac's "sickly" and swampy environs, Dickson constructed a fort on higher ground twelve miles northward at Baton Rouge. His plan required tactful negotiation with Stephen Watts, Loyalist owner of the Baton Rouge property, who expected ample compensation for the site, which he esteemed "as the first in Value, of any in this part of the Province." Watts had acquired his plantation in 1775 after fleeing Philadelphia, where American rebels had confiscated his property. Three years later, he suffered yet another blow when James Willing plundered his Mississippi estate and seized "twenty-six Slaves of prime quality, who would now sell for 10,000 dollars." Watts's case for payment was still pending when Dickson surrendered on September 21, 1779.[9]

One cannot imagine Bernardo de Gálvez dickering with a Louisiana planter over land requisite for wartime defense. Unlike British army commanders, Gálvez held supreme civil and military power in his province—and he was not averse to exercising it. For example, he directed white immigration in accordance with military requirements. In 1779, he ordered newly arriving Canary Islanders to settle in the bayou country fronting British West Florida. The Gálvez family had a major hand in this operation from the outset since Bernardo's father, Matías, was governor of the Canaries. The immigrants paid a heavy price in flooding, disease, and death—the consequence of being thrust into an unhealthful locale.[10]

Oliver Pollock accompanied Gálvez during the Spanish march from New Orleans to Manchac and the capture of Baton Rouge. The day after Manchac's surrender, Pollock addressed an open letter to the "Inhabitants of the Natchez District," admonishing them "to give every assistance to his most Catholick Majesty's Arms." Written at Gálvez's request, the message had a beguiling tone as if directed to American Whigs rather than to a district whose white inhabitants included many British Loyalists. Pollock announced that Spain had declared in favor of the "Independency" of the United States—thereby repeating the governor's propagandistic call to New Orleans residents. Most important, the letter conveyed Gálvez's intent to secure Anglo Natchez by liberal concessions, including guarantees of religious freedom and property rights. The Spanish crown would, moreover, pay Natchez tobacco growers the same price for their crop as the king offered Louisiana planters.[11] These privileges betokened Spanish military priorities. Gálvez wanted no trouble from upcountry Natchez while concentrating his forces for assaults on the Gulf ports.

Pollock had a piece of good fortune a few days after he penned his appeal to Natchez. His privateer, the *Morris*, attacked and captured the *West Florida*, a British war sloop on Lake Pontchartrain.[12] Pollock covertly used this episode to claim that the United States had sovereign rights within the Mississippi-Manchac-Pontchartrain artery wrested from British West Florida. (It mattered little in this view that Spanish forces had actually carried that ground.) Concealing matters from Gálvez, Pollock ordered William Pickles, captain of the *Morris*, to administer U.S. oaths of allegiance to French residents on Lake Pontchartrain's northern shore between Bayou Lacombe and Tangipahoa—an area where Pollock himself had a vested interest through a West Florida land grant.[13]

Self-interest and nationalistic interest were all of a piece. In early 1780 Pollock urged Robert Morris's commerce committee to maximize U.S. navigational and territorial rights in the Lower Mississippi Valley: "I am still at a loss respecting who is to possess the Province of West Florida, but at all events I strongly presume you'll not give Up that part of it on the Mississippi (with the free navigation on the River) which has already been reduced by Capt. Willing, and consequently guaranteed by the Treaty with France, as also from the pass of the Rigolets to the pass of Manchaque [sic] which runs along the Lake Pontchartrain, and was taken the 21st September last by Capt. Pickles."[14] Pollock hereby intrigued to expand U.S. conquests to territories traversed by American raiders but scarcely occupied by them. All might still work according to his plan if the United States could get France to support its cause and to restrain Spanish ambitions.[15] Congress applauded Pickles's military success by paying him $6,146 in August 1780 and sending news of his triumph to John Jay, U.S. emissary in Madrid. But the Pollock-Pickles coup about Lake Pontchartrain failed to budge Spain whatsoever on the Mississippi issue.[16]

American military possession might be fleeting, but geographic facts were seemingly immutable. Oliver Pollock treasured the same Gulf Coast–Mississippi corridor from the Rigolets to Manchac so strongly coveted by George Johnstone, Montfort Browne, Elias Durnford, and other Britons. To Pollock, the United States had an unquestionable right to navigation of the Mississippi even if Spanish forces took Mobile and Pensacola. In his public letter to Natchez of September 22, 1779, he stated that Gálvez would uphold "the Spirit of Liberty" guaranteeing the district's American citizens "an uninterrupted Commerce with New Orleans." Pollock mistakenly presumed Spanish complaisance in wartime leading to an open commercial régime during peace.[17]

Madrid's colonial officers in upriver zones extended the royal domain through pronouncements paralleling Pollock's maneuvers for the United

States. On November 22, 1779, Captain Balthazar de Villiers, commandant of the small Arkansas garrison, declared Carlos III sovereign of all territories on the Mississippi's eastern bank across from the Arkansas, White, and St. Francis Rivers in Louisiana. To support his Majesty's right, the captain sealed his proclamation, and a royal insignia, in a tin box and then buried the cache fifty paces east of the Mississippi and just below a particular tree. Claims of sovereignty were all that could be made in lieu of actual imperial occupation.[18]

Spanish victory in the Lower Mississippi Valley far exceeded what Madrid hoped to accomplish by acquiring Louisiana from France in 1762. A province obtained solely for defensive purposes had become a base for successfully attacking an English colony. Gálvez's conquest owed something to the relaxation of barriers prohibiting commerce between Louisiana and bordering regions of New Spain, notably Texas. During the summer of 1779, Gálvez ordered 2,000 head of Texas cattle as a mobile food source for his troops on the move toward Manchac and Baton Rouge. Payment went to missions and ranches about San Antonio, and at La Bahía inland from the Texas Gulf Coast.[19]

Cattle drives again helped Spanish forces during the siege of Mobile in 1780 and boosted the Pensacola campaign the following year. Robert Thonhoff, historian of this frontier exchange, has declared a fitting headline: "Longhorns Helped Win American Independence."[20] By implication, Texas beef shored up Spanish Gulf Coast conquests that led to victory at Yorktown. While this claim may be exaggerated, it is still fascinating to consider the connection between Texas colonial ranches and the Spanish conquest of British West Florida. Not all livestock herded over several hundred miles reached the battle zone. During the summer of 1780, Comanche raiders in Texas plundered cattle and horses on their way eastward.[21]

Allegiance in Indian Country and the Gulf Region

From the beginning of his governorship, Gálvez believed it essential to gain Indian support on both sides of the Mississippi. Prior to war, he assiduously courted the Choctaws through deft diplomacy, gift-giving, and the assistance of French frontier commandants in the Spanish service. This approach certainly served Gálvez well during his campaign of 1779, when native peoples in the Lower Mississippi Valley either aided him or stayed out of the fighting.[22] Disgruntled by Spanish success, General

Campbell complained to Germain that the Indians "are a mercenary Race, and are the Purchase and Slaves of the highest Bidder without Gratitude or Affection; However, my Lord, I'm afraid that Europeans themselves have taught them these Principles."[23]

Campbell's frank assessment was insightful to a point. His one glaring error was to conceive of exchanges between giver and recipient entirely in monetary terms. From an Indian perspective, such relationships ideally created reciprocal obligations modeled on kinship, which encompassed security and respect as well as goods. It is undeniable, however, that the flow of trade goods and presents was crucial in shaping native loyalties during Anglo-Spanish Gulf warfare.[24]

Alexander Cameron, British agent to the Choctaws and Chickasaws, was repeatedly frustrated by Campbell's personal incapacity to gain native trust. Gálvez shined by comparison even though he had fewer gifts to bestow on Indians. As Cameron put matters, "Gálvez will even humble himself so low as to kiss their warriors from ear to ear and pay them every respect that is due to great chiefs. He sends for them to visit him even to Orleans."[25] At one gathering in October 1779, Gálvez treated with no less than seventeen Choctaw chiefs who were accompanied by 480 warriors. Though his visitors denounced the English, they coyly held back from any commitment to enter the war. Privately condescending toward Indians, Gálvez observed that "savages" coveted large medals—the grander the better. In early 1780, José de Gálvez ordered Mexico City's royal mint to make silver medals for Louisiana's Indians precisely according to samples furnished by Don Bernardo in New Orleans.[26]

Despite Spanish efforts, Great Britain gained the lion's share of Indian support as the struggle for the Gulf Coast peaked in 1780–1781. Though natives fought on both sides, their tilt in Britain's favor became obvious as the conflict progressed. Gálvez became so leery of Choctaw attacks after taking Mobile in March 1780 that he pledged to forswear the use of Indian auxiliaries if Campbell promised the same. No deal resulted from this proposal. Campbell rejected Spanish complaints of native atrocities by distinguishing between Indians who were legitimately attached to his army and those who committed "depredations" without license. He also protested Gálvez's use of Indians, who plundered British traders in Choctaw country and committed other attacks before finding safety on Spanish ships in Mobile Bay.[27]

The proffer of trade goods was the linchpin of growing Choctaw-British collaboration. At least some Choctaws who served Gálvez during the war's first six months became so upset by the Spanish failure to furnish merchandise that they vowed loyalty to England once again. These Indians counted the Spaniards as enemies because the latter were intent on taking Pensacola—an event that would "shut up the Path" between themselves and the English, "who still had Goods." One pro-British warrior mocked his fellows in the Spanish camp: "You who love them go and partake [of] their [body] lice and palmetto matts [*sic*] with them."[28]

The Creeks moved decisively to defend British Pensacola against Spanish attack in 1780 because of similar concerns. By that time, many Muscugolge were already committed to the English through their conflict with American frontiersmen. Just one month after the Spanish occupation of Mobile, Indian warriors gathered in great numbers about the British camp in Pensacola. By mid-April, these fighters included 1,235 Creeks, 236 Choctaws, and 31 Chickasaws—probably the largest gathering of native warriors during the entire America Revolutionary War.[29] Since Indian men disliked prolonged camp service—and General Campbell was chary of supporting them—many went back to their villages within a few months. By the autumn of 1780, a substantial Choctaw force again gathered to assist the British near Mobile Bay. The Spanish responded to persistent Indian attacks by sending free black and mulatto militiamen from New Orleans to the combat zone. The reinforcements were soon tested. Just before daybreak on January 7, 1781, some 180 British, Loyalist, and German Waldeck soldiers launched a fierce assault on Spanish troops east of the bay. Four hundred Choctaws and other Indians aided the attackers by cutting off retreating foes. The Spanish suffered heavy losses, though managing to hold their stockade.[30]

A lack of British naval support—and not the want of Indian auxiliaries—was the decisive military shortfall contributing to Pensacola's surrender in May 1781. Several hundred Choctaws fought in the garrison's defense after categorically rejecting diplomatic entreaties sent by their pro-Spanish brethren. Alexander McGillivray, Creek leader and British Loyalist, led forty warriors to the besieged fort—and another forty arrived soon thereafter. Many more might have joined the fight if the ineffectual Campbell had not hesitated to provide supplies and gunpowder well in advance of battle. Ironically, the British commander regarded the Creeks as vital to Pensacola's defense. In all, Indian warriors inflicted perhaps one-third of all Spanish casualties during the siege.[31] Native military involvement by no means ended after the battle. Two hundred Choctaws served in the British defense of Savannah prior to the town's evacuation in July 1782. These men were more than twelve months in service, and at a distance of some five hundred miles. Their long journey home began by ship from Tybee Island on the Georgia coast to St. Augustine and then westward overland.[32]

For the Choctaws, whose environment was severely scarred by overhunting, a pro-British stance brought food and other necessities besides liquor. In February 1781, Campbell complained to Whitehall of "the immense Consumption of Provisions by Indians" at Pensacola.[33] The Indian quest for weaponry, gunpowder, and lead matched the desire for food and raiment. Emisteseguo of the Upper Creeks was killed by Georgia Whigs in 1782 as he led a war band toward English-occupied Savannah, where ammunition might be had for deerskins.[34] His path eastward doubtless appeared to be the only viable route once Pensacola and Mobile had fallen to Spain.

Gálvez had considerable success in winning French colonial support along the coastal zone well east of the Mississippi. By the fall of 1779, French residents of Mobile supplied him with covert intelligence on British military positions in their town. Gálvez was most pleased by assistance from local allies. "They love us" was his gleeful commentary.[35]

When Spanish forces commenced their siege of Mobile in early 1780, they continued to receive useful information from French residents living within the battle zone. Other creoles fled to the woods to escape Spanish cannon fire and English demands for assistance. After the fall of Mobile on March 13, Gálvez assumed the mantle of French protector in his correspondence with General Campbell, who was ensconced at Pensacola during the recent fighting. In Gálvez's view, local residents should not be judged harshly because some of their "Friends and Relations" were among his own troops from Louisiana.[36]

Campbell was not pleased by Gálvez's justification of French behavior. While rejecting the idea of collective punishment, the British general declared that those who aided the enemy could be fairly judged as traitors. Above all, such malefactors merited trial for violating the laws "that gave them Peace Plenty and Security" for years under British rule. This threat was rendered moot because England did not recapture Mobile in the war.[37] The Franco-Spanish alliance in the Gulf region transcended the putative boundary between Louisiana and West Florida.

Gálvez showed liberality to Mobile's British subjects by offering royal protection for eight months to those who swore loyalty to the Spanish crown. On March 17, one hundred and twenty Britons took the oath by giving their word under God and the Bible. Five days later, sixty-seven French male residents swore fidelity as Catholics under the sign of the cross.[38] Because of Mobile's strategic coastal position, Spanish authorities declined to grant permanent residency to the district's English subjects.

The American Revolutionary War in the southern theater spread chaos in many spheres. Thousands of enslaved blacks took advantage of the upheaval by fleeing farms and plantations. A considerable if unknown number passed into Indian territories. For many fugitives, life and death hung in the balance. Runaways endured physical exhaustion and illness, and also hazarded meeting foes instead of friends. Indians often had a material incentive for capturing fugitives and reaping payment from whites for their return. This cold fact did not necessarily operate as colonial slaveholders desired. From 1781 to 1783, some Upper Creek men sold the blacks they apprehended to Spanish-occupied Pensacola rather than dealing with white claimants in the southern states. In other cases, Indians acted as slave brokers for British Loyalists disposing of blacks during their flight through Georgia to East Florida.[39]

The Creeks and Seminoles kept numerous blacks for themselves during the war. In 1777, John Stuart reported that Seminole headmen backed the crown on condition that whatever horses, cattle, and slaves they took would be theirs. Creek warriors notoriously regarded captured blacks as "the king's gifts."[40] The consequences were often felt long after the war's end. Juan Gros, a free black militiaman of New Orleans who was captured by Indians near Pensacola in 1781, was not released for eight years—and then only after a Spanish captain paid a healthy ransom to a Seminole chief.[41]

Had Gálvez not taken the British Mississippi in 1779, England's imperial position in the Floridas might have endured long after U.S. independence. From 1774 through 1778, there was an influx of Loyalist immigrants and refugees to West Florida from the Atlantic states. Notwithstanding fragmentary records, these persons can be estimated at a few hundred whites and probably a good many more enslaved blacks. Since the colonial population was perhaps 4,900 in 1774 (approximately 3,700 whites and 1,200 blacks), the arrival of even a small body of migrants represented a noteworthy increase.[42] Provincial records disclose one persistent fact: white newcomers greatly preferred land along the Mississippi and its tributaries to any other locale. In the years 1780 to 1782, there was a notable uptick in migration across southern borderlands. Several hundred settlers from the Carolina-Georgia backcountry drifted westward into Indian country or moved to the Mississippi simply to escape the chaos of war. The surprising point is not the limits of the wartime migration to West Florida and neighboring Indian districts, but rather the fact that settlers and slaves traversed long distances and survived perilous voyages.[43]

The war brought a quick end to the British policy of curbing provincial land grants in West Florida. On November 11, 1775, Governor Chester issued a proclamation of asylum and bounty to all faithful subjects coming to the province. Immigrants benefited under this ruling, as did previous settlers who had not been able to acquire valid land titles. In November 1778, Captain Thaddeus Lyman obtained a 450-acre family right and a 1,000-acre bounty on the Big Black River that he had scouted for the Company of Military Adventurers five years before. He made this successful bid after leading Loyalists in the fight against James Willing's raiders.[44]

Natchez's Anglo settlers were just recovering from American pillaging when Gálvez captured Baton Rouge in September 1779. Diehard Loyalists felt betrayed after receiving news that British commander Dickson had unilaterally conceded their upriver district in his surrender. Some Natchez whites felt "Sorrow Rage and distraction . . . to be thrown thus away" without being allowed to fight "for one of the finest Countries in the World!"[45] Rumor weakened the motive of resistance: false reports that Gálvez had one thousand Indians in his army, including four hundred nearby Choctaws, and that eight hundred Americans were supposedly coming down the Mississippi to join the Spanish for an attack on Pensacola. Under these circumstances, fifty-nine Natchez residents publicly thanked Dickson for securing honorable terms on their behalf.[46]

Gálvez remained true to his word by respecting Anglo property rights and purchasing Natchez tobacco with royal specie. Notwithstanding this generous treatment, some local Britons seethed at Spanish governance and plotted to restore English rule at the first opportunity. In 1780 the conspirators secretly informed General Campbell of their plan and asked for his blessing.[47] The general was initially wary of a backdoor insurgency, but consented months later when Gálvez's armada immediately threatened Pensacola. On March 17, 1781, Campbell confidentially dispatched officers' commissions to Natchez men and called on the faithful to overthrow Spain's "Tryannick despotism." The commissions were issued in blank form, with the volunteers filling in their own names as officers. Campbell's approval was a crucial legitimizing measure since the insurgents wanted to act as British soldiers, and not as rebels.[48]

The Natchez conspirators quickly gathered 100 to 200 men under arms, and began a siege of the district's Spanish fort on April 22, 1781. One Spaniard was killed in the exchange of gunfire and cannon shot. The defenders' resolve weakened as the rebels spread rumors of mining the fort with explosives. On May 4, Captain Juan de la Villebeuvre capitulated; the defeated were allowed passage downriver on pledging to abstain from any further fighting in Natchez during the war. Fifty insurgents under Captain John Blommart entered the fort and raised the Union Jack. Their triumph proved brief.[49] The Natchez revolt was eclipsed within days by the fall of Pensacola, which foreclosed any chance that British Mississippi insurgents could hold on to their gains. The drama on the Gulf Coast intersected with Mississippi Valley intrigues and also with imperial rivalries of transatlantic scope.

Pensacola, Natchez, and Frontier Disquiet

The Spanish victory at Pensacola was the result of intensive planning, bold leadership, and good fortune. Gálvez's advance force set sail from Havana on February 8, 1781, with over 1,300 troops gathered on thirty-one transports and accompanied by five warships. On March 18, Louisiana's intrepid governor blazed the way into Pensacola Bay on the brig *Galveztown*, which somehow escaped the fire of British shore batteries. Success came when Admiral José Solano's Spanish-French armada arrived from Havana a month later. Gálvez now had 7,000 soldiers besieging Pensacola besides overwhelming naval superiority. Campbell and his roughly 1,300 soldiers fought gamely with Indian support but finally had no chance. The white flag was raised from Pensacola's battered Fort George on May 8, with formal surrender ceremonies coming two days later. Anglo colonists were shocked by events—and would have been even more aghast had they known that the British navy was pursuing Dutch and French Caribbean targets rather than coming to their aid. In London, Germain lamented "the little attention ... shown to the Protection of Pensacola" even before receiving definite news of the surrender.[50]

Gálvez offered generous terms to vanquished Britons because he wanted to avoid a prolonged fight that would delay preparations for a Spanish and French strike on Jamaica. While yielding all claim to West Florida, Campbell secured the right to determine his men's outbound destination, provided the evacuees did not ship for Jamaica or St. Augustine. Campbell chose New York City for his point of arrival—and Gálvez

(top) Bernardo de Gálvez, (Lithograph, 1903, based on an earlier original painting). Courtesy of The Historic New Orleans Collection, no. 1991.34.15. This portrait depicts Gálvez as the victor of Pensacola, and now viceroy of New Spain. He is identified as being thirty-eight years old, which would place the portrait's inscription as being written in 1785.

(bottom) Coat of Arms and Patent of Nobility awarded to Bernardo de Gálvez by Carlos III of Spain (bound illuminated manuscript, 1783). Courtesy of The Historic New Orleans Collection, no. 74-78-L.1. The lower right portion of the shield shows Gálvez standing athwart the brig *Galveztown*, the flagship that he led into Pensacola Bay on March 18, 1781.

acquiesced.⁵¹ British soldiers and sailors were barred from any further service against Spain and its allies during the war—or until a prisoner exchange was made. This guarantee was absolutely useless to the United States, which was not formally allied to Madrid. By mid-July 1781, many of Pensacola's former defenders arrived at New York after a brief stay in Cuba.⁵²

American leaders in Philadelphia understandably viewed the released soldiers and sailors—about one thousand in number—as British reinforcements in a critical war zone. One Maryland delegate, who was especially bitter in tone, remarked that "the Success of the Spaniards" at Pensacola "will be more prejudicial to our Operations, than their failure would have been." Delegates were both perplexed and upset because many of them held Bernardo de Gálvez in such high esteem. Samuel Huntington, president of Congress, expressed this mood in a letter to Washington: "I cannot . . . perswade [sic] myself that Governor Gálvez who commanded the Expedition, & hath manifested the most Friendly Sentiments, & attachment for us, would admit of terms so apparently detrimental to these States."⁵³

Simply put, Spanish military objectives diverged from U.S expectations. In March 1780, the Spanish had taken Mobile when American forces in South Carolina waited vainly for assistance from Havana to break the British siege of Charleston. Madrid was hardly responsible for this setback, but it did not score political leverage as France did through joint military operations with the Continental Army. In May 1782, South Carolina ships aided Spain in the conquest of the Bahamas, but this affair had little impact since the islands were returned to Britain in the peace treaty.⁵⁴

Gálvez had his own trials to endure at Pensacola in May 1781. Having treated Campbell with distinction, he was furious upon learning that his British counterpart had licensed the Natchez uprising. From a Spanish perspective the insurgents were rebels, no matter that some held commissions as British officers. They had sworn loyalty to Carlos III in September 1779, and could not legitimately go back on their word because the war continued elsewhere. Campbell attempted to win a pardon for the insurgents by good-will gestures, including his explicit declaration that Natchez incontestably belonged to Spain. Gálvez took this overture as an insult since British authorities had already conceded all West Florida to his Catholic Majesty. With resounding pride, he shot back: "Natchez, being part of West Florida, belongs to me."⁵⁵ Had Gálvez accepted Campbell's proposal, Spain would have gained British confirmation of territorial gains that were subsequently disputed by the United States. But this last difficulty was not foreseen.

From the onset of the Natchez uprising, Anglo insurgents believed they would carry the day through British triumph at Pensacola. They knew that Gálvez had failed in previous attempts to take the port. Moreover, Campbell had given them word that British naval assistance from Jamaica was forthcoming. Given these expectations, the insurgents were dumbstruck by Gálvez's triumph, and were soon beset by bitter infighting. Rebel leader John Blommart insisted on holding the fort and negotiating honorable terms when Spanish forces came upriver to reclaim possession. His more radical confederates vowed to destroy the garrison rather than hand it back to the enemy.[56] A good many Loyalist dissidents fled to the Chickasaw country, while other Anglo diehards made their way to British forces in Georgia and South Carolina.

On June 23, 1781, a Spanish detachment of Louisiana militia and Indian auxiliaries reoccupied Natchez's Fort Panmure without opposition. Captain Étienne Robert de la Morandière, a Quebec native, efficiently led this mission. Blommart and three other insurgents were quickly sent to prison in New Orleans.[57] Apart from this show of force, Spain renewed its governance of Natchez by accommodation more than iron hand. Two hundred and forty white males, largely of Anglo background, renewed oaths of allegiance to Carlos III, and thereby retained their place in the Mississippi Valley. Spanish authorities meanwhile prosecuted leading insurgents for treason. Twenty-one men, a good number of whom remained at large, were found guilty and had their property confiscated. Six imprisoned insurgents, including Blommart, were sentenced to death, but ultimately reprieved by Gálvez in 1783 at the personal request of Prince William Henry, Duke of Lancaster. The pardoned men were exiled to Jamaica.[58]

The Spanish treatment of Natchez insurgents was far more lenient than the sentences meted out to the New Orleans rebels of 1768, five of whom were executed for ousting Governor Ulloa. In the latter case, Alejandro O'Reilly made an unflinching statement that Spain governed Louisiana—and that the province was no longer French. In 1781, Gálvez saw to the punishment of Anglo ringleaders but avoided overly harsh measures that could stir a general upriver rebellion. Blommart and his imprisoned comrades had a reasonable if not unassailable legal defense against the charge of treason. Since they had British military commis-

acquiesced.[51] British soldiers and sailors were barred from any further service against Spain and its allies during the war—or until a prisoner exchange was made. This guarantee was absolutely useless to the United States, which was not formally allied to Madrid. By mid-July 1781, many of Pensacola's former defenders arrived at New York after a brief stay in Cuba.[52]

American leaders in Philadelphia understandably viewed the released soldiers and sailors—about one thousand in number—as British reinforcements in a critical war zone. One Maryland delegate, who was especially bitter in tone, remarked that "the Success of the Spaniards" at Pensacola "will be more prejudicial to our Operations, than their failure would have been." Delegates were both perplexed and upset because many of them held Bernardo de Gálvez in such high esteem. Samuel Huntington, president of Congress, expressed this mood in a letter to Washington: "I cannot . . . perswade [sic] myself that Governor Gálvez who commanded the Expedition, & hath manifested the most Friendly Sentiments, & attachment for us, would admit of terms so apparently detrimental to these States."[53]

Simply put, Spanish military objectives diverged from U.S expectations. In March 1780, the Spanish had taken Mobile when American forces in South Carolina waited vainly for assistance from Havana to break the British siege of Charleston. Madrid was hardly responsible for this setback, but it did not score political leverage as France did through joint military operations with the Continental Army. In May 1782, South Carolina ships aided Spain in the conquest of the Bahamas, but this affair had little impact since the islands were returned to Britain in the peace treaty.[54]

Gálvez had his own trials to endure at Pensacola in May 1781. Having treated Campbell with distinction, he was furious upon learning that his British counterpart had licensed the Natchez uprising. From a Spanish perspective the insurgents were rebels, no matter that some held commissions as British officers. They had sworn loyalty to Carlos III in September 1779, and could not legitimately go back on their word because the war continued elsewhere. Campbell attempted to win a pardon for the insurgents by good-will gestures, including his explicit declaration that Natchez incontestably belonged to Spain. Gálvez took this overture as an insult since British authorities had already conceded all West Florida to his Catholic Majesty. With resounding pride, he shot back: "Natchez, being part of West Florida, belongs to me."[55] Had Gálvez accepted Campbell's proposal, Spain would have gained British confirmation of territorial gains that were subsequently disputed by the United States. But this last difficulty was not foreseen.

From the onset of the Natchez uprising, Anglo insurgents believed they would carry the day through British triumph at Pensacola. They knew that Gálvez had failed in previous attempts to take the port. Moreover, Campbell had given them word that British naval assistance from Jamaica was forthcoming. Given these expectations, the insurgents were dumbstruck by Gálvez's triumph, and were soon beset by bitter infighting. Rebel leader John Blommart insisted on holding the fort and negotiating honorable terms when Spanish forces came upriver to reclaim possession. His more radical confederates vowed to destroy the garrison rather than hand it back to the enemy.[56] A good many Loyalist dissidents fled to the Chickasaw country, while other Anglo diehards made their way to British forces in Georgia and South Carolina.

On June 23, 1781, a Spanish detachment of Louisiana militia and Indian auxiliaries reoccupied Natchez's Fort Panmure without opposition. Captain Étienne Robert de la Morandière, a Quebec native, efficiently led this mission. Blommart and three other insurgents were quickly sent to prison in New Orleans.[57] Apart from this show of force, Spain renewed its governance of Natchez by accommodation more than iron hand. Two hundred and forty white males, largely of Anglo background, renewed oaths of allegiance to Carlos III, and thereby retained their place in the Mississippi Valley. Spanish authorities meanwhile prosecuted leading insurgents for treason. Twenty-one men, a good number of whom remained at large, were found guilty and had their property confiscated. Six imprisoned insurgents, including Blommart, were sentenced to death, but ultimately reprieved by Gálvez in 1783 at the personal request of Prince William Henry, Duke of Lancaster. The pardoned men were exiled to Jamaica.[58]

The Spanish treatment of Natchez insurgents was far more lenient than the sentences meted out to the New Orleans rebels of 1768, five of whom were executed for ousting Governor Ulloa. In the latter case, Alejandro O'Reilly made an unflinching statement that Spain governed Louisiana—and that the province was no longer French. In 1781, Gálvez saw to the punishment of Anglo ringleaders but avoided overly harsh measures that could stir a general upriver rebellion. Blommart and his imprisoned comrades had a reasonable if not unassailable legal defense against the charge of treason. Since they had British military commissions, they claimed to be enemy combatants and prisoners of war—and not traitors against the Spanish crown. Though Gálvez rejected this argument, he finally chose to show magnanimity at a time when Anglo-Spanish hostilities were drawing to a close.[59]

As Spanish authorities investigated the Natchez uprising, it became clear that the conspirators were a varied lot of erstwhile British subjects. Blommart, a Swiss Protestant by birth, was a wealthy merchant and landowner who boasted a library of 150 volumes and operated two whiskey stills at the time of the rebellion. Jacob Winfree, one of his closest confederates, had migrated from Virginia to the Mississippi in 1773 and had become a leading planter-slaveholder.[60] Other rebels were debtors said to have jumped into the fray to better their lot. Anglo traders in Indian country aided the uprising, especially by serving as couriers between Natchez and Pensacola. Disorders in the southern backcountry were felt along the Mississippi. Rebel ringleader Kit Marr was a former Georgia renegade who was notorious for horse stealing and cattle rustling.[61]

The Natchez insurgency occurred amidst Anglo-Spanish warfare, highly unsettled colonial-Indian relations, and tensions between British Loyalists and U.S. partisans. Two leading rebels—brothers John and Philip Alston—headed a faction that raised the American flag for a few days at Natchez after the Spanish surrender of May 4. Pro-U.S. settlers were an opportunistic group that evidently viewed Philadelphia, and no longer London, as their surest protector. Philip Alston had formerly assisted the British defense of Natchez against Willing's raiders in 1778.[62]

Some insurgents engaged in outlawry from the moment they took up arms against Spain. On the morning of April 22, 1781, John Turner and about twenty armed freebooters boarded a merchant barge just below Natchez as it was headed up the Mississippi to the Ste. Genevieve in the Illinois country. Demanding surrender in the name of George III, the raiders seized four French colonial merchants, the barge's crew, and several slaves.[63] Luis Bolduc, one of the captives, had a disquieting moment when held at the house of insurgent Jack Ellis. The elderly matron there boasted that General Campbell would defeat Gálvez at Pensacola, take New Orleans, and then send his troops and Indian allies to settle matters in Natchez. This scenario offers a sense of how ordinary frontier folk felt the vagaries of war.[64]

The initial Spanish investigation of the Natchez revolt from May to July 1781 was itself a work of transnational cooperation. Lt. Colonel Jacinto Panis presided at much of the questioning, with the aid of French and English interpreters. At Blommart's interrogation, Panis had the assistance of Lt. Colonel Zenon Trudeau, a New Orleans creole who entered the Spanish service at a young age and fought at Baton Rouge and Pensacola.[65]

Royal authorities in New Orleans were alert to any signs that the Natchez troubles were part of a larger conspiracy. Panis repeatedly questioned Anglo witnesses whether they harbored prejudices against Spain. None answered in the affirmative. Panis probed further whether English settlers from Opelousas to Arkansas were in cahoots with the insurgents. In fact, Britons and Anglo-Americans were of such diverse backgrounds—and spread over such disparate territories—that there was no such coalescence. Differences in personal outlook and political temperament existed within particular families. During the Natchez uprising, one Anglo resident of Opelousas protected his stake in Spanish territory by implicating his brother-in-law Jacob Winfree as a leading rebel. A few Anglo families left Natchez with the intent of resettling with their slaves in Louisiana as the uprising neared collapse.[66]

The war in the South and its many frontiers did not end at Yorktown. James Colbert, a Scots Indian trader who styled himself a British captain, was Spain's chief nemesis on the Mississippi in 1782–83. Roughly sixty years old at the time, he was a vigorous man whose family was a veritable clan in its upriver stronghold 120 miles east of the Mississippi. Colbert had sired eleven children by three native women over four decades and amassed wealth and slaves in the process. Along with several sons, he fought for England near Mobile in 1780 and took a few captured Spanish soldiers back to the Chickasaw country; he returned to fight at Pensacola the next year.[67] Securing connections to the Gulf Coast was critical for a trader living deep in the interior.

In May 1782, Colbert and forty Anglo backwoodsmen commandeered the boat of Silvestre Labbadie, a St. Louis merchant moving upriver with a plentiful cargo, including Spanish presents for several Indian groups. The Anglo marauders had a French Louisiana ally who helped spring the trap by deceptively telling Labbadie that there was no danger along his northward passage.[68] Colbert held the white passengers and their slaves as hostages but released a Spanish officer's wife, her children, and several others after three weeks. The guerilla chief refused to release his remaining captives until the Spanish freed all imprisoned Natchez insurgents. In a defiant letter to New Orleans, he tongue-lashed Spaniards for castigating him for outlawry when they had "Upheld Mr. Willing in Rob[b]ing

& plundering the Inhabitants On the Missisippy [*sic*] before war was Ever declared between the Crown of great Brittain & his Catholick majesty." Past wrongs demanded satisfaction.⁶⁹

Though creating havoc, Colbert was unable to gain the release of imprisoned Britons. He still remained a force, however, because the Spanish and their Illinois Indian allies could not corral him. In April 1783, Colbert stormed the Spanish fort at Arkansas with roughly eighty men—about sixty whites, five blacks, and eleven Indians—the latter being mostly his sons and nephews. This attack yielded additional captives, but not control of the shaken outpost.⁷⁰ Although Colbert died after a fall from a horse in late 1783, his sons and their progeny were a potent force among the Chickasaws for generations. The Colbert family's Revolutionary War experience was itself a sign of rising mestizo influence among southern Indian peoples.⁷¹

The Chickasaws were divided by Colbert's militancy and disturbed by the movement of Anglo refugees and other whites into their neighborhood. Paya Mattaha, a headman who had close ties to British officials through 1781, entertained Spanish peace overtures and received badly needed gifts the next year. The Chickasaws were so economically straitened that one group of warriors trekked to British St. Augustine to receive presents in early 1783. Some two thousand Indians, including groups from above the Ohio, were then huddled by the East Florida garrison in quest of alliance and succor.⁷²

Esteban Miró, Louisiana's interim governor after Gálvez's departure, viewed a military campaign against Colbert's partisans as costly and impractical. After all, the guerillas were operating in Indian country three hundred leagues (nearly eight hundred miles) north of his capital.⁷³ Miró's initial adjustment of Natchez-Mississippi difficulties established precedents for his governorship lasting through 1791. Rejecting severity toward Anglo Natchez, the governor resolved to gain popular respect through mild governance (*"un Trato suave"*) whenever possible.⁷⁴ In fact, he showed this disposition even before officially gaining his post. Newly arrived in New Orleans from Pensacola's battlefield in May 1781, Miró upbraided Baton Rouge commandant Pedro Favrot for planning to emancipate Natchez slaves who informed on their rebellious masters.⁷⁵

Unrest in the Mississippi Valley was heightened by the uncertainty of the war's final outcome—and rumors of invasion from various points of the compass. Upper Louisiana was edgy ever since St. Louis villagers withstood an attack on May 26, 1780, by a British irregular force, composed chiefly of Indian warriors from the Great Lakes and a French Canadian contingent. Two summers later, the town feared a similar invasion, which might possibly be supported by Colbert and his Anglo Loyalist allies moving westward from Georgia. Though an attack did not materialize, Spanish officials in New Orleans did not rest assured for some time.[76]

Fervent British partisans in the southern theater were striving to keep the war alive even as peace negotiations were about to begin in Paris in 1782. Robert Ross, former New Orleans merchant and West Florida landholder, felt a keen commitment this way because of losses and suffering at Spanish hands. In 1777, he was stung by Gálvez's confiscation of two of his ships for smuggling. The next year Ross spent fifty-five days in a New Orleans jail for pro-British activities.[77] After his release, he reentered the fray by passing messages between Natchez's Anglo conspirators and General Campbell in Pensacola. In early 1782, Ross journeyed from Natchez to Charleston, where he presented the Earl of Dunmore with a lengthy memorandum on Louisiana's economic value and the precise military routes available to take New Orleans. His enthusiasm was as broad as the river he treasured: "The Mississippi is in America, what the Nile is in Africa." And "there is not an Individual who has left it [the Mississippi] since the [Spanish] Conquest, who does not Ardently Wish to return."[78] Ross's assessment was tinctured by a belief that French Louisiana residents would much prefer an open English commerce to their present condition under Spanish rule. In short, the Mississippi-Gulf region was still ripe for imperial transformation through the application of force and adroit politics. The future, too, held great promise through incipient Spanish American rebellions, which could open an English pathway to New Mexico's mines.[79]

Dunmore enthusiastically forwarded Ross's report to London and volunteered to lead the conquest of Louisiana with two thousand British soldiers.[80] Several months later when in London, he presented a still more audacious plan—the Loyalist conquest of New Orleans and all the territory upriver to the Ohio. Anglo American royalists would wage an autonomous struggle "on their own Continent," choosing their commander, who would wield military and civil power under the crown.[81] Through Indian alliances, the Loyalist enclave would possess the power "to drive the Thirteen united Provinces into the Sea." The object was British continental mastery from the Gulf to Canada, with the harvest of all the rich agricultural lands and the peltry trade of the Mississippi Valley. Dunmore bypassed any discrepancy between his previous plans of arming southern blacks with his conception of white Loyalist predominance in Louisiana. In fact, Tory diehards and their British friends regarded slavery as a mainstay throughout the Floridas.[82] A still greater obstacle loomed—the British government's negative to adventurist schemes at odds with an imperial pullback from a failed North American war.

Diplomacy and the Imperial Peace Settlement

Dunmore forged his plan of Tory empire several months after American commissioners Jay, Franklin, and Adams began peace negotiations with British representatives in Paris. Jay came to Paris from his failed diplomatic mission to Madrid, which deeply prejudiced him against Spanish interests.[83] Franklin was also wary of Madrid's objectives. In October 1780, he advised Jay neither to expect much from Spain nor to yield the principle of free navigation on the Mississippi. "Poor as we are, yet as I know we shall be rich, I would rather agree with them [the Spanish] to buy at a great Price the whole of their Right on the Missisipi [sic] than sell a Drop of its Waters.—A Neighbour might as well ask me to sell my Street Door." As a budding U.S. imperialist, Franklin esteemed the Mississippi as highly as he had when lobbying for a British Illinois colony in 1767 and imagining western settlers aiding the mother country against Spain.[84]

Though Jay did not hoodwink his colleagues, he was unquestionably the driving force for U.S.-British détente at Spanish expense. If he had his way, Spain's victories along the Gulf Coast would be entirely overthrown by a renewed English military offensive. In October 1782, he proposed just this idea to Richard Oswald, British diplomatic emissary. Jay's plan was a Spanish nightmare: Britain would embark troops from New York City and Charleston for the recapture of West Florida. Oswald, a wealthy merchant and absentee East Florida plantation owner, embraced the proposal as an opportunity for British merchants to gain a large share of North American trade through the Gulf ports. Whitehall chose not to take up the project, however, since the king's government was winding down the American war and concentrating its formidable naval arsenal against the Bourbon powers.[85]

By the time Jay and Oswald pushed their West Florida intrigue, the American peace commissioners had already made progress toward a peace settlement with Britain—thereby thwarting Spanish and French efforts to keep an independent United States east of the Appalachians and as far above the Gulf as possible. The conde de Aranda, Spanish ambassador at Paris, worked tirelessly toward this end but to no avail.[86] The preliminary U.S.-British treaty of November 30, 1782, was a severe blow to Madrid. Gálvez's conquests were effectively confined, at least on paper. Britain recognized the Mississippi as the U.S. western boundary as far south as the 31st parallel, well below Natchez. Both the British and U.S. governments acknowledged each other's right of free navigation along the entire river, whose southerly portion happened to be under Spanish control. At least on paper, the United States stood as continental successor to Great Britain south of Canada.[87]

The U.S.-British accord had its share of intrigue, notably a secret article on West Florida, designating alternative boundaries depending on the outcome of still continuing Anglo-Spanish warfare. The American commissioners strongly favored Britain if it recovered West Florida by the war's end. In that case, the United States acknowledged English possession from the Gulf northward through Natchez, and still higher up to the confluence of the Mississippi and Yazoo (32° 28° N. latitude). Jay, Franklin, and Adams showed no such generosity to Spain. The United States claimed southward to 31st parallel, including the entire Natchez district, if the English did not recover West Florida and, by implication, if Spain retained Pensacola and Mobile. In sum, the American commissioners were ready to take more from Spain than Britain when establishing national boundaries.[88]

Congress wisely rejected the secret West Florida treaty provision as an unseemly complication to a favorable peace accord. Foreign secretary Robert R. Livingston was disturbed by Jay's maneuvers, which he regarded as dishonorable for favoring the British foe over Spain, "a nation engaged in the same cause with us, and closely connected to our ally [France]." Though pleased by the treaty as a whole, he chided the peace commissioners for sowing "the seeds of enmity" toward Spain. Jay and his colleagues held their ground, justifying the secret article as necessary to secure Britain's relinquishment of territorial claims from Canada to the region far below the Ohio. The commissioners also derided Spain's "extravagant and improper designs" on the "whole Country" between the Floridas and Lake Superior.[89]

Although the final U.S.-British treaty omitted the separate article on West Florida, the accord was still galling to Madrid. The two English-speaking powers, neither of which possessed any territory in the Mississippi's southernmost course, still mutually guaranteed their navigational rights on the entire river. Though Great Britain had surrendered Natchez to Spain in Mississippi-Gulf warfare, it awarded that district and lands as far south as the 31st parallel to the United States. Whitehall furthered its interests by implicitly stoking postwar controversy between Spain and the American Union over the Mississippi Valley.[90] The British government, meanwhile, decided that East Florida was not worth keeping since it had already lost the Gulf Coast–Mississippi corridor to Spain. Whitehall's resolve to cede East Florida to Madrid by treaty in 1783 was a result of cost-and-benefit analysis in which the empire paid scant regard to East Florida's Anglo settlers, five thousand of whom had fled south of Georgia in the war's final year. George Johnstone, West Florida's first governor, was one of the few M.P.'s who spoke against the cession.[91]

With the Paris peace settlement of 1783, East Florida had a clearly specified northern boundary along the St. Marys River—a point that neither Spain nor the United States contested. West Florida was a quite different and more muddled case. In the British-Spanish treaty, Great Britain conclusively ceded West Florida to Spain but without specifying that colony's boundaries. Three factors worked to Spanish detriment here. First, British negotiators preferred territorial ambiguity rather than any concession contradicting what was already promised the United States (a Mississippi to Chattahoochee border along the 31st parallel). Second, Spain lost bargaining power in 1782–83 because of military reverses suffered at Gibraltar and in the Caribbean. Third, Spain had no alliance with the American Confederation by which it could have bolstered its leverage. Had Madrid been willing to acknowledge U.S. navigational rights on the Mississippi, it could have most probably obtained undisputed possession of Natchez. Congress was resolved to acknowledge Madrid's rights to the Floridas if the United States was allowed unrestricted commercial access on the great river.[92] But Spain desired exclusive sovereignty of the Mississippi's east bank as far north as the Ohio. The impetuous American republic had to be kept at bay. Writing to Aranda in late September 1782, foreign minister Floridablanca remarked contemptuously on U.S. pleadings, which he pithily summarized: "*Spain, recognize our independence, and Spain, give us money.*"[93] These sentiments exemplify imperial frustration, giving no hint of the very considerable sums that Spain actually expended for the United States toward the larger goal of humbling Britain.

In the last stages of European peace negotiations, Madrid rejected

French proposals aimed at resolving U.S.-Spanish differences over the Mississippi. On March 17, 1783, Floridablanca wrote Aranda that he was unalterably opposed to making New Orleans a free port, as Vergennes had suggested, lest the Americans dominate the trade of "all New Spain and the Islands and of our gold and silver and other valuable products." Floridablanca caustically remarked that the French proposition was so obnoxious that "it would be better" by comparison "to return the Floridas to England and renounce the idea of keeping the Mexican gulf for ourselves alone."[94] U.S. commercial adventurism, not territorial ambition alone, was Spain's great bugbear. Ironically, U.S.-Spanish wartime collaboration peaked when Madrid—and its overseas officials—countenanced foreign trade that would have been illicit in peacetime. The shipment of flour and other foodstuffs from Philadelphia and Baltimore to Havana contributed significantly to Spanish victories at Mobile and Pensacola. Similarly, Bernardo de Gálvez welcomed American flatboats bearing provisions down the Mississippi to Louisiana.[95] These openings would be restricted and even shut after the war ended.

In 1782, Louis Brion de la Tour, a notable French cartographer, completed an exquisitely detailed map illustrating scenes of warfare culminating in French, American, and Spanish victories over Great Britain. In the map's upper-left quadrant, we see a picture of a British general, and his troops, surrendering to an American commander and his countrymen at Yorktown. The map's legend states that Cornwallis is handing his sword to Washington—which has a certain symbolic truth even if their seconds conducted the actual surrender. Most important for our purposes, the map's lower-right portion heralds Spain's Gulf Coast triumph. By this account, Pensacola, "one of the world's most beautiful ports," fell to Gálvez and Admiral Joseph Solano after twelve days of bombardment. The defeated garrison was said to number 1,700 men, "not including a multitude of Negroes and Indians [*Sauvages*]."[96]

Brion de la Tour's map artfully joins Gulf Coast warfare to the climactic battle by the Chesapeake. This juxtaposition helps us to visualize two

(opposite) Louis Brion de la Tour, *Suite du Théatre de la Guerre dans l'Amérique Septentrionale y Compris le Golfe du Méxique* (Paris: Chez Esnauts y Rapilly, 1782). Courtesy of the DeGolyer Library, Southern Methodist University, call no. G3300n 1782.B7. This map links the Spanish conquest of British Pensacola in 1781 to the Franco-American victory at Yorktown. It also shows the Spanish colony of *Floride Occidentale* (West Florida) bordering smaller Georgia to the east.

distinct, if overlapping conflicts—the American War of Independence and the Bourbon powers' war against Britain. The map fittingly depicts two substantial Spanish colonies (*Florida Occidentale* and *Florida Orientale*) seemingly blocking Georgia's reach to the Gulf Coast and Lower Mississippi Valley. These uncertain boundaries would soon be tested in the war's aftermath.

CHAPTER 5

Bidding and Conspiring for Access to the Realm, 1783–1787

The British cession of both Floridas to Spain is one of the more significant if often overlooked consequences of the American Revolutionary War on a continental scale. English imperial visions of unrivaled power from the Gulf to the Upper Mississippi were suddenly eclipsed. Bonds of monarchical protection and allegiance were thrown into disarray for native groups and colonials from St. Augustine to Pensacola and across southern interior lands. The new international scene was rife with tension. On June 26, 1784, Carlos III officially closed the Mississippi to foreign traffic wherever the river passed between Spanish territories.[1] Since the American Congress was weak and ineffectual, U.S. expansionists looked to states such as Georgia to license aggressive forays toward the Mississippi.

A multiplicity of intrigues stirred the Florida-Louisiana borderlands after the Revolutionary War. From within and beyond Spanish territory, British Loyalists and U.S. nationals bid for residency rights, economic privileges, and other benefits under the Castilian flag. While some Anglos devised colonizing projects to Spain's advantage, others plotted to seize crown territories through subterfuge or armed attack. Still others moved opportunistically between collaborative and adversarial designs. Spanish authorities had no easy time in distinguishing between trustworthy and wholly self-serving foreigners seeking their place within the realm.

East Florida: Upheaval and Exodus

In the Revolutionary War's latter stages, East Florida was transformed by a large influx of white Loyalist refugees and blacks fleeing South Carolina and Georgia. From July 1782 through April 1783, more than 5,000 whites, accompanied by 8,200 slaves, entered the province. East Florida now had a far larger population of colonials and enslaved blacks than had ever dwelt there at any single point from 1565 to 1780. Many of the whites expected Britain to remain their sovereign. They were appalled by word of the peace treaty in 1783, which gave George III's subjects eighteen months to settle their affairs and depart.[2] The colony's new Spanish governor, Vicente Manuel de Zéspedes, did not arrive at St. Augustine until July 1784. The presiding British governor, Patrick Tonyn, meanwhile remained until late 1785 to safeguard English interests during what proved a prolonged and testy evacuation.[3]

Zéspedes was beset by difficulties in his early days at St. Augustine. While warmly greeted by Minorcan, Italian, and Greek settlers, he feared an uprising by disgruntled Britons and Anglo refugees. In the St. Marys–St. Johns frontier below Georgia, Anglo-American armed bands thieved and feuded, routinely stealing slaves and committing violence against each other. Patrick Tonyn viewed the roughnecks as "a pestiferous banditti" threatening any semblance of civil society.[4] With few royal troops at his disposal, Zéspedes offered clemency to troublemakers who agreed to leave the province. This measure failed, however, to solve the outlaw problem, which was compounded by misunderstandings between Spanish officers and Anglo militiamen.[5]

By the fall of 1785, the great majority of British colonists had departed East Florida. The evacuees most often relocated to the Bahamas and the Caribbean, while others journeyed to Nova Scotia, Europe, or moved overland into the southern Appalachians or onward to the Mississippi. Departing British and Loyalist slaveholders sold many African American refugees to Georgia and other states. Many other blacks were subjected to bondage in the Caribbean or the Bahamas. But slavery's chains did not hold all. Black refugees who had gained British pledges of freedom in wartime did their utmost to maintain their liberty in new and precarious settings.[6]

The American Revolutionary War weighed heavily on East Florida well after the peace treaty of 1783. Many Loyalist refugees had come from the southern backcountry, where internal violence was endemic. In the Carolinas and Georgia, it was common for inhabitants to move back and forth between Whig and Tory allegiances, or to maneuver cautiously between warring factions simply to avoid harm. The Revolution had radical consequences in redefining the relationship between citizens and the state.[7] Once unmoored from customary allegiances, some Anglo colonists were prepared to accept the status of Spanish subjects, especially if they could pursue liberty and property under the House of Bourbon.

Zéspedes strengthened his hand against malefactors by defending law-abiding British subjects as long as the latter remained in East Florida. In early 1785, Anglo settlers of the St. Johns River fulsomely thanked the governor for arresting outlaws Daniel McGirtt and William Cunningham and thereby safeguarding "our Lives and Property."[8] The idea of Anglo-Spanish accommodation did not sit well in all quarters. Some Britons in the Bahamas worried that their Florida brethren would remain under Spanish rule rather than join the Loyalist exodus to the islands. One Bahamian publicly appealed to Anglo Floridians to be true to their native faith and flag: "Do not be deceived free men of Britain.... Do not trust in [the] Spanish.... Doubtless you are unable to consider foregoing the inestimable blessings which are your birthright and most invaluable inheritance, to establish yourselves under a government where even your property and your lives depend upon the will of one man whose religion instructs him that to persecute heretics is meritorious before God."[9]

Contrary to this propaganda, Zéspedes countenanced permanent residency for a small number of trustworthy Britons voluntarily pledging loyalty to Spain. Two leading beneficiaries of this indulgence were William Panton and John Leslie, Scots Loyalists who transferred their Indian trading business from Georgia and South Carolina to East Florida during the Revolutionary War. Petitioning Zéspedes in July 1784, they offered to serve Spain through their "capital and credit," which they contended would strengthen Madrid's influence among native peoples and thereby stave off U.S. intrusions. The partners still voiced scruples, requesting the Spanish crown to respect "our religious persuasions until perhaps a conviction of the errors of Protestant doctrine shall cause our conversion to the Catholic faith." No such change was forthcoming or expected—even though non-Catholics did not possess the legal right of residency in the Indies. Zéspedes accommodated Panton, Leslie, and Company for quite practical reasons—no Spanish firm, whether Iberian or colonial, had a role in supplying the region's Indian peoples and shipping deerskins to Europe. Besides, both Panton and Leslie had the backing of Creek leader Alexander McGillivray, whom Spanish authorities regarded as their primary and most powerful friend in southern Indian territories. By early 1785, the Scots' firm had extended its operations to Pensacola, and it would grow still more in time.[10]

While Panton and Leslie excelled in political finesse, other Anglo Loyalists moved erratically in quest of Florida riches. John Cruden, former South Carolina Tory, was a wartime opportunist managing slave labor for the British crown but finally advocating the massive use of black troops as a last resort to escape defeat. Fleeing to East Florida, he plotted resistance to Spanish takeover in early 1784, only to take a new tack once Zéspedes secured St. Augustine that summer.[11] Bowing to the Castilian flag now seemed the route to self-advancement. On October 28, 1784, Cruden addressed an extraordinary petition to his "Dread Sir"—"Charles the Third ... King of Spain and the Indies," purportedly on behalf of fellow East Florida Loyalists. He requested no less than a proprietary grant of the colony's entire northern rim between the St. Johns and St. Marys Rivers, including "the Islands on the Sea Shore." If allowed "sole direction" of the region's "internal Government," his association would pay "a reasonable Tribute" to the king and "defend the Frontier. . . . Against Every power but our Mother Country," Great Britain. Humility may have marked the petition's outward form, but hardly its substance.[12]

Cruden's plan was brazen but not simply idiosyncratic. In the two decades following the peace of 1783, a bevy of foreigners bargained for concessions from the Spanish crown in weakly held or disputed borderland regions. Without following any fixed formula, petitioners observed the politics of quid pro quo by offering services in return for landholding or commercial privileges. Cruden proposed, for example, to defend the royal domain in return for the opportunity to remake his fortune, recoup slaveholdings lost during war, and escape Whig vengeance.[13] His petitions are also noteworthy for expressing stereotypical Anglo attitudes toward Spain. He confessed great unease at denying "the Religion of our Fathers"—Protestantism—for the privilege of living as a Catholic under Spanish rule. In yet another plea, he lauded Bernardo de Gálvez "as a Soldier and a Gentleman"—a man he professed to "love" as "the Real Spaniard." By inference, the Spanish cavalier was an admirable figure a cut above his common countrymen. None of this flattery worked. In 1786, Cruden abandoned his Florida scheming for life in the Bahamas.[14]

East Florida Anglo refugees had a hankering for relocating to Louisiana or the Mobile region, where there was more fertile land and less internecine violence. William ("Bloody Bill") Cunningham, a former Tory guerilla in the Carolinas, wreaked havoc along Florida's northern frontier in the war's aftermath before requesting Zéspedes's permission to migrate with his slaves to Louisiana. Rebuffed by the governor, he remained a troublesome spirit and was eventually deported by Spanish authorities to the Bahamas.[15]

Unlike Cunningham, John Linder was a Tory refugee who moved from renegade status to respectability through skillful adaption to Spanish governance. Along with his son John Jr., he violently feuded with other British Loyalists along the St. Johns frontier in 1784. Seeking a new start, the Linders, who were of Swiss background, negotiated successfully with Zéspedes to resettle in West Florida. By May 1785, father and son were leaders of some sixty white families that migrated from East Florida to the Tensaw River above Mobile Bay. The younger Linder alone had eighty-five slaves in his household. Pedro Favrot, commandant of Mobile, welcomed well-to-do newcomers who were anti-U.S. in political leanings. Himself a Louisiana creole, he appreciated the Linders, whom he described as German (*"allemand"*), fluent in French, and free of "fanatical" English ways.[16]

John Linder Sr., a justice in Tensaw, saw to it that the civil disorders that plagued the Georgia-Florida frontier did not recur in his district. In late 1785, he apprehended a drifter named Nuson who had killed two men and committed several robberies the previous spring in Georgia. The malefactor was banished rather than executed. Nuson's white female companion now gained custody of three slaves—a man and two children—whom she had entrusted to him during the war.[17]

Colonial venturing into southern borderlands had consequences for Indian peoples who encountered white newcomers in various guises as settlers, traders, and drifters. In the spring of 1785, Alibamon headmen near the Tensaw complained of the growing white presence on their lands and the colonial habit of killing deer and bear without regard to season. Commandant Favrot, who had little patience for these complaints, lectured the chiefs that the settlers were English royalist refugees and not Americans as alleged, and therefore fully entitled to his Catholic Majesty's protection.[18]

Alexander McGillivray shared Favrot's stance on Tensaw colonization. His position was especially delicate since he was both a former British Loyalist and a kinsman to the Alibamons through his maternal lineage. Viewing the United States and especially Georgia as an immediate threat, he regarded the Tensaw settlement as a useful barrier against American encroachment. He still urged John Linder Sr. to avoid antagonizing the Alibamons by excessive hunting or settling outside certain bounds. McGillivray thereby arrested a small problem that might compromise his larger goal of building a pan-Indian alliance with Spanish assistance. On May 16, 1785, he warned Esteban Miró that U.S. commissioners were about to survey the disputed international boundary line at the 31st parallel—and that 2,500 American troops were massing by the Ohio's mouth under George Rogers Clark and John Montgomery "to take possession by Force" in the Lower Mississippi Valley.[19] In reality, there was no such invasion plan, but McGillivray wanted the Spanish to be prepared for hostilities.

Natchez and the Bourbon County Crisis

Unlike the Tensaw settlement, which budded in Spanish territory, the Natchez district was at the heart of the postwar border dispute between Spain and the United States. When Congress did little to press its stake, the state of Georgia moved to the forefront with fervid ambitions and old claims from its colonial past. On February 15, 1785, the Georgia legislature established a new jurisdiction—the "County of Bourbon"—with its government seat at Natchez. The name Bourbon was here a token of aggrandizement and hardly an honor to the ruling house of Spain. Georgia intended to occupy Natchez and to annex fertile Mississippi lands from the Yazoo River southward to the 31st parallel, along with interior territory far eastward to the Chattahoochee. In sum, the state put itself forward as the lawful enforcer of U.S. rights under the Treaty of Paris.[20]

Georgia's adventurist reach far exceeded its power to dispossess the Spanish, let alone the Creeks, Choctaws, and Chickasaws. Besides, the state was entering shaky constitutional territory by acting without congressional authorization. Georgia therefore adopted a subtle approach, in which intrigue came into full play. Instead of assembling militiamen, the legislature appointed thirteen commissioners, as justices of the peace, to attempt a non-violent coup d'état. Four commissioners, who were destined to dominate events, traveled from Georgia to the Mississippi. The other appointees were mostly Natchez men who were encouraged to collaborate in the takeover.[21] Georgia ordered its deputies to avoid any dispute "with either the Spaniards or the Indians" about "Territorial claims—the navigation on the Mississippi, or any matter whatsoever which may eventually involve this State in a contest." How, then, did the state expect to commandeer a region that Madrid had recently won through war with Britain? The presumption was facile: Spanish officers were expected "voluntarily" to relinquish "Forts Towns and places."[22]

Natchez's Anglo inhabitants would presumably rally behind Georgia, swear a state loyalty oath, and obtain land grants in the process. Spanish authority would be eviscerated with little or no violence.

The plan's architect was Thomas Green, a native Virginian of over sixty years whose ambitions did not slow with age. He had relocated from the southern backcountry to Natchez in 1782, leading twelve white families owning several hundred slaves. Within two years, he returned east after running afoul of Spanish officials over Indian affairs and his friendship with an Anglo fugitive living among the Chickasaws.[23]

Once back in Natchez in June 1785, Green dispatched a curt declaration to commandant Lt. Felipe Treviño: "the district of Natchez" lay within the "County of Bourbon" in the state of Georgia. Though not demanding immediate Spanish surrender, Green spread word to local households that 1,500 Georgia soldiers were marching overland to Natchez, with additional support coming up the Mississippi. Even though Treviño did not believe these rumors, which were in fact lies, he feared the news would agitate inhabitants and push them to rebellion.[24]

Spanish authorities in Louisiana had little military force to spare for Natchez. It proved an ordeal to send reinforcements from New Orleans to the crisis point. After a month's journey, Lt. Governor Francisco Bouligny arrived at Natchez with forty-six grenadiers, bringing the frontier garrison's strength to roughly one hundred men. Miró's written report of the Mississippi crisis reached Mexico City before Bouligny traveled 240 miles upriver with his soldiers.[25]

Despite Georgia's bluster, most Anglo settlers in the Lower Mississippi Valley were not prepared to risk another violent episode after the revolt of 1781. The unfinished business of British-Spanish peace was still of paramount importance. Three months before Green returned to the Mississippi, twelve Anglo settlers traveled from Natchez to New Orleans on a delicate mission. Their time to remain as British subjects was drawing to a close through a Spanish allowance of extended residency. Meeting with Miró, the Natchez men courteously petitioned that they and their neighbors be admitted as Spanish subjects with civic rights and an exemption from fighting in a future war against Britain. Their plea was one of simple humanity. If forced into exile, they would be lost: "Where will we go?"[26] The petition was granted, though without any special dispensation in case of Anglo-Spanish hostilities.

In purely economic terms, Anglo settlers were quite aware of living in a plantation district offering advantages they were unlikely to find elsewhere. Once Natchez came under Madrid's administration, it was included within a royal program subsidizing tobacco production, which boomed in the war's aftermath. Bounties paid in specie enabled planters to develop a way of life founded on expansive credit and slave labor.[27] Significantly, Spanish authorities regarded the Natchez-Manchac corridor to be part of Louisiana and eligible for the same privileges as settlements west of the Mississippi. In jurisdictional terms, Louisiana's governor had authority on both sides of the Mississippi, and his purview included West Florida, whose loosely defined limits extended well past Pensacola to Apalachee Bay.[28]

Though Georgia's commissioners pronounced Natchez to be part of that state, most Anglo residents had quite tangible reasons for being loyal to the Spanish crown. Green made few converts, and he dared not take up Miró's invitation to present himself in New Orleans. Fearing arrest, he retired to Indian country even before Bouligny took command at Natchez in late July 1785.[29] Though Green left the scene, three other Georgia commissioners entered Natchez during the summer of 1785 and made it their home for several months. Imperial considerations set the parameters for a borderlands contest in which neither side wanted an armed confrontation. Viceroy Gálvez in Mexico City anticipated a diplomatic solution with Congress and sent military stores but no troops or heavy cargoes to Louisiana during hurricane season. Miró finally ordered the Georgia envoys to leave in November 1785 when he clearly held the upper hand.[30]

Bouligny's military force was small, but it had a definite impact on a frontier district of about 1,100 white settlers and 900 enslaved blacks.[31] Dissent was punishable, even though Spanish officials were disinclined to severity. Three prominent settlers who purportedly opposed Madrid's governance were subjected to house arrest, imprisonment for a few months, or exile. (Tacitus Galliard, the banished man, returned to Natchez within a year of being convicted.) Rather than being Georgia stalwarts, the dissenters were local autonomists favoring regional statehood, possibly as a way station toward joining the American Union.[32] The public pulse, in so far as it may be measured, reveals a society torn from British colonial allegiance, but by no means Spanish in any cultural or national sense.

Miró was a realist searching for effective ways to administer frontier regions where Anglo Protestants lay in the pathway of U.S. southwestern expansion. Unable to chart imperial policy, he urged his superiors toward flexibility. In June 1785, he advised Gálvez that Spain's closure of the Mississippi was dangerously provoking the American West, whose disgruntled settlers might seize Louisiana within a few years and then extend their "conquests and forays" (*conquistas y correrias*) to New Spain.[33]

Miró's pragmatic approach had closely related political and religious dimensions. Under his régime, former British subjects were secure if they took an oath of allegiance to the crown and abstained from non-Catholic public worship. This policy became the rule at Natchez, Baton Rouge, and Tensaw well before Madrid signaled its endorsement in 1786. The royal treasury subsidized Irish Catholic priests to proselytize in Louisiana and West Florida, though the clerics brought few Anglo Protestants into the fold.[34] Miró showed his preference for well-to-do foreign colonists when dispensing land grants. In October 1785, he approved the petition of brothers Benjamin and James Smith to settle with their slaves on a tract of 2,100 acres near Baton Rouge previously occupied by a departed English Loyalist.[35]

Miró was inclined to strike deals with Anglo elites that had a vested interest in Spanish success. In 1785, he authorized James Mather, an English merchant of New Orleans, to oversee Mobile's Indian commerce. When Pedro Favrot criticized this choice, Miró bitingly asked whether the commandant could find "some Spaniard or Frenchman to run the place [the Mobile store]?" The trade "cannot be conducted with merchandise other than . . . English, both because the savages prefer it and because it is cheaper." British-Indian commerce was, moreover, the only viable alternative to U.S. traders operating from the north.[36]

In an even riskier move, Miró permitted Colonel Anthony Hutchins, the foremost British Loyalist in Natchez during the Revolution, to return to his plantation in 1785 after a political exile of nearly four years. Hutchins had fled the Mississippi for South Carolina after coming under Spanish scrutiny for allegedly inciting the British Loyalist revolt of 1781. Once back at White Apple Village in the heart of Natchez, he quietly cooperated with Spanish authorities against Georgia's commissioners. He passed intelligence to Lt. Governor Bouligny, who was pleased to invite Mrs. Hutchins to a dinner hosted for ladies of the district. At Bouligny's recommendation, Hutchins was appointed a militia officer of the Second Creek district. Louisiana authorities deftly dispensed such honors in a community where military rank was a prestigious matter. [37]

Anthony Hutchins, a man of some sixty years in 1785, was a New Jersey native who became a substantial North Carolina landowner before migrating to Natchez in 1772. His younger brother, Thomas, had already developed a keen interest in the Mississippi as a British military engineer, cartographer, and aspiring land claimant. Anthony Hutchins rose to the fore as a plantation owner, militia colonel, and a staunch Loyalist in wartime. Robbed and arrested by Willing's raiders in 1778, he exacted revenge by breaking his parole in New Orleans, heading upriver, and turning his home district into a Tory stronghold. He appears to have quietly abetted the Anglo uprising against Spain in 1781 but managed to hide his tracks and to escape arrest. The Spanish recapture of Natchez forced him to flee, but it did not diminish his attachment to the Mississippi. Bernardo de Gálvez, who suspected Hutchins of duplicity even before the rebellion, aptly described him as "a restless character . . . capable of plotting all sorts of schemes."[38]

Anthony Hutchins tested new allegiances immediately after the war during his exile in the United States. Putting aside past British loyalty, he petitioned Congress in May 1783 to take control of all territory on the Mississippi's east side, including Natchez, "as low down as the 31st Degree." Hutchins turned to the United States in the hope of recouping his place in the "rich and opulent Country" by the Mississippi. He even imagined his district becoming in due time an "Independent State, which may hereafter join the Confederacy of America."[39]

To heighten his chances of success, Hutchins laced his petition with anti-Spanish invective. Had he fallen into Spain's grasp in the war's final stage, he would have been shipped "in chains" to New Orleans, with all likelihood of being sentenced "to the Mines" or made a galley prisoner for life. The Spanish were "a Mercyless [sic] Set of Men, whose mode of Government is more to be dreaded than any other civilized Nation upon the Earth." One would scarcely know from this harangue that Hutchins's wife was still in possession of the Natchez family estate under a quite moderate régime.[40] The petition was welcomed by a congressional committee, which recommended that Oliver Pollock, now U.S. agent in Havana, intervene with Spanish authorities on Hutchins's behalf.[41] Little came of this proposal, which ironically pinned Hutchins's hopes on Pollock, his bitter wartime foe.

Unable to gain U.S. assistance, Hutchins finally made his own peace with Spanish Louisiana. He did so at a propitious time, when Madrid needed influential Anglo allies during the Bourbon County crisis. Returning to Natchez while Georgia was pressing its claims, Hutchins courted Miró in a lengthy discourse denying any personal involvement in the Natchez uprising of 1781, and blaming that affair on pro-U.S. rabble-rousers.[42] The past would be set aright and the door opened to personal prosperity and power. Hutchins enhanced his standing with Miró by relaying covert intelligence on Natchez that was beyond Spanish earshot. While the Georgia threat still loomed in October 1785, he described an unsettled community: "the best of the people are happy & satisfied in their present situation & dread a revolution, some others are easy about the matter whatever way the scale shall turn, the residue appear to be divided (i.e.) some for the American cause, & some for Anarchy only."[43] By implication, Georgia was the stalking horse for an American takeover.

Hutchins artfully disclosed Natchez's innermost political discourse in his own inimitable and intriguing manner. As he explained to Miró, "I some times have opportunities of hearing by chance many things that are not intended to reach my ear." Though such words might be harmless, he thought it best "to hint" at "the substance" of information "only obliquely expressed, and which carries with it something of a hostile meaning." His sense of matters was not reassuring to Spain. The situation was rife for danger because of likely collusion between local residents and American freebooters invading from the north:

> The volunteers will come down . . . as free booters, & pay themselves out of the property of such inhabitants as shall refuse to take arms in their favor, together with that of others down the River, which is a matter of no wonder . . . as what better can be expected from such a number of lawless people as are up these waters, incapable of restraint, destitute of principle, void of feeling, long enured [sic] to rapine & ravage, that can lack nothing but a word from the mischievous to prompt them to execute any act or design, however direful or unwarrantable.[44]

There is little reason to doubt Hutchins's contempt for footloose frontier folk in American territory. His exegesis was also designed to build his political clout with Miró, who was, after all, concerned about a hostile downriver attack. Close to home, Hutchins duplicitously told Miró which local dissidents were penitent and which troublemakers. Sutton Banks "is said to be very cautious of either imprudent actions or expressions"; Tacitus Galliard "it is said boasts greatly that he has not taken an oath [to Spain] at all, not even that of fidelity." Miró was thankful for Hutchins's information, but wary about using hearsay in a court proceeding.[45]

Spanish conciliation of Anglo Natchez may be viewed from various perspectives, depending on whether our judgments are based on the mid-1780s or extended to subsequent decades. In Miró's flexible model of Spanish colonialism, crown officials permitted British and Anglo-American Protestants to become Spanish subjects and to share responsibility for public order. Considered in a more critical light, the reforms instituted in the Natchez district had little chance of strengthening Madrid's authority unless supported by sufficient military force. Once concessions were granted to individualistic Anglo colonists, the latter would inevitably push for greater autonomy over time. Would militia posts, for example, finally satisfy men still lacking electoral privileges, representative government, or the right of public worship? The Natchez district may even be considered the first Anglo-American "Texas"—a locale where a permissive colonial order allowed foreigners to take control from within while the U.S. government generated growing pressure from without.

One should not press the analogy between Natchez and Texas too far, though the comparison is illustrative of important tendencies. The American confederation of the mid-1780s was not equivalent to the more robust federal union of the 1820s and 1830s. (And the Mexican state of the latter era differed in important respects from the previous Spanish régime.) Whether the young American confederation could remain a whole—let alone control the trans-Appalachian West—still persisted as an issue beyond the establishment of the first government under the Constitution in 1789. Aranda's often-cited prediction of 1783—that the United States was born "a pygmy" but would one day become a "giant"—has an air of inevitability that was not obvious at the time. Madrid had more to fear then from a weak American union, which was unable to stanch military adventurism on its own frontiers, than a strong national authority insisting on its citizenry's respect for law.[46]

Congress Responds to Events at Natchez

Rumors reached Philadelphia and New York City of tensions between Georgia and Spain about the time that Thomas Green arrived at Natchez. The first reports were not necessarily accurate. The marquis de Barbé-Marbois, French emissary to the United States, sent word to George Washington on June 12, 1785, that several persons had been killed in a clash between the Spanish at "fort Natchez" and local inhabitants. Washington replied that he feared "disagreeable" events from disputes regarding the

Mississippi's closure. Emigration to the river "is astonishingly great, & chiefly from a description of people who are not very subordinate to the Laws & Constitution of the States they go from; whether the prohibition of the Spaniards therefore is just or unjust, politic or impolitic, it will be with difficulty that a people of this class can be restrained from the enjoyment of natural advantages."[47] Washington was not at all looking for a clash with Spain, whose monarch had just graciously favored him with a gift of two mules ("Jacks of the first race") that he greatly prized. Still, his letter to Barbé-Marbois conveyed a subtle message quite probably meant for Diego de Gardoqui, the newly arrived Spanish ambassador to Congress. Unless Spain accommodated U.S. boundary and navigational rights, it would invite problems as American western settlement grew. In 1780, James Madison had aired a similar idea, writing that Madrid would be unwise to retain "vacant" lands in the Lower Mississippi Valley because the area lay in the path of U.S. frontier migration.[48]

Madison did not repeat this view during the Natchez crisis nearly five years later. While greatly valuing the Mississippi, he was disgusted by Georgia's attempted coup as a token of unbridled state adventurism. Suspecting Georgia of planning to seize the Gulf ports, Madison hoped that "no State could be guilty of either so flagrant an outrage on the federal Constitution, or so imprudent a mode of pursuing their claims against a foreign nation."[49] Congress should alone resolve U.S. boundary claims and rights to the Mississippi through diplomatic negotiations.

Gardoqui complained of Georgia's actions in a firm but courteous manner, reminding Congress that the Spanish had an incontestable title to Natchez by conquest. In response, the delegates adopted a conciliatory tone without giving ground on the boundary question itself. The United States had "an undoubted right" to all territories specified by peace treaty with Britain—and therefore a southern boundary on the Mississippi's east bank at the 31st parallel. The delegates, meanwhile, expressed their concern over "unwarrantable attempts" by persons undermining peaceful relations with Spain. Georgia's congressional representatives gave ground by disavowing Green's conduct and disclaiming the least intention of disturbing Spanish subjects on the Mississippi. The state's volte-face set matters aright for the time being.[50] Congress found it expedient to scold a single offender without backing down on controversial issues before serious negotiations ensued with Madrid.

John Jay's role in Spanish negotiations in 1785–86 was a far cry from the hard line he had taken at the Paris peace negotiations just a few years before. Unable to budge Gardoqui on the Mississippi, he took a conciliatory posture promoting American commercial interests in a time of economic hardship. In his scenario, the United States would forbear navigation of the great river south of national territory for twenty-five to thirty years, in return for Madrid's permitting American ships and goods to enter Iberian ports and the Canary Islands. Jay's proposal notoriously provoked a fierce sectional divide that placed the Union in peril. Many southern and western citizens cried betrayal as they learned of the debate in Congress, which pitted seven northern state delegations against those from Maryland to Georgia. Though the southern bloc was in the minority, it was able to foil Jay's plan since the approval of nine states was necessary to carry a foreign treaty under the Articles of Confederation.[51]

The sacrifice of the Mississippi did not sit well among many Northerners, despite the sectional divide in Congress. In early 1787, New Jersey's legislature rescinded the state's congressional vote for Jay's proposal. Speculative interest in Mississippi lands influenced this political reversal. Other U.S. citizens who were involved in the Mississippi during wartime were loath to see any concessions to Spain. James Willing, former American marauder, was a hardliner even before Jay's scheme became public. Writing to fellow Pennsylvanian James Wilson in early 1785, he lauded Georgia's Mississippi claims: "The Spaniards are Encroaching by rapid Strides on our Territory and wish to dispossess these States [of] a Valuable Country and with it, the Navigation of the River, of so much importance to the Western Settlements."[52]

Besides the navigation issue, the United States and Spain remained at loggerheads over their territorial boundary from the Mississippi to the Chattahoochee. Jay counseled an amicable settlement of differences, even advising Congress that "it would be better even to yield a few Acres, than to part in ill humour."[53] James Madison, then in Congress, was so frustrated with Jay that he thrust himself into negotiations. Meeting with Gardoqui in March 1787, he winced at Spanish territorial claims on the Mississippi as far north as the Ohio. The Virginian worried that congressional weakness would drive frustrated western settlers into British hands.[54]

Spanish diplomacy unwittingly abetted the American citizenry's drive to forge its own path to the Gulf, whether with or without a national treaty. In 1786, foreign minister Floridablanca still clung to the idea of opposing American navigation on the Mississippi below the Ohio; he would admit as far south as the Yazoo only if absolutely necessary to reach an accord. A year later he instructed Gardoqui to offer the 31st parallel as the limit of American navigation by treaty. Left unanswered was why the United States would accept any restriction short of New Orleans at the least.[55]

Floridablanca inched toward retreat on the boundary question, though no more effectively than on the Mississippi. His territorial stance of 1786 advocated a vast Indian neutral ground between the Yazoo River and the mouth of the Ohio—with neither Spain nor the United States permitted to settle the region. By September 1787, Floridablanca abandoned this idea, which depended on royal commitment to native defense beyond Madrid's capability. His new draft proposal conceded American sovereignty to the 31st parallel—with the exception of the Natchez district and a corridor leading southward to Spanish areas below the proposed boundary line. The foreign minister's moderation, quickened by fear of American frontiersmen, came too late to break diplomatic stalemate.[56]

Western Disaffection and the Freebooting Threat

Floridablanca and other royal councilors were aware of the remarkable growth of white settlement in the trans-Appalachian United States. Though Madrid did not know the precise extent of American population, it had good cause for concern. Kentucky had some 8,000 colonial inhabitants in 1782, about 50,000 five years later, and over 73,000 in 1790. White settlers also pushed westward along the Cumberland and Holston Rivers in the region that became Tennessee. That area had perhaps 25,000 non-Indian residents by 1788 and more than 35,000 two years later.[57]

The American West was so disaffected from Congress that some frontier leaders were reputedly considering separation from the Union. To appreciate the depth of popular discontent, two points are worth noting. First, nearly all whites in the region regarded the Mississippi as vital to prosperity in the here and now—and not a claim that could be bartered away for decades and then somehow recovered. Second, Congress had the political standing of a plural executive, safeguarding the country's vital interests in peace and war. If Congress abandoned this fundamental role, it could forfeit the citizenry's allegiance, especially in frontier districts where life was precarious because of endemic clashes between settlers and native peoples.[58] The political uncertainty brought on by Jay's negotiations lingered because the foreign secretary did not foreclose a Spanish accord that might conceivably give way on both navigational and boundary issues. In the absence of good news from Congress, many western settlers continued to fear the worst.[59]

Thomas Green, already stung by his failure to wrest Natchez from Spain, likened Jay's proposed treaty to a "worse Slavery than ever Great Britain presumed." Writing to Georgia's government from Louisville in December 1786, he pleaded for license to mount a military expedition to seize the Natchez district. Rather than depending on state militia, Green offered to recruit volunteers under the renowned George Rogers Clark, now a Virginia militia general in Kentucky. Freebooting had a payoff. According to Green's plan, the troops would proceed "at their own risk and expense" if Georgia simply offered Natchez lands to the volunteers. In his fever-pitch call, "hundreds are now awaiting to join us with their families seeking an Asylum for liberty & Religion."[60] Adventurism was patriotism when citizen-soldiers championed the United States over Spain. In Green's folk speech, the Spanish were said to be building their defenses at "pencecoly" and New Orleans. They were "Drawin[g] the Intrust of the Indens from us" and supplying the Creeks with arms for attacks on Cumberland and Cantuck [Kentucky]." There was no recourse but the sword: "If the natches is not give up [by Spain] or taken our Weston Cuntery is nothing."[61]

Green's plan is the first notable instance of a conspiracy formed in the United States for the armed takeover of Spanish territory. His venture certainly has the hallmark of a "filibuster"—a freebooting military expedition conceived and directed by individuals acting beyond the purview of their own country's government. Moreover, Green planned to recruit volunteers for battle against Spain—a nation officially at peace with the United States. His plan was not wholly autonomous, however, since it hinged on Georgia's authorization. Then, too, the chief conspirator expected support in the disputed Natchez borderlands where his own kin resided.[62]

The rhetoric of conspiracy suggested all or nothing—the conquest of Natchez under Georgia's claim or the Green clan's departure with all its slaves from Spanish territory. Instead of any high drama, however, the invasion plan suddenly collapsed because of frontier factionalism. Before Green raised any volunteer force, his message was divulged to a group of Kentucky politicos who were foes of George Rogers Clark. James Wilkinson, former American brigadier, led the way in sabotaging Clark at a convention held in Danville, Kentucky, in December 1786.

The Clark-Green venture was effectively dead once it became a matter of public dispute and notoriety.[63]

Wilkinson and friends lambasted Clark for loose and undisciplined conduct on several fronts. The general was criticized for abusing French settlers in the Illinois country and arbitrarily confiscating the property of Louisiana merchants as a retributory act against Spain for its seizure of American boats on the Mississippi. Pressed on the freebooting question, Clark denied rather unconvincingly that he had any knowledge of Green's invasion plan. He supposedly wished no harm to Spaniards but only peaceful settlement and a small land grant at Natchez.[64]

Gardoqui, a suave diplomat who cultivated congressional allies, was greatly troubled by the federal government's inability to restrain its citizens' violent tendencies against Spanish and Indian territories. From his Manhattan residence, he advised Floridablanca in May 1787 that the impending federal convention in Philadelphia was unlikely to produce any political remedy. The United States was not only badly divided in opinion but also had many destitute persons who, having nothing to lose, would venture (*aventurarian*) to better their fortunes by shaking the pillars of state. Adventurism was a dangerous habit, especially among western settlers seething over Spain's closure of the Mississippi and plotting to open "a path to the sea" by force if necessary.[65]

Gardoqui's education in American democracy grew exponentially one day in 1786 when Lt. John Sullivan, formerly of the Continental Army, appeared at the diplomat's house. The lieutenant announced himself an Irishman and a Catholic and requested an officer's rank in a Spanish regiment in America. Gardoqui told his unwelcome visitor to leave, only to have Sullivan bedevil him in a more serious way a year later. In August 1787, American newspapers published Sullivan's letter blasting Gardoqui for not giving him the desired military post. Because of this slight, the lieutenant refused to accept "any rank or degree in the service of his Catholic Majesty."[66] Moving from rebuke to gasconade, Sullivan pronounced himself "a soldier of fortune" ready to unite with thousands of former American officers sharing the patriotic motive of opening trade to the Gulf. His comrades would not be stopped by "the narrow policy of any foreign court": "From the Natches to the Kaskaskies—from Pittsburg to St. Mary's river, they are prepared to pour forth with the greatest ease 50,000 veterans in arms, in defense of their *commercial* rights, throughout the navigable rivers of the southern parts of this empire.... The Americans are amphibious animals. They cannot be confined to the land alone. Tillage and commerce are their elements. Both, or neither will they enjoy. Both they will have, or perish."[67]

What was a diplomat to do when encountering personal declamations from obscure men threatening Spain's downfall from the Mississippi to the Atlantic? Disdaining any direct reply, Gardoqui brought the Sullivan letter to John Jay's attention so that the American government would take appropriate measures. Jay mollified Gardoqui as best he could. On October 8, 1787, Congress resolved that the United States viewed Sullivan's conduct as "very reprehensible"—and accordingly pledged to frustrate his designs.[68]

A month later, Jay had to allay Gardoqui's concerns once more. The American foreign secretary had just received a copy of a letter recently written by Sullivan to Major William Brown of Philadelphia. In the message, Sullivan admonished Brown to migrate to the Tennessee River: "There will be work cut out for you in that Country—I want you much—By God—take my Word for it that we will be speedily in Possession of New Orleans." Sullivan's letter came into the hands of Oliver Pollock in Philadelphia, who in turn gave a copy to Robert Morris and Gouverneur Morris, who then passed all to Jay. Pollock, who was hardly pro-Spanish, saw personal benefit from divulging political intelligence in this case.[69]

Secretary of War Henry Knox was troubled by frontier lawlessness well before the Sullivan affair erupted. Highly critical of George Rogers Clark's rampages in Illinois, he advised Congress of the need for countermeasures in April 1787. Knox identified two general problems: "the spirit of adventure"—a type of reckless individualism in his view—and "the supposed imbecillity [sic] of government." He warned that the United States was more liable to lose "the great national advantages resulting from a wise administration of the western territory, by the evils of usurpation and intrusion, than by any other causes whatever." In November 1787, Knox ordered General Josiah Harmar, stationed along the Ohio, to supervise an investigation of frontier districts where Sullivan's message was rumored to take hold.[70] The inquiry was placed in the hands of a solitary officer, Lt. John Armstrong, who found no evidence of anti-Spanish plotting on a journey to the Holston River settlements. Rather than conspiring against Natchez, whites of the Holston battled each other over whether they should remain part of North Carolina, or instead join the frontier state of Franklin. Internecine frontier discord—and concurrent Indian conflict—blunted aggressive settler movements targeting the Mississippi.[71]

Martín Navarro, intendant of Louisiana, received various reports of western intrigues during the early months of 1787. While knowing that Clark was under investigation by Congress, he doubted the capacity of the American government to stanch frontier disorders. According to Navarro's sources, Clark had gathered as many as 2,000 men at Vincennes for a descent on the Yazoo. This judgment correctly identified the projected point of attack though exaggerating the number of freebooters encamped about the Wabash and Ohio. Navarro declared that Louisiana stood alone against "a troop of bandits, without discipline, without law, and without humanity, animated by no other principle than robbery."[72] The danger to royal interests could not be overstated by provincial officers anxious for Madrid's assistance.

Navarro was attuned to the adventurist threat but rather contemptuous of the United States, which he perceived as helpless in various quarters. Britain excluded U.S. ships from its West Indian colonies while France also restricted American commerce. Spain kept up the Mississippi's closure to all but a smattering of American traffic. British agents stirred Indian attacks on U.S. settlers from the Wabash and the Great Lakes. The Cherokees and Creeks kept colonists in alarm from the Ohio to Florida.[73]

Navarro was far from complacent, notwithstanding his summation of U.S. woes. By the summer of 1787, he had come to share Miró's judgment that Spain could not retain Louisiana without conciliating leading men in the trans-Appalachian West, particularly Kentucky, where Madrid was the target of growing popular resentment. Both Miró and Navarro were impressed by James Wilkinson's role in opposing Clark's machinations about the Ohio. Kentucky powerbrokers quite possibly shared common interests with the Spanish crown. Wilkinson had his eye on opening Kentucky-Louisiana commerce for profit and power. Both Miró and Navarro wished to strengthen Louisiana—and weaken the United States—by using trade and immigration as political instruments. The path was being readied for Wilkinson's journey to New Orleans in the summer of 1787. The freebooting threat to Louisiana opened Mississippi passageways for Americans who thirsted for lucre more than military glory.

PART II

New Empires, New Republics, 1787–1803

PROLOGUE

Wilkinson and the Imperial Self

James Wilkinson of Lexington, Kentucky, made his own bold entry into Louisiana by pledging loyalty to Spain while still a U.S. citizen and a supposed patriot. He did so in a remarkable "Declaration" of August 21, 1787, transmitted in person to Miró and Navarro in New Orleans.[1] His pronouncement may be interpreted as a bid for imperial selfhood—an attempt to place his own person at the center of a new continental order. Wilkinson was exceptionally influential in this guise, though hardly singular in envisioning new political arrangements sweeping across Indian territories and regions where Madrid's governance was tenuous or in dispute.

Wilkinson's declaration was no standard political oath respecting Spanish monarchical norms. It was instead a philosophical creed justifying his conduct on the principle of "Interest," i.e., self-interest—"the ruling Passion of Nations, as well as of Individuals." These words would have meant little had not Miró and Navarro shared a similar discourse as educated gentlemen versed in Enlightenment precepts. They clearly understood their visitor when the latter wrote of "silencing every passion & every prejudice," and following "the dictates of Reason, Honour & conscience." Most strikingly, Wilkinson conceived of his military service during the Revolution as entitling him to choose a new national loyalty. He had done his duty by America, and helped her "until She triumphed over Her Enemy." Now that she was free, he was also "at Liberty, after having contended for Her happiness, to seek for my own." Tossing off the United States as if he had the right to seek a new mistress, Wilkinson declared allegiance to the Spanish monarch on his own terms: "I am persuaded, my Conduct will be directed, by such principles of loyalty to my Sovereign ... as will ... transmit my Name unsullied to posterity."[2]

Wilkinson was a master at posing as the champion of borderlands comity amidst frontier violence and invasion threats. Late in 1786 he

James Wilkinson. Lithoprint after portrait of Charles Willson Peale of 1796–97. Courtesy of Edward Alexander Parsons Collection, di_07450, The Dolph Briscoe Center for American History, the University of Texas at Austin. This portrait shows Wilkinson, then about forty years old, about a decade after his first visit to New Orleans in 1787.

warned Louisiana officials that Colonel Thomas Green, along with "other desperadoes," were planning to attack Natchez "in violation of the Laws of their own Country, of the Faith of Treaties, & of the usage of Nations." In a subsequent letter, Wilkinson took credit, "along with the leading Characters in Kentucky," for squelching Green's enterprise.[3] For the next seventeen years, Louisiana's Spanish governors closely heeded Wilkinson's voluminous correspondence about frontier machinations.

Wilkinson was just as much an adventurer as George Rogers Clark or Thomas Green, though his risk-taking differed in kind from freebooting conspiracies intended to overthrow Spanish colonialism. Taking a broad view, we can discern overlapping elements between ostensibly lawful and illicit Anglo-American maneuvering toward Louisiana and the Floridas. For example, U.S. commercial penetration of Louisiana commonly blurred the lines between legitimate commerce and smuggling. Military adventurers developed their own colonizing and commercial strategies founded on intrigue and diplomacy besides armed force. In fact, adventurist scheming often hinged on intrigue precisely because private interests had insufficient power to gain their way without persuasion, bluff, or outright deception.

The wars of the French Revolution were an accelerant for projected assaults launched from the United States on Madrid's exposed North American possessions. As Spain moved unsteadily from being at war with France (1793–1795) to being France's ally against Britain (1796–1802), U.S. adventurers variously sought French or British license for anti-Spanish campaigns. Borderlands contestation in the Mississippi Valley and Gulf had a volatile transatlantic dimension, influenced by Saint Domingue's slave revolution as well as European upheaval.

British Loyalist ambitions continued to roil the Spanish realm well after the Revolutionary War. The quintessential North American adventurer of the late eighteenth century was Tory William Augustus Bowles, self-proclaimed leader of the Creek nation, who waged a persistent fight for independent Indian statehood in the Florida Gulf Coast and adjoining territories. Bowles's opponents—whether Spanish or U.S. by nationality—invariably dubbed him an "adventurer," a term conjuring images of unlicensed banditry and piracy to those aligned against him.

Adventurist schemes turned on the capacity of private individuals to mold imperial and national powers to serve their interests. The struggle for the Louisiana-Florida borderlands inverted mercantilist and metropolitan-centered conception of empire. In the mercantilist model, metropoles defined the parameters of war, trade, and transnational interchange for peripheral colonial regions. During the late eighteenth century, individuals operating beyond state control endeavored to enlist imperial governments to back their own schemes of frontier development and political transformation. This tendency exemplifies Charles Maier's idea that "empire grows from the outside in and as well as from the inside outward."[4]

Louisiana and the Floridas witnessed multiple possibilities of being drawn into new republics or empires. Indian peoples had a central part in this struggle since their lands and way of life were at stake. There is an irony to the widespread European and colonial perception that Indian allegiance could be bought by the highest bidder. Interchange between Spanish Louisiana officialdom, foreign settlers, and merchants hinged on the idea that self-interest was the governing principle of human society. That idea was put to the test as Spain attempted to woo Anglo settlers and U.S. newcomers to its standard in the Mississippi Valley. By an economic twist of fate, Spanish Louisiana's defense was funded by royal Mexican silver, some of which found its way into the pockets of foreign colonizers and traders with highly individualistic ambitions.

CHAPTER 6

License to Venture

Colonization and Commercial Adventurism

The year 1787 was a turning point in borderlands contention between Spain and the United States. It was also a high point for Esteban Miró and Martín Navarro, whose recommendations shaped Madrid's new initiatives for coopting and countering American frontiersmen. The results were paradoxical—a helmsmanship of carrot and stick. Spain ended its closure of the downriver Mississippi trade but without conceding general navigation rights on the river to the United States. Louisiana and neighboring West Florida were meanwhile opened to U.S. immigrants—the very group presenting the gravest danger to Spanish colonialism. Royalist thinking rested on self-interest and calculated risk. The new immigrants would supposedly be so grateful for Spanish largesse that they would become loyal subjects defending the soil against foreign threats, even those emanating from the United States.[1]

Spain's new initiatives had a paradoxical character. Fear and vulnerability brought forth adaptability and imagination. Louisiana's continuing viability required population growth and economic development overriding any simple model of an imperial buffer zone where foreigners were kept at bay. Madrid's policies for the Mississippi Valley countenanced a multi-ethnic borderlands society though not a multi-confessional one—at least with respect to public worship.[2]

Changing borderland conditions coincided with shifting imperial leadership. The deaths of leading men—Bernardo de Gálvez in November 1786 and José de Gálvez in June 1787—were significant losses, compounded by the passing of Carlos III the following year. Miró, himself a protégé of the younger Gálvez, had to do without a steady mentor, while finding greater room to advocate policy changes in his own right.[3] It is an intriguing if unanswerable question if the formidable Gálvez duo—both uncle and nephew—would have approved a growing Kentucky–New Orleans trade and opened the door to U.S. colonization in a provincial gateway bordering Northern New Spain and the Gulf. During his last months in office, José de Gálvez was certainly leaning to a liberalized immigration régime for Louisiana and West Florida districts where Anglo colonists already resided. Antonio Váldes, his successor as minister of the Indies, forwarded this policy at Miró's behest. Floridablanca, too, went along as foreign minister.[4]

The Spanish imperial government proceeded carefully while admitting foreigners to Louisiana and the Floridas. Different rules applied to particular regions, depending on pressures generated from the United States. For example, Madrid did not officially open East Florida to non-Catholic settlement until 1790——three years after similar license was permitted for Louisiana and West Florida.[5] The Mississippi Valley outdistanced all regions in attracting foreign interest because of its huge agricultural and commercial potential.

Because nearly all large-scale colonization projects for Spanish Louisiana failed to pan out, it is all too easy to overlook the province's potential as a regional competitor to the western United States for immigration and economic growth. Louisiana's social order was still malleable in many regions. The prevalence of slavery—as opposed to free European labor—had yet to be determined in Natchez, let alone northward. Numerous colonizers believed they could benefit Spain—and not least themselves—by plotting settlement and commerce in the continent's fertile interior.

Pierre Wouves d'Argès—Aspiring French Colonizer

Imperial Spain licensed a French colonial promoter to oversee the official opening of Louisiana to Protestant settlers from the western United States. The steward of this enterprise was Pierre Rezard Wouves d'Argès, former army captain and chevalier of the order of St. Louis. Wouves left France by 1783 to pursue his fortune in faraway Louisville by the falls of the Ohio. Three years later, he arrived at New Orleans where he presented a petition on behalf of 1,582 Kentucky families requesting Spanish permission to settle close by Natchez. Encouraged by Miró and Navarro, he next journeyed to Paris, and eventually Spain, to secure royal authorization. On August 23, 1787, Antonio Valdés approved the project in the king's name. By this order, immigrant laborers and artisans were invited to settle the Mississippi either above or below Natchez, and to receive land gratis on condition they behaved as loyal vassals. The Spanish court vaguely pledged religious toleration, provided that only Roman Catholics were eligible for military or civil office. Irish Catholic priests would minister to the colonists, just as previously mandated for Natchez.[6]

The new royal edict was innovative, if executed in a guarded manner through a single colonial sponsor. Wouves d'Argès had several weighty tasks as a semi-official Spanish agent. While recruiting colonists, he was charged with announcing a new royal commercial policy for trans-Appalachian trade with Louisiana. Kentucky residents were to be informed that they could lawfully market their produce in New Orleans on payment of a 25 percent duty. Madrid thereby backed away from its closure of the Mississippi to foreigners wherever the river's banks fell within Spanish territories. Two caveats should be noted. First, this license applied only to downriver shipments. Second, the westerners were to sell their produce for cloth and other dry goods, wines, rum, and liquors. Spain maintained its policy of prohibiting the export of specie from its American dominions to foreign lands.[7]

Imperial authorities put such a premium on shoring up Natchez that they tolerated certain anomalies in Wouves's settlement project. When the chevalier initiated his plan, he claimed that the majority of his prospective colonists were German by birth or ancestry. This appears highly improbable given Kentucky's overwhelmingly Anglo-American settler population. One cannot help but think that Wouves sugarcoated his proposal in order to allay Madrid's concerns about Kentucky frontiersmen entering the realm. He later dropped the pretense of German colonization once assured of Spanish royal support.[8] Aranda backed the chevalier's project and likened foreign militiamen safeguarding Louisiana's frontier to loyal Muslim troops then defending Spain's North African enclaves in Ceuta and Oran. The Spanish court anticipated an Anglo-American influx by insisting that Natchez's district governor be fluent in English. The British presence in the Lower Mississippi Valley also necessitated this measure.[9]

Wouves d'Argès presented himself to Spanish officials as a trustworthy gentleman with an expert knowledge of the western United States. Sensitive to being labeled an intriguing foreigner, he assured Floridablanca that he was no "*Proyectista*" (schemer) with an "over-excited imagination." The chevalier thereby tailored his petition to a particular Spanish outlook of enlightened reform. *Proyectistas* in Bourbon Spain were civil servants and intellectuals who actively promoted a more rational and efficient economic order. To be dubbed a *proyectista* might appear a compliment, but it was a term that senior ministers commonly used to mock proponents of ambitious but fanciful schemes that were politically and financially unfeasible.[10]

A projecting spirit was certainly a key element of Louisiana colonization proposals during the late eighteenth century. In the case of Wouves d'Argès, however, political maladroitness outstripped acumen. The Spanish court's approval was a heady start, but it meant little after the chevalier reached New York City in January 1788 and plotted his return to Kentucky. Dependent on Gardoqui's cooperation, Wouves alienated the Spanish envoy by asserting powers beyond his station. Badly short of funds, he next journeyed by sea to New Orleans, where he found Miró as recalcitrant as Gardoqui had been. Notwithstanding grand plans, Wouves never reached Kentucky let alone brought any western colonists to Natchez.[11]

The chevalier's failure reflected a lack of coordination between Madrid and its overseas officials in New York City and New Orleans. Neither Gardoqui nor Miró appreciated a French visitor interfering in their management of U.S. relations. Gardoqui was miffed when Wouves loosely spread word that the Spanish government was committed to free trade with the United States.[12] Miró himself preferred granting commercial concessions to a few Western magnates, especially James Wilkinson, rather than opening the Mississippi trade to the generality of American frontier folk. Frustrated at New Orleans, Wouves ultimately returned to France in 1789 rather than accept a Spanish commandant's post in Upper Louisiana.[13]

Martín Navarro—Political Economist

Veteran intendant Martín Navarro saw Louisiana's fate as hinging on timely incentives for population and commercial growth. Taking his case directly to Madrid in the fall of 1788, he penned a lengthy memorandum extolling industrious and respectable immigrants who would stimulate shipbuilding, manufacturing, agricultural improvement, and technological invention. Navarro, much like Adam Smith, was a believer in private economic ambition as a public virtue. Months before welcoming Wilkinson to New Orleans, he lauded Natchez's Anglo tobacco planters as loyal vassals with a stake in Louisiana's success. As he sardonically confided to

José de Gálvez, those colonists worshipped the king's silver "as much as the Indians venerate their idols."[14]

Though Navarro never returned to Louisiana after leaving the province in 1788, his thought is highly important for understanding the evolution of Spanish policy in the Mississippi Valley over a twenty-year span. First coming to New Orleans with Ulloa in 1766, he witnessed the trials of French colonial revolt two years later and the challenges of governing Louisiana after O'Reilly's invasion. Gálvez's wartime triumphs brought unprecedented opportunities but did not secure economic prosperity. Navarro took a broad view of his responsibilities as the province's chief administrative and financial officer. The king's revenues mattered to him, but so did the more general issue of economic growth. He consistently held that Louisiana required special dispensation because it had almost no trade with Spain itself. Madrid's policy of *comercio libre* within the empire was therefore insufficient for provincial needs. As Navarro wrote in 1787, "the wings of progress" would be clipped if Louisiana were forced into a unitary imperial commercial régime. His mantra was the relaxation or elimination of government restrictions, especially those limiting the colony's economic ties to the French Caribbean.[15]

A *proyectista* by temperament, Navarro had the habit of generalizing from particular circumstances to universal truths. In his "Political Reflections" of 1780, he opined that human nature itself inclined toward migration wherever profit beckoned: "Self-interest and the increase of wealth overcome all barriers, and draw men to a locale from the remotest regions."[16] Royal subsidies could be useful for directed ends. In 1780, Navarro suggested that the crown establish an annual fund of 20,000 pesos to finance the settlement of poor families (all presumably Catholic) from France, Germany, and Ireland. His model immigrants were Germans, whom he considered industrious and self-reliant.[17]

Navarro became disenchanted with subsidized immigration after it proved too expensive to settle any substantial number of indigent European Catholics in Louisiana. The turning point came in 1785–86, when the royal treasury made huge expenditures while bringing nearly 1,600 Acadian refugees from France to the Mississippi. Considerable planning went into this joint public-private venture. French ship owners contracted to transport the Acadians on condition of respecting Spanish regulations requiring all passengers to receive adequate food and raiment. Besides transportation costs, government obligations mounted because of the newcomers' travails in a disease-ridden environment. Madrid never again assumed such a major role in financing Mississippi-Gulf colonization.[18]

While interested in European colonization, Navarro put far greater emphasis on the importation of African slave labor. In 1780, he observed that Louisiana had enjoyed its greatest prosperity when British merchants were unencumbered in bringing blacks to the province. As Navarro looked ahead to peace, he recommended that Louisiana's commerce with the French Caribbean be encouraged to maximum extent.[19] A royal *cédula* of January 22, 1782, followed suit, allowing Spanish subjects in Louisiana a ten-year period for trade with France and the French West Indies if certain conditions were met. (In deference to Havana, commerce with the French islands was only permitted if urgently necessary, though this clause was mainly honored in the breach.) Significantly, slaves could be imported duty-free into Louisiana. Although the export of specie from the province was generally prohibited, it was allowed for the purchase of slaves from friendly or neutral European colonies. Navarro would have ideally liberalized trade still further so that French ships and even other foreign vessels could directly traffic in Louisiana.[20]

Navarro never lost sight of satisfying French colonial planters and merchants who constituted Lower Louisiana's social elite. Besides, he had a personal stake with French merchants in the slave trade. In 1787, he lobbied vigorously, if unsuccessfully, that Louisiana ship owners should be licensed for direct commerce with Africa. While arguing mainly on economic grounds, he also wrote of redeeming Africans from "slavish idolatry" and bringing them to the threshold of the church.[21] Unless the slave trade was boosted, he warned that Louisiana would lose all hope of becoming "one of the most consequential" American colonies, and instead be reduced to "the poorest and most miserable."[22]

Colonial growth in Louisiana came at an enormous human cost. Slaves continued to outnumber free persons in the province during the 1780s. Together with West Florida, Louisiana had 16,544 slaves, 1,303 free people of color, and 14,215 whites in 1785. Three years later, the ranks of the enslaved had climbed to 21,645. The white population also showed a marked increase to 19,445; free persons of color numbered 1,701. Martín Navarro's reports, putting economic considerations to the fore, seriously underplayed the danger of slave insurrection.[23] Smuggling resumed its central role in Louisiana's slave trade much as had been the case before the Revolutionary War. The British ports of Kingston Jamaica, and Roseau in Dominica accounted for a huge share of Louisiana's slave importation between 1783 and 1791.[24]

The Spanish crown's Louisiana tobacco purchase program, for which Navarro assumed responsibility in 1781, spurred the growth of plantation agriculture and slavery in Natchitoches as well as in the Mississippi Valley. To Navarro, royal tobacco subsidies were a political and economic investment, bringing specie into the province, spurring population growth, and also securing the loyalty of French creole producers and Natchez's Anglo planters. José de Gálvez lent crucial support by mandating the purchase of Louisiana tobacco in Veracruz or at Cádiz.[25]

Slavery and commercial agriculture occupied the attention of western U.S. elites as well as Spanish officialdom. In James Wilkinson's memorial to Miró and Navarro of September 1787, the Kentucky magnate requested permission to make a shipment of "Negroes, Live Stock, Tobacco, Flour, Bacon, Lard, Butter, Cheese, Apples & Tallow" in "the amount of fifty or sixty thousand Dollars" to New Orleans. By the time this request was put in writing, Miró and Navarro quickly approved it since they had already reached an implicit understanding with Wilkinson after weeks of discussion. In a display of measured generosity, Louisiana's governor and intendant authorized their guest to ship merchandise amounting to $30,000 in value to New Orleans until the king might permit additional commercial privileges to Kentucky's leading citizens. While Wilkinson's proposal is most notorious for raising the issue of Kentucky's separation from the Union, it also furthered the idea of Anglo-American migration to Louisiana, along with the downriver sale of western produce. Miró and Navarro were as eager as Wilkinson to advance these aims—and they doubtless respected his idea that U.S. colonists should be admitted to Louisiana only if arriving with "visible property" or giving "ample security" for "good behavior."[26]

Madrid broadened its tentative allowance of Anglo-American colonization in the Mississippi Valley a little more than one year after Wilkinson's personal visit to New Orleans. By royal order of December 1, 1788, the Spanish crown opened Louisiana and neighboring West Florida to settlers from Kentucky and bordering western regions. Only vagabonds were explicitly excluded. Shortly after this order reached New Orleans, Miró issued his own land regulations for foreign colonists. Similar to the English headright system, the governor's rule entitled immigrants to receive anywhere from 240 to 800 acres depending on the number of workmen per household. Land was deliberately awarded without charge, so that settlers would be properly grateful to the king. Colonists were required, moreover, to swear an oath of allegiance to "his most Catholic Majesty" and to bind themselves "to take up arms only in defense of this Province." In keeping with policy already instituted for Natchez, the newcomers would "not be molested in religious matters," though only Catholic worship was publically allowed.[27]

The royal order of December 1, 1788 was more generous to foreign immigrants than allowances offered to Wouves d'Argès's prospective colonists. Western U.S. newcomers were now exempt from all duties on property and produce brought to Louisiana and then sold within the province. If such goods were exported via the Gulf, they were subject to a 6 percent tariff. Madrid not only enhanced the scope of foreign immigration, but it also granted extensive commercial privileges to westerners remaining within the United States. The new royal order reduced the tariff from 25 to 15 percent on produce that Kentuckians and other Ohio Valley inhabitants exported to Louisiana. The New Orleans market beckoned more strongly than ever before.[28]

Oliver Pollock Returns to New Orleans

Oliver Pollock was undoubtedly the most experienced merchant renewing his ties to New Orleans during the late 1780s. His case is especially important because it mirrors the ups and downs of U.S.-Spanish ties since the Revolutionary War. Departing New Orleans for North Carolina, Virginia, and then Philadelphia in 1782, Pollock carried a heavy burden of indebtedness incurred as U.S. agent and military supplier in Louisiana. His thoughts immediately turned to recouping his fortune through Spanish trade—in this case with Cuba. All seemed promising once he gained the post of U.S. commercial agent for Havana. But Pollock faced embarrassment as soon as he entered that port in August 1783 when customs officers seized a stash of contraband goods on his incoming ship.[29] His woes mounted the next year since he was prohibited from leaving Cuba until satisfying creditors. Though stripped of some property in court processes, Pollock was not in as bad circumstances as the rest of his countrymen in Cuba. Spanish authorities ordered all U.S. merchants out of Havana in March 1784, subjecting them to imprisonment if they remained. Ironically, the new régime was enforced by Luis de Unzaga, Cuba's captain-general, and former benefactor of the United States in New Orleans.[30]

Pollock was eventually reprieved after his old friend Bernardo de Gálvez took command as captain-general at Havana in the spring of 1785. Gávez's act was not pure generosity since Pollock still owed him for war loans and could hardly repay when confined in Cuba. The American agent was accordingly permitted to return to Philadelphia on condition he would make good on his debts.[31] Diego de Gardoqui, the new Spanish envoy to the United States, not only accompanied Pollock on the voyage, but also had the responsibility of seeing that his fellow passenger fulfilled his financial obligations once ashore. On June 3, 1785, Gardoqui stood as sponsor in Philadelphia at the baptism of Pollock's newborn son, appropriately named Bernard Galvez Pollock. This honorable gesture did not translate into good will toward Spain itself. On the very day of the child's baptism, Pollock wrote John Jay that Madrid had no rightful claim to Natchez, and that Georgia's title to disputed Mississippi territories was sound. Having been humiliated in Havana, Pollock was not well disposed to Spanish colonialism. He even predicted that Cuba's inhabitants would in time rebel against Spain, and "eagerly embrace the earliest favorable opportunity, to shake off the galling chain." Pollock's financial situation did not quickly ease. Congress lent but partial help, paying $9,606 of interest due on his loan from Gálvez but not the principal of $74,087.[32]

As much he detested past slights, Pollock could no more forswear business with Spanish colonies than stop breathing. After all, he made his initial entry to New Orleans as supplier to O'Reilly's invasion force in 1769. Nearly two decades later, he angled to restore his privileged standing with Madrid's officialdom. In September 1787, he earned Gardoqui's good will by helping to expose Lt. John Sullivan's freebooting designs on Spanish territories. Sharing this news with Miró and Navarro by letter, Pollock took pride in his undercover agency saving Louisiana from "a *Banditti*" thirsting after "blood & plunder." Within a few months he headed to New Orleans by sea, most eager to gain a place in Louisiana commerce. He meanwhile carried political intelligence to Miró regarding Kentucky's political disaffection from the Union.[33]

Pollock planned his Louisiana venture before a natural disaster magnified the colony's need for external assistance. On Good Friday, March 21, 1788, a terrible fire devastated New Orleans, consuming 856 houses—the overwhelming number of the town's dwellings, stores, and public buildings. Miró quickly sent $24,000 to Gardoqui for the purchase in Philadelphia of 3,000 barrels of flour and other necessities, medicines, and tools. The governor dispatched three ships from New Orleans to carry the provisions—and another three ships to New York City for similar purpose. Gardoqui was given special authority to license U.S. merchant vessels to carry foodstuffs to Louisiana.[34]

In October 1788, Miró was greatly relieved to learn that Pollock's ship had arrived at the Balize. The governor sent a barge to convey the visiting merchant to town. Pollock sincerely desired to help New Orleans, where he had resided for thirteen years. His visit also turned on profit. On February 12, 1789, he petitioned Miró for a five-year contract to supply New Orleans annually with 3,000 barrels of superfine Philadelphia flour and 4,000 barrels of good Kentucky flour, along with 200 casks of tobacco via the Ohio and Mississippi Rivers. Pollock set his prices—ten pesos for each barrel of flour, and ten pesos per 100 pounds of tobacco. As shrewd as ever, he insisted on selling directly to the royal treasury for specie. Notwithstanding Spanish sensitivities about silver outflows, Pollock requested allowance to carry half of what he gained duty-free out of the province. Miró accepted the general plan, and recommended the export privileges pending Madrid's determination. Rather than requiring the regular 15 percent import duty on Pollock's goods shipped downriver, the governor consented to a 6 percent tariff.[35]

Pollock's venture—along with Miró's emergency measures—strengthened Louisiana's economic ties to Philadelphia and more generally to the Atlantic economy. This process was well underway before the New Orleans fire, but accelerated in its aftermath. Pollock's financial standing had a clear uptick since his New Orleans business helped him to liquidate wartime obligations that neither Virginia nor Congress had covered.[36] Before returning to Philadelphia in 1790, Pollock managed to repurchase his former land at Tunica, just above Baton Rouge, that he had owned as a British subject before the Revolution. He was meanwhile honored by the New Orleans *cabildo* (municipal council) for his gift of a new "fire pump" brought from Philadelphia.[37] Though he would not again come back to the Mississippi Valley until old age, his timely visit of the late 1780s signaled the growth of Atlantic–Gulf Coast commercial connections that originated from adventurist trade outside the parameters of imperial law. Pollock's mercantile risk-taking invariably involved careful political calculation. To his dying day, he lobbied the United States to assume financial responsibility for all the losses he had incurred as congressional commercial agent in New Orleans and Havana. Congress did him justice but never to the extent he demanded.[38]

Foreign Settlement and Legal Pretexts

The settlement of Spanish territories from the United States proceeded mainly through hundreds of individual journeys, undertaken voluntarily by single white men and families, and by enslaved blacks through compulsion. Some U.S. nationals quickly exploited opportunities founded on prior illicit trade with Louisiana. Thomas Irwin, recently of Pennsylvania, imported a shipload of slaves from Dominica for sale at New Orleans and Natchez in 1788. His vessel, the *Navarro*, was undoubtedly named after Martín Navarro, who usually turned a blind eye toward such smuggling.[39] One of the enslaved men on board was Ibrahima, a Fulbe prince who had been seized by African raiders in his native village and eventually sold to an English slaver bound for the West Indies. During the *Navarro*'s voyage from Dominica to New Orleans, fourteen among fifty-seven slave passengers perished. Ibrahima's journey to Louisiana was harrowing in ways defying words. His adventure was the product of mercantile adventurism over which he had no control.[40]

Irwin moved quickly from slave trading to other Louisiana initiatives. Writing to his Pennsylvania kinsmen in May 1789, he enthused over money to be made by shipping flour and other goods down the Ohio and Mississippi. But more profit could be had if "a few Family" came to settle at Natchez. The colonists would then enjoy the status of Spanish subjects and be able to bring goods and merchandise with them free of duty.[41] Irwin confessed that it was under "the pretext" of sponsoring colonization that he had just obtained Miró's permission for his brother, Matthew, to migrate to Louisiana. If no family members could be persuaded, "the Boatmen must say when they arrive" at Natchez "that they mean to settle themselves in this Country. . . . Lands are Granted to all new comers down the River Gratis, and I believe about 400 Acres for each in a Family."[42] The bogus colonists could then be paid off as necessary so that all assigned acreage went to Irwin and his relatives alone. Whether or not this scheme was actually executed, its planning indicates the broader American motive of penetrating the Spanish realm for maximum economic gain. Adventurism and intrigue were at play in this relatively minor episode just as they were present in James Wilkinson's grand machinations. License to venture meant operating under the veneer of legality, whether or not one stayed within the law.

To ensure success, Irwin urged his agent and kin to consult Captain Stephen Minor, serving under the Castilian flag at Natchez. Minor was a former Pennsylvanian who had journeyed to the Lower Mississippi Valley and joined the Spanish military during the conquest of British West Florida. Irwin clearly regarded Minor as an officer who would help fellow Pennsylvanians wheedling their way into Louisiana.[43] Profit was the goal, and not any political takeover. Irwin soon became a Natchez planter, gaining Spanish specie for tobacco harvested by slaves.[44]

Just as in the pre-Revolutionary era, the Louisiana–West Florida borderlands beckoned northern white adventurers as well as southern colonists. In early 1790, Ezekiel Forman of Philadelphia headed down the Ohio and Mississippi for Natchez with his family and sixty-five slaves, including men, women, and children. Nearly all of the blacks came from the household of Ezekiel's brother, General David Forman of Freehold, Monmouth County, New Jersey.[45] On the river voyage from Pittsburgh, whites and house servants embarked on a seventy-foot keelboat, while black field hands huddled together on a trailing craft loaded with tobacco. Blacks were pained by leaving their familiar ground but had no say in the matter. The Mississippi had special promise for a wealthy Jersey slaveholder when state action on emancipation appeared on the horizon.[46]

The Formans were courteously received at Natchez by Manuel Gayoso de Lemos, whose fluency in English facilitated his appointment as governor over a largely Anglo district. Ezekiel Forman came well recommended, carrying a reference from Gardoqui in New York City. Wilkinson added his encomium, advising Miró that "the happiest effects may be expected from the emigration of such Characters as this Gentleman." Forman purchased a plantation along St. Catherine's Creek in the heart of Natchez. His nephew, Samuel, obtained 800 acres several miles south near the White Cliffs above the Mississippi. Recalling his good fortune years later, Samuel wrote that such a sizeable grant was unexpected, since a single man (*soltero*) such as himself was entitled to 240 acres under provincial regulations. He clearly scored a premium by Gayoso's desire to have affluent Anglo settlers on his side.[47]

Samuel Forman felt quite at home during his time in Natchez. Captain Minor, whom Forman later remembered as a "Jersey man," helped in dealings with Spanish officers. Another accommodating resident was Mrs. Hutchins, wife of Anthony Hutchins, one of the district's wealthiest planters who hailed from Monmouth County, New Jersey. Benjamin Monsanto and his wife, "Spanish Jews" by Forman's reckoning, "were the most kind and hospitable of people." Jews were officially proscribed from the Spanish realm, but at least a few lived comfortably in the Lower

Mississippi Valley. Though Samuel Forman did not remain long in the Natchez district, it was not because of any difficulties with Spanish authority. He remembered that Gayoso had permitted a Baptist minister to preach one Sunday at Colonel Hutchins's home.[48]

At the time the Forman family came to the Lower Mississippi Valley, a steady stream of flatboats bearing tobacco, flour, barreled meats, and sundries put into Natchez. A few boats carried well-to-do whites, accompanied by blacks, migrating to Spanish territory. In most river craft, white deck hands were the majority of passengers. Some of these sojourners applied to become Spanish subjects and landowners.[49] During the early 1790s, the town of Natchez had a commercial center and boisterous "under-the-hill" neighborhood by the Mississippi, where ferrymen and workmen lived in ramshackle dwellings. Gayoso, an able planner, set aside space for a hospital and church besides town lots for merchants, planters, and artisans on the town's bluffs. The district's rural areas included not only plantations where slavery predominated, but also farms or smallholdings possessed by whites raising livestock and planting corn for sustenance.[50]

Martín Navarro was correct when writing of Anglo Natchez's worship of silver. In April 1791, one planter enthused: "The Kings Ship, With Five hundred & fifty thousand Dollars, is but six leagues below this Town. We wait for her very impatiently. The Inspection of Tobacco is not severe; they [the Spanish] receive all that is any way tolerable, & Governor Miró declares that Hard Dollars should be given for it, when the Vessel gets up."[51] Madrid's decision to cut Louisiana tobacco purchases to a minimum that very year was a severe blow to the entire colonial economy—and especially stunning to Natchez. At Gayoso's request, the provincial government responded to the district's plight by instituting a three-year moratorium on the collection of debts in 1792. Disputes between debtors and merchant-creditors mounted as the relief period came to a close.[52]

Anglo-American exploitation of Spanish liberality was at its height during the tobacco boom. Ezekiel Forman admitted the same in a letter to Miró by which he differentiated himself from his less honest countrymen. The "general system" of colonization, he declared, was "that of making speculative incursions, and reaping the advantages the country afforded, under the pretence of becoming, at some future day, a Settler."[53] Though Forman may have exaggerated the extent of subterfuge, he certainly touched on a common social phenomenon. In 1808, Charles Wilkins, a merchant of Lexington, Kentucky, recalled the Mississippi trade of the early 1790s, when "various modes were adopted to evade the payment of the [customs] duties by adventurers to New Orleans, & it was practiced by others as well as by myself to petition the Governor for a grant of Land, under the pretence of becoming an inhabitant."[54] The economic benefit of taking an oath of allegiance to the crown was sufficiently powerful to blur distinctions between genuine immigrants as opposed to adventurers of nominal and deceptive political profession.

Far north of Natchez, Upper Louisiana witnessed a steady, if not spectacular colonization surge during the 1790s. Older villages grew and new ones sprouted, attracting Anglo-American newcomers, French *habitants* of American Illinois, and others. Most white newcomers were small farmers, though the wealthier brought slaves with them. Emigrant Indian peoples meanwhile entered the region seeking refuge from the United States. The Shawnees and Delawares were especially numerous; others included the Miamis, Ottawas, Potawatomis, and Peorias. Collectively these groups found a measure of peace and autonomy in Spanish territory that no longer existed in their native ground east of the Mississippi. They were not free of trouble, however, for they encountered difficulty from the powerful Osages who regarded the newcomers as poaching on their domain.[55] With a multiplicity of immigrants, Louisiana was being transformed in ways that neither Spanish provincial officials nor ambitious colonial promoters anticipated.

A Preference for Self-Sufficiency

By 1788, the Spanish imperial government pulled back from funding additional immigration to Louisiana and the Floridas. This resolve was consistently maintained in Madrid, though it was not clearly understood by entrepreneurs across the Atlantic. As a result, colonization proposals initiated in North America were frequently out of sync with Spanish fiscal realities. To the colonial sponsor, it seemed only sensible that Spain would invest in frontier settlements, especially for transportation and start-up costs. If immigrants succeeded, they would more than repay the crown by the agricultural bounty produced. Moreover, loyal settlers in the borderlands would bolster imperial defense against the United States. These arguments were logical, though of limited efficacy in impressing Madrid, where royal councilors undervalued Louisiana and the Floridas compared to core colonial zones in the Americas.

Spanish authorities strongly preferred self-supporting newcomers to poor immigrants—even among Catholics. Consider, for example, David Carroll Franks and Bryan Bruin—native Irishmen presenting distinct colonization proposals to royal officers in 1787. Appealing to Gardoqui, Franks petitioned on behalf of seventy Catholic families desiring to leave Ireland for East Florida.[56] Bruin, a former Virginia landowner who had recently settled in Louisiana, asked Miró's permission to allow his son Peter and several Catholic families from the Old Dominion to settle with him in the fertile Natchez-Manchac corridor. The governor trusted Bruin and granted his request. Arriving in Natchez in June 1788 after journeying down the Ohio and Mississippi, Colonel Peter Bryan Bruin brought twenty slaves with him along with his wife and three children. The group accompanying him included a few married couples and small slaveholders, fourteen single white men, and two unmarried women. Bryan absorbed considerable expenses but required minimal government aid.[57] In contrast, David Carroll Franks desired the crown to pay the oceanic passage of Irish tenant-farming families who were his kin or neighbors. The Spanish court rejected the project as impractical, costly, and likely offensive to British sensitivities over Ireland.[58]

Agustín Macarty, scion of an Irish-French family of New Orleans, formed an ambitious plan in 1787 of bringing 2,000 to 3,000 Irish Catholics from the United States to Louisiana. Citing anti-Catholicism in American society, he logically claimed his prospective settlers would become faithful Spanish subjects. Miró strongly agreed but was unable to convince Madrid to support Irish Catholic colonization from the United States. In fact, the imperial government rejected Macarty's proposal for threatening financial outlays similar to the royal subsidies recently given Acadian immigrants. Though Macarty would have been hard-pressed to recruit such a large group of colonists, he was never granted the chance.[59]

In retrospect, Spanish plans of harnessing Anglo-American colonials for Louisiana's defense were tenuous and short-lived. Francisco Luís Hector, barón de Carondelet, took a sharply critical view of U.S. immigration once assuming the governor's office in New Orleans on December 30, 1791. Writing to Floridablanca, he noted that some Natchez planters were considering returning to Kentucky since the imperial government had curtailed tobacco purchases. Carondelet concluded that there was no counting on such people "accustomed to changing their domicile just as they do a shirt." Significantly, the governor calibrated political loyalty by class and not simply nationality. Dismissing poorer whites as untrustworthy, Carondelet argued that U.S. immigrants should be allowed into

Louisiana only if possessing considerable wealth or owning at least ten slaves.[60] Once back in Spain, Miró admitted that there was no guarantee of Anglo-American good behavior and that skeptics might view the crown as nourishing foreign enemies at its breast. He still believed, however, that there was no alternative: Louisiana could neither be populated nor defended without risk-taking.[61]

Putting a new agenda to the fore, Carondelet urged that the Natchez district be populated at all cost with Spanish, Flemish, and German colonists. Within a few months of taking office, he sent two deputies to Philadelphia to coordinate immigration affairs with Josef de Viar and Josef de Jáudenes, royal envoys to the United States. The lead agent was Henri Peyroux de la Coudrienère, an army captain and colonial promoter who had steered Acadian migrants from France to the Lower Mississippi Valley in 1784–85. Carondelet counted on Peyroux's mission to draw several thousand Irish Catholics and French, German, and Flemish settlers from the United States to the Natchez–Baton Rouge corridor. Little was accomplished, however, partly because Peyroux showed more interest in shipping flour than settlers to Louisiana.[62]

Successive governors at New Orleans naturally emphasized Louisiana's importance to the defense of Mexico. No point was more apt to gain imperial attention. To combat Anglo-American adventurism, Carondelet turned to colonial promoters whose roots were in Europe rather than the United States. He did not have to scramble to find willing partners since several European émigré entrepreneurs had their own immigration schemes in mind. Barthélemi Tardiveau, a Frenchman who settled in Kentucky about 1780, was involved in various Mississippi Valley ventures well before developing a plan in 1792 to colonize Upper Louisiana with Europeans dislocated by the French Revolution. Formulating his proposal with Carondelet's blessing, he asked to be commissioned as a paid immigration agent who would journey to Europe and recruit as many as 300,000 colonists as he made his way across France, the Netherlands, and Swiss cantons. Since the Spanish government was most unlikely to foot the bill, Tardiveau proposed that wealthy colonists absorb costs in exchange for receiving land commensurate with the number of poorer folk they transported. Well schooled in business and politics, the émigré promoter vaunted the philosophical basis for success: "Self-interest is indisputably the first motive of human conduct."[63] Carondelet paid his own respect to this principle by permitting Tardiveau to transport tobacco and other produce duty-free to New Orleans in order to pay for his voyage to

Europe. All grand plans were aborted, however, by the outbreak of war between France and Spain in 1793.[64] Tardiveau was himself a politically savvy character with flexible national loyalties. Just a few years before devising his colonization project for Spain, he had drafted a secret memorandum calling on France to resume its sovereignty over Louisiana.[65]

Though Tardiveau's grand scheme led nowhere, Carondelet achieved a small-scale success by aiding beleaguered French exiles who had fled revolution and landed in the United States only to be ensnared in poverty at Gallipolis on the Ohio frontier. J. B. Didier, Catholic priest and émigré leader, brought the group's struggles to Carondelet's attention. In a plaintive letter of June 1792, Didier told the governor how "Gentlemen Adventurers" in New York City had exploited the refugees by supplying goods and credit at high cost. In the priest's words, his countrymen were the dupes of illusory tales and sheer fakery. American liberty appeared a chimera. If the Spanish crown lent aid, Didier believed that as many as 1,800 of his exiled compatriots would leave various U.S. locales for Louisiana.[66] Carondelet was pleased to help. A Flemish Catholic with a strong sense of noblesse oblige, he competed with the United States on the cultural front. Besides spurring Louisiana's growth, he wished to demonstrate the king's mercy and to counteract American "falsehoods" that the Spanish government was a despotic régime "oppressed by friars and imposts." Once Louisiana received its fair due, foreigners would be disabused of any concerns they might have about alleged "tribute, inquisition, persecution," and the want of colonial property rights.[67] Carondelet's vision might have been realized in a stable international climate, but it could scarcely be achieved while Louisiana was jolted by French provincial disaffection, invasion threats from the United States, and uncertainty brought on by European warfare.

Louisiana's relationship to the Caribbean was meanwhile thrown into confusion by political turmoil and slave revolution in Saint-Domingue. In May 1790, the Spanish monarchy prohibited the entry of slaves and free black or mulatto refugees from French colonies into Madrid's overseas dominions. Two years later, Carondelet took the New Orleans cabildo's advice by banning slave importation from either the French Caribbean or Jamaica. Louisiana planters held to the idea that creole slaves drawn from the West Indies were more prone to rebellion than *bozales* (blacks imported directly from Africa). Beset by a slowing economy and a recent slave rebellion, the cabildo barred the introduction of slaves altogether from 1796 to 1800. This order did not stop slave smuggling or the overland migration of enslaved blacks from the United States.[68] The colonial vision of a stable, secure, and prosperous plantation régime was far from realized.

Ethnicity and Immigration Proposals—European Influences

Among all European groups, Germans enjoyed the best reputation among Spanish officials at New Orleans. Martín Navarro once commented that a colonization contract bringing 1,000 German families to Louisiana "would be cheap at any cost"—and preferable to any dependence on Canary Islanders.[69] German immigration figured in a number of Louisiana colonization proposals. In 1788, Baron von Steuben, former Prussian officer in the Continental Army, unsuccessfully petitioned for a royal grant of 2.4 million acres in Louisiana, to be settled largely by colonists and soldiers recruited in Germany.[70] In early 1789, Peter Paulus, a Dutch emigré in Philadelphia, came to New Orleans seeking approval for the admission of 3,000 families, most of whom were said to be of German origin. Miró objected to the plan's provision for local self-governance but still pledged to appoint Paulus to a commandant's post if the latter brought 1,000 law-abiding settlers to Louisiana. For unknown reasons, Paulus dropped his interest in Mississippi Valley colonization after returning to Pennsylvania.[71]

During the 1790s, Spanish officials at New Orleans and Philadelphia tended to see German colonists as one element among several European nationalities that were vital to Louisiana's defense and development. In one plan of October 1792 Carondelet advocated European settlement in particular geographic zones in light of immigrant capabilities. He believed French colonists to be well-adapted to Upper Louisiana, especially the Mississippi's west bank from the area just below the Ohio to the Missouri River. He favored German, Dutch, and Flemish settlement in the Lower Mississippi Valley for the immediate defense of New Orleans. The governor envisioned Galveztown, on the Iberville River's south bank, as an ideal locale for German immigrants, whether the latter came from the United States or Europe. Echoing Navarro's ethnic prejudices whether intentionally or not, he contended that Canary Islanders had previously failed at settling Galveztown because of their "natural laziness" (*desidia natural*). This was scarcely a fair or accurate judgment.[72]

While wholeheartedly supportive of Germans, Carondelet distinguished between desirable French royalists and unwanted political radicals who were to be excluded or expelled. The governor assiduously enforced this last policy during Spain's war with France from 1793 to 1795.[73] The idea of attracting Europe's war refugees still lingered. In June 1795, Louis de Villemont, scion of a distinguished Louisiana family, developed an elaborate proposal of drawing European refugees to the Mississippi. Much to Carondelet's liking, he denigrated Anglo-Americans as "the new Vandals" that had to be stopped.[74] Villemont's planning went for naught, however, since Manuel de Godoy, duque de Alcudia and the king's first minister, opposed the project. The imperial government was again apprehensive lest Spanish tampering with European refugees complicate diplomatic relations. Madrid was also coming to view Louisiana as expendable in a crisis. (Godoy quipped of the province's allegedly defenseless condition: "You can't lock up an open field.") When the council of state dismissed Villemont's proposal in November 1795, it *rejected* any presumption "that Louisiana was the key to the Mexican Empire, and more important than the island of Cuba."[75] This judgment came just a few weeks after Madrid reduced its stake on the Mississippi by the Treaty of San Lorenzo, ceding all claims to the river's east bank above the 31st parallel to the United States. The agreement also admitted the U.S. right of unimpeded navigation from the river's source to the Gulf. Spain further conceded the American right to deposit or store goods at New Orleans for duty-free export for a three-year period. (Madrid pledged to renew this allowance at the term's end if the privilege was exercised in a manner consonant with national interest.) U.S. merchant vessels could now lawfully enter the Mississippi from the Gulf and serve as the seaborne carriers of agricultural produce arriving downriver from the Ohio.[76]

Imperial Spain's waning interest hardly stayed Carondelet's resolve to promote European colonization in Louisiana. In fact, he was already resolved to strengthen his province's southwestern frontier through immigration projects before disheartening news of the treaty arrived. In the spring of 1795, he welcomed the petition of Joseph Piernas, a former Spanish lieutenant and a ranch owner living near the Sabine River in Texas, to establish a colony of five hundred Irish and German families, all to be brought from Europe, along the Calcasieu River, which flows southward into the Gulf near modern St. Charles, Louisiana. Piernas, who had extensive business contacts in the Mississippi Valley, hoped to profit by overcoming economic barriers separating Texas from Louisiana.[77] Though the Calcasieu project was never realized, it is significant for combining entrepreneurship with Enlightenment ideals of social progress transcending national bounds. Piernas's proposal, which received Carondelet's backing, declared that a member of the "body politic" (*cuerpo politico*) could serve no higher purpose than "to better the society to which he belongs" by developing "an invention or new device facilitating mechanical, agricultural, or scientific activities (*operaciones*) beneficial to humanity." Judging by this lofty rhetoric, it seems most probable that Carondelet had a hand in drafting the proposal, which was formally addressed to himself as governor.[78]

In conjunction with the Calacasieu project, Carondelet amplified defensive plans for the scarcely colonized Ouachita River Valley on the Mississippi's southwestern flank. His policy again depended on initiatives by private colonial sponsors working in tandem with the provincial government. In 1795-96, Carondelet authorized the Marquis de Maison Rouge and Baron de Bastrop, both European exiles, to establish settlements along the Ouachita. Each promoter brought a small number of immigrants to the region, unlike most foreign *proyectistas* whose schemes never bore fruit.[79]

Maison Rouge and Bastrop had similar plans but were individuals of markedly different temperament. The former was a rather imperious French royalist, and the latter a politically savvy Dutchman who claimed noble status upon arriving in the United States. Bastrop was by far the cleverer in adapting to the North American frontier. The prospect of Ouachita colonization was itself highly pleasing to Captain Juan (Jean-Baptiste) Filhiol, a native Frenchman who had long served in the backwater district. He described the area's smattering of settlers as untamed hunters, "lacking religion and morals," and living "more poorly than the Indians" (*Sauvages*).[80]

Louisiana's colonial economy ran the gamut from backwoods hunting to plantation slavery. Immigration measures were therefore bound to reflect regional considerations. Carondelet finalized a colonization contract with Maison Rouge at the same time his government was brutally suppressing an incipient slave revolt at Point Coupée. Not coincidentally, the governor exhibited a clear preference for whites as defenders of Louisiana's Ouachita frontier. Settlers in Maison Rouge's tiny colony, which fell far short of its initial allotment of thirty families, were supposed to receive land and monetary assistance based on the number of white agriculturists or skilled laborers per household. Two prominent French residents in the settlement were nonetheless slaveholders.[81] Carondelet discouraged slavery in Bastrop's colony, where white newcomers received modest land grants so as to exclude planters who might think of converting land to indigo cultivation and slave labor. Bastrop pledged to encourage wheat production and to build a flour mill within the colony. Carondelet had visions of Ouachita flour being exported to Havana, thereby reducing Cuba's economic dependence on the United States.[82]

Bastrop promised far more than he could ultimately deliver. Short of capital and with little government funding, he never came close to realizing his projected aim of bringing five hundred European families to the Ouachita. The Dutch "baron" also failed to construct a sustainable flour mill. Nature hardly cooperated. The Ouachita River lacked sufficient depth and flow during summer and autumn for a steady operation.[83] Political obstacles arose besides environmental limitations. In 1797, Louisiana intendant Juan Ventura Morales suspended Bastrop's commission because of concerns that U.S. citizens were illicitly joining the settlement. Carondelet remained supportive of the Ouachita project, but he could do little to redeem it after leaving Louisiana for good that year. Bastrop managed to hang on through skillful politicking at New Orleans. In 1800, he gained Governor Casa Calvo's permission to introduce slaves for cotton production. An adventurer at heart, Bastrop plunged into capitalistic entrepreneurship rather than being beholden to a simple agrarian colony.[84] By the time the United States took possession of Louisiana, he had already turned to land speculation and intrigue as his primary business. Through a convoluted series of transactions in 1804–5, he parted with the greater part of his purported Ouachita holdings, now alleged to encompass 900,000 acres, to two purchasers: Abraham Morhouse of Louisiana and Charles Lynch of Kentucky. The fact that Lynch subsequently sold part of his share to Aaron Burr has made "the Bastrop grant" a staple for historical accounts of western land speculation and conspiracy. Burr's supposed plan of invading Spanish territory from the Ouachita is an ironic twist on Carondelet's purpose only a decade before to build a defensive barrier for Mexico in that frontier district. In 1807, Bastrop himself received Spanish permission to settle in Texas, where he became a prominent San Antonio resident, trader, and landowner. He was of immense service to the Austin family during the opening of Texas to Anglo-American settlement and slavery from 1820 until his death in 1827.[85]

Disjunctions between Policy and Practice

Spanish Louisiana was in many ways a series of outposts and garrisons tied militarily and politically to New Orleans. The province was too vast in extent and diverse in population to function as a coherent administrative whole. While Carondelet was promoting European colonization in 1796, Pierre Charles Dehault Delassus de Luzières, commandant of New Bourbon in Upper Louisiana, published a pamphlet in Kentucky fulsomely welcoming U.S. settlers to his district. Carondelet was alarmed that this notice could spread, especially since the author's son, Carlos Dehault Delassus, was commandant at New Madrid. The governor let the younger Delassus know that royal officers would be fined 150 *piastres* for admitting U.S. immigrants to Spanish territory without his permission. Carondelet made one exception by approving the entry of American settlers growing wheat—since flour was in so much demand at New Orleans.[86]

Manuel Gayoso de Lemos, Carondelet's successor, took a staunchly anti-U.S. colonization stance after being badly stung by the Spanish cession of Natchez to the American republic. In 1798, he prohibited foreigners from being admitted to the province unless they agreed that their children would be reared as Catholics. This requirement was a thin reed against U.S. predominance since it presumed restrictions could be imposed on future generations that were not incumbent on the present. Gayoso's policy had more wiggle room than his orders implied. While striving to hold back U.S. immigration, he encouraged faithful Anglo-American subjects to migrate from Natchez southward into Spanish territory once the Treaty of San Lorenzo took effect.[87]

Lt. Governor Zenon Trudeau, presiding at St. Louis, complained to Gayoso that stringent regulations would preclude non-Catholic settlement and thereby retard Louisiana's growth. A native of New Orleans, Trudeau strongly supported "projects for large settlements ... founded on a mixed population." To do otherwise would stifle economic progress, invite Indian attacks, and confine colonists to their "wretched villages." Louisiana would then be unable to compete for settlers with "the American side of the Mississippi," which would flourish by comparison.[88] Trudeau had his own regional perspective, but he was perfectly in step with New Orleans by favoring wealthy newcomers irrespective of their Anglo Protestant background. In January 1797, he extended his hospitality to Moses Austin, recently of Virginia, who arrived in Upper Louisiana with the intention of establishing a large lead-mining operation.

Carondelet favored the enterprise by awarding Austin one-square league of land (or 4,428 acres) at Mine à Breton. Ordinary western Americans meanwhile crossed into Spanish territory with little concern about official religious orthodoxy. Daniel Boone was among the most renowned of hundreds of such individuals. Worn out by misfortunes in Kentucky, he vowed never to look back when he took his family across the Mississippi to the Femme Osage district of Upper Louisiana in 1799.[89]

The idea that Spanish Louisiana could vie successfully with the United States for immigrants did not stop suddenly with the Treaty of San Lorenzo. Nor did crown officials easily give up the idea of detaching Kentucky, and possibly other frontier areas, from the American Union. Carlos Martínez de Yrujo, Spanish envoy at Philadelphia, reported in 1797 that the people of Kentucky and Tennessee "hate the federal government." Gayoso informed Madrid a year later of the urgency of Spain maintaining its "connection with Kentucky." His immigration regulations of 1798 stipulated that Louisiana's borders should remain open to men who held public office in the United States. This provision was doubtless intended to welcome influential Americans into the service of Spain. By inference, General James Wilkinson, a secret royal agent, had the right to settle in Louisiana if he needed to do so.[90] Spain's goal of resisting and weakening the United States gave vent to political intrigues with American frontier magnates.

CHAPTER 7

Frontier Separatism and Integration

Decoding cyphers was sometimes a difficult task for Esteban Miró and James Wilkinson in their confidential correspondence. At one point in 1789 or 1790, Miró confessed that he could "only guess at the meaning of the first five lines" of the Kentucky powerbroker's recent letter. In another note, the governor complained that he had not heard from Wilkinson in several months.[1] To illustrate a clear cipher, Miró wrote a coded note for Wilkinson: "War with England will produce some alterations in the pending negotiations & so our communication ought to be more frequent." This message was as much about the substance as the medium of correspondence. Fluid political circumstances necessitated frequent exchanges about the international and regional scene.[2]

Miró's quest for a workable cipher is a small facet of what U.S. historians once called "the Spanish conspiracy"—the attempt by Madrid's officers to stoke western American secession from the Union. In Spain's ideal scenario, Kentucky and other frontier districts would seek Madrid's protective guidance rather than remain under a feckless federal government. Louisiana's Spanish governors did in fact promote this agenda for roughly a decade with the intent of containing U.S. expansionism. And why should they not? The American republic strove in numerous ways, short of war, to undermine Spain's hold in southeastern North America.

Separatist intrigues constituted part of a diplomatic process by which U.S. citizens negotiated with Madrid's surrogates outside the federal government's purview. Rather than western secession being the sole question, the issue of frontier integration was also at stake: whether Spain and western Americans might find mutually satisfactory ways of linking interior continental regions to the Gulf. Madrid's colonial officials gambled that Anglo-American frontier entrepreneurs and powerbrokers could be won to their side by self-interest alone. Negotiations along these lines raised various possibilities of political and economic association.

Separatist scheming was not necessarily an all-or-nothing proposition—one leading inevitably to the West's lasting attachment to Spain rather than an indissoluble Union with the Atlantic states. In fact, transnational diplomacy was a means of securing tangible if often short-term benefits for western U.S. powerbrokers and Spanish officials in lieu of formal treaty-making. Small intrigues could pay dividends even if grand schemes went awry. This is not to say that such interchange was equal; it heavily tilted toward U.S. exploitation of Spanish vulnerability over time. James Wilkinson and a few cronies milked Louisiana's governors for all the silver they could direct northward for years.[3]

Gardoqui's Perspective on the West

During the summer of 1787, Diego de Gardoqui guardedly watched the American political scene from his Manhattan residence. Congress held its sessions in New York City while the federal Convention gathered in Philadelphia to remedy the Articles of Confederation. The Spanish envoy surmised that "Anarchy, or Convulsion" would likely prevail until government reforms inched ahead over years. He was contemptuous of his host nation's weakness, especially its inability to control the "innumerable vagabonds" (*infinitos Vagos*) gathered about the Ohio, and others already camped on the Mississippi.[4]

Months later Gardoqui perceived the debate over the Constitution as presaging political fragmentation—a trend he clearly welcomed. Writing to Floridablanca in April 1788, he predicted that the failure of ratification would result in anarchy "or what is better"—the formation of two confederations. Western Americans were still seething about Jay's failed Mississippi diplomacy and considering new political options. The State of Franklin, a breakaway region of North Carolina, was said to be eager for a Spanish connection. North Carolina itself rejected the new federal Constitution at the time, throwing its western regions into political limbo. Kentucky, which was struggling to achieve independence from Virginia, also appeared poised for radical political realignment.[5]

In July 1788, Gardoqui entered a critical stage in his separatist gambit through discussions with John Brown, Kentucky delegate to Congress. The Spanish envoy's message had a political catch: Kentuckians could receive access to the New Orleans market only by becoming entirely "separate and sovereign" (*separados y soberanos*), and independent of the United States. Gardoqui, a careful student of political geography, reasoned that

Spain could safely grant commercial privileges to Kentucky as an interior district with no economic reach beyond New Orleans. Frontiersmen lacking a merchant marine could not possibly engage in the contraband trade from the Mississippi to the Caribbean. The Spanish envoy was adamant about holding Madrid's line against U.S. commercial penetration, whether via the Ohio-Mississippi downriver passage or from the Gulf to the Mississippi.[6]

Brown was encouraged by Gardoqui's overtures and disgusted with Congress, which put off Kentucky's repeated appeals for separation from Virginia and admission to the Union via statehood. Before leaving New York City for home in the summer of 1788, he confidentially wrote a political ally of Spain's readiness to open the New Orleans market once the district declared full independence.[7] Brown wavered, however, when finally attending the Kentucky convention in Danville that November. Sensing fierce opposition to the mere suggestion of a Spanish alliance, he rode the political mainstream and won election to represent the Kentucky district in the first Congress under the new federal Constitution.[8] Brown still kept his Spanish contact in reserve. In early 1789 he wrote Gardoqui that Kentucky would harken to Spain as long as the latter held the Mississippi and thereby kept the British at bay.[9]

Ironically, Gardoqui's intrigues were a step behind Madrid's rapidly evolving Mississippi policies, which headed toward freer trade with the American West without requiring that region to break first with the United States. In December 1788, the imperial government ruled that Kentucky and Ohio Valley residents could ship their produce to Louisiana on paying a 15 percent import duty, which could be further reduced for politically influential shippers. This measure was itself a means to draw trans-Appalachian settlers closer to Spain outside the formalities of alliance.

Gardoqui's western contacts aired regional disaffection with Congress, but they exaggerated the prospect of a Spanish alliance in order to gain particular advantages. John Sevier, governor of Franklin, is a prime example. While his mini-state neared collapse in September 1788, he wrote Gardoqui that he could carry Franklin out of the Union if his Catholic Majesty furnished some military supplies and whatever specie could be spared. All aid could be paid back once Franklin had the right to send agricultural produce from "our rivers" to the Gulf ports "below." In this cagey message Sevier deceptively declared that his district's frontier folk were "unanimously determined" on "an Alliance and Commercial

Connection" with Spain.[10] His overtures to Gardoqui were actually a last resort, coming after the State of Franklin failed to win Georgia's support for its own claim to Muscle Shoals on the Tennessee River's Great Bend—a bridge toward the Alabama-Tombigbee watershed and the Gulf. Various speculative interests fixed their gaze on this site, which Congress recognized as Cherokee territory under the Treaty of Hopewell of 1785.[11]

Gardoqui held back from directly aiding Franklin, but he lent encouragement through talks with Dr. James White, Sevier's ally and a native-born American Catholic whose European education and suave manner impressed the Spanish chargé. By the fall of 1788, Gardoqui authorized White, whom he had known for two years, to transmit his western separatist plans in person at Havana and New Orleans. Before the year's end, White arrived in Cuba under the alias Jacques Dubois. Captain-general José de Ezpeleta welcomed the secret agent and endorsed the proposition of Franklin placing itself under Spanish "protection," in return for countenancing the district's expansion into the Tennessee Valley and the shipment of its agricultural produce to Mobile and New Orleans. The captain-general saw a great payoff in the dismemberment of the American Union. In fact, he mistakenly believed that Kentucky and Franklin were already independent of the United States.[12] His endorsement of Anglo-American frontier interests brushed past the problem of how Spain could simultaneously satisfy a white settler agenda and uphold Indian territorial rights. After concluding talks in Havana, White embarked for New Orleans with Manuel Gayoso de Lemos, Natchez's newly appointed governor, who was intrigued by trans-Appalachian politics though wary of Franklin's incipient strides toward the Gulf.[13]

Miró was less sanguine than Ezpeleta upon Dr. White's arrival in Louisiana. In his judgment, Franklin was too weak and internally divided to assume the independent sovereignty White suggested was within reach. The governor would go no further than to offer commercial privileges to the Franklinites at New Orleans. Negotiations of political association would need to await the clear establishment of Franklin's independence.[14] Miró was strongly interested in western separatism but he deliberately stopped short of an adventurist policy that would expose Spain to confrontation with the United States. In July 1789, he shunned meddling in trans-Appalachian politics by denying Gayoso's request to travel northward for direct talks with Franklin's leaders. A vibrant officer, Gayoso obeyed, though he was disappointed not to be able to explore American frontier districts for himself.[15]

(top) Esteban Miró. Lithograph of portrait, undated. Courtesy of The Historic New Orleans Collection, no. 1991.34.16. This portrait shows Miró as a youthful cadet or officer, probably before he saw his first American military service in New Spain in 1767, when he was twenty-three years old.

(bottom) Manuel Luis Gayoso de Lemos. Photograph of miniature portrait, undated. Courtesy of The Historic New Orleans Collection, no. 1979.325.2577. This portrait shows a youthful Gayoso, doubtless well before he assumed the post of Natchez district governor at age forty-two in June 1789.

Miró's judgment was sound in this instance. The State of Franklin was dead by the time Dr. White made his entreaty at New Orleans. In February 1789, Sevier mended his fences with North Carolina and joined other politicians working for the state's ratification of the Constitution and the cession of its western land claims to the federal government. His separatist politics—and dalliance with Spain—came to a halt as soon as he chose other means of advancing his interests as a frontier magnate and land speculator.[16] Assessing the collapse of Franklin-Louisiana diplomacy, one historian has written of "the Spanish farce" rather than conspiracy as the governing reality in Trans-Appalachia. In this view, wily frontiersmen played the Spanish card for political leverage and profit without any genuine commitment to the separatist politics they seemingly favored.[17] One suspects this was the case with Sevier. But certain individuals found it politic to collaborate with Spain in mutually supportive if not wholly consistent ways. Dr. James White is a case in point. Through his private diplomacy with Havana and New Orleans, he established bona fides that served him well over years. In 1796, he moved from the Cumberland district to live under the Castilian flag in the far more fertile Natchez district. Three years later he was moving south of the new international boundary at the 31st parallel and into Spanish territory once more. Dr. White remained alert to new opportunities the rest of his days. After the Louisiana Purchase, he retained lands in Spanish West Florida while becoming a U.S. judge in Attakapas, Orleans Territory, where he died in in 1809. Living in the borderlands could be quite profitable, not least if one had a knack of adapting to a changing political world.[18]

Wilkinson and Intrigue

James Wilkinson was a vigorous thirty-three year old—a veteran military officer and a suave gentleman—when he first visited New Orleans in August 1787. Neither Miró nor Navarro had precise knowledge of Wilkinson's tempestuous time in the Continental Army, when contention and intrigue marred his service. The governor and intendant saw their visitor as a brigadier, no matter that he had held that rank for but a brief time. They certainly appreciated his penchant for geopolitical strategizing and for incorporating a Spanish perspective within his analysis.[19]

Wilkinson was a tireless lobbyist with a consistent message, whether delivered personally in New Orleans or, far more commonly, by lengthy letters that stood as political essays. In his view, the American Union was beset by a fatal flaw—an irreconcilable clash of interests between the Atlantic states and the trans-Appalachian West. In February 1789, Wilkinson advised Miró that Spain "ought to assert every Power & every Art" to "increase the animosity of the Eastern and Western People of America." This policy depended on Madrid maintaining "the exclusive right" to navigation of the Mississippi and thereby continuing to demonstrate the federal government's weakness to frustrated western citizens.[20] Wilkinson made it seem that Spain had no option except to undermine the United States in order to win the trans-Appalachian West. Unless Madrid demonstrated unquestioned strength, Kentucky would necessarily look to the British to open the Mississippi.[21] One should emphasize that Miró could not afford to ignore these warnings or bypass borderlands stratagems when his military hand was weak. In 1787, the sole Spanish regiment in Louisiana had little more than 400 men—far short of its mandated level of over 1,800. Two years later the regiment had just over 600 men—scarcely a sufficient number for a province of Louisiana's vast extent.[22]

Spanish imperial policy did not follow Wilkinson's formulations lest the crown raise western U.S. anger to the boiling point. Madrid instead played to frontier powerbrokers in the hope they would steer their districts in a pro-Spanish direction. Under the royal order of December 1, 1788, Louisiana's governor had discretionary authority to reduce the import duty below 15 percent for "notables," western U.S. shippers with political clout.[23] The royal stamp was implicitly given to Wilkinson's special place in downriver Mississippi trade. His was not a monopoly, but rather an oligarchical premium exacted through political services.

Wilkinson's primary object was the sale of Kentucky tobacco for Mexican silver drawn from Louisiana's royal treasury. In 1788, he and his partner, Isaac Dunn, netted $10,887 in specie by one large government purchase.[24] Miró and subordinate officers treated Wilkinson's tobacco as if it had been produced in Louisiana and thereby entitled to government bounty. In fact, the governor wanted to increase purchases of Kentucky tobacco but could not go as far he wished lest he strain the royal treasury.[25] By elevating one frontier powerbroker as top dog, Miró had to limit rewards for others. In April 1789, he officially invited Cumberland and Franklin settlers to sell their tobacco and other produce in the New Orleans market, though not directly to the king's agents. The governor's policy remained elitist by promising a reduced import tariff to "men of influence."[26] Miró saw the frontier as the very opposite of a democratic order, but instead a society where strong leaders could bend ordinary folk toward their ends.

Wilkinson would have lost all credibility in Kentucky had his fellow citizens known how strenuously he opposed U.S. navigational rights on the Mississippi and even the lowering of the Louisiana import duty from 25 to 15 percent in his secret correspondence with Miró.[27] Paradoxically, his personal feat of opening New Orleans commerce had the consequence of furthering Kentucky-Louisiana connections beyond his control. On September 9, 1789, Spanish customs agents arrested five Kentucky men on the brig *Navarro* thirty miles below New Orleans for attempting to carry a considerable portion of specie out of the province on an intended voyage to Saint-Domingue and then to the United States. Confessing their guilt before Miró, the accused explained that they had not come to Louisiana mainly for business but rather to view the country before bringing their families to settle at Natchez. Since money was needed for their return trip by sea, they had brought with them "a small adventure in the produce of Kentucky" for sale in Louisiana. Earning over $5,000, they felt safe until a Spanish customs barge unexpectedly headed their way as they boarded a brig for passage to the Gulf of Mexico. The Kentuckians quickly skedaddled in a small rowboat toward shore, throwing some silver in the river and then hiding the remainder in nearby woods. Customs men discovered the ruse and recovered $3,474 of the cache though another $1,526 sunk without a trace in the Mississippi. The Kentucky smugglers did not explain why they had concealed some silver in their clothing in light of their alleged "total Ignorance" of the law and of any wrongdoing on their part. Desperate for pardon, they asked for Miró's clemency, adding that they had no greater desire than becoming "Good and usefull [sic] Subjects to his Majesty."[28]

Wilkinson, who was in New Orleans at the time, immediately came to the defense of the culprits, who had come to Louisiana with his avowed encouragement. If the men were severely punished, he warned that American newspapers would attack Spain "with gross misrepresentations & the vilest Calumny," thereby destroying any hope of western U.S. colonization in Louisiana. Wilkinson also declared that his own reputation was at stake, since he would be seen as complicit in the men's punishment. With typical grandiloquence, he reminded Miró that "the most important revolutions" in history were frequently "produced by incidents, in themselves, frivolous & contemptible." The governor not only freed the arrested men, but also had their confiscated money restored on condition they would pay a 6 percent export duty on the proceeds. He even ordered one treasury official put under arrest for twelve hours for exceeding his authority in the episode.[29]

Though Wilkinson predicted dire consequences for Spanish power if he was not backed to the hilt, he gave Miró a quite unrealistic sense of his command of Kentucky politics. The governor was therefore stunned to receive Wilkinson's admission in 1790 that there was but a single prominent Kentuckian—Benjamin Sebastian—squarely in the separatist camp. Wilkinson had implied a wholly different outcome when recently visiting New Orleans and receiving a loan of $7,000 that amounted to a political payoff. Embarrassed by an unexpected turn in Kentucky affairs, Miró was compelled to write Madrid that he could scarcely judge events fifteen hundred miles from his capital. He would have been even more chagrined if he had dispensed the king's money to Kentucky as loosely as Wilkinson recommended.[30]

Palliating this disappointment, Miró resolved that Wilkinson was an asset even if the latter failed to bring Kentucky out of the Union. The flow of political intelligence from the western United States to Louisiana was itself valuable. In early 1789, Miró was impressed by Wilkinson's report of British agent John Connolly's visit to his Lexington home. By this account it appeared that the English in Canada were poised to equip a Kentucky freebooting strike against Louisiana. In actuality there was no such operation underway at the time. But Miró could scarcely know British plans, and he was thankful that Wilkinson furnished an advance warning.[31] Connolly was himself a character worthy of frontier intrigue. A former Tory stalwart in Kentucky, he spent most of the Revolutionary War as a prisoner of war. When peace came, he fled to London where he petitioned Spanish ambassador Bernardo del Campo for allowance to found a Mississippi colony for Irish and Maryland Catholics under Madrid's auspices. Failing in this endeavor, he returned to the British service in Canada.[32] With a penchant for changing sides, Connolly quite probably believed that Wilkinson's loyalty was for sale.

Wilkinson was himself adept at bribery, routinely feathering the nests of royal officers to maximize profit. In March 1791, he offered a lengthy lesson in evading customs duties to Hugh McIlvain, his business partner, before the latter embarked on a Louisiana trading venture. McIlvain was to impress Spanish authorities at Natchez by putting on his "best Bib &

Tinker" and vowing allegiance to his Catholic Majesty. His boat hands, too, would make a show of settling in Louisiana since western U.S. immigrants in Louisiana were entitled to bring in marketable produce free of duty.[33] All would be smoothed by McIlvain's gift to Natchez's commandant—and later by a large gratuity to provincial secretary Gilberto Leonard at New Orleans. If all went well, the royal treasury would pay good silver for McIlvain's tobacco. Unsurpassed in effrontery, Wilkinson had previously cautioned Miró not to fall for the confidence games of U.S. traders. As he put matters: "The sanguine Spirit of an American leads Him to interpret every doubtful Measure to His own advantage."[34]

If Wilkinson had been as adept in business as he was in deception, he would have made a fortune. But commercial success escaped him after early gains. By 1791, his enterprises were tottering because of shipping accidents, speculative losses, the curtailment of royal tobacco purchases, and other misfortunes, both self-imposed and beyond his control. McIlvain's venture itself achieved little, showing that intrigue was hardly a fail-safe method of cornering the New Orleans market.[35] In light of financial reverses, Wilkinson renewed his U.S. military career as his surest path to influence over borderlands diplomacy and intrigue. In October 1791, he obtained the rank of lieutenant colonel—a position that heightened his leverage with Spanish officialdom. Within weeks of his appointment, he boasted to Gayoso: "I am now in the high Road to Military preferment, & to Glory, which I flatter myself will give you much pleasure." Early the next year Wilkinson was promoted to brigadier general, an office he employed to great effect with barón de Carondelet, who paid handsomely for the brigadier's services. The barón fully appreciated the Kentuckian's mercenary motives, and characterized him as a talented but wholly self-interested man who could turn from friend to enemy in a moment. Wilkinson was paid a 2,000 peso annual pension not simply for the aid he could give, but the harm he could inflict if neglected or wronged.[36]

Wilkinson was adroit at boosting himself above other American claimants for New Orleans commerce. During his first visit to New Orleans, he assured provincial secretary Andrés Armesto that he was "not one of the many Impostors who have disgraced America & Injured the Subjects of Louisiana, by coming to this City."[37] Wary of competitors, he relied greatly on Daniel Clark Sr., a former Pensacola resident and one of the most experienced Anglo merchants in New Orleans, to further his relations with senior Spanish officials. Wilkinson was not the only

American citizen to do so. In 1787, Oliver Pollock obtained a timely infusion of credit from Clark as he looked to reenter Louisiana trade from Philadelphia.[38]

In August 1788, Clark entered a business arrangement with Wilkinson and partner Isaac Dunn for receiving downriver shipments, converting produce sales to cash and conveying European and Caribbean commodities northward. Clark's role was so significant that his profit share by contract was 50 percent while Wilkinson and Dunn each had a 25 percent stake. Wilkinson referred to Clark's upriver shipment as "an Adventure of Merchandize," which he would invest to purchase tobacco for the former's account in New Orleans.[39] Commercial risk-taking and political adventurism were inseparable. In August 1788, Miró advanced $6,000 to Clark, ostensibly to assist Mississippi commerce but actually to reward Wilkinson for pushing a Kentucky separatist agenda.[40]

Though Clark's partnership with Wilkinson proved short-lived, his political influence with Louisiana's Spanish officials continued through the 1790s. His nephew, Daniel Clark Jr., was an apt pupil, becoming an aspiring merchant after leaving Ireland for New Orleans in 1786. He also followed his uncle's entrepreneurial example, rising in commercial circles and amassing land and slaves in the Manchac-Natchez corridor. The younger Clark invested heavily in Louisiana's trade with the United States and the Caribbean. In 1793, he formed a partnership with Philadelphia merchants John Reed and Standish Forde in order to exploit loosened customs enforcement during Spain's war with France. With his talent for intrigue and close ties to Louisiana governors, Clark became Wilkinson's most important link to New Orleans and Natchez in the mid- to late 1790s. Outwardly respecting Spanish authority, he opportunistically maximized his political and economic connections to the United States.[41]

Although Wilkinson continually wrote Spanish governors of sectional discord between the Atlantic and western states, he had crucial family and financial ties to the East—not least through his wife, Ann Biddle, and her prominent Philadelphia family. In 1792, he advised Gayoso to convey secret messages to him by sea to his brother-in-law Clement Biddle in Philadelphia if overland routes were blocked by Indian hostilities.[42] Two years before Wilkinson had requested Gayoso to be hospitable to Standish Forde when the latter was at Natchez, in light of the visiting merchant's "extensive" credit. The brigadier enthused that Forde had the idea of introducing "the Steam Boat, which may certainly be employed, to great public as well as private advantage, in the Navigation of the Mississippi." Wilkinson, an erstwhile western separatist, was in this instance an integrationist furthering Philadelphia's capital investment in Louisiana's development. Economic connections proliferated in complex yet intimate ways. Reed and Forde—"merchant adventurers," as historian Arthur P. Whitaker aptly described them—obtained a Spanish permit for their Mississippi trade and New Orleans outbound shipments through one of Oliver Pollock's associates. The Philadelphia partners were suitably grateful to Spanish officialdom to name one of their vessels *Gayoso*, besides dispensing gifts to the king's surrogates at New Orleans.[43]

As Madrid's position in Louisiana and West Florida weakened after the Treaty of San Lorenzo, Daniel Clark Jr. took to passing confidential insights on Spanish policy to the U.S. government. Writing to Secretary of State Timothy Pickering in 1798, he reviewed Louisiana's relations with the western United States over the previous dozen years. He described Miró, who departed Louisiana for Spain in late 1791, as "a weak man, unacquainted with the American Government, ignorant even of the position of Kentucky with respect to his own province, but alarmed at the very idea of an iruption [sic] of Kentucky men, whom he feared without knowing their strength." In Clark's view, Wilkinson's first mission to New Orleans of 1787 was most memorable for encouraging "emigrants and speculators" settling in Louisiana or selling goods there.[44]

Was Clark's assessment of Miró just? The governor appeared weak in retrospect because he permitted Wilkinson to define his province's relations to Kentucky—the most strategic and rapidly growing trans-Appalachian settler district of the time. But this retrospective view seriously understates Spanish political acumen. After all, Miró cultivated relations with western powerbrokers during the late 1780s when the United States was weak and trans-Appalachian separatism appeared quite possible. He was, if anything, more astute in this respect than Carondelet, who strived for a compact with western separatists through huge territorial concessions and other emoluments. In September 1795, the barón lobbied Madrid to provide funds for his secret negotiation of a commercial treaty with Kentucky deputies in New Orleans. In this hopelessly unrealistic scenario, a trade agreement was conceived as the foundation for alliance between Spain and an independent American West. Though Carondelet invited Wilkinson to his capital for discussions, the brigadier declined since he had too much to lose by disclosure. Stationed in Ohio, he was then awaiting a payment of $9,000 from the governor. Later that year, Wilkinson advised Carondelet to be as discrete as ever: "I must hope that my correspondence may be placed beyond the reach of treachery or intrigue."[45]

Wilkinson's example emboldened a small clique of Kentucky allies, who played the separatist political card with New Orleans for their own enrichment. Benjamin Sebastian, a key emissary for this group, falsely portrayed himself as authorized to negotiate for Kentucky in meetings with Carondelet and Gayoso in 1795–96. Carondelet subsequently recommended that a group of Kentucky bigwigs, including Sebastian, receive a ten-million-acre grant in Louisiana on condition of establishing 4,000 families within a six-year term. The imperial government nixed this proposal.[46] Louisiana's highest magistrates simply could not fathom that American federalism might work across an extended, loosely joined nation with serious sectional cleavages. In 1794, Gayoso wrote Harry Innes of Kentucky that the eastern states would view western separatism "with indifference if not pleasure," because they would no longer bear the expense of supporting armies for Indian warfare. Innes made his own personal calculations, responding that he expected "*unequivocal assurances of Indemnity*" for bringing his state into alliance with Spain.[47] Gayoso and Carondelet believed monetary inducements and guaranteed access to the Mississippi would finally compel western settlers to view collaboration as their sole path to prosperity. They underestimated Anglo-American ethnic unity and resentment of Spain for arming Indian peoples in borderland conflicts against white settlers. Though Kentucky was no longer a "dark and bloody ground" of Indian-white clashes by the mid-1790s, its white inhabitants closely identified with settler folk in Tennessee, Georgia, and Ohio.[48]

The ultimately irreconcilable nature of U.S. frontier and Spanish Indian policies did not obviate short-term accords. In early 1789, Miró was highly pleased by amicable letters received from Colonel James Robertson and Brigadier Daniel Smith of the Cumberland River settlements nominally under North Carolina's jurisdiction.[49] A foremost leader in Nashville, Robertson paid his respects to New Orleans by referring to the Cumberland district as "Mero," a name adopted in the governor's honor. The colonel's letter, along with Smith's, expressed friendship with Spain for a dual purpose. First, Cumberland's leaders wanted Madrid's officers to prevent Creek and Cherokee raids by halting the flow of arms and munitions to Indian peoples. Second, Robertson declared an overriding economic rationale: "Every thinking person in this Country is fully convinced it is our interest to be on good terms if possible with troops in possession of the mouth of [the] Mississippi." This pronouncement tellingly indicated a greater commitment to the New Orleans trade than Spanish control itself. Robertson also aired a personal motive. His son-in-law desired Miró's passport to visit Louisiana as a step toward settling there. The colonel, too, was thinking of moving with his own family if his son-in-law had a favorable reception. As a sign of good will, Robertson denied all reports that Cumberland or Kentucky settlers were plotting an invasion of Louisiana. Miró responded in kind. He pledged to counsel peace to McGillivray of the Creeks, but he admitted that he had little sway over the Cherokees.[50] From a Spanish perspective, Miró's negotiation with the western U.S. bought time and fended off recurrent danger. The division of the Union was an optimal goal in 1787–1790, but it was not the sole objective.

Cumberland's economic woes and Indian conflicts had a sobering effect on Thomas Green, erstwhile anti-Spanish conspirator who settled in that district after his abortive Natchez takeover of 1785. Grasping at Spanish Louisiana's liberal immigration régime just a few years later, he prepared to swear another oath of allegiance to the crown. In April 1789, Green confessed his rationale to U.S. Indian commissioner Richard Winn. Though believing Creek and Cherokee attacks were "Set in Motion by the Spaniards," he did not simply blame Madrid. Congress should take action or face the consequences: "Unless Something is done for us, we must work out Salvation for ourselves." Since navigation of the Mississippi was still restricted, "we live at the Mercy of the Spaniards Unprotected, Unsupported Invaded and Harrass'd at every quarter." Green made his peace with Spanish officialdom and was back at his family estate in Natchez by late 1789. Once again a royal subject, Green put aside his rebellious politics—at least for a time—for the immediacy of profit and security.[51]

The Colonization Track

One cannot easily overstate the degree to which Miró's plans for Louisiana emphasized lawful Anglo-American Mississippi Valley colonization. Had he not needed Wilkinson so much for Kentucky politicking, he would have been glad to see his friend settle in Louisiana. The governor clearly wished his chosen frontier powerbroker to lead the way for influential Americans to embrace opportunities in Spanish territory. Wilkinson had a hankering for land in the Lower Mississippi Valley, though he and his closest Kentucky associates did not follow through on their petition of early 1789 for a Spanish land grant of 600,000 acres between the Yazoo and Big Black Rivers.[52] Significantly, Wilkinson advised Miró against broadening colonization opportunities for ordinary western Americans. Most U.S. emigrants to Louisiana, he warned, "are generally Debtors & fugitives from Justice—poor & without principle . . . dangerous Subjects and ought to be guarded against." Wilkinson then boasted of his power "to carry the great body of our most opulent & respectable Citizens, wherever I may lead in Person." But political success was not guaranteed. Wilkinson imagined a Yazoo grant as "an asylum for myself & my adherents" if his Kentucky plans met unexpected opposition from Congress.[53] By this rhetorical grandstanding, Wilkinson implicitly told Miró that he was keeping options open in both U.S. and Spanish territory. Though not organizing any large-scale American settlement of Louisiana, he was in the habit of recommending acquaintances and friends as worthy colonists in his correspondence with New Orleans. This practice added to his own sources of information and credit in Louisiana. He meanwhile warned against particular "adventurers" as "impostors" feigning Louisiana settlement but aiming at trade and land engrossment alone.[54]

Wilkinson's ambition allowed for allies to share in the spoils, though he recoiled against American rivals who threatened his regional hold. Not coincidentally, he ridiculed poor western immigrants just at the time that Colonel George Morgan of New Jersey projected a large Anglo-American settlement under Spanish auspices in Upper Louisiana. In early 1789, Wilkinson turned to Miró to kill Morgan's scheme, which was strongly supported by Gardoqui in New York City. In the resulting competition, Miró battled strenuously against Gardoqui for butting into his provincial domain. Although Morgan and Gardoqui eventually lost the contest, their collaboration is important for showing possibilities of Anglo-American emigration and frontier integration in the Mississippi region.

A Choice of Power-Brokers

Similar to Oliver Pollock, George Morgan's experience in the Louisiana-Florida borderlands evolved over several decades. A founding partner of the Illinois Company in 1766, Morgan advocated British colonization at mid-continent before pledging his fortunes to the American revolutionary cause. As a merchant and frontier entrepreneur, he nearly succeeded in gaining congressional approval for a military offensive aimed at the

British Mississippi and Gulf ports in 1777. In that episode, he showed a propensity for intrigue by seeking Spanish collaboration while concurrently coveting Mobile and Pensacola for the United States alone. In 1788, Morgan renewed western colonizing plans as head of the New Jersey Land Society—a company seeking to purchase two million acres in the Illinois country from the federal government. The project ran afoul, however, when encountering unexpectedly strong opposition from the area's French settlers, who hired merchant Barthélemi Tardiveau to defend their land rights before Congress. Morgan then decided to shift his attention from the U.S. to the Spanish side of the Mississippi. The change was well considered and no sudden leap in the dark. Morgan worked out the details of Upper Louisiana colonization with Gardoqui, who was thrilled with the prospect of enticing a prominent American to develop crown territories to U.S. detriment.[55]

The Spanish chargé did not approach Morgan directly in making his initial overtures. That course appeared too risky, as it was likely to raise congressional hackles if it became public knowledge. Gardoqui instead contacted Morgan through a mutual friend—Thomas Hutchins—geographer of the United States and a highly knowledgeable authority on the Mississippi-Gulf Coast. A former British military engineer and West Florida landowner, Hutchins earned plaudits as author of *An Historical Narrative and Topographical Description of Louisiana and West-Florida*, published in Philadelphia in 1784. Gardoqui greatly respected Hutchins's knowledge of the west. By early 1788, he elicited the geographer's analysis of frontier conditions, which he then passed on to Madrid. All seemed to confirm Gardoqui in his view that Spain could induce respectable Anglo-American migrants into crown territories as a barrier against "the licentious, the needy, [and] adventurous"—men who were predictably dangerous.[56]

Hutchins was especially susceptible to Spanish influence because he was a British West Florida land claimant whose properties were now under Madrid's sovereignty. In February 1788, Gardoqui helped the geographer by urging Miró to honor Hutchins's grants totaling more than 5,000 acres in the Manchac-Natchez corridor. One of the properties adjoined the Natchez estate of Anthony Hutchins—Thomas's elder brother and a local bigwig who was then in good standing with Spanish authority.[57] Nagged by financial difficulties, Thomas Hutchins gladly lent his services to Morgan, who paid tuition for the geographer's son at the College of New Jersey in Princeton. Assisting Morgan's Illinois project,

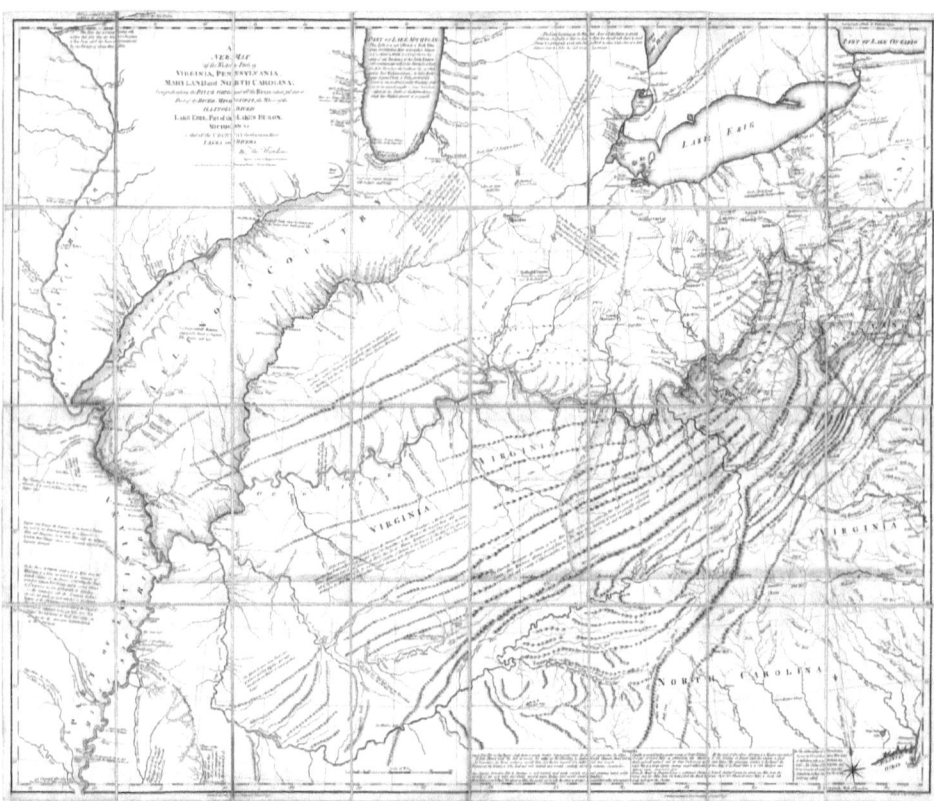

Thomas Hutchins, *A New Map of the Western Parts of Virginia, Pennsylvania, Maryland and North Carolina*... (London, Published According to Act of Parliament Nov. 1, 1778). Courtesy of David Rumsey Map Collection, no. 5044000. This map, later published in Philadelphia, served Spanish officials as a guide to the trans-Appalachian West.

Hutchins quickly turned to a Spanish option when his patron's land purchase proposal failed to win congressional approval.[58]

On August 30, 1788, Morgan took a big leap toward Spanish Louisiana by formally petitioning Gardoqui for a royal concession empowering him to supervise colonization within a vast region, extending two degrees of longitude (110 miles), as measured westward from the Mississippi's bank at Cape Cinque Hommes just south of Ste. Genevieve, Missouri. Morgan projected his colony's southern limit at the confluence of the San Francisco or St. Francis River and the Mississippi, some 280 miles below Cape Cinque Hommes along the great river's winding course. Gardoqui approved the proposal within days, pending royal confirmation.[59]

The Gardoqui-Morgan plan followed a decidedly liberal model of Anglo-American colonization in the Spanish domain. As soon as Morgan arrived in Louisiana and swore allegiance to the crown, he would be allowed to dispose of land—to whichever persons and at whatever price—that he and Governor Miró agreed on. Lawful settlers would enjoy, both for themselves and their posterity, free navigation of the Mississippi, along with the duty-free sale of their produce in Louisiana just as other Spanish vassals there did. They would also receive equivalent rights of exportation to his Catholic Majesty's dominions. Morgan's colonists were not to be molested in "the exercise" of religion—a phrase implying freedom beyond private worship.[60]

Why did Gardoqui approve such broad authority for a foreign entrepreneur? Like Morgan, the Spanish envoy was a merchant who respected commercial acumen, especially when applied to public purpose. Other factors likely came into play. Gardoqui knew of Miró's favors to Wilkinson and calculated that Louisiana's governor would be generous to a distinguished U.S. citizen settling within his province. The Spanish chargé still viewed the United States as a fragmented and dangerously turbulent country. He aimed for a bold counterstroke and believed he could carry the day with Floridablanca's backing. Indeed, he wrote the foreign minister that Morgan's demands were "moderate" in light of his project's importance. The colonel himself vowed he could build a colony of more than 100,000 inhabitants within a decade![61]

Besides boosting Louisiana's economic development, Gardoqui invited responsible U.S. citizens to sponsor Anglo-American settlement in East Florida. He even supported Protestant as well as Irish immigration there before the crown opened the colony to non-Catholic immigrants in 1790. Though he had little success in these Florida endeavors, his efforts reflect an experimental willingness to incorporate propertied foreigners into Spanish border colonies.[62]

George Morgan was eager to move to Spanish territory, provided that Anglo-American liberties, notably trial by jury, followed in his path. He also emphasized the importance of settlers forming their own local laws through representative assemblies. Without endorsing these ideas, Gardoqui did not discourage Morgan from believing colonial autonomy was possible under Spanish frontier governance. Morgan's project embraced the principle of free movement by free men. His native Pennsylvania expressed this ideal in its first state constitution: "That all men have a natural inherent right to emigrate from one State to another that will receive them, or to form a new State in vacant countries, or in such countries as they can purchase, whenever they think that thereby they may promote their own happiness."[63]

Gardoqui gained certain favors in return for his imprimatur. Morgan agreed to spread word of Spanish good will toward American frontier settlers. He also carried a letter from Gardoqui to John Brown of Kentucky, pledging support for that district should its leaders declare independence from both Virginia and the United States. U.S. separatism was to be forwarded on two levels: by siphoning American settlers to Louisiana and detaching trans-Appalachian regions from the Atlantic states.[64] While Gardoqui could hardly advance this project without western cooperation, he deliberately exploited the centrifugal tendencies in American society both east and west of the mountains.

In November 1788, Isaac Dunn, Wilkinson's associate in New Orleans trade, sent his partner an urgent note from Pittsburgh. Colonel George Morgan was busily recruiting colonists in town for a new settlement on the Mississippi's west bank below the Ohio. Moreover, the colonel had the backing of Gardoqui, who was said to be licensing several other Louisiana colonization projects. Dunn was nearly apoplectic in addressing his "dear Wilkiy": "All the Atlantic world are in Treaty with the Spaniard, we have no time to lose."[65]

Dunn felt panicky because Morgan's prospective colony appeared poised to grow rapidly and to dominate the Kentucky-Mississippi trade. Gardoqui was reported to have awarded Morgan a land concession "with liberal and extraordinary indulgences." Dunn's warning for Wilkinson admitted no middle ground: "Unless we can succeed in our politicks in Kentucke [sic]," Morgan's "scheme goes to our Ruin." Once becoming Spanish subjects, American settlers in Upper Louisiana would possess numerous advantages, notably fertile land and duty-free access to the New Orleans market. By early 1789, Wilkinson learned that Morgan's infant settlement, called New Madrid, stood on high ground overlooking the Mississippi about thirty miles below the Ohio. The new post would have a river landing and its own customs post if Morgan had his druthers. Any craft moving down the Ohio and Mississippi might be inspected there. In short, Morgan and New Madrid stood in the way of Wilkinson's pretensions as foremost intermediary between the western United States and New Orleans. Wilkinson immediately let Miró know that Morgan's project must be stopped.[66]

Though Morgan managed to bring some seventy colonists to begin the settlement of New Madrid in early 1789, his grand colonizing plans met political rebuff. Steeled by Wilkinson's resolve, Miró took strong exception to the New Jersey colonel's project. The governor had his own cause for alarm since he was greatly disturbed by Gardoqui's cavalier grant of colonial privileges within his jurisdiction. Though not personally hostile to Morgan, he would not countenance the American entrepreneur's ideas of local self-governance, public religious freedom, and privately managed land sales to settlers. In Miró's view, colonists had to receive land grants directly from the king to feel proper gratitude for residence under crown protection.[67]

Morgan and Miró found little common ground during discussions in New Orleans during the spring of 1789. Returning to New Jersey that summer, the colonel poured out his disappointment to Gardoqui, who was himself responsible for many of the misunderstandings that compromised the colonization project. Miró did not actually want to exclude Morgan, but rather moderate his plans according to Spanish political requirements. As the governor put the case to Madrid in May 1789, he could not tolerate "the establishment of a republic in the midst of His Majesty's dominions."[68] Anglo-American settlers could not be admitted to landholding and commercial privileges without proper respect for Spanish political authority.

Thomas Hutchins had great hopes for Morgan's colony, though he fell ill in Pittsburgh and died in early 1789 without ever seeing New Madrid. In one of his last letters, he asked Daniel Clark Sr. of New Orleans to assist Morgan when the latter came to visit Miró. Hutchins expected a huge onrush of settlement: "Should Colonel Morgan find Encouragement . . . he will depopulate New Jersey, this [the Ohio], and the Kentuckey [sic] Country of all its best Inhabitants, Farmers, Tradesmen, and Mechanics, who will take the Oath of Allegiance to the King of Spain and become most excellent Subjects."[69]

Land and trade were motivating forces far outweighing national allegiance in this scenario. Pleading for Clark's support, Hutchins expressed his intention of resigning his post as geographer to the United States if Miró appointed him to a similar position in Louisiana. Now fifty-eight years old, he envisioned a new and flourishing chapter in life: "I am resolved myself to become a Spanish Subject—You know I have some good Lands near Natchez which the Governor of New Orleans I am told has generously directed to be preserved for me." Hutchins died just when on the verge of personally separating from the American Union and becoming a Spanish subject. Having shifted allegiance from Britain to the United States in 1780, he was finally prepared to serve any imperial government that would pay for his services at mid-continent.[70]

The movement of Anglo-Americans to the Louisiana-Florida borderlands did not occur in isolation from other frontier zones. In May 1789, Miró complained to Alexander McGillivray that a Creek war party had attacked Americans moving westward through the Chickasaw country toward the Mississippi. The assailants were even rumored to be planning to destroy Morgan's settlement at *l'Ance à la Graisse* or New Madrid. The governor was angered by this report, since he believed the crown's Indian friends bound to respect all settlers who came to live in Spanish territory with royal permission.[71] Denying involvement in the raids, McGillivray informed Miró of a rumor that most Illinois settlers were decamping to Morgan's colony of their own accord. Sharing similar reports with William Panton, he only wished that the Creeks had the power to drive all Americans from the Ohio and Cumberland Valleys to their "New Asylum" west of the Mississippi.[72]

During his discussions with Gardoqui, Morgan sold himself as a man as skillful at managing colonial-Indian relations as bringing eastern farmers and tradesmen to a new Mississippi homeland. This talk was not an idle boast. As U.S. Indian agent in the Ohio country from 1776 through 1778, he gained the friendship of the Delawares, who in turn honored him with the title "Tamamend" (the affable one).[73] On his journey from Fort Pitt to the Mississippi in early 1789, he recruited ten deputies from five native peoples, including the Delawares, to accompany his party of about seventy colonists to the Mississippi's western bank. Meeting with Delaware, Shawnee, and Cherokee representatives at New Madrid in April, he assured the assemblage that he now was their "father" and that all of his settlers had become subjects of the king of Spain. "My People will improve the Lands," he declared, while establishing trade for beaver pelts and deerskins. Had Morgan succeeded in initiating mass colonization, he would have been hard put to maintain amicable Indian relations. Instead, New Madrid's emergence as a small settlement in the 1790s proceeded quite peaceably.[74]

Though Morgan's colony had a modest beginning, his project still disturbed U.S. observers who sensed a threat to American interests. James Madison was especially suspicious of Spanish intentions. On November 5, 1788, he apprized Monroe of Gardoqui's support of Morgan's "scheme," which was said to involve Spain granting "a large tract of several hundred miles extent on the West side of the Mississippi . . . to emigrants from the U.S." Suspecting that Gardoqui was manipulating Morgan, Madison added a warning: "A watchful eye ought to be kept on the machinations of Spain." Strict confidentiality was important since a fair portion of his information was "received . . . under bla[c]k veil."[75] Once receiving a copy of Morgan's recruiting handbill, Madison sent President Washington a duplicate and warned of the need to be on guard against "the Spanish project."[76] Ironically, Gardoqui was then preparing to leave the United States for Spain within a few months. Josef Ignacio de Viar and Josef de Jáudenes, his assistants who succeeded him as royal commissioners to the United States, were competent diplomats but by no means prone to ambitious political scheming as was their more distinguished predecessor.[77]

The outcome of Morgan's collaboration with Gardoqui appeared quite open-ended in early 1789. John Dawson, a Virginia congressman, predicted the new Louisiana settlement "will probably produce a remarkable Era in the American history, as a door will be opend [sic] through which the United States will lose many thousands of her best citizens." Morgan was attracting "the most respectable characters, and the most useful farmers and tradesmen" who would enjoy "freedom in religious matters" and "a free navigation of the Mississippi to New Orleans clear of all duties and taxes." Dawson praised Morgan's method of reconnoitering and surveying land as "far superior to that of Congress."[78]

Concerns about Morgan's project were evident in Trans-Appalachia as well as in Congress. James Cole Mountflorence, who visited Kentucky in 1789 on behalf of North Carolina land investors, deliberately enlisted "people of influence" to discourage movement to Morgan's colony, which he believed "Settles very fast." He then posed a troubling question: "What Can be the New Policy of Spain, I am at a loss to find out—they Continue to give great Encouragement to the American Settlers thro'out all Louisiana."[79] Other U.S. citizens were not the least anxious about New Madrid. One Philadelphia commentator rather blandly remarked that "Col. Morgan is commencing a settlement on the Spanish territory, opposite the mouth of the Ohio, which, no doubt, will be in time, united to this part of America."[80]

Lardner Clark, a New Jersey native who was a leading Nashville merchant, was keenly aware of New Madrid's beginning as he considered doing business with New Orleans in May 1789. He observed that Spain's new liberal policies had a "real motive" of political import—"to encourage Emigration from this Country [the United States] into that [Louisiana]." Clark astutely elaborated on this point. "I suppose it [New Madrid] intended as a Counter Settlement to those of the Americans and meant to form a Barrier against them, which probably will at some period be very necessary." Spain was said to be offering "many indulgences" to the "Adventurers to Col. Morgan's New Settlement."[81]

Lardner Clark's analysis is found in the Spanish archives—a fact strongly suggesting that his correspondent, Senator Benjamin Hawkins of North Carolina, shared the letter with Gardoqui, who happened to be a good friend.[82] Most important, Clark conceived of "adventurers" as men legitimately pursuing economic advantage by migrating across national boundaries. Adventurism in this sense was not any preconceived plan of conquest, but rather the sum of disparate individual choices about where to live and under which flag to prosper. The United States did not have anything resembling an inevitable hold at mid-continent when George Washington took his first oath as president in New York City in April 1789.

CHAPTER 8

Conspiracies and International Turmoil

In December 1787, Governor Vicente Manuel de Zéspedes of East Florida welcomed Thomas Powell of Charleston, South Carolina, to St. Augustine. The visitor was no ordinary guest since he had been corresponding for several months with Zéspedes about an alleged anti-Spanish conspiracy in his home state. Powell managed this undercover business by dispatching secret messages to St. Augustine via a Catholic priest in Charleston. Once in Florida, he told Zéspedes of anti-Spanish plotting aimed at Natchez's conquest and the spread of revolution in South America.[1]

Like other conspirators turned informers, Powell expected a reward for his services, in this case permission to settle in Florida as a loyal vassal. Failing in this quest, his name fades rather quickly from Spanish records.[2] Powell's intrigue may have been brief but it reveals conspiratorial currents surging across South Carolina, Georgia, and southern frontier regions. Zéspedes found it hard to fathom the crown's foes—men whom he described as "needy adventurers" prone to "idleness" and "greed"—and who suffered from the delusion that they "need only scratch the soil in the Spanish American dominions to find fistfuls of gold and silver; and for that goal they are capable of committing whatever lawless act, however crazy or extreme, to realize their nonsensical dreams."[3] Zéspedes went so far as to identify three hostile pretenders to the Mississippi: "Great Britain, the United States, and the Adventurers."[4] Freebooters acting outside state authority were seemingly as dangerous as hostile nations. Interestingly, Zéspedes distinguished between politically motivated adventurers and less dangerous "crackers"—white frontier drifters who "were nomadic like Arabs," and mainly interested in poaching on Indian land and moving beyond the reach of law.[5]

Conspiratorial designs on Spanish Louisiana and the Floridas germinated following the Revolutionary War and blossomed during the wars of the French Revolution. As various plots rose and fell, U.S. national authority was being tested alongside Spanish control. If American citizens could form their own volunteer armed forces, they might move from conquest to the creation of new frontier empires or republics. Freebooting in the early republic combined privatistic quests for power and an adventurist impulse to refashion continental affairs.[6]

The South Carolina Yazoo Company

Georgia's abortive Natchez coup of 1785 did not diminish its enormous territorial claims founded in the colonial past. On December 21, 1789, the Georgia legislature allotted 25 million acres of its purported western domain among three private entities—the South Carolina Yazoo, Tennessee Yazoo, and Virginia Yazoo companies. Each firm was obligated to make purchase within two years in order to secure full title.[7]

By licensing the Yazoo companies, Georgia unilaterally asserted control over Chickasaw, Choctaw, Cherokee, and other native lands reaching from the Mississippi to the Tombigbee and stretching 150 miles on a north-south plane from the 35th parallel to the area just above Natchez. State legislators intended to boost revenues and land settlement but without directly assuming the costs of colonization. The Yazoo companies took on the incongruous duties of preserving peace in frontier areas and "extinguishing" Indian land claims whenever possible.[8] Georgia clung to the idea that it could absorb a large portion of the Mississippi's east bank without provoking war with Madrid. In making the Yazoo grants, the legislature deliberately sold lands above Natchez but not between that town and the 31st parallel—the core region under dispute between Spain and the United States. Still, Georgia's act was bound to stir the pot. Spanish-Indian alliances could scarcely hold if private companies commandeered the Mississippi's east bank from Chickasaw Bluffs to Natchez's northern fringe.[9]

The South Carolina Yazoo Company, whose grant encompassed ten million acres, proved the most active and aggressive of the firms operating under Georgia's license. Headquartered in Charleston, the Carolina associates possessed the most southerly Yazoo grant—an area seemingly open to colonization via the Ohio-Mississippi river passage. Moreover, the South Carolina firm's titular domain immediately bordered Natchez, a settler district with fertile soils and ready access to the New Orleans market. The company began with but four shareholders, but then looked to expand its ranks by including investors of sizeable fortunes and political influence.[10]

Dr. James O'Fallon, an Irish émigré and American revolutionary war veteran, became the South Carolina Yazoo Company's principal colonizing agent by the spring of 1790. An opportunistic bachelor of forty-one years, he had already developed a talent for scheming well before that time. Like other ambitious Charleston men, he toyed with befriending Spain as his first golden pathway to the Floridas.[11] In May 1788, O'Fallon sent Gardoqui a proposal to found a Catholic colony on East Florida's northern frontier that would arrest any U.S. or British invasion. Touting his Irish origins and aversion to England, he asked Madrid for no less than £250,000 to support his project.[12] In correspondence with Zéspedes, O'Fallon emphasized the urgency of the moment. By his account, Warren Hastings, former British governor-general in Bengal, was on the verge of leaving England to lead an Anglo-American adventurist push to the Spanish Mississippi Valley. O'Fallon even claimed to have seen one of Hastings's letters disclosing the plot. This tale might well be a lie, but how could that be proven? Hastings was a renowned figure who had recently been impeached by the House of Lords and might be tempted by a grand Mississippi project. Zéspedes took this idea seriously, though he was quite skeptical of O'Fallon's trustworthiness.[13]

Failing at entering Florida by Spanish permission, O'Fallon offered his talents to the South Carolina Yazoo Company—a group specializing in backdoor politicking and bribery. In February 1790, company director Alexander Moultrie unsuccessfully attempted to buy off Alexander McGillivray with an offer of 400,000 acres within the firm's grant.[14] With no possible route across Creek country, the Yazoo partners reckoned Kentucky as the surest pathway to the Lower Mississippi Valley. The group accordingly courted James Wilkinson, who seemed to have a magical touch at New Orleans, to become one of their "solid Adventurers" or investors.[15] By April 1790, O'Fallon established his base of operations cheek-by-jowl beside Wilkinson in Lexington, Kentucky. Taking a page from his host, the doctor sought to ingratiate himself with New Orleans by playing up his antipathy to the American Union. In May, he wrote Miró of his company's plan to establish an "independent" frontier colony whose success would set in motion the "gradual secession" of all U.S. trans-Appalachian districts from "the Atlantic Confederacy." Combined with this heady goal was a desire for an alliance with Spain—or with another supportive European power. While keeping political options open, O'Fallon aired pro-Spanish sentiments in the hope that Miró would invite him for direct negotiations in New Orleans.[16] Wilkinson initially favored the Yazoo scheme and assumed an advisory role with the company's directors for several months. His friendship was characteristically opportunistic and lasted only so long as he believed the Charleston associates might carry off their design.[17]

Miró was himself unsure about countering the Yazoo scheme. Though intrigued by O'Fallon's anti-U.S. posture, he was wary of a group that could become antagonistic unless Spain met its demands for political recognition and access to the New Orleans market. Moreover, O'Fallon was already claiming that his company could place "ten thousand fighting Men" by the Mississippi within eighteen months of initial settlement. Miró necessarily weighed Indian concerns, especially McGillivray's hostility to the Yazoo scheme. The Choctaws and Chickasaws were ready to go to war if necessary to stop a colonial surge in their vicinity. Miró was opposed to allowing the South Carolina company to make any settlement at Nogales (Walnut Hills), strategic ground just south of the Yazoo, which he wished to be colonized by loyal settlers. The governor concluded that it was best to play for time and not yet to invite O'Fallon to New Orleans.[18]

Impatient for satisfaction, O'Fallon assumed an intimidating posture within a few months. On July 16, 1790, he advised Miró that his company was determined to plant a colony of "three to five thousand well armed Men" on the Yazoo River under any circumstances. While O'Fallon's imagined legion varied in size, his threats were unambiguous. If either the Spanish or Indians chose violence over peace, they would be met with force. O'Fallon would even call on the United States for assistance in that event. His vaunted anti-unionism was hardly consistent, but instead a ploy toward creating an autonomous colonial domain with or without Spanish acquiescence.[19]

Oblivious to Indians as beings with their own will, O'Fallon chided Miró for allegedly inciting Choctaw and Chickasaw resistance. In a blustery series of letters, he warned that the Choctaws were geographically caught "between two cross-fires"—their Creek enemies to the east and his own prospective Mississippi colony. Any Choctaw resistance would spark a devastating war, for which Spain would be held accountable. O'Fallon's diplomacy amounted to a frenetic game of borderlands bluff. Miró was meanwhile hard-pressed to establish a defensive posture on the high ground at Nogales above Natchez. He could not secure that site for Spanish fortification before obtaining Choctaw permission through lengthy negotiations.[20]

While Miró brooded over a likely attack, O'Fallon adjusted plans as he grew disillusioned with Wilkinson. In December 1790, the doctor privately derided his erstwhile confederate as "mysterious, intriguing, circuitous & meandering. . . . He cannot move but in zig-zaggs [sic]." O'Fallon was an apt judge of character in this respect, but badly mistaken that he could beat Wilkinson at his own game: "I will convince the court of Spain . . . that, *in one year* I will do that Court more vital & important service, if it will suffer me—; than ten thousand W[ilkinson]s could have affected *in a century*."[21] In the daunting task of empire-building, O'Fallon operated quite independently of his Charleston associates. Breaking free of Wilkinson, too, he found a commander in George Rogers Clark of Louisville, a frustrated old general irresistibly drawn to anti-Spanish campaigning. Like other freebooters hungering for Mississippi soil, O'Fallon attempted to recruit soldier-settlers with land bounties. In September 1790, he described such awards as "plantation rights"—a phrase strongly suggesting opportunity for ordinary white freemen. Not forgetting females, he stipulated that "every woman, married or marriageable," should receive 100 acres for accompanying troops to the settlement. His "encouragement to female adventurers" was a matter of questionable taste. The first woman to "land" in the colony was promised a bounty of 500 acres; "and five hundred more to her who shall bring forth in it the first live child, bastard or legitimate."[22] Adventurers—male and female—were those who risked life and limb for the prospect of enjoying liberty and property in a new society.

O'Fallon's only recorded enumeration of his Yazoo Battalion has a lopsided cast, listing thirty-nine officers by name but without reference to any ordinary rank-in-file. His implicit strategy was to recruit gentlemen who would then bring foot soldiers into the ranks. From small beginnings, he imagined an irresistible "Yazoo fever" swelling his colonial recruits by the hundreds. Wilkinson closely observed matters and forwarded O'Fallon's confidential correspondence to Miró.[23] In February 1791, Clark was reportedly readying river barges near Louisville for a descent to the Yazoo and Nogales. Just one month later, however, Wilkinson boasted to Miró of undercutting O'Fallon's operation so that the latter's followers dwindled from five hundred to a mere fifty. Whether O'Fallon ever had so many enlistees is extremely doubtful. By magnifying the supposed invasion force, Wilkinson raised his political standing in New Orleans.[24]

O'Fallon's alliance with Clark had an important private dimension. In February 1791, the doctor wed Frances ("Fanny") Clark, the general's eighteen-year-old sister. Reports of the marriage spread widely—and not always in a decent light. Visiting Natchez about that time, Colonel John Pope of Virginia sarcastically remarked that the O'Fallon-Clark liaison was delaying Yazoo colonization: "Doctor O'Fallan [sic], Agent for the *Yazous* [sic] Company, ardently pants for the Cultivation of this delicious Soil; but by Connoisseurs, it is shrewdly conjectured, that having pitched his Tent in the Grotto of Miss *Clarke* [sic], his Ardency, like his Constitution, will turn into downright Frigidity."[25]

If subject to private ridicule, O'Fallon's scheming was certainly viewed seriously by the Washington administration, which saw the Yazoo companies as a threat to national authority over Indian relations and foreign policy. The federal government acted cautiously, waiting to learn what was exactly afoot in Kentucky before putting its own prestige on the line. On March 22, 1791, Thomas Jefferson called on Kentucky's district attorney to prosecute O'Fallon if the latter persisted in raising an independent army. In dramatic rhetoric, the secretary of state declared it intolerable that a "whole nation" was exposed to "the calamities of war" with Indian nations, "and perhaps others ... merely that a few adventurers may possess themselves of lands." By "others" Jefferson meant the Spanish; the sensitivity of ongoing negotiations with Madrid probably explains his decision not to mention Spain directly.[26]

Instead of arresting O'Fallon, Washington isolated him from his Charleston confederates. During a visit to South Carolina and Georgia in the spring of 1791, the president tactfully affirmed federal law prohibiting states and individuals from negotiating Indian treaties apart from national authority. The South Carolina Yazoo company was meanwhile unable to raise sufficient funds to make good its land title, let alone to undertake colonization. Thomas Washington, a principal shareholder, had already tarnished the group's name by being convicted of counterfeiting, and hung for that crime in Charleston.[27]

The South Carolina Yazoo scheme plummeted from imagined imperial heights to embarrassment. Expected thousands of settlers failed to materialize—and Miró was not browbeaten into compliance. Nor did the company come close to securing a European loan or engrossing the African slave trade as planned. Director Alexander Moultrie had enthused over the Mississippi as a more promising slave country than South Carolina: "I have near Two Hundred Negroes here but can have as many as I want at the Yazoo."[28] Greed and callousness went hand-in-hand.

Miró's initial response to the South Carolina Yazoo project was exploratory rather than staunchly oppositional. Attempting to budge imperial policy, the governor suggested opening New Orleans to European and U.S. merchant vessels in order to spur Louisiana's economic growth and to assuage western American discontent. Miró's advice may be likened to Madison's famous dictum for constitutional balance: "Ambition must be made to counteract ambition." Spanish countenance of legitimate U.S. immigrants would undercut an intrusive border colony controlled by foreign adventurers and beholden to no national government.[29]

Beyond special pleading for free trade, Miró showed discomfort with the far-flung imperial boundaries that he was obligated to defend. Since Gálvez's wartime triumphs, Madrid claimed possession of the Mississippi's east bank all the way to the Ohio.[30] Miró looked for territorial wiggle room as O'Fallon threatened to descend on his doorstep. In dispatches to Madrid and Havana in 1791, he suggested that West Florida's northern boundary reached no further than the mouth of the Yazoo—the same provincial line that the Privy Council had drawn at George Johnstone's behest in 1764. By this reckoning, the Mississippi's east bank northward from the Yazoo to the Tennessee belonged to the Choctaws and Chickasaws, whom the crown was obliged to arm for defensive purposes. As pragmatic as ever, Miró expected Indian peoples to take the lead in safeguarding theoretical royal territories that Spain could not realistically hold against invasion.[31] Luis de Las Casas, captain-general at Havana, had alternatively tough and cautious advice for New Orleans. On the one hand, Miró should not yield an inch of territory from Natchez to the Yazoo—territory that indisputably belonged to his Catholic Majesty by conquest from Great Britain. On the other, the governor should attempt a peaceful resolution of the crisis if possible. Wary of an uncontrollable frontier clash, Las Casas advised Natchez's royal garrison not to fire first on incoming Yazoo colonists; the king's soldiers should even refrain from shooting altogether unless their fort was directly attacked.[32] Had Clark or O'Fallon somehow managed to lead a substantial armed group to the Yazoo but not gone further south, it is not clear that Spanish authorities would have attempted to stop the settlers by force.

Miró was on guard for internal subversion in Natchez as long as the invasion threat lingered. The governor had less to worry over than he believed. Throughout the Yazoo crisis of 1790–91, the Natchez district's Anglo-American settlers kept their distance from intrusive land companies. Pleading for continued Spanish purchases of tobacco, white inhabitants did not identify with strangers who might cause difficulty in their neighborhood. Colonel Peter Bryan Bruin of Bayou Pierre, whom O'Fallon assiduously courted as an Irish Catholic ally, cooperated with Spanish authorities by forwarding the doctor's letters directly to Governor Gayoso in Natchez.[33]

International politics impinged on the diplomatic jousting between O'Fallon and Miró. While the South Carolina company plotted its course in 1790, it appeared likely that Great Britain and Spain would go to war over rival claims to the Pacific Northwest. The specific locale of contention was Nootka Sound—an inlet on the western perimeter of Vancouver Island. Though Anglo-Spanish controversy was resolved diplomatically to British advantage in October 1790, it took some months for this news to reach the Lower Mississippi Valley. O'Fallon warned Miró that the Pacific crisis was but a prelude to the catastrophe that Spain would suffer if his company's demands were unmet: "The affair, the trifling affair of Nootka Sound is, yet, recent before the eyes of your Excellency." With this melodramatic pronouncement, the conspirator bluffed that he could summon British military power at will along the Mississippi.[34]

Louisiana's highest officials were relieved when news came of an Anglo-Spanish diplomatic settlement. At Natchez, Gayoso put aside concerns about a British invasion from Canada. He also took comfort from word that Congress had resolved to admit Kentucky as a state. Although Gayoso desired the Union's dismemberment, he was now gratified by President Washington's steady hand.[35]

As long as an Anglo-Spanish war loomed, the U.S. administration feared an unstoppable British descent from the Great Lakes and across American territory to Louisiana. Washington wrote alarmingly in late August 1790 of western settlers being "seduced" by British power—being tempted to support a British military offensive opening the Mississippi-Gulf corridor. Jefferson counseled American neutrality for the time being, though he believed the United States ought to intervene militarily if there was no peaceful means of preventing "the calamity" of English conquest of Louisiana and the Floridas. But this position did not gain the cabinet's approval.[36] Washington's government held back from any clear decision as it waited to see how an Anglo-Spanish conflict would affect the continental balance of power.

Imperial England—and not the fledgling American government—seemed the most likely metropolitan power to bring down Spanish colonialism in 1790. Within a few years that presumption was undone by European conflagration brought on by the French Revolution. It was now France that appeared the stoutest enemy of Spanish colonialism—and the most likely nation that Anglo-American adventurers might ally with for their own purposes.

The French Revolution and American Filibustering

The French Revolution shook the old international order based on dynastic alliances. In 1790 the French national assembly declined to invoke the Bourbon Family Compact during the Nootka-Sound crisis. Franco-Spanish relations deteriorated over the next two years and reached a nadir with the execution of Louis XVI on January 21, 1793. On March 7, France declared war on Spain with the intent of spreading revolution on both sides of the Atlantic. From 1793 to 1795, Spain collaborated with its traditional British foe in the fight against revolutionary France.[37]

In late 1792, French government leaders debated the optimal means of undermining Spanish rule in the Americas. While ideologically committed to revolutionary change, the Girondin republicans then in power were divided over expending military and monetary resources in the American theater. Pierre Lebrun, minister of foreign affairs, threw his weight behind largely clandestine operations targeting Louisiana rather than supporting Venezuelan revolutionary Francisco de Miranda's ambitious plan for an invasion of the South America.[38]

French officials were influenced by various Louisiana schemes proposed by individuals with direct knowledge of the North American scene. In October 1792, James Cole Mountflorence, a Paris resident who had lived in Trans-Appalachia for years, offered to raise a North American legion of 10,000 men in the name of France. His ideal fighters were an assemblage of frontiersmen, Canadians, and Illinois *habitants*—"all sworn enemies of Spanish despotism."[39] Though Mountflorence did not gain the appointment, his plan epitomized the republican agenda of enlisting diverse nationalities in the battle for liberty. Individual volunteers would reap material rewards by seizing the property of Spanish royalists and clergy—whose wealth would also pass to the French republic. Hardy trans-Appalachian settlers were seemingly perfect candidates for this work because of their independent spirit and hatred of Spain.[40]

In late 1792, Edmond Charles Genet, newly appointed emissary to the United States, received the broad charge of expanding "the Empire of Liberty" by stirring the American populace against both Britain and Spain. Though formally instructed to respect U.S. national authority, he believed himself empowered to conduct operations beyond federal purview as necessary. With the intent of revolutionizing Canada and Louisiana, he carried blank military commissions and letters of marque to be distributed where useful. His objective of opening U.S. ports to French privateering coincided with adventurist scheming targeting the Mississippi Valley and the Floridas.[41] Genet was to proceed by covertly dispatching French agents to Kentucky with the mission of recruiting five hundred armed volunteers for a descent on the Lower Mississippi Valley and New Orleans. Little opposition was expected. French settlers and Anglo-Americans in the Mississippi Valley were seen as natural allies devoted to economic progress—unlike Spaniards purportedly envious of such achievement.[42] Ideas of Hispanic backwardness colored French republican policy of the 1790s just as similar prejudices had underscored the New Orleans revolt of 1768.

French conceptions of a Mississippi campaign took shape from ideas passing freely across the Atlantic. For example, it was commonly assumed in Paris that trans-Appalachian settler districts were ripe for freebooting because of their tenuous ties to the Atlantic states. Western leaders would therefore embrace the idea of mounting a military campaign against Spanish territory.[43] Pierre Lyonnet, a former Louisianan living in Paris, had a notable influence on French government thinking. He glowingly described American volunteers as *"filibustiers des Bois"*—woodland freebooters who were also dubbed "adventurers by principle and habit" in a related anonymous report.[44] French government sources offer what is probably the first documented reference to *filibustering* (*"un coup de filibustiers"*) as a weapon to be employed against Spain in the trans-Appalachian West. Such rhetorical flourishes harkened back to sixteenth-century Franco-Spanish rivalry, and also heralded a militant republicanism destroying the *ancien régime*.[45] Michel-Ange-Bernard Mangourit, Genet's confederate and French consul in Charleston in 1793–94, lauded Colonel William Tate, South Carolina freebooter, in just these terms: "He has all the virtues of the adventurers who conquered the two Indies, without having their vices and ignorance."[46]

At roughly the same time that Lyonnet was at work, several American conspirators were contemplating a French alliance for related purposes.

Knowing that France and Spain were headed toward war in early 1793, George Rogers Clark forwarded a confidential message offering his military services to the French minister to the United States. Not being a skilled penman, the general doubtless called on the literary talents of comrade O'Fallon, who now viewed France as his beacon for realizing Yazoo ambitions. Clark beheld the prospect of "humbling Spain in her vital parts," conquering New Mexico and Louisiana, and opening the way to "all Spanish America, with its mines." France would thereby obtain "the whole Fur, Tobacco and Flour Trade of this western world, and a great consumption of her manufactures."[47] The union of maritime and continental power was a staple of imperial projections toward the Mississippi Valley for decades—whether British, French, or Anglo-American by design.

The renowned Thomas Paine was in the midst of revolutionary Paris, but still sufficiently interested in American affairs to urge on O'Fallon through a friendly correspondence. The author of *Common Sense* and *The Rights of Man* lauded the Yazoo cause and advised the doctor to assume a French officer's command in the conquest of Louisiana. Paine contended that France would honor the Yazoo Company's proprietary claims and the land bounties that soldiers earned in battle. He saw no difficulty if the French government decided to cede conquered Spanish territories to the United States. The demise of monarchism was Paine's prime concern, not the rebirth of French imperialism in the Mississippi Valley.

If American filibustering had operated as planned in Paris, Kentucky would have had first place as a base for striking Spanish Mississippi and Gulf territories. Instead, the Georgia-Florida frontier, where U.S. authority was notoriously weak, became the most active arena of conspiracy and strife. Several factors were at play here. In 1790, the Spanish imperial government opened East Florida to Protestant settlers from the United States. Most newcomers clustered in the region between the St. Johns and St. Marys Rivers and cultivated ties on both sides of the international border. Georgia's intense conflict with the Creek nation meanwhile spilled into anti-Spanish intrigues. Many of the state's citizens were disgusted by federal policies restraining white movement into Indian territories. Popular discontent aroused sympathy for filibustering, though not mass participation in attempted Florida invasions.

Genet's first days in the United States were in Charleston, whose citizenry feted him as a representative of the French republic. William Moultrie, governor of South Carolina, conversed amiably with Genet and approved the latter's privateering and filibustering agenda. The governor was an enthusiast for Mississippi lands and commercial connections, similarly trumpeted by his brother Alexander, former director of the South Carolina Yazoo Company.[48] Once in Philadelphia, Genet lobbied Jefferson to countenance his plans. The secretary of state was in sympathy with the French minister's goals while careful not to endorse his means. In his notes on conversations with Genet, Jefferson recalled stating that he did not mind if there were "insurrections" excited against Spanish rule within Louisiana. If Kentucky men invaded, however, they would be "putting a halter about their necks" for committing hostilities "against a nation [Spain] at peace with the US." The supposed threat of the hangman's noose was hyperbole, as Jefferson doubtless knew. The national government could not have impaneled a western jury that would have found citizens guilty of a capital offense for taking on despised Spaniards.[49]

On July 12, 1793, Genet forwarded a military commission to George Rogers Clark, named "Commander-in-chief of the independent and revolutionary army of the Mississippi."[50] The French minister continued this course well after the Washington administration demanded his recall later that summer. By October, Genet appointed William Tate to head the "American revolutionary legion" in the southern theater. A former Yazoo company investor, Tate had visions of forming a volunteer army that would push westward, unite with Clark's force, and share the spoils of Louisiana land. Despite Mangourit's support in Charleston, this heady plan fizzled because of inadequate funds as well as Genet's political indiscretions.[51]

Genet explicitly authorized both Clark and Tate to raise their volunteer forces "outside the territory of the United States." This phrase was the French minister's bow to political proprieties and international law. By asking expeditionary soldiers to gather beyond U.S. boundaries, Genet was attempting to bring down Spanish colonialism without appearing to violate U.S. national authority.[52] Apart from political legerdemain, the phrase "outside the territory of the United States" had a significant measure of truth in regard to projected filibuster strikes. The American republic might have a western boundary at the Mississippi and a southeast border along the St. Marys, but it hardly had secure command of those frontiers. The Washington administration moved to uphold national sovereignty by pressuring governors in Kentucky, South Carolina, and Georgia to discountenance foreign volunteer enlistment in their jurisdictions.[53]

George Washington's prestige was of utmost importance in countering the freebooting phenomenon. Congress heeded the president's call for remedial legislation by an act of June 5, 1794, which instituted fines and prison sentences for American citizens who exercised a foreign military commission within the United States, or who went beyond U.S. territories to enlist "in the service of any foreign prince or state."[54] The bill boosted national sovereignty, though it omitted a proposed clause giving the president explicit power to use land and sea forces, and to call out the militia, to interdict any hostile enterprise mounted from U.S. territory against a foreign nation with which the United States was at peace.[55] Secretary of State Edmund Randolph was quite uncertain about the government's power to restrain western freebooting against Spain. In August 1794, he feared the government was caught between the unenviable choices of supporting a Kentuckian invasion of Spanish territory—or instead disavowing such aggression and risking that state's separation from the Union.[56]

Barón de Carondelet had little confidence that his province could withstand a filibuster assault launched in the name of France. As he informed Madrid in late October 1793, a joint Franco-American invasion of Louisiana would gather strength because the area "is largely French in population." Besides hostile military movements, the governor feared the infiltration of "pernicious" revolutionary maxims of liberty and equality.[57] He was quite anxious about his capital, where colonial disaffection surfaced well before news of French-Spanish hostilities reached Louisiana. When definite reports of war came that summer, Carondelet expelled sixty-eight colonists for suspected disloyalty. The banished individuals were transported to Havana—to be shipped from there either to U.S. ports or else Saint-Domingue. Significantly, the governor deliberately struck at men of little property, who appeared especially dangerous because they had the least to lose by siding with an enemy attack. The expulsions hardly calmed matters. Within a few weeks, Carondelet reported "mysterious gatherings and assemblies" being held outside the city by suspected French republicans.[58]

Carondelet's fear of internal subversion was directly proportional to his perception of external threats. Though disturbed by Genet's revolutionary manifesto circulating in Louisiana, he was more alarmed by reports from New York City that a French naval squadron could be heading for the Mississippi's mouth. Indeed, he suspected Genet had the ulterior purpose of luring Spanish galleys far upriver to fend off freebooters while the main enemy invasion force would move from the delta to New Orleans. In November 1793, Carondelet made a secret downriver visit to Plaquemine in the Lower Valley for the preparation of regional defense. The trip's covert nature suggests the governor's lack of trust in city residents who might conspire in his absence.[59]

In January 1794, Carondelet breathed somewhat easier once it became evident that no maritime strike was forthcoming. In the battle for hearts and minds, Louisiana's governor took the offensive, issuing a proclamation of February 12, 1794, warning inhabitants of slave insurrection and devastation if they made common cause with French radicals and American vagabonds poised to invade from Kentucky.[60] While Carondelet propagandistically exploited colonial fears, his message was not so far-fetched. Auguste Lachaise, a former republican officer of Saint-Domingue, was one of Genet's principal agents in Kentucky. Informants in Trans-Appalachia claimed that "the adventurers" intended to plunder plantations, seize slaves, and take land for themselves.[61] Carondelet was well informed of the situation in the western United States through Wilkinson and other sources. He publicly reassured Louisiana's inhabitants that Washington's government opposed the filibuster. Besides, the freebooters were so poorly funded that their letters of credit were protested in Kentucky.[62]

Carondelet was not without resources. Because of troop reinforcements, he had many more soldiers than Miró generally had, if never the strong and disciplined force he wished. Spanish regulars in Louisiana and West Florida amounted to some 1,500 to 1,600 in 1793–94, with troop concentrations at New Orleans and Pensacola, and a rather thin distribution elsewhere.[63] Since 1768, most French Louisianan army officers stood strongly behind Spanish authority. There was none more stalwart than Pedro Rousseau, Gálvez's former pilot, and the most intrepid commander of royal river galleys patrolling the Mississippi during the 1790s. Ready to do battle against invaders, he was no less dedicated to arresting the disloyal among his own countrymen.[64] The royal galley *La Flecha*, commanded by Juan Barnó y Ferrúsola, scored a coup on February 5, 1794, by arresting Jean-Pierre Pisgignoux on the Mississippi near New Madrid. The captured man was unmistakably French by nationality, but his political leanings were hardly obvious. Formerly part of Genet's circle in

Philadelphia, he turned double-agent by ratting on his comrades. First covertly divulging his story to Madrid's envoys in New York City, he later charted his own southwestward path with the intent of disclosing all to Carondelet. Pisgignoux's motives are uncertain beyond his hope of the informer's reward. His machinations failed miserably in this respect. Subject to Spanish interrogation at Nogales and New Orleans, he was finally sent to prison in Havana.[65]

Carondelet did not trust Pisgignoux but he was too suspicious of creole intentions to dismiss the informer's loose accusations of conspirators lurking in high places. Just to be safe the governor transferred alleged plotter Captain Pedro Favrot from duty in Natchez to New Orleans. Favrot, a loyal veteran of Gálvez's victorious army, was not pleased. Sometime in 1794–95, he penned an unsigned letter pleading with Carondelet for cool-headedness: "Stop speaking to us of intrigues and conspiracies. . . . All the people are terrified. Distrust springs up between the colony and its governor. It spreads even among families, between friends."[66]

French allegiances were quite diverse if measured from the North American interior, the Caribbean, or U.S. port cities. Pisgignoux was himself a Saint-Domingue refugee who was desperate to recoup lost ground. Other native Frenchmen maneuvered far more adeptly across the U.S.-Spanish divide. Barthélemi Tardiveau, émigré merchant in the Ohio Valley, was an unofficial French agent during the late 1780s but stayed aloof from Kentucky filibustering in 1793 when he had business ventures dependent on Carondelet's good will. His brother Pierre, meanwhile, served as an interpreter for Genet's surrogates in Kentucky. Michel Lacassagne, another émigré merchant, worked effectively as a Spanish agent in Louisville.[67] Loyalties differed among individuals based on their views of the French Revolution and their sense of which imperial power, if any, would be worth backing in uncertain circumstances.

In contrast to jittery New Orleans, Natchez's conservative Anglo settlers were strongly cooperative with Spanish authority. Gayoso successfully rallied colonials to the royal standard against what seemed an impending Jacobin and adventurist attack. The Natchez militia—three hundred strong—marched southward under Esteban Minor to reinforce New Orleans in the fall of 1793. Though these men did not have to draw their swords, their conduct appreciably boosted Spanish morale and discouraged creole disaffection.[68]

The Clark-O'Fallon-Genet plan finally collapsed because of weak trans-Appalachian support more than Spanish strength in Louisiana.

O'Fallon himself died in early 1794—the apparent victim of injuries from a horse-fall.[69] Clark's lack of funds seriously crimped operations. The Washington administration's stance against the attempted expedition was also crucial, though the slowness of communication between Philadelphia and Trans-Appalachia left things unsettled for some time. Dr. James White, an influential Cumberland settler of pro-Spanish leaning, wrote Gayoso in early 1794 that French agents were sending military commissions to his locale, along with "large promises, but hitherto not a denier of money," without which he believed the enterprise would have no chance. Colonel John Montgomery, a well-respected officer, was the point man for recruitment in Cumberland.[70]

Clark, Montgomery, and friends attempted a military solution to the Mississippi issue at a time when westerners were sharply criticizing the U.S. government for failing to induce Spain to recognize American navigational rights from the river to the Gulf. French agent Lachaise took on the dual cause of free trade and unimpeded river traffic as his surest way to gain recruits. On May 19, 1794, he declaimed to Lexington's Democratic Society: "The Spaniards who defend the Mississippi are more worthy of Contempt than the Ottomans." In a fiery peroration, he summoned citizens and patriots to join a "Holy Expedition" to oust Spain from the region.[71]

Lachaise's rhetoric did not produce an army. Though western Americans had no hesitancy about criticizing U.S. Mississippi policy, they were ambivalent on the legitimacy and usefulness of filibustering. On February 8, 1794, the *Kentucky Gazette* printed Clark's call for volunteers in the very same issue that it included General Arthur St. Clair's proclamation warning citizens against enlisting in any unauthorized expedition against Spanish Louisiana![72] General Anthony Wayne's troops in Ohio had a significant regional role in showing the American flag. Wayne staunchly opposed freebooting, though he admitted that he could not recruit sufficient Kentucky volunteers when the latter thirsted for "*Lawful plunder*" in Spanish Louisiana. In the new federal empire, the nation's leaders required both political strength and discretion in bringing frontier districts under law. Knox ordered Wayne to use force if necessary to thwart a Louisiana invasion, but only after "every peaceable effort" of persuasion was exhausted.[73]

Clark, O'Fallon, and their French allies did make converts, but also raised hackles among those who opposed their enterprise for assorted reasons. Genet's contentiousness with Washington's government did not sit well with some Kentuckians. John Bradford, editor of the *Kentucky Gazette*, refused to publish the French emissary's circular for recruits even though he was personally sympathetic to an invasion of Louisiana. Governor William Blount of the Southwest territory ordered General James Robertson of Nashville to do his utmost to stop "that Jacobin Incendiary Genet." Robertson aired his own sentiments against the filibuster to Gayoso.[74] Some western American leaders wanted to manage their own expansionist agenda independently of French influence. Carondelet knew no rest after Genet's project collapsed since Blount and Robertson continued their drive to amass Indian lands and to control key points of communication and trade, most notably Muscle Shoals and Chickasaw Bluffs.

Filibuster Intrigues on the Florida Frontier

Filibuster leaders by the Georgia-Florida frontier devoted far more attention to Indian relations than their counterparts in Kentucky. Geography accounted for much of the difference. Kentucky conspirators planned a Mississippi strategy as the key to Louisiana's takeover. Their plans centered on capturing Spanish forts and rallying colonials to their side as they descended the great river from New Madrid to Natchez for an assault on New Orleans. No such leapfrogging was possible by overland route from Georgia into Florida. Creek acquiescence therefore appeared essential to both French agents and American volunteer officers.

Colonel Samuel Hammond of Georgia, the most influential southerner to assume a French military commission, had a powerful economic motive for a Florida invasion. Together with his brother Abner, he headed an Indian trading firm that competed against the rival house of Panton, Leslie, and Company operating in the Floridas under Spanish license.[75] The Hammonds collaborated with French consul Mangourit, who had idealistic notions of dealing with Indian peoples on a basis of equality. In this case, Franco-American cooperation depended on bypassing differences in outlook between allied parties.[76] Mangourit had already experienced political embarrassment in Charleston because of the local citizenry's fears that French republicanism could incite slave insurrection. Saint-Domingue's white exiles in Charleston were among Mangourit's harshest critics.[77]

Filibuster campaigns were vulnerable to internal dissension and collapse whenever volunteers became skittish about the resort to arms. The Georgia push toward Florida was compromised in just this fashion. In a dramatic twist, Abner Hammond turned against brother Samuel in December 1793 by unveiling the invasion plot to Carlos Howard, veteran Spanish Florida officer, in secret talks held on Georgia's Cumberland Island and nearby Amelia Island within Spain's jurisdiction. The informer's purported motive was "to reclaim his brother" from a "wild" and unlawful project. Abner Hammond was also profit-minded, as he requested Spanish compensation for the war supplies he brought into Florida "as property of the French Republick [sic]." Governor Juan Nepomuceno de Quesada was unmoved by this plea and sent Hammond from St. Augustine to prison in Havana.[78] Astonishingly, clumsy plotters and turncoats believed they could hoodwink Spaniards at will. They were proven wrong on a good many occasions.

The Hammond affair exacerbated an already tense situation within East Florida. In mid-January 1794 Quesada summoned a council of war in St. Augustine to consider disturbing information. On the basis of testimony from loyal settlers, it appeared that several U.S. immigrants were either collaborating with Georgia plotters or else had learned of the conspiracy without reporting it to royal authorities. East Florida's Anglo-American settlers were restive because Spanish officials balked at their demands for an open Indian commerce and for free trade with the United States. These complaints coincidentally arose just two years after Thomas Jefferson imagined the lawful movement of U.S. settlers into East Florida leading toward the colony's peaceful absorption by the American republic.[79] Futurity appeared not so rosy in Spanish St. Augustine.

Quesada's fear of internal subversion led to draconian measures. On January 21, the East Florida council of war ordered all colonists living above the St. Johns—and in proximity to Georgia—to move south of the river with their possessions, and to burn their houses and other buildings so that the enemy could make no use of them. Many settlers were uprooted, though some left their homes intact rather than setting a torch to them. Quesada's policy enraged colonists arrested for insurgent activity. The invasion scare of 1794—and the harsh Spanish response—intensified rather than diminished frontier disorder and insecurity.[80]

Notwithstanding Quesada's fears, Samuel Hammond was in no condition to push from Georgia into Florida. Freebooting suffered a political reversal in the southern United States as the Washington administration exerted pressure on state officials. In December 1793, Governor Moultrie of South Carolina issued a proclamation prohibiting the raising of volunteers in the state for French military service. Though Hammond was still recruiting in Georgia at the time, his opportunity for success was diminishing even before his brother turned informant.[81] In February 1794, Antoine Fauchet, the new French minister to the United States, ordered a halt to all military activity authorized by his predecessor on American soil. Mangourit, who had imagined as many as 4,000 volunteers descending on East Florida, was soon ousted from his duties in Charleston. U.S. adventurers along the St. Marys lost the French naval support they required for supplies. What seemed a volunteer surge proved but an ebb tide.[82]

Public debate over adventurism was heated even as military adventurism lost steam. In a libertarian reading of Rousseau, the Franklin Society of Pendleton, South Carolina—William Tate's neighborhood—protested the state's investigation of filibuster leaders. "Man is born free," the society declaimed, and "may remove out of the limits of these United States" as he pleased.[83] As Kentucky governor Isaac Shelby had recently maintained, this right included the citizen's privilege of bringing arms with him when he voluntarily left the state. Freebooting appeared justifiable from this perspective because of Spain's dual policies of restricting Mississippi navigation and supporting Indian resistance against Anglo-American settlement.[84] After a lively exchange with Jefferson, Shelby received a verbal upbraiding from the new secretary of state, Edmund Randolph: "And, indeed, what Government can be destitute of the means of self-defence, as to suffer, with impunity, its peace to be drawn into jeopardy by hostilities levied within its territory, against a foreign nation in order to be prostrated at the will of tumultuous individuals, and scenes of bloodshed and civil war to be introduced[?]"[85] Randolph's emotional rhetoric again suggests how fragile the frontier seemed from Philadelphia's vantage point in the mid-1790s.

Military adventurism comingled with plans for creating a political transformation in the Florida-Louisiana borderlands. By a formal contract of July 1793 negotiated in Savannah, Samuel Hammond and French consul C. M. F. de Bert plotted a new order once victory was achieved over Spanish forces. East Florida was to become part of the French Republic until the war's end, when "the said country is to become independent to all intents & purposes" under a "strictly democratic republican government." It was even suggested that the new republic might form a union with West Florida and Louisiana once Spain lost its grip on those provinces.[86] Once again, freebooting suggested political realignments of continental scope. The Hammond-Bert scheme made no mention of the United States, but rather deferred to the French republic. In this informal borderlands treaty, France was allotted one-half of all proceeds from the sale of the East Florida's vacant lands. In apparent deference to French concerns, colonial purchases were to be executed without intruding on territories "reserved to the Indians for their hunting grounds."[87] U.S. freebooters and their French backers had quite distinct interests in conquest.

The most aggressive freebooting along the Georgia-Florida frontier was linked to white settler forays into Indian territory. General Elijah Clarke, veteran Georgia militia commander, accepted a commission as a French officer in the fall of 1793 after the Washington administration blocked an expedition that he was about to lead against the Creeks. As an apparent prelude to a Florida campaign, Clarke assembled volunteers during the next half-year by the Oconee River—the border between Georgia and the Creek nation as mandated by federal treaty. Violating national law, Clarke intentionally led a few hundred soldiers and settlers to the river's west bank—and into Indian land beyond U.S. jurisdiction. By July 1794, he formed a fledgling government that was effectively independent of both Georgia and the United States. Fittingly, his colonial outposts were called Fort Advance and Fort Defiance. Not all was bellicose, however. As a practical matter, Clarke strived to avoid clashes with the Creeks.[88]

With Henry Knox as point man, the Washington administration called on Georgia authorities to douse the trans-Oconee movement. Governor George Mathews, who respected the president, responded to intense federal pressure by deploying state militia to block supplies to Clarke's settlement and finally to break up the colony in late September 1794. No blood was spilled in this episode, but feelings ran high. Clarke declared Knox's orders "unconstitutional." The general was a hero to many Georgians, and therefore escaped state prosecution.[89]

Though the Oconee venture had been thwarted, the Georgia-Florida frontier remained combustible. In the late spring of 1795, a filibustering band from Georgia at last made its way into Florida. The invasion was an outgrowth of Quesada's arrest of some half-dozen Anglo colonists the previous year. After being released from prison in piecemeal fashion, the embittered men gathered in Georgia to plot revenge. The architects of invasion were Richard Lang and William Plowden, influential settlers who were among the first to regain their freedom. Disregarding the fact that the United States and Spain were at peace, the filibusters went on the offensive through volunteer recruitment, unofficial French assistance, and collaboration between Anglo-American settlers operating on both sides of the St. Marys.[90]

On June 29, 1795, a force of sixty to seventy Georgia and Florida irregulars overran a small Spanish garrison along the road to St. Augustine. (Anglo-Americans from Georgia led the assault with assistance from their Florida confederates.) On July 9, this same contingent, now grown to over one hundred, attacked a royal outpost just below the St. Johns. The attackers killed three Spanish soldiers and took more than twenty prisoners. When a Spanish fleet counterattacked with the aid of a British corsair, the Anglo freebooters and insurgents escaped northward to Amelia Island and ultimately found refuge in Georgia. Hostilities came to a halt before the year's end, but East Florida's travails continued. It was not until 1798 that the trials of rebels—whether in person or *in absentia*—were concluded at St. Augustine.[91] The invasion of 1795 represented the sole instance when anti-Spanish plotting in a U.S. border region actually led to armed conflict in Louisiana or the Floridas during the decade.

Georgia-Florida contention spilled very little blood compared to hostilities between whites and Indians from the Tennessee to the Oconee. Georgia's continual push into Creek country may have even reduced pressures that would have been otherwise directed toward Florida. As Tate and Hammond were mustering volunteers in 1793–94, a plethora of armed white groups, including Georgia militiamen, attacked the Creeks on Indian ground. Wanton murders and retaliatory violence were all too common. Federal army officers did their best to counter lawless forays, but they had too few troops to control the situation. Their most important act was to report events unstintingly to Philadelphia and to call on Georgia's government for restraint.[92]

Given continual tensions with Georgia, Indian leaders proceeded carefully when Quesada called for assistance in early 1794 to ward off filibusters threatening his province. An assembly of Seminoles and others, led by Payne ("the Oconee king"), affirmed their friendship but without offering immediate aid, and instead asking to be supplied with arms and munitions just as had been the case when England held the Floridas. Downplaying the invasion threat, Payne observed that the United States stood against the freebooters who were but "a Sett of Lawless Vagrants." His people were not to be cowed by such a group. Payne's perspective on frontier lawlessness was quite similar to the outlook of U.S. and Spanish authorities that scorned undisciplined freebooters.[93] In subsequent discussions, Quesada attempted to disabuse Seminoles and Creeks of any trust in Frenchmen—a people that had descended so low as to "kill" their king. The governor deceptively told Indians that the Spanish and English together had defeated the French in their own country. Such talk had little effect when Spain's military might was scarcely in view. The Hallooing King of the Lower Creeks subsequently rebuffed Quesada's entreaties by declaring "it is the Wish of us all not to have any thing to Do in a Warr [sic] that is between White people."[94]

When Florida rebels and Georgia filibusters again threatened Florida in 1795, both the Spanish and their foes again appealed for Creek and Seminole assistance or friendship. Payne once more stood aloof from the fighting, sending a friendly message to St. Augustine but also complaining of a lack of weapons and munitions. When Quesada finally beat back the rebel advance in August, he did so with reinforcements from Cuba along with assistance from loyal Anglo settlers and free black militiamen.[95]

Elijah Clarke, erstwhile Indian fighter, assumed the guise of a self-proclaimed "citizen" of the French republic when furthering Georgian freebooting into Florida in 1795. Planning to retake the offensive against the Spanish that fall, he sent messages of good will to the Creeks and Seminoles. Desiring Indian neutrality in the coming fight, he directed two letters to John Kinnaird, an influential Lower Creek headman of Scots-Indian ancestry who had gained considerable wealth in slaves and cattle during the Revolutionary War and its aftermath. Though illiterate, Kinnaird was an important intermediary between his people and U.S. and Spanish authorities. Forwarding Clarke's letters to St. Augustine, he asked for Quesada's understanding: "I am still your friend as Ever and will always be in any thing but war which I think it is not your wish to involve our Nation in a war with any power, as you [know] us to be but a weak people & not able to stand against America or france."[96]

Kinnaird did not want to become embroiled in the battle for new empires and new republics that was being waged by external forces impinging on his people. Though he was wealthy, he still occupied a tenuous position in a factionalized Creek world where sharp divisions existed among centralizers and localists, the propertied elite and the poor, and those who favored political accommodation with the United States, as opposed to violent resistance, as the optimal means to keep their hold on the land. Other southern Indian peoples faced similar dilemmas. In the late eighteenth century, native and colonial spheres overlapped to an unprecedented extent, with whites and their offspring occupying significant roles on Indian ground.

CHAPTER 9

Intrigues across Creek Country and Beyond

Arturo O'Neill, Spanish commandant at Pensacola, strongly admired Alexander McGillivray for leading the Creeks into an alliance with Spain in 1784. Much had changed since both men had been on opposing sides in the battle of Pensacola three years before. Though McGillivray had been a steadfast British partisan in wartime, he was outraged by the English cession of much of his people's lands to the United States. Moreover, Britain had surrendered the Floridas to Spain, thereby giving Madrid the opportunity to defend its regional position through native alliances. O'Neill was at the forefront of seizing this advantage. In October 1783, he advised Havana of the importance of gaining McGillivray's friendship and also the good will "of other creoles living in the [Indian] nations and of such Englishmen as are married and have Indian children."[1]

O'Neill's comments were prescient. Following the Revolutionary War, southern Indian peoples had a numerically small but increasingly influential group of mestizo chiefs, especially those born of unions between Scottish colonial traders and native women. Children in such families gained their status through matrilineal descent and paternal economic power. Alexander McGillivray was himself the son of the wealthy trader-landowner Lachlan McGillivray; his mother, Sehoy Marchand, was the child of a Kosati woman and a French military officer. Educated in Charleston as a youth, Alexander was highly versed in Anglo-American culture. A master diplomat but no warrior, he built power outward from his home at Little Tallassee in Upper Creek country. Hardly living in typical Muscogulge fashion, he had a fine wood-frame house and a plantation with some fifty slaves by the early 1790s.[2]

The Creeks had a primary place in the Spanish strategy of containing the United States because of their considerable numbers, prowess in war, and their geographic position between the Gulf Coast and Georgia. Then, too, McGillivray's political savvy and honored status as a Creek "beloved man" appeared a godsend to Madrid's colonial officers. Writing in early 1786, O'Neill described McGillivray as "a Mestizo Indian of the Wind House, or Tribe, and a Chief of great standing." The commandant was impressed later that year when Upper Creek war parties drove Georgia settlers off Indian lands. Other warriors joined the Cherokees to expel whites from Muscle Shoals on the Tennessee. The victors achieved their success with gunpowder, ball, and flints covertly furnished from the king's storehouse in Pensacola.[3]

Within months of hailing McGillivray, O'Neill became suspicious of his foremost Creek ally. At issue was McGillivray's collaboration with the mercantile firm of Panton, Leslie, and Company, which had Madrid's license to monopolize the importation of Indian trade goods, and the export of deerskins, from the St. Johns River to San Marcos de Apalache and Pensacola. The company's privileges did not sit well with O'Neill, who knew that its commercial power had tipped the political scales in its favor. William Panton, the company's head on the Gulf, was O'Neill's *bête noire* for professing friendship to Spain but declining to swear allegiance to its monarch. In fact, Panton swore an oath to the Spanish monarch that applied only so long as he resided in the royal domain.[4] O'Neill could not fathom why a foreigner should enjoy royal privileges on such loose terms. A veteran of Spain's Hibernia regiment, he had an Irish Catholic's distrust of British Protestants. Besides, he could hardly ignore Panton, who made Pensacola his chief residence and place of business in 1785.[5] O'Neill's complaints did not persuade higher-ranking Spanish officials, either his own superior, Esteban Miró, or Vicente Manuel de Zéspedes in St. Augustine. Both men believed that Spain could not do without Panton, Leslie, and Company in the Florida Indian trade. Both regarded McGillivray's friendship as vital to Spain's broad goal of restraining the United States.[6]

Powerbrokers and intermediaries of diverse backgrounds seized upon commerce as a crucial nexus of political and military influence in Indian country. For example, Alexander McGillivray was highly pleased in 1787 by news that Coushatta (Kosati) warriors had killed William Davenport, a Georgia Indian agent, and several other U.S. citizens who were attempting to establish trade in the Chickasaw country. As McGillivray explained to Miró, he had deliberately targeted Davenport because of the latter's "intrigues" aimed at bringing the Choctaws and Chickasaws into "the American interest" through commercial ties. In the same letter the Creek leader urged that Panton, Leslie, and Company be permitted to extend their Gulf Coast operations from Pensacola to Mobile. Madrid granted this request in 1789 after strenuous lobbying by Miró and Navarro.[7] McGillivray had strong reasons for aiding the Scots merchant house in the battle against U.S. territorial and commercial expansion. After all, Panton and Leslie were anti-U.S. in politics and trade. But the issue was still more complex because McGillivray reaped personal benefits and power from association with private merchants whose interests often clashed with the Indian peoples that they supplied.

McGillivray and Bowles

In the spring of 1788, McGillivray's strategic compass received a jolt. On orders from Madrid, Miró reduced Creek military supplies because of imperial concerns that frontier conflict could provoke the United States to war with Spain. Since the Creeks were hard-pressed on the Georgia front, McGillivray considered a new source of military assistance. That summer he secretly met in Lower Creek country with William Augustus Bowles, a visitor from the Bahamas, about new routes of trade and military supply. Alternatives to Spanish aid—and possibly to Panton, Leslie, and Company—were now under consideration.[8]

Bowles, a retired half-pay British officer, had a most colorful past. As a lad of fourteen, he left his Maryland home in 1777 to fight for the king in Pennsylvania. Two years later, he was an ensign in a Loyalist regiment assigned to Pensacola's defense. Feisty and independent, he deserted his unit after a row with an officer, and after some weeks found shelter with Perryman, a Lower Creek mestizo headman living by the Chattahoochee River. Bowles became familiar with Muscogulge ways in the household of an English-speaking chief who stood with the British against American rebels. By the war's end, the newcomer may have had a son by Perryman's daughter Mary—though the evidence on this point is limited. Bowles was too restless to remain under one roof for long. After joining Creek war parties against the Spanish, he managed to regain his place with British forces to fight in the battle of Pensacola. Like many Tory exiles, he found a home in the Bahamas after the war.[9]

The facts of Bowles's early life are not easily corroborated because his story is largely known through propagandistic biographies written by English friends. There is no doubt, however, about the importance of the Bahamas, especially Nassau on New Providence, as his link to the Floridas in the postwar period. After stints as a portrait painter and stage actor in Nassau, Bowles sought high adventure by association with the

Earl of Dunmore, former Virginia governor and relentless intriguer who became chief magistrate of the islands in 1786. Building on his wartime experience, Dunmore reasserted British influence by operations in which his hand would not directly show. He did so by collaborating with the Nassau merchants John Miller and Broomfield Bonnamy, who intended to oust Panton, Leslie, and Company from Florida's Indian trade. In this internecine struggle, Britons took opposing sides depending on whether they earned their keep under the Union Jack or the Castilian flag.[10]

Enlisting for Miller and Bonnamy, Bowles prepared for a Florida military strike in 1788. His object was not to attack the Spanish, but rather to lead a small band of hired guns from the Bahamas that would seize and destroy Leslie's storehouse on the St. Johns River and perhaps Panton's by San Marcos if conditions proved right. Before launching the raid, Bowles made a preliminary visit to the Chattahoochee in order to share his plans with McGillivray. He clearly wanted the Creek beloved man on his side.[11]

Rumors spread wildly in Pensacola and the Creek country prior to Bowles's armed landing in September 1788. Commandant O'Neill heard from several traders that McGillivray was collaborating with a British-sponsored invasion. O'Neill had labeled McGillivray as a closet British Loyalist for some time—and now his fears appeared justified. According to several informants, a heavily armed ship had come from the Bahamas to Florida's Atlantic coast bearing munitions and gifts for the Creeks. Six hundred white soldiers under Bowles had supposedly put ashore, too, with the intent of joining the Creek fight against Georgia and opening a free port for the Indian trade.[12]

In reality, Bowles was readying an expedition, though he had not yet sailed at the time initial reports circulated of his arrival. While bringing gifts for the Creeks, he landed with a much smaller force than rumored. In September 1788, two schooners with about fifty men put into the Indian River north of Cape Canaveral. The motley group included former Tories, English sailors, and a few convicts recruited by the lure of capturing slaves, horses, and other loot in their path.[13] Physically imposing and confident, Bowles dressed in a gold-laced British uniform to impress Indians of his bona fides. Boasting to white companions, he announced that "Aleck McGillivray . . . had ceded to him (Bowles) all the authority and influence he possessed among the Creek Indians." Tales of assured victory were the youthful adventurer's stock in trade.[14]

Bowles never came close to success during his Florida foray of 1788.

As his recruits trudged northward, they struggled to carry their swivel guns and blunderbusses across lowlands and rivers. No Indians joined the ranks. Exhausted and short of food, the volunteers were unnerved by news that Spanish troops and Anglo militiamen stood ready to defend Leslie's storehouse. Bowles headed northwestward, hoping to resume the offensive in short order. His men proved unwilling. Many deserted and rather pathetically gave themselves up to the Spanish or asked for mercy from Leslie's storekeeper.[15] Bowles's first Florida invasion was a raid across Indian country, but not at all an Indian raid.

In the wake of defeat, Bowles and a few companions journeyed toward the Gulf Coast and found shelter among Lower Creek friends. During the winter of 1788–89, Bowles stayed once more at Perryman's home, just as he done years earlier during his British military service. Other headmen were pleased to receive him.[16] Bowles returned to the Bahamas with confidence that his plans could succeed if better executed. His recent failure had been largely a geographic miscalculation. Panton and Leslie would have to be weakened in their Gulf Coast operations before struck to the east.[17]

While Bowles contemplated a new offensive with British backing, Secretary of War Knox considered a strategy of bringing McGillivray to the peace table and ending Georgia-Creek hostilities that had raged for years. The Creeks—unlike the Cherokees, Chickasaws, and Choctaws—had never entered a treaty with the United States. True, minority chiefs had made several territorial cessions to Georgia, but their acts were scarcely enforceable considering the intense opposition from McGillivray and the lion's share of the nation. Knox's challenge was to draw McGillivray to the U.S. interest and thereby to prevent a southern Indian union under Spanish auspices that would be "an impassible barrier" to American expansion. No less important, the secretary was determined to assert national authority by reining in Georgia's aggressive westward movement. The upshot was Washington's decision of August 1789 to appoint commissioners to attempt a Creek treaty.[18]

Though U.S.-Creek negotiations initially stalled, an agreement was reached the next year after McGillivray traveled to New York City to negotiate directly with Knox. While the Creek leader was accompanied by a substantial delegation of chiefs, mostly from the Upper Towns, he worked out the treaty's details without divulging secret articles to his entourage. Under one covert provision, McGillivray gained an American brigadier's rank with an annual salary of $1,200. Just one week after signing the treaty, he took an oath of allegiance to the United States administered by Supreme Court justice John Blair and witnessed by Knox.[19]

Secrecy governed the crucial commercial aspects of the McGillivray-Knox accord. The Treaty of New York stipulated a two-year period in which the Creeks and the United States could reach a mutually satisfactory trade agreement. McGillivray thereby gained time to test a U.S. commercial option at a time that Anglo-Spanish enmity escalated to the brink of war. The U.S.-Creek accord took this danger into account by allowing an unnamed individual, by inference McGillivray, to designate persons allowed to conduct duty-free commerce from the United States into Creek territory should current Florida trade be interrupted by war or by Madrid's obstructive regulations. Here was a formula for a paramount leader to guarantee his hand in trade if Panton and Leslie were forced to leave the scene as Britons in Spanish territory.[20]

McGillivray was so accustomed to intrigue that he did not see the inclusion of secret treaty articles as problematic. But he erred by ceding more land than most headmen accompanying him believed was the case when putting their marks on an English-language document. Though the Creeks wished to retain full control of Oconee River hunting grounds, McGillivray agreed to a boundary line on the river's western Apalachee fork—a fact that greatly bothered many Creeks once the treaty's terms became fully known. In October 1790, several disgruntled Creek men threw their tobacco into the fire on hearing McGillivray's rendition of events at the Upper Creek Town of Tuckabatchee.[21] The treaty was even less popular in Georgia, where it was virulently denounced for curbing the state's boundaries. The accord effectively nullified all previous Creek land cessions that the state had wheedled from compliant chiefs. One Georgia newspaper condemned the treaty as a giveaway to Indians who were but "a *dispicable* [sic] horde of savage free-booters" encroaching on state land.[22] In truth, freebooting was itself a Georgia enterprise par excellence.

The New York treaty exposed Spanish vulnerability in the Floridas. Governor Zéspedes had sent his trusted associate Captain Carlos Howard from St. Augustine northward to track McGillivray's every step in Philadelphia and New York City, but to little effect. The United States was meanwhile a seeming beneficiary, though the treaty's execution was far from guaranteed given Creek opposition. James Seagrove, appointed U.S. agent to the Creeks in October 1791, found it safer to operate from the Georgia frontier than to establish residence in Muscogulge territory.

Earlier that year, Knox called on John Heth, a trustworthy junior officer, to be his courier to McGillivray, relaying the U.S. commitment to protect the Creeks against "all lawless white adventurers." This message was of dubious value, since the United States had little control over Georgia frontiersmen. McGillivray sent Heth back to New York in October 1791 just as he was confronting a new challenge from William Augustus Bowles.[23]

Bowles the Pretender

At the time McGillivray negotiated the Treaty of New York, Bowles was on his way to England, where he arrived in the October 1790. His journey was itself a drama of personal bravado. Outfitting a schooner in the Bahamas the previous year, he first headed to Halifax and Quebec, where he sounded out Lord Dorchester, Canada's governor-general, on a British alliance with southern Indian nations. Though Dorchester was noncommittal, he provided a schooner and some funds for his enterprising visitor to make his case in London.[24]

Bowles attracted some native followers, but only glimmerings of power in the Indian world when he reached London in the fall of 1790. Richard Justice and Moses Price, Cherokee mestizos, accompanied him to both Canada and England. Bowles also had three Creek followers. He was not at all what he claimed to be: "Ambassador from the United Nations of Creeks, and Cherokees, to the Court of London." Physical distance from North America definitely expanded on the pretender's fictitious authority. Benjamin Baynton, a London biographer, called Bowles "the *Beloved Warrior*"—an "appellation" by which "he is universally known to the [Indian] nations."[25] If modern historians debate the reality of eighteenth-century Creek nationhood, how can we measure the absurdity of a non-Indian claiming that he represented the Creek and Cherokee nations combined? Wearing a feathered headdress in London, Bowles publicized himself as the warrior and lawgiver destined to civilize the "barbarous." He posed in an elegant open-collared shirt with Indian-style neckband held in place by a royal officer's silver gorget. All seemed appropriate to a man whose bearing and countenance exuded self-assurance.[26]

Showy public appearances were the prelude to unconventional diplomacy. In January 1791, Bowles presented an audacious plan of operations to Lord Grenville, royal foreign minister. Asking the British government for "arms and military stores," he declared his intention of leading a com-

William Augustus Bowles, photograph of original painting by Thomas Hardy, 1790–91. Courtesy of Florida Photographic Collection, RC06489, State Library and Archives of Florida. This portrait shows Bowles, in his physical prime at about age twenty-seven, during his visit to England.

bined force of Indian warriors and U.S. frontiersmen to drive Spain out of "the whole country of the Floridas," New Orleans, and the Lower Mississippi Valley—all of which "will belong completely to the Creek & Cherokee Nation." His victorious army would then "proceed without delay to Mexico, & in conjunction with the natives, declare it independent of the Spaniards." In Bowles's judgment, imperial troops were insufficient to subdue distant continents without native auxiliaries. That maxim, he observed, was "as good in America as Indostan [Hindustan]."[27]

Bowles's declaration is striking for its audacious vision of aligning Anglo-American settler ambitions with Indian statehood. In a boast that might have been lifted from an O'Fallon letter, Bowles said he could recruit at least 6,000 fighting men from U.S. western districts, whose people hungered "for a situation near the sea in our country." The political economy of unifying maritime and interior zones was again an adventurist model, now imagined in a mindboggling conjunction of Creeks and Cherokees with their customary Anglo-American foes.[28]

In the adventurist environment following the Revolution, freewheeling frontier powerbrokers believed they could pressure imperial states to back their agendas or face dire consequences. Bowles did not hesitate to warn Grenville what would occur if Whitehall rejected his plan. The Creek Nation would then "unite with their old enemies"—"the Americans"—and proceed to assail Canada with the assistance of "all the Northern Indians." This threat was a crude version of Wilkinson's ploy of suggesting a Kentucky-British alliance if Spain rejected his overtures. Grenville responded coolly, though without dismissing his presumptuous guest altogether. Bowles next badgered Spanish ambassador Bernardo del Campo, who characterized his guest as a "daring rascally rogue" (*un Tuno picarón osado*) for threatening war unless Carlos IV consented to his demands for an open Florida trade. Campo did not believe Bowles had British government support, but was still wary because of the "hundreds of American-Loyalist Families" and other Englishmen living among the Creeks and Cherokees.[29]

Distinguishing the genuine from the outright fake is no simple task in examining Bowles's endeavors. While a putative Indian leader, he was no more wedded to traditional native ways than McGillivray. Instead of imagining him as either Creek savior or fraud, he is best understood as an Anglo adventurer striving in mercurial fashion to bridge the colonial-native divide and to remake Indian life through transformations in domestic, international, and transatlantic spheres. For all his avowed commitment to Indian statehood, he kept his English associations alive for good reason. Britain ruled the waves. Nothing could be achieved or sustained without secure and profitable oceanic trade.

Bowles was impolitic to Grenville, but brazenly deceptive in his Spanish diplomacy—expressed in a series of declamations to worthies such as Zéspedes, Ezpeleta, and Floridablanca himself. While preparing to depart the Bahamas for Canada in August 1789, Bowles sent letters to all three men in which he implausibly denied any connection with Dunmore, mouthed only good will toward Spain, and wrote the king's first minister of his intention to visit his Catholic Majesty's ambassador in London.[30]

Adventurist diplomacy had bipolar tendencies. Built on intrigue, it often blazed forth with the confessional, cutting through standard niceties with the frank admission of ambitious aims. In Bowles's telling, the Spanish crown's most dangerous enemies were not so much hostile nations as private adventurers (*aventureros particulares*)—men whose zeal and ambition were unbounded.[31] This advice was uttered as if the writer had nothing to do with the adventurist danger—which was hardly the case. Bowles's repeated threats were ultimately self-defeating because they aroused Madrid's officers to treat him as a dangerous foe who must be arrested if not killed.[32] Spanish power was so thin along the Florida Gulf Coast, however, that royal authorities had no easy time when the adventurer once more appeared in their vicinity.

Unlike his fifty-man invasion force of 1788, Bowles had no more than a handful of companions when embarking from the Bahamas for the Florida Gulf Coast in August 1791. He sailed in a well-worn schooner with a few followers, including Moses Price, three other Indians, at least one black man, and perhaps a half-dozen sailors.[33] The ship hoisted newly designed flags of Bowles's Muskogee nation. As depicted in Spanish records, each flag bore the emblem of a sun with facial features—mouth, nose, eyes and eyebrows. Each also had a cross—one like the British St. George's and another displaying two stick-like objects crossing diagonally. This was a rather fitting symbol for a man who was a Tory as well as a self-made Indian leader.[34]

Bowles brought gifts of weapons and other goods to attract Creeks and Seminoles to his standard. The schooner also carried a large canoe to navigate shallow coastal waterways and to avoid Spanish detection. After a brief landing on Florida's Atlantic shore, Bowles and company sailed to the upper Gulf with its labyrinth of bays and inlets. The adventurers

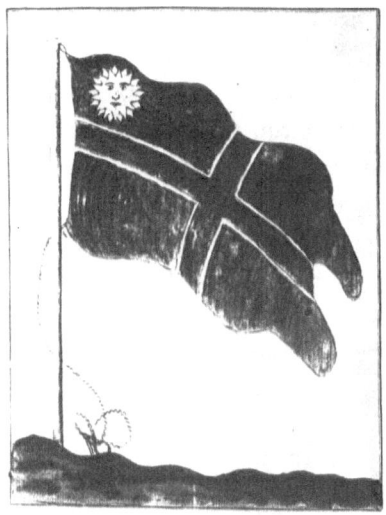 

Flag of William Augustus Bowles (1791–1792), Archivo Histórico Nacional, Estado, legajo 3889, p. 333. Photostat courtesy of Library of Congress.

Flag of William Augustus Bowles (1791–1792), Archivo Histórico Nacional, Estado, legajo 3889, p. 334. Photostat courtesy of Library of Congress.

navigated inland on the Ochlockonee River, whose tributary branches, swamps, and forests provided shelter west of San Marcos de Apalache and William Panton's nearby storehouse.[35]

For all of Bowles's impetuosity, there was a geopolitical shrewdness to his planning. The Ochlockonee, Apalachicola, and other rivers of Florida's Gulf shore were backdoor waterways within the panorama of colonial-native relations in North America. This fact worked to Bowles's advantage, since he could operate where there were few Spanish vessels and but a smattering of soldiers. Besides, his landing took him to the Lower Creek and Seminole country, where many natives desired new British connections, distrusted Spain, and resented dependency on the House of Panton and Leslie. McGillivray, who had never lorded over the Lower Creeks, was in an especially vulnerable position since signing the Treaty of New York. Bowles exploited these circumstances to the hilt. His calculus of power progressed through commercial access to the Gulf, mastery in the Creek country, and then an expansive reach across the continent's southeastern frontiers. The adventurer's familiarity with a particular locale and his knowledge of native customs and language contributed not a little to his confidence. Even an obscure region might suddenly acquire imperial significance in a continent where the locus of power seemed pliable and subject to radical and rapid transformation.

Bowles had an intimate knowledge of the Ochlockonee and regional waterways. In the early fall of 1791, Spanish captain Luis Bertucat and Panton's hired men could not find the adventurer as they searched the region in schooners and small craft. When Bertucat shifted his reconnaissance to the Apalachicola, he finally discovered a clearing that Bowles and company had frequented but was now deserted. Lower Creek men told the captain that no Spaniards had been in the locale for a century. Bowles had meanwhile spent some time at his old patron Perryman's house, where he was said to be under "Indian protection." He also renewed his acquaintance with Perryman's daughter Mary, who was by this time married to Edward Forrester, one of Panton's employees.[36]

By early December 1791, Bowles was confident enough to assume the rank of general when initiating correspondence with O'Neill and Carondelet. By his own deserts, he was also a civil officer—"Director" of the Creek Nation. Spanish officers took note lest the intruder live up to his titles and make good on his claim of having 650 warriors in his service by or near the Gulf Coast. Bowles asked Carondelet for "a noble peace" guaranteeing his nation "free Navigation in the sea coast bordering on their native country, to what they . . . have a better right than any other people." If meeting resistance, he vowed war: "We shall be obliged to commence the hostilities, joining us with the Americans, who are continually offering us their hands."[37] Bluff was again coupled to the threat of a sudden political realignment unless the adventurer got his way. Bowles shrewdly boasted British credentials and told natives that he acted with George III's blessing to right wrongs. He courted the Lower Creeks and Seminoles by gifts and promises of still greater presents to be brought from the sea. He would defeat McGillivray's Treaty of New York, supplant the outworn Creek leader, and destroy the House of Panton and Leslie.[38]

Though Bowles had by far his strongest following among the Lower Creeks, he also encountered opposition there. Two influential mestizo chiefs—Tom Perryman and Jack Kinnaird—stood against the adventurer for undermining economic and social order. Kinnaird reported Bowles's activities to Spanish authorities and to U.S. agent James Seagrove, who cultivated him in turn.[39] Lower Creek mestizos took individual stances rather than observing any group solidarity. John Galphin, a staunchly anti-U.S. headman, shared Bowles's animus against Panton and Leslie even though he did a substantial business with that trading house just as Kinnaird and Tom Perryman did.[40]

McGillivray was stunned by Bowles's challenge and desperate to eliminate a rival whom he had badly underestimated. In October 1791, he sent three Tuckabatchee warriors to kill Bowles, but his hired guns failed to locate their target. McGillivray now counted on Spanish authorities, including his old rival O'Neill, to capture Bowles and to stop all "Knaving Vagabonds" from reaching the Florida Gulf Coast. Feeling unwell and uncertain, the once vital Creek leader withdrew from Little Tallassee to his plantation at Little River, a safer locale to the southwest. Back home in March 1792, McGillivray was still at wits' end, besides suffering rheumatism from his travel in January's snow, rain, and high water. He wrote Panton that Bowles, a "mad desperado," "has used great art & Cunning to wean the lower Indians [the Lower Creeks] from my Influence" by telling them he would restore past English favor. To McGillivray's consternation, Bowles derided Panton to his native allies as "no Englishman but a Damned Spaniard."[41] The revival of British friendship and material bounty were powerful weapons in Bowles's arsenal.

A revolution is not often commenced by robbery, but such was the plan in Florida in early 1792. Bowles and company sent tremors along the Gulf by seizing Panton's Wakulla River trading house on the night of January 16, 1792. The capture was not difficult. Two white clerks were at the storehouse but had no guard. William Cunningham, "major general" in Bowles' army, led the way with about nine Indians, almost certainly Lower Creeks or Seminoles. Bowles soon arrived with a reported "great many" others—perhaps above seventy native men in all.[42]

Pilfering the storehouse over several days, Bowles now had the wherewithal to attract Creeks to his cause. Though pledged to Indian independence, he did not come to Florida as a liberator of slaves. A number of blacks near Panton's storehouse fled the intruders for fear of capture. Five of the escapees accompanied the store's clerk in flight to the Spanish fort of San Marcos. A greater number went to the Seminole village of Miccosukee, which had sheltered maroons for years. African American quests for security and freedom did not simply align with Bowles's mission.[43] Fear spread wherever random violence threatened to upset a fragile colonial order. East Florida's Anglo planters imagined Bowles bursting into their neighborhood to plunder, capture blacks, and to instigate an Indian war. They strongly backed Spanish authorities during the crisis.[44]

New Orleans responded slowly to Bowles's incursion, partly because

Carondelet was just succeeding Miró as governor-general of Louisiana and West Florida. With minimal assistance from Cuba, the new governor had to improvise and stretch his limited resources to meet the threat. In late January 1792, Carondelet had *La Galga*, the Havana mail ship, outfitted into an armed schooner to make a show of force at San Marcos.[45] Captain Pedro Rousseau commanded all twenty-four soldiers on board while naval lieutenant Josef Evia piloted *La Galga* to the Florida Gulf Coast in early February. Evia carried Carondelet's message to McGillivray asking for cooperation in taking Bowles "alive or dead." This request was unavailing since McGillivray kept his distance from the Spanish operation.[46] Captain-general Luis de Las Casas, who happened to be Carondelet's brother-in-law, lent cautious advice from Havana. He approved the plan of capturing Bowles, but argued against assassination.[47]

Once at San Marcos, Evia played his part well, knowing that sheer force was out of the question. Bowles had at least twenty armed Indian supporters—and probably more out of Spanish view—encamped within short distance of the weak royal garrison. In keeping with Carondelet's instructions, Evia respectfully contacted Bowles on February 22, offering to show him a letter by Floridablanca in response to the adventurer's overtures to the Spanish court. Though Bowles was wary, he decided to meet with Evia to size up the situation. His vanity was touched—Madrid seemed at last ready to deal with him as a head of state. Floridablanca's letter was instead a false front, fabricated by Carondelet who added his own courteous missive inviting Bowles for direct talks in New Orleans.[48] Swayed by Spanish offers, Bowles voluntarily embarked on Evia's ship on February 29 for a voyage to Louisiana's capital. Some two hundred Indians watched the scene, placated for the moment by Spanish gifts and liquor. Bowles came ashore in New Orleans on March 12 and was hustled to quarters in army barracks. The titular Creek head of state was a prisoner even if formally a well-treated guest.[49]

Bowles's ensuing talks with Carondelet reached a climax on March 17, when the adventurer made a desperate stab for a Spanish alliance—and his personal freedom. The Americans were poised "to get possession of tombecbe and Missisipy, if they were knowing, that I was absent of the Creek nation." His people would turn against Spain if they knew "I am considered a prisoner." "Catastrophe" was certain unless he was released. A Creek alliance was "the only means to save the Spanish Colonies in Amerique."[50]

Carondelet was impressed with his prisoner, describing him as "an extraordinary young man," seemingly "savage" by appearance but with "a lively and resolute spirit." The governor listened carefully to Bowles's condemnation of McGillivray and his insistent plea for a pan-Indian confederation in alliance with Spain and against the United States. This argument had a strong appeal in New Orleans, though it failed to bring reprieve. Bowles was held in New Orleans for just ten days before being sent to Havana for questioning. Carondelet dared not hold him longer lest any Creek visitors be outraged to find their leader in prison.[51]

Spanish officials regarded a renewed British connection to the Gulf Coast to be nearly as threatening as U.S. advances from the north. Carondelet urged Havana to cut off all communication between Dunmore, his Bahamian merchant friends, and Bowles's Indian supporters. Las Casas feared that Bowles would break jail in Havana or somehow smuggle papers to his English associates. The captain-general shipped his dangerous charge to Spain, where the adventurer's next resting place was a Cádiz prison.[52] Bowles's threats and lies came back to haunt him as Carlos IV's councilors doused his continuing entreaties for alliance. Bernardo del Campo voiced the prevailing view that the prisoner could not be trusted considering all his attempts to do Spain "the greatest harm possible."[53]

Bowles's life is an improbable story for the remainder of the decade. Transported to a distant Manila jail in 1795, he was shipped back to Spain two years later—Cádiz was his supposed destination. Determined to be free, Bowles jumped ship at Gorée on the West African coast, vaulted aboard a French vessel and then to an American merchantman, and eventually made his way to London. By 1799, he was once again in the Bahamas and sailing for the Florida Gulf to renew his vision of uniting the Creeks and other southern Indians toward independence under his leadership.[54]

Colonial Intrigues and Creek-Seminole Strivings

Bowles vaunted into the role of Creek paramount leader, but his two closest associates during his Florida venture of 1791–92 were British Loyalists: William Cunningham and George Wellbank. Their stories are important for showing disparate tendencies evident in adventurist scheming. Whereas Cunningham turned from Bowles's supporter to betrayer, Wellbank continued as a faithful ally in Indian country after the general's capture. Most probably an English agent, Cunningham took up Bowles's cause after a lengthy journey from British-occupied Detroit to the Creek country. Though he became Bowles's chief lieutenant for a few months, he quarreled bitterly with his commander after the capture of Panton's storehouse. Franco, a slave witness, told Spanish authorities that the dispute was over the division of spoils.[55] Whatever the precise cause of contention, Cunningham did his utmost to damn Bowles and to save himself after fleeing to the Spanish at San Marcos. In the process, the informer divulged a plot in which Bowles was allegedly conspiring with U.S. frontier leaders as well as with Dunmore to conquer Louisiana and the Floridas.[56] Cunningham finally gained nothing by betrayal. Carondelet judged him a security danger and deported him to Havana. From there he, too, was sent to prison in Spain.[57]

Unlike Cunningham, Wellbank was a volunteer officer genuinely committed to a new colonial-Indian alliance under British auspices. No radical, he tried to persuade Lower Creek and Seminole headmen to return items pilfered from Panton's storehouse. The chiefs displayed their own sense of fairness by returning some loot but keeping deerskins and most goods for themselves.[58] Aiming his sights on larger goals, Wellbank sent Lower Creek chief Little Prince (Tustanagee Hopoy) to forward his letters northward to the Cherokees and ultimately to Canada. Spanish authorities were disturbed by this news, which they took as further evidence of English intrigue to rouse all southern Indian nations against Spain.[59]

In the wake of Bowles's capture, McGillivray attempted to quash Wellbank and to restore his claim to paramount Creek leadership. In May 1792, he sent one hundred Upper Creek warriors on a mission to warn the Lower Towns against fighting either the Spanish or Panton, Leslie, and Company. The head of this force was Louis Le Clerc de Milford, a French adventurer who became something of a Creek war leader through personal ambition and marriage to McGillivray's sister.[60] Robert Leslie, manager for Panton at San Marcos, wrote his boss that it was impossible to capture Wellbank since any attempt that way could incite "a Fresh revolt of the Indians."[61]

Bowles's influence did not die when he was imprisoned in Spain. Wellbank found shelter in Lower Creek–Seminole lands for almost a year before heading northward to spread Bowles's message to the Cherokees. From there he traveled to Detroit and Niagara to make his case for British alliance with southern and western Indian peoples. In August 1793, he was back among the Cherokees and relaying ideas of British-sponsored free trade to Indians via the Gulf. Such talk was dangerous as was any association with Bowles. In 1794, Wellbank was clubbed to death by Indian assailants in Upper Creek country.[62]

The Lower Creeks were divided about Bowles, though it is unquestionable that the latter had many ardent supporters. Pedro Olivier, Spanish commissary to the Creeks, listened soberly in July 1792 as Lower Town headmen grieved over the absence of "Our beloved Friend & Father, (Gen'l Bowles)." Rejecting Olivier's overtures of friendship until Bowles was sent to them, they voiced their need for dual protection: "We hold the English by one hand & the Spanish by the other. . . . The Land your People live on at St. Augustine, St. Marks & Pensacola is ours & only lent by us to you."[63]

Besides fairer trade than offered by Panton and Leslie, many Lower Creeks and Seminoles clearly wanted to revive British military and political connections. In October 1791, McGillivray vainly attempted to lure Bowles from the house of Philatouche, a headman of Chiaha, a Lower Creek town by the Chattahoochee. Philatouche, known as "the Factor," was a middleman in the deerskin trade who had fought alongside the British during the Revolution. He was also son-in-law to Perryman, and thereby connected to Bowles's first Creek patron. Coweta chief Ochillase Chopka was another headman who demanded an open British commerce and rejected Panton's blandishments that Bowles was the "Prince of Liars" and no true Englishman. Many Creeks believed they could judge that matter for themselves.[64]

Francisco Montreuil, royal commandant at San Marcos de Apalache, reported in February 1793—nearly one year after Bowles's capture and imprisonment—that there were as many as four hundred Indians gathering about the mouth of the Ochlockonee River just four leagues from his fort. Their purpose was to build a trading house (*Casa de Comercio*) where they might be supplied with goods dispatched from New Providence in the Bahamas. Wellbank promoted this project, along with Indians who wanted it for their own reasons. Referring to the native plan, Montreuil used the same word—"*proyecto*"—commonly employed by Spanish authorities to describe colonization proposals and other entrepreneurial schemes.[65]

To conduct trade on their own terms was a native goal no less than it was for George Morgan, James Wilkinson, and other U.S. nationals seeking commercial access via the Mississippi to New Orleans and the Gulf. This was especially important because of escalating native indebtedness and impoverishment caused by imbalances in the deerskin trade. Philatouche and other Lower Creek chiefs warned the Spanish that they could not count on peace without allowing free trade along the coast. Native headmen objected to Panton's high prices and also complained of the scarcity of supplies since Panton and Leslie had expanded their traffic to the Choctaws, Chickasaws, and Cherokees. The Creeks worried, too, about international turmoil that could adversely affect them. One colonial observer reported in November 1792 that the Creeks "are at this Moment greatly distressed and alarmed on account of the Scarcity of Goods in their land, and say they are sure the Spanish War with England will bring real poverty among them." Anglo-Spanish rivalry appeared dangerously explosive by the Gulf, though it was more tempered in Europe. England and Spain were not at war in 1792—and they were about to become allies against France the next year.[66]

About the beginning of 1793, Philatouche traveled to the Bahamas with a small party of Indians and returned with a commission from Dunmore, who appointed him "head warrior" of his town. Interestingly, this document praised the honoree for his "Extraordinary Valour" displayed in the past war against American rebels.[67] The return voyage ended abruptly on March 2, 1793, when a Spanish corsair captured the sloop carrying the Creeks at the Ochlockonee's mouth. Madrid's officers did not dictate to Philatouche and friends but rather opened negotiations and dispensed gifts toward appeasing Indian grievances. Robert Leslie, who supervised the talks on his company's behalf, warned the Creeks that they needed Spanish friendship since "the Americans were at this Instant coming against them."[68] A crisis in Spanish-Creek relations was averted, but broader problems remained. More than a decade after Gálvez's conquest of Pensacola, Madrid's colonial officers had a most tenuous standing in Creek country.

U.S. influence among the Creeks was even more precarious than Spanish standing during Bowles's incursion of 1792 and its denouement. Agent James Seagrove suspected the Spanish were playing "a double game" with Bowles—arresting and deporting him but secretly plotting with their prisoner to strengthen Creek resistance to the United States. Frustrated with McGillivray for rekindling his Spanish ties in 1792, Seagrove wrote Henry Knox of trying conditions: "A Spaniard, or an Englishman, is respectable all through the Creek nation, but it is very dangerous for any person, known to belong to the United States, to travel, or be in that country." The agent dreaded that Shawnee visitors among the Creeks would draw the Muscogulge and other southern Indian nations into a general war against the United States. He was similarly alarmed that Panton held McGillivray in his economic clutches. Seagrove's apprehensions grew when he learned that Panton had headed northward in May 1792 from Upper Creek to Cherokee country in order to foment an anti-U.S. alliance founded on his Gulf Coast trading power.[69]

In fact, Panton was determined to recoup his firm's prestige and economic standing after blows suffered at Bowles's hands. His answer was to revamp the supply of weaponry to native peoples in the fight against U.S. territorial and commercial expansion. Carondelet strongly encouraged this course. The governor had already adopted a far more aggressive policy than Miró of arming Indian peoples to resist the United States and concurrently promoting confederation among the Choctaws, Chickasaws, Cherokees, and Creeks.[70] In May 1792, Panton furthered this policy by meeting with John Watts, a militant Cherokee chief, for the ostensible purpose of settling the issue of Indian debts to his firm. In actuality, the visiting trader discussed military supply routes and invited several chiefs to visit Pensacola and then meet with Carondelet in New Orleans. Watts traveled to Pensacola but did not accompany the other Cherokee chiefs to New Orleans. The New Orleans conference took place in November 1792 but was undermined by recent events far northward. In late September, American frontier militia defeated a large Chickamauga, Creek, and Shawnee offensive near Nashville. Carondelet's plan of extending the Spanish defensive shield to the Tennessee and Cumberland was compromised, though far from undone. The governor fully intended that military aid be passed to Indian peoples under cover (*"bajo mano"*) so as not to antagonize the United States.[71]

William Blount, governor of the sprawling Southwest Territory, felt hard-pressed in Knoxville for information about Panton's business and Spanish-Indian ties along the Gulf. In September 1792, he appointed James Alexander Douglass as a spy to ferret events about Pensacola. Douglass appeared suitable because he was "a Scotchman by birth" who "will get ready access to Panton, and all the Scotch." Moreover, the agent "has been bred a Jesuit, and understands the Spanish Language; [and] has lived several Years among the Indians." Though Douglas reached Pensacola, he was killed by Chickasaws on his return journey to Knoxville. Blount noted with frustration that the death had occurred by a "mistake." The offending Chickasaws, themselves on friendly terms with the United States, admitted to confusing Douglass with a horse-rustler. If frontier whites commonly suspected all Indians as enemies who ventured near their settlements, the converse was sometimes the case in native territory.[72]

In the struggle for paramountcy in Indian country, various parties vied to control events on a broad geographic plane. McGillivray frequently directed his sights on the Tennessee frontier and the Chickasaw country for fear that U.S. predominance in those sectors would leave the Creeks isolated and defenseless. By the mid-1790s, William Panton became intent on eliminating competitors in Indian trade as far west as Chickasaw Bluffs. William Augustus Bowles envisioned military power and an open trade as the foundations of Indian statehood. Carondelet pressed his ambitious plan of Indian confederation under Spanish auspices. What all grand visionaries discovered, however, is that southern Indian spheres were too decentralized and factionalized—and too replete with multiple actors—to allow one single nation or leader to control native societies as imagined. Young warriors often followed their own course of raiding, scalping, and plundering irrespective of elders. Middlemen living in contested geographic space made choices as to which imperial nation and merchants they should cultivate on the calculus of profit and risk. Benjamin James, a white trader of West Yazoo, confidentially wrote William Blount in June 1792 of his willingness to supply pro-U.S. Chickasaws with arms and munitions. John Forbes, Panton's associate at Mobile, did not know of this development when he recommended James to serve as Spanish liaison to the Choctaws. In fact, Forbes mistakenly believed that James was "now entirely detached" from the American camp. Many Creeks, including McGillivray, remained more doubtful. A few months later, a Creek war party set out to kill James but failed when the intended victim received timely assistance from a Choctaw man. All this did not mean that James was committed to one side in borderlands struggles. In 1792, he assumed a significant role in Spanish-supported talks aimed at mediating a Chickasaw-Creek peace.[73]

As Louisiana's governor-general, Carondelet put great stock in McGillivray's leadership, notwithstanding the Creek leader's humiliation at Bowles's hands. On July 6, 1792, the barón entered a pact with McGillivray at New Orleans in which Spain was the senior party. Hurtling past Miró's previous caution, the governor affirmed his king's determination to arm the Creeks for immediate war against all Americans refusing to leave Indian territories. McGillivray was now awarded a Spanish annual stipend of $3,500—a whopping increase over the $2,000 given the previous year. He was still ready to fight and continued the battle against U.S. settlement and commercial inroads along the Tennessee, Tombigbee, and other western waters. He also targeted Piomingo, his principal Chickasaw nemesis, for the latter's pro-American stance. Creek-Chickasaw clashes waxed hotly, undermining the chances of pan-Indian union.[74]

Piomingo found allies among the Colbert clan, the leading Chickasaw mestizo family, which had moved from being strongly British Loyalist during the Revolution to becoming U.S. allies. In February 1792, James Colbert sent a panicked note to General James Robertson, commander in Tennessee's Mero district. Creek raiders had just struck: "Now Brothers the Day has come they have Spilled our Blood. I hop[e] you will Exert your Selves and Jone [join] us so that whe [we] might give the lads [a] Drubbin[g] for they have encroach[ed] on us this great while." Colbert was a Chickasaw whose words had a decided Scottish brogue. McGillivray, of similar Scots-Indian ancestry, wrote later that year of Piomingo's warriors as the probable killers of "Three of our people Young Lads."[75]

Though McGillivray resumed the appearance of paramount leader in the summer of 1792, he was too physically and mentally spent to command as he once did. In his final letter to Carondelet, he displayed a pitiful servility to Panton by opposing a rival trader's entry to Choctaw territory via Mobile. Forty-three years old, McGillivray died at Panton's Pensacola residence on February 17, 1793—near the man whose callous embrace he could not escape.[76]

For all McGillivray's flaws, his death weakened the Creeks because no unifying leader emerged in his wake. In July 1793, his closest Creek allies decided for peace and called on Washington to restrain Blount from mounting a suspected attack against them. The president heeded Knox's advice to pursue a peaceful solution to southern frontier hostilities. Washington had no desire for a Creek war while U.S. forces were contending with the Shawnees, Miamis, Delawares, and other Indians in the Ohio country.[77]

The Unraveling of Carondelet's Policy

Carondelet had cause for optimism during his early months in office. In January 1792 he was heartened by news of a decisive Indian victory over Arthur St. Clair's army in Ohio. James Wilkinson, who was secretly delighted by the U.S. setback, reported the battle's bloody outcome to New Orleans. Carondelet quickly sent agents northward to further Shawnee collaboration with southern Indian peoples. Stopping the Americans appeared quite possible.[78]

Diplomatic success on the Mississippi front meanwhile augured well for Louisiana's defense. On May 14, 1792, Manuel Gayoso de Lemos secured Choctaw and Chickasaw acquiescence at Natchez for the Spanish purchase of strategic ground at Nogales where a royal garrison had recently been built.[79] This treaty was achieved through careful negotiation aided by several intermediaries—such as white trader Turner Brashears, who served as Choctaw chief Franchimastabé's interpreter. French colonial influence remained vital in Spanish-Indian diplomacy. Juan de la Villiebeuvre, long an intermediary with the Choctaws, obtained that nation's consent in 1792 for the Spanish to construct a fort on the Tombigbee, where a French garrison had once stood. Simon Favre, who had aided the British in Indian parlays, was an effective Spanish aide through his deft knowledge of the Choctaw language.[80]

Gayoso's successful negotiations for the construction of Spanish forts were as notable as his most ambitious diplomatic project—the Treaty of Nogales of October 28, 1793. By this agreement, the Chickasaw, Creek, Alibamon, Cherokee, and Choctaw nations formally entered into an offensive and defensive alliance to protect one another's lands. Moreover, Spain guaranteed native territories within his Catholic Majesty's domain and pledged to represent and safeguard Indian peoples in boundary negotiations with the United States.[81] The treaty had a grand intent, though it had less substance than indicated in formal provisions. One glaring weakness was the thinness of Creek ties to the Choctaws and Chickasaws. The Creeks had minimal representation and no leading chiefs at the treaty proceedings. Chickasaw headman Piomingo did not enter the Nogales accord and remained in enmity with the Creeks.[82] Gayoso was a gifted diplomat and a man of good will, though quite cynical about the gift-giving necessities of Spanish Indian policy. Just a few months after the Nogales treaty, he advised Carondelet that Indians were devoted to Spain only so long as they received presents and that natives would desert the crown "without the least return of gratitude" if believing that they could gain more from other quarters.[83]

Native peoples could not afford to be trusting in an environment where betrayals and imperial reversals were commonplace. In June 1795, for example, a Chickasaw assembly parlaying with Gayoso by the Mississippi became suspicious when a Spanish river barge failed to appear with pledged gifts. Rumors circulated that the Spaniards had deceptively lulled the Chickasaws for talks so that their villages would be open to Creek attack. A crisis was averted when Gayoso ordered a hurried search for the barge, which happened to be delayed downriver when the craft sprung a leak. Sufficient goods were finally distributed to allay Chickasaw discontent.[84]

Carondelet's conception of a grand Indian union finally fell victim to imperial constraints. Madrid buckled under multiple strains, fiscal woes, and war with France from 1793 to 1795. The situation of Indian peoples in Trans-Appalachia scarcely mattered to Carlos IV's councilors. Aranda cautioned Carondelet in March 1794 not to give material aid to the Cherokees in their conflict with the United States. In his judgment, the Indians had forfeited any claim to assistance because they had commenced hostilities "with neither our consent nor advice." Spain might mediate with the United States on behalf of native groups, but it would not fight for them. Aranda insisted that Spanish colonial officers warn the Creeks and Cherokees to remain purely on the defensive and refrain from attacking Georgia or Carolina settlements.[85]

The Spanish retreat became most obvious through the Treaty of San Lorenzo of October 27, 1795, by which Madrid admitted U.S. rights to free navigation on the Mississippi and also yielded all its territorial claims between the river's east bank and the Chattahoochee above the 31st parallel. The treaty's fourth article obligated each of the parties to prevent Indian nations living in either U.S. or Spanish zones from engaging in cross-border attacks. Both countries further agreed "to make the advantages of the Indian trade common and mutually beneficial to their respective subjects and citizens." This last provision was a stunning break with the past. Warding off U.S. commercial inroads into Indian country had been at the forefront of Spanish policy in the Louisiana-Florida borderlands for the previous twelve years.[86]

Godoy's territorial giveaway was a devastating blow to native peoples living from the Alabama-Tombigbee watershed westward to the Mississippi. This entire region, apart from a rather thin Gulf littoral below the 31st parallel, now belonged to the United States by European diplomatic convention. Fort Confederation, which was Carondelet's chosen site for pan-Indian unity, lay within U.S. territory. Gayoso's Treaty of Nogales was a dead letter, especially its pronouncement that the crown would be a protector of Indian rights in negotiation with the United States. Spain lost this capacity because it had little left with which to bargain. Indendant Juan Ventura Morales wrote of intense Indian disgust with the treaty—and anger at Spain for leaving natives "in the mouth of the wolf."[87]

Imperial decision making undid Gayoso's success in winning Indian consent for Spanish fortification of the Mississippi's east bank as far north as Chickasaw Bluffs. In 1795, Gayoso supervised the establishment of fort San Fernando de las Barrancas at the bluffs through negotiation with Ugulayacabé (Wolf's Friend), the Chickasaw leader most trusting of Spanish assistance to stop American advances. Two years later, Ugulayacabé joined with old rivals Piomingo and William Colbert in warning the Spanish commandant at New Madrid not to block the downriver shipment of U.S. presents to his people. Wolf's Friend did not like Americans but he could not afford to reject their supplies.[88]

The Creeks were also compromised by San Lorenzo, though in a less severe way than the Chickasaws and Choctaws. Unlike those peoples, they still had sufficient numbers and military strength to resist white movement into their heartlands. However, they gave some ground in light of new conditions. By the Treaty of Coleraine of June 29, 1796, Upper and Lower Town headmen agreed to abide by the New York treaty of 1790—including its previously contentious Oconee boundary provision. They also consented to the establishment of a U.S. trading or military post on the Altamaha River. For these concessions, the Creeks received $6,000 in goods and a restatement of existing boundaries. As customary in such agreements, the treaty committed the Creeks to the return of blacks who had been captured in American territory or, by implication, who had fled the United States into Indian land.[89]

The Treaty of Coleraine alluded to one boundary issue for future resolution—the surveying of the newly designated U.S.-Spanish boundary line along the 31st parallel, which happened to cut across Lower Creek territory. Recognizing the need of Indian cooperation, the agreement stipulated that the Creeks were to provide two principal chiefs and twenty hunters to assist the U.S.-Spanish boundary team. Each chief was promised a half-dollar a day for his work and each hunter a quarter-dollar besides payment for meat that Indians provided the surveyors.[90]

Had the Treaty of San Lorenzo been quickly put into effect as stipulated, the movement to U.S. empowerment would have been far clearer than it proved to be. The accord's implementation was delayed, however, because of resistant Spanish colonial officials, an unstable international environment, and Lower Creek and Seminole opposition. Above all, there was the real possibility that European warfare and related Caribbean conflict would spill into Louisiana and the Floridas, thereby superseding U.S-Spanish treaty arrangements. Colonial adventurism and freebooting schemes once more came to the fore at the close of the eighteenth century.

CHAPTER 10

The Imperial Question at Century's End

Captain Isaac Guion, U.S. army officer at Fort Massac on the Ohio, had the honor of leading the first detachment of soldiers down the Mississippi in the summer of 1797 to take charge of Spanish posts on the river's east bank ceded by treaty to the American republic. Though the U.S.-Spanish accord had been finalized nearly two years previously, the transition from one national flag to another had been delayed by diplomatic formalities, logistical preparations, and the need for favorable weather and river conditions. Following the War Department's instructions, Guion took care to perform his duties in a courteous manner. On June 15, 1797, he sent a junior officer to give advance notice of his mission to Lt. Colonel Carlos Dehault Delassus, commandant of New Madrid, whose post on the Mississippi's west bank was to remain under the Castilian flag.[1]

Guion's gesture did not have its intended outcome. As his boat *Chickasaw* went just below New Madrid, Delassus accused the American vessel of "unprovoked aggression" for sailing past his station without his consent.[2] This complaint must have struck Guion as odd since the treaty of 1795 guaranteed the United States the right of free navigation along the Mississippi's entire length. Delassus was himself acting under orders from New Orleans. Carondelet had decided to postpone the treaty's execution until Spain and the United States settled a sticky legal question over the terms by which garrisons were to be transferred. In reality, the governor's rationale was a pretext for delaying and even stopping the cession from taking effect altogether.[3]

Carondelet adopted his temporizing posture on receiving Madrid's instructions, suggesting a new imperial resolve on Louisiana. On October 29, 1796, Manuel de Godoy, duque de Alcudia, ordered the governor to suspend indefinitely the evacuation of Mississippi posts, but to cooperate with American commissioners on running the new boundary line at the 31st parallel from the river's east bank to the Chattahoochee. This

233

order was ambiguous—amounting to a scaling back, though not an open repudiation, of Madrid's treaty obligations to the United States. Alcudia justified the suspension by maintaining that the Jay Treaty—the U.S. British accord ratified in 1795—violated international law by guaranteeing English and American navigation on the Mississippi's entire length. By Spanish judgment, the United States had no authority to bestow navigational rights that it did not possess in the first place.[4]

Madrid's revamped Louisiana policy was a slap at Britain even more than at the United States. In fact, it came about through a radical political realignment in a war-torn Europe. On October 5, 1796, the Spanish monarchy threw its weight behind republican France by declaring hostilities against England. Madrid and Paris had been moving toward alliance since reaching their own peace settlement the previous year. The vainglorious Alcudia acquired the title "the prince of the peace" for ending the French war. His mercurial policies proved disastrous. Spain's war against Albion became a long and costly failure. The conflict's first phase lasted from 1796 to 1802 and the second from 1804 to 1808. British naval might struck hard by cutting the Spanish lifeline to the Americas. Spain's political subordination to France induced the secret cession of all Louisiana to Bonaparte's government in 1800. Alcudia's previous order that Carondelet hold the line on the Mississippi was dead well before then.[5]

Besides British-Spanish rivalry, there were additional sources of international instability unsettling southeastern North America. From 1798 to 1800, France and the United States waged an undeclared naval war that threatened to erupt into full-fledged hostilities, and thereby ignite a U.S.-Spanish conflict over Louisiana and the Floridas. Intrigue was at a premium since private schemers vied alongside governments to shape the course of empire. Adventurers and secret agents traversed a murky political landscape where neither peace nor war reigned and where imperial and ethnic borders appeared as permeable as quicksand.

Espionage and Conspiracy

Pierre-Auguste Adet, French minister to the United States, had no stronger wish than to see his host country humiliated for the Jay Treaty, which in his view broke from the Franco-U.S. alliance of 1778. Early in 1796 he found a willing aide in General Victor Collot, former French commander on Guadeloupe, who had come to Philadelphia after surrendering the island to British forces in 1794. The general was no stranger to the United

States, having served as an officer under Rochambeau's victorious army at Yorktown.⁶

A proud Frenchman, Collot embraced Adet's charge to make a tour of the Ohio and Mississippi Valleys for gathering military, political, and geographic intelligence. His mission was essentially one of espionage, performed in eighteenth-century gentlemanly style. By exploring in quite open fashion, Collot intended to disarm suspicious U.S. and Spanish officials, even while coyly gauging whether the southern states would secede from the Union. French diplomats appeared to be on the verge of prying Louisiana from Spain by voluntary cession. Collot eagerly anticipated how his mission would contribute to French "military communications, both by land and water, between Louisiana and Canada."⁷

When Collot left Philadelphia for Pittsburgh in March 1796, he carried passports authorizing him to tour U.S. and Spanish territories for scientific purposes. Secretary of War James McHenry suspected espionage and looked for a legal pretext to seize Collot's papers. American military bumbling, however, allowed the French general to make his way from the Ohio to the Mississippi.⁸ In August Collot reached Upper Louisiana, where he conversed with French residents on both sides of the Mississippi. Here he found a place in what one historian has called "a creole corridor"—the pathway of French colonials up and down the great river. Not surprisingly Collot remarked on the Mississippi scene from a metropolitan perspective. Describing *habitants* of American Illinois as an "ignorant" and "indolent" people speaking a crude "jargon," he was still impressed by their abiding attachment to France. He praised St. Louis villagers as "excellent [French] patriots" burdened by Spanish misgovernment.⁹ Heading south to Cape Girardeau, he was hosted by Louis Lorimier, a native French Canadian and a Spanish captain well versed in Indian trade and diplomacy.¹⁰ Lorimier jolted his guest with intelligence that British forces in Canada were readying an invasion of Spanish Louisiana.¹¹ Collot was himself fearful of being cut down by foes—whether English, Spanish, or American. His suspicions intensified when Joseph Warin, his second, was badly beaten by two Chickasaw warriors near the confluence of the Arkansas and White Rivers. The general wondered whether the attackers might be hired assassins mistaking his adjutant for himself.¹²

Collot's journey had begun as a wholly French espionage affair, but became more complicated as he went down the Mississippi. Instead of gleaning western U.S. separatism, he heard of the British threat from the north. Though believing Spanish rule in Louisiana to be ineffectual,

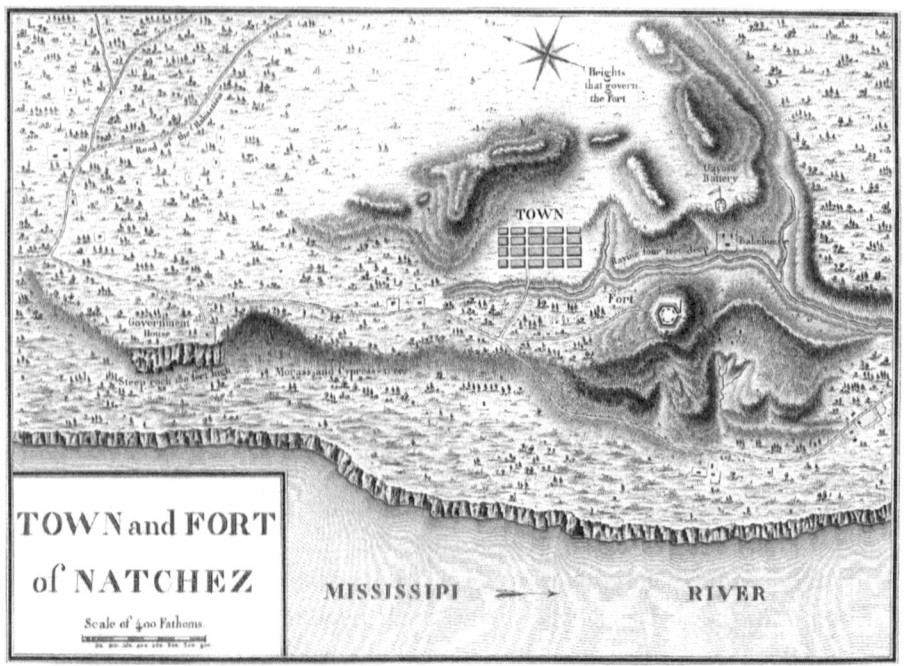

Town and Fort of Natchez (1796), in Georges Victor Collot, *Voyage dans l'Amérique Septentrionale*... (Paris, 1826). Courtesy of David Rumsey Map Collection, no. 4664024.

he could not help but take Madrid's interests into account. An English assault on the colony would not simply oust Spain, but also foreclose French control. Collot told Elias Beauregard, commandant at Nogales, that France was ready to send 12,000 troops if necessary to fortify Spain's Mississippi posts for defense against an American invasion.[13]

Collot's thorough Mississippi tour was finally interrupted on October 27, 1796, when the general was staying at a sugar plantation below New Orleans. Carondelet, who was scarcely pleased by Collot's unauthorized reconnaissance, sent a military guard to apprehend Collot and bring him to the capital for questioning.[14] A testy encounter ensued over the next few days. Carondelet scolded his distinguished guest but took no punitive action apart from appropriating some of the general's papers, notably his survey of St. Louis. Collot cried foul when deprived of Thomas Hutchins's map of the Illinois country. He remarked that simple fairness would permit Carondelet to take only the portion of the map sketching Spanish possessions! The general indignantly refused the governor's request that he travel incognito during his sea voyage to Philadelphia. With

Plan of Nogales (1796), in Georges Victor Collot, *Voyage dans l'Amérique Septentrionale*... (Paris, 1826). Courtesy of David Rumsey Map Collection, no. 4664022.

words and gestures, he signified that France was Louisiana's true master, and Spain a mere provisional caretaker.[15]

Collot's mission began with French imperial visions but took on a more complex character when the general reached Philadelphia in February 1797. It was now known that Spain had joined France in war against Britain. Collot accordingly shared intelligence on the English threat in Canada and Trans-Appalachia with Carlos Martínez de Yrujo, Spanish minister to the United States. Not revealing all at once, he recommended a gifted and knowledgeable officer, himself by inference, for military command in Upper Louisiana.[16] Six weeks later, Collot gave Yrujo a written report disclosing a conspiracy with loose strands of Tory, Indian, British, and western U.S. involvement. The name Chisholm came to the fore as an English agent, Tennessee resident, and frontier ringleader in cahoots with Robert Liston, British minister to the United States.[17] Though Collot's information was not entirely accurate, it was on the mark in identifying Tennessee as a conspiratorial nexus.

Conspiracy moved suddenly from backdoor diplomacy to center stage in Philadelphia during the summer of 1797. On July 3, the Adams administration transmitted recently obtained documents to Congress showing that Senator William Blount of Tennessee, and a certain Chisholm, were colluding with Ambassador Liston in a grand but hidden enterprise. In the incriminating message, Blount cryptically stated that he had met with Liston and was prepared to take the lead in "business on the part of the British." He then urged his confidant, Indian agent James Carey, to "read this letter over three times, then burn it."[18] But Carey neglected this advice, and the telltale document eventually came to the government's attention. Congress acted with extraordinary speed once it had evidence revealing a U.S. senator to be a secret British ally. The House of Representatives impeached Blount on July 7, 1797—and the Senate expelled its accused member the next day.[19]

Blount's conspiracy was real, though it was not so advanced as Congress initially feared. In contrast to what was rumored, the British government had not licensed its Canadian forces to sweep down on Louisiana. The conspiracy was actually in its formative stage—a case of scheming still absent any organized military apparatus. But that point was still unknown to congressmen who quite plausibly believed that a British plot could unhinge a continent. Blount was a formidable Tennessee leader who might very well bring discontented frontiersmen into league with him.[20]

Blount's scheme turned on his belief that Spain was about to return Louisiana to French rule. The senator accordingly turned to the British as his best bet for removing Spain—and especially its powerful ally France—from the Mississippi and the Gulf. In the process, he pushed for commercial access to New Orleans and the preservation of his enormous western landholdings, which were tottering because of bankrupt partnerships, insistent creditors, and a panicky market.[21] If all came out as hoped, the British Empire might be said to be serving Blount's interests rather than the Tennessee magnate bowing to London.

Blount's motives may be inferred through his secret correspondence with Dr. Nicholas Romayne of New York City, his friend, business associate, and confederate angling for British military intervention. In one letter, the senator remarked that he would be quite content to see Spain retain Louisiana if a French takeover could be prevented. Romayne urged Blount to spread word in the western country of a "hostile and warlike" French republic that would emancipate all slaves, shut the Mississippi to Americans, and destroy the value of land and property.[22] Some westerners indeed worried that France's abolition of slavery in 1794 could spread to Louisiana if that colony came under Paris's sway once more. Writing to Gayoso in November 1796, Kentucky intriguer Benjamin Sebastian observed that "negro property" was "repugnant to the French Constitution." This prospect troubled Sebastian, but it did not did not lead him to shelve his plans for acquiring Louisiana land.[23]

George Washington's recent departure from the presidency had an impact on conspiratorial projections. As Romayne pondered a British connection, he derided the Adams administration as weak and contemptible. As he pithily wrote Blount: "With respect to the United States we are to be pissed upon and degraded, or I am deceived."[24] These words caused Romayne some embarrassment when Congress later investigated the conspiracy. Blount himself fled Philadelphia posthaste for his Knoxville home after his expulsion from the Senate. Though tarnished, he remained a respected man among fellow frontier folk who held grievances against a distant federal authority perceived as overly sympathetic to Indian interests.[25]

Secretary of State Timothy Pickering, a Massachusetts Federalist and Anglophile, had no desire to see his friend Liston take the blame for a freebooting conspiracy centered in the trans-Appalachian West. The secretary was content with the ambassador's explanation that the English government was not itself involved. Pickering did not probe his British colleague's belated admission that he had indeed received conspiratorial visitors, but he had discountenanced their project.[26] This was simply not the case.

In the winter of 1796–97, Liston met in Philadelphia with Captain John Chisholm, a rough-hewn character whom the ambassador described as more comfortable talking about land than putting thoughts "into proper stile and shape on paper."[27] Chisholm had an obscure if colorful background. Claiming to have journeyed from New York City to Pensacola during the Revolutionary War, he later migrated to Tennessee, where he became a trader, tavern keeper, and Blount's liaison to the Cherokees, among whom he had a mistress or wife.[28] He was among the many white men who remade their lives in Indian country toward the close of the eighteenth century.

As ambitious as Bowles, Chisholm regaled Liston with a plan for an Anglo-American filibuster aimed at Pensacola, New Orleans, New Madrid, and New Mexico's imagined silver mines. Indian support was expected, especially for attacks along the Gulf Coast. Chisholm requested British naval assistance and other unspecified aid.[29] Liston was initially noncommittal but warmed to the scheme within a few months. In mid-March 1797, the ambassador arranged Chisholm's passage to England and gave him a letter of introduction to his Majesty's government.[30] In Liston's view, Britain dare not stand idle while Madrid was on the verge of ceding Louisiana to France. The ambassador regarded Chisholm's proposal as an "Enterprize" of "Adventurers" with every prospect of success. Volunteers would carry the battle, while the British government incurred inconsiderable risk and a small measure of financial aid.[31]

Liston was an enabler of conspiracy rather than a first mover in the plan, which produced schisms among the conspirators as it developed. Blount was put off when Chisholm departed for England because he believed his associate ill suited for a sensitive diplomatic mission. The senator also counted on Chisholm as his liaison to southern Indian peoples—a task that could hardly be advanced in Britain.[32] Blount did not take native assistance for granted and worried over Cherokee perceptions that he was too hard-nosed in pressing for land in recent treaty negotiations. His doubts are ironic given his many years of wheedling as much native territory as possible into settler society. The Creeks derisively labeled Blount "the Dirt King" (*Tucke-mico*) because of his insatiable appetite for land.[33]

Adventurist expectations had the habit of racing ahead of political realities by presuming imperial backing well before it was secured. Chisholm believed he could not fail in England, but he gained no interview with any British worthy. We may never know how much of his tale was true—or the extent to which it conformed to Blount's or Romayne's thinking. Chisholm imagined Louisiana and Florida becoming British possessions through conquest. Plunder taken from Spaniards was to be divided between volunteers and the crown, and "each private Soldier" was to receive one thousand acres of land. Frontier contention would be settled once and for all when New Orleans and Pensacola were made free ports and the Mississippi's navigation forever opened to the British and American peoples. The recurrent image of unifying the Gulf and interior was presented here in alluring and illusory finality.[34]

Examining the Blount conspiracy in even a limited way tells us that the plan was no brainchild of a single leader. Its components were as multifarious as the known parties who served as sub-captains and aides. Plausible hopes mixed indiscriminately with grotesquely unrealistic ambitions, confidence games, and lies. Disentangling the credible from the outrageous is nearly impossible. Romayne desired a British-directed campaign while Chisholm had a far more hell-bent sense of frontier warfare.

Blount was open to both propositions as long as he could win. However much acreage he had on paper, he neither had the resources nor will to mount a filibuster campaign without an imperial ally and guarantor providing maritime support. That much seems clear.

In April 1797, British officials in Canada were alarmed by rumors that Spanish and French agents were conspiring in the Mississippi Valley to instigate Indian attacks into their territory, and also to stir French Canadian rebellion. Though these rumors were unfounded, there were connections between southwestern conspiratorial movements and Canadian Indian affairs.[35] Chisholm courted Joseph Brant, the astute Mohawk chief residing in Canada, to lead Anglo irregulars from the Great Lakes region in an attack on Upper Louisiana. Though it is not clear that Brant received the invitation, there is little doubt that Chisholm aimed at a broad transnational alliance involving white freebooters and Indians.[36] Conspiratorial movements in disparate continental zones arose at roughly the same time, indicating the breadth of adventurist gambits for geopolitical realignment. In July 1797, the Adams administration dealt with political fallout from the *Olive Branch* affair—an abortive attempt by Vermonter Ira Allen to connive with the French for the liberation of Canada from British rule, and the creation of a new northern independent republic.[37]

Spanish Louisiana authorities calibrated their diplomacy in accordance with Madrid's fluctuating position vis-à-vis France and Britain. While Franco-Spanish war raged in 1794, Carondelet appealed to John Graves Simcoe, Upper Canada's governor, to assist in defending Louisiana against pro-French Kentucky freebooters. Simcoe courteously declined since he was then absorbed in strengthening Ohio Indians as the latter faced a U.S. offensive.[38] In March 1797, Carondelet cited the English invasion threat from the north as his rationale for holding onto Mississippi forts that Madrid was obligated by treaty to deliver to the Americans. The governor's concern was genuine, though clearly directed toward his larger goal of thwarting the United States.

Spanish Stratagems and the U.S. Takeover in Natchez

Appalled by the Treaty of San Lorenzo, Manuel Gayoso de Lemos was too resourceful to accept his district's cession to the United States without attempting to recast the political field. His prompt advice to Madrid on this issue in 1796 was largely responsible for Alcudia's subsequent order postponing the evacuation of Mississippi posts. But Gayoso wanted to go further by stopping the new boundary line from being run at the 31st parallel below Natchez.³⁹ Soon after making his case to Madrid, Gayoso wrote his confidant Daniel Clark Jr. that the U.S.-Spanish boundary accord "will never be accomplished." He expected the British to keep the Great Lakes forts within U.S. territory, thereby violating the Jay Treaty and compelling Madrid to retract its own territorial cession to the United States. Moreover, the governor believed it "more than probable" that several states would secede from the Union. In short, Spain would be "absolved from her engagements" to the United States "if this Union is dissolved . . . [and] exists no longer."⁴⁰

Gayoso had come to perceive U.S. internal weakness, and not Spanish strength, as the key to saving Louisiana for his king. Carondelet, too, had a similar sense after San Lorenzo. In February 1797 he expressed unmitigated joy at the news of General Anthony Wayne's death. Wayne, senior U.S. commander and a tough adversary, would now give way to James Wilkinson, who was of course in the king's pay. In late April 1797 the governor wrote in cipher to Wilkinson, offering him a pension of 4,000 pesos and a land grant in Upper Louisiana. These benefits came with the understanding that the general would show his "true adhesion" to Spain by suspending further U.S. military movement down the Mississippi. Wilkinson accepted the money in due course, but he did not jeopardize his rising American career by heeding Carondelet's request.⁴¹

The imperial underpinnings of Spanish Louisiana were precarious whether viewed from the Gulf or the Ohio-Mississippi corridor. British naval dominance in the Caribbean cut New Orleans from its Havana lifeline, halting shipment of royal subsidies sustaining Louisiana's governance and defense. Deprived of communication with Cuba for months, Carondelet grasped at sudden deliverance. He badly wished to believe reports that 12,000 Spanish troops had arrived in Havana. His thoughts turned to impressing "our friends in Kentucke" who were supposedly waiting for just the right moment to take their state out of the Union. There was no more substance to the rumored Cuban resurgence than to the phantom of Kentucky separatism.⁴²

Spanish delaying tactics did not sit well with U.S. boundary commissioner Andrew Ellicott, who eagerly anticipated the task of running the new international borderline upon his arrival at Natchez on February 24, 1797. By character and intellect, he was a meticulous and resolute man, whose technical expertise went along with a streak of political shrewdness and underhandedness. An accomplished astronomer and surveyor, he assumed a central role in laying out the new federal city on the Potomac in 1791. Though a Quaker by family background, Ellicott was not a pacifist. A Maryland militia officer during the Revolutionary War, he placed a premium on order and discipline.[43]

Ellicott was not appeased by Gayoso's tactful but still obvious manner of hampering his mission. On March 13, 1797, the U.S. boundary commissioner remained at his tent on Natchez's outskirts rather than accept Gayoso's invitation to lodge in his house. A serious dispute followed later that month when Spanish soldiers remounted cannon in the district fort. After Ellicott complained of this seemingly aggressive step, Gayoso replied that he required the weaponry for defense against possible Choctaw attacks. Ellicott encouraged Lt. Percy Pope, heading a U.S. military detachment approaching Nogales, to proceed to Natchez as soon as possible. With tensions rising, Gayoso finally consented to Pope's stationing his men near town on April 17. Confrontation appeared likely. Pope, a brash officer without patience for Spanish demurral, inflamed the situation. It would be mistaken, however, to think that Pope and Ellicott were simply manufacturing a crisis from above. A host of Anglo inhabitants in Natchez wanted to see a Spanish withdrawal forthwith, come what might.[44]

Gayoso nurtured the hope that Natchez settlers would come to their senses and realize that they would be better off under Spanish than U.S. governance. He counted on local opposition to Georgia, which was once again stirring unrest by another Yazoo Act selling vast portions of western acreage to private land companies.[45] But the diminution of Spanish authority could not be stayed. Some leading residents maneuvered to secure their full rights under Madrid's rule before any sudden change in government. William Dunbar, one of Natchez's wealthiest planters, obtained Gayoso's permission in April 1797 to take lawful possession of a town lot in recompense for his past services as a district surveyor.[46] Gentlemanly deal-making did not bring public peace. By June many of Natchez's white residents were openly carrying arms and readying to oust the Spanish by force. On the sixth, Gayoso sent an urgent plea to Alcudia, recounting all that Natchez meant for imperial defense. Once retreat was signaled, a chain of reverses would be set in motion. The loss of Louisiana would lead ultimately to the loss of Mexico. The painful truth could not be concealed when defeat appeared imminent. No royal minister could ever say that Gayoso had not been true to his sovereign.[47] But the governor did not dwell on the question of personal honor when battle loomed.

During the evening of June 11, 1797, Captain Esteban Minor, veteran of Louisiana's royal regiment, brought disturbing news to Gayoso. Having just conversed with Ellicott and Pope, he explained that virtually all Anglo-American inhabitants in the district were now in a "state of revolution" and declaring themselves citizens of the United States.[48] Just two days before, Anglo-American townsmen cried foul when Spanish guards arrested Barton Hannon, a firebrand Baptist preacher, who got into a row with a few Irish Catholic men. This episode was the trigger for disturbances that had more serious causes. Many inhabitants felt unmoored as their district swung erratically between the Spanish past and the American future. Rumors and intrigues swelled as the Mississippi's spring floodtide. The discontented took their complaints to Ellicott and Pope, who fanned the rising chorus for U.S. rule.[49]

Ellicott does not seem to have wanted an actual armed conflict, but instead intensified local pressure that would compel Gayoso and Carondelet to back down. His anger at Spanish authorities grew hotter on June 4, when he learned that Thomas Power was headed from Natchez as Carondelet's secret agent to alleged Kentucky separatists. Ellicott correctly informed the State Department that Power intended to visit General Wilkinson in Ohio. No additional inference was yet made from this point. In fact, Power was carrying news to Wilkinson and his Kentucky coterie that Carondelet was prepared to offer $100,000 if the group brought the state out of the Union and agreed to a peaceful border settlement with Spain. According to Power's letter, Carondelet would allow a western separatist government to expand as far south as the Yazoo—and to a parallel point on the Tombigbee—if events transpired as he wished.[50]

Gayoso hunkered down in his fort on the night of June 11 with just over seventy soldiers and militia. An imminent assault was expected. Sentinels guarded the palisades; artillerymen stood at their posts with lit matches. And yet no attack followed either that night or during the next nine days. A tense standstill held.[51] A breakthrough in the crisis occurred on June 21, when Gayoso left the fort to enter negotiations with leading citizens at his government house. On the 22nd, he concluded a formal truce with a district committee of seven men, chosen at a public meeting controlled, in Ellicott's words, by "gentlemen of property and influence." The committee's head was Anthony Hutchins, now well over seventy years old, and still directing affairs in much the same manner as he had formerly done as a British provincial colonel, a Tory turned Spanish subject, and finally a planter potentate about to seek his place under the stars and stripes.[52]

The accord of June 22, a type of local treaty in lieu of a definitive imperial settlement, provided that no inhabitants were to be prosecuted for any recent actions they had taken "under the belief and persuasion that they were citizens of the United States." Though the citizenry recognized the continuance of Spanish law until U.S. sovereignty took effect, they were released from militia service during the interim—except if called to combat an Indian invasion or to suppress riots. As for political allegiance, the inhabitants were declared "to be in an actual state of neutrality, during the continuance of their [present] uncertainty." The committee acted with the approval of Ellicott and Pope, who attended the negotiations though they were not signatories to the agreement. While Gayoso saw his authority ebb away, his remaining time in Natchez was brief. In late July, he headed for New Orleans to assume the post of Louisiana's governor-general, taking the place of Carondelet who departed for royal service in Ecuador's highlands.[53]

Most of Natchez's white inhabitants turned warmly toward the United States and expressed contempt for the Spanish flag under which many had prospered. Consider, for example, Peter Bryan Bruin, who made his fortune by migrating from Virginia to "the Natchez" in 1788, where he obtained ample lands, served as a militia colonel, and lived quite well at Castle Bruin, his home at Bayou Pierre. In July 1796, he acquired two additional Spanish land grants totaling nearly 2,000 acres in his neighborhood.[54] Faithfulness faded quickly after the Treaty of San Lorenzo. In early 1797, Bruin confidentially befriended Andrew Ellicott, a fellow Mason, when the latter came down the Mississippi. By November he declaimed: "I have as little opinion of Spanish, as the Romans had of Punic faith.... There is no dependence to be plac'd on a People, who laugh at truth, as an antiquated Value and with whom Honor has no tye [sic]." Bruin was soon a territorial judge under the United States.[55]

Unlike many of his countrymen, James Wilkinson very seldom indulged in negative stereotyping of Spaniards. In fact, he elevated himself above ordinary citizens by courteous correspondence with Madrid's colonial officers over years. Wilkinson's penchant for Spanish connections was not entirely materialistic, however much he cherished silver dollars. His love of pomp in language and military dress paralleled his desire to be on a par with cavaliers of aristocratic bearing. Gaining the respect of

Miró, Gayoso, and Carondelet satisfied his pretensions even as it fed his pocketbook.

After obtaining a U.S. brigadier's rank in 1792, Wilkinson spent most of the next five years posted in the Ohio Valley—with timely political visits to Philadelphia as needed. Still stationed in the northwest during the Natchez crisis of 1797, he had the luxury of personally avoiding the troubled frontier zone, while supervising his troops and passing word of Spanish military measures to U.S. officials. Wilkinson did not of course reveal that his knowledge came via his own backdoor correspondence with Carondelet and Gayoso.[56]

Intrigue was a useful instrument by which individual powerbrokers navigated their own paths amidst borderlands confusion. Wilkinson delighted in casting suspicions on various parties to deflect attention from his own machinations. In late May 1797, he informed Winthrop Sargent, secretary of the Northwest Territory, of "the serious consequences" arising from "the refusal of the Spaniards in Louisiana, to execute the Treaty of Friendship, Limits and Navigation." Now was a time for every officer "to guard against the Intrigue and Enterprize [sic] of Foreigners and Aliens." This last warning concerned Louis Philippe—the youthful exiled duc d'Orleans—then in route with his two younger brothers from Kentucky to New Orleans. Wilkinson believed "suspicion is warranted" that "Mr. D' Orleans" could be plotting "to debauch and detach the people of the Western Country from their Obligations . . . to the United States, and to embark them in the mad Projects of the French."[57] The brothers had no such motive—a fact that Wilkinson probably understood.

Wilkinson's intrigues were as astounding for their geographic range as their cunning exploitation of U.S.-Spanish tensions. Throughout the 1790s, he was a sponsor of Philip Nolan, the youthful Irish-born adventurer who specialized in the roundup of Texas mustangs and their sale in Louisiana and the United States. In January 1797, Nolan was in the mid-Mississippi Valley after completing his third venture to the distant southwest—what he called "the unknown land." Traveling on the Ohio, he shared information with Ellicott, then heading downriver, on Spanish plans to thwart the U.S. occupation of Mississippi posts. A few months later Nolan sounded out Gayoso on forming a business partnership to ship dry goods to Texas. The district governor seems to have been interested, though the deal never came off. Most important, Nolan secured Carondelet's special permission for yet another journey to Texas—a province still officially off-limits to Louisiana trade. The young adventurer had his mentor's knack for playing both sides, obtaining a sextant from Gayoso and receiving Ellicott's instruction in astronomy and telescopic use.[58]

In January 1798, Gayoso at last received positive orders from court that the evacuation from Natchez and all ceded territory should move ahead. With typical graciousness, he pledged his cooperation to Ellicott. He could do no more. By the end of March 1798, U.S. troops were in sole command of Nogales and Natchez. On May 31, Gayoso embraced Ellicott when the two men met along the Mississippi at the 31st parallel to begin running the new boundary line. Ellicott responded stiffly, evidently not forgetting his trials of the previous year. He wrote his wife of being startled by Gayoso's gesture: "We met and saluted in the Spanish manner by kissing! I had not been shaved for two days—Men's kissing I think a most abominable custom."[59]

The Spanish position on the Mississippi and in West Florida was badly compromised by the loss of Natchez—and all else north of the 31st parallel. In late November 1798, Gayoso laid bare his misfortunes in a lengthy dispatch to Alcudia. He complained about being without troops, resources, or information necessary for his task. Rather than fearing the U.S. government, he was most wary of "the intrigues" of influential Americans who "form independent parties and projects . . . with the view of settling within our territory," and whose eyes were fixed on "the Mines of Mexico, which they already consider a part of their future imaginary Empire." The American president was almost bound to tolerate aggressive inroads into Spanish territory lest dissatisfied western citizens form "independent states" prejudicial to the Union.[60] Spain would have no relief from the American republic whether that nation acted as a sovereign empire or gave license to its restless citizenry.

Andrew Ellicott and Daniel Clark Jr.

Having begun his task of running the boundary line in 1798, Ellicott rested in New Orleans early the next year to renew his strength after an exhausting period of traversing swamps, creeks, canebrakes, and piney uplands from the Mississippi to the Pearl River. Writing once more to Pickering, he credited Daniel Clark Jr. and Wilkinson's friend Philip Nolan with being extraordinarily supportive of his mission in Natchez. Indeed, he believed Clark's "financial arrangements . . . would have carried us thro,' had violent measures become necessary."[61]

Clark's assistance to Ellicott in 1797 undoubtedly involved intelligence on Spanish political intentions. A close associate of Wilkinson and Nolan, Clark also had a good rapport with Carondelet and Gayoso. Intensely ambitious, he befriended Ellicott as he saw U.S. power rise relative to Spain. The boundary commissioner responded in kind, naming Clark U.S. vice-consul in New Orleans well before the State Department officially approved the appointment. American shipowners and merchants benefited as a result. Clark had a masterful knowledge of Spanish commercial regulations and strong personal ties to the French mercantile community of New Orleans. Gaining the cabildo's support and gubernatorial assent, he helped to minimize bureaucratic delays that foreign vessels encountered in passing from the Gulf to New Orleans—and out to sea again. In June 1798, he proudly announced his success in gaining a tariff reduction from 21 percent to 6 percent on goods shipped "in American Bottoms" to U.S. Mississippi settlements. He gained the same favorable rate for U.S. merchant vessels importing goods to New Orleans during the remainder of the Anglo-Spanish war.[62]

Eager to profit from the new boundary line, Clark hoped that the United States and Spanish governments would build new fortifications in the vicinity of Clarksville, his plantation along the Mississippi's east bank just three miles above the border. He was somewhat anxious of a full-fledged war between the United States and France, but still believed the situation might have redeeming qualities. If "the British an[d] Americans are in Alliance," he wrote Ellicott, "it will be impossible, nay it will be idle in Spain, ever to attempt to repossess her Self of the mouth of this great River." This same letter conveyed "Pleasure inexpressible" at a report that British ships had destroyed a Spanish squadron in "the Bay of Mexico." Just three weeks after passing this message to Ellicott, Clark scored his coup with the Gayoso administration on the tariff issue.[63] Spain might be damned in private, but its colonial officials were to be courted with the utmost pleasantness—and doubtless some gratuity to boot.

The principal actors in frontier intrigues had many contacts but seldom formed political friendships of enduring and stable tenor. Options of association and allegiance were common currency; ruin could come without wariness of possible betrayal. There is little doubt, for example, that Clark supplied evidence to Ellicott in November 1797 of Wilkinson's Spanish pension and his western separatist schemes. Clark did so for purposes that may be surmised but not fully known. Perhaps he wanted leverage vis-à-vis Wilkinson should the latter, who was now a friend, turn against him one day. More obviously, he desired to boost his standing with Ellicott, the federal officer best positioned to benefit him. The eventual enmity between Clark and Wilkinson lay well in the future; it came full blast with the collapse of the Burr conspiracy in 1807.[64] Borderland intrigues ran their own course alongside the jockeying for power among nations.

Ellicott passed his information regarding Wilkinson's underhanded Spanish dealings to Pickering. The report was astonishing. According to Ellicott's informant, Wilkinson and his American friends were plotting the secession of Kentucky and Tennessee from the Union and the conquest of New Mexico—to be aided by "corrupted" Spanish officers and Louisiana troops. This tale was not itself true, though Wilkinson's Spanish stipend was of course a fact.[65] Pickering chose not to launch any serious investigation of Wilkinson. Anticipating war with France, he was probably averse to igniting a domestic political firestorm by exposing the nation's senior army officer. The secretary of state had endured enough political criticism over his closeness to British minister Liston during the Blount fiasco. When Alexander Hamilton, himself a Pickering ally, guided U.S. military policy in the summer of 1798, he approved Wilkinson's command of the southwestern frontier.[66]

Hamilton was no advocate of freebooting, but he was as eager as Blount to arrest the dangers arising from France's political dominance over Spain—and the very possible Spanish cession of Louisiana and the Floridas to the French republic. Months before he won appointment as Inspector General of the Army in July 1798, the former treasury secretary believed the American republic could secure its rank among nations only by a firm policy toward France—a nation he detested for propagating "atheism, conquest, and anarchy," and for wantonly seizing U.S. merchant vessels en route to British ports.[67]

Louisiana and the Floridas occupied a central place in Hamilton's thinking of how the United States should wage war against France, and also quite possibly Spain—the latter being reduced in his view to little more than a proxy of the French Directory. In early 1798, his agenda featured collaboration with Great Britain outside any formal alliance. If the United States and France came to "an open Rupture," England could best cooperate by applying naval force against "the Floridas [,] Louisiana & [the] South American possessions of Spain." Hamilton maintained a friendly correspondence with Venezuelan revolutionary Francisco de

Miranda, then in England, about their common objectives. While in sympathy with Miranda, he informed his friend that he could not assist any British campaign aimed at South America liberation unless approved by the U.S. government.[68]

Hamilton's military projections differed from Blount's by contemplating operations by U.S. regular troops—and not adventurers. In a strategic sense, however, his ideas paralleled the adventurist conception of relying on Britain's maritime power to advance an American continental agenda. Hamilton was confident of anticipated war gains: "All on this side the Mississippi must be *ours* including both Floridas."[69] New Orleans was, of course, on the river's east bank.

While U.S.-French relations deteriorated, Carlos IV's government anticipated negative repercussions for Spain. During the summer of 1798, Juan Manuel Álvarez, minister of war, learned through French sources that William Pitt's "gold and intrigues" had gained ascendancy over the U.S. Congress. According to this intelligence, Britain was secretly urging the United States to embark on the seizure of Louisiana and the Floridas. The English would then likely attempt the conquest of Havana with Anglo-American assistance—just as had occurred in 1762.[70]

Because historians have devoted so much attention to the Louisiana Purchase, they have tended to underplay the international ramifications of hostility between the U.S. and French governments in 1797–99. North America's imperial fate appeared to hang in the balance.[71] U.S. leaders had their own sense of international events spiraling beyond control, especially as France appeared poised for North American aggrandizement. Hamilton feared French control of the Mississippi and the Gulf as a prelude to "despoiling Spain of the riches of Mexico and Peru."[72] George Washington imagined that France would invade south of the Potomac in the event of war. The southern states were most vulnerable for several reasons: "because they are the weakest; 2. because they [the French] will expect . . . to find more friends there; 3. because there can be no doubt of their arming the Negros [sic] against us; and 4. because they would be more contiguous to their Islands, & to Louisiana & the Floridas, if they can obtain possession of them."[73]

French intervention appeared a genuine threat to Blount, Washington, and many others. In September 1798, Daniel Clark Jr. cheered reports that Washington was "to head our Armies." He then passed a rumor that the French republic had just sent "1,500 armed black troops" to Cuba, "with a view to disseminate the Doctrine of emancipation." Clark deplored this action, though he added a note of moral self-reflection: "Until Slavery is done away among the human Species God will not be reconciled to us."[74]

Because U.S.-French hostilities never moved beyond an undeclared naval war, it is all too easy to overlook the significance of the projections and forebodings of Hamilton, Pickering, and Washington in 1798. The international crisis that year led Congress, politically divided though it was, to authorize the formation of a provisional army of 10,000 men, to increase the number of regular regiments, and to approve naval construction for the defense of shallow southern rivers as well as oceanic combat.[75] In early 1799, Inspector General Hamilton fumed at Adams's attempts at diplomatic settlement. Rather than allowing France to dictate North American affairs, he wanted the United States to preempt Paris by "taking possession of the Floridas and Louisiana"—"countries . . . essential to the permanency of the Union."[76] There was no reference here to British assistance in the Gulf-Mississippi theater, but an unmistakable sense of direct American military power.

Wilkinson Takes Command

In October 1798, Wilkinson at last took personal charge of some 300 to 400 U.S. troops at Loftus Heights in the Lower Mississippi Valley. Overlooking the river's east bank, his encampment was but six miles above the 31st parallel. Thirty-five years earlier, this portion of the great river had witnessed a successful attack by Tunica warriors on British soldiers, commanded by Major Arthur Loftus, then attempting a northern movement to the Illinois country. Now the area was astir in a wholly different way. Accustomed to being indulged by Louisiana's governors, Wilkinson was miffed when Gayoso requested an explanation for the U.S. troop placement so near Spanish territory. The general responded that his military position actually aided Spain by allowing the United States to curb "her own licentious Citizens" in the frontier region.[77]

Wilkinson had recently shown his own credentials as a guardian of frontier order. On his way down the Mississippi in the summer of 1798, he demanded the arrest of Zachariah Cox, a Tennessee adventurer leading a small group of frontiersmen downriver with the intent of colonizing Spanish territory. Because the group had a reputation for intruding on Indian land, it was rumored to be disorderly and violent. In compliance with Wilkinson's request, Governor Sargent had Cox jailed when the latter reached Natchez. But the prisoner escaped and made his way to

New Orleans, where Gayoso listened courteously to his plan of forming a company to develop a commercial route between the Tennessee River and the Tombigbee-Alabama water passage to Mobile Bay. Cox was more of an entrepreneur than a reckless scoundrel as denounced by Wilkinson, whose fury was unleashed at another rival for Spanish favor. The general's idea of borderland comity was one where he was the kingpin controlling U.S. access to Louisiana and the Gulf. Gayoso undoubtedly derived some pleasure from showing that he could not be bossed by the almighty Wilkinson, who lectured him on the evils of Cox's monopolistic proposal and the sordid motives of western Americans.[78]

Notwithstanding Spanish vulnerability, the United States hardly commanded the Lower Mississippi Valley during its first military entry to the region. Wilkinson did not hide American weakness in messages to the War Department. He was disturbed by the willingness of some Natchez district residents to move southward into Spanish territory. One noteworthy émigré was Dr. James White, and another was the son of "Old [Anthony] Hutchins." Others might follow, Wilkinson warned, if swayed "by the Arts of a few Mal-Contents." He fretted over the desertion of soldiers drawn away by "the bounties of land to Emigrants and the high wages to labourers offered by the Spaniards" in Louisiana. With no hint of irony, Wilkinson admitted that this information "cannot be concealed from the Troops and will have influence on men of loose morals and unsettled dispositions."[79] A few months later he shared similar insights with Hamilton. His command was situated in the most exposed point of the Union because of its "distance" from "National succour & its proximity to a foreign Power." An entrenched enemy could open "a Communication with the Southern Indians & greatly facilitate foreign Intrigue & the Acts of Corruption among our wide extended Western Settlements." Besides, he had little faith in the Mississippi Territory's free citizenry, whose national allegiance had changed so often through recent wars and international treaties that they lacked "any permanent attachments to Government."[80]

For all these negative remarks, Wilkinson still imagined he might launch an offensive "should events compel us to attack." If properly reinforced, his army could execute "a Coup-de-main" against New Orleans, or even follow a "direct route into the Mexican provinces of Texhas & St. Afee [Santa Fe] & St. Andero [Nuevo Santander]." The general was becoming more familiar with Mexican geography but still superficially knowledgeable—as his tortuous spelling of place names alone indicates.[81]

Speculation about foreign incursions and far-flung U.S. military campaign came readily to Wilkinson. It was a practice that suited his ambivalent posture toward war, as opposed to political intrigue, as a course of action. In fact, Wilkinson knew that any U.S. offensive to the southwest was not possible under present circumstances. He had only a few hundred men under his command in the Lower Mississippi Valley. A good many of them were sick. The general was soon to leave the Mississippi for consultations in Philadelphia before returning to the region in early 1800.[82]

Ellicott, the Boundary Issue, and Empire

Andrew Ellicott met repeated delays in running the U.S.-Spanish borderline along the 31st parallel in 1798. After nine months of trudging through woods and morass, Ellicott returned from the Pearl River to New Orleans for a respite and supplies in January 1799. Once in the city, he caught up on news of the wider world where much was in turmoil.[83] Surveying the New Orleans scene for his good friend Timothy Pickering, Ellicott longed for the day when Louisiana would be annexed to the American republic. Yet he mused: "For my own part I cannot see any advantages the U.S. could derive from the possession of this province at present. They are already possessed of its commerce and draw from it annually a very large sum in specie—and that perhaps with more ease than if it was in our possession." Similar to British observers in previous decades, Ellicott countenanced Spanish governance in Louisiana so long as Mexican silver had a way of reaching his countrymen's pocketbooks.[84]

Though pleased with U.S. commercial predominance, Ellicott still voiced uncertainties. The American republic could accept Louisiana's situation only so long as a debilitated Spanish régime was in place. The United States, he declared, should "lay hold of" Louisiana rather than allow Spain to transfer it to "any other European nation." Ellicott urged similar action if the region instead should become "part of a new empire"—apart from the United States or European powers. In his estimation, "many gentlemen of respectable talents" in the region were "looking forward with pleasure" to political changes magnifying their personal importance.[85] Though not divulging any names, Ellicott presumably had the likes of Wilkinson, Clark, and other powerbrokers in mind. Privatistic forces appeared capable of empire building in their own right.

Indian allegiances were hardly settled where so much imperial contention remained alive. Ellicott worried about native opposition to the running of a new boundary line from the beginning of his mission. After all, U.S. territorial acquisition at Spanish expense came without Indian consent. Ellicott soothed potential problems among the Choctaws by collaborating with John Pitchlyn, an influential mestizo chief who was a firm U.S. ally. "Liberal presents" were dispensed to impoverished Indians, who were told that the new boundary line was "not intended to steal their land," but instead "to divide the Virginia[ns] . . . from the Spanish." In June 1798, Captain Isaac Guion reported that one Choctaw group was setting horses to trample its own corn fields in light of American encroachments, and moving south to the Chickasawhay River in Spanish territory. Many others had already migrated west of the Mississippi, where they came into frequent conflict with the Caddos and the Arkansas nation.[86] Spanish assistance eased the pathway of some Indian migrants toward security. In June 1797, Red Shoes of the Alibamons led four hundred of his people to New Orleans to obtain royal permission to settle far from the Americans. This quest led to Alibamon-Coushatta settlement on the Red River in Louisiana.[87]

Indian emigrants were settling Louisiana's southwestern frontiers just as a new international border was being drawn east of the Mississippi. Ellicott's boundary survey was a joint U.S.-Spanish affair in which Gayoso fully cooperated once receiving Madrid's orders to go ahead. The governor appointed Captain Minor, one of his most experienced officers, as royal commissioner to assist the work. In August 1799 Ellicott, Minor, and their small party encountered Seminole and Lower Creek resistance as they headed up the Chattahoochee. Seminoles not only freely plundered the commissioners' camp, but also threatened to stop the survey from continuing. Ellicott took the path of safety by leaving camp along the Flint River on September 19 and heading by schooner down the Apalachicola to the Gulf Coast, and then toward the Spanish fort of San Marcos de Apalache.[88]

The Florida Gulf Coast felt the winds of change from sea as well as land. While Ellicott struggled in Seminole country, he received warnings that William Augustus Bowles was once more on his way to Florida's shore. This news came from various sources, including William Panton, Bowles's old nemesis, who denounced his foe's "talents of deception" aimed at "deluded" Indians. The renowned adventurer was indeed nearing, being on the last leg of a voyage from Jamaica and the Bahamas, if hardly arriving in imposing manner. On September 18, 1799, Bowles's schooner, H.M.S. *Fox*, and its small crew ran aground on St. George's

Island at the entrance of Apalachee Bay. Never out of stratagems, the self-styled Creek director-general sent a message to Ellicott, who was on the nearby mainland. Bowles graciously requested a meeting: "Altho' we may differ in politics yet as Gentlemen we may associate, and be friends." Ellicott, who was not one to skip an intriguing encounter, made his way by boat to the island. Both men conversed freely for eight days. Negotiation bent to nature. Neither party could leave as long as strong headwinds prevented safe passage to the mainland. Ellicott provided food for Bowles and his shipwrecked crew during the interim.[89]

While exchanging pleasantries, Ellicott and Bowles realized they were political opponents. Ellicott's mission was to demarcate a boundary line distinguishing U.S. and Spanish territory. By his reckoning, native peoples living on either side of the international border were necessarily subject to either the American republic or to Spain. Bowles directly told Ellicott that the Creeks were a free and independent people. The U.S.-Spanish treaty of 1795 was in his words "an atrocious violation" of Indian sovereignty.[90]

Though Bowles realized that he could not win Ellicott to his side, he had no hesitancy about using him to send his recent proclamations to the American press. These pronouncements were made in the name of "the State of Muskogee"—an independent Indian government. The name "Muskogee" was itself significant, for it represented the use of Muscogulge speech for designating a Native state. Bowles thereby gave expression to Creek aspirations through a political ideal of nationhood that was more European than American Indian in character.[91]

Ellicott's friendly encounter with Bowles yielded useful, if not surprising political intelligence, which the boundary commissioner himself passed to Spanish authorities. Bowles was planning to attack the fort of San Marcos and to seize Panton's nearby store.[92] Though not in support of Bowles, Ellicott still saw him as a man of "enterprize and address"—a figure with a dexterous and bold sense of command. He doubted, however, whether the adventurer's Gulf Coast landing could possibly succeed once it was discovered that the British government was not behind him. In Ellicott's judgment, the absence of imperial support spelled certain defeat, since Bowles's individual prowess "will be of as little use to him ... as the wings of [a] Butterfly are to their owner in a vacuum."[93] Other U.S. observers were less sure. At Natchez in May 1800, Wilkinson wrote Hamilton that Bowles's influence would be "extensive and pernicious" only on two conditions—if the British either came to war with the United States or "contemplate[d] an attack on New Orleans and Pensacola, which from Jamaica would be readily practicable and certain of success."⁹⁴ Wilkinson's sense of contingency—the notion of a sudden and transformative imperial irruption—was a constant presence in the Gulf-Mississippi region at century's close.

Conclusion
The Impermanence of Boundaries

Intrigues proliferated in frontier regions where diverse interests contended for power, but where no single nation or imperial power predominated. As a result, individuals and groups commonly grasped for advantage by masking motives, angling for allies across ethnic or territorial borders, and exaggerating their strength or concealing vulnerability. The Louisiana-Florida borderlands of the late eighteenth century epitomized these tendencies because of successive imperial crises intersecting with changing local and regional circumstances.

Political and social adaptability were certainly at a premium in Louisiana and the Floridas. One cannot overstate the consequences of French imperial withdrawal from North America in 1763–66, and the British government's loss and abandonment of the Floridas in 1781–85. Spain's slow and unsteady entry into Louisiana after the Seven Years War incited French colonial disaffection and the New Orleans revolt of 1768. The gradual English evacuation of East Florida in 1784–85 gave time for British Loyalists to bargain with Spanish officials for residency rights and commercial privileges under the new régime. It was in this period that McGillivray rose to prominence and that Panton and Leslie expanded their trade from St. Augustine to San Marcos and then Pensacola. Loyal subjects who were unloosed by king and country often felt little choice except to negotiate new bonds of allegiance and protection. Some individuals, of course, turned the art of being political chameleons into a profitable and wholly self-serving habit.

Was there a British and Anglo-American tendency to deceive Spanish authorities? Certainly the British contraband trade with Spanish American colonies over many decades fed into similar U.S. exploits. Ohio Valley and Kentucky traders of the late eighteenth century mastered the arts of smuggling and mouthing nominal professions of Spanish allegiance for their own emolument. Economic opportunism was at work here more clearly than ethnic or religious prejudice. The king's governors in New

Orleans generally tolerated a fair degree of illicit trade because strict legal enforcement would have stirred colonial resentment by depriving Louisiana of flour, other merchandise, and slaves. Ties of mutual self-interest on an interregional level dictated events more clearly than Madrid's imperial mandates.

The rise of western U.S. frontier elites after the Revolutionary War was both threatening and alluring to Spanish authorities in New Orleans. Crown officials desperately wanted reliable allies within Kentucky, Cumberland, Franklin, and other districts where citizens threatened to solve the Mississippi question by force. James Wilkinson exploited Spanish vulnerability for maximum personal gain, and without coming close to fulfilling the separatist political agenda that Louisiana's governors secretly promoted. With all his chicanery, Wilkinson provided one useful service to Spain—intelligence on prospective filibusters and U.S. troop movements.

Anglo-American military adventurers of the 1790s assumed that either France or Great Britain would reenter North American affairs in a decisive manner. Whether conspirators were pro-French or pro-British, they expected to harness imperial military might and sea power to their advantage. Belligerent empires were so deeply engaged in European and Caribbean struggles, however, that they were not in any simple position to transfer forces from the islands to the continent. British expeditions to the Caribbean from 1793 to 1802 were massive enterprises in their totality. In 1797—the year of Blount's conspiracy—the English sent 30,000 soldiers across the Atlantic in a futile attempt to subdue French and black revolutionary armies in Saint-Domingue, and to wage related campaigns.[1] London's imperial priorities reduced the chance of an offensive against Spanish Louisiana.

The riverine geography of southeastern North America had a profound influence on colonial adventurism, imperial rivalries, and white-Indian relations. In February 1765, Governor George Johnstone informed London that opening a viable Gulf-Mississippi passage through British territory was essential because of the difficulty of navigating Florida's "shallow Rivers, where Ships of Force cannot go," and where Indian peoples tenaciously held interior lands.[2] The Natchez district became the core British and Anglo-American settlement zone in the Lower Mississippi Valley because of fertile soils and comparative ease of access to New Orleans and the Gulf. The region between the Apalachee Bay and the Apalachicola River had a slight imperial presence, opening the way for

William Augustus Bowles to plot continental transformations through a new maritime base supported by Creeks and Seminoles.

As Bowles's case exemplifies, Anglo-American adventurism in the late eighteenth century had a Tory pedigree and not simply Whig and republican proclivities. The most ambitious adventurers of the era overleapt governmental restraints and attempted to reshape continental affairs through new currents of transnational politics, commercial exchange, and colonization. The Spanish borderlands were as yet more permeable to foreign settlement and trade than military conquest. Andrew Jackson's sword had still to appear with its fateful power, forcing Spain's final retreat from Florida in 1821.

Bowles maneuvered in a milieu in which boundaries were impermanent and subject to dramatic and thoroughgoing change. Shortly after making landfall in Florida in the fall of 1799, he castigated the U.S. government for "the intrigue and knavery" of its Indian treaties, successively broken as the new republic gained the strength to override and to renegotiate existing boundaries. The American Revolution was the decisive event of his lifetime. In the aftermath of conflict, frontier regions became "receptacles for men of every class . . . among whom a spirit of libertinism prevailed from the want of laws to curb their licentiousness. A spirit of speculation in land, originated among these people which like a ravaging flame extended itself over the whole of the United States, which reached your members of Congress, and even your grave Senators."[3] It is ironic that Bowles denounced frontier "libertinism" when he was part of a British and Anglo-American adventurist movement into southern Indian country that began before the Revolution and accelerated during and after the war.

Bowles's Florida incursion of 1799 proved his longest and most remarkable. In a creative burst of nation building, he laid the ideological groundwork for a Muskogee state as soon as he made camp among the Lower Creeks. Proclamations issued from his pen with lightning speed and a royal flourish. "We the Director General of Muskogee" was his standard preamble, and he closed with a rousing "God Save the State of Muskogee."[4] The arch-Tory adventurer displayed a British cultural sensibility more obviously than an Indian understanding of nationhood founded on common kinship.

Bowles was an adventurer in all the principal meanings of his era. He was not only a freebooter, but also a colonial and commercial promoter whose Anglo comrades viewed the Floridas as a ripe venue for land acquisition and profiteering. Free trade was his constant rallying cry. On November 16, 1799, Bowles declared the Muskogee ports of Apalachicola, Ochlockonee, and Tampa open "to all Nations not at war with us."[5] In reality, those waterways did not yet have active harbors, but that scarcely troubled a director general with a penchant for futurity.

Had Bowles not been a charismatic figure with personal ties to Creek society, his incursion of 1799 would have been hopeless from the beginning. He brought only two white comrades and a few others with him from the Bahamas, and he was wholly dependent on Lower Creek and Seminole warriors. He found a potent ally in Kinache, Seminole chief of Miccosukee, who raised warriors for Bowles's single military success against Spanish colonialism—the capture of San Marcos de Apalache on May 19, 1800, after a one-month siege. Tomás Portell, the garrison's commandant, estimated that Bowles had only nine or ten white freebooters alongside four hundred Indian fighters during the campaign, in which several Spanish soldiers and sailors were killed or wounded. The fort had fewer than seventy soldiers at the time of surrender.[6]

The capture of San Marcos evinced Indian disgust with Spaniards and with Panton's trading house rather than an abiding commitment to Bowles or to his titular Muskogee state. After winning booty in arms and goods, most warriors retired to their villages within a short time. In late June 1800, Bowles and his allies abandoned the fort and escaped into forests and marshlands when a Spanish naval squadron under Vicente Folch sailed up the Apalachee (St. Marks) River and approached the garrison.[7] Indians generally wanted a plentiful supply of goods from coastal areas, but they had little interest in maritime power in the way Bowles envisioned. While operating within Florida in 1800–1801, the director general commissioned Bahamian privateers for service in the Muskogee navy. Several ships, flying his independent banner, captured Spanish merchant and fishing vessels. A British admiralty court in Nasaau dealt a blow to this campaign in 1802 by freeing a captured Spanish vessel brought into port under the Muskogee flag. John Kelsall, the presiding judge, issued a stinging rebuke at Bowles and his "unprincipled adventurers" for waging unrestrained violence that was contrary to "public War in all its legitimate forms." Time was running out for Bowles when British authority swung strongly against him. The English truce with France and Spain of 1802 left him more isolated than ever.[8]

The astonishing point is not that Bowles was eventually captured by the Spanish with Creek and U.S. assistance in 1803, but rather that he remained at large in Florida for so long. Upper Creek headmen, drawn into the U.S. economic orbit, wanted him dead for threatening to engulf their region in war.[9] For all the enemies Bowles made, there were still Creeks and Seminoles who hoped he could somehow bring his promised British merchantmen, and perhaps soldiers, to their shore. Spaniards viewed him as an inveterate British agent; a good many natives supported and sheltered him for precisely that reason.

Though Bowles attracted some black supporters and spread fear among white slaveholders, he did not voice any principled opposition to African bondage. African American loyalties were diverse in the Floridas. In 1801, General Jorge Biassou, a black exile from Saint Domingue's slave revolution, headed St. Augustine's free black militiamen who took up arms against Bowles and his Miccosukee allies.[10] Bowles's Seminole friends engaged in slave raiding even while harboring black runaways and gradually incorporating them into their society—if not as equal members. Some blacks looked to Bowles as a guardian of their personal freedom. At his final arrest in 1803, Spanish authorities took into custody eleven blacks and four mulatto men who stood with him. The African American quest for freedom in Seminole country later emerged in sharper profile in 1814–15 when blacks aligned with British forces arrayed against Andrew Jackson's army.[11]

Spanish officials paid Indian allies for Bowles's capture in May 1803, which was made after the director general was lured to an assembly in the Upper Creek heartland. U.S. agent Benjamin Hawkins, along with Panton's successor John Forbes, had a major role in these proceedings. Fittingly, the capture took place at the Hickory Ground—a site where Bowles's former rival Alexander McGillivray had once held sway. Bowles was sent under Spanish guard to New Orleans and then Havana, where he died in Morro prison on December 23, 1805.[12] His optimistic vision of Creek nationhood, born in the American Revolution's aftermath, appeared a distant chimera in the decade following his death. Deepening Creek poverty and factional discord triggered a religious nativist movement that erupted in the Redstick War of 1813–14. Muscogulge dissidents then struck against the Creek national council's insistence on strict internal discipline, respect for private property rights, and accommodation with the United States.[13]

The U.S. campaign to quash Bowles coincided with the federal government's resolve to establish social order and clear-cut boundaries in southern borderlands. On April 24, 1802, the Jefferson administration settled the longstanding Georgia boundary issue by negotiation without any Indian input. By this accord, Georgia relinquished to the United States all territorial claims from the Chattahoochee River westward to the Mississippi. In turn, the U.S. government paid $1,250,000 to Georgia and pledged to "extinguish the Indian title to all the other lands" within the state.[14] The seeds of the Trail of Tears were now planted.

The U.S.-Georgia accord was part of a process of Indian dispossession that was the work of private commercial interests and not only government dictate. For example, John Forbes and associates reaped an eventual windfall from a succession of U.S. treaties negotiated in 1805 with the Creeks, Choctaws, Chickasaws and Cherokees. These agreements, amounting to a buyout of about eight million acres of native land, were accompanied by understandings that the federal government would compensate Forbes and Company for the cancellation of native indebtedness owed the firm.[15] Forbes meanwhile sought Spanish approval to create a semi-autonomous Gulf Coast fiefdom where he would monopolize the deerskin trade, open the region to British Loyalists and poor European immigrants, and expand African slave importation. Though this project died like so many other schemes, it shows how private entrepreneurs continued to believe they could manipulate Spanish borderland territories for their own aggrandizement.[16]

Personal transformations were commonplace amidst imperial contestation in the Louisiana-Florida borderlands. David Bradford, Pennsylvania political radical and leader in the Whiskey Rebellion, escaped federal arrest by fleeing down the Ohio in the fall 1794, remaking his fortune as a planter and slaveholder at Bayou Sara in Spanish West Florida within a few years. Anticipating France's takeover of Louisiana in early 1803, Bradford believed the transfer of national sovereignty at New Orleans would have little economic impact, except that the French would likely transact business in paper money rather than in Spanish gold. Unsure how his neighborhood would be divided between French and Spanish jurisdictions, he was elated when apprised of the Louisiana Purchase, which he hailed as "a grand Speculation." Bradford's relief was understandable since he was a U.S. nationalist, though a nominal Spanish subject.[17]

The Louisiana Purchase opened a new era of U.S. predominance that overrode European decision making for North America. France's acquisition of Louisiana from Spain in 1800 was undone in quite rapid fashion by disparate forces—French military defeat in Saint-Domingue and the Jefferson's administration's diplomatic skill, strengthened by the threat of war unless the American citizenry got their way. The Purchase elicited widespread U.S. rejoicing along with innumerable political commentaries. Louisiana's acquisition appeared to strike a finishing blow to foreign intrigues targeting the Mississippi Valley and the Gulf region. Allan B. Magruder, a Kentucky politico, urged Americans to compare their country's present good fortune with a host of recent dangers: "Who does not recollect the intrigues of Sir Robert Liston, his intercepted letters to governor Simcoe [of Canada], the bribing of Blount, and Bowles's embassy of Muskogee Indians, to the court of London?" In this view, Britain had plotted for years to turn Louisiana into a weapon against the United States and "a rod over Spain and her Mexican mines." France's occupation was perhaps even more threatening. Had that government retained Louisiana, Magruder imagined that it would have incited Indian attacks on the American frontier and quite likely stirred 500,000 slaves to rebellion in the southern states.[18]

The fear of foreign intrigue and upheaval was genuine, however prone to exaggeration and self-deception. British minister Liston had hardly bribed Blount, but rather had been courted by the Tennessee senator and his agents. Bonaparte was scarcely planning to liberate North American slaves when his troops were battling to suppress black freedom in the Caribbean. Louisiana's colonials were strongly attached to slavery and not about to obey any imperial power—even France—that did not safeguard their interests. Slavery did not simply spread from east to west in North American history. It established roots in the Lower Mississippi Valley, reaching as far northward as Illinois, well before the United States furthered the cotton kingdom to the detriment of human freedom.[19]

Intrigues and rumors were widely felt in Louisiana when that colony hung in the balance on the eve of Jefferson's Purchase. Pierre Clément de Laussat, Louisiana's prefect during the few weeks the colony was under French sovereignty, wrote Pierre Favrot, commandant at Plaquemine, not to worry about Western American invasion threats. Such talk was "fodder" fed by "little schemers" (*petits intrigans*) to ordinary frontier folk. Laussat had his own grand scheme of strengthening French power through Indian alliances and European immigration to the Mississippi Valley.[20] The prefect's colonization plans closely resembled Carondelet's previous conception of building Louisiana as a bulwark against U.S. expansion. The Jeffersonians were justifiably alarmed by a French Louisiana for reasons transcending control of New Orleans.

Jefferson's geographic understanding of the Louisiana Purchase was predicated on U.S. aggrandizement at Spanish expense in the near term and potentially well into futurity. Jefferson asserted that Louisiana encompassed a portion of Spanish West Florida, notably the strategic region between the Isle of Orleans and the Perdido River, just west of Pensacola.[21] This contention was plausible, if not foolproof, because French Louisiana had formerly included the Gulf shore as far eastward as Mobile Bay. Jefferson's boldest territorial claim was his assertion that the Louisiana Purchase comprised lands extending southwestward to the Rio Grande. As a legalistic justification, Jefferson relied on the wording of the Spanish-French convention by which France received Louisiana with the same boundaries the colony had when it was transferred to Spain in 1762. Those bounds were most indefinite—and the president took full advantage of this point.

Jefferson's management of the Louisiana boundary question attests to his penchant for deliberate ambiguity in his statecraft toward Spain. Keeping varied territorial options alive was as important to him as it was to his arch-foe Aaron Burr when plotting to raise a private army and naval force for operations in the Gulf region and even Mexico. This is not to equate Jefferson the public statesman with Burr the conspirator acting outside the bounds of national authority. What should be emphasized is that some citizens saw U.S. policy as a virtual invitation to take up arms on their own against the Spanish. If the Louisiana Purchase included Texas and much of West Florida, how could Americans be guilty of a crime for intruding into territories that their nation already claimed for itself?

The Spanish policy of admitting Anglo-Americans into royal borderlands might have worked for an extended period in a stable international environment, but it was vitiated by rising U.S. power, the Bourbon monarchy's political ineptness under Carlos IV, and finally the onset of Hispano-American revolution in 1808. Not surprisingly, Anglo-American settlers in West Florida's Baton Rouge district cast off Spanish rule in 1810 when crown officials balked at supporting colonial demands for full autonomy. As a result, white inhabitants declared an independent West Florida republic, which was incorporated within a few months into the United States. President Madison adroitly held to international legalities in this instance by maintaining the need to restore order in a region that was already part of the United States by the Louisiana Purchase. Federal authorities had a more difficult time restraining zealous American settlers on the Tombigbee River from exploiting West Florida confusion by launching freebooting assaults on Spanish Mobile.[22]

The American citizenry's drive toward Spanish territories was a diffuse movement not clearly under U.S. government control. Uncertain federal command was evident during East Florida's Anglo-American revolt in 1812, which drew support from Georgia freebooters and some U.S. military personnel until the Madison administration took an unequivocal stand against the filibuster. Spanish forces in Florida stood their ground, with support from Seminoles and blacks as well as loyal settlers.[23]

Jeffersonians had a habit of testing Spanish frontier control where it was weakest. Though not countenancing filibustering, Secretary of State James Monroe was quite interested in developing contacts with the Mexican independence movement. During the summer of 1812, Anglo-American freebooters used Louisiana as a base to invade Spanish Texas and to assist Mexican and Tejano insurgents in battle. That particular campaign failed, but it marked a significant point in burgeoning U.S.-Mexican ties. Hispano-American wars of independence spawned involvement by a host of adventurers of diverse nationalities.[24]

In 1821, Mexico emerged as an independent nation, with quite uncertain relations with its northern neighbor. No sooner had the Mexican eagle taken wing than U.S. and English adventurers swooped down on Mexico City with the intent of obtaining colonization contracts in Texas. James Wilkinson was among the most fervent bidders, employing the same tactics as frontier mediator and self-seeking profiteer he first displayed at New Orleans in 1787. He died in the Mexican capital on December 28, 1825, without fulfilling his last quest. Mexican authorities faced a conundrum in Texas similar to the one the Spanish previously confronted in Louisiana and the Floridas. Was the goal of developing and defending a frontier region worth the risk of a foreign takeover of national territory? This question was hardly straightforward given economic ties overriding simple ethnic loyalties. Tejano and Mexican elites commonly embraced foreign trade and speculative opportunities that went along with growing U.S. investment in their homelands.[25]

Adventurism and intrigue were not simply leading elements of U.S. imperialism; they were vital forces shaping cross-border and transnational interchange among numerous historical actors and ethnicities in the Louisiana-Florida borderlands. That legacy of multiplicity would endure in many human struggles—both bloody and peaceful—shaping the Americas far into the future.

NOTES

ABBREVIATIONS

AH	*The Papers of Alexander Hamilton*, ed. Harold C. Syrett. 27 vols. New York: Columbia University Press, 1961–1987.
AHN	Archivo Histórico Nacional
AMT	Aileen Moore Topping Collection concerning a Spanish Diplomatic Mission to the United States, 1777–1785, Library of Congress
ASP	American State Papers
ASPFR	American State Papers, Foreign Relations
ASPIA	American State Papers, Indian Affairs
BF	*The Papers of Benjamin Franklin*, ed. Leonard W. Labaree et al. 40 vols. New Haven, Conn.: Yale University Press, 1959–2011.
BN	*Biblioteca Nacional* (Madrid)
BOURBON	"Papers Relating to Bourbon County, Georgia, 1785–1786," ed. Edmund C. Burnett. *American Historical Review* 15 (October 1909): 66–111; (January 1910): 297–353.
C.O.	Great Britain, Colonial Office
CONSP	*¿Conspiración española? 1787–1789: Contribución al estudio de las primeras relaciones históricas entre España y los Estados Unidos de Norteamérica*, ed. José Navarro Latorre and Fernando Solana Costa. Zaragoza: Institución Fernando el Católico del C.S.I.C., 1949.
DAR	*Documents of the American Revolution, 1770–1783 (Colonial Office Series)*, ed. K. G. Davies. 21 vols. Shannon and Dublin: Irish University Press, 1972–1981.
DRAPER	Draper Manuscript Collection
EF	East Florida Papers
FAVROT	*The Favrot Family Papers: A Documentary Chronicle of Early Louisiana*, ed. Guillermo Náñez Falcón, vols. 1–3, and Wilbur E. Meneray, vols. 4–5. New Orleans: Howard-Tilton Memorial Library, 1988–2001.
FONDO	*Fondo Floridas* (*Archivo Nacional de Cuba*)
GDQUI	Dispatches, Diego de Gardoqui y Arriquibar, Durrett Codex 74, Special Collections Research Center, University of Chicago Library
GWLC	George Washington Papers, Library of Congress
HPLCAN	Haldimand Papers, Library and Archives Canada
HPMSS	*Sir Frederick Haldimand: Unpublished Papers and Correspondence, 1758–84.* [Add. Mss. 21661–21892.] London: World Microfilm Publications, 1977.
HSP	Historical Society of Pennsylvania

JCC	*Journals of the Continental Congress, 1774–1789*, ed. Worthington Chauncey Ford et al. 34 vols. Washington, D.C.: Government Printing Office, 1904–1937.
JWCHM	James Wilkinson Papers, Chicago History Museum
LC	Library of Congress
LCAN	Library and Archives Canada (Ottawa)
LDC	*Letters of Delegates to Congress, 1774–1789*, ed. Paul H. Smith. 26 vols. Washington, D.C.: Government Printing Office, 1976–2000.
JMLC	James Madison Papers, Library of Congress
LOCKEY	Joseph Byrne Lockey Documents Related to the History of Florida, University of Florida Libraries (Gainesville)
MPAED	*Mississippi Provincial Archives, 1763–1766: English Dominion*, vol. 1, ed. Dunbar Rowland. Nashville: Brandon Printing Co., 1911.
MPASD	Mississippi Provincial Archives: Spanish Dominion, 1759–1820
NARA	National Archives and Records Administration
NYPL	New York Public Library
PC	*Papeles procedentes de la isla de Cuba* (Archivo General de Indias)
PCC	Papers of the Continental Congress
PLC	Papers of Panton, Leslie, and Company
PRO	Great Britain, Public Records Office
SD	*Audiencia de Santo Domingo* (Archivo General de Indias)
SMV	*Spain in the Mississippi Valley, 1765–1794*, ed. Lawrence Kinnaird. 3 parts. Annual Report of the American Historical Association for the Year 1945, vols. 2–4. Washington, D.C.: Government Printing Office, 1946–49.
THNOC	The Historic New Orleans Collection
TJLC	Thomas Jefferson Papers, Library of Congress
YONGE	P. K. Yonge Library of Florida History, University of Florida (Gainesville)

INTRODUCTION

1. Weber, *The Spanish Frontier in North America*; Smith and Hilton, *Nexus of Empire*; Brown, *Coastal Empires*.

2. Elliott, *Empires of the Atlantic World*, 237; Michael Braddick, "Civility and Authority," and Elizabeth Mancke, "Empire and State," in Armitage and Braddick, *The British Atlantic World*, 129–30, 212–13. For the process of incorporation and differentiation, see Burbank and Cooper, *Empires in World History*, 8–11. For colonialism, see Meinig, *The Shaping of America*, 7, 65-66.

3. Adelman and Aron, "From Borderlands to Borders," 815–16. See also Hämäläinen and Truett, "On Borderlands"; Gould, "Entangled Histories."

4. The theme of national sovereignty is cogently addressed in Gould, *Among the Powers of the Earth*. For similar issues in the antebellum era, see May, *Manifest Destiny's Underworld*.

5. For a survey of this broad subject, see Wright, *Anglo-Spanish Rivalry in North America*.

6. Richard Hakluyt, "The Principal Navigations," in *Hakluyt's Collection of the Early Voyages*, 3:593; 4:26. In these quotations, I have changed the letter "u" to "v" in accordance with modern spelling. John Smith, *The Generall Historie of Virginia*, 94. See also Jones, "The Colonial Impulse," 141.

7. See Mancke, "Empire and State," 199–200; Black, *The British Seaborne Empire*, 7. The "privatization of colonization" is discussed in Sarson, *British America, 1500–1800*, xiv.

8. Bottigheimer, "English Money and Irish Land," 13.

9. Hume, *The History of England*, 6:97 (quotation). Hume characterized diverse groups as "adventurers": ancient Saxon colonizers, Scandinavian invaders, Norman conquerors, medieval crusaders, English settlers of Ireland, and Francis Drake's comrades in arms. 1:25–26, 136, 246, 253, 295–98; 2:23; 5:275, 396.

10. Campbell, *An Account of the Spanish Settlements in America*, 179 (second quotation), 251 (first quotation).

11. Franklin to Kames, February 25, 1767, BF, 14:67–68.

12. For the domination of "cultural space," see Greene, *Imperatives, Behaviors, and Identities*, 4–7. See also Wright, *William Augustus Bowles*; Din, *War on the Gulf Coast*.

13. *The British Sailor's Discovery* 29 (quotation), 67–68. English colonial ideology was anti-Spanish at its core. See Cañizares-Esguerra, "Entangled Histories," 788.

14. Elliott, *Spain, Europe, and the Wider World*, 47–49, 190–91; Kamen, *Empire*, 458–59, 479–80; Weber, *Bárbaros*, 5.

15. Powell, *Tree of Hate*, 51–52. Powell falsely attributes the expulsion of the Jews from Spain to what he calls their "treason" against Catholic monarchs. He belittles the Jewish victims of persecution, and their descendants, by the wholly unconvincing idea that "Christian Spain deserves some recognition for unusual restraint in the face of what other Europeans [i.e., Christians] obviously viewed as provocation." Powell's discourse is profoundly antisemitic—as exemplified by the analogy he draws between the castigation of Jews in fifteenth- and sixteenth-century Spain and the execution of Julius and Ethel Rosenberg for nuclear espionage in the 1950s. See *Tree of Hate* (reprint, 2008), 175.

16. Talleyrand characterized the diplomat's art as dependent upon dissimulation: "*La parole a été donnée à l'homme pour disimuler sa pensée.*" Talleyrand is quoted in Abarca, "Classical Diplomacy and Bourbon 'Revanche' Strategy," 317.

17. Meinig, *The Shaping of America*, xvii.

18. For geography and environmental influences, see Morris, *The Big Muddy*; Powell, *The Accidental City*. For a historical synthesis emphasizing multiple geopolitical and cultural vantage points, see Countryman, *Americans*, 23–26.

PART I PROLOGUE

1. Egremont to Amherst, January 13, 1762, Correspondence and Papers of Sir Jeffrey Amherst, reel 9, 041/16. George III's declaration of war of January 2, 1762, is enclosed in

Egremont to Amherst, January 7, 1762, Correspondence of Amherst, reel 9, O 41/14A. For the Spanish background, see Lynch, *Bourbon Spain*, 317–18.

2. Egremont to Amherst, January 13, 1762, Correspondence of Amherst, reel 9, 041/16.

3. George III to Albemarle, C.O. 117/1.

4. Anderson, *Crucible of War*, 501.

5. Amherst to Egremont, September 23, 1762, Correspondence of Amherst, reel 9, 042/8.

6. Lyon, *Louisiana in French Diplomacy*, 21; Gayarré, *History of Louisiana*, 2:87–89; Villiers du Terrage, *Les dernières années de la Louisiane française*, 122–23, 142–45; Ekberg, "The Flour Trade in French Colonial Louisiana," 279.

7. Mapp, *The Elusive West*, 399. For British conceptions of maritime empire, see Gould, *The Persistence of Empire*, 68.

8. Gipson, *The British Empire before the American Revolution*, 8:300–304.

9. Aiton, "The Diplomacy of the Louisiana Cession," 713–14; Anderson, *Crucible of War*, 503–6. For the broad historical context, see Black, "Britain's Foreign Alliances in the Eighteenth Century"; Abarca, "Classical Diplomacy," 324–25.

10. Aiton, "Diplomacy of the Louisiana Cession," 714–16. For French geographic understandings of Louisiana, see Mapp, *The Elusive West*, 148–61, 265.

11. Shepherd, "The Cession of Louisiana to Spain," 445–47.

12. Gipson, *The British Empire before the American Revolution*, 8:305–7. For the Spanish stake in Florida, see Hoffman, *Florida's Frontiers*; Weber, *The Spanish Frontier in North America*, 179–83. See also Bolton, "The Debatable Land."

13. Hoffman, *A New Andalucia*; Weddle, *Spanish Sea*.

14. Aiton, "Diplomacy of the Louisiana Cession," 717–19. For a full text of the definitive Treaty of Paris, February 10, 1763, in French and in English translation, see Shortt and Doughty, *Documents Relating to the Constitutional History of Canada*, 1:97–112. For the peace articles with respect to Florida, see Gold, *Borderland Empires in Transition*, 13–28, 193–95.

15. Pearce, *British Trade with Spanish America*, 27–30; Liss, *Atlantic Empires*, 61; Christelow, "Economic Background of the Anglo-Spanish War of 1762," 22–36; Stein and Stein, *Silver, Trade, and War*, 62–65, 139–41; Rice, "Great Britain, the Manila Ransom, and the First Falklands Dispute," 386–409.

16. Rousseau, *Règne de Charles III*, 1:98; Lyon, *Louisiana in French Diplomacy*, 23; Bute to Bedford, September 28, 1762, in Sedgwick, *Letters from George III to Lord Bute*, 138–39n.

17. Journal of Abbadie, July 1763, in Alvord and Carter, *The Critical Period*, 162–63; Kerlérec to Choiseul, May 2, 1763, in Galloway, *Mississippi Provincial Archives: French Dominion* 5:284. For Creek concerns, see Hahn, *The Invention of the Creek Nation*, 265–66.

18. Pagden, *Lords of All the World*; Calloway, *The Scratch of a Pen*.

19. Royal notice of Louisiana's cession was evidently the first broadside printed in New Orleans. See McMurtrie, *The Earliest Known Louisiana Imprint*. Choiseul confidentially relayed Louisiana's cession to the British ambassador in Paris. See Neville to the Earl of Halifax, October 24, 1763, State Papers Foreign (SP 78/258), National Archives, Kew.

20. Le Page du Pratz, *The History of Louisiana*, 2:202. French understandings of western Louisiana and New Mexico are analyzed in Mapp, *The Elusive West*, 150–63. For

the Mississippi issue in 1763, see Pease, "The Mississippi Boundary of 1763," 284-85; Brecher, *Losing a Continent*, 178-82.

21. Bellin's map is beautifully reproduced in Lemmon, Magill, and Wiese, *Charting Louisiana*, 73. Geographer Thomas Hutchins correctly understood that New Orleans was not clearly situated on an island since mud and trees often blocked water channels in the Lower Mississippi Valley. Besides, bayous creating the so-called island were apt to be dry in late summer and early fall. See Hutchins, *An Historical Narrative and Topographical Description of Louisiana and West-Florida*, 25-26, 43, 61. See also Morris, *The Big Muddy*, 27-30.

22. Pittman, *The Present State of the European Settlements on the Mississippi*, 10.

23. Bedford to Egremont, September 19, 1762, in Bedford, *Correspondence of John, Fourth Duke of Bedford*, 3:101-2; Aiton, "Diplomacy of the Louisiana Cession," 715-16.

24. Shortt and Doughty, *Constitutional History*, 1:97-126 (quotation, p. 116); Bedford to Egremont, December 24, 1762, in Bedford, *Correspondence of Bedford*, 3:178-79.

25. Brown, "The Iberville Canal Project," 492-93.

26. Shortt and Doughty, *Constitutional History*, 1:117.

27. Villiers du Terrage, *Les dernières années de la Louisiane française*, 152. See also Dawdy, *Building the Devil's Empire*, 108; Surrey, *The Commerce of Louisiana during the French Régime*, 42-54, 80-81, 218-21, 386-87. In 1761, Choiseul was willing to cede Louisiana to Spain if a suitably large loan were provided by Madrid. See Lyon, *Louisiana in French Diplomacy*, 20-21; Mapp, *The Elusive West*, 362-64, 378-79.

28. The company's undated proposal, and a subsequent modified version, are in BN, THNOC, microfilm 83-20-L. The French company was based in La Rochelle. See Christelow, "Proposals for a French Company," 603-11.

29. Rodríguez Casado, *Primeros años de dominación española en la Luisiana*, 99-100; Gayarré, *History of Louisiana*, 2:163.

30. For the British arrival at Pensacola and Mobile, see Rea, *Major Robert Farmar*, 33-36. For the entry at St. Augustine, see Siebert, "The Port of St. Augustine," 250.

CHAPTER 1

1. Johnstone's lobbying piece, "Thoughts concerning Florida," bears no date, probably written in late 1762 or early 1763. See PRO 30/47/14. See also Fabel, "George Johnstone," 165-66. Johnstone's source on Pensacola Bay was Le Page du Pratz, *The History of Louisiana, or the Western Parts of Virginia and Carolina*, 1:xliv-xlv.

2. "Thoughts concerning Florida," PRO 30/47/14. For Spanish taxation of colonial commerce, see Stein and Stein, *Silver, Trade, and War*, 85, 191-93.

3. Fabel, *Bombast and Broadsides*, 7-8. The War of Jenkins' Ear carried over into the broader War of the Austrian Succession, 1744-1748. See Pares, *War and Trade in the West Indies*, 110-26.

4. Elliott, *Empires of the Atlantic World*, 23-26, 231-34; Brading, "Bourbon Spain and Its American Empire," 410-12; Márquez, "Commercial Monopolies and External Trade," 409-11; Parcero Torre, "Comercio y contrabando en Cuba," 257-58.

5. Campbell, *An Account of the Spanish Settlements*, 422.

6. Johnstone to Bute, June 16, 1763, in Jucker, *The Jenkinson Papers*, 158-59. See also

Fabel, "George Johnstone," 164–75. Johnstone was officially commissioned on November 21, 1763; West Florida Papers, reel 1, LC.

7. "Thoughts concerning Florida," PRO 30/47/14.

8. *The North Briton*, 2:119–20 (No. 35, January 29, 1763). For the idea of empire in British public consciousness, see Greene, "Empire and Identity," 215–18; Gould, *The Persistence of Empire*, 37.

9. Johnstone physically struck one of Wilkes's friends, but not his chief critic. See *An Appeal to the Public, in Behalf of George Johnstone, Esq.*, 22, 37–42. Fabel, *Bombast and Broadsides*, 4–16. For the Scottish upsurge, see Colley, *Britons*; Snapp, *John Stuart and the Struggle for Empire*, 45–53.

10. See Ignotus, *Thoughts on Trade in General . . . and the Preliminary Articles of Peace*, 75; *The True State of the Case*, 34; *Reflections on the Terms of Peace*, 32.

11. Nobleman, *A Review of the Arguments for an Immature Peace*, pt. 2, 30.

12. *The Freeborn Englishman's Unmasked Battery*, 36–37; Nobleman, *A Review of the Arguments for an Immature Peace*, pt. 2:33.

13. For the report of June 8, 1763, see Shortt and Doughty, *Constitutional History of Canada*, 1:144–45.

14. For the Proclamation of October 7, 1763, see ibid., 1:163–68.

15. Board of Trade to Egremont, June 8, 1763, ibid., 1:144.

16. Ibid., 1:138 (last quotation), 142–43.

17. This regulation assumed immigrant households to be headed by men without specifying that fact. See Fabel, *The Economy of British West Florida*, 7–9.

18. The East Florida notice of October 31, 1764 is in the *South-Carolina Gazette*, December 3, 1764; Prevost to Secretary of War, September 7, 1763, MPAED, 1: 136.

19. Mowat, *East Florida as a British Province*, 11–12.

20. Lords Eglinton and Elibank were the helpful friends. In 1766, Eglinton successfully transferred his grant near Pensacola to Natchez. See Howard, *The British Development of West Florida*, 37–38, 65, 80–81. See also Fabel, *Bombast and Broadsides*, 4–16, 28, 47.

21. The Board of Trade's recommendation is in C.O. 5/599. The boundary change won royal approval on June 6, 1764. See West Florida Papers, reel 1, LC. See also Fabel, *Bombast and Broadsides*, 28.

22. "Thoughts concerning Florida," PRO 30/47/14. For the peace treaty, see Shortt and Doughty, *Constitutional History of Canada*, 1:115, 117, 120.

23. For the Florida evacuation, see Gold, *Borderland Empires in Transition*, 66–73, 100–102; Landers, *Black Society in Spanish Florida*, 28–30, 59.

24. Cited in Rea, "Lieutenant Colonel James Robertson's Mission to the Floridas," 39.

25. For Farmar's list, see MPAED, 1:121–22. See also Gold, *Borderland Empires in Transition*, 106–14; Usner, *Indians, Settlers, and Slaves*, 129.

26. The passage from the Gulf into Pensacola Bay was not simple, but much preferable to the situation at Mobile Bay. See Report of Major William Forbes, January 30, 1764, MPAED, 1:113; Lt. Col. Prevost to the Secretary of War, September 7, 1763, MPAED, 1:136; Major Robert Farmar to the Secretary of War, January 24, 1764, MPAED, 1:10. Master James Cook remarked on Pensacola's barren surroundings. See Robert R. Rea, "Master James Cook," 301–2.

27. Of forty property transactions during this period, at least thirty-one (77.5 percent) involved sales by French residents to British subjects, including three Jewish merchants. C.O. 5/601.

28. Farmar acquired Tensaw River plantations from Francis Daran and Joseph Millon, respectively, on June 11 and August 3, 1764. He purchased the Dauphin Island lands from Agatha Arnaut, widow of New Orleans, on August 8, 1764. See C.O. 5/601. See Alden, *John Stuart and the Southern Colonial Frontier*, 194–96; Rea, *Major Robert Farmar*, 120–22.

29. For the Coxe patent, see Crane, *The Southern Frontier*, 48–60. The postwar British and Anglo-American push for frontier land grants is discussed in Bailyn, *Voyagers to the West*, 23. In 1663, Charles II's privy council voided the "Carolana" grant by nullifying any "Letters Patent" that may have been issued to Heath. See Wood, *Black Majority*, 13.

30. *An Impartial Enquiry into the Right of the French King*.

31. Ibid., 56.

32. Ibid., 11–12, 20–22. Other British publicists feared French control of New Orleans and western Louisiana for similar reasons. See *The Expediency of Securing Our American Colonies*, 32.

33. Skemp, *William Franklin*, 41–42; Wright, *Franklin of Philadelphia*, 129; Hutson, "Benjamin Franklin and the West," 433–34. William Coxe of Philadelphia was a grandson of Doctor Daniel Coxe of London. Daniel Coxe VI of New Jersey (1739–1826) was the doctor's great-grandson. See Cary, "The American Dream," 184–85.

34. Fabel, *The Economy of British West Florida*, 14–18, 87–88, 92, 103–5, 181–84; Clark, *New Orleans*, 164–65.

35. Franklin to Jackson, March 8 and April 17, 1763, BF, 10:208 (first quotation), 255 (second quotation).

36. Jackson to Franklin, November 12, 1763, ibid., 10:369–70; Jackson to Franklin, [April 13, 1764], ibid., 11:175–76 (quotation).

37. See Benjamin Franklin to William Franklin, September 12, 1766, BF, 13:414. Lyman's efforts are discussed in greater detail in chapter 2.

38. The growing literature on this subject is only suggested here. Important titles include Usner, *Indians, Settlers, and Slaves*; Braund, *Deerskins and Duffels*; Wright, *Creeks and Seminoles*; Atkinson, *Splendid Land, Splendid People*; Gibson, *The Chickasaws*; Reeves, *The Choctaw before Removal*; O'Brien, *Choctaws in a Revolutionary Age*; White, *The Roots of Dependency*.

39. Some Chickasaws migrated from the Upper Tombigbee to the Creek country fronting South Carolina in the 1710s and 1720s. See Atkinson, *Splendid Land, Splendid People*, 18–20. For the Chickasaw role as slave suppliers, see Gallay, *The Indian Slave Trade*, 129–32, 170–71, 296–97; Gibson, *The Chickasaws*, chap. 2; White, *The Roots of Dependency*, chap. 3; Patricia K. Galloway, "Choctaw Factionalism and Civil War, 1746–1750," in Reeves, *The Choctaw before Removal*, 120–56.

40. De Vorsey, *The Indian Boundary in the Southern Colonies*, 20–23.

41. These units were the 3rd Battalion of the 60th Regiment, destined for Pensacola, and the 22nd and 34th Regiments bound for Mobile. See MPAED, 1:128–31. For an estimate of the initial military force and population figures, see Fabel, *The Economy of*

British West Florida, 18. George Johnstone wrote that his "feeble" province had 1,800 or 2,000 inhabitants and two regiments in 1766. See Johnstone to the Board of Trade, April 1, 1766, C.O. 5/583.

42. Major Farmar's Instructions to Officers, October 24, 1763, MPAED, 1:93; Farmar to the Secretary of War, January 24, 1764, MPAED, 1:11. See also Rea, *Major Robert Farmar*, 36–38; Pittman, *The Present State of the European Settlements on the Mississippi* (edited by Rea), x–xi; Alvord and Carter, *The Critical Period*, xxxiii–xl.

43. Abbadie to Kerlérec, November 6, 1763, in Galloway, *Mississippi Provincial Archives: French Dominion*, 5:293. Farmar instructed his officers to be on the outlook for French emissaries "seducing the Native Indians." See Instructions, October 24, 1763, MPAED, 1:93. See also Gold, *Borderland Empires in Transition*, 106–14.

44. Robertson to Amherst, November 15, 1763, quoted in Rea, "Lieutenant Colonel James Robertson's Mission," 43. The conference proceedings with the Choctaws are in MPAED, 1:83–91.

45. Speech to the Indian Nations, November 14, 1763, MPAFD, 5:295–96.

46. Usner, *Indians, Settlers, and Slaves*, 123–26; Gold, *Borderland Empires in Transition*, 169–72.

47. For native migrations, see Usner, *Indians, Settlers, and Slaves*, 131; Gold, *Borderland Empires in Transition*, 165.

48. Adair, *The History of the American Indians*, 310. Johnstone's remarks to Gage are quoted in Rea, "'Graveyard for Britons,'" 349. Elias Durnford, "A Description of West Florida with the State of It's [sic] Settlements," in Durnford to Dartmouth, January 15, 1774, C.O. 5/591.

49. Lt. Ford to Farmar, November 24, 1763, MPAED, 1:23; Farmar to the Secretary of War, January 24, 1764, MPAED, 1:12, 17 (quotation); Major William Forbes to the Secretary of State, MPAED, 1:142–43.

50. See the letter of Major Loftus to Major General Thomas Gage, April 9, 1764, in Alvord and Carter, *The Critical Period*, 237–39; Rea, *Major Robert Farmar*, 38, 45–46; Pittman, *The Present State of the European Settlements on the Mississippi*, xiii–xvi. For Tunica motivations, see Fabel, *Colonial Challenges*, 95–96.

51. Loftus to Gage, April 9, 1764, and Journal of Abbadie, March–April 1764, both in Alvord and Carter, *The Critical Period*, 238 and 174–82, respectively.

52. Journal of Abbadie, April 1764, ibid., 180–81.

53. Johnstone to the Board of Trade, October 31, 1764, MPAED, 1:168. For French Louisiana's illicit trade prior to 1763, see Dawdy, *Building the Devil's Empire*, 109–15.

54. Johnstone's notice, along with Choiseul's proclamation, is printed in the *South-Carolina Gazette*, Dec. 17, 1764.

55. Johnstone to Pownall, February 19, 1765, PRO, Treasury 1, vol. 437 (1765). Since Johnstone did not communicate his correspondents' names or include transcripts of their messages, one cannot be certain that he received quite so many letters as implied. See Fabel, *The Economy of British West Florida*, 78.

56. *An Impartial History of the Late Glorious War*, 310.

57. Johnstone to the Board of Trade, February 19, 1765, PRO, Treasury 1, vol. 437. See also Halifax to the Lords of Trade, February 9, 1765, PRO, State Papers, 37/4.

Johnstone also wanted an exemption for the admission of Spanish dyewoods, which were imported to West Florida in the absence of any clear prohibition. See Fabel, *The Economy of British West Florida*, 78–83.

58. For the governor's plans for "Point Iberville," see Johnstone to Archibald Robertson, February 9, 1765, MPAED, 1:280–83; Johnstone to Pownall, May 4, 1765, MPAED, 278–79. Johnstone was at Mobile in the fall of 1766. See Johnstone to Elias Lagardere, November 21, 1766, C.O. 5/574.

59. Johnstone to John Lindsay, December 10, 1764, quoted in Rea, "A Naval Visitor in British West Florida," 144. See also Johnstone to Archibald Robertson, February 9, 1765, MPAED, 1:280–83; Johnstone to Pownall, May 4, 1765, MPAED, 1: 278–79. See also Brown, "The Iberville Canal Project," 494.

60. Johnstone to the Board of Trade, February 19, 1765, MPAED, 1:271–73. See also Johnstone to Sir John Lindsay, December 10, 1764, MPAED, 1:263–64. For the problem of the "barricado" and "rubbish," see Pittman, *The Present State of European Settlements on the Mississippi*, 31.

61. *Plan of Point Ibberville*, 1765, Louisiana—Maps, William L. Clements Library, University of Michigan. The "Anatamaha" literally meant "the fishplace" in native speech. See Pittman, *The Present State of European Settlements on the Mississippi*, 30. See also Brown, "The Iberville Canal Project," 496–97.

62. For the Alibamon and Houma attack, see Archibald Robertson to George Johnstone, September 2, 1765, C.O. 5/574. See also Rea, *Major Robert Farmar*, 63–64; Conover, "British West Florida's Mississippi Frontier Posts," 178.

63. MPAED, 1: 221, 232 (last quotation).

64. *Mémoire de Monsieur le Comte de Montault de Monberaut* [1765], C.O. 5/587. Montault's lengthiest plea to British authorities is available in translation. See Howard and Rea, *The Memoire Justificatif of the Chevalier Montault de Monberaut*, 25–28, 43–51. For accusations of French "intrigue" with Indian peoples, see Johnstone and Stuart to the Earl of Halifax, June 12, 1765, MPAED, 1:184.

65. See Johnstone's speech, March 26, 1765, MPAED, 1:222. Johnstone told the Choctaw and Chickasaw headmen of Montault's cooperation with the British during this speech. For a slightly different wording of this speech, see De Vorsey, *The Indian Boundary in the Southern Colonies*, 208.

66. For speech of Tomatly Mingo, April 1, 1765, see MPAED, 1:237–39. See also the speech of Alibamo Mingo, MPAED, 1:239–41. For the issue of medals, see White, *The Roots of Dependency*, 72–73.

67. Robert Farmer to Gage, December 16–19, 1765, in Alvord and Carter, *The New Régime*, 127–28; O'Brien, *Choctaws in a Revolutionary Age*, 72.

68. For a measurement of distances, see Journal of Captain Harry Gordon, 1766, in Alvord and Carter, *The New Régime*, 291–98, 310. For British military observations, see Captain Stirling to General Gage, December 15, 1765; Lt. Fraser to Gage, December 16, 1765, in Alvord and Carter, *The New Régime*, 124–25, 130–31.

69. See "The humble Address of the first British settlers . . ." to Robert Farmar, January 21, 1764, printed in the *Georgia Gazette*, February 23, 1764.

70. Johnstone to Elias Lagardere, November 21, 1766, C.O. 5/574.

71. The exchange between Topoye and Stuart was recorded by the latter at Mobile, June 23, 1766, C.O. 323/24. For a brief mention of the Coosadas, see Saunt, *A New Order of Things*, 167.

72. "Shouloushamastabé alias red Shoes his Talk...," July 4, 1766; "Tomatle [Tomatly] Mingo Great Medal Chief of Sesseacha [Seneacha] his Talk...," July 12, 1766; Charles Stuart's "answers" attached, C.O. 323/24. For the murder, see White, *The Roots of Dependency*, 74.

73. Piker, "'White & Clean' & Contested," 315–47.

74. For the complaint of Georgia merchants and related issues, see Braund, *Deerskins and Duffels*, 114 (quotation), 130–38, 146–47. For the rum traffic, see Johnstone to Elias Lagardere, November 21, 1766, C.O. 5/574. The Chickasaw trade is discussed in Adair, *The History of the American Indians*, 370.

75. This report came via a Choctaw war party that assailed the Creeks shortly after the latter had killed the two Britons. See Charles Stuart to John Stuart, October 1, 1766, Board of Trade, microfilm B-3501, LCAN.

76. Johnstone to Conway, June 23, 1766, MPAED, 1:511–13.

77. Johnstone to John Stuart, September 30, 1766, C.O. 323/24. For the trial of one John Plumb for murdering an Indian, see Johnstone to Elias Lagardere, November 21, 1766, C.O. 5/574. This episode is very probably the same that is discussed in Adair, *History of the American Indians*, 294–95.

78. Johnstone to Conway, June 23, 1766, MPAED, 1:512. Johnstone had the support of his provincial council, but not the royal military.

79. See Gage to Tayler, December 18, 1766, FHMSS.

80. Shelburne's rebuke of Johnstone is in his recall order of February 19, 1767, C.O. 5/618. For Johnstone's plan of destroying the Creeks, see Johnstone to Conway, June 23, 1766, MPAED, 1:513. Johnstone's request for a six-month leave was granted on September 22, 1766. See C.O. 5/618.

81. Fabel, *Bombast and Broadsides*, 28, 53–56, 60.

CHAPTER 2

1. John Thomas to John Stuart, December 12, 1771, HPMSS.

2. Moore, *Revolt in Louisiana*, 199–208.

3. "A Description of West Florida with the State of It's [sic] Settlements," in Durnford to Dartmouth, January 15, 1774, C.O. 5/591. For immigration trends, see Fabel, *The Economy of British West Florida*, 6–20, 32–38, 173–75.

4. "A Description of West Florida," in Durnford to Dartmouth, January 15, 1774, C.O. 5/591.

5. Ekberg, *French Roots in the Illinois Country*, 88–99. See also DuVal, *The Native Ground*, 120–41; Calloway, *One Vast Winter Count*, 356–63.

6. Usner, *Indians, Settlers, and Slaves*, 108.

7. Including Arkansas and the Illinois country, the Louisiana census of 1777 enumerates 8,381 whites, 273 free mulattoes, 263 free blacks, 545 mulatto slaves, and 8,464 "Negro" slaves (a total of 17,926 individuals). See "*Padrón General de todos los Individuos de la Provincia de Louisiana,*" May 12, 1777, PC, legajo 2351. For the diverse range of Loui-

siana's colonial economy, see Usner, *Indians, Settlers, and Slaves,* 106–7, 119–20, 158–64; Morris, *The Big Muddy,* 56–67; Clark, *New Orleans,* 54–57.

8. On January 20, 1767, Ulloa and Aubry made a formal declaration of their joint administration pending the arrival of additional Spanish troops. See Moore, *Revolt in Louisiana,* 48–49. Denis-Nicolas Foucault, French Louisiana's administrative chief (*commissaire-odinnateur*), remained in office. See Brasseaux, *Denis-Nicolas Foucault,* 9–10, 51–57.

9. Ulloa to Johnstone, April 1, 1766, and Johnstone to Ulloa, May 3, 1766, C.O. 5/583. Johnstone's derogatory remarks are in his letter of July 19, 1766, to John Pownall (Secretary to the Board of Trade), C.O. 5/583.

10. Bolton, *Texas in the Middle Eighteenth Century,* 104–6.

11. Din, "Protecting the 'Barrera,'" 187–92; Moore, *Revolt in Louisiana,* 70–79.

12. Haldimand signed the proclamation at Pensacola on January 14, 1768. For a reproduction, see McMurtrie, *A Newly-Discovered Broadside Printed at New Orleans in 1768.* Haldimand's proclamation brought in about forty deserters after he extended the deadline for their return. See Rea, "Military Deserters from British West Florida," 134–35.

13. An exception to loose customs enforcement came in 1773, with the Spanish seizure of a Rhode Island vessel for smuggling. See Fabel, *The Economy of British West Florida,* 85–94.

14. Ulloa's optimistic views about immigration to Louisiana are expressed in an undated official report of 1767, SMV, 2, pt. 1:17. See also Ulloa to Grimaldi, September 29, 1766, in Chandler, "Ulloa and the Acadians," 89–91; Brasseaux, *The Founding of New Acadia,* 73–88; Faragher, *A Great and Noble Scheme.*

15. Ulloa's instructions for Walker's tour are documented in Chandler, "Odyssey Continued,"454–55. See also Jerningham to Ulloa, December 14, 1767, SMV, 2, pt. 1, 39.

16. Jerningham to Ulloa, November 28, 1767, in Robertson, "A Projected Settlement of English-speaking Catholics," 323–24; Ulloa to Grimaldi, February 11, 1768, SMV, 2, pt. 1, 41.

17. Captain James Campbell to Johnstone, December 12, 1764; Lt. Maclellan to Johnstone, December 10, 1764, MPAED, 1:267–69. See the Earl of Halifax to George Johnstone, September 8, 1764; Caminade to Halifax, February 18, 1765; Caminade to Johnstone, June 15, 1765, MPAED, 1:284–88; Johnstone to Halifax, February 19, 1765, MPAED, 1:151, 178–83, 255–56.

18. For Browne's critic, see the untitled broadside, December 12, 1766, Charles-Town [S.C.], Early American Imprints, First ser., no. 10252. Browne's abuse of the Irish and his quarrels with French Huguenot immigrants are discussed in Fabel, *The Economy of British West Florida,* 12–14; Starr, "Campbell Town," 532–47. The 17,400 acres represented most of a 20,000-acre mandamus grant that Browne held from the crown. See Howard, *The British Development of West Florida,* 87, 105.

19. The bayous were Lacombe and Grand Coquille. See Browne to Hillsborough, July 6. 1768, C.O. 5/557. Two Tangipahoa men did not take the loyalty oath because they were also Louisiana landowners. See Lt. Alexander Fraser to Frederick Haldimand, July 12, 1768, HPLCAN (microfilm H-1438).

20. Browne to Hillsborough, July 6, 1768, C.O. 5/557. For critical comments on Browne, see Lt. Alexander Fraser to Haldimand, June 29, 1768, HPLCAN (H-1438).

21. Narrative of Edward Mease [1770–1771], in Rowland, *Publications of the Mississippi Historical Society*, 5:77. For the defeat of the Natchez in 1730, see Usner, *Indians, Settlers, and Slaves*, 73.

22. Browne to Hillsborough, July 6, 1768, C.O. 5/557. For the historical context, see Usner, *Indians, Settlers, and Slaves*, 70–82.

23. The Louisiana Superior Council appealed to France for support. See "Memoir of the October 29 Revolt in Louisiana, for Presentation to His Royal Highness, His Lordship the Duke of Orleans," in Meneray, *The Rebellion of 1768*, 34–35. For the nationalist slogan on wines, see Moore, *Revolt in Louisiana*, 161.

24. Noyan to Haldimand, August 18, 1768, HPLCAN (H-1438). See also Moore, *Revolt in Louisiana*, 173; Rodríguez Casado, *Primeros años de dominación española en la Luisiana*, 142.

25. The chevalier de Noyan to Haldimand, August 18, 1768, HPLCAN (H-1438).

26. Caminade to Haldimand, August 13, 1768, with postscript, August 20, 1768, ibid.

27. Masan also sent assurance that Ulloa's removal had followed a strictly legal form. See Masan to Haldimand, November 2 and 7, 1768, HPMSS. For Ulloa's perspective on the Pensacola talks, see Gayarré, *History of Louisiana*, 2:232.

28. Saintelette, who received several West Florida land grants in 1767, was another Louisiana resident with close ties to Pensacola. See Howard, *The Economic Development of British West Florida*, 86.

29. Haldimand's criticism of both Ulloa and the rebels is expressed in a confidential assessment to French magistrate Aubry at New Orleans. See Haldimand to Aubry, January 10, 1769 (quotation), HPMSS.

30. Memoir of the October 29 Revolt in Louisiana, in Meneray, *The Rebellion of 1768*, 26, 36 (quotation).

31. Statement of Lafrénière, October 29, 1768, translated in Gayarré, *History of Louisiana*, 2:379. For the decree of March 23, 1768, see Moore, *Revolt in Louisiana*, 111–13; Clark, *New Orleans*, 166–68.

32. *Mémoire, des Habitans et Négocians de la Louisiane*, 7, 16. Montfort Browne forwarded a printed copy of this memorial to Whitehall. See Browne to Hillsborough, February 28, 1769, C.O. 5/577. For Haldimand's rejection of the rebels' plea, see Rodríguez Casado, *Primeros años de dominación española en la Luisiana*, 221–24.

33. *Représentations... par tous les Habitans, Négocians, Artizans & autres Peuples*, October 29, 1768 (New Orleans, 1768), in Browne to Hillsborough, December 1, 1768, C.O. 5/579. For a translation of the *Représentations*, adopted by the Superior Council, see Gayarré, *History of Louisiana*, 2:378.

34. According to Browne, fifty of Louisiana's "principal Inhabitants" were readying a statement for him requesting that they be allowed to settle at "the Natchez." Browne to Hillsborough, December 1, 1768, C.O. 5/586.

35. Gage to Haldimand, June 27, 1768, HPMSS.

36. Ibid.

37. Browne to Haldimand, August 14, 1768, HPMSS. For his warnings of an Indian attack, see Browne to Hillsborough, August 16 and August 25, 1768, C.O. 5/585.

38. "The Memorial of the Council and Assembly of His Majesty's Province of West Florida," August 24, 1768, West Florida Papers, reel 1, LC. The petition of West Florida

inhabitants, signed by twenty-two men, was forwarded by Browne to Haldimand by a letter of August 14, 1768, HPMSS.

39. Memoir from the Planters and Merchants of Louisiana to His Majesty [Louis XV], [1768], in Meneray, *The Rebellion of 1768*, 19.

40. See Observations of the Louisiana Superior Council to the Parliament of Paris [1769?], ibid., 38.

41. Hillsborough suggested to the Spanish ambassador at London that Carlos III might cede Louisiana to Britain, but he did not pursue this idea when rebuffed. See Moore, *Revolt in Louisiana*, 175, 188.

42. Rodríguez Casado, *Primeros años de dominación española*, 282–91 (for quotations, see pp. 287–88); Boulle, "French Reactions to the Louisiana Revolution of 1768," 148–50.

43. Moore, *Revolt in Louisiana*, 195.

44. Browne to Hillsborough, "The State & Condition of New Orleans and Louisiana," February 28, 1769 (quotations). See also a second letter of the same date by Browne to Hillsborough, C.O. 5/577. Browne incorrectly identified Natchitoches as a German settlement in his description of Louisiana.

45. Browne to Hillsborough, February 28, 1769. I have quoted the New Orleans remonstrance, which Browne copied verbatim, with one spelling error. See *Mémoire, des Habitans et Négocians*, 4.

46. Hillsborough to Browne, July 17, 1769, C.O. 5/586. Browne was quite hopeful after receiving this message. See Browne to Hillsborough, October 8, 1769, C.O. 5/587.

47. Campbell wrote his report after returning to Pensacola. See Campbell to Browne, October 9, 1769, C.O. 5/587. Browne moved politically ahead of his provincial council, which was more cautious about granting land to French Louisiana newcomers without royal approval. See Padgett, "Minutes of the Council of West Florida," 375.

48. Montfort Browne to Gage, August 19, 1769; Browne to Hillsborough, August 20–21, 1769; James Campbell to Browne, July 30, 1769, C.O. 5/577. O'Reilly's official report specifies the occupying force as including *"compañias de milicias de Blancos, Pardos, y Morenos,"* "Oficio de D. Alejandro O'Reilly a D. Julián Arriaga," August 30, 1769, BN, THNOC. For another report magnifying the Spanish force, see John Fitzpatrick to McGillivray and Struthers, August 4, 1769, in Dalrymple, *The Merchant of Manchac*, 465.

49. The executed men were Nicolas Chauvin de Lafrénière, Jean-Baptiste de Noyan, Pierre Marquis, Pierre Caresse, and Joseph Milhet. One additional individual died before he was pronounced guilty of treason. Five others found guilty were sentenced to imprisonment in Cuba. See Moore, *Revolt in Louisiana*, 198–209.

50. Proclamation of August 21, 1769, BN, THNOC. (This proclamation was issued in the French language.) The taking of the loyalty oath by Acadian and German settlers is in "Oficio de D. Alejandro O'Reilly a D. Julián de Arriaga," August 30, 1769, BN, THNOC. O'Reilly soon permitted Acadians living at a remote upriver post to join their compatriots to the south. See Brasseaux, *Founding of New Acadia*, 89.

51. For Gage's friendly note, translated into Spanish, see Gage to O'Reilly, November 18, 1769, PC, legajo 2370. Gage's interest in invading Louisiana in wartime is discussed below.

52. José Melchior de Acosta, a Spanish captain in Louisiana, claimed that three prominent rebels were employing slaves to clear ground near the Pearl River in West Florida

in advance of O'Reilly's mission. Ringleader Lafrénière allegedly planned to do so as well. For Acosta's claim, see his testimony given at Havana, May 22, 1769, BN, THNOC. See also Moore, *Revolt in Louisiana*, 166, 205–6.

53. Jones to Haldimand, March 14, 1770, HPLCAN, (H-1439). British military engineers George Gauld and Thomas Hutchins shared Jones's view that creole flight was held back by the absence of English troops by the Mississippi. See George Gauld, "A General Description of the Sea Coasts, Harbours, Lakes, Rivers &c. of the Province of West Florida, 1769," American Philosophical Society, Philadelphia; Hutchins Draft report to Thomas Gage, [1773], Thomas Hutchins Papers (Box 2), HSP.

54. The legislation allowed local persons to choose up to twelve magistrates who would decide certain civil and criminal cases and "make rules and order for the good of their community." For the act of June 28, 1769, see Rea and Howard, *The Minutes, Journals, and Acts of the General Assembly of British West Florida*, 360. For the crown's veto of West Florida legislation, see Hillsborough to Chester, December 11, 1770, C.O. 5/587; Richard Jackson, Esq., July 30, 1770, to the Board of Trade, C.O. 5/577. Jackson's legal opinion objected to the establishment of "a Subordinate Province" within West Florida where a "proscribed" religion, i.e., Catholicism, would be sanctioned.

55. Browne landed a governor's post in the Bahamas in 1774. After arriving in the islands, he journeyed to West Florida and toured his Mississippi holdings in preparation for new profiteering. See Fabel, "An Eighteenth Colony," 652–61 (quotation, p. 661).

56. Hillsborough to Gage, January 2 and 22, 1771, in Carter, *Correspondence of General Thomas Gage*, 2:22–26.

57. Gage to Hillsborough, April 2, 1771, in Carter, *Correspondence of General Thomas Gage*, 1:294–96 (quotation, p. 295); Gage to Haldimand, March 28 and 29, 1771, HPMSS; Haldimand to Gage, February 13, 1771, HPMSS.

58. Hutchins to Gage, draft report [1773], Hutchins Papers, Box 2-80, HSP. See also Treagle, "British Spy along the Mississippi." Unzaga sent his own spy, French planter Juan de Surriret, to Pensacola and New York City in 1772, to observe British military movements. See Cummins, *Spanish Observers and the American Revolution*, 22–23.

59. Hutchins's report of 1773 echoed ideas of Elias Durnford. See Hutchins, "Remarks relating to the Rivers Mississippi, Ibberville [sic], Amit & Lakes Maurepas & Pontcha[r]train," Hutchins Papers, Box 1, HSP; Chester to Hillsborough, September 28, 1771, C.O. 5/578.

60. "The Communication Between the Iberville & the River Mississippi," in Durnford to Hillsborough, June 11, 1770, C.O. 5/587; Durnford, "Estimate of the Expence [sic] which will attend making the proposed Cut from the River Mississippi to the River Ibberville [sic]," in Chester to Hillsborough, September 28, 1771, C.O. 5/578 (this letter included five Durnford maps). See also "Estimates for the Necessary Posts in West Florida," in Durnford to Hillsborough, March 25, 1770, C.O. 5/587. His "Plan of the proposed New Town also the proposed Cut from the Mississippi to the Iberville," British Museum, is reprinted in Dalrymple, *The Merchant of Manchac*, illustration between pp. 196–97.

61. Gage to Haldimand, May 18 and June 10, 1772, HPMSS. See also Chester to Hillsborough, September 28, 1771, C.O. 5/578.

62. Chester to Hillsborough, August 28, 1771, C.O. 5/588; Elias Durnford, "Some

Thoughts on the Indian Trade," in Durnford to Hillsborough, February 18, 1770, C.O. 5/587. See also Greg O'Brien, "Supplying Our Wants: Choctaws and Chickasaws Reassess the Trade Relationship with Britain, 1771–72," in Brown, *Coastal Encounters*, 60.

63. For complaints of rum sales, see the speech of Captain Ouma, January 2, 1772, in Rowland, *Publications*, 5:150. Mingo Emitta pointedly asked John Stuart: "What can our White Brethren think of us by giving such narrow Flaps, they don't cover our Secret parts, and we are in danger of being deprived of our Manhood, by every Hungry dog That approaches us." See Speech of Mingo Emitta, January 2, 1772, in Rowland, *Publications*, 5:148.

64. John Thomas to Chester, November 26, 1772, C.O. 5/589. See also Dalrymple, *The Merchant of Manchac*, 17; Fabel, *The Economy of British West Florida*, 57; Fabel, *Colonial Challenges*, 126–28. Thomas was acquitted of murder in October 1772, but he was still rebuked by the West Florida council. See Rea, "Redcoats and Redskins on the Lower Mississippi," 5–35.

65. John Thomas to John Stuart, December 12, 1771, HPMSS; Fitzpatrick to Miller, Swanson, and Company, May 8, 1773, in Dalrymple, *The Merchant of Manchac*, 147.

66. Charles Stuart was cousin to John Stuart and held the post of deputy superintendent under him. See Alden, *John Stuart*, 212. For Stuart's diplomacy and the situation of the small nations, see Fabel, *Colonial Challenges*, 131–32; Usner, *Indians, Settlers, and Slaves*, 165–69. In 1770, General O'Reilly sent one James O'Kelley to spy on Lt. Thomas at Manchac. See Cummins, *Spanish Observers*, 14–15.

67. Stuart to Hillsborough, February 7, 1771, DAR, 5:37. Two French interlocutors were Jean (Juan) de la Villebeuvre and Esteban Trudeau, both officers in Spain's Louisiana battalion. See Din, "'For Defense of Country and Glory of Arms,'" 11. For Stuart's report conveying Creek attitudes, see his letter to Hillsborough, February 6, 1772, DAR, 5:35; Chester to Hillsborough, September 10, 1771, C.O. 5/578.

68. See, for example, Emisteseguo's speeches of October 29–31, 1771, in Rowland, *Mississippi Historical Society Publications*, 5:115–29. For Stuart's concerns about Escochabey, see Alden, *John Stuart*, 325–27. David Taitt, British Indian agent, had strong concerns of Creek-Spanish collusion. See Taitt to John Stuart, September 9, 1772, HPLCAN (H-1430).

69. McIntosh to Charles Stuart, September 3, 1772, encl. in Peter Chester to Hillsborough, November 16, 1772, C.O. 5/579. For the Shawnee-Cherokee-Creek communications, see Dowd, *A Spirited Resistance*, 43–44.

70. Braund, *Deerskins and Duffels*, 161. For British responses to Creek-Choctaw warfare, see Taitt to John Stuart, January 3 and 12, 1774; Stuart to Haldimand, January 5, 1774, HPLCAN (H-1430).

71. Chester to the Earl of Dartmouth, March 7, 1774, C.O. 5/591.

72. John Bradley to Elias Durnford, February 1, 1770; Account of John Fergy [February 5, 1770], in Durnford to Hillsborough, February 6, 1770, C.O. 5/577. For frontier turmoil and banditry, see Usner, *Indians, Settlers, and Slaves*, 126–30.

73. Testimony of Daniel Huay, August 25, 1770, enclosed with John McIntire to Peter Chester, July 19, 1770, C.O. 5/588.

74. For the West Florida provincial grants, see "A State of all, Grants of Land which have passed the Great Seal of the Province of West Florida on Family Right and Pur-

chase since the Arrival of His Excellency Governor Chester at Pensacola on the 10th day of August 1770 to the 4th day of November 1773," in Chester to Dartmouth, December 20, 1773, C.O. 5/591. The Privy Council made 114 grants totaling 1.4 million acres in East Florida between 1766 and 1775, but only a small fraction of these mandamus grants, which were issued by royal command, resulted in settlement. See Mowat, *East Florida as a British Province*, 54–65. See also Johnson, *British West Florida*, 119.

75. Gage to Haldimand, October 31, 1770, HPMSS.

76. Hillsborough to Chester, February 11, 1771, C.O. 5/588.

77. Three Jewish traders and some Frenchmen were expelled for suspected commerce with Veracruz and Campeche—an offense against the inviolability of New Spain. For O'Reilly's policy, see Bjork, "The Establishment of Spanish Rule," 215; Fabel, *The Economy of British West Florida*, 89; O'Reilly to Arriaga, October 17, 1769, SMV, 2, pt. 1:97. See also Korn, *The Early Jews of New Orleans*, 31–33.

78. Cummins, "Oliver Pollock," 198–218; Cummins, "Oliver Pollock's Plantations," 35–48. On December 2, 1772, the West Florida council approved a grant of 400 acres for Pollock at Tangipahoa. See C.O. 5/589.

79. Romans, *A Concise Natural History of East and West Florida*, 113. See also Fabel, *The Economy of British West Florida*, 92–94. For the Havana trade, see John Fitzpatrick to George Morgan, September 12, 1770; Fitzpatrick to John Ritson, February 22, 1771, in Dalrymple, *The Merchant of Manchac*, 95, 103. For the Spanish prohibition of Louisiana's trade with the French West Indies, see Julián de Arriaga to Luis de Unzaga y Amezaga, June 20, 1771, PC, legajo 174.

80. Fabel, "The Letters of R," 402–27. Three letters of "R," written from New Orleans on December 22, 1772, January 8, 1773, and January 24, 1773, were published in New York on September 13, September 27, and October 18, 1773, respectively.

81. Fabel, "Letters of R," 417 (January 8, 1773), 427 (quotation of January 24, 1773). These letters may have stimulated New York and New Jersey interest in Mississippi colonization. On July 18, 1773, the packet *New Jersey and Mississippi* left Elizabeth Town with seventy persons bound for West Florida. See Fabel, "An Eighteenth Colony," 667.

82. Mézières to Unzaga, February 1, 1770, in Bolton, *Athanase de Mézières and the Louisiana-Texas Frontier, 1768–1780*, 1:142–43.

83. Durnford to Hillsborough, February 3, 1770, C.O. 5/587; Durnford to Hillsborough, June 12–13, 1770, C.O. 5/587; Juan Fernando de Palacio to John Chaloner Jackson, March 21, 1770, encl. in Durnford to Hillsborough, June 12, 1770, C.O. 5/587.

84. For the absolute prohibition on Louisiana's commerce with New Spain, see O'Reilly to Bucareli, April 3, 1770, PC, legajo 1055.

85. The East Texas frontier regulations followed the recommendations of the marqués de Rubí, who made a grand visitation of the Interior Provinces in 1766–67. See Weber, *The Spanish Frontier in North America*, 205–20; Chipman, *Spanish Texas*, 186–87; La Vere, "Between Kinship and Capitalism," 209; J. Edward Townes, "The Nature of Loyalty: Antonio Gil Ibarvo and the East Texas Frontier," in Smith and Hilton, *Nexus of Empire*, 164–82.

86. John, *Storms Brewed in Other Men's Worlds*, 383–84; Burton, "Vagabonds along the Spanish Louisiana-Texas Frontier," 460–61.

87. Lyman's petition stated his intention to cultivate indigo, hemp, and tobacco.

"The Memorial of Phineas Lyman" to the Board of Trade, received February 16, 1770, C.O. 5/577. For detailed accounts of the Military Adventurers, see Fabel, *The Economy of British West Florida*, chap. 7; Bailyn, *Voyagers to the West*, 484–88.

88. See "Plan Proposed by Genl. Phineas Lyman, for Settling Louisiana, and erecting New Colonies between West Florida and the Falls of St. Anthony" [ca. 1766], Shelburne Papers, 48:3, William L. Clements Library, University of Michigan.

89. "The Memorial of Phineas Lyman" to the Board of Trade, received February 16, 1770, C.O. 5/577. For the fear of "Hot Climates," see "General Lyman's Reasons for a Settlement on the Mississippi" [1766], in Alvord and Carter, *New Régime*, 272.

90. See Memorial of Colonel Israel Putnam, Captain Roger Enos, Mr. Thaddeus Lyman, and Lt. Rufus Putnam, March 5, 1773, C.O. 5/590. In July 1773 Chester and council reserved nineteen townships, each of 23,000 acres, for the Military Adventurers pending royal approval—and on condition that settlement begin by March 5, 1774. See Memorial of Major Timothy Herlihy et al., March 5, 1774, C.O. 5/591.

91. See the journal of Rufus Putnam in Bates, *The Two Putnams*, 165, 192–97. For the scouting expedition, see Fabel, "Encounters Up the Mississippi, Yazoo, and Big Black Rivers," 95–103. The precise number of New Englanders arriving in 1774 is not known. Five leaders stated that 104 persons of their group had already arrived, or were on their way to West Florida, along with family members. See Memorial of Timothy Herlihy et al., March 5, 1774, C.O. 5/591.

92. For "the Jersey Settlement," see Claiborne, *Mississippi, as a Province, Territory and State*, 107. The West Florida council reserved Swayze's grant on condition of settlement by May 1, 1774. See Council minutes, April 19, 1773, C.O. 5/590. About this time Amos Ogden of New Jersey sold 19,000 acres of his 25,000 royal grant near Natchez to Samuel Swayze. See Haynes, *The Natchez District and the American Revolution*, 15. For the supply of flour, see John Fitzpatrick to Jesse Lum, October 7, 1773, in Dalrymple, *The Merchant of Manchac*, 161.

93. Chester to Dartmouth, May 16, 1773, and August 28, 1773, C.O. 5/590. For migration trends, see Fabel, *The Economy of British West Florida*, 15, 34, 174–75. A contemporary view is in Elias Durnford, "A Description of West Florida with the State of It's Settlements," January 15, 1774, C.O. 5/591. Durnford wrote of "Families entering the Province not only by Sea, from New England, New York, Georgia & East Florida but by the River Ohio, from the Back Settlements of Maryland Virginia & Carolina's."

94. Washington to James Wood, March 13, 1773; Washington to William Crawford, September 25, 1773 (quotation), GWLC. Philip Livingston, of New York's elite family, obtained the West Florida provincial secretary's office in 1770, and soon thereafter amassed fees and huge land grants through his privileged position at Pensacola. See Robin F.A. Fabel, "Philip Livingston, Chameleon 'Premier' of West Florida," in Smith and Hilton, *Nexus of Empire*, 183–97.

95. Dartmouth to John Stuart, March 3, 1773, in DAR, 6:95. See also the Board of Trade's report of January 23, 1773, opposing Montfort Browne's scheme to establish an interior colony on the Mississippi. DAR, 6:5. For the Order in Council of April 7, 1773, see DAR, 6:118. For the Board of Trade's growing apprehensions about interior colonies, see its report of April 29, 1772, DAR, 5:79–89. See also Bailyn, *Voyagers to the West*, 31–32, 49–55; Sosin, *Whitehall and the Wilderness*, 208–10.

96. Gage to Haldimand, November 28, 1773, HPMSS.

97. Fabel, *The Economy of British West Florida*, 183–88.

98. By spring of 1774, two of the gang were tried and executed, but others remained at large. For details of the murders, see E. R. Wegg to Governor Peter Chester, November 25, 1773, C.O. 5/591; Chester to Dartmouth, August 28, 1773, C.O. 5/590 and June 6, 1774, C.O. 5/591.

99. Urquhart to Chester, July 1, 1773, encl. in Chester to Dartmouth, August 28, 1773, C.O. 5/590.

100. Lt. John Campbell to Dartmouth (quotation), May 1774, C.O. 5/592; Chester to Dartmouth, November 20, 1775. For the congressional overture, see Starr, *Tories, Dons, and Rebels*, 44–45.

CHAPTER 3

1. Quoted in Oltra and Pérez Samper, *El conde de Aranda y los Estados Unidos*, 122.

2. Aranda to Grimaldi, January 13, 1777, in Yela Utrilla, *España ante la independencia de los Estados Unidos* (cited hereafter as Yela Utrilla), 2:46–47.

3. Floridablanca replaced Grimaldi as minister of state in February 1777. For a detailed discussion of Floridablanca's policy, see Ruigómez de Hernández, *El gobierno español del despotismo ilustrado ante la independencia de los Estados Unidos de América*, 214–16, 225–30.

4. My interpretation, emphasizing the interplay of U.S.-Spanish rivalry and cooperation, differs from that of Thomas E. Chávez, whose worthwhile book tends to downplay the mutual competition between Spain and the United States during the Revolutionary War. See Chávez, *Spain and the Independence of the United States: An Intrinsic Gift* (Albuquerque: University of New Mexico Press, 2002).

5. Chester to Germain, October 26, 1776, C.O. 5/593.

6. The gunpowder amounted to some 100 quintals or 10,000 lbs. See Unzaga to Navarro, September 20, 1776, SMV, 2, pt. 1:234; James, *Oliver Pollock*, 64–69.

7. For the seizures, see Francis Duplessis to Robert Morris, August 12, 1776, Levis Collection, HSP; Pollock to the president of Congress, September 18, 1782, Oliver Pollock Papers, LC; Pollock to Andrew Allen and Robert Morris, October 10, 1776, LC.

8. The Virginia committee of safety wrote Louisiana's governor of Gibson's mission without specifying what the captain would propose in person. The committee's letter of May 22, 1776, is enclosed in Unzaga to José de Gálvez, September 7, 1776, SD, legajo 2596. For a Spanish-language transcription, with English translation, of Unzaga's letter, see Robertson, "Spanish Correspondence Concerning the American Revolution," 300–304. Gibson's written questions (in English) on the Pensacola campaign are enclosed in Unzaga to Gálvez, September 30, 1776. For a transcription, see Caughey, *Bernardo de Gálvez in Louisiana*, 135.

9. Patrick Henry kept informed of Gibson's mission. See Henry to Edmund Pendleton, November 22, 1776, Executive Communications, Misc. reel 5372, Library of Virginia (Richmond).

10. Lee to the governor of Louisiana, May 1776, PC, legajo 2370.

11. Unzaga to José de Gálvez, September 7, 1776, SD, legajo 2596; Robertson, "Spanish Correspondence," 300–301. See also James, *Oliver Pollock*, 64–70.

12. Unzaga to Lee, September 4, 1776, SD, legajo 2596; Robertson, "Spanish Correspondence," 305–6.

13. Gálvez to the captain general of Cuba [the marqués de la Torre], December 23–24, 1776, in Robertson, "Spanish Correspondence," 304–5 [SD, legajo, 2596]. For Spanish contributions to the American war effort, see José A. Armillas Vicente, "*Ayuda secreta y deuda oculta: España y la independencia de los Estados Unidos*," in López-Chicheri, *Norteamérica a finales del siglo XVIII*, 177, 181; Rodríguez, *La revolución americana*, 84.

14. Oliver Pollock to Committee of Congress, [April?] 1777, Pollock Papers, LC. Commerce committee to Pollock, October 24, 1977, ibid., LC.

15. Chester to Germain, October 26, 1776, and Chester to Unzaga, November 4, 1776, C.O. 5/593. For the situation of British forces, see Chester to Germain, September 14, 1776, C.O. 5/593; Germain to Chester, August 7, 1776, C.O. 5/592. By June 1777, British soldiers in the Gulf ports amounted to 800, and were still consumed in garrison duty. See "Return of His Majesty's Forces," June 3, 1777, C.O. 5/593.

16. Germain to Chester, February 7, 1777, C.O. 5/593.

17. For the proposal of a campaign launched northward from Mobile, see Stuart to Henry Clinton, May 9, 1776, in Davies, DAR, 12:135–36. See also Wright, *Florida in the American Revolution*, 34. For the use of Pensacola, see Stuart to Gage, October 24, 1775, DAR, 11:164; John Stuart to Henry Stuart, October 24, 1775, DAR, 11:162–64. For the necessity of Indian unity, see Stuart to Clinton, March 15, 1776, DAR, 12:79 (quotation). For British policy, see Corkran, *The Creek Frontier*, 254–58, 268–75, 284–87, 299–300.

18. John Stuart to Germain, August 23, 1776, DAR, 12:188–91; Stuart to Germain, November 24, 1776, DAR, 12:253–54. Stuart described the refugees as men, women, and children—a group "entirely naked and destitute." See Stuart to Germain, January 23, 1777, DAR, 14:35. See also Calloway, *The American Revolution in Indian Country*, 198–99.

19. Charles Stuart to John Stuart, August 19, 1776, and David Taitt to John Stuart, August 26, 1776, West Florida Council, September 4, 1776, C.O. 5/593.

20. Emisteseguo conveyed his "talk" to Stuart through agent Alexander Cameron. See Emisteseguo to John Stuart, November 19, 1776, DAR, 12:250–51.

21. Stuart to Germain, October 26, 1776, DAR, 12:241.

22. JCC, December 30, 1776, 6:1055–57. Congress aspired to annex Nova Scotia and Cape Breton and to divide Newfoundland in equal measure with France.

23. Ibid., 1057. Congress responded to the Portuguese government's pro-British stance and the closure of Portuguese ports to American ships. See Ródriguez, *La revolución americana*, 21.

24. On November 16, 1776, the Secret Committee of Trade mandated that Morris receive a cargo recently arrived from New Orleans courtesy of Oliver Pollock. Gibson was a courier on that ship. See Secret Committee Minutes, LDC, 5:504 (November 16, 1776).

25. Morgan was initially a captain at Fort Pitt, but was promoted to colonel by early 1777. See Savelle, *George Morgan: Colony Builder*, 73, 143. For Morgan's Illinois business of the early 1770s, see the George Morgan Mss. (microfilm), HSP.

26. Virginia opposed George Morgan's attempt to establish a land office for his company, and began to take countermeasures in May 1776. See Order of the Virginia Convention, [May 20, 1776], in Rutland, *The Papers of George Mason*, 1:273.

27. Savelle, *George Morgan*, 141.

28. Morgan to the Governor of Louisiana, April 22, 1777, George Morgan Papers, LC.

29. ibid.

30. Gálvez worked with a secret agent to transmit goods received from Havana for the American war effort. See Bernardo de Gálvez to José de Gálvez, August 9, 1777, SD, legajo 2547. See also Cummins, *Spanish Observers*, 78–80.

31. Morgan to Benedict Arnold, June 28, 1777, copy to the Board of War, July 6, 1777, PCC, NARA, Record Group 360, Microcopy 247, roll 157.

32. Ibid.

33. José de Gardoqui, Diego's father, had long-established commercial ties to New England merchants, and shipped military supplies to Massachusetts in 1775. See Calderón Cuadrado, *Empresarios españoles*, 190–97, 205–13. For Lee's mission to Spain, see Rodríguez, *La revolución americana*, 90–101.

34. The Board of War recommended that General Edward Hand, commander at Fort Pitt, lead the expedition of 1,000 men. See JCC, July 19, 1777, 8:566–67. Arnold to the Board of War, July 5, 1777, PCC, Microcopy 247, roll 157.

35. Charles Thomson's notes summarized the debate of July 24 and 25. See Burnett, *Letters of Members of the Continental Congress*, 2:421–23. For Harrison's relationship to Morris, see Ver Steeg, *Robert Morris*, 14–15, 33–34; Abernethy, *Western Lands and the American Revolution*, 213–15.

36. Burke cited in notes of debates, in Burnett, *Letters of Members of the Continental Congress*, July 25, 1777, 2:422–23; Laurens to Rutledge, August 12, 1777, in Hamer and Chesnutt, *The Papers of Henry Laurens*, 11:445. For Laurens's investment in East Florida, see Bailyn, *Voyagers to the West*, 441.

37. Burnett, *Letters of Members of the Continental Congress*, 2:424–25. For the broader military picture, see Mackesy, *The War for America*, 123–25.

38. Caughey, *Bernardo de Gálvez*, 71–72; Gálvez's expulsion order of April 18, 1777, in French and in English translation, is in C.O. 5/593. For José de Gálvez's tacit approval of U.S. maritime entry to Louisiana, see Cummins, *Spanish Observers*, 46–47, 67.

39. Report of Dickson and Stephenson to Chester, West Florida Council minutes, September 29, 1777, C.O. 5/594. The two pro-American shipmasters were William Pickles and Joseph Calvert, whom Pollock aided through his ties to Gálvez.

40. Gálvez referred to Pollock as *"un honrado Mercador, nacido en Irlanda."* Gálvez to Alexander Dickson and John Stephenson, August 26, 1777, SD, legajo 2547; the same letter is in C.O. 5/594.

41. Lloyd to Gálvez, April 27, 1777, C.O. 5/593.

42. Chester to Gálvez, June 10, 1777, C.O. 5/593; Dickson and Stephenson to Gálvez, August 17, 1777, and Gálvez to Dickson and Stephenson, August 26, 1777, C.O. 5/594. This quotation is translated precisely as given in English documents. For the original Spanish, see Gálvez to Dickson and Stephenson, August 26, 1777, SD, legajo 2547.

43. Pittman, *The Present State of the European Settlements on the Mississippi*, 6.

44. Gálvez was willing to tolerate some measure of French contraband, which he

considered unavoidable. See Bernardo de Gálvez to José de Gálvez, January 28, 1777, SD, legajo 2547. Daunnoy (also spelled d'Aunoy) was commissioned by Versailles on October 3, 1776, and in Saint-Domingue on January 7, 1777. See Bernardo de Gálvez to José de Gálvez, July 10, 1777, with attached authorization, SD, legajo 2547. For the change in Spanish commercial policy, see Caughey, *Bernardo de Gálvez*, 70–71; Din, *Spaniards, Planters, and Slaves*, 72–73.

45. For Gálvez's position, see his letter to Dickson and Stephenson, August 19, 1777, SD, legajo 2547. See also the report of Dickson and Stephenson, West Florida Council minutes, September 19, 1777, C.O. 5/594.

46. Gálvez to Dickson and Stephenson, August 19, 1777, C.O. 5/594 (first quotation); Gálvez to Lloyd, May 11, 1777, C.O. 5/593 (second quotation). See also Gálvez to the marqués de la Torre, May 6, 1777, PC, legajo 1146. See also Din, "Protecting the 'Barrera,'" 204.

47. Ordinary sailors on the confiscated British ships were in jail for two months. Dickson and Stephenson estimated total English losses at 70,000 dollars. See West Florida Council minutes, C.O. 5/594. See also Fabel, *The Economy of British West Florida*, 97–98.

48. See James Willing to Haldimand, January 3, 1772, July 6, 1772, and November 11, 1772; Thomas Willing to Haldimand, June 30, 1773, HPLCAN (H-1439).

49. Starr, *Tories, Dons, and Rebels*, 82–85; Haynes, *The Natchez District and the American Revolution*, 56–64; Caughey, "Willing's Expedition down the Mississippi, 1778," 5–36.

50. Morris drafted this proposal for the Marine committee. According to plan, Jones would have four warships and a sloop for his force. See Clark, *Naval Documents*, 7:1110. This series includes transcriptions and translations of relevant Spanish documents. See also Morison, *John Paul Jones*, 87–93.

51. Willing to General Edward Hand, January 7, 1778, Society Collection, HSP; Committee of Commerce to Oliver Pollock, Pollock Papers, LC; George Morgan to James Willing, January [ ], 1778, HSP. For Morgan's account for boat building, see George Morgan Mss. (microfilm), HSP. The crew's officers and soldiers came from one Virginia regiment in Continental service. See NDAR, 11:780.

52. Chester to Germain, March 25, 1778, C.O. 5/594; Willing's order, March 3, 1778, Gratz Mss., HSP.

53. Rowland, *Life, Letters and Papers of William Dunbar*, 61–62; DeRosier, *William Dunbar*, 40–41.

54. William Wilton to Governor Chester, March 8, 1778, C.O. 5/594.

55. Germain to Chester, July 25, 1777, C. O. 5/593.

56. Chester to Germain, March 25, 1778, C.O. 5/594.

57. The fifty slaves, valued at 15,000 dollars by their owner, belonged to David Ross, one of the wealthiest British merchants of New Orleans. See Ross & Co. to Bernardo de Gálvez, April 11, 1778, C.O. 5/594; Pollock to Committee of Congress, April 2, 1778, Pollock Papers. For an estimate of the captured slaves, see Din, *Spaniards, Planters, and Slaves*, 74.

58. Robert Morris and William Smith to Bernardo de Gálvez, October 24, 1777, and November 21, 1777, SD, legajo 2547; Bernardo de Gálvez to José de Gálvez, March 11, 1778, SD, legajo 2547.

59. Bernardo de Gálvez to José de Gálvez, March 11, 1778, ibid.

60. Proclamation (*Bando*) of Bernardo de Gálvez, March 11, 1778, ibid. See also Fergusson to Gálvez, March 14 and March 15, 1778, C.O. 5/594. Governor Chester advised Gálvez against permitting any Spanish subjects to aid the American raiders. See Chester to Gálvez, March 5, 1778, SD, legajo 2547; Chester to Gálvez, May 28, 1778; Germain to Chester, July 1, 1778, C.O. 5/594.

61. Alexander to Gálvez, March 5, 1778, SD, legajo 2596. Anonymous to John Campbell, March 1, 1778, West Florida Council minutes, March 18, 1778, C.O. 5/594.

62. The Manchac residents' letter, in Spanish translation, was probably written in early April 1778. This letter and Gálvez's reply of April 11, 1778, are in SD, legajo 2596. See also Bernardo de Gálvez to José de Gálvez, April 12, 1778, SD, legajo 2596.

63. Anonymous to John Campbell, March 1, 1778, West Florida Council minutes, March 18, 1778, C. O. 5/594.

64. For the executions, see Rowland, *Life, Letters and Papers of William Dunbar*, 27; Grand Jurors for Manchac to Governor Chester, February 4, 1778, copy in C.O. 5/580; Petition of "the Gentlemen, Freeholders and Principal Inhabitants" of West Florida to the King [1779], received August 14, 1779, C.O. 5/580. The description of "slaves scattered about in the Country" is in James Mather et al. to Fergusson, March 27, 1778, C.O. 5/594.

65. James Mather et al. to Fergusson, March 27, 1778, C.O. 5/594. The Loyalist signers included Mather, David Ross, William Dunbar, Alexander Ross, John Campbell, and George Ross. For these individuals, see Fabel, *The Economy of British West Florida*, 31, 45, 101-7.

66. Gálvez to Fergusson, March 29, 1778; Fergusson to "loyal subjects," March 23, 1778; Fergusson to British subjects, April 3, 1778; C.O. 5/594. The captain's directive unfortunately does not indicate the number of blacks that he held.

67. West Florida council minutes, April 27, 1778; Chester to Germain, May 7, 1778, C.O. 5/594.

68. Fitzpatrick to William Weir, September 16, 1778, in Dalrymple, *The Merchant of Manchac*, 307.

69. Gálvez's summons of April 15, in English translation, is enclosed in Chester to Germain, May 7, 1778, C.O. 5/594, as is "Translation of an Oath tendered by the Governor of Louisiana." See also Gálvez to Chester, March 29, 1778, C.O. 5/594.

70. Gálvez to Willing, March 16, 1778, enclosed in Bernardo de Gálvez to José de Gálvez, June 9, 1778, SD, legajo 2547. English boat owner Stephen Shakespear was repeatedly put off by Pollock for the return of confiscated property. See Deposition of Stephen Shakespear, (Pensacola) May 6, 1778, SMV, 2, pt. 1:273-76. Shakespear's claim was still outstanding after the war. See Starr, *Tories, Dons, and Rebels*, 92n.

71. Bernardo de Gálvez to Juan de la Villebeuvre, March 20, 1778, enclosed in Bernardo de Gálvez to José de Gálvez, March 24, 1778, SD, legajo 2547. The elder Gálvez had written his nephew on August 15, 1777, that Spain might establish a protectorate over Britain's Mississippi posts following an American conquest—as long as such an action did not provoke war with England. See Cummins, *Spanish Observers*, 82.

72. Bernardo de Gálvez to José de Gálvez, April 12, 1778, SD, legajo 2596.

73. Caughey, *Bernardo de Gálvez*, 140-47.

74. Bernardo de Gálvez to José de Gálvez, May [ ], 1778, Santo Domingo, legajo 2596. This letter includes Willing's and Pollock's joint statement, May 2, 1778, acknowledging indebtedness to Gálvez for a large quantity of goods, including three hundred guns. See also Cummins, *Spanish Observers*, 80–88; James, *Oliver Pollock*, 81–82.

75. Bernardo de Gálvez to José de Gálvez, June 9, 1778, SD, legajo 2547.

76. For the issue of confiscated ships and slaves, see Willing to Gálvez, March 24, April 1 and 5, 1778, SMV, 2, pt. 1, 260–63. The Manchac raid was proposed in Willing to Gálvez, May 24, 1778, SMV, 2, pt. 1, 278. British troops occupied Manchac by May 30, perhaps forcing Willing to reconsider his plan. See Barker to Gálvez, May 30, 1778, SMV, 2, pt. 1, 283. For Willing's plea to go upriver, see his letter to Robert Morris, William Smith, and the Gentlemen of the Navy Board, July 29, 1778, PCC, Microcopy 247, Roll 104.

77. For the change in American command, see "Resolves of the officers," August 12, 1778, DRAPER, Series J, George Rogers Clark Papers, J-48; Pollock to Lt. George, August 20, 1778, DRAPER, Series J, George Rogers Clark Papers, J-48; Lt. George to Gálvez, August 14 and 18, 1778, and Gálvez to Lt. George, August 18, 1778, both enclosed in Bernardo de Gálvez to José de Gálvez, September 2, 1778, SD, legajo 2596.

78. Thomas Willing was co-owner of the plantation. Little Page Robertson did not sign, but marked his sworn statement of September 24, 1778, C.O. 5/595. H.M.S. *Ardent* captured Willing on December 2, 1778. See Willing to George Washington, January 25, 1781, GWLC.

79. Testimony of John Watkins, March 5, 1778, and of Alexander McIntosh, March 17, 1778 (quotation), West Florida Council minutes, C.O. 5/594. See Savelle, *George Morgan*, 153–60.

80. Testimony of John Watkins, March 5, 1778 (Speech of Lt. Strodders). See also Watkins's testimony, March 2, 1778, West Florida Council minutes, C.O. 5/594.

81. "Terms of Accommodation," February 21, 1778, Council minutes, March 17, 1778, C.O. 5/594.

82. Farquhar Bethune to John Stuart, June 16, 1778, DAR, 15:145. Gálvez to Antonio Bucareli y Ursua, March 24, 1778, NDAR, 11:778–79; Bernardo de Gálvez to Juan de la Villebeuvre, March 20, 1778, SD, legajo 2547. For implications of the gun trade, see O'Brien, *Choctaws in a Revolutionary Age*, 47–48.

83. Grand Pre to Gálvez, July 8 and 13, 1778; Villebeuvre to Gálvez, July 13, 1778, SD, legajo 2596.

84. Henry Atkins (Indian Interpreter), Choctaw Nation, to Charles Stuart, September 7, 1778, C.O. 5/595.

85. Willing to the Navy Board, April 14, 1778, PCC, Microcopy 247, Roll 104. For Leyba's substantial aid to Clark in 1778–1779, see McDermott, "The Myth of the 'Imbecile Governor,'" in McDermott, *The Spanish in the Mississippi Valley*, 329–31.

86. Clark wrote Pollock on July 18, 1778—thirteen days after taking control of Kaskaskia. Pollock also hoped for an American offensive against Pensacola. See Pollock to Lt. George (message for Clark, with James Willing's approval by signature), August 20, 1778, DRAPER, J-48. See also Gitlin, *The Bourgeois Frontier*, 36–37.

87. Pollock to Lt. George (message for Clark, with James Willing's approval by signature), August 20, 1778, DRAPER, J-48.

88. Pollock to Secret committee, March 6, April 1, and May 7, 1778, Pollock Papers, LC. To maintain his agency for the United States, Pollock had to take out loans from Gálvez. See James, *Oliver Pollock*, 174–76, 269–72. Pollock took out a loan of 6,294 pesos at the height of the Willing crisis. See Pollock to Bernardo de Gálvez, May 9, 1778, enclosed in Bernardo de Gálvez to José de Gálvez, June 9, 1778, SD, legajo 2547.

89. Willing to Robert Morris, William Smith, and the Gentlemen of the Navy Board, July 29, 1778, PCC, Microcopy 247, Roll 104.

90. See Henry to the Governor in chief of Louisiana, October 20, 1777, PC, legajo 2370. For the idea of annexing West Florida, see Henry to Gálvez, January 14, 1778, PC, legajo 2370. Henry sent this last message in French translation as well as in English, though he confessed the translation was imperfect. See also Gálvez to Henry, May 6, 1778, PC, legajo 2370.

91. The Board was so ambivalent that it drafted but then rejected a resolve "to take possession of and secure ... the country on the Mississippi ... as the other parts of the Floridas" still in British hands. JCC, October 31, 1778, 12:1083. For payment to soldiers and officers, see JCC, 12:1291 (December 14, 1778); JCC, 13:291–92 (March 8, 1779).

92. See claim of Betty, age fifty, November 28, 1783, Adams County Records, Mississippi Department of Archives and History, microfilm 5327. This reference is courtesy of Professor Charles Weeks of Jackson, Mississippi. Willing was in Arkansas in 1782. See the testimony of several Louisiana residents, July 8, 1782, SMV, 3, pt. 2:32–39.

93. Miralles, who inherited a stake in Florida trade from his father, was a leading merchant in the sale of slaves to the Spanish Caribbean in the 1760s and 1770s. See Vicente Ribes-Iborra, "La era Miralles: El momento de los agentos secretos," in López-Chicheri, *Norteamérica*, 145–54. For Miralles's diplomatic mission, see Cummins, *Spanish Observers*, chap. 5; McCadden, "Juan de Miralles," 359–75.

94. Miralles to José de Gálvez, August 20, 1778, AMT, LC. For Brétigny's background, see *Papers of Henry Laurens*, 12:17n, 14:237n. For the receipt of Brétigny's letter to Congress, see JCC, 11:808. Brétigny's memorial was presented on August 26. See JCC, 11:837. His name is also spelled Brétigney.

95. Miralles to José de Gálvez, August 20, AMT, LC. In this letter, Miralles asserted that a small Spanish flotilla could readily capture St. Augustine because the crown would have the support of the Yuchis, a Florida Indian group. See Cummins, *Spanish Observers*, 95–98.

96. Laurens to William Livingston, August 21, 1778, *Papers of Henry Laurens*, 14:196; Miralles to José de Gálvez, August 20, 1778, AMT, LC.

97. Laurens admitted that he was having difficulty convincing congressional delegates of his suspicions of Spain. See Laurens to William Livingston, *Papers of Henry Laurens*, August 21, 1778, 14:195–96.

98. On November 2, 1778, Congress resolved that General Benjamin Lincoln at Charleston should advance against St. Augustine if the strategic situation allowed for invasion. By Laurens's stipulation of November 10, officers and soldiers were to be awarded lands within East Florida. See JCC, 12:1091, 1116–21. See also Laurens to Richard Caswell, November 14, 1778, LDC, 11:210; Henry Laurens's notes on a Georgia Campaign, January 20, 1779, 11:494–95.

99. For occasions in which Miralles raised the issue of territorial transfer, see Mira-

lles to José de Gálvez, December 20, 1778, Miralles to Diego José Navarro, February 14, 1779; Miralles to Gálvez, May 16, 1779, AMT, LC.

CHAPTER 4

1. See "Relación de la campaña que hizo Don Bernardo de Gálvez, contra los ingleses, en la Luisiana," September 1779, in Serrano y Saenz, *Documentos históricos de la Florida y la Luisiana*, 344–45. See also Caughey, *Bernardo de Gálvez in Louisiana*, 149–50.

2. For Gálvez's "pretext" ("pretesto"), see "Relación," 345. For an overview of the war, see Chávez, *Spain and the Independence of the United States*, 175–97.

3. Campbell to Germain, December 15, 1779, C.O. 5/597. For West Florida–Louisiana "clandestine trade," see "Extract of a letter from Pensacola," September 10, 1779, in the *Royal Gazette* (New York), February 26, 1780.

4. Campbell to Germain, December 15, 1779, C.O. 5/597.

5. Germain to Campbell, June 25, 1779; Campbell to Germain, December 15, 1779, C.O. 5/597. See also Hutchins to Germain, January 24, 1779, C.O. 5/595.

6. Campbell to Germain, December 15, 1779, C.O. 5/597. See also "Relación de la campaña," in Serrano y Saenz, *Documentos históricos*, 347–48; Caughey, *Bernardo de Gálvez*, 153–54. Gálvez received reinforcements from Cuba after his Mississippi offensive was underway. See Kuethe, *Cuba*, 98.

7. Favrot to Gálvez, July 15, 1779, FAVROT, 1:236. See also Caughey, *Bernardo de Gálvez*, 154.

8. Dickson to Campbell, March 12, 1779, C.O. 5/597.

9. Watts to Dickson, March 16, 1779. C.O. 5/597. Dickson urged royal compensation for Watts, and his neighbor, Samuel Flowers, as he reported the surrender of Baton Rouge. See Dickson to Campbell, September 22, 1779, C.O. 5/597.

10. Din, *The Canary Islanders of Louisiana*, 16–21, 31–35.

11. See Pollock to the Inhabitants of the Natchez District, September 8, 1779, Oliver Pollock Papers, LC.

12. William Pickles, captain of the *Morris*, shared honors with his second, Pedro Rousseau, a native of France. See Caughey, *Bernardo de Gálvez*, 159.

13. For the Tangipahoa affair, see Pollock to Pickles, January 20, 1780, Pollock Papers; Pollock to the commercial committee, January 20, 1780, Pollock Papers; Committee report, July 10, 1780, JCC, 17:600. Pollock obtained a grant of 400 acres at Tangipahoa from the West Florida council on December 2, 1772. See Council minutes, C.O. 5/589.

14. Pollock to the commercial committee, January 20, 1780, Pollock Papers.

15. Pollock misleadingly used the terms "Capitulation" and "submission" to describe the oaths of allegiance sworn by inhabitants residing along Lake Pontchartrain. See Pollock to commercial committee, January 20, 1780, Pollock Papers; Report of commercial committee, July 10, 1780, JCC, 17:600.

16. For Congress's praise for Pickles and his payment, see JCC, 17:600 (July 10, 1780); JCC, 17:700 (August 5, 1780). Pickles was subsequently captured by the British on the high seas when captaining a ship bound for Amsterdam and carrying Henry Laurens on an important diplomatic mission. By the time Pickles returned to Philadelphia in 1782, Congress had lost interest in the Tangipahoa–Lake Pontchartrain claims. See Robert

Morris to the president of Congress (John Hanson), February 21, 1782, in Ferguson et al., *The Papers of Robert Morris*, 4:285.

17. Pollock to the "Inhabitants of the Natchez," September 22, 1779, Pollock Papers.

18. SMV, 1, pt. 2:401. See also Din, "Arkansas Post in the American Revolution," 11.

19. Thonhoff, *The Texas Connection with the American Revolution*, 47–52; Chipman, *Spanish Texas*, 204–5.

20. Thonhoff, *Texas Connection*, 46.

21. Ibid., 65–66.

22. Bernardo de Gálvez to José de Gálvez, January 28, 1777, SD, legajo 2547. For Gálvez's assessment of the Choctaws, see his letter to José de Gálvez, December 30, 1777, SD, legajo 2547.

23. Campbell to Germain, December 15, 1779, C.O. 5/597.

24. Braund, *Deerskins and Duffels*, 168; Cashin, *William Bartram and the American Revolution on the Southern Frontier*, 224–25; White, *The Roots of Dependency*, 79–82.

25. Cameron to Germain, August [ ], 1780, DAR, 18:158–59. See also O'Donnell, *Southern Indians in the American Revolution*, 96–105.

26. Bernardo de Gálvez to José de Gálvez, October 16, 1779, AHN, legajo 3884bis; José de Gálvez to Fernando José Mongino, January 20, 1780; Mongino to José de Gálvez, May 11, 1780, AHN, legajo 3884bis.

27. Gálvez to Campbell, April 9, 1780; Campbell to Gálvez, April 20, 1780, C.O. 5/597; Durnford to Campbell, March 2, 1780, C.O. 5/597. The Choctaws leaned toward Britain, but some aided the Spanish. See Campbell to Germain, August 6, 1780, C.O. 5/597.

28. Alexander Cameron to Gen. John Campbell, August 29, 1780 (first quotation), in Campbell to José de Ezpeleta, August 29, 1780, C.O. 5/597. Farquhar Bethune to Cameron, August 27, 1780, quoted in Holland, "The Anglo-Spanish Contest for the Gulf Coast," 95 (final quotation in sequence). For Choctaw antagonism to the Spanish at Mobile, see also O'Brien, *Choctaws in a Revolutionary Age*, 46.

29. Campbell only enumerated the warriors at the point they were most numerous in camp. See Campbell to Germain, August 6, 1780, C.O. 5/597.

30. Ezpeleta to Bernardo de Gálvez, January 20, 1781, BN, THNOC. For the role of Louisiana's free black and mulatto militia, see Pedro Piernas to Bernardo de Gálvez, December 9, 1780, and Piernas to Gálvez, September 24, 1780, FONDO, leg. 2, reel 2, THNOC. See also Kathryn Holland, "The Anglo-Spanish Contest for the Gulf Coast as Viewed from the Town Square," in Coker and Rea, *Anglo-Spanish Confrontation on the Gulf Coast during the American Revolution*, 98. For a British account, see John Campbell to Germain, January 11, 1781, C.O. 5/597. For the Spanish perspective, see Holmes, "Alabama's Bloodiest Day of the American Revolution," 208–35.

31. There were 744 Choctaw fighters at Pensacola in February 1781—and some 400 there during the final weeks of battle in April and early May. Creek fighters numbered perhaps 120 during this last stage. See Holland, "The Anglo-Spanish Contest for the Gulf Coast," 98–101; James H. O'Donnell III, "Hamstrung by Penury: Alexander Cameron's Failure at Pensacola," in Coker and Rea, *Anglo-Spanish Confrontation*, 82–87. Michael Green, "The Creek Confederation in the American Revolution: Cautious Participants," all in Coker and Rea, *Anglo-Spanish Confrontation*, 98–101, 82–87, and 69–72,

respectively. For Campbell's high regard for Creek fighters, see his letter to Colonel Thomas Brown, November 15, 1780, PRO 30/11/4.

32. John Graham, Superintendent of Indian Affairs, Western Division, to Guy Carleton, October 20, 1782, PRO 30/55/52.

33. Campbell to Germain, February 15, 1781, C.O. 5/597. See also White, *The Roots of Dependency*, 87-89.

34. Braund, *Deerskins and Duffels*, 168; O'Donnell, *Southern Indians in the American Revolution*, 121-23.

35. Medina Rojas, *José de Ezpeleta*, 33. Gálvez is quoted in Fabel, "Reflections on Mobile's Loyalism," 38.

36. Gálvez to Campbell, April 9, 1780; Campbell to Gálvez, April 20, 1780, C.O. 5/597. See also Coker and Coker, *The Siege of Mobile, 1780*.

37. Campbell to Gálvez, April 20, 1780. C.O. 5/597. The temporary flight of French colonists is mentioned in Navarro to Mayorga, February 7, 1780, SMV, 2, pt. 1, 372.

38. Medina Rojas, *José de Ezpeleta*, 38-39. See also Fabel, "Reflections on Mobile's Loyalism," 41.

39. Saunt, *A New Order of Things*, 59, 120-22; Snyder, *Slavery in Indian Country*, 182-86. For the general condition of blacks in the southern states, see Frey, *Water from the Rock*.

40. Riordan, "Finding Freedom in Florida," 34. See also Braund, "The Creek Indians, Blacks, and Slavery," 618; Braund, *Deerskins and Duffels*, 182-83.

41. Francisco Cruzat to Zéspedes, January 21, 1789, PC, legajo 120. For details of this case, see Snyder, *Slavery in Indian Country*, 184-85.

42. For a general assessment, see Siebert, "The Loyalists in West Florida and the Natchez District." J. Barton Starr estimates the Tory refugees to West Florida at 1,300-1,600, while Robin F.A. Fabel suggests a more modest count without offering a precise estimate. See Starr, *Tories, Dons, and Rebels*, 46-50, 230-31; Fabel, *The Economy of British East Florida*, 20-21.

43. See West Florida Council minutes, September 16 and 29, 1777, C.O. 5/594; November 13-20, 1778, C.O. 5/595.

44. Chester's proclamation of November 11, 1775, is in C.O. 5/592. For the Lyman grant, see West Florida Council minutes, November 9, 1778. For Lyman's wartime service, see Haynes, *The Natchez District and the American Revolution*, 88.

45. Isaac Johnson to Anthony Hutchins, October 5, 1779 (quotation), C.O. 5/595. For the Baton Rouge surrender terms of September 21, 1779, see Dent, ed., "West Florida—The Capture of Baton Rouge by Gálvez," 258-62.

46. Inhabitants of Natchez to Lt. Col. Dickson, [October] 1779, in Scott, "Britain Loses Natchez, 1779," 45-46. The signers included John Blommart, William Eason, John Alston, and others who would rebel against Spain in April 1781. The Choctaw threat is mentioned in West Florida Council minutes, October 25, 1779, C.O. 5/580. See also Haynes, *The Natchez District and the American Revolution*, 124-25.

47. Robert Ross to the Earl of Dunmore, March 8, 1782, Chalmers Papers, NYPL. For the royal shipment of Louisiana tobacco to Veracruz, see Martín Navarro to José de Gálvez, April 12, 1780, PC, legajo 593.

48. For Campbell's commissions, see Caughey, "The Natchez Rebellion," 58. See also

Ross to the Earl of Dunmore, March 8, 1782, Chalmers Papers, NYPL. Christopher (Kit) Marr was an insurgent firebrand bringing the commissions to Natchez. See the testimony of John Blommart, July 4, 1781, in "Testimonio del Proceso de Juan Blommart uno de los Principales Gefes de la Revelion de Natchez [1781]," SD, legajo 2548. This document discloses the Spanish investigation of the Natchez uprising after the insurgency's collapse.

49. This summary is based on evidence in "Testimonio del Proceso," SD, legajo 2548. For an overview, see Caughey, "The Natchez Rebellion," 57–83; Holmes, "Juan de la Villebeuvre," 108–11; Haynes, *The Natchez District and the American Revolution*, 135–44.

50. Beerman, "José Solano and the Spanish Navy," in Coker and Rea, *Anglo-Spanish Confrontation*, 125–44. For British naval priorities, see Fabel, "Ordeal by Siege," 289–91. See also Germain to Campbell, July 4, 1781, C.O. 137/80.

51. The Spanish even accepted the cost of transporting the British to their designated port. The Pensacola surrender terms, in English translation, are found in "Bernardo de Gálvez: Diary of the Operations against Pensacola," 76–82. Gálvez wrote that 1,137 soldiers surrendered at Pensacola. These did not include, he noted, 300 men who headed for Georgia as surrender terms were being discussed. See Porrúa Turanzas, *Diario de las operaciones contra la plaza de Panzacola, 1781*, 67.

52. Germain cited this point when explaining why English troops surrendering to Spanish arms were not excluded from the American war, except in battles where French or Spanish forces were engaged. See Germain to Campbell, September 15, 1781, C.O. 5/597. See also Campbell to Germain, July 21, 1781, PRO, C.O. 5/597. For the arrival of the British prisoners in New York City, see Padgett, "Bernardo de Gálvez's Siege of Pensacola in 1781," 327; Porrúa Turanzas, "Diary of Operations," 75.

53. Richard Potts to Samuel Hughes, July 24, 1781, LDC, 17:440–41; Huntington to Washington July 2, 1781, LDC, 17:367.

54. George Washington was glad to learn of the Spanish capture of Mobile, but disappointed by the lack of assistance from Havana. See Washington to Miralles, February 27, 1780, GWLC. For the Bahamas campaign, see Beerman, "The Last Battle of the American Revolution," 85–90, 94–95; Chávez, *Spain and the Independence of the United States*, 206–9.

55. Campbell to Gálvez and Gálvez to Campbell, June 3, 1781, SD, legajo 2548. This correspondence also includes Campbell's proposed peace articles regarding Natchez. The original English documents are in C.O. 5/597. The English translation in British records is as follows: "And the Natchez being part of West Florida belongs to me." The original Spanish reads: ". . . y siendo parte de la Florida occidental, Natchez me pertenece." The British capitulation of Pensacola and all West Florida was signed on May 9, 1781.

56. See the testimony of John Blommart, July 4, 1781, in "Testimonio del Proceso," SD, legajo 2548.

57. Caughey, "The Natchez Rebellion," 62–68; Holmes, "Juan de la Villebeuvre," 109–10; Starr, *Tories, Dons, and Rebels*, 217.

58. Blommart was sentenced to death by hanging on July 6, 1781. See "Testimonio del Proceso." Gálvez granted the pardon in gracious style before Prince William at Cap Français in Saint-Domingue. See "Extract from the Havana *Gazette*," April 25, 1783, in the *Pennsylvania Evening Post, and Public Advertiser* (Philadelphia), June 6, 1783. See also

Caughey, "Natchez Rebellion," 79–81. The sale of rebel estates was recorded on May 6, 1782, SMV, 3, pt. 2:12.

59. Caughey, "Natchez Rebellion," 66–67.

60. Blommart was born in Geneva and Protestant in religion. See the testimony of John Blommart, July 4, 1781, in *"Testimonio del Proceso."* For background information on Winfree, see Fabel, *The Economy of British West Florida*, 34, 175. For Blommart, see Howard, *The British Development of West Florida*, 91; Johnson, *British West Florida*, 169, 182.

61. See the testimony of Mays Gray, May 9, 1781; Abraham Ellis, June 15, 1781; John Bell, June 15, 1781; William Bell, June 15, 1781, in "Testimonio del Proceso." William Bell estimated that the insurgents had about two hundred armed supporters in Natchez and environs.

62. Testimony of John Blommart, July 4, 1781, in *"Testimonio del Proceso."* For the raising of the American flag, which flew four days, see deposition of Juan Baptista Datchurut, Francisco Valle, and R. Rapicaut [June 1781], as recorded in the same judicial process. See also William Eason's testimony of July 2, 1781, in the above record. For Philip Alston's service to British Loyalism, see Blommart to Colonel John McGillivray, August 5, 1778, SMV, 2, pt. 1:301.

63. Testimony of Juan Baptista Datchurut and Francisco Valle, July 2, 1781, in "Testimonio del Proceso."

64. Ibid.

65. For Trudeau, see Nasatir, *Spanish War Vessels on the Mississippi*, 59–60n.

66. See the testimony of Mays Gray, May 9, 1781; Abraham Ellis, John Bell, William Bell, William Penrose, June 15, 1781, in "Testimonio del Proceso."

67. Din, "Loyalist Resistance after Pensacola," 158–60; Corbitt, "James Colbert and the Spanish Claims to the East Bank of the Mississippi," 457–72; Atkinson, *Splendid Land, Splendid People*, 93–94.

68. Declaration of Labbadie, July 5, 1782, SMV, 3, pt. 2:21–34. Colbert's Louisiana ally was one Monsieur Meson (or Mason), who had previously served as a conduit for British Natchez Loyalists. See Blommart to John McGillivray, August 5, 1778, SMV, 2, pt. 1:301.

69. Declaration of Labbadie, July 5, 1782, SMV, 3, pt. 2:21–34; Colbert to Miró, October 6, 1782, Louisiana Papers, Bancroft Library, University of California; Din, "Loyalist Resistance after Pensacola," 162–65; Corbitt, "James Colbert and the Spanish Claims to the East Bank of the Mississippi," 458–65; Haynes, *The Natchez District and the American Revolution*, 140–50.

70. Corbitt, "James Colbert," 466–68.

71. By the early 1790s, the Colbert family took a pro-U.S. stance in Chickasaw politics. See Atkinson, *Splendid Land, Splendid People*, 148–52.

72. Cruzat to Miró, August 8, 1782, SMV, 3, pt. 2:52; Calloway, *The American Revolution in Indian Country*, 225–33; Gibson, *The Chickasaws*, 65–66, 74–75; Atkinson, *Splendid Land, Splendid People*, 124. For the Indian presence at St. Augustine, see O'Donnell, *Southern Indians*, 129–30.

73. Miró to Bernardo de Gálvez, November 7, 1782, FONDO, legajo 3, reel 4.

74. Miró to Bernardo de Gálvez, June 5, 1782, ibid.

75. Favrot to Piernas, May 16, 1781 (two letters); Miró to Favrot, May 22, 1781. Favrot's

public letter was sent to Natchez on May 18. See Favrot to *"Messieurs Les habitant[s] Du District, et fort, Des Natchez."* See also Favrot to Piernas, May 17, 1781. All documents are in PC, legajo 198A. For Favrot's background, see FAVROT, 1:xvii–xxii.

76. For the attack on St. Louis, see McDermott, "The Myth of the 'Imbecile Governor,'" in McDermott, *The Spanish in the Mississippi Valley*, 339–48. See also the declarations of Pedro Picoté de Belestre, Francisco Vallé, and Silvestre Labbadie, July 8, 1782, SMV, 3, pt. 2:34–39; Miró to Bernardo de Gálvez, November 7, 1782, FONDO, legajo 3, reel 4.

77. While in Pensacola in 1779, Ross wrote a letter castigating Willing, and also criticizing Gálvez for his "antipathy and rancor . . . against the English nation." "Copy of a letter from Mr. Robert Ross, of Pensacola . . . ," March 27, 1779, in *Royal Gazette* (New York City), May 5, 1779. See also Fabel, *The Economy of British West Florida*, 31, 55, 99–102. For Ross's arrest, trial, and imprisonment in 1778, see the documents in C.O. 5/580. See also Ross to the Earl of Dunmore, March 8, 1782, Chalmers Papers, NYPL.

78. [Robert Ross], "Observations on the Importance of Louisiana to Great-Britain, with a state of the Force now actually in it, & some hints which may be useful, should an attempt be made to reduce that Colony & to annex it to his Majestys Dominions" [1782], PRO 30/55/52. Dunmore enclosed Ross's "Observations" to London from Charleston. See Dunmore to Germain, March 30, 1782, March 30, 1782, PRO/C.O. 5/175.

79. [Ross], "Observations." Ross pointed to current rebellions in Spain's "southern provinces"—a possible reference to the Tupac Amaru revolt in Peru, or more likely to unrest in New Granada (now Colombia). For the impact of South American events on Gálvez's military plans, see Chávez, *Spain and the Independence of the United States*, 204.

80. Dunmore to Germain, March 30, 1782, C.O. 5/175.

81. Dunmore to Thomas Townshend, August 24, 1782, Chalmers Papers, NYPL. Dunmore's plan is recently discussed in David, *Dunmore's New World*, 133–36.

82. Dunmore to Thomas Townshend, August 24, 1782, Chalmers Papers. See also Wright, "Lord Dunmore's Loyalist Asylum in the Floridas," 371–72. This article could be more precise on one key point—Dunmore urged massive slave recruitment for war in the southern states, but not directly for Louisiana. See Dunmore to Henry Clinton, February 2, 1782, C.O. 5/175.

83. Jay's mission was mandated by congressional resolution of September 17, 1779, followed by confirmation on September 28, 1779. See JCC, 15:1084, 1118–20.

84. Franklin to Jay, October 2, 1780, BF, 33:357. For Franklin's previous pro-British ideas on the Mississippi, see his letter to William Franklin, August 28, 1767, BF, 14:242.

85. Oswald to Thomas Townshend, October 2, 1782, in Morris, *John Jay*, 373–74. See also Schafer, "'A Swamp of an Investment'?" 30–31. For Oswald's ideas, see Hancock, *Citizens of the World*, 394.

86. For Aranda's diplomacy, see *"Continuación del Diario sobre los limites con los americanos,"* September 1, 1782, in Yela Utrilla, 2:360; Oltra and Pérez Samper, *El conde de Aranda y los Estados Unidos*, 204–14.

87. The preliminary accord was not to go into effect until Britain and France reached a peace treaty. For the U.S.-British peace articles of November 30, 1782, see JCC, 24:243–51. The Chattahoochee River was called the Apalachicola in the treaty's text—a common reference at the time.

88. Ibid., 250–51.

89. Livingston to the President of Congress, March 18, 1783, in Wharton, *The Revolutionary Diplomatic Correspondence of the United States*, 6:314 (quotation); Livingston to Peace Commissioners, March 25, 1783, *Revolutionary Diplomatic Correspondence*, 6:339 (second quotation); Joint Ministers (Peace Commissioners) to Livingston, July 18, 1783, The Papers of John Jay, Columbia University Libraries.

90. The British rejected Aranda's proposal for a treaty provision explicitly including Natchez and vicinity within West Florida. See Alleyne Fitz-Herbert to Charles James Fox, May 3, 1783, in Lockey, *East Florida, 1783–1785*, 75–76.

91. Mowat, *East Florida as a British Province*, 141–42.

92. Congress emphasized its readiness to guarantee Spain's rights to the Floridas if Madrid succeeded in war—and acceded to U.S. navigation on the Mississippi. See congressional resolution of September 17, 1779, followed by confirmation on September 28, 1779. See JCC, 15:1084, 1118–20.

93. Jay to Floridablanca, September 22, 1781, in Yela Utrilla, 2:342–50; Floridablanca to Aranda, September 20, 1782, Yela Utrilla, 2:364–65. See also Rodríguez, *La revolución americana*, 129.

94. Floridablanca to Aranda, March 17, 1783, in Lockey, *East Florida*, 69.

95. See Gálvez to Favrot, May 26, 1780, FAVROT, 1:263. For the substantial U.S.-Havana trade, see Cummins, *Spanish Observers*, 171–75.

96. Brion de la Tour, *Suite du Théatre de la Guerre dans l'Amérique Septentrionale y Compris le Golfe du Méxique* (Paris: Chez Esnauts y Rapilly, 1782), DeGolyer Library, Southern Methodist University.

CHAPTER 5

1. Whitaker, *Documents Relating to the Commercial Policy of Spain in the Floridas*, xxvi. For the prohibition's intent, see Sánchez-Fabrés Mirat, *Situación histórica de las Floridas en la segunda mitad del siglo XVIII*, 52–54.

2. A British report listed East Florida arrivals between July 1782 and April 20, 1783, at 5,090 whites and 8,285 slaves. See Siebert, *Loyalists in East Florida*, 1:130–31. See also Troxler, "Loyalist Refugees and the British Evacuation of East Florida, 1783–1785," 1–28.

3. The Loyalist influx began early in the war, grew substantially in 1778–79, and then reached new heights in 1782–83. See Troxler, "Refuge, Resistance, and Reward," 567–84.

4. Tonyn to the Lords Commissioners of the Treasury, December 6, 1784, in Lockey, *East Florida, 1783–1785*, 424. See also Troxler, "Refuge, Resistance, and Reward," 589–90.

5. Tanner, *Zéspedes in East Florida*, 41–47. Zéspedes had about 450 troops under his command in 1785. See Hoffman, *Florida's Frontiers*, 238. See also Johnson, "The Spanish St. Augustine Community."

6. For black evacuees, see Frey, *Water from the Rock*, 182, 199–200; Quarles, *The Negro in the American Revolution*, 175–77; Troxler, "British Evacuation of East Florida," 15, 24–25; David, *Dunmore's New World*, 149–54; Marshall, *Remaking the British Atlantic*, 206–8.

7. Calhoon, "The Floridas, the Western Frontier, and Vermont," 1–15. For an important collection of essays, see Hoffman, Tate, and Albert, *An Uncivil War*.

8. "The Humble Address of the Inhabitants of the River St. John[s]," January 25, 1785, EF, reel 16. All but one of the fifty signatories of this address had a British surname. The sole exception was Lewis Fatio, of Swiss Protestant parentage and an English subject. See Parker, "Men without God or King," 144.

9. Extract from the *Providence Gazette*, February 5, 1785, in Lockey, *East Florida*, 453.

10. Memorial of Panton and Leslie, July 31, 1784, in Lockey, *East Florida*, 257–61. For a thorough and important examination of Panton, Leslie, and Company, see Coker and Watson, *Indian Traders of the Southeastern Spanish Borderlands*. A royal order of March 8, 1786, permitted British settlers to remain in East Florida if they swore allegiance to Spain and accepted the Catholic faith. See Murdoch, "Governor Céspedes and the Religion Problem in East Florida," 327–28. The obligation of Catholic adherence was soon discarded. See Sanchez-Fabrés Mirat, *La situación histórico de las Floridas*, 149.

11. Cruden conceived of black military recruits, serving the king for life, as a means to control plantation slaves after the war. See Cruden to the Earl of Dunmore, January 5, 1782, Chalmers Papers, NYPL. See also Troxler, "British Evacuation of East Florida," 10–14; Tanner, *Zéspedes in East Florida*, 47–48; Siebert, *Loyalists in East Florida*, 1:169, 190; 2:361.

12. Cruden to Charles III, October 28, 1784, EF, reel 82.

13. Ibid.

14. Ibid. For Cruden's praise of Gálvez, see his letter to Carlos Howard, December 8, 1784, in Lockey, *East Florida*, 431; Cruden to Howard, March 18, 1785 and Howard to Cruden, March 22, 1785, EF, reel 16; "Manifesto que hace don Juan Cruden," November 8, 1785, EF, reel 16. See also Wright, *Florida in the American Revolution*, 137; Tanner, *Zéspedes in East Florida*, 47–48; Siebert, *Loyalists in East Florida*, 1:169, 190; 2:361.

15. Cunningham et al. to Zéspedes, July 15, 1784, in Lockey, *East Florida*, 235–36; Siebert, *Loyalists in East Florida*, 1:126–28, 174; 2:314–15; Tanner, *Zéspedes in East Florida*, 45–46.

16. See Zéspedes to Arturo O'Neill, October 25, 1784; Favrot to Miró, May 12, 1785, PC, legajo 198B. For the reference to English fanaticism, see Favrot to Miró, September 12, 1785, PC, legajo 198B.

17. Linder petitioned that Favrot expel Nuson, who was imprisoned in Mobile. See Linder to Favrot (with affidavits), December 7, 1785; Petition of Mary [Marcy] Love and Favrot's judgment, January 6–7, 1786, PC, legajo 198B.

18. "*Chefs des Villages*" to Lt. Colonel Grimarest, May 30, 1785; Favrot to "*Grands Chefs*," June 10, 1785, PC, legajo 198B.

19. McGillivray to Miró, May 16, 1785, PC, legajo 198B.

20. Act of February 7, 1785, BOURBON, 70–71. An original copy of the act is in PC, legajo 198A. A Georgia legislative act of February 17, 1783, justified the state's territorial claims. See FONDO, reel 1, legajo 1.

21. Thomas Green, William Davenport, Nicolas Long, and Nathaniel Christmas were the justices journeying from Georgia to the Mississippi. See Act of February 7, 1785, BOURBON, 70–71. For a helpful article, see Din, "War Clouds on the Mississippi," 51–76.

22. Instructions to Justices, February 11, 1785, BOURBON, 72–73 (quotations).

23. Miró to the conde de Gálvez, June 20, 1785, BOURBON, 92; Din, "War Clouds on the Mississippi," 52; Abernethy, *Western Lands and the American Revolution*, 312.

24. Green to Treviño, June 12, 1785, PC, legajo 198A; Green to Treviño, June [ ], 1785, BOURBON, 72–73; Treviño to Miró, June 15, 1785, BOURBON, 82. For reports of invasion, see McGillivray to Zéspedes, May 22, 1785, and Favrot to Miró, June 3, 1785, BOURBON, 73–75.

25. Bouligny arrived at Natchez on July 23 after a month's journey, followed by his troops four days later. See Din, *Francisco Bouligny*, 146; Bernardo de Gálvez received Miro's reports of June 14 and 20, 1785, on July 16. See Gálvez to Miró, August 2, 1785, BOURBON, 312.

26. See Petition, March 1, 1785, MPASD, 2:256 (quotation).

27. For the beginnings of Natchez tobacco production, see Robert Ross, "Observations on the Importance of Louisiana to Great Britain," enclosed in Dunmore to Germain, March 30, 1782, PRO 30/55/52. By 1786, tobacco production had exploded to 589,920 pounds. See Holmes, *Gayoso*, 90–92.

28. Barón de Carondelet, who became governor of Louisiana and West Florida in late 1791, believed that Lower Louisiana (south of the Iberville) extended some sixty leagues, or about 150 miles, east of the Mississippi when Spain acquired the province from France. See report of December 21, 1794, in "Carondelet on the Defense of Louisiana, 1794," 476.

29. Miró to Green, June 19, 1785, BOURBON, 90–91. See also Din, "War Clouds on the Mississippi," 54–56; Din, *Francisco Bouligny*, 146–47. Green was in the Chickasaw country in September 1785. See BOURBON, 333–34.

30. Gálvez to Miró, August 2, 1785, BOURBON, 312–14; Gálvez to Zéspedes, December 30, 1785, EF, reel 16. Miró's order of November 10, 1785, gave the Georgia commissioners fifteen days to leave Natchez. See BOURBON, 342; Din, "War Clouds on the Mississippi," 60–61.

31. Bouligny estimated the population as noted above. A Spanish census of 1784 listed 1,121 white men and women and 498 slaves of all ages. See Holmes, *Gayoso*, 16n.

32. [Richard] Ellis, [Tacitus] Gaillard, and [Sutton] Banks to the Citizens of Natchez, June [ ], 1785 (document translated into English from Spanish record), BOURBON, 77. See also Din, "War Clouds on the Mississippi," 62–65; Din, *Francisco Bouligny*, 154–55.

33. Miró to Gálvez, June 14, 1785, BOURBON, 79.

34. Din, "The Immigration Policy of Governor Esteban Miró," 157–58; Sánchez-Fabrés Mirat, *Situación histórica de las Floridas*, 149–50. For the limits of Catholic evangelization, see Din, "The Irish Mission to West Florida," 325–26; Holmes, *Gayoso*, 69–77.

35. The Smiths' petition and Miró's approval, both of September 1, 1785, are in the Kuntz Collection, Tulane University. In 1786, the Baton Rouge district had 279 slaves compared to only 74 free persons. See Tate, "Spanish Census of the Baton Rouge District For 1786," 70–84.

36. Miró to Favrot, May 11, 1786, FAVROT, 2:42. Martín Navarro strongly supported Miró in this matter. See Sánchez-Fabrés Mirat, *Situación histórica de las Floridas*, 118–19; Fabel, *The Economy of British West Florida*, 94, 106–7.

37. Bouligny to Miró, August 17 and 28, 1785, BOURBON, 325, 327. For the militia appointment, see Bouligny to Miró, August 22, 1785, SMV, 3, pt. 2:142.

38. For Hutchins's role in hunting down the bandits, two of whom were executed at Pensacola, see George Urquhart to Chester, July 1, 1773, C.O. 5/590; E. R. Wegg to Chester, November 25, 1773; Chester to Dartmouth, June 6, 1774, C.O. 5/591. For the Revolutionary era, see Starr, *Tories, Dons, and Rebels*, 85–87, 108–12; Gálvez to Pierre Joseph Favrot, May 26, 1780, FAVROT, 1:263.

39. Hutchins to Congress, May 22, 1785, PCC, Microcopy No. 247, roll 50.

40. Ibid. See also Grant, "Anthony Hutchins," 413; Claiborne, *Mississippi, as a Province, Territory and State*, 1:131–35.

41. Congress appointed Pollock as agent at Havana on June 2, 1783. See JCC, 24:266–67.

42. For Hutchins's account of the rebellion, see his letter to Miró, July 10, 1785, PC, legajo 198. His account, which was highly self-serving though not wholly false, has shaped historical accounts of the Natchez uprising. See, for example, Caughey, *Bernardo de Gálvez*, 216–23.

43. Hutchins to Miró, October 20, 1785, PC, legajo 198A.

44. Ibid.

45. Ibid. See also Tacitus Gaillard to Miró, September 15, 1785, and Sutton Banks to Miró, September 25, 1785, PC, legajo 198A; Miró to Hutchins, November 12, 1785, PC, legajo 198A.

46. Aranda's *dictamen* (official judgment) of 1783, expressing his profound disappointment with the Treaty of Paris, is in Rodriguez, *La revolución americana*, 64.

47. Barbé-Marbois to Washington, June 12, 1785; Washington to Barbé-Marbois, June 21, 1785, GWLC. See also Washington to Richard Henry Lee, August 22, 1785, GWLC.

48. For the Spanish gift of mules, see Washington to William Carmichael, June 10, 1785, GWLC. Madison's view of southwestern migration is found in his draft of a congressional committee report of October 16, 1780, which Congress approved the next day as a guide for Jay's diplomatic mission to Spain. See *The Papers of James Madison*, 2:127–35. A nearly identical printed version is in JCC, 18:935–47 (quotation on 939).

49. Madison to Monroe, June 21, 1785, James Madison Papers, Library of Congress. Madison received his information concerning Natchez via Kentucky.

50. Gardoqui to Congress, September 23, 1785, NARA, RG 360, PCC, M247, roll 142; JCC, October 13, 1785, 29:829–30.

51. Delaware did not vote with either the northern or southern block on the major vote to change Jay's instructions. See JCC, August 25, 1786, 31:569–70. A classic historical account is in Bemis, *Pinckney's Treaty*, 85–94.

52. Jonathan Dayton, Burr's future associate, headed the New Jersey legislative committee arguing for the U.S. Mississippi claim. See McCormick, *Experiment in Independence*, 227–29. James Willing specifically asked Wilson to share his views with southern members of Congress. See Willing to Wilson, February 12, 1785 (quotation), Society Collection, HSP. See also Willing to Wilson, February 20, 1785, Dreer Collection, HSP.

53. Speech of Jay, August 3, 1786, JCC, 31:482.

54. Madison joined William Bingham of Pennsylvania for discussions with Gardoqui on March 13, 1787. Madison's notes of these discussions are in Papers of James Madison, 9:309–11. Interestingly, Madison based U.S. rights on the Treaty of Paris of 1763 and not only of 1783.

55. Floridablanca to Gardoqui, September 1, 1786, in Gómez del Campillo, *Relaciones diplomaticas entre España y los Estados Unidos*, 1:382. Floridablanca hinted at additional concessions in his proposal of September 5, 1787—if the United States and Spain formed a joint commission treating the question of navigation between the 31st parallel and the Mississippi's mouth. See Floridablanca to Gardoqui, in Gómez del Campillo, *Relaciones diplomaticas entre España y los Estados Unidos*, 1:394-97.

56. The change in Floridablanca's negotiating position can be seen by comparing his letters to Gardoqui of September 1, 1786, and September 5, 1787. See *Relaciones diplomaticas*, 1:382, 392-95. See also Whitaker, *Spanish-American Frontier*, 84. The Council of State, which Floridablanca headed, accepted the possibility of concession on the boundary question, while holding fast to the idea of excluding the United States from the Gulf. See "Instrucción reservada de la junta de estado . . . 8 de julio de 1787," in Ferrer del Rio, *Obras originales del conde de Floridablanca*, 228.

57. For population figures, see Rohrbough, *The Trans-Appalachian Frontier*, 16.

58. Abernethy, *Western Lands and the American Revolution*, 320-21.

59. George Muter of Kentucky clearly expressed the western viewpoint on the Mississippi: "Our people here are greatly alarmed at the prospect of the navigation of the Mississippi being given up. And I have not met with one man, who would be willing to give the navigation up, for ever so short a time, on any terms whatever." See Muter to Madison, February 20, 1787, JMLC.

60. Green to the Governor, Council, and Legislature of Georgia, December 3, 1786, DRAPER, J 54.

61. Green to Col. Anthony Bledsoe, September 10, 1785, Louisiana Papers, Bancroft Library, University of California. He wrote this letter from the Chickasaw country to Bledsoe in Cumberland.

62. For defining characteristics of filibustering in the early American republic, see May, *Manifest Destiny's Underworld*, 6-7.

63. The Danville committee assembled on December 19, 1786, and the next day reviewed Clark's testimony as collected by James Wilkinson. The testimony represents the committee's summary of Clark's statement, but not apparently a verbatim account. See Report of Committee, Danville, Ky., December 20, 1786, DRAPER, J 54.

64. Report of Committee, Danville, Ky., December 20, 1786, DRAPER, J 54.

65. Gardoqui to Floridablanca, May 12, 1787, *Relaciones diplomaticas*, 1:516; Gardoqui to Floridablanca, May 12, 1787, *Relaciones diplomaticas*, 1:377 (quotation), 379.

66. According to Gardoqui, Sullivan visited him about one year before the envoy formally notified Jay of his concern. See Gardoqui to Jay, August 28, 1787,PCC, M247, roll 125. Sullivan addressed his letter of March 1, 1787, to Gardoqui from "the Frontier of the Creek Nation." The letter was published in the *Columbian Herald* (Charleston, S.C.), August 6, 1787. Miró chided Green in a letter of June 19, 1785, BOURBON, 90-91.

67. Sullivan to Gardoqui (March 1, 1787), in the *Columbian Herald* (Charleston), August 6, 1787.

68. Gardoqui to Jay, August 25, 1787; Jay to Congress, October 4, 1787; Jay to Gardoqui, October 11, 1787, PCC, M247, roll 142. For the congressional resolution, see JCC, 33:631, October 8, 1787.

69. John Sullivan to Major William Brown, September 24, 1787, enclosed in Jay to

Gardoqui, November 10, 1787, PCC, M247, roll 142. Robert Morris and Gouverneur Morris attested to Oliver Pollock's showing them "a true copy" of Sullivan's letter on November 6, 1787. See PCC, M247, roll 165. Gardoqui made a duplicate copy of Sullivan's letter along with the intelligence from Robert and Gouverneur Morris via Pollock. See PC, legajo 1409.

70. Henry Knox to Congress, April 19, 1787, JCC, 32:222 (quotations); Knox to Harmar, November 14, 1787, PCC, M247, roll 142.

71. Lt. Armstrong to Major John P. Wyllys, April 28, 1788, PCC, M247, roll 142. See also Major Wyllys to Colonel Harmar, February 6, 1787, PCC, M247, roll 164. In his letter to Major Brown of September 24, 1787, Sullivan stated his intention of returning "to the state of Franklin." See Jay to Gardoqui, November 10, 1787, PCC, M247, roll 142; General Harmar to Henry Knox, January 10, 1788, PCC, M247, roll 165.

72. Navarro to the marqués de Sonora, June 7, 1787, BN, THNOC.

73. Ibid.

PART II PROLOGUE

1. James Wilkinson, "Declaration," August 21, 1787, PC, legajo 2373.
2. Ibid.
3. Wilkinson to [ ], December 20, 1786, PC, legajo 2373. Based on a reference in a subsequent letter, it is highly probable that Wilkinson sent this message to Francisco Cruzat. He asked the officer to pass his message to Miró. For Wilkinson's boast of suppressing Green's projected invasion, see his letter to Cruzat, May 15, 1787, PC, legajo 2373.
4. Maier, *Among Empires*, 69.

CHAPTER 6

1. Din, "The Immigration Policy of Governor Esteban Miró in Spanish Louisiana," 155–75; Weber, *The Spanish Frontier in North America*, 279–82; Whitaker, *The Spanish-American Frontier*, 21–23; Sánchez-Fabrés Mirat, *Situación histórica de las Floridas*, 163–66; Hilton, "*Movilidad y expansión en la construcción política de los Estados Unidos*," 63–96.
2. For the challenges confronting Spanish authority, see Hilton, "Being and Becoming Spanish in the Mississippi Valley, 1776–1803," in Smith and Hilton, *Nexus of Empire*, 8–36; Din, "Empires Too Far." For the significance of imperial distinctions among subject groups, see Burbank and Cooper, *Empires in World History*, 11, 20.
3. Weber, *Spanish Frontier in North America*, 258.
4. Sonora to Floidablanca, June 2, 1787, AHN, Estado, legajo 3889.
5. For East Florida, see Hoffman, *Florida's Frontiers*, 244–45.
6. The royal order indicated that land could be granted either above or below Natchez. See Valdés to Miró, August 23, 1787, AHN, Estado, legajo 3889. For a useful analysis, see Din, "Pierre Wouves d'Argès in North America."
7. Valdés to Miró, August 23, 1787, AHN, Estado, legajo 3889.
8. Wouves d'Argès to Aranda, February 18, 1787, AHN, Estado, legajo 3889. In his

formal petition to the Spanish court, Wouves made no mention of German immigrants. See Wouves d'Argès to Floridablanca, August 1, 1787, AHN, Estado, legajo 3889. In another appeal that same day, the chevalier referred to only "two or three good German Catholic families" accompanying him to Natchez. See *Observaciones necesarias para la inteligencia del Memorial embiado al Excelisimo Sr. conde de Floridablanca*, August 1, 1787, AHN, Estado, legajo 3889. The petition of August 1, 1787, is printed in CONSP, 225–26.

9. Aranda to Floridablanca, April 2, 1787, AHN, Estado, legajo 3889; Floridablanca to Antonio Valdés, August 3, 1787, AHN, Estado, legajo 3889.

10. Stanley J. Stein and Barbara H. Stein write of the Spanish *proyectistas* as "political economists" who were "were not businessmen, although they often drew upon business expertise." See Stein and Stein, *Silver, Trade, and War*, 153, 267. *Projectictas* included civic-minded individuals promoting social betterment. See TePaske, "Spanish America," 516.

11. Din, "Pierre Wouves d'Argès in North America," 360–70.

12. Gardoqui to Wouves d'Argès, January 30, 1788, AHN, Estado, legajo 3889.

13. Din, "Pierre Wouves d'Argès in North America," 367–69.

14. For Navarro's assessment of Louisiana's situation relative to the United States, see his letter to Valdés, November 11, 1788, in CONSP, 311–22. Navarro to the marqués de Sonora (José de Gálvez), June 7, 1787, BN, THNOC.

15. Navarro to Valdés, December 19, 1787, BN, THNOC. Lt. Governor Francisco Bouligny was also keen on Louisiana's economic development, but put greater emphasis than Navarro did on luring Spanish merchants to participate in provincial commerce. See Din, *Louisiana in 1776: A Memoria of Francisco Bouligny*, 14–16, 57–64, 70–77.

16. Martín Navarro, "Reflexiones políticas sobre el estado actual de la provincia de la Luisiana," in Serrano y Saenz, *Documentos históricos de la Florida y la Luisiana*, 368. (Quotation: "El interés y aumento de maior fortuna atropella todos los inconvenientes, y atrae á un punto hombres de las mas remotos regiones." Navarro's *Reflexiones* are dated September 24, 1780 [and not 1782 as indicated in Serrano].)

17. Navarro, ibid., 366–67, 371 (quotation).

18. Solano Costa, "La emigración acadiana a la Luisiana española"; Mouhot, "The Emigration of the Acadians," 147–49. The expenses associated with Acadian entry in 1786 approached the annual military budget for all Louisiana and West Florida. See Cunningham, "Financial Reports Relating to Louisiana, 1766–1788," 385–90. See also Din, *The Canary Islanders of Louisiana*, 17–27.

19. Navarro, "Reflexiones políticas," 366–67, 371–72.

20. Ibid., 374–75. Under the cédula of January 22, 1782, specie exported for purchasing slaves was subject to a six percent duty. Louisiana imports and exports were taxed at the same rate. The cédula is analyzed and printed in both Spanish and English translation in Whitaker, *Documents Relating to the Commercial Policy of Spain*, xxvii–xxx, 32–35.

21. Navarro to the marqués de Sonora (José de Gálvez), June 7, 1787, PC, legajo 593. For Navarro's personal investment, see Ingersoll, "The Slave Trade and the Ethnic Diversity of Louisiana's Slave Community," 146–47.

22. Besides desiring increased slave importation, Navarro also wanted to attract French planters to migrate from the islands to the Mississippi Valley. See Navarro to

Valdés, December 19, 1787, BN, THNOC. In 1789, Navarro toured France and England to study manufacturing for the Indian trade. See Whitaker, "The Commerce of Louisiana and the Floridas at the End of the Eighteenth Century," 194, 199-200.

23. Din, *Spaniards, Planters, and Slaves*, 124. See also "Census for Louisiana in the Year 1785," American State Papers, House of Representatives, 8th Congress, 1st Session, Miscellaneous: Vol. 1:381. For slave resistance, see Bell, *Revolutions, Romanticism, and the Afro-Creole Protest Tradition in Louisiana*.

24. Martinique had a leading role in Louisiana's slave importation in 1789-90. See Jean-Leglaunec, "Slave Migrations in Spanish and Early American Louisiana," 188-94.

25. For the growth of Natchitoches tobacco production and slavery, see Burton, "Spanish Bourbons and Louisiana Tobacco," 167-86. The imperial dimensions of the purchase program are analyzed in Náter, "Fiscalidad imperial y desarrollo regional en el siglo XVIII," 79-87. See also Brian E. Coutts, "Boom and Bust." For Navarro's early encouragement of Natchez tobacco production, see his letters to José de Gálvez, October 13, 1779, and April 30, 1782, PC, legajo 593.

26. Wilkinson to Miró and Navarro, [September 5, 1787], PC, legajo 2373. Miró and Navarro referred to the memorial as presented the day before they approved it. See Miró and Navarro to Wilkinson, September 6, 1787, PC, legajo 2373. For the amount of $30,000, see Miró and Navarro to Armesto and Leonard, September 6, 1787, PC, legajo 2373. For reference to Wilkinson's arrival in New Orleans on July 2, 1787, see Miró and Navarro to Valdés, September 25, 1787, in CONSP, 208.

27. Miró delivered the regulations, written in English, to Peter Paulus, an aspiring colonizer from Pennsylvania. See Miró to Paulus, March 12, 1789, PC, legajo 120. The regulation allowed families of two or three workmen to receive at least 400 acres. Families with ten to fifteen workers were to obtain "above" eight hundred acres. The royal order of December 1, 1788, is found in CONSP, 323-25.

28. Miró to Paulus, March 12, 1789, PC, legajo 120. The reduction of the tariff from 25 percent to 15 percent was included in the royal order of December 1, 1788.

29. Lewis, "Anglo-American Entrepreneurs," 115-18. Congress appointed Pollock as agent at Havana on June 2, 1783. See JCC, 24:266-67.

30. See Lewis, "Anglo-American Entrepreneurs," 121-23. For Pollock's legal difficulties in Havana, see the affidavit of John Mourett and Ebenezer Rees, sworn in Havana, May 27, 1784, in Woodward, *A Representation of the Case of Oliver Pollock*, 10-12. See also Pollock to Robert Morris, August 28, 1784, in Ferguson, *The Papers of Robert Morris*, 9:507-8.

31. Pollock to Jay, June 3, 1785, Jay Papers. Gálvez wrote a reference letter for Pollock lauding the latter's patriotism in wartime. Certificate of Gálvez, May 1, 1785, enclosed in Pollock to Jay, July 7, 1785, Jay Papers.

32. Pollock to Jay, June 3, 1785, Jay Papers. For the congressional resolve, see committee report, JCC, July 12, 1785, 29:531-32.

33. Pollock to Miró and Navarro, November 12, 1787, PC, legajo 1409. For Pollock's contacts with Gardoqui and Brown, see James, *Oliver Pollock*, 325-32; Watlington, "John Brown and the Spanish Conspiracy," 55-59. For Pollock's trade in tobacco, see Andrew Bayard to Harry Innes, November 14, 1790, Innes Papers, Ayer MS 439, Newberry Library.

34. Ermus, "Reduced to Ashes," 307–8; DeRojas, "The Great Fire of 1788 in New Orleans," 578–81; Pritchard, "An Account of the Conflagration." See also Din, *Francisco Bouligny*, 161–62.

35. Pollock to Miró, February 10, 1789, AHN, Estado, legajo 3889. In his acceptance letter, Miró observed that Louisiana did not have suitable goods for export to the United States that would be an alternative to specie. See Miró to Pollock, February 12, 1789, PC, legajo 2370; Miró to Valdés, February 12, 1789, AHN, Estado, legajo 3889. For Pollock's welcome in New Orleans, see James, *Oliver Pollock*, 327–33.

36. Pollock to Miró, February 10, 1789, AHN, Estado, legajo 3889. For a helpful overview of Pollock's life, see Cummins, "Oliver Pollock," 198–218. Louisiana's broadening commerce after the fire is discussed in Ermus, "Reduced to Ashes," 309–13.

37. For the repurchase of the Tunica property, see Cummins, "Oliver Pollock's Plantations," 41–47. See also Arena, "Philadelphia-Spanish New Orleans Trade in the 1790s," 429–45 (the "fire pump" reference is from p. 432).

38. *Report of the Committee . . . on the Petition of Oliver Pollock* [1814]. *Report of the Committee on the Petition of Oliver Pollock. December 21, 1818.*

39. Alford, *Prince among Slaves*, 34–38. For Irwin's participation in the slave trade at Natchez, see Buckner, "Constructing Identities on the Frontier of Slavery," 60–64.

40. Alford, 41–42. Irwin sold Ibrahima to Thomas Foster, a Natchez planter, on August 18, 1788.

41. Thomas Irwin to General William Irvine [*sic*], May 20, 1789, Irvine Papers, HSP. Miró's written permission to Matthew Irwin, written in English, is dated May 25, 1789, and may be found in the same collection.

42. Ibid.

43. Thomas Irwin to General William Irvine, May 20, 1789, Irvine Papers, HSP. For Stephen Minor's background, see Holmes, *Documentos inéditos*, 186n.

44. Thomas Irwin's name appears among a group of Natchez planters petitioning Esteban Miró to lobby the Spanish crown to resume the purchase of Louisiana tobacco in large quantities. The undated petition was probably written in 1790. See Inhabitants of the District of Natchez to Stephen Miró [1790?], PC, legajo 120.

45. The size of Forman's party is indicated in his undated letter to James Wilkinson [1790], PC, legajo 2374. Ezekiel Forman's river journey was later recounted by his nephew Samuel. See Forman, *Narrative of a Journey Down the Ohio and Mississippi in 1789–90*, 20–26. Forman's memoir, written sometime before his death in 1862, was annotated by Lyman Draper.

46. Forman, *Narrative*, 20–26. On April 22, 1790, Lt. Col. Carlos de Grand-Pré in Natchez informed Governor Miró of the arrival of Ezekiel Forman, his wife and four children, white servants and passengers, and sixty-seven slaves. See SMV, 3, pt. 2:326–27. On November 24, 1789, Samuel Forman had contracted with his uncle, General David Forman, to assist in bringing the latter's slaves and servants to Fort Pitt for the first part of the journey to Natchez. David Forman agreed to pay Samuel a salary of $100 per year in "Spanish Mill'd Dollars." See Articles of agreement, November 24, 1789, Fairchild Collection, Box 3, NYPL. Samuel Forman carried legal papers attesting to the fact that the blacks were only passing through Pennsylvania—and therefore not to be judged free under that state's gradual emancipation act of 1780.

47. For Wilkinson's recommendation, see Wilkinson to Miró, February 22, 1790, PC, legajo 2374. For Natchez events, see Forman, *Narrative*, 53–56. On June 1, 1791, Miró signed a certificate declaring Samuel Forman a Spanish subject of good standing. He issued a passport to him the same day. Both documents are in the Fairchild Collection, Box 3, NYPL.

48. Forman, *Narrative*, 56–58.

49. Carlos de Grand Pré reported the arrival of some fifty-five American flatboats and two *berchas*—the latter craft resembling keelboats—at Natchez from February 23 through July 31, 1790. Apart from Ezekiel Forman, only two white boat owners came to settle with more than an incidental number of slaves. One owner came with twenty-five blacks while the other arrived with seven. The overwhelming majority of flatboat employees came as single men. See SMV, 3, pt. 2:299–300, 313–14, 323–31, 333–37, 342–56, 368.

50. The name "under-the-hill" may not have been used before 1800. See Elliott, "City and Empire," 279–99; Morris, *Becoming Southern*, 24–28; Holmes, *Gayoso*, 37–43, 101–4; Buckner, "Constructing Identities on the Frontier of Slavery," 50–55.

51. Chandler Rice to Samuel Forman, April 3, 1791, Samuel Forman Papers, Fairchild Collection, NYPL.

52. The Spanish council of state ruled on December 21, 1790, that two million pounds of Louisiana tobacco would be admitted for the 1790 crop, but only 40,000 pounds for 1791. The quota was only temporarily raised in 1794 and 1796. See Holmes, *Gayoso*, 90–95.

53. "A representation . . . by Ezekiel Forman" to Miró [1790], PC, leg. 120.

54. Affadavit of Charles Wilkins, October 7, 1808, Harry Innes Papers, Ayer Mss., Newberry Library. See also Connelley and Coulter, *History of Kentucky*, 1:466–68.

55. For the growth of Upper Louisiana, see Aron, *American Confluence*, 77–105; DuVal, *The Native Ground*, 162–64; Foley, *The Genesis of Missouri*, 65; Din and Nasatir, *The Imperial Osages*, 240–46.

56. Gardoqui to Zéspedes, July 5, 1787, EF, reel 38; Zéspedes to the marques de Sonora, July 28, 1787, EF, reel 17. Tanner, *Zéspedes in East Florida*, 145.

57. After arriving at Natchez, Bruin settled at Bayou Pierre north of the town. See the passenger list of Spanish commandant Carlos de Grand-Pre, June 20, 1788, Parsons Collection, University of Texas at Austin. See also Coker, "The Bruins and the Formulation of Spanish Immigration Policy in the Old Southwest," 61–71; Holmes, *Gayoso*, 37.

58. The tenants, living on the lands of Franks's father, grandfather, and uncle, authorized him to be their spokesman in America. See *Traducción de carta escrivia desde Irlanda*, September 22, 1786, EF, reel 17. For the court's judgment, see Valdés to Floridablanca, September 3, 1787, AHN, Estado, legajo 3889.

59. Macarty's memorial of August 14, 1787, is printed in Solano Costa, "La colonización irlandesa de la Luisiana española," 201–8. The royal court rejected Macarty's plan on May 14, 1789, long after it had been forwarded to Madrid. See Solano Costa, "La colonización irlandesa de la Luisiana española," 202–3.

60. Carondelet to Floridablanca, February 25, 1792, AHN, Estado, legajo 3898. ("Lo poco, o nada que se debe contar sobre aquellas gentes acostumbradas a mudar de domi-

cilio, como de camisa.") Carondelet believed newly returned Kentuckians would assist their American compatriots if the latter attacked Spanish territory.

61. In a report written during the summer of 1792, Miró welcomed the idea of European colonization, but also proposed the establishment of a royal fund to pay the transportation costs of American settlers and their families who desired to move to the Spanish Mississippi. Only "vagabonds" need be explicitly kept out. See *"Descripción de la Luisiana, 1792,"* in Holmes, *Documentos inéditos*, 27.

62. Carondelet to Floridablanca, February 25, 1792, AHN, Estado, legajo 3898. For the Philadelphia colonization mission, see Din, "Spain's Immigration Policy in Louisiana and the American Penetration," 256–58.

63. Tardiveau to Carondelet, July 17, 1792, AHN, Estado, legajo 3898. In Tardiveau's words: "El interes personal es sin disputa el principal movil de las operaciones del hombre." For biographical background, see Rice, *Barthélemi Tardiveau*, 1–2, 25–26, 42–44.

64. Rice, *Barthélemi Tardiveau*, 44–47. See also Din, "Spain's Immigration Policy and Louisiana," 259–61; Aron, *American Confluence*, 83–84.

65. Tardiveau authored a report on Louisiana for the come de Moustier, French minister to the United States. See Rice, *Barthélemi Tardiveau*, 13–15; Lyon, "Moustier's Memoir."

66. For Didier's appeal to Carondelet (as translated into Spanish), see Andreu Ocariz, "El proyecto de Louis de Villemont," 48–49.

67. Carondelet to Floridablanca, May 8, 1792, PC, legajo 177.

68. In 1789, Miró limited the importation and sale of black creole slaves from the British and French Caribbean. In 1792–1793, Louisiana merchants could only lawfully import native Africans—and that with the cabildo's permission. For a detailed explanation of royal and provincial regulations, see Din, *Spaniards, Planters, and Slaves*, 124–25, 151–54, 186–87, 206–7.

69. Navarro, "Reflexiones políticas," 369. ("Una contrata de mil familias alemanas, casadas y de buena robustez, a qualquiera costo serian baratas.")

70. For the German component of von Steuben's proposal, see his memorial in CONSP, 239.

71. Burson, *The Stewardship of Don Esteban Miró*, 128–29; Din, "Proposals and Plans for Colonization in Spanish Louisiana," 206–7.

72. Carondelet is cited in Andreu Ocariz, "El proyecto de Louis de Villemont," 52–53. (Villemont is also spelled Vilemont in contemporary records.)

73. Whitaker, *The Spanish-American Frontier*, 185–200.

74. Not ruling out slave importation, Villemont intended to allow only *bozales* into the province. See Andreu Ocariz, "El proyecto de Louis de Villemont," 45–48 (quotation, p. 45); Din, "Spain's Immigration Policy," 264–65.

75. Godoy's aphorism, in English translation, is in Whitaker, *The Mississippi Question*, 34–35. For Godoy's and the council's negative judgment, see Andreu Ocariz, "El proyecto de Louis de Villemont," 55.

76. Whitaker, *The Mississippi Question*, 85–90. In 1798, American ships were permitted to sell imported goods in Louisiana, but at a duty of 21 percent that had the unintended impact of encouraging smuggling.

77. Joseph Piernas, "Proyecto de una nueva población en el río de Calcasieu en la provincia de la Luisiana," April 24, 1795, in Holmes, *Documentos, inéditos*, 144–69. Knowing the imperial government's financial concerns, Piernas made no demand on the royal treasury. The imperial government finally approved his proposal in 1798, almost three years after it was initiated! See Holmes, "Joseph Piernas and a Proposed Settlement"; Holmes, "Joseph Piernas and the Nascent Cattle Industry"; Holmes, "The Calcasieu Promoter."

78. Piernas's formal address to Carondelet is dated April 25, 1795, while his colonization proposal to the crown was signed the previous day. See Holmes, *Documentos inéditos*, 147, 169.

79. Andreu Ocariz, "Los últimos proyectos inmigratorios en la Louisiana española," 41–43; Mitchell and Calhoun, "The Marquis de Maison Rouge," 289–462. See also Moore, "The Role of the Baron de Bastrop," 606–81.

80. Filhiol to Miró, September 1, 1784, PC, leg. 197. See also Hardin, "Juan Filhiol"; Dickinson, "Don Juan Filhiol." Lt. Governor Bouligny developed an elaborate plan of Ouachia colonization in 1778, though the project was not implemented. See Din, "Francisco Bouligny's 1778 Plans for Settlement in Louisiana," 211–24.

81. European indentured servants were also permitted, with the proviso that they be allotted land after completing a six-year term. A translation of the contract is in Mitchell and Calhoun, "The Marquis de Maison Rouge," 303–4. The two well-to-do colonists were Alexandre Montseraud, a Saint-Domingue refugee who had three slaves, and the chevalier d'Anemours, former French consul-general to the United States who was the master of six slaves. For the list of colonists, see Mitchell and Calhoun, "The Marquis de Maison Rouge," 326.

82. Moore, "The Role of the Baron de Bastrop," 613–15.

83. In May 1797, Bastrop's settlement had ninety-nine persons, including fourteen white families, ten single white men, and one slave. See Moore, "The Role of the Baron de Bastrop," 616–27; Din, "Spain's Immigration Policy," 268–70. For the Ouachita, see Darby, *A Geographical Description of the State of Louisiana*, 178–85. Darby wrote that excellent wheat had been cultivated in the past within Bastrop's grant, but he did not give evidence of any current production.

84. The marqués de Casa Calvo supported Bastrop against provincial intendant Ramón de López y Angulo, who argued that the colonization contract should be canceled. See Casa Calvo's letter to Spanish secretary of state Mariano Luís de Urquijo, August 8, 1800, AHN, Estado, legajo 3901; López y Angulo to Urquijo, August 12, 1800, AHN, Estado, legajo 3888. See Din, "Spain's Immigration Policy," 268–70.

85. After the sales of 1804–5, Bastrop retained 100,000 acres of what he claimed by grant. See Mitchell and Calhoun, "The Marquis de Maison Rouge," 387–90, 399–406. For Bastrop's Ouachita sales and Texas settlement, see Moore, "The Role of the Baron de Bastrop," 627–75.

86. [Dehault Delassus de Luzières], *An Official Account of the Situation*. Delassus signed this report on May 17, 1796. For the penalty prescribed for admitting U.S. immigrants, see Carondelet to Charles (Carlos) du Hault de Lassus, July 1, 1796, Parsons Collection. This letter was written in French. The surname Delassus was spelled various ways in contemporary records.

87. Holmes, *Gayoso*, 219–20, 226–28.

88. Trudeau to Gayoso, May 6, 1798, in Nasatir, *Before Lewis and Clark*, 2:559. See also Din, "Spain's Immigration Policy in Louisiana," 271.

89. Gracy, *Moses Austin*, 59–66; Faragher, *Daniel Boone*, 274–80. See also Brown, *Frontiersman*, 226–37.

90. Yrujo to Godoy [Prince of the Peace], August 5, 1797, cited in Loomis and Nasatir, *Pedro Vial and the Roads to Santa Fe*, 162; Gayoso to Francisco Saavedra, November 22, 1798, in Nasatir, *Before Lewis and Clark*, 2:583. The exception for public officers in the United States is mentioned in Din, "Spain's Immigration Policy in Louisiana," 271.

CHAPTER 7

1. Miró's notes in these instances include the day and month, but not the year of communication. The quotation is from a note dated February 28. Miró's complaint about Wilkinson's not being clear in cipher carries the date of January 14. There is a strong possibility that this last message was drafted in 1790. See Miró to Wilkinson, draft notes, PC, legajo 2373.

2. The draft cipher letter, mentioning possible hostilities with England, ends with the notation March 4. See PC, legajo 2373. It may have been written in 1790, when hostilities loomed between Britain and Spain.

3. Narrett, "Geopolitics and Intrigue."

4. Gardoqui to Miró, June 22, 1787 (quotations), and August 4, 1787, PC, legajo 1409. In the letter of August 4, Gardoqui wrote of the "shameless arrogance" of American "vagabonds" migrating to the Mississippi.

5. Gardoqui to Floridablanca, April 18, 1788, in Gómez del Campillo, *Relaciones diplomaticas entre España y los Estados Unidos*, 1:532–37 (quotations, p. 532).

6. Gardoqui to Miró, October 2, 1788; George Morgan to Gardoqui, October 7, 1788, GDQUI, 1:319, 365. Gardoqui refused a passport to two merchants who requested permission to ship goods by riverboat from Fort Pitt via Spanish Illinois to New Orleans. See Gardoqui to Ezpeleta, October 22, 1787, PC, legajo 1409.

7. Gardoqui to Miró, October 2, 1788, GDQUI, 1:319–20. See John Brown to George Muter, July 10, 1788, in LDC, 25:222. For an important analytical and documentary source, see CONSP.

8. Brown to Madison, May 12, 1788, LDC, 25:96; Brown to John Breckenridge, August 5, 1788, LDC, 271. See also Watlington, "John Brown and the Spanish Conspiracy," 65–67; Harrison, *Kentucky's Road to Statehood*, 68–72.

9. Watlington, "John Brown and the Spanish Conspiracy," 66.

10. John S[evier] to Gardoqui, September 12, 1788, PC, legajo 2370. Sevier initially opposed the formation of Franklin as an independent state in December 1784, but soon linked himself to Franklin statehood. See Whitaker, "The Muscle Shoals Speculation," 371; Whitaker, "Spanish Intrigue in the Old Southwest," 158–62.

11. See Whitaker, "The Muscle Shoals Speculation," 365–70; Finger, *Tennessee's Frontiers*, 113–24. Private speculative and colonizing interests allied with Georgia because that state claimed that the bend of the Tennessee lay within its boundaries. See Nichols, "Land, Republicanism, and Indians," 204–5.

12. White to Ezpeleta, December 26, 1788, CONSP, 271–74; Ezpeleta to Valdés, December 29, 1788, CONSP, 122–25 (AHN, Estado, leg. 3888). White assumed the role of intermediary between Sevier and the Spanish chargé. See Conrad, "The Indefatigable Dr. James White," 12–23; Henderson, "The Spanish Conspiracy in Tennessee," 229–43.

13. Holmes, *Gayoso*, 28–29.

14. Royal order of December 1, 1788, CONSP, 323. White to Miró, April 18, 1789, PC, legajo 2370; Miró to White, April 20, 1789; Miró to Valdés, April 30, 1789, PC, leg. 177 (YONGE).

15. The Spanish supreme council of state approved Gayoso's proposed frontier tour, but not in sufficient time to sway Miró. See CONSP, 145; Gayoso to Floridablanca, May 8, 1789, in CONSP, 275–84; Holmes, *Gayoso*, 28–29, 39–40.

16. Finger, *Tennessee's Frontiers*, 122–24; Abernethy, *From Frontier to Plantation*, 85–90, 99–100.

17. Conrad, "The Indefatigable Dr. James White," 24.

18. Ibid., 24–36.

19. Jacobs, *Tarnished Warrior*, 47–59. For a recent biography, see Linklater, *An Artist in Treason*.

20. Wilkinson to Miró, February 12, 1789, PC, legajo 2373.

21. Ibid. Wilkinson starkly declared Kentucky's choice as one of alliance with either Spain or Britain during his first visit to New Orleans. See his memorial to Miró and Navarro of September 1787, PC, legajo 2373.

22. Din, *Francisco Bouligny*, 167–68.

23. The royal order is printed in CONSP, 323–25.

24. "Sales . . . by Major Dunn and Disposed of for Account of James Wilkinson Esquire Kentucky" [1788], NARA, RG 107, Letters Received by the Secretary of War, Unregistered Series, 1789–1861, Microcopy 222, roll 1, W-1788.

25. Miró to Wilkinson, August 6, 1788. The governor defended excessive purchases of Kentucky tobacco simply on the grounds of preserving Wilkinson's political friendship. See Miró to Valdés, Spr. 11, 1789, PC, legajo 177 (YONGE).

26. Stephen Miró [Message to Franklin and the Cumberland District], April 20, 1789, PC, legajo 2370. This message was transmitted in English.

27. Wilkinson to Miró, February 12, 1789, PC, legajo 2373.

28. Memorial of John Duncan, William Leavey, James Reynolds, Philip Bush, and John Pickett to Stephen Miró, September 9, 1789, PC, legajo 2373. For the Spanish account of the incident, see Josef Evia [José de Evia] to Miró, September 10, 1789, PC, legajo 177 (YONGE).

29. Miró to Manuel Gregorio de Texada, September 12, 1789 (two letters of that date), PC, legajo 177 (YONGE).

30. See Wilkinson's "List of Characters in Kentucky, worthy to be engaged in the Interest of his Catholic Majesty," January 4, 1790, PC, legajo 2374. Miró had solicited this list when Wilkinson was visiting him in New Orleans. For the loan of $7,000, see Miró to Wilkinson, September 22, 1789, PC, legajo 177 (YONGE); Miró to Valdés, May 22, 1790, PC, legajo 177; Miró to Wilkinson, September 20, 1790, PC, legajo 2374.

31. Wilkinson to Miró, February 12, 1789, PC, legajo 2373. See also Wright, *Britain and the American Frontier*, 44.

32. Memorial of John Connolly in Bernardo del Campo to Floridablanca [1783], AHN, Estado, legajo 4246, LC; Campo to Floridablanca, September 29, 1783, AHN, Estado, legajo 4246, LC. See also Burton, "John Connolly," 70–105.
33. Wilkinson to McIlvain, March 17, 1791, Ayer Ms. 439/Box 1, Newberry Library.
34. Wilkinson to Miró, February 12, 1789, PC, legajo 2373.
35. For the shift in Spanish policy, see Coutts, "Boom and Bust," 306–7. Wilkinson's troubled financial position is discussed in Jacobs, *Tarnished Warrior*, 106–7.
36. Wilkinson to Gayoso, November 4, 1791, PC, legajo 2374. Carondelet's assessment is in his letter to Floridablanca, February 25, 1792, AHN, Estado 3898. For Wilkinson's pension, which was retroactive to January 1, 1789, see Carondelet to Floridablanca, February 16, 1792, AHN, Estado 3898. Wilkinson was appointed brigadier general on March 5, 1792, after receiving the lieutenant colonel's rank on October 22, 1791. See Jacobs, *Tarnished Warrior*, 114–18.
37. Wilkinson to Andrés Armesto, August 1, 1787, PC, legajo 2373.
38. On March 21, 1787, Clark assumed an obligation of $22,519 (including interest) that Pollock had contracted with Peter Le Bourgeois and his wife, Margaret Renne[?], of New Orleans in 1780. See notarized agreement of May 27, 1788, indicating Clark's fulfillment of the debt, along with certification by Governor Miró on May 4, 1790, Coxe Family Papers (Oliver Pollock folder), HSP. Daniel Clark Sr. was provincial secretary and a deputy customs collector in Pensacola in 1765. See Fabel, *The Economy of British West Florida*, 138–39; Cummins, "Anglo Merchants and Capital Migration."
39. Articles of Agreement, August 7, 1788, Letters Received by the Secretary of War, Unregistered Series, 1789–1861, NARA, RG 107, M222, roll 1, W-1788; Wilkinson's acknowledgment of Clark's shipment, or "Adventure," is dated September 18, 1788, NARA, RG 107, M222, roll 1, W-1788.
40. The governor felt so bound to Wilkinson that he described their collaborative political scheme as "our plan." See Miró to Wilkinson, August 6, 1788, PC, legajo 2373.
41. See Elizabeth Urban Alexander, "Daniel Clark: Merchant Prince of New Orleans," in Smith and Allen, *Nexus of Empire*, 241–67.
42. Wilkinson to Gayoso, December 21, 1792, PC, legajo 2374.
43. Wilkinson to Gayoso, December 17, 1790, PC, legajo 2374. Clement Biddle had an economic stake in Wilkinson's move from Philadelphia to Kentucky in 1783–84. For links between Biddle, Reed and Forde, and Pollock, see Whitaker, "Reed and Forde, Merchant Adventurers of Philadelphia," 237–62 (especially pp. 245–52).
44. Clark to Pickering, April 18, 1798, Annals of Congress, 10th Congress, 1st session, Appendix: 2372 (1st quotation), 2374. After breaking with Wilkinson years later, Clark condemned his former associate as a selfish monopolist filching Spanish silver while scheming at Kentucky's secession. See Clark, *Proofs of the Corruption of Gen. James Wilkinson*, 12, 15.
45. For the negotiations of a possible treaty, see Carondelet to Wilkinson, July 1795; Wilkinson to Carondelet [October 16, 1795?], PC, legajo, 2374. For the advice on discretion, see Wilkinson to Carondelet, September 22, 1796, PC, legajo 2375.
46. George Nicholas, Harry Innes, William Murray, and Benjamin Sebastian to Carondelet, November 19, 1795, in Las Casas to Alcudia, February 16, 1796, MPASD, 6:167–70; Carondelet to Alcudia, September 25, 1795, ibid., 6:33–42. See Din, "Spain's

Immigration Policy in Louisiana," 267. For Gayoso's involvement in separatist diplomacy, see Nasatir, *Spanish War Vessels on the Mississippi, 1792–1796*, 120–31.

47. Gayoso to Innes, July 27, 1794, PC, legajo 2371; Innes to Gayoso, December 11, 1794, quoted in Whitaker, "Harry Innes and the Spanish Intrigue," 239.

48. For "dark and bloody ground" as a Kentucky metaphor, see Brown, *Frontiersman*, 44; Aron, *How the West Was Lost*, 56–57, 111–12. Kentucky militia joined Cumberland whites, for example, in attacking Chickamauga towns in 1794. See Dowd, *A Spirited Resistance*, 112.

49. Miró to Wilkinson, PC, legajo 2370.

50. Robertson to Miró, January 29, 1789 (postscript February 18, 1789), and Smith to Miró, March 11, 1789, in Whitaker, "Letters of James Robertson and Daniel Smith," 409–12 (quotation, pp. 410–11); Miró to Robertson, April 20, 1789, in "Correspondence of General James Robertson," 87–88; McGillivray to Robertson, December 1, 1788, "Correspondence of General James Robertson," 85–86.

51. Green to Richard Winn [also spelled Wynn], April 15, 1789, PC, legajo 120.

52. James Wilkinson, John Brown, Harry Innes, Benjamin Sebastian, and Isaac B. Dunn to Gardoqui, January 15, 1789, AHN, Estado, legajo, 3894; Wilkinson to Miró, February 14, 1788, AHN, Estado, legajo, 3888bis.

53. Wilkinson to Miró, February 12, 1789, PC, legajo 2373.

54. Wilkinson to Gayoso, March 16, 1790, April 2, 1790, and May 4, 1790 (quotation), PC, legajo 2374.

55. Tardiveau's services came with a fee—one-tenth of all lands that Congress guaranteed to his clients, who were mostly of French descent but also included some Anglo-Americans. See the agreement between Cahokia inhabitants and Tardiveau, August 27, 1787, in Alvord, *Cahokia Records*, 591–93. Similar agreements were made between Tardiveau and other Illinois settlers. See Rice, *Barthélemi Tardiveau*, 1–2, 7–9. For the congressional ruling of August 29, 1788, confirming the French inhabitants' land rights, see JCC, 34:472–74. See also Morgan to Commissioners of the Treasury, September 9, 1788, NARA, RG 360, PCC, microcopy M247, roll 153; Gardoqui to Morgan, September 2, 1788, GDQUI, 1:329, 331–32. See also Savelle, *George Morgan*, 204.

56. Hutchins, *An Historical Narrative and Topographical Description of Louisiana and West-Florida*. See Gardoqui's Spanish translation of Hutchins's "*Reflexiones concernientes al Territorio del oeste de los Estados Unidos*" [1788], AHN, Estado, legajo 3889bis. This document quotes Hutchins at length and includes Gardoqui's own gloss.

57. Gardoqui even sent Miró one of Thomas Hutchins's maps demarcating the land claims. As explained below, Miró did not follow Gardoqui's recommendation. For the envoy's request, see Gardoqui to Miró, February 13, 1788, AHN, Estado, legajo 3889.

58. Hutchins supported Morgan's bid for an Illinois governorship at the same time he asked for Morgan's help in paying a debt of £300 in 1786. See Hutchins to Morgan, February 24, 1786, George Morgan Papers, LC. For tuition payments of July 5, 1787, to October 6, 1788, see George Morgan Account Book, Princeton University Library (Rare Books and Special Collections). For collaboration on the Illinois project, see Hutchins to the Board of Treasury, May 27, 1788; Hutchins to committee of Congress, March 5, 1788, PCC, Microcopy M247, roll 96.

59. Gardoqui to Morgan, October 4, 1788, GDQUI, 1:362–63. Gardoqui authorized Morgan to reconnoiter the land between Cape Cinque Hommes and the confluence of the St. Francis River and the Mississippi—and extending two degrees of longitude to the west. See Gardoqui to Morgan, October 4, 1788, GDQUI, 1:362. Distances are calibrated according to Captain Harry Gordon and Lt. Thomas Hutchins's measurements of 1766. See "Journal of Capt. H. Gordon, 1766," in Alvord and Carter, *The New Régime*, 310–11.

60. Gardoqui to Morgan, October 4, 1788, GDQUI, 1:362–63. In his petition to Madrid of September 1788, Morgan requested a still vaster concession as far south as the *"río rojo o Colorado"*—the Red River. See proposal of Morgan, September [ ], 1788, GDQUI, 1:348.

61. Morgan's proposal, September [ ], 1788, CONSP, 245; Gardoqui to Floridablanca, October 24, 1788, GDQUI, 1:317.

62. For East Florida colonization projects, see Gardoqui's passport to Henry Ellison, April 19, 1789, EF, reel 38. Gardoqui approved the plan of William Eugene Imlay, a New Jersey physician, to establish a 600-square mile colony in East Florida. See Gardoqui to Imlay, June 2, 1789; Imlay to Zéspedes, July 29, 1789; Zéspedes to Gardoqui, July 29 and 30, 1789, EF, reel 38.

63. Morgan's proposal, September [ ], 1788, CONSP, 243. See also *The Constitution of the Common-Wealth of Pennsylvania*, 9.

64. Morgan to Gardoqui, October 7, 1788, and Gardoqui to Morgan, October 10, 1788, GDQUI, 1:365–68.

65. Dunn to Wilkinson, November [ ], 1788, JWCHM.

66. Wilkinson to Miró, February 14, 1789. The letter is transcribed in Spanish in CONSP, 261–65. See also Wilkinson to Miró, February 12, 1789, PC, legajo 2373.

67. Din, "Immigration Policy of Governor Esteban Miró," 168–70.

68. Miró to Valdés, May 20, 1789, MPASD, 3:377. Miró's warning of "a Republic in the midst of His Majesty's Dominions" (*una República en medio de los dominios de S.M.*) referred specifically to Peter Paulus's colonization proposal, but was similarly relevant to Morgan's plan, which the governor discussed at length in the same letter.

69. Hutchins to Clark, December 20, 1788, PC, legajo 2370.

70. Ibid.

71. Miró to McGillivray, May 22, 1789, in Caughey, *McGillivray of the Creeks*, 232–33.

72. McGillivray to Miró, May 26 and June 24, 1789, ibid., 234–36, 239–40; McGillivray to Panton, August 10, 1789, ibid., 247 (quotation).

73. Savelle, *George Morgan*, 137–39.

74. George Morgan, Speech to the Delawares, Shawnees, and Cherokees, April [?], 1789, Wayne Mss., HSP. For emigrant Indians in Spanish Illinois or Missouri, see Aron, *American Confluence*, 80–81, 101–4; Foley, *The Genesis of Missouri*, 65. Spanish commandant Manuel Perez stated that Morgan was accompanied by seventy heads of families, about twenty of whom began a settlement while the others returned to bring back family members. See Perez to Miró, March 2, 1789, PC, legajo 120.

75. Madison to Monroe, November 5, 1788, JMLC. For Madison's general distrust of Spain, see Stagg, *Borderlines in Borderlands*, 30.

76. Coxe to Madison, March 18, 1789, JMLC; Madison to Washington, March 26,

1789, GWLC. In this letter, Madison described Morgan's settlers as "adventurers," a term that was firmly rooted in the Anglo-American understanding of voluntary colonial migration.

77. Jáudenes returned to Spain before joining Viar as a Spanish commissioner to the United States in 1791. See Whitaker, *The Spanish-American Frontier*, 72, 145.

78. Dawson surmised that Morgan's colonists had received "the most sound assurances of freedom in religious matters—a free navigation of the Mississippi to New Orleans clear of all duties and taxes; besides being entitled to all the commercial priviledges [sic] which the citizens of New Orleans enjoy in any of the King of Spain's rich dominions." See John Dawson to Beverley Randolph, January 29, 1789, LDC, 25:485. See also Dawson to Madison, January 29[?], 1789, LDC, 25:483.

79. James Cole Mountflorence to Benjamin Hawkins, May 11, 1789, PC, leg. 120. Mountflorence, who was of Anglo-French parentage and grew up in Paris, served as a foreign volunteer in the American Revolutionary War before becoming involved in trans-Appalachian affairs. See Campbell, "The French Intrigue of James Cole Mountflorence," 781–83.

80. "Letter respecting the state of American manufactures, &c.," May 8, 1789, *The American Museum, or Universal Magazine* 6 (September 1789): 238.

81. Lardner Clark to Hawkins, May 9, 1789, PC, leg. 120. Though Hawkins was a nationalist rather than a western separatist, he cultivated a personal rapport with Gardoqui. See Masterson, *William Blount*, 158, 162.

82. Clark to Hawkins, May 9, 1789, PC, leg. 120. Lardner Clark remained a Nashville resident for some years. Financial difficulties in the 1790s induced him to relocate to Illinois and then Ste. Genevieve in Upper Louisiana, where he died in 1801. See Provine, "Lardner Clark."

CHAPTER 8

1. Powell was questioned by Captain Carlos Howard, Zéspedes's secretary, who served as interpreter and translator in this case. See "Copia de la Traducción del Interrogatorio hecho á Don Thomas Powell," December 21, 1787, in Zéspedes to Ezpeleta, January 16, 1788, PC, legajo 1395, LOCKEY, Transcripts. See also Powell to Zéspedes, August 28, 1787; Zéspedes to Powell, September 12, 1787; Powell to Zéspedes, November 9, 1787, Zéspedes to Powell, November 21, 1787, LOCKEY, Transcripts. For details of the Powell intrigue, see Tanner, "Zéspedes and the Southern Conspiracies," 15–28.

2. "Interrogatorio hecho á Don Thomas Powell," December 21, 1787, in Zéspedes to Ezpeleta, January 16, 1788, PC, legajo 1395, LOCKEY, Transcripts; Powell to Carlos Howard, March 11, 1788, EF, reel 82.

3. Zéspedes to Antonio Valdés, March 24, 1788, AHN, legajo 3901, LOCKEY, Transcripts. (Quotation: "Puede mas vien considerarse el mero prematuro parto de la ociosidad, y codicia de aventureros necesitados, quienes no conociendo mas Ley, ó caveza, que las que les dicta su propio capricho, se han dexado aluzinar [?] de la creencia tan errada, como ridicula (pero que sin duda les acompaña) de que en los Dominios Hispano-Americano, con solo escarbar la tierra, se encuentra oro, y Plata, apuñados llenos; y por

lo mismo son capses de emprender qualquiera atentado, por loco, y extravagante que sea, para realizar sus disparatados sueños."

4. Zéspedes to Valdés, March 24, 1788, ibid.

5. Zéspedes to Luis de Las Casas, June 20, 1790, translated in Lewis, "*Cracker*—Spanish Florida Style," 191.

6. For freebooting or filibustering in the 1850s, see May, *Manifest Destiny's Underworld*.

7. "An Act for disposing of certain vacant lands or territory within this State," December 21, 1789, ASPIA, 1:114-15. See also Haskins, *The Yazoo Land Companies*, 8. The act of 1789 was a precursor to the Georgia's notorious "Yazoo" scheme of 1795. See McGrath, *Yazoo: Law and Politics in the Early Republic*, 5-7.

8. ASPIA, 1:114.

9. The Georgia act followed the state's failure to reach a satisfactory land cession agreement with Congress by which it would cede a large portion of its western land claims to national authority. See the report of Committee of Congress, July 14, 1788, JCC, 34:320-23.

10. Haskins, *The Yazoo Land Companies*, 7. Alexander Moultrie, scion of one of South Carolina's leading families, was the company's director and most prestigious founding shareholder.

11. Born James Fallon on March 11, 1749, the doctor changed his name to O'Fallon in the late 1780s when negotiating with Spanish authorities. See Parish, "The Intrigues of Doctor James O'Fallon," 230-63.

12. Ibid., 236-37.

13. Zéspedes to Ezpeleta, October 1, 1788, PC, legajo 1395, LOCKEY, Transcripts. See also Marshall, *The Impeachment of Warren Hastings*.

14. For the Yazoo company's offer to McGillivray, see Alexander Moultrie to McGillivray, February 19, 1790, in Whitaker, "The South Carolina Yazoo Company," 393.

15. Thomas Washington, a Yazoo company founder, desired Wilkinson to be among his group's "solid Adventurers." See Washington to Wilkinson, February 21, 1789 [1790?], PC, legajo 2373.

16. O'Fallon to Miró, May 24, 1790, PC, legajo 2371.

17. Wilkinson to Miró, April 30, 1790, PC, legajo 2374; Wilkinson to Gayoso, June 20, 1790, PC, legajo 2374. For Wilkinson's change of mind, see his letter to Alexander Moultrie, November 4, 1790, PC, legajo 2374. See also Parish, "The Intrigues of Doctor James O'Fallon," 246; Weeks, *Paths to a Middle Ground*, 58.

18. Miró to Antonio Valdés, August 10, 1790, PC, legajo 177 (LOCKEY, Transcripts). For O'Fallon's claim of 10,000 fighting men, see his letter to Miró, May 24, 1790, PC, legajo 2371.

19. O'Fallon to Miró, July 16, 1790, SMV, 3, pt. 2:359-60.

20. O'Fallon to Miró, January 15, 1791, PC, legajo 2371; Miró to Las Casas, December 20, 1790, PC, legajo 1446. For Spanish defensive preparations for Nogales, see Weeks, *Paths to a Middle Ground*, 58-59.

21. O'Fallon to Colonel Bryan Bruin, December 21, 1790, PC, legajo 2371.

22. The size of grants was proportionate to rank. The colonel-commandant, heading the troops, was to be awarded 6,000 acres. Infantry captains had a right to 3,000 acres

while privates were each offered 200 acres. See "Military Articles of contract, &c. entered into between the South Carolina Yazoo Company and their troops, of the Yazoo Battalion" [1790], ASPIA, 1:115–17.

23. See "Officers of the Yazoo Battalion, commissioned as well as warranted [1790]," ASPIA, 1:117. For O'Fallon's boast of progress in recruitment, see his letter to Colonel John Holder, February 3, 1791, PC, legajo 2374; O'Fallon to William Morton, February 3, 1791, PC, legajo 2374.

24. Wilkinson to Miró, February 14, 1791, PC, legajo 2374. In this letter, Wilkinson boasted that he would soon destroy O'Fallon's enterprise. See also Wilkinson to Miró, March 17, 1791, PC, legajo 2374; Miró to Luis de Las Casas, April 30, 1791, PC legajo 151B; Parish, "The Intrigues of Doctor James O'Fallon," 249–52.

25. Pope, *A Tour through the Southern and Western Territories of the United States of America*, 29. See also Parish, "The Intrigues of Doctor James O'Fallon," 252. O'Fallon wrote of Fanny Clark as "an amiable Girl." See his letter to William Morton, February 3, 1791, PC, legajo 2374.

26. Jefferson to Kentucky district attorney, March 22, 1791, TJLC.

27. Washington to Alexander Moultrie, November 7, 1791, GWLC. For Washington's concerns about the Tennessee Yazoo Company, see his letter to Edmund Randolph, October 10, 1791, GWLC. Thomas Washington's actual surname was Walsh; "Washington" was his alias. See Haskins, "The Yazoo Land Companies," 7.

28. Moultrie to Benjamin Farrar, January 24, 1790, in Whitaker, "The South Carolina Yazoo Company," 390. See also O'Fallon to Miró, February 18, 1791, SMV, 3, pt. 2:403.

29. Miró to Valdés, August 10, 1790, PC, legajo 177, Transcripts (YONGE). Madison's dictum is in *Federalist*, no. 51.

30. While claiming to the Ohio, Bernardo de Gálvez authorized Gardoqui to yield lands as far south as the Tennessee River if necessary to reach an accord with the United States. See Gálvez to Gardoqui, April 28, 1785, AHN, Estado, legajo 3888bis. He was open to additional concessions provided Indian rights were protected above the Yazoo River. See Bemis, *Pinckney's Treaty*, 62–66.

31. Miró to Valdés, August 10, 1790, PC, legajo 177 (YONGE); Miró to Las Casas, February 24, 1791, PC, legajo 1446.

32. Las Casas to Miró, April 4, 1791, PC, legajo 151B. See also Las Casas to Miró, April 13 and 29, 1791, PC, legajo 151B. Las Casas had previously advised Miró to defend royal territory by force if necessary but also to attempt a negotiated solution with the South Carolina company. See Las Casas to Miró, November 20, 1790, PC, legajo 151B.

33. O'Fallon to Bruin, December 17 and 21, 1790, SMV, 3. pt. 2:393–98; Miro to Las Casas, February 24, 1791, PC, legajo 1446.

34. O'Fallon to Miró, January 15, 1791, PC, legajo 2371.

35. Gayoso to Miró, April 16, 1791, MPA: Spanish Dominion, 3:595–602; Weber, *The Spanish Frontier in North America*, 285–86. Spanish officials had a printed copy of the congressional act of February 4, 1791, authorizing Kentucky's admission as a state as of June 1, 1792. See PC, legajo 151B.

36. Washington to Jefferson, August 27, 1790; Jefferson to Washington, [August 28, 1790], TJLC.

37. Lynch, *Bourbon Spain*, 377–78, 388–91.

38. Campbell, "The Origin of Citizen Genet's Projected Attack on Spanish Louisiana," 515–44.

39. Mountflorence, a man of Anglo-Irish parentage, had grown up in Paris, later served in the American Revolutionary War, and thereafter became William Blount's land agent. See Campbell, "The French Intrigue of James Cole Mountflorence," 779–96 (quotation on 795), as well as Mountflorence's plan of October 26, 1792, as presented to the French foreign ministry, 794–96. See also Masterson, *William Blount*, 212–13.

40. The French foreign ministry considered George Rogers Clark and James Willing as potential volunteers leaders based on their achievements in the Revolutionary War. See Lyonnet, "Considerations sur la Louisiane" [1792], in Turner, "Documents on the Relations of France to Louisiana, 1792–1795," 501. In one anonymous draft plan, Wilkinson was identified as an essential ally. See "Plan proposé pour faire une Revolution dans la Louisiane," in Turner, "Selections from the Draper Collection," 948, 952.

41. For extending the "empire of liberty" and privateering, see Genet's Instructions, December 1792, in Turner, "Selections," 960 (quotation), 964–65.

42. "Plan proposé pour faire une Revolution dans la Louisiane" [fin 1792 et 4 premiers mois de 1793], in Turner, "Selections," 946–47.

43. "Plan proposé pour faire une Revolution dans la Louisiane," in Turner, "Selections," 951–52.

44. For "filibustiers des Bois," see Pierre Lyonnet, "Considerations sur la Louisiane" [1792], in Turner, "Documents on the Relations of France to Louisiana," 501. The phrase "adventurer by principle and habit" is taken from a related report. See "Plan proposé pour faire une Revolution dans la Louisiane," in Turner, "Selections," 948.

45. "Plan proposé pour faire une Revolution dans la Louisiane," in Turner, "Selections," 948. For the repudiation of monarchical diplomacy, especially under Louis XVI, see Genet's Instructions [1792], in Turner, "Selections," 959.

46. For the consul's praise of Tate, see Mangourit to Fauchet, March 30, 1794, in Turner, "The Mangourit Correspondence," 646.

47. Clark to the French minister, February 5, 1793, in Turner, "Selections," 967–71 (quotation on 970). For O'Fallon's probable authorship, see Parish, "The Intrigues of Doctor James O'Fallon," 258–59.

48. Klein, *Unification of a Slave State*, 207–9. See also Elkins and McKitrick, *The Age of Federalism*, 354–65; DeConde, *Entangling Alliances*, 183–86, 197–203.

49. Notes of Cabinet Meeting and Conversation with Edmond Charles Genet, July 5, 1793, *The Papers of Thomas Jefferson*, 26:438–39.

50. For Genet's charge, see *Supplement aux instructions donnés au Citoyen Genet*, endorsed December 23, 1792, in Turner, "Selections," 967; Genet to Clark, July 12, 1793, in Turner, "Selections," 986.

51. Tate's commission was issued in September or October 1793. See Genet to Tate, 1793, in Turner, "Mangourit Correspondence," 599; Mangourit to Tate, October 1, 1795, in Turner, "Mangourit Correspondence," 673–75. See also Ahlstrom, "Captain and Chef de Brigade William Tate."

52. Genet transmitted Clark's commission via André Michaux, French botanist and secret agent. See Turner, "Selections," 995–96. See also Genet to Tate, September 7, 1793, in Turner, "Mangourit Correspondence," 599.

53. Washington had Jefferson issue warnings on this ground in 1793 to Governors Isaac Shelby of Kentucky and William Moultrie of South Carolina. See Papers of George Washington, 14:379n. See also Jefferson to William Moultrie, November 13, 1793, TJLC; Henry Knox to George Mathews [governor of Georgia], May 11, 1794, GWLC.

54. Each offense was considered "a high misdemeanor" meriting a prison term not exceeding three years. The act prescribed a higher fine (up to $2,000) for an individual who acted under a foreign commission than for an enlistee, whose maximum fine was set at $1,000. See ASP, Statutes at Large, 3rd Congress, 1st session, 382–84.

55. A proposal along these lines was presented in the Senate, March 13, 1794. See Annals of Congress, Senate, 3rd Congress, 1st Session, 68.

56. Randolph to Jefferson, August 28, 1794; Jefferson to Randolph, September 7, 1794, TJLC.

57. Carondelet to the duque de Alcudia (Manuel de Godoy), October 25, 1793 (quotation); Carondelet to Gayoso, October 29, 1793, AHN, Estado, legajo 3898.

58. Carondelet to Alcudia, April 26, 1793, July 12 and July 31, 1793 (quotation), AHN, legajo 3898. For political unrest and the expulsions, see Liljegren, "Jacobinism in Spanish Louisiana," 49–64.

59. Carondelet to Gayoso, October 29, 1793, Carondelet to Alcudia, November 6, 1793, AHN, legajo 3898; Carondelet to Francisco Bouligny, November 20, 1794, Rosemonde E. and Emile Kuntz Collection, Louisiana Research Collection, Tulane University.

60. *Circulaire, Adressée par le Gouvernement à tous les Habitans de la Louisiane*, Kuntz Collection, Louisiana Research Collection, Tulane University.

61. M. Mitchell to Carondelet [1793] in Carondelet to Las Casas, December 30, 1793, PC, legajo 152B, LOCKEY, Transcripts. For Mitchell's background, see Gayoso to Carondelet, April 18, 1793, in Houck, *The Spanish Régime in Missouri*, 2:4–8. Mitchell sought payment for his services from Spanish envoys Viar and Jáudenes in New York City. See Mitchell to Gayoso, June 20, 1793, PC, legajo 2371.

62. *Circulaire, Adressée par le Gouvernement à tous les Habitans de la Louisiane,* Kuntz Collection, Louisiana Research Collection, Tulane University, 3–4. For Wilkinson's reports, see Carondelet to Gayoso, October 29, 1793, legajo 3898.

63. Din, "'For Defense of Country and the Glory of Arms,'" 34–35; Din, *Francisco Bouligny*, 192–95; Carondelet to Alcudia, November 24, 1794, in "Carondelet on the Defense of Louisiana, 1794," 498–99, 505.

64. Din, *Francisco Bouligny*, 82, 89; Nasatir, *Spanish War Vessels on the Mississippi*, 32–34, 62–65, 89–94, 109–12.

65. For Pisgignoux's arrest, see Nasatir, *Spanish War Vessels on the Mississippi*, 74–75, 82–83. Gayoso's interrogation of Pisgignoux, on March 7–8, 1794, is in PC, legajo 152B. See also Declaration of Pisgignoux, March 5, 1794, in Carondelet to Las Casas, March 20, 1794, PC, legajo 152B, LOCKEY, Transcripts. For the questionable nature of Pisgignoux's accusations, see Liljegren, "Jacobinism in Spanish Louisiana," 81–82.

66. Anonymous letter to Carondelet [1794–1795], in the handwriting of Pierre-Joseph Favrot, FAVROT, 2:162. For political tensions in Upper Louisiana, see Ekberg, *François Vallé*, 147–48.

67. Pierre Tardiveau to George Rogers Clark, November 23, 1795, in Turner, "Selections," 1096. See also Rice, *Barthélemi Tardiveau*, 10–15, 25–26, 41–46. For Lacassagne's work for Spain, see Gayoso to Lacassagne [1794], PC, legajo 2371.

68. Liljegren, "Jacobinism in Spanish Louisiana," 79–81; Holmes, Gayoso, 170–73; Holmes, *Honor and Fidelity*, 60. Gayoso tended to river defense and did not himself accompany the militia to New Orleans. See Gayoso to Alcudia (Godoy), February 18, 1794, in Turner, "Selections," 1042–45.

69. Parish, "The Intrigues of Doctor James O'Fallon," 258–61.

70. White to Gayoso, February 1, 1794, PC, legajo 2371. Harry Innes of Kentucky believed the filibuster would "unquestionably fail" since it lacked "two essential ingredients Money & Influence." See Innes to Gayoso, February 14, 1794, PC, legajo 2371.

71. Auguste Lachaise, "To the Democratic Society of Lexington," Harry Innes Papers, Ayer MS 439, Newberry Library.

72. Clark's declaration was first published in the *Centinel of the Northwestern Territory* (Cincinnati), January 25, 1794. St. Clair's proclamation was issued on December 7, 1793.

73. Wayne to Knox, March 3, 1794, in Knopf, *Anthony Wayne*, 307. Knox ordered Wayne to prevent any "hostile inroads into the dominions of Spain." See Knox to Wayne, March 31, 1794, in Knopf, *Anthony Wayne*, 317–18.

74. Blount to Robertson, January 18, 1794, in Turner, "Selections," 1037; Robertson to Gayoso, February 1, 1794, PC, legajo 2371. For Bradford's stance, see Connelley and Coulter, *History of Kentucky*, 1:331.

75. Samuel Hammond accepted a French commission as brigadier general, with his brother Abner as colonel. See Bennett, *Florida's "French" Revolution*, 26–27. This book includes an invaluable series of documents regarding Florida affairs.

76. For Mangourit's plan for a Creek Treaty [1794], see Turner, "Mangourit Correspondence," 591–93. See also Mangourit to Hammond, March 6, 1794, and Hammond to Mangourit [March, 1794], in Turner, "Mangourit Correspondence," 594–96.

77. Murdoch, "Citizen Mangourit," 530; Alderson, *This Bright Era of Happy Revolutions*, 39–40, 73, 94–99, 161; Alderson, "Charleston's Rumored Slave Revolt of 1793," 93–111. See also Klein, *Unification of a Slave State*, 211–12.

78. For the idea of reclaiming his brother, see the deposition of Abner Hammond, January 7, 1794, in Bennett, *Florida's "French" Revolution*, 40; see also there the request for compensation in Hammond's written declaration of January 6, 1794, 42.

79. Ibid., 47–48; Miller, "The Struggle for Free Trade in East Florida," 54–59.

80. Bennett, *Florida's "French" Revolution*, 72–75; Landers, *Black Society in Spanish Florida*, 206–7. The order to burn homesteads was enforced only to a limited extent. See Murdoch, *The Georgia-Florida Frontier*, 135.

81. Bennett, *Florida's "French" Revolution*, 21, 33–34, 49–50. See also Murdoch, "Citizen Mangourit," 525, 531.

82. Alderson, *This Bright Era of Happy Revolutions*, 117–19, 169–71; Hammond to Mangourit [March, 1794], in Turner, "Mangourit Correspondence," 594–96; Mangourit to Citizen Minister (Department of Foreign Affairs), December 10, 1793, in Murdoch, "Correspondence of French Consuls," 10–11.

83. Quoted in Link, *Democratic-Republican Societies*, 137. See also Klein, *Unification of a Slave State*, 208.

84. Shelby was disinclined to appease Spain, whose ruler "withholds from us an invaluable right, and who secretly instigates against us a most savage and cruel enemy." Shelby to Jefferson, January 13, 1794, ASPFR, 1:456.

85. Edmund Randolph to Isaac Shelby, March 29, 1794, ASPFR, 1:456–57. For a printed copy, see Dunlap's *American Daily Advertiser* (Philadelphia), June 3, 1794.

86. The Bert-Hammond contract came to light when Abner Hammond recorded its contents from memory for Spanish officials in St. Augustine. The document appears credible even if not a literal version of the original agreement. See Bennett, *Florida's "French" Revolution*, 94–97 (quotation, p. 96). A photostat of Abner Hammond's rendition is in the LOCKEY, Box 8.

87. Quoted in Bennett, *Florida's "French" Revolution*, 96.

88. Coulter, "Elijah Clarke's Foreign Intrigues," 260–79.

89. See Clarke's letter to his Committee of Safety, September 5, 1794, in ASPIA, 1:501. Coulter, "Elijah Clarke's Foreign Intrigues," 270–76 (quotation, p. 276).

90. Bennett, *Florida's "French" Revolution*, 172–76; Miller, "Rebellion in East Florida in 1795," 173–86.

91. Miller, "Rebellion in East Florida," 177–86; Bennett, *Florida's "French" Revolution*, 185–98.

92. For the murders of innocent Creeks, see Major Gaither to Henry Knox, Constant Freeman to Henry Knox, January 1, 1794, ASPIA, 1:472; Major Richard Brooke Roberts to Knox, May 10, 1794, ASPIA, 1:482; Freeman to Knox, May 9–10, 1794, ASPIA, 1:483–84.

93. The Oconee King Called Payne and others to the Governor, January 31, 1794, EF, reel 43. For the Creek desire to avoid a war "between White people," see "A Talk from the Hallooing King ... & other principal Headmen of the Lower Creek Nation," May 19, 1794, EF Papers, reel 43.

94. Quesada to Las Casas, February 18, 1794, PC, legajo 152B, LOCKEY, Transcripts; "A Talk from the Hallooing King ... & other principal Headmen of the Lower Creek Nation," May 19, 1794, EF, reel 43.

95. Payne to Quesada, July [ ], 1795, EF, reel 43; Bennett, *Florida's "French" Revolution*, 193–95; Landers, *Black Society in Spanish Florida*, 206–7.

96. Clarke to Kinnaird, September 9 and September 14, 1795 (quotation), EF, reel 43. The second letter is more legible in Spanish translation than in English. See also Kinnaird to Quesada, October 13, 1795, EF, reel 43. For Kinnaird's background, see Braund, *Deerskins and Duffels*, 174, 182; Saunt, *A New Order of Things*, 56, 107–10. (I have used the spelling Kinnaird because it reflects the Scottish spelling of that family name.)

CHAPTER 9

1. O'Neill to Ezpeleta, October 19, 1783, in Caughey, *McGillivray of the Creeks*, 62. For O'Neill's life, see Beerman, "Arturo O'Neill," 29–41. The indispensible study of Panton, Leslie, and Company is Coker and Watson, *Indian Traders of the Southeastern Spanish Borderlands*.

2. Langley, "The Tribal Identity of Alexander McGillivray," 231–39; Davis, "The Founding of Tensaw," 81–98; Cashin, *Lachlan McGillivray, Indian Trader*; Frank, *Creeks*

and Southerners, 33–36; Braund, *Deerskins and Duffels*, 83–86; Saunt, *A New Order of Things*, 54–55. See also O'Brien, *Choctaws in a Revolutionary Age*, 90.

3. O'Neill to Gardoqui, April 19, 1786, AHN, Estado, legajo. 3893; ONeill's report of Creek military success is in his letter to the marqués de Sonora [José de Gálvez], August 10, 1786, in Caughey, *McGillivray of the Creeks*, 127–28. For the supply of munitions, see McGillivray to O'Neill, August 12, 1786; Miró to O'Neill, June 20, 1786, in Caughey, *McGillivray of the Creeks*, 117–18; Coker and Watson, *Indian Traders*, 80–81. For Spanish diplomacy, see Sánchez-Fabrés Mirat, *Situación histórica de las Floridas*, 64–78.

4. The Spanish court required Zéspedes to administer an oath "of fidelity and obedience" to Panton, Leslie, and Company. See *Minuta de Indias* to Bernardo de Gálvez, May 8, 1786, AHN, Estado, leg. 3898. On August 30, 1786, Zéspedes reported that John Leslie had taken the oath in his own name and for the associates and dependents of his commercial house. See Zéspedes to the marqués de Sonora (José de Gálvez), East Florida Papers, reel 17.

5. O'Neill to Miró, May 21, 1787, in Caughey, *McGillivray of the Creeks*, 153. Panton began trade at San Marcos in 1783 and at Pensacola in 1785. See Coker and Watson, *Indian Traders*, 47–50, 68–71; Watson, "Continuity in Commerce."

6. Coker and Watson, *Indian Traders*, 79, 86–87, 94, 102–11.

7. Ibid., 101. For McGillivray's aid to Panton and Leslie, see Coker and Watson, *Indian Traders*, 54–69, 102–12, 127–29.

8. In response to Spanish inquiries, McGillivray admitted meeting with a British Loyalist in July 1788, though he did not initially name Bowles or indicate that the latter had come from the Bahamas. See McGillivray to O'Neill, August 12, 1788, in Caughey, *McGillivray of the Creeks*, 192–93; Coker and Watson, *Indian Traders*, 116–18.

9. See Baynton, *Authentic Memoirs of William Augustus Bowles*, 8–9, 22–36; *The Life of General W. A. Bowles*. J. Leitch Wright contends that Bowles had a son by Mary Perryman and another child by a Cherokee woman living among the Creeks. For biographical details, see Wright, *William Augustus Bowles*, 6–16. For skepticism of the children's paternity, see Sturtevant, "The Cherokee Frontiers, the French Revolution, and William Bowles," 71–72.

10. Wright, *William Augustus Bowles*, 19–28; Coker and Watson, *Indian Traders*, 115–18; David, *Dunmore's New World*, 161–64.

11. J. Leitch Wright conjectures that Bowles was already considering supplanting McGillivray in 1788. See Wright, *William Augustus Bowles*, 30.

12. Declaration of Henry Snell, August 6, 1788, PC, legajo 1394, LOCKEY, Transcripts; Declaration of Thomas Miller, August 11, 1788; Declaration of John Linder Jr., August 12, 1788, PC, legajo 1394, LOCKEY, Transcripts.

13. "Substance of a voluntary declaration made by Sundry [foreign] Banditti at St. Augustine," November 21, 1788, FONDO, legajo 1, reel 1, THNOC. This document is the joint statement of five of Bowles's captured followers to Spanish officials. See also Wright, *William Augustus Bowles*, 28–33. John Hambly, storekeeper for John Leslie, reported Bowles's arrival and the latter's meeting with Payne, a Seminole chief of mestizo background. See Hambly to John Leslie, September 14, 1788, EF, reel 8. See also Tanner, *Zéspedes in East Florida, 1784–1790*, 90.

14. For Bowles's boast of acting with McGillivray's approval, see "Substance of a

voluntary declaration made by Sundry [foreign] Banditti at St. Augustine," November 21, 1788, FONDO, legajo 1, reel 1.

15. Ibid.; Wright, *William Augustus Bowles*, 32. Zéspedes sent nine of Bowles's men in custody to Havana. See Zéspedes to Ezpeleta, February 4, 1789, PC, legajo 1395, LOCKEY, Transcripts.

16. McGillivray to Panton, January 12, 1789, in Caughey, *McGillivray of the Creeks*, 215.

17. Wright, *William Augustus Bowles*, 34. Two Cherokee and four Creek men evidently accompanied Bowles on his return to the Bahamas in 1789. See Zéspedes to Domingo Cabello, July 23, 1789, EF, reel 8. For Perryman's pro-British stance, see Searcy, *The Georgia-Florida Contest in the American Revolution*, 137.

18. Knox to Washington, July 7, 1789, Papers of the War Department, 1784 to 1800, wardepartmentpapers.org (this project is sponsored by George Mason University). Bennett, *Florida's "French" Revolution*; Knox to Lincoln, Griffin, and Humphreys, August 29, 1789, ASPIA, 1:65–68.

19. The accord, ratified by the Senate on August 12, 1790, is in The Papers of George Washington, Presidential Series: 6:249–54. For McGillivray's signed oath of allegiance, see Affidavit, August 7, 1790, Papers of the War Department. The original is in the Henry Knox Papers, Pierpont Morgan Library.

20. Papers of George Washington, Presidential Series: 6:249–54.

21. Lt. Colonel James Casey, who was present at the Tuckabatchee meeting on October 20, 1790, reported that McGillivray met a decidedly mixed response: "Some seemed pleased others threw their Tobacco into the fire in disgust." See Report, Casey to Knox [1791], Papers of the War Department. The Apalachee fork of the Oconee is not to be confused with Apalachee Bay on the Gulf Coast.

22. Cited in Nichols, "Land, Republicanism, and Indians," 215.

23. Knox to Ensign John Heth, May 31, 1791, ASPIA, 1:126; McGillivray to Panton, October 28, 1791, in Caughey, *McGillivray of the Creeks*, 299n. Seagrove gained some credibility among the Muscogulge when he sent food to relieve famine conditions in the Creek country in 1792. See Downes, "Creek-American Relations," 359–61.

24. Bahamian merchant John Miler supported Bowles's trip to Canada, which was encouraged by Dunmore. Bowles met with Dorchester at Quebec in July 1790. See Wright, *William Augustus Bowles*, 38–45.

25. See Baynton, *Authentic Memoirs of William Augustus Bowles*, title page and 19 (quotations). See also Bowles to Lord Grenville, January 3, 1791, in Turner, "English Policy toward America in 1790–1791," 727. In this letter, Bowles spoke for himself and fellow "Representatives from the United Nation [sic] of Creeks and Cherokees." For details of Bowles's London visit, see Sturtevant, "The Cherokee Frontiers," 65–71.

26. Baynton, *Authentic Memoirs of William Augustus Bowles*, 71–72.

27. Bowles to Grenville, January [ ], 1791, PC, legajo 2372. This letter is transcribed in Turner, "English Policy toward America," 728–33.

28. Bowles to Grenville, PC, legajo 2372.

29. Grenville was formally willing to support Creek trade with the British West Indies, "supposing that they should find themselves in a situation to avail themselves of this indulgence." See Turner, "English Policy toward America," 733. See also Bernardo del Campo to Floridablanca, April 15, 1791, AHN, Estado, 3889bis. Grenville denied any

British support for Bowles's maneuvers. See Grenville to Campo, July 16, 1792, AHN, Estado, 3889bis.

30. William Augustus Bowles, "To the Printer of the *Lucayan Herald*" [Nassau], August 19, 1789, enclosed in Bowles to Zéspedes, August 21, 1789; EF, reel 8; Bowles to Ezpeleta, August 21, 1789, PC, legajo 1425, LOCKEY, Transcripts; Bowles to Floridablanca, August 30, 1789, PC, legajo 3889bis.

31. Bowles to his Catholic Majesty, March 25, 1791, MPASD, 3:493–502.

32. On July 19, 1791, captain-general Luis de Las Casas ordered Governor Quesada of East Florida to arrest Bowles and to send him to Havana if possible. See Las Casas to Quesada, EF, reel 1.

33. Declaration of Eduardo Londres [Edward London], August 9, 1791, EF, reel 8. London, a ship captain who had just come to St. Augustine from the Bahamas, stated that Bowles was accompanied on his voyage to the Floridas by his own brother and "a Mestizo named Price, who speaks good English." Evidence about Bowles's brother is limited. See also Luis Bertucat to O'Neill, November 14, 1791, in Holmes and Wright, "Luis Bertucat and William Augustus Bowles," 58–59.

34. The designs of two flags are in AHN, Estado, legajo 3889. These flags differed in design from the standard that Bowles later designed for the State of Muskogee in 1799–1800. A common element remained the sun with facial features. See McAlister, "William Augustus Bowles and the State of Muskogee," 323–24.

35. Luis Bertucat to O'Neill, November 14, 1791, in Holmes and Wright, "Luis Bertucat and William Augustus Bowles," 55–59.

36. For the hunt for Bowles, see Bertucat to O'Neill, November 14, 1791, in Holmes and Wright, "Luis Bertucat and William Augustus Bowles," 57–58. See also Bertucat to O'Neill, September 24, 1791, enclosed in O'Neill to Miró, October 3, 1791, PLC, reel 6; Bertucat to O'Neill, October 12, 1791, PLC, reel 6.

37. Bowles to Carondelet, December 4, 1791, PLC, reel 6. Bowles to O'Neill, December 4, 1791, PLC, reel 6. Bowles showed his apparent good will toward Spain by sending O'Neill evidence of the "dangerous enterprise" of James O'Fallon's South Carolina Yazoo company.

38. Bowles to Carondelet, December 4, 1791, PLC, reel 6. Here Bowles signed as "General William August Bowles, Director of the Talapuche Nation." Talapuche was the Spanish name for the Creeks.

39. For Tom Perryman's defection from Bowles, see Robert Leslie to Panton, January 30, 1792, PLC, reel 6. For Kinnaird's anti-Bowles stance, see Seagrove to McGillivray, January 14, 1792, in Caughey, *McGillivray of the Creeks*, 303.

40. For Galphin's threats, see John Forrester to Quesada, October 1, 1792, AHN, Estado, legajo 3889bis. Galphin had aided Bowles in 1788, when he was still McGillivray's ally. See Wright, *William Augustus Bowles*, 31. For Kinnaird's, Perryman's, and Galphin's business dealings, see "A List of debts due by Indians traders & factors to Panton Leslie & Co. at their Store at Applachy . . ." [1792–1800], PLC, reel 6. Kinnaird was the largest purchaser of goods at Panton's store by the Apalachee.

41. For the assassination attempt, see McGillivray to O'Neill, October 28, 1791, PLC, reel 6. For the subsequent letter and quotations, see McGillivray to Panton, May 12, 1792, FONDO, legajo 1, reel 1. McGillivray also wrote of his failure to induce Coweta

and Cussita chiefs to kill Bowles in this letter. For the warning against "Knaving Vagabonds," see McGillivray to O'Neill, January 1, 1792, PC, legajo 2371.

42. For Cunningham's initial entry, see Statement of Edward Forrester, February 28, 1792, in Lawrence Kinnaird, "The Significance of William Augustus Bowles' Seizure of Panton's Apalachee Store in 1792," 171–72. John Hambly, another Panton and Leslie employee, informed a Spanish officer that Bowles had taken the storehouse with seventy-four Indians. See Fernando Eduardo de la Puente to Juan Nepomuceno de Quesada, January 25, 1792, EF, reel 47. See also Cunningham's testimony before Spanish officials in New Orleans, April 2, 1792, PC, legajo 2371. For his appointment as Bowles's major-general, see Carondelet to Floridablanca, March 22, 1792, PLC, reel 7.

43. Franco's escape account was reported by Lt. Eduardo de la Puente to Quesada, February 9, 1792, EF, reel 47. For Seminole opposition to Bowles, see Puente to Quesada, February 11, 1792, EF, reel 47. See also Wright, *Creeks and Seminoles*, 87–88; Saunt, *A New Order of Things*, 126, 134.

44. Richard Lang, East Florida planter and local officer, organized inhabitants for the defense of John Leslie's storehouse. For Anglo-Spanish collaboration against Bowles, see Richard Lang to Quesada, February 18, 1792, EF, reel 47. Francis Philip Fatio, a Swiss Tory and Florida settler, was an important Spanish ally in the area. For his warnings against Bowles, see Fatio to Quesada, January 15, 1792, EF, reel 47.

45. Din, *War on the Gulf Coast*, 47.

46. Carondelet to McGillivray, January 19, 1792, PLC, reel 6. See also Din, *War on the Gulf Coast*, 47–48; Sánchez-Fabrés Mirat, *Situación histórica de las Floridas*, 184.

47. Las Casas to Carondelet, February 16, 1792, PC, legajo 152A, LOCKEY, Transcripts.

48. Carondelet to Bowles, February 2, 1792, PLC, reel 6. For Carondelet's preference to capture Bowles by "stratagem" [*estratagema*], see his letter to Luis de Las Casas, March 13, 1792, PLC, reel 7; Carondelet to Floridablanca, March 22, 1792, PLC, reel 7; Evia to Bowles, February 22, 1792, and Bowles to Evia, February 22, 1792, EF, reel 43.

49. Evia to Francisco Xavier Guessy, and Guessy to Evia, February 27, 1792, in Holmes, *José de Evia*, 214, 217; Evia, "Diario," in Holmes, *José de Evia*, 228–29. Bowles believed his letters "to the King and Ministers of Spain" had brought him Carondelet's invitation. See Bowles to an unnamed recipient, February 29, 1792, PC, legajo 2371.

50. Evia, "Diario," in Holmes, *José de Evia*, 229–30; Bowles to Carondelet, March 17, 1792, PLC, reel 7.

51. Carondelet did not rule out the idea of Bowles's return to Florida, if that step was judged consistent with Spain's interests. See Carondelet to Floridablanca, March 22, 1792, PLC, reel 7. For the death sentence, see Bowles to Carondelet, PC, legajo 2371.

52. Las Casas to Carondelet, April 12 and April 14, 1792, PC, legajo 152A LOCKEY, Transcripts. The Wellbank-Bowles connection was again troubling to Las Casas. Bowles was sent from Cádiz to a Madrid jail in September 1792. See Din, *War on the Gulf Coast*, 53, 57.

53. Bernardo del Campo, to Aranda, June 8, 1792, AHN, Estado, legajo 3889bis. Campo received Grenville's assurance that his government did not approve Bowles's Florida mission. For Bowles's entreaties while in Spain, see Wright, *William Augustus Bowles*, 80.

54. Wright, *William Augustus Bowles*, 81–109.

55. Franco's master was Robert Leslie, John Leslie's younger brother. Franco (or Frank) obviously spoke English very well since Bowles and Cunningham conversed in their native tongue. Franco's observations are in Fernando Eduardo de la Puente to Quesada, February 9, 1792, EF, reel 47. For Cunningham's statement to Spanish officials at Fort San Marcos, see *Traducción de la Declaración de Gulliermo Cun[n]ingham, socio que fue del Aventurero Bowles*, February 12, 1792, EF, reel 43.

56. [Statement and Interrogation of William Cunningham], April 2, 1792, PC, legajo 2371. This document is transcribed in Kinnaird, "Bowles' Seizure of Panton's Apalachee Store," 177–92. British influence is discussed in Braund, "The Creek Indians and the Coming of the War of the Revolution," 39–62.

57. For Cunningham's deportation to Cuba, see Carondelet to Las Casas, April 16, 1792, PC, legajo 152A, LOCKEY, Transcripts. See also Wright, *William Augustus Bowles*, 82. Royal officials in Spain suspected Cunningham to be the same man (with the identical name) whom Zéspedes had exiled from East Florida in 1785. This identity is not clear, however. See "Nota para la Secreatria del Estado," May 28, 1792, PC, legajo 2371.

58. Wellbank to Bowles, March 6, 1792; Wellbank to Carondelet, March 8, 1792, enclosed in Carondelet to Las Casas, March 26, 1792, PC, legajo 152A, LOCKEY, Transcripts.

59. The Spanish learned about Little Prince's mission through Wellbank's letter to Bowles, which the latter received while he was a prisoner in New Orleans. See Las Casas to Floridablanca, April 21, 1792, SMV, 4, pt. 3:30–31. Wellbank had faithfully served with Bowles in 1788, and gained valuable experience while hiding out among the Lower Creeks. See Wright, *William Augustus Bowles*, 31, 34.

60. Milford's name is rendered in various ways in records. Milfort was the French spelling—as opposed to Milford, which appears in Spanish archives. Milford's mission is discussed in Quesada to Las Casas, May 8, 1792, AHN, Estado, legajo 3889bis.

61. Robert Leslie to Panton, March 22, 1792, FONDO, legajo 1, reel 1. Robert Leslie was John Leslie's brother.

62. For Wellbank's stay among the Cherokees, see a report by Beverley Randolph, August 13, 1793, Papers of Washington, Presidential Series, 14:147–50; Charles Storer to Timothy Pickering, October 4, 1793, in Papers of Washington, Presidential Series, 14:219–21. For Wellbank's mission and death, see Wright, *Britain and the North American Frontier*, 80–81, 100–101.

63. A Talk from the Kings, Chiefs & Warriors of the Lower Creek nation to Captn. Pedro Olivier, July 3, 1792, PC, legajo 2371. Cunningham testified that Bowles had his strongest support at Coweta, Broken Arrow (Hlekatchka), Ushita [Usiche], and Hitchiti. See Cunningham's testimony in New Orleans, April 2, 1792, PC, legajo 2371. See also Quesada to Las Casas, May 10, 1792, PC, legajo 2371.

64. For McGillivray's unsuccessful attempt to lure Bowles from Philatouche's house, see Alexander McGillivray to William Panton, October 28, 1791, PLC, reel 6; See also the Spanish translation of Ochilasse Chopka's "Talk" to Governor Quesada, October 23, 1792, EF, reel 43; Panton to the Kings, Warriors, & Headmen of the Cussitaws, Cowetas, Broken Arrow . . . , February 19, 1792, in Caughey, *McGillivray of the Creeks*, 308–9.

65. Quesada to Montreuil, February 9, 1793; Montreuil to Quesada, February 19, 1793, EF, reel 43. See also Robert Leslie to John Leslie, March 17, 1793, EF, reel 43.

66. Montreuil to Quesada, February 19, 1793, EF, reel 43. Daniel McGillivray to

William Panton, November 12, 1792, FONDO, legajo 1, reel 1. Daniel McGillivray was a kinsman of Alexander McGillivray.

67. For Philatouche's commission, see Dunmore to Philatouche Upaiahatche, February 5, 1793, EF, reel 43. Thomas Forbes, associate of Panton and Leslie in the Bahamas, gathered information on "Old Philatouche the Factor." Not crediting that Indians were managing their own diplomacy, Forbes believed "they must be directed & managed by some White Banditee [sic] among them." He observed that Philatouche's group had the assistance of Tom Lewis, "the half breed," serving as "their Conductor & Interpreter here." See Thomas Forbes to John Leslie, February 19, 1792, EF, reel 43.

68. Robert Leslie to John Leslie, March 17, 1792, EF, reel 43; Francisco Montreuil to Quesada, January 19, 1793, and March 15, 1793, EF, reel 43. Philatouche's visit to the Bahamas followed a previous Creek delegation that had gone there in the fall of 1792 under Wellbank's sponsorship. See Galphin to James Seagrove, October 15, 1792, ASPIA, 1:321.

69. For Seagrove's suspicion of Spanish double-dealing, see his letter to Washington, July 5, 1792, ASPIA, 1:305. Soon after writing this letter, Seagrove received information about Shawnee meetings with Spanish officials in New Orleans and Pensacola. See James Leonard to Seagrove, July 24, 1792, ASPIA, 1:308. For the danger to Americans in Creek country, see Seagrove to Knox, May 24, 1792, ASPIA, 1:296.

70. Carondelet was not initially wedded to Panton and Leslie, but came to support them because of immediate strategic needs that could not wait the formation of a new Indian trading firm. See Coker and Watson, *Indian Traders*, 162–66.

71. For Carondelet's report of the conference, see Carondelet to Aranda, November 28, 1792, AHN, legajo 3898. For the Indian defeat, see Dowd, *A Spirited Resistance*, 109–10.

72. Blount to Knox, September 15, 1792, and Blount to Knox, April 9, 1793, in Carter, *Territorial Papers*, 6:183, 6:251, respectively.

73. Ben James to Blount, June 30, 1792, in Carter, *Territorial Papers*, 6:284; Forbes to McGillivray, June 30, 1792, Fondo: Floridas, legajo 1, reel 1. Forbes urged the Spanish to send an emissary to the Chickasaws because "the mountain leader [Piomingo], the Colberts, and their Guang [sic]" were setting out for Cumberland to strengthen their U.S. ties. See also Weeks, *Paths to a Middle Ground*, 108–9, 174–75; SMV, 4, pt. 3:164–65, 253–54; O'Brien, *Choctaws in a Revolutionary Age*, 88.

74. The Carondelet-McGillivray accord of July 6, 1792, is in AHN, Estado, legajo 3898. For a translation, see Caughey, *McGillivray of the Creeks*, 329–30. McGillivray expressed his gratitude for the increased pension and his determination to fight the Americans. See McGillivray to Carondelet, July 22, 1792, PC, legajo 2371.

75. Colbert to General James Robertson, February 10, 1792, William Blount Papers, LC. Several Colberts as well as Piomingo's warriors assisted the United States in Ohio Indian warfare in 1791. See Atkinson, *Splendid Land, Splendid People*, 152–54. See also McGillivray to Carondelet, November 15, 1792, in Caughey, *McGillivray of the Creeks*, 345.

76. On McGillivray's death, see Panton to Carondelet, February 20, 1793, in Caughey, *McGillivray of the Creeks*, 354. See also McGillivray to Carondelet, January 15, 1793, in Caughey, *McGillivray of the Creeks*, 351–52.

77. See Talk by the heads of the Creek Nation, July 3–July 21, 1793, in Papers of Washington, Presidential Series, 13:171. Washington and Knox asked Blount to submit a war plan against the Creeks, but both the president and secretary of war urged a

peaceful solution for the time being. Knox to Washington, August 7, 1793, Papers of Washington, Presidential Series, 13:375. See Blount and Pickens to Knox, August 1, 1793, Papers of Washington, Presidential Series, 13:359-61.

78. Carondelet to Floridablanca, January 18, 1792, and February 25, 1792, AHN, Estado, legajo 3898. Carondelet first received word of the battle through an American deserter and then obtained a more detailed account from Wilkinson, who exaggerated American casualties. See Wilkinson to Miró, November 4, 1791, AHN, Estado, legajo 3898. See also Hurt, *The Ohio Frontier*, 114–18.

79. The Natchez treaty is translated and printed in Weeks, *Paths to a Middle Ground*, 119–25, 201–2.

80. Weeks, *Paths to a Middle Ground*, 73–80, 88–94, 120.

81. The principal Creek signatory was Suluchemastabé, an Alibamon chief. The Cherokees were not immediately present because of conflict with America settlers. A Cherokee delegation affirmed the proceedings after the treaty was concluded. For an analysis of the treaty and a translation of the accord, see Weeks, *Paths to a Middle Ground*, 119–25, 230–32.

82. The slightness and marginal influence of the Creek delegation is discussed in Cotterill, *The Southern Indians*, 107. For Piomingo's absence and Chickasaw-Creek clashes, see Weeks, *Paths to a Middle Ground*, 99–100, 110–11, 114–16; Atkinson, *Splendid Land, Splendid People*, 151–79; O'Brien, *Choctaws in a Revolutionary Age*, 91–97.

83. Gayoso to Carondelet, September 9, 1794, quoted in in Holmes, *Gayoso*, 159.

84. Nasatir, *Spanish War Vessels on the Mississippi*, 115–16.

85. Aranda [*ministro de Estado*] to Luis de Las Casas, March 5, 1794, enclosed in Las Casas to Carondelet, June 14, 1794, PC, legajo 152B, LOCKEY, Transcripts. Aranda conveyed the royal order of March 5, 1794, to Havana, where it was communicated to Florida. See Las Casas to the Governor of Pensacola, June 14, 1794, PC, legajo 152B, LOCKEY, Transcripts.

86. A text of the treaty is in ASPFR, 1:546–49. For the treaty text in Spanish and English see Bemis, *Pinckney's Treaty*, 343–62.

87. Morales to Gardoqui, March 3, 1797, AHN, Estado, legajo 3902.

88. Weeks, *Paths to a Middle Ground*, 134–41, 236–42; Holmes, *Gayoso*, 166–67; Nasatir, *Spanish War Vessels*, 110–16. Mountain Leader, Wolf's Friend and General [William] Colbert to Carlos Dehault Delassus, July 2, 1797; Ugulyacabé to Delassus, July 3, 1797, PC, legajo 2372. See also Atkinson, *Splendid Land, Splendid People*, 177–79.

89. The text of the treaty is in ASPIA, 1:586–87.

90. Ibid. The Indian boundary scouts were also to receive ammunition for hunting.

CHAPTER 10

1. Guion to Delassus, June 15, 1797, PC, legajo 2372.

2. Protestation by Carlos Dehault Delassus, received by Isaac Guion, July 16, 1797, PC, legajo, 2374. Carondelet received advance word of Guion's mission from Wilkinson, the captain's superior. See Wilkinson to Carondelet, May 25, 1797, PC, legajo 2375; Wilkinson to Carondelet, April 30, 1797, PC, legajo 2372.

3. Carondelet admitted that the issue of fortifications was a pretense in his correspon-

dence with Wilkinson. See Carondelet to Wilkinson, April 20, 1797, PC, legajo 2375. See also Sánchez-Fabrés Mirat, *Situación histórica de las Floridas*, 225.

4. The royal order of October 27, 1795, is found in Carondolet to Gayoso, March 5, 1797, MPASD, 6:332-42.

5. Lynch, *Bourbon Spain*, 367-70, 390-95, 405-6; Elliott, *Empires of the Atlantic World*, 372-73.

6. The general's full name was Georges Henri Victor Collot. For his role on Guadeloupe, see Dubois, *A Colony of Citizens*, 24-25, 135-49. For biographical details, see Martin, "George Victor Collot," 7-9, 15-16, 115-18.

7. Collot to Adet [1796], in Echeverria, "General Collot's Plan for a Reconnaissance of the Ohio and Mississippi Valleys," 516-20 (quotation p. 519). Adet admired Genet's previous collaboration with American adventurers. See Adet to the Minister of Foreign Relations, February 9, 1796, in Turner, "Correspondence of the French Ministers to the United States, 1791-1797," 2:826-31 (quotation, 831). For the diplomatic background, see Lyon, *Louisiana in French Diplomacy*, 81-98.

8. McHenry to St. Clair, May [ ], 1796, *The St. Clair Papers*, ed. Smith, 2:395-96. Collot was stopped and questioned at Fort Massac, but then permitted to proceed by Captain Zebulon Pike, father of the famed explorer. See Kyte, "A Spy of the Western Waters," 435-36.

9. Collot, *Voyage dans l'Amérique Septentrionale*, 1:318-19 (first quotation), 339 (second quotation). The idea of a "Creole Corridor" is examined in Gitlin, *The Bourgeois Frontier*, 26-28.

10. Collot, *Voyage dans l'Amérique Septentrionale*, 2:16 -17. For Lorimier's background, see Nasatir, *Spanish War Vessels on the Mississippi*, 71-72n, 297-98n; Brown, *Frontiersman*, 105-6, 127-28, 182-83, 244.

11. According to Lorimier's report, the British Canadian expedition was alleged to include 2,000 regulars, 1,500 militia, and several Indian groups. See Collot, *Voyage*, 2:16-17.

12. Warin continued the journey after being beaten, but later died in New Orleans. See Collot, *Voyage*, 2:36-39; Kyte, "A Spy on the Western Waters," 431; Martin, "George Victor Collot in the Mississippi Valley," 100.

13. Elias Beauregard to Gayoso, PC, legajo 2364. For the sharing of intelligence with Trudeau and Gayoso, see Collot, *Voyage*, 2:16-17, 88-92.

14. Collot, *Voyage*, 2:124, 153-61.

15. Collot to Carondelet, December 1, 1796, *Voyage*, 2:404-5; Collot to Carondelet, October 31, 1796, *Voyage*, 2:402.

16. Collot to Yrujo, March 1, 1797, in Turner, "Documents on the Blount Conspiracy," 578-79; see Collot to Yrujo, March 1, 1791, in Turner, "Documents on the Blount Conspiracy," 580 (second letter of that date). Collot recommended French Canadians and Indians for the defense of Upper Louisiana. See Collot to Yrujo, April 15, 1797 (endorsed by Adet), in Turner, "Documents on the Blount Conspiracy," 585-87; Yrujo to Carondelet, March 13, 1797, PC, legajo 2365.

17. See Collot to Yrujo, April 15, 1797 (endorsed by Adet), in Turner, "Documents on the Blount Conspiracy," 585-87. Collot had received intelligence on the plot from an unnamed source in Natchez. See Collot, *Voyage*, 2:88-91.

18. Blount wrote: "I shall myself have a hand in the business, and probably shall be at

the head of the business on the part of the British." See Blount to Carey, April 21, 1797, Annals of Congress, Senate, 5th Congress, 3rd Session, 2350.

19. For a helpful overview, see Melton, *The First Impeachment*, 98–125. For the senate process, see Annals of Congress, Senate, 5th Congress, 1st Session (July 8, 1797), 34–35, 43–44.

20. For an insightful essay on the affair, see Cayton, "'When Shall We Cease to Have Judases?,'" 156–89.

21. Masterson, *William Blount*, 298–302.

22. Blount to Romayne, March 17, 1797; Romayne to Blount, March 15, 1797, Annals of Congress, Senate, 5th Congress, 3rd Session, 2345–46. Though Blount did not directly mention emancipation in this letter, he did warn of French political pressure through control of the Mississippi.

23. Sebastian did not sign the letter, but gave his secret code number—1325. [Sebastian to Gayoso], November 5, 1796, PC, legajo 2375. The French Constitution of 1795 strengthened the National Convention's emancipation decree of February 1794. See Dubois, *A Colony of Citizens*, 25, 279–82.

24. Romayne to Blount, March 15, 1797, ibid., 2345.

25. Blount died of illness in 1800. See Masterson, *William Blount*, 325–31, 346–47. Congress itself engaged in a lengthy and tortuous debate over the Blount affair. The Senate constituted itself into a court to try the impeached officer, but finally decided on January 14, 1799, that it lacked jurisdiction in the case. See Melton, *The First Impeachment*, 231–32.

26. Pickering to Liston, July 1, 1797; Liston to Pickering, July 2, 1797, ASPFR, 2:70–71. Blount's divulged letter referred to Chisholm meeting with Liston in Philadelphia. See Blount to Carey, April 21, 1797, Annals of Congress, Senate, 5th Congress, 3rd Session, 2349. See also Lycan, *Alexander Hamilton and American Foreign Policy*, 370–71.

27. Liston to [George Hammond?], March 16, 1797, in Turner, "Documents on the Blount Conspiracy," 584.

28. Chisholm, who claimed to be a native Englishman, remembered Pensacola's conquest as occurring in 1778—three years before it actually happened. See "The Declaration of John D. Chisholm," November 29, 1797, in Turner, "Documents on the Blount Conspiracy," 595. This declaration was made to Rufus King, American ambassador to England. During the 1810s, Chisholm had a significant place among Cherokees in Arkansas. See Myers, "Cherokee Pioneers in Arkansas," 131.

29. Chisholm only put his plan to paper in London in late 1797 after the conspiracy was dead. He then unburdened himself to American ambassador Rufus King. See "The Declaration of John D. Chisholm"; "The General Outlines of the Plan," November 29, 1797, and "Questions proposed by Rufus King and Answered by John D. Chisholm," December 5, 1797 [attested to by Chisholm on December 9, 1797], in Turner, "Documents on the Blount Conspiracy," 595–605.

30. Pickering to Liston April 28, 1797; Liston to Pickering, April 29, 1797, ASPFR, 2:69–71; Robert Liston to John D. Chisholm, March 17, 1797, in Turner, "Documents on the Blount Conspiracy," 584–85. For Chisholm's connection to Blount, see Masterson, *William Blount*, 276–77, 302–7; Melton, *The First Impeachment*, 90–95.

31. Liston to Grenville, March 16, 1797, in Turner, "Documents on the Blount Conspiracy," 582–83 (quotations, p. 582).

32. In his statement to Rufus King, Chisholm remarked that Blount wanted him to "be gone into the Indian Country and mind the business there" rather than journey to England. See "The Declaration of John D. Chisholm," November 29, 1797, in Turner, "Documents on the Blount Conspiracy," 599.

33. Blount to Carey, April 21, 1797, Annals of Congress, Senate, 5th Congress, 3rd Session, 2349–50. For Blount's rubric as "Dirt King," see Benjamin Hawkins to William Faulkner, November 25, 1797, in *The Collected Works of Benjamin Hawkins, 1796–1810*, ed. Foster, 9.

34. "The General Outlines of the Plan" [1797], in Turner, "Documents on the Blount Conspiracy," 600–601. Chisholm offered this outline in connection with his statement to Rufus King of November 29, 1797.

35. For British Canadian fears of French and Spanish collusion, see Taylor, *The Divided Ground*, 335–37.

36. In October 1796, Collot received word at Natchez of Chisholm's alleged alliance with Brant. See Collot, *Voyage*, 1:88–89. Chisholm told Rufus King that he contacted Brant by letters in 1796 and 1797. See Declaration of John D. Chisholm (followed by outline of his plan), November 29, 1797, in Turner, "Documents on Blount's Conspiracy," 598, 600–601. See also Questions proposed by Rufus King and Answered by John D. Chisholm, December 5, 1797, in Turner, "Documents on Blount's Conspiracy," 603–4.

37. Pickering to Andrew Ellicott, July 28, 1799, Ellicott Papers. Allen and his ship, the *Olive Branch*, were seized by the British navy on November 20, 1796. See Graffagnino, "'Twenty Thousand Muskets!!!,'" 419–23.

38. Nasatir, *Spanish War Vessels on the Mississippi*, 79.

39. Gayoso was more resolute than Carondelet on this issue, perhaps because his own post was at stake. See Holmes, *Gayoso*, 178–79.

40. Gayoso to Daniel Clark, Parsons Collection. Gayoso made the same case to Carondelet. See Gayoso to Carondelet, June 7, 1796, PC, legajo 2364.

41. For the offer of the pension and land grant, see Carondelet to Wilkinson, April 20, 1797, PC, legajo 2375. See also Carondelet to Gayoso, April 23, 1797, MPASD, 6:423. Four days later, Carondelet informed Gayoso of his cipher letter to Wilkinson making the pension conditional on a delayed American troop movement. See MPASD, 6:429 (April 27, 1797). Carondelet wrote that Wayne's death was a "very happy" occasion "for us." See Carondelet to Gayoso, February 21 1797, MPASD, 6:394–95.

42. Carondelet to Gayoso, April 27, 1797, MPASD, 6:431–32. In this letter, Carondelet observed that he had received nothing from Havana in three months. He also remarked British corsairs had caused more than 90,000 pesos in losses to the province and the crown.

43. Mathews, *Andrew Ellicott*, 12–13; McGroarty, "Major Andrew Ellicott and His Historic Border Lines," 98–111.

44. Gayoso to Ellicott, March 12, 1797; Ellicott to Gayoso, March 13, 1797; Ellicott to Gayoso, March 23, 1797; Gayoso to Ellicott, March 23, 1797; Ellicott to Pope, March 25, 1797; Gayoso to Ellicott, March 31, 1797, ASPFR, 2:22–27. Pope arrived at Natchez on April 24, 1797. See Gayoso to Pope, March 25 and April 1, 1797; Pope to Captain Burguard [Beauregard], April 13, 1797; Pope to Gayoso, April 15, 1797; Gayoso to Pope, April 17, 1797, ASPFR, 2:73–74.

45. Gayoso to Carondelet, June 7, 1796, PC, legajo 2364. In his proclamation to Natchez of March 29, 1797, Gayoso raised the issue of protecting resident land rights. The proclamation is printed in ASPFR, 2:25. For the Yazoo act of 1795, see McGrath, *Yazoo*, 5–19.

46. See the correspondence between Dunbar and Gayoso, April 4–19, 1797, in Rowland, *Life, Letters and Papers of William Dunbar*, 76–78.

47. Gayoso wrote to Godoy on June, 6, 1797. See Sánchez-Fabrés Mirat, *Situación histórica de las Floridas*, 228.

48. Manuel de Lanzós, "Diario de la revolución de Natchez, 1797," in Holmes, *Documentos inéditos*, 322–23.

49. Haynes, *The Mississippi Territory and the Southwest Frontier*, 5–17; Holmes, *Gayoso*, 188–92.

50. Ellicott to Pickering, June 4 and 5, 1797, ASPFR, 2:709–10. According to Carondelet's proposed settlement with the Kentuckians, Spain would retain its forts at Chickasaw Bluffs and on the Tombigbee River above the new boundary line. See letter of Thomas Power, Louisville, July 19, 1797, Harry Innes Papers, Newberry Library. This offer came after Carondelet had approved, in principle, a land grant of ten million acres in Spanish territory to William Murray, Harry Innes, Benjamin Sebastian, John Holingsworth, and others. See Din, "Spain's Immigration Policy in Louisiana," 267.

51. Lanzós, *"Diario de la revolución de Natchez,"* 325–26.

52. Holmes, *Gayoso*, 193–95. According to Ellicott's account, Gayoso agreed to the talks only after conferring secretly with him two days before at Captain Minor's residence. See Ellicott, *Journal of Andrew Ellicott*, 109–10, 113 (quotation), 115–16; See also Gayoso to Ellicott, June 13, 1797, and Ellicott to Gayoso, June 15, 1797, *Journal of Andrew Ellicott*, 105–9.

53. For the committee resolutions, see Ellicott, *Journal of Andrew Ellicott*, 114–16. See also Holmes, *Gayoso*, 200–201.

54. Land grants, issued by Carondelet, July 20, 1796, PC, legajo 2364. One grant was for 500 arpents (432 acres) and the other for 1,800 arpents (1523 acres).

55. Peter Bryan Bruin to Ellicott, November 3, 1797, Ellicott Papers, LC. For initial Bruin-Ellicott collaboration, see Ellicott, *Journal of Andrew Ellicott*, 40. For Bruin's appointment, see Pickering to Ellicott, May 11, 1798, in Carter, *Territorial Papers*, 5:34.

56. Wilkinson to McHenry, June 2, 1797, Papers of the War Department, 1784 to 1800 (wardepatmentpapers.org).

57. Wilkinson to Sargent, May 28, 1797, Winthrop Sargent Papers, Massachusetts Historical Society. See Childs, *French Refugee Life*, 29–30, 113–14.

58. For Nolan's assistance to Ellicott, see Ellicott, *Journal of Andrew Ellicott*, 29–35. For comments on "the unknown land," see Nolan to Wilkinson, January 6, 1796, JWCHM. For Gayoso's gift of the sextant, see Nolan to Wilkinson, May 6, 1797, JWCHM. Nolan discussed Ellicott's instruction to him in a letter to Wilkinson of April 24, 1797. See James Wilkinson, *Memoirs of My Own Times*, 2: Appendix II. For Nolan's dealings with Gayoso and Carondelet, see Loomis and Nasatir, *Pedro Vial and the Roads to Santa Fe*, 207–12.

59. Andrew Ellicott to Sarah Ellicott, June 19, 1798, in Mathews, *Andrew Ellicott*, 159.

60. Gayoso to Alcudia, November 30, 1797, AHN, Estado, leg. 3900.

61. Ellicott to Wilkinson (postscript marked "Confidential"), following letter to Wilkinson, January 17, 1799, Ellicott Papers, LC.

62. For Clark's report of successful lobbying, see his letter to Andrew Ellicott and Isaac Guion, June 13, 1798, Ellicott Papers, LC. For Clark's maneuvers, see Alexander, "Daniel Clark"; McMichael, "William Dunbar, William Claiborne, and Daniel Clark."

63. Clark to Ellicott, May 20, 1798 (quotations); Clark to Ellicott and Guion, June 13 and 14, 1798, Ellicott Papers, LC.

64. For the Clark-Wilkinson feud, see the statement of Daniel Clark, January 11, 1808, in ASP, Misc. 1:704-5; Wilkinson, *Memoirs*, 2:133-38. See also Daniel Clark, *Proofs of the Corruption of Gen. James Wilkinson and of His Connexion with Aaron Burr*.

65. Ellicott to Pickering, November 14, 1797, in Wilkinson, *Memoirs*, 2:170-71. Ellicott did not deny this letter's authenticity when it was revealed when the House of Representatives—and finally a military board of inquiry—undertook an investigation in 1808 of Wilkinson's Spanish dealings of the previous decade. See Andrew Ellicott's deposition, May 22, 1808, ASP, Misc. 2:87-90. (See answer to interrogatory no. 15, p. 90).

66. McHenry to Wilkinson, July 8, 1798, Papers the War Department. Secretary of War McHenry initially ordered Wilkinson to proceed southward from Ohio and to take post at Walnut Hills and Natchez. See McHenry to Wilkinson April 20, 1798, Wilkinson Papers, JWCHM; Wilkinson to McHenry, July 20, 1798, JWCHM.

67. Hamilton to Pickering, March 22, 1797, AH, 20:545. See also Chernow, *Alexander Hamilton*, 546.

68. Hamilton to McHenry, [January 27-February 11] 1798, AH, 21:345. See also Lycan, *Alexander Hamilton*, 383-89.

69. Lycan, *Alexander Hamilton*, 383-89. See also Harper, *American Machiavelli*, 221-23.

70. Álvarez to the conde de Santa Clara (captain-general of Cuba), June 26, 1798 (quotation), and July 22, 1798, FONDO, leg. 2, reel 2, THNOC.

71. Lyon, *Louisiana in French Diplomacy*, 91-98.

72. Alexander Hamilton, "The Stand No. IV" [April 12, 1798], in Lyon, *Louisiana in French Diplomacy*, 21:414-15. See also Pickering to Hamilton, March 25, 1798, AH, 21:374-75.

73. Washington to Hamilton, July 14, 1798, AH, 22:20.

74. Clark to Ellicott, September 10, 1798, Ellicott Papers, LC. Clark wrote two letters to Ellicott that day. One praises Washington as quoted above; the other has a long postscript denouncing France for its supposed antislavery campaign on Cuba.

75. For the military preparations of 1798, see Elkins and McKitrick, *The Age of Federalism*, 589-90, 598-99.

76. Hamilton to Harrison Gray Otis, January 26, 1799, AH, 22:441.

77. Wilkinson to Gayoso, November 19, 1798; Gayoso to Wilkinson, PC, legajo 2375.

78. Cox protested the fact that he was not accorded habeas corpus. See Cox to Sargent, September 3 and 20, 1798, Sargent Papers. See more generally Cox, "Documents Relating to Zachariah Cox," 29-114, esp. therein the testimony of William Cumpton, February 1, 1799, 88-91, and Cox, *An Estimate of the Commercial Advantages by Way of the Mississippi and Mobile Rivers, to the Western Country* (Nashville, 1799), 37-50.

79. For emigration and the problem of "Mal-Contents," see Wilkinson to James McHenry, November 6, 1798, Papers of the War Department. For Wilkinson's appre-

hensions about soldiers deserting to Spanish territory, see his letter of January 10, 1799, to McHenry, Papers of the War Department. See also his letter to Hamilton, April 15, 1799, Wilkinson Papers, JWCHM.

80. Wilkinson to Hamilton, April 15, 1799, JWCHM.

81. Ibid. This letter is reproduced, with minor variation in spelling and capitalization, in AH, 23:45–49.

82. Ibid. For Wilkinson's return to the Mississippi, see his letter to Hamilton of February 12, 1800, AH, 24:233–34.

83. For Ellicott's secret political intelligence, see his letter to Timothy Pickering, November 14, 1797, in James Wilkinson, *Memoirs*, 2:170–71. For his journey to New Orleans, see Ellicott, *Journal of Andrew Ellicott*, 186–88.

84. Ellicott to Pickering, January 13, 1799, in Ellicott Papers, LC.

85. Ibid.

86. John Pitchlyn to Ellicott, August 9 and September 22, 1797; Guion to Ellicott, June 24 and 25, 1798, Ellicott Papers, LC. The letter of June 25 includes the cited quotations, while the June 24 letter reports southward migration.

87. The Alibamon request is discussed in Morales to Pedro Varela y Ulloa, June 30, 1797, AHN, Estado, legajo 3902. See also Hook, *The Alabama-Coushatta Indians*, 28–29.

88. Declaration of Andrew Ellicott and Stephen Minor, August 15, 1799, PC, legajo 2371. See also Holmes, "The Southern Boundary Commission," 312–41; Minor to Gillespie, September 22, 1799, Ellicott Papers, LC.

89. Panton to Ellicott, August 23, 1799, Ellicott Papers, LC; Bowles to Ellicott, September 22, 1799, PC, legajo 2371. Bowles remarked that it was four days since his ship ran aground. The letter is printed in Ellicott, *Journal of Andrew Ellicott*, 227–28 (quotation); Ellicott to Benjamin Hawkins, October 9, 1799, ibid., 230.

90. Ellicott to Benjamin Hawkins, October 9, 1799, in Ellicott, *Journal of Andrew Ellicott*, 231.

91. See Proclamation by Wm. A. Bowles, Director Genl. of Muskogee, October 31, 1799, PC, legajo 2371.

92. Ellicott to Folch, October 9, 1799, Ellicott Papers, LC. Ellicott provided food to Bowles and crew. For quotations, see Ellicott to Hawkins, October 9, 1799, *Journal of Ellicott*, 230; Ellicott to Minor, October 9, 1799, Ellicott Papers, LC. For the proclamations, see the *Carolina Gazette* (Charleston), January 23, 1800. Both decrees were dated October 31, 1799, and issued at Wekiva, Bowles's base by the Chattahoochee River.

93. Ellicott to Esteban Minor, October 9, 1800, Ellicott Papers, LC.

94. Wilkinson to Hamilton, March 7, 1800, AH, 24:303–4.

CONCLUSION

1. Duffy, *Soldiers, Sugar, and Seapower*, 191. In 1798, Toussaint Louverture rejected a proposal by French agent Gabriel Hédouville for an assault on the United States. See Girard, "*Rêves d'Empire*," 400–401.

2. Johnstone to John Pownall (secretary to the Board of Trade), February 19, 1765, MPAED, 1:273.

3. [Bowles to President John Adams?], October 31, 1799, Ayer MS 100 (transcript),

Newberry Library. This letter, evidently extant only in transcript, appears by its argument and rhetoric a genuine exposition by Bowles. It is addressed to "Sir," rather than by name to Adams. It is unsigned but ends with Bowles's motto, "God save the State of Muskogee," and is dated October 31, 1799, at Wekiva.

4. Proclamations, October 31 and November 16, 1799, PC, legajo 2371. On October 26, 1799, twenty-seven chiefs in assembly appointed Bowles "to continue & direct the Affairs of our Nation and support our Dignity." The chiefs' names appear in Bowles's hand, and without the markings that customarily appeared when native leaders signed agreements with colonial powers. See PC, legajo 2371.

5. Bowles proclaimed that he took action pursuant to the Muskogee supreme council's directive of October 25, 1799. See Proclamation, November 16, 1799, PC, legajo 2371. The proclamation established an import duty on foreign merchandise of 2.5 percent as of January 1, 1800. The duty on imported "Spiritous Liquors" was set at 6 percent.

6. Bowles obtained passage to the Florida Gulf from Jamaica via the Bahamas. The Earl of Balcarres, Jamaica's governor, lent crucial aid in this instance. See Wright, *William Augustus Bowles*, 108–15. About twenty-five Spanish sailors were present when San Marcos fell. For the fort's capture, see Din, *War on the Gulf Coast*, 113–27.

7. Din, *War in the Gulf Coast*, 134–40; Wright, *William Augustus Bowles*, 128–38.

8. Kelsall's decision, rendered in the court's term of March 31–May 29, 1802, is found in McAlister, "The Marine Forces of William Augustus Bowles," 15n, 23–27. In 1801, John Halkett, new governor of the Bahamas, took a strongly antagonistic approach to Bowles and Dunmore's old associates. See Wright, *William Augustus Bowles*, 156–58.

9. For Upper Creek perspectives, see the speech of Efau Hadjo, before Benjamin Hawkins, November 25, 1799. See also the speech of Creek chiefs to Governor of Pensacola and Mr. Panton. Both speeches are in "A Talk of the Creek Nation Respecting William Augustus Bowles." For the Redstick War, see Saunt, *A New Order of Things*, 254–66.

10. Landers, *Atlantic Creoles*, 72–79, 105–6.

11. Only three of the blacks were clearly identified as slaves, implying that the others were free persons. Sixteen whites were also captured. For the list of prisoners, see Relación de los Presos del Partido del Aventurero Guillermo Augusto Bowles, January 20, 1804, JWCHM. For the African American role along the Gulf during the War of 1812, see Smith, *The Slaves' Gamble*. See also Snyder, *Slavery in Indian Country*, 217–24.

12. See Forbes, "A Journal of John Forbes," 287; Wright, *William Augustus Bowles*, 162–71.

13. Saunt, *A New Order of Things*, 249–64; Hudson, *Creek Paths and Federal Roads*, 96–104.

14. For the Georgia-U.S. agreement of April 24, 1802, see ASP, Public Lands, 1:114. See also Hudson, *Creek Paths and Federal Roads*, 46.

15. Forbes and Company reaped over $77,000 by this process through 1814. The sum amounted to one-fifth of annuities pledged to Indians in the treaties. See Coker and Watson, *Indian Traders*, 243–72; Kennedy, *Mr. Jefferson's Lost Cause*, 156–65.

16. Forbes to the marqués de Casa Yrujo [1804], in Coker, *John Forbes' Description of the Spanish Floridas, 1804*.

17. David Bradford to David Reddick, February 9, 1803; Bradford to unknown recipi-

ent, October 10, 1803 (quotation), David Bradford Letters, Louisiana State University Libraries. See also Rothman, *Slave Country*, 48; Slaughter, *The Whiskey Rebellion*, 218, 267.

18. Magruder, *Political, Commercial, and Moral Reflections*, 18, 39–40. See also Lewis, "A Tornado on the Horizon," 117–40.

19. Pierre Clément de Laussat, prefect of Louisiana, attempted to restore the colony's former *Code Noir* in 1803 at the insistence of New Orleans municipal authorities. See Din, *Spaniards, Planters, and Slaves*, 230. For slavery's growth, see Rothman, *Slave Country*.

20. Laussat to Favrot, April 6, 1803, Favrot Papers, Louisiana Research Collection, Tulane University. See also Faber, "The Passion of the Prefect," 270–75; Paul Lachance, "The Louisiana Purchase in Demographic Perspective," in Kastor and Weill, *Empires of the Imagination*, 161–63. Laussat intended to win over western Americans—and thereby strengthen the colony against possible U.S. invasion. See Kukla, *A Wilderness So Immense*, 313.

21. DeConde, *This Affair of Louisiana*, 214–20. For the implications of Jeffersonian policy, see Onuf, "'Empire for Liberty,'" 310.

22. Haynes, *The Mississippi Territory and the Southwest Frontier*, 249–59, 267–82; Stagg, *Borderlines in Borderlands*, 69–86; McMichael, *Atlantic Loyalties*, 154–68.

23. Cusick, *The Other War of 1812*, 180–81, 211–12; Owsley and Smith, *Filibusters and Expansionists*, 66–81; Stagg, *Borderlines in Borderlands*, 126–29; Landers, *Atlantic Creoles*, 113–20.

24. Narrett, "José Bernardo Gutiérrez de Lara"; Narrett, "Liberation and Conquest"; Ramos, *Beyond the Alamo*, 27–49; Blaufarb, "The Western Question," 742–63.

25. Narrett, "Geopolitics and Intrigue," 143; Reséndez, *Changing National Identities at the Frontier*, 93–123.

BIBLIOGRAPHY

ARCHIVAL COLLECTIONS
(MANUSCRIPTS AND MICROFILM)

Ann Arbor, Michigan
   William L. Clements Library
      Louisiana—Maps
      William Petty, 1st Marquis of Lansdowne 2nd Earl of Shelburne Papers
Austin, Texas
   University of Texas at Austin, Dolph Briscoe Center for American History
      Edward Alexander Parsons Collection
Baton Rouge, Louisiana
   Hill Memorial Library
      David Bradford Letters
      Great Britain, Public Records Office (microfilm)
      Phillip Hicky Papers
      John Smith and Reuben Kemper Papers
Berkeley, California
   Bancroft Library, University of California
      Louisiana Papers
Chicago, Illinois
   Newberry Library
      Edward E. Ayer Manuscript Collection
      Harry Innes Papers
   Chicago History Museum, Research Center
      James Wilkinson Papers
   University of Chicago Library, Special Collections Research Center
      Dispatches, Diego Gardoqui y Arriquibar
      Reuben T. Durrett Collection
Dallas, Texas
   DeGolyer Library, Southern Methodist University
      Map Collection
   Fondren Library Center
      Draper Manuscript Collection
Fort Worth, Texas
   Mary Counts Burnett Library
      East Florida Papers
      Papers of Panton, Leslie, and Company

Gainesville, Florida
    P. K. Yonge Library of Florida History
        Joseph Byrne Lockey Documents Related to the History of Florida
Jackson, Mississippi
    Mississippi Department of Archives and History
        Mississippi Provincial Archives: Spanish Dominion, 1759–1820
Kew, Great Britain
    The National Archives
        Colonial Office
        Public Record Office
        Treasury Office
New Orleans, Louisiana
    The Historic New Orleans Collection
        Archivo Histórico Nacional (Spain)
        Archivo Nacional de Cuba: Fondo Floridas
        Bernardo de Gálvez Collection
        Documents from the National Library (*Biblioteca Nacional*) of Spain
    Tulane University, Howard-Tilton Memorial Library
        Rosemonde E. and Emile Kuntz Collection, Louisiana Research Collection
New York, New York
    Columbia University Libraries
        Correspondence of Sir Jeffrey Amherst
        The Papers of John Jay
    New York Public Library
        Fairchild Collection
        George Chalmers Papers
Ottawa, Canada
    Library and Archives Canada
        Great Britain. Colonial Office
        Haldimand Papers
Philadelphia, Pennsylvania
    Historical Society of Pennsylvania
        Dreer Autograph Collection
        Simon Gratz Collection
        Thomas Hutchins Papers
        Levis Collection
        George Morgan Manuscripts
        Society Collection
        William Irvine Papers
    American Philosophical Society
        George Gauld, "A General Description of the Sea Coasts, Harbours, Lakes, Rivers &c. of the Province of West Florida, 1769."
        Benjamin Vaughan Papers

Tallahassee, Florida
  Strozier Library, Florida State University
    Sir Frederick Haldimand: Unpublished Papers and Correspondence, 1758-84
Washington, D.C.
  Library of Congress
    William Blount Papers
    Andrew Ellicott Papers
    Bernardo de Gálvez Papers
    Thomas Jefferson Papers
    James Madison Papers
    George Morgan Papers
    Oliver Pollock Papers
    Aileen Moore Topping Collection concerning a Spanish Diplomatic Mission
      to the United States, 1777-1785
    George Washington Papers
    West Florida Papers
    James Wilkinson Papers
  Library of Congress—Photostat Collections
    Archivo General de Indias
    Archivo Histórico Nacional (Spain)
    Papeles procedentes de la isla de Cuba, 1665-1821

RESEARCH GUIDES

Beers, Henry Putney. *French and Spanish Records of Louisiana: A Bibliographical Guide to Archive and Manuscript Sources*. Baton Rouge: Louisiana State University Press, 1989.

Hill, Roscoe R. *Descriptive Catalogue of the Documents relating to the History of the United States in the Papeles Procedentes de Cuba deposited in the Archivo General de Indias at Seville*. Washington, D.C.: Carnegie Institution of Washington, 1916.

Jiménez Codinach, Estela Guadalupe. *The Hispanic World, 1492-1898: A Guide to Photoreproduced Manuscripts from Spain in the Collections of the United States, Guam, and Puerto Rico*. Washington, D.C.: Library of Congress. 1994.

PUBLISHED PRIMARY SOURCES

Adair, James. *The History of the American Indians*. London, 1775.

Alvord, Clarence Walworth, ed. *Cahokia Records, 1778-1790, Collections of the Illinois State Historical Library, Vol. 2*. Springfield: Illinois State Historical Library, 1907.

Alvord, Clarence Walworth, and Clarence Edwin Carter, eds. *The Critical Period, 1763-1765*. British Series (Volume 1). *Collections of the Illinois State Historical Society* 10. Springfield: Illinois State Historical Library, 1915.

———. *The New Régime, 1765-1767*. British Series (Volume 2). *Collections of the Illinois State Historical Society* 11. Springfield: Illinois State Historical Library, 1916.

An Appeal to the Public, in Behalf of George Johnstone, Esq.; Governor of West Florida. London, 1763.

An Impartial Enquiry into the Right of the French King to the Territory West of the Great River Mississippi, in North America . . . London, 1763.

An Impartial History of the Late Glorious War . . . Manchester, 1764.

Bates, Albert C., ed. *The Two Putnams: Israel and Rufus in the Havana Expedition 1762 and in the Mississippi River Exploration 1772–1773 with some account of the Company of Military Adventurers*. Hartford: Connecticut Historical Society, 1931.

Baynton, Benjamin. *Authentic Memoirs of William Augustus Bowles, Esquire, Ambassador from the United Nations of Creeks and Cherokees, to the Court of London*. London, [1791].

Bedford, John Russell. *Correspondence of John, Fourth Duke of Bedford*. 3 vols. London, 1842–46.

Bolton, Herbert E., ed. *Athanase de Mézières and the Louisiana-Texas Frontier, 1768–1780: Documents Published for the First Time, from the Original Spanish and French Manuscripts, Chiefly in the Archives of Mexico and Spain*. 2 vols. Cleveland: Arthur H. Clark, 1914.

Bolton, Herbert E., ed. "The Debatable Land: A Sketch of the Anglo-Spanish Contest for the Georgia Country." Addendum to *Arredondo's Historical Proof of Spain's Title to Georgia*, edited by Bolton. Berkeley: University of California Press, 1925.

The British Sailor's Discovery, or the Spanish Pretensions Confuted. London, 1739.

Brugger, Robert J., et al., eds. *The Papers of James Madison. Secretary of State Series*. 9 vols. Charlottesville: University Press of Virginia, 1986–2011.

Burnett, Edmund C., ed. *Letters of Members of the Continental Congress*. 8 vols. Washington, D.C.: Carnegie Institute, 1921–1936.

———. "Papers Relating to Bourbon County, Georgia, 1785–1786." *American Historical Review* 15 (October 1909): 66–111; (January 1910): 297–353.

Campbell, John. *An Account of the Spanish Settlements in America*. Edinburgh, 1762.

"Carondelet on the Defense of Louisiana, 1794." *American Historical Review* 2 (April 1897): 474–505.

Carter, Clarence Edwin, ed. *The Correspondence of General Thomas Gage*. 2 vols. 1931. Reprint, [Hamden, Conn.]: Archon Books, 1969.

Carter, Clarence Edwin, et al., eds. *The Territorial Papers of the United States*. 28 vols. Washington, D.C.: Government Printing Office [and other government publishers], 1934–1975.

Chandler, Richard E., trans. and ed. "Odyssey Continued: Acadians Arrive in Natchez." *Louisiana History* 19 (Fall 1978): 446–63.

Clark, Daniel. *Proofs of the Corruption of Gen. James Wilkinson and of His Connexion with Aaron Burr*. Philadelphia: Wm. Hall, Jr., and Geo. W. Pierie, 1809.

Clark, William Bell, et al., eds. *Naval Documents of the American Revolution*. 11 vols. Washington, D.C.: Department of the Navy, 1964–2005.

Coker, William S., ed. *John Forbes' Description of the Spanish Floridas, 1804*. Pensacola: Perdido Bay Press, 1979.

Coker, William S., and Hazel P. Coker. *The Siege of Mobile, 1780, in Maps: With Data on Troop Strength, Military Units, Ships, Casualties, and Prisoners of War*. Pensacola: Perdido Bay Press, 1982.

———. *The Siege of Pensacola, 1781, in Maps: With Data on Troop Strength, Military Units, Ships, Casualties, and Related Statistics*. Pensacola: Perdido Bay Press, 1981.

Coker, William S., and G. Douglas Inglis. *The Spanish Censuses of Pensacola, 1784–1820: A Genealogical Guide to Spanish Pensacola*. Pensacola: Perdido Bay Press, 1980.

Collot, (Georges-Henri-Victor). *Voyage dans l'Amérique Septentrionale*. 2 vols. Paris: A. Bertrand, 1826.

The Constitution of the Common-Wealth of Pennsylvania. Philadelphia: John Dunlap, 1776.

Correspondence of General James Robertson," *American Historical Magazine* 1 (January 1896): 80–88, 107–12.

Cox, Isaac Joslin, ed. "Documents Relating to Zachariah Cox." *Quarterly Publication of the Historical and Philosophical Society of Ohio* 8 (1913): 29–114.

Dalrymple, Margaret Fisher, ed. *The Merchant of Manchac: The Letterbooks of John Fitzpatrick, 1768–1790*. Baton Rouge: Louisiana State University Press, 1978.

Darby, William. *A Geographical Description of the State of Louisiana, the Southern Part of the State of Mississippi, and the Territory of Alabama*... 2nd ed. New York: James Olmstead, 1817.

Davies, K. G., ed. *Documents of the American Revolution, 1770–1783 (Colonial Office Series)*. 21 vols. Shannon and Dublin: Irish University Press, 1972–1981.

[Dehault Delassus de Luzières, Pierre Charles]. *An Official Account of the Situation, Soil, Produce &c. of that Part of Louisiana which Lies between the Mouth of the Missouri and New Madrid*... Lexington: J. Bradford, [1796?].

Dent, Harry P., ed. "West Florida—The Capture of Baton Rouge by Gálvez, September 21st, 1779." *Louisiana Historical Quarterly* 12 (April 1929): 258–62.

Din, Gilbert C., trans. and ed. *Louisiana in 1776: A Memoria of Francisco Bouligny*. New Orleans: Jack D. L. Holmes, 1977.

Echeverria, Durand, trans. "General Collot's Plan for a Reconnaissance of the Ohio and Mississippi Valleys, 1796." *William and Mary Quarterly*, 3rd ser., 9 (October 1952): 516–20.

Ellicott, Andrew. *The Journal of Andrew Ellicott, Late Commissioner on Behalf of the United States During Part of the Year 1796, the Years 1797, 1798, 1799, and Part of the Year 1800: For Determining the Boundary Between the United States and the Possessions of His Catholic Majesty in America*... Philadelphia: William Fry, 1814.

The Expediency of Securing Our American Colonies by Settling the Country Adjoining the River Mississippi, and the Country upon the Ohio, Considered. Edinburgh, 1763.

The Favrot Family Papers: A Documentary Chronicle of Early Louisiana. Edited by Guillermo Náñez Falcón, vols. 1–3, and Wilbur E. Meneray, vols. 4–5. New Orleans: Howard-Tilton Memorial Library, 1988–2001.

Ferguson, E. James, et al., eds. *The Papers of Robert Morris, 1781–1784*. 9 vols. Pittsburgh: University of Pittsburgh Press, 1973–1999.

Ferrer del Rio, Antonio. *Obras originales del conde de Floridablanca, y escritos referentes a su persona*. Madrid: M. Rivadeneyra, 1867.

Forbes, John. "A Journal of John Forbes, May 1803: The Seizure of William Augustus Bowles." *Florida Historical Quarterly* 9 (April 1931): 279–89.

Ford, Worthington Chauncey, et al., eds. *Journals of the Continental Congress, 1774–1789.* 34 vols. Washington, D.C.: Government Printing Office, 1904–1937.

Forman, Samuel S. *Narrative of a Journey down the Ohio and Mississippi in 1789–90.* Cincinnati: R. Clarke and Co., 1888.

Foster, Thomas H. II, ed. *The Collected Works of Benjamin Hawkins, 1796–1810.* Tuscaloosa: University of Alabama Press, 2003.

The Freeborn Englishman's Unmasked Battery: Containing Remarks on the Preliminary Articles of Peace... London, 1762.

Galloway, Patricia Kay, ed. *Mississippi Provincial Archives [Vol. 5]: French Dominion, 1749–1763. Collected, Edited, and Translated by Dunbar Rowland and A. G. Sanders.* Baton Rouge: Louisiana State University Press, 1984.

Gálvez, Bernardo de. "Bernardo de Gálvez: Diary of the Operations against Pensacola." *Louisiana Historical Quarterly* 1 (January 1917): 44–84.

Gómez del Campillo, Miguel. *Relaciones diplomaticas entre España y los Estados Unidos según los documentos del Archivo Histórico Nacional.* 2 vols. Madrid: Consejo Superior de Investigaciones Cientificas, 1944–45.

Hakluyt, Richard. "The Principal Navigations, Voyages, Traffiques, and Discoveries of the English Nation." In *Hakluyt's Collection of the Early Voyages, Travels, and Discoveries of the English Nation.* 5 vols. London, 1809–1812.

Hamer, Philip M., David R. Chesnutt, et al., eds. *The Papers of Henry Laurens.* 16 vols. Columbia: University of South Carolina Press, 1968–2003.

Holmes, Jack D. L., ed. *Documentos inéditos para la historia de Luisiana, 1792–1810.* Madrid: Ediciones José Porrúa Turanzas, 1963.

———. *Honor and Fidelity: The Louisiana Infantry Regiment and the Louisiana Militia Companies, 1766–1821.* Birmingham, Ala.: Jack D. L. Holmes, 1965.

———. *José de Evia y sus reconocimientos del Golfo de México, 1783–1796.* Madrid: José Porrúa Turanzas, 1968.

———, ed. and trans. "O'Reilly's 1769 Commission: A Personal View." *Louisiana History* 24 (Spring 1983): 307–13.

Houck, Louis. *The Spanish Régime in Missouri.* 2 vols. 1909. Reprint, New York: Arno Press, 1971.

Howard, Milo B. Jr., and Robert R. Rea, trans. and eds. *The Memoire Justificatif of the Chevalier Montault de Monberaut: Indian Diplomacy in British West Florida, 1763–1765.* University, Ala.: University of Alabama Press, 1965.

Hume, David. *The History of England, from the Invasion of Julius Caesar to the Revolution in 1688.* 8 vols. Edinburgh, 1792.

Hutchins, Thomas. *An Historical Narrative and Topographical Description of Louisiana and West-Florida, A Facsimile Reproduction of the 1784 Edition.* Edited by Joseph G. Treagle Jr. Gainesville: University of Florida Press, 1968.

Hutchinson, William T., et al., eds. *The Papers of James Madison: Congressional Series.* 17 vols. Chicago: University of Chicago Press; Charlottesville: University of Virginia Press, 1962–1991.

Ignotus. *Thoughts on Trade in General... and the Preliminary Articles of Peace.* London, 1763.

Jackson, Donald, and Dorothy Twohig, eds. *The Papers of George Washington: The Diaries*. 6 vols. Charlottesville: University of Virginia Press, 1976–1979.

Jucker, Ninetta S., ed. *The Jenkinson Papers, 1760–1766*. London, Macmillan, 1949.

Kinnaird, Lawrence. *Spain in the Mississippi Valley, 1765–1794*. 3 parts. Annual Report of the American Historical Association for the Year 1945, vols. 2–4. Washington, D.C.: Government Printing Office, 1946–49.

Knopf, Richard C., ed. *Anthony Wayne, A Name in Arms: Soldier, Diplomat, Defender of Expansion Westward of a Nation; the Wayne-Knox-Pickering-McHenry Correspondence*. Pittsburgh: University of Pittsburgh Press, 1960.

Labaree, Leonard W., et al., eds. *The Papers of Benjamin Franklin*. 40 vols. New Haven, Conn.: Yale University Press, 1959–2011.

Le Page du Pratz, (Antoine-Simon). *The History of Louisiana, or of the Western Parts of Virginia and Carolina*. 2 vols. London, 1763.

Lewis, James A. "*Cracker*—Spanish Florida Style." *Florida Historical Quarterly* 63 (October 1984): 184–204.

The Life of General W. A. Bowles... From "Public Characters, for 1802." London, [1803]).

Lockey, Joseph Byrne. *East Florida, 1783–1785: A File of Documents Assembled, and Many of Them Translated*. Edited by John Walton Caughey. Berkeley: University of California Press, 1949.

Lyon, E. Wilson, ed. "Moustier's Memoir on Louisiana." *Mississippi Valley Historical Review* 22 (September 1935): 251–66.

Magruder, Allan B. *Political, Commercial and Moral Reflections, on the Late Cession of Louisiana, to the United States*. Lexington, Ky., 1803.

Mathews, Catherine Van Cortlandt. *Andrew Ellicott: His Life and Letters*. New York: Grafton Press, 1908.

McAlister, Lyle N., ed. "The Marine Forces of William Augustus Bowles and his 'State of Muskogee.'" *Florida Historical Quarterly* 32 (July 1953): 3–27.

McMurtrie, Douglas C., ed. *The Earliest Known Louisiana Imprint*. New Orleans, privately printed, 1938.

———, ed. *A Newly-Discovered Broadside Printed at New Orleans in 1768 by Dennis Braud....* Chicago: Ragner H. Johnson, 1941.

Mémoire, des Habitans et Négocians de la Louisiane, sur l'Événement du 29 Octobre 1768. New Orleans, 1768.

Meneray, Wilbur E., ed. *The Rebellion of 1768*. Trans. Philippe Seiler. New Orleans: Howard-Tilton Memorial Library, 1995.

Morales Padrón, Francisco, ed. *Journal of Don Francisco Saavedra de Sangronis during the commission which he had in his charge from 25 June 1780 until the 20th of the same month of 1783*. Trans. Aileen Moore Topping. Gainesville: University of Florida Press, 1989.

Morris, Richard B., et al., eds. *John Jay: The Making of a Revolutionary, Unpublished Papers, 1745–1780*. New York: Harper and Row, 1975.

———. *John Jay: The Winning of the Peace: Unpublished Papers, 1780–1784*. New York: Harper and Row, 1975.

Murdoch, Richard K. "Correspondence of French Consuls in Charleston, 1793–1797." *South Carolina Historical Magazine* 74 (January 1973): 1–17; (April 1973): 73–79.

———, ed. "Documents Pertaining to the Georgia-Florida Frontier, 1791–1793." *Florida Historical Review* 38 (April 1960): 319–38.
———, ed. "Mission to the Creek Nation in 1794." *Florida Historical Quarterly* 34 (January 1956): 266–84.
Nasatir, Abraham P., ed. *Before Lewis and Clark: Documents Illustrating the History of the Missouri, 1785–1804*. 2 vols. St. Louis: St. Louis Historical Documents Foundation, 1952.
Navarro Latorre, José, and Fernando Solana Costa. *¿Conspiración española? 1787–1789: Contribución al estudio de las primeras relaciones históricas entre España y los Estados Unidos de Norteamérica*. Zaragoza: Institución Fernando el Católico del C.S.I.C., 1949.
Nobleman. *A Review of the Arguments for an Immature Peace . . .* London, 1763.
The North Briton. 3 vols. London, 1763.
Oberg, Barbara B., general ed. *The Papers of Thomas Jefferson*. 40 vols. Princeton, N.J.: Princeton University Press, 1950–2014.
Padgett, James A., ed. "Bernardo de Gálvez's Siege of Pensacola in 1781 (As Related in Robert Farmar's Journal)." *Louisiana Historical Quarterly* 26 (April 1943): 311–29.
———. "Minutes of the Council of West Florida, April 3–July 22, 1769." *Louisiana Historical Quarterly* 23 (April 1940): 353–404.
Pittman, Philip. *The Present State of the European Settlements on the Mississippi. A Facsimile Reproduction of the 1770 Edition*. Edited by Robert R. Rea. Gainesville: University of Florida Press, 1973.
Pope, John. *A Tour through the Southern and Western Territories of the United States of America; the Spanish Dominions on the River Mississippi, and the Floridas; the Countries of the Creek Nations; and Many Uninhabited Parts*. 1792. Reprint, New York: Charles L. Woodward, 1888.
Porrúa Turanzas, José, ed. *Diario de las operaciones contra la plaza de Panzacola, 1781*. 2nd ed. Madrid, 1959.
Rea, Robert R., with Milo Howard Jr., comps. *The Minutes, Journals, and Acts of the General Assembly of British West Florida*. University, Ala.: University of Alabama Press, 1979.
Reflections on the Terms of Peace. London, 1763.
Report of the Committee on Pensions and Revolutionary Claims, on the Petition of Oliver Pollock. Washington, D.C., 1814.
Report of the Committee on Pensions and Revolutionary Claims, on the petition of Oliver Pollock. December 21, 1818. Washington, D.C., 1818.
Robertson, James A. "Spanish Correspondence Concerning the American Revolution." *Hispanic American Historical Review* 1 (August 1918): 299–316.
Romans, Bernard. *A Concise Natural History of East and West Florida . . .* New York: Printed for the author, 1775.
Rowland, Dunbar, ed. *Mississippi Provincial Archives, 1763–1766: English Dominion*, vol. 1. Nashville: Brandon Printing Co., 1911.
———. *The Mississippi Territorial Archives, 1798–1803: Executive Journals of Governor Winthrop Sargent and Governor William Charles Cole Claiborne*. Nashville: Brandon Printing Co., 1905.
———. *Publications of the Mississippi Historical Society*. Vol. 5. Jackson, Miss., 1925.

Rowland, Mrs. Dunbar (Eron Rowland), comp. *Life, Letters and Papers of William Dunbar of Elgin, Morayshire, Scotland, and Natchez, Mississippi: Pioneer Scientist of the Southern United States*. Jackson: Mississippi Historical Society, 1930.

Rutland, Robert A., ed. *The Papers of George Mason, 1725-1792, Volume 1, 1749-1778*. Chapel Hill: University of North Carolina Press, 1970.

Scott, Kenneth, ed. "Britain Loses Natchez, 1779: An Unpublished Letter." *Journal of Mississippi History* 26 (February 1964): 45-46.

Sedgwick, Romney, ed. *Letters from George III to Lord Bute, 1756-1766*. London: Macmillan, 1939.

Serrano y Sanz, Manuel, ed. *Documentos históricos de la Florida y la Luisiana, Siglos XVI al XVIII*. Madrid: Librería General de Victoriano Suárez, 1912.

———. *España y los Indios Cherokis y Chactas en la segunda mitad del siglo XVIII*. Seville: Tip. de "Guia Oficial," 1916.

Shortt, Adam, and Arthur G. Doughty, eds. *Documents Relating to the Constitutional History of Canada, 1759-1791*. 2 vols. 2nd rev. ed., Ottawa: J. de L. Taché, 1918.

Siebert, Wilbur Henry. *Loyalists in East Florida; The Most Important Documents Pertaining Thereto, Edited with an Accompanying Narrative*. 2 vols. 1929. Reprint, Boston: Gregg Press, 1972.

Smith, John. *The Generall Historie of Virginia, New-England, and the Summer Isles*. London, 1625.

Smith, Paul H., et al., eds. *Letters of Delegates to Congress, 1774-1789*. 26 vols. Washington, D.C.: Government Printing Office, 1976-2000.

Smith, William Henry, ed. *The St. Clair Papers*. 2 vols. 1881. Reprint, Freeport, N.Y.: Books for Libraries Press, 1970.

Syrett, Harold C., et al., eds. *The Papers of Alexander Hamilton*. 27 vols. New York: Columbia University Press, 1961-1987.

"A Talk of the Creek Nation Respecting William Augustus Bowles." *Florida Historical Quarterly* 11 (July 1932): 33-39.

The True State of the Case, In an Address to the Good People of England. From a Well-Wisher to His Country. London, 1763.

Turner, Frederick J. "Correspondence of the French Ministers to the United States, 1791-1797." In *Annual Report of the American Historical Association for the Year 1903*. Vol. 2. Washington, D.C.: Government Printing Office, 1904.

———. "Documents on the Blount Conspiracy, 1795-1797." *American Historical Review* 10 (April 1905): 574-606.

———. "Documents on the Relations of France to Louisiana, 1792-1795." *American Historical Review* 3 (April 1898): 490-516.

———. "English Policy toward America in 1790-1791." *American Historical Review* 7 (July 1902): 706-35; 8 (October 1902): 78-86.

———. "The Mangourit Correspondence in Respect to Genet's Projected Attack upon the Floridas, 1793-1794." In *Annual Report of the American Historical Association for the Year 1897*, 569-679. Washington, D.C.: Government Printing Office, 1898.

———. "Selections from the Draper Collection in the Possession of the State Historical Society of Wisconsin, to Elucidate the Proposed French Expedition under George Rogers Clark against Louisiana, in the Years 1793-1794." In *Annual*

Report of the American Historical Association for the Year 1896. Vol. 1: 930–1107. Washington, D.C.: Government Printing Office, 1897.

Twohig, Dorothy, et al., eds. *The Papers of George Washington: Presidential Series*. 17 vols. Charlottesville: University of Virginia Press, 1987–2013.

Wharton, Francis, ed. *The Revolutionary Diplomatic Correspondence of the United States*. 6 vols. Washington, D.C.: Government Printing Office, 1889.

Whitaker, Arthur Preston, trans. and ed. *Documents Relating to the Commercial Policy of Spain in the Floridas*. Deland, Fla.: Florida State Historical Society, 1931.

———. "Letters of James Robertson and Daniel Smith." *Mississippi Valley Historical Review* 12 (December 1925): 409–12.

Wilkinson James. *Memoirs of My Own Times*. 3 vols. Philadelphia: Abraham Small, 1816.

Woodward, Augustus Brevoort. *A Representation of the Case of Oliver Pollock*. Carlisle, Pa.: George Kline, 1806.

Yela Utrilla, Juan F. *España ante la independencia de los Estados Unidos*. 2 vols. Lérida: Gráficos Academia Mariana, 1925.

BOOKS, ARTICLES, AND DISSERTATIONS

Abarca, Ramon E. "Classical Diplomacy and Bourbon 'Revanche' Strategy, 1763–1770." *Review of Politics* 32 (July 1970): 313–37.

Abernethy, Thomas Perkins. *From Frontier to Plantation in Tennessee A Study in Frontier Democracy*. 1932. Reprint, University, Ala.: University of Alabama Press, 1967.

———. *Western Lands and the American Revolution*. 1937. Reprint, New York: Russell & Russell, 1959.

Adelman, Jeremy, and Stephen Aron. "From Borderlands to Borders: Empires, Nation-States, and the Peoples in Between in North American History." *American Historical Review* 104 (June 1999): 814–41.

Ahlstrom, John D. "Captain and Chef de Brigade William Tate: South Carolina Adventurer." *South Carolina Historical Magazine* 88 (October 1987): 183–91.

Aiton, Arthur S. "The Diplomacy of the Louisiana Cession." *American Historical Review* 36 (July 1931): 701–20.

Alden, John Richard. *John Stuart and the Southern Colonial Frontier: A Study of Indian Relations, War, Trade, and Land Problems in the Southern Wilderness, 1754–1775*. 1944. Reprint, New York: Gordian Press, 1966.

Alderson, Robert J. Jr. "Charleston's Rumored Slave Revolt of 1793." In *The Impact of the Haitian Revolution in the Atlantic World*, edited by David P. Geggus, 93–111. Columbia: University of South Carolina Press, 2001.

———. *This Bright Era of Happy Revolutions: French Consul Michel-Ange-Bernard Mangourit and International Republicanism in Charleston, 1792–1794*. Columbia: University of South Carolina Press, 2009.

Alexander, Elizabeth Urban. "Daniel Clark: Merchant Prince of New Orleans." In *Nexus of Empire: Negotiating Loyalty and Identity in the Revolutionary Borderlands, 1760s–1820s*, edited by Gene Allen Smith and Sylvia L. Hilton, 241–67. Gainesville: University Press of Florida, 2010.

Alford, Terry. *Prince among Slaves*. New York: Harcourt Brace Jovanovich, 1977.

Ammon, Harry. *The Genet Mission*. New York: Norton, 1973.
Anderson, Fred. *Crucible of War: The Seven Years' War and the Fate of Empire in British North America, 1754–1766*. New York: Knopf, 2000.
Anderson, Fred, and Andrew Cayton. *The Dominion of War: Empire and Liberty in North America, 1500–2000*. New York: Viking, 2005.
Andreu Ocariz, Juan José. "El proyecto de Louis de Villemont para la colonización de Luisiana." *Estudios* (Zaragoza, 1976): 41–59.
——. "Los últimos projectos inmigratorios en la Luisiana española." *Estudios* (Zaragoza, 1983): 33–50.
Arena, C. Richard. "Philadelphia-Spanish New Orleans Trade in the 1790s." *Louisiana History* 2 (Autumn 1961): 429–45.
Armitage, David, and Michael J. Braddick, eds. *The British Atlantic World, 1500–1800*, 2nd ed. New York: Palgrave Macmillan, 2009.
Aron, Stephen. *American Confluence: The Missouri Frontier from Borderland to Border State*. Bloomington: Indiana University Press, 2006.
——. *How the West Was Lost: The Transformation of Kentucky from Daniel Boone to Henry Clay*. Baltimore: Johns Hopkins University Press, 1996.
Atkinson, James R. *Splendid Land, Splendid People: The Chickasaw Indians to Removal*. Tuscaloosa: University of Alabama Press, 2004.
Babcock, Matthew. "Roots of Independence: Transcultural Trade in the Texas-Louisiana Borderlands." *Ethnohistory* 60 (Spring 2013): 245–68.
Bailyn, Bernard. *Voyagers to the West: A Passage in the Peopling of America on the Eve of the Revolution*. New York: Knopf, 1986.
Beerman, Eric. "Arturo O'Neill: First Governor of West Florida during the Second Spanish Period," *Florida Historical Quarterly* 80 (July 1981): 29–41.
——. *España y la independencia de Estados Unidos*. Madrid: Editorial MAPFRE, 1992.
——. "The Last Battle of the American Revolution: Yorktown. No, the Bahamas! (The Spanish-American Expedition to Nassau in 1782)." *The Americas* 45 (July 1988): 79–95.
Bell, Carolyn Cosse. *Revolutions, Romanticism, and the Afro-Creole Protest Tradition in Louisiana, 1718–1868*. Baton Rouge: Louisiana University State Press, 1997.
Bemis, Samuel Flagg. *The Diplomacy of the American Revolution*. 1935. Rev. ed., Bloomington: Indiana University Press, 1957.
——. *The Hussey-Cumberland Mission and American Independence: An Essay in the Diplomacy of the American Revolution*. 1931. Reprint, Gloucester, Mass.: Peter Smith, 1968.
——. *Pinckney's Treaty: America's Advantage from Europe's Distress, 1783–1800*. 1926. Reprint, New Haven, Conn.: Yale University Press, 1960.
Bennett, Charles E. *Florida's "French" Revolution, 1793–1795*. Gainesville: University Presses of Florida, 1981.
Bjork, David Knuth. "The Establishment of Spanish Rule in the Province of Louisiana, 1762–1770." Ph.D. diss., University of California, 1923.
Black, Jeremy. "Britain's Foreign Alliances in the Eighteenth Century." *Albion* 20 (Winter 1988): 573–602.
——. *The British Seaborne Empire*. New Haven, Conn.: Yale University Press, 2004.

Blaufarb, Rafe. "The Western Question: The Geopolitics of Latin American Independence." *American Historical Review* 112 (June 2007): 742–63.

Bulmer-Thomas, Victor, John H. Coatsworth, and Roberto Cortés Conde. *The Cambridge Economic History of Latin America, Volume I: The Colonial Era and the Short Nineteenth Century*. Cambridge: Cambridge University Press, 2006.

Bolton, Herbert Eugene. *Texas in the Middle Eighteenth Century: Studies in Spanish Colonial History and Administration*. 1915. Reprint, New York: Russell & Russell, 1962.

Bottigheimer, Karl S. "English Money and Irish Land: The 'Adventurers' in the Cromwellian Settlement of Ireland." *Journal of British Studies* 7 (November 1967): 12–27.

Boulle, Pierre H. "French Reactions to the Louisiana Revolution of 1768." In *The French in the Mississippi Valley*, edited by John Francis McDermott, 143–57. Urbana: University of Illinois Press, 1965.

Brading, D. A. "Bourbon Spain and Its American Empire." In *The Cambridge History of Latin America, Volume I: Colonial Latin America*, edited by Leslie Bethell, 389–439. Cambridge: Cambridge University Press, 1984.

Brasseaux, Carl A. *Denis-Nicolas Foucault and the New Orleans Rebellion of 1768*. Ruston, La.: McGinty Publications, 1987.

———. *The Founding of New Acadia: The Beginnings of Acadian Life in Louisiana, 1765–1803*. Baton Rouge: Louisiana State University Press, 1987.

Brasseaux, Carl A., and Richard E. Chandler. "The Britain Incident, 1769–1770: Anglo-Hispanic Tensions in the Western Gulf." *Southwestern Historical Quarterly* 87 (April 1984): 357–70.

Braund, Kathryn E. Holland. "The Creek Indians, Blacks, and Slavery." *Journal of Southern History* 57 (November 1991): 601–36.

———. *Deerskins and Duffels: The Creek Indian Trade with Anglo-America, 1685–1815*. Lincoln: University of Nebraska Press, 1993.

Brecher, Frank W. *Losing a Continent: France's North American Policy, 1753–1763*. Westport, Conn.: Greenwood Press, 1998.

Brown, Douglas Stewart. "The Iberville Canal Project: Its Relation to Anglo-French Commercial Rivalry in the Mississippi Valley, 1763–1775." *Mississippi Valley Historical Review* 32 (March 1946): 491–516.

Brown, Meredith Mason. *Frontiersman: Daniel Boone and the Making of America*. Baton Rouge: Louisiana State University Press, 2008.

Brown, Richmond F., ed. *Coastal Encounters: The Transformation of the Gulf South in the Eighteenth Century*. Lincoln: University of Nebraska Press, 2007.

Buckner, Timothy Ryan. "Constructing Identities on the Frontier of Slavery: Natchez, Mississippi, 1760–1860." Ph.D. diss., University of Texas at Austin, 2005.

Burbank, Jane, and Frederick Cooper. *Empires in World History: Power and the Politics of Difference*. Princeton, N.J.: Princeton University Press, 2010.

Burson, Caroline. *The Stewardship of Don Esteban Miró, 1782–1792*. New Orleans: American Printing Co., 1940.

Burton, Clarence Monroe. "John Connolly: A Tory of the Revolution," *Proceedings of the American Antiquarian Society* 95 (October 1909): 70–105.

Burton, H. Sophie. "Spanish Bourbons and Louisiana Tobacco: The Case of Natchitoches, 1763–1803." In *Coastal Encounters: The Transformation of the Gulf South in the Eighteenth Century*, edited by Richmond F. Brown, 167–86. Lincoln: University of Nebraska Press, 2007.

———. "Vagabonds along the Spanish Louisiana-Texas Frontier, 1769–1803: 'Men Who Are Evil, Lazy, Gluttonous, Drunken, Libertinous. Dishonest, Mutinous, etc. etc. etc.—And Those Are Their Virtues.'" *Southwestern Historical Quarterly* 113 (April 2010): 438–67.

Burton, H. Sophie, and F. Todd Smith. *Colonial Natchitoches: A Creole Community on the Louisiana-Texas Frontier*. College Station: Texas A&M University Press, 2008.

Calderón Cuadrado, Reyes. *Empresarios españoles en el proceso de independencia norteamericana; La casa Gardoqui e hijos de Bilbao*. Madrid: Unión Editorial, 2004.

Calhoon, Robert M. "The Floridas, the Western Frontier, and Vermont: Thoughts on the Hinterland Loyalists." In *Eighteenth-Century Florida: Life on the Frontier*, edited by Samuel Proctor, 1–15. Gainesville: University Presses of Florida, 1976.

Calloway, Colin G. *The American Revolution in Indian Country: Crisis and Diversity in Native American Communities*. Cambridge: Cambridge University Press, 1995.

———. *One Vast Winter Count: The Native American West before Lewis and Clark*. Lincoln: University of Nebraska Press, 2003.

———. *The Scratch of a Pen: 1763 and the Transformation of North America*. New York: Oxford University Press, 2006.

Campbell, Wesley J. "The French Intrigue of James Cole Mountflorence." *William and Mary Quarterly*, 3rd ser., 65 (October 2008): 779–96.

———. "The Origin of Citizen Genet's Projected Attack on Spanish Louisiana: A Case Study in Girondin Politics." *French Historical Studies* 33 (Fall 2010): 515–44.

Cañizares-Esguerra, Jorge. "Entangled Histories: Borderland Historiographies in New Clothes?" *American Historical Review* 112 (June 2007): 787–99.

Cary, Catherine Snell. "The American Dream: John Tabor Kempe's Rise from Poverty to Riches." *William and Mary Quarterly*, 3rd ser., 14 (April 1957): 176–95.

Cashin, Edward J. *Lachlan McGillivray, Indian Trader: The Shaping of the Southern Colonial Frontier*. Athens: University of Georgia Press, 1992.

———. *William Bartram and the American Revolution on the Southern Frontier*. Columbia: University of South Carolina Press, 2000.

Caughey, John Walton. *Bernardo de Gálvez in Louisiana, 1776–1783*. 1934. Reprint, Gretna, La.: Pelican Publishing Co., 1972.

———. *McGillivray of the Creeks*. Norman: University of Oklahoma Press, 1938.

———. "The Natchez Rebellion of 1781 and Its Aftermath." *Louisiana Historical Quarterly* 16 (January 1933): 57–83.

———. "Willing's Expedition Down the Mississippi, 1778." *Louisiana Historical Quarterly* 15 (January 1932): 5–36.

Cayton, Andrew R. L. "'When Shall We Cease to Have Judases?' The Blount Conspiracy and the Limits of the 'Extended Republic.'" In *Launching the "Extended Republic": The Federalist Era*, edited by Ronald Hoffman and Peter J. Albert, 156–89. Charlottesville: University Press of Virginia, 1996.

Chandler, R. E. "Ulloa and the Acadians." *Louisiana History* 21 (Winter 1980): 87–91.

Chávez, Thomas E. *Spain and the Independence of the United States: An Intrinsic Gift*. Albuquerque: University of New Mexico Press, 2002.

Chernow, Ron. *Alexander Hamilton*. New York: Penguin, 2004.

Childs, Frances Sergeant. *French Refugee Life in the United States: An American Chapter of the French Revolution*. Baltimore: Johns Hopkins University Press, 1940.

Chipman, Donald E. *Spanish Texas, 1519–1821*. Austin: University of Texas Press, 1992.

Christelow, Allan. "Economic Background of the Anglo-Spanish War of 1762." *Journal of Modern History* 18 (March 1946): 22–36.

———. "Proposals for a French Company for Spanish Louisiana, 1763–1764." *Mississippi Valley Historical Review* 27 (March 1941): 603–11.

Claiborne, J. F. A. *Mississippi, as a Province, Territory and State*. 2 vols. 1880. Reprint, Baton Rouge: Louisiana State University Press, 1964.

Clark, John G. *New Orleans, 1718–1812: An Economic History*. Baton Rouge: Louisiana State University Press, 1970.

Coker, William S. "The Bruins and the Formulation of Spanish Immigration Policy in the Old Southwest." In *The Spanish in the Mississippi Valley, 1762–1784*, edited by John Francis McDermott, 61–71. Urbana: University of Illinois Press, 1974.

Coker, William S., and Robert R. Rea, eds. *Anglo-Spanish Confrontation on the Gulf Coast during the American Revolution*. Pensacola: Gulf Coast History and Humanities Conference, 1982.

Coker, William S., and Thomas D. Watson. *Indian Traders of the Southeastern Spanish Borderlands: Panton, Leslie and Company and John Forbes and Company, 1783–1847*. Pensacola: University of West Florida Press, 1986.

Colley, Linda. *Britons: Forging the Nation, 1707–1837*. New Haven, Conn.: Yale University Press, 1992.

Connelley, William Elsey, and E. M. Coulter. *History of Kentucky*, 5 vols. Chicago: American Historical Society, 1922.

Conover, Bettie Jones. "British West Florida's Mississippi Frontier Posts, 1763–1779." *Alabama Review* 29 (July 1976): 177–207.

Conrad, Glenn R. "The Indefatigable Dr. James White." *Southern Studies* 6 (Fall 1995): 1–55.

Corbitt, D. C. "James Colbert and the Spanish Claims to the East Bank of the Mississippi." *Mississippi Valley Historical Review* 24 (March 1938): 457–72.

Corkran, David H. *The Creek Frontier, 1540–1783*. Norman: University of Oklahoma Press, 1967.

Cotterill, R. S. *The Southern Indians: The Story of the Civilized Tribes before Removal*. Norman: University of Oklahoma Press, 1954.

Coulter, E. Merton. "Elijah Clarke's Foreign Intrigues and 'the Trans-Oconee Republic.'" *Proceedings of the Mississippi Valley Historical Review* 10, pt. 1 (1918–1919): 260–79.

Countryman, Edward. *Americans: A Collision of Histories*. New York: Hill and Wang, 1996.

Coutts, Brian E. "Boom and Bust: The Rise and Fall of the Tobacco Industry in Spanish Louisiana, 1770–1790." *The Americas* 42 (January 1986): 289–309.

Crane, Verner W. *The Southern Frontier, 1670–1732*. 1929. 2nd ed., 1956. Reprint, New York: Norton, 1981.
Cummins, Light Townshend. "Anglo Merchants and Capital Migration in Spanish Colonial New Orleans, 1763–1803." *Gulf Coast Historical Review* 4 (Fall 1988): 6–27.
———. "An Enduring Community: Anglo-American Settlers at Colonial Natchez and the Felicianas, 1774–1810." *Journal of Mississippi History* 55 (May 1993): 133–54.
———. "Oliver Pollock and the Creation of an American Identity in Spanish Colonial Louisiana." In *Nexus of Empire: Negotiating Loyalty and Identity in the Revolutionary Borderlands, 1760s–1820s*, edited by Gene Allen Smith and Sylvia L. Hilton, 198–218. Gainesville: University Press of Florida, 2010.
———. "Oliver Pollock's Plantations: An Early Anglo Landowner on the Lower Mississippi, 1769–1824." *Louisiana History* 29 (Winter 1988): 35–48.
———. *Spanish Observers and the American Revolution, 1775–1783*. Baton Rouge: Louisiana State University Press, 1991.
Cunningham, Charles H. "Financial Reports Relating to Louisiana, 1766–1788." *Mississippi Valley Historical Review* 6 (December 1919): 385–90.
Cusick, James G. *The Other War of 1812: The Patriot War and the American Invasion of Spanish East Florida*. Gainesville: University Press of Florida, 2003.
David, James Corbett. *Dunmore's New World: The Extraordinary Life of a Royal Governor in Revolutionary America—with Jacobites, Counterfeiters, Land Schemes, Shipwrecks, Scalping, Indian Politics, Runaway Slaves, and Two Illegal Royal Weddings*. Charlottesville: University of Virginia Press, 2013.
Davis, Karl. "The Founding of Tensaw: Kinship, Community, Trade, and Diplomacy in the Creek Nation." In *Coastal Encounters: The Transformation of the Gulf South in the Eighteenth Century*, edited by Richmond F. Brown, 81–98. Lincoln: University of Nebraska Press, 2007.
Dawdy, Sharon Lee. *Building the Devil's Empire: French Colonial New Orleans*. Chicago: University of Chicago Press, 2008.
DeConde, Alexander. *Entangling Alliances: Politics and Diplomacy under George Washington*. Durham, N.C.: Duke University Press, 1958.
———. *This Affair of Louisiana*. New York: Scribner's, 1976.
DeRojas, Lauro. "The Great Fire of 1788 in New Orleans." *Louisiana Historical Quarterly* 20 (1937): 578–81.
DeRosier, Arthur H., Jr. *William Dunbar: Scientific Pioneer of the Old Southwest*. Lexington: University Press of Kentucky, 2007.
De Vorsey, Louis. *The Indian Boundary in the Southern Colonies, 1763–1775*. Chapel Hill: University of North Carolina Press, 1961.
Dickinson, Samuel Dorris. "Don Juan Filhiol at Écore à Fabri." *Arkansas Historical Quarterly* 46 (Summer 1987): 133–55.
Din, Gilbert C. "Arkansas Post in the American Revolution." *Arkansas Historical Quarterly* 40 (Spring 1981): 3–30.
———. *The Canary Islanders of Louisiana*. Baton Rouge: Louisiana State University Press, 1988.
———. "Empires Too Far: The Demographic Limitations of Three Imperial Powers

in the Eighteenth-Century Mississippi Valley." *Louisiana History* 38 (Summer 2009): 261–92.

———. "Father Jean Delvaux and the Natchitoches Revolt of 1795." *Louisiana History* 40 (Winter 1999): 5–33.

———. "'For Defense of Country and the Glory of Arms': Army Officers in Spanish Louisiana, 1766–1803." *Louisiana History* 43 (Winter 2002): 5–40.

———. *Francisco Bouligny: A Bourbon Soldier in Spanish Louisiana*. Baton Rouge: Louisiana State University Press, 1993.

———. "Francisco Bouligny's 1778 Plans for Settlement in Louisiana." *Southern Studies* 16 (Summer 1977): 211–24.

———. "The Immigration Policy of Governor Esteban Miró in Spanish Louisiana." *Southwestern Historical Quarterly* 63 (October 1969): 155–75.

———. "The Irish Mission to West Florida." *Louisiana History* 12 (Autumn 1971): 315–34.

———. "Loyalist Resistance after Pensacola: The Case of James Colbert." In *Anglo-Spanish Confrontation on the Gulf Coast during the American Revolution*, edited by William S. Coker and Robert R. Rea, 158–76. Pensacola: Gulf Coast History and Humanities Conference, 1982.

———. "Pierre Wouves d'Argès in North America: Spanish Commissioner, Adventurer, or French Spy?" *Louisiana Studies* 12 (Spring 1973): 354–75.

———. "Proposals and Plans for Colonization in Spanish Louisiana, 1787–1790." *Louisiana History* 11 (Summer 1970): 197–213.

———. "Protecting the 'Barrera': Spain's Defenses in Louisiana, 1763–1779." *Louisiana History* 19 (Spring 1978): 183–211.

———. "Spain's Immigration Policy in Louisiana and the American Penetration, 1792–1803." *Southwestern Historical Quarterly* 76 (January 1973): 255–76.

———. *Spaniards, Planters, and Slaves: The Spanish Regulation of Slavery in Louisiana, 1763–1803*. College Station: Texas A&M Press, 1999.

———. "War Clouds on the Mississippi: Spain's 1785 Crisis in West Florida." *Florida Historical Quarterly* 60 (July 1981): 51–76.

———. *War on the Gulf Coast: The Spanish Fight against William Augustus Bowles*. Gainesville: University Press of Florida, 2012.

———, ed. *The Spanish Presence in Louisiana, 1763–1803*. The Louisiana Purchase Bicentennial Series in Louisiana History, vol. 2. Lafayette, La.: Center for Louisiana Studies, University of Southwestern Louisiana, 1996.

Din, Gilbert C., and Abraham P. Nasatir. *The Imperial Osages: Spanish-Indian Diplomacy in the Mississippi Valley*. Norman: University of Oklahoma Press, 1983.

Dowd, Gregory Evans. *A Spirited Resistance: The North American Indian Struggle for Unity, 1745–1815*. Baltimore: Johns Hopkins University Press, 1992.

Downes, Randolph C. "Creek-American Relations, 1790–1795." *Journal of Southern History* 8 (August 1942): 350–73.

Dubois, Laurent. *A Colony of Citizens: Revolution and Slave Emancipation in the French Caribbean, 1787–1804*. Chapel Hill: University of North Carolina Press, 2004.

Duffy, Michael. *Soldiers, Sugar, and Seapower: The British Expeditions to the West Indies and the War against Revolutionary France*. Oxford: Clarendon Press, 1987.

Dull, Jonathan R. *A Diplomatic History of the American Revolution.* New Haven, Conn.: Yale University Press, 1985.

DuVal, Kathleen. *The Native Ground: Indians and Colonists in the Heart of the Continent.* Philadelphia: University of Pennsylvania Press, 2006.

Ekberg, Carl J. "The Flour Trade in French Colonial Louisiana." *Louisiana History* 37 (Summer 1996): 261–82.

———. *François Vallé and His World: Upper Louisiana before Lewis and Clark.* Columbia: University of Missouri Press, 2002.

———. *French Roots in the Illinois Country: The Mississippi Frontier in Colonial Times.* Urbana: University of Illinois Press, 1998.

Elkins, Stanley, and Eric McKitrick. *The Age of Federalism: The Early American Republic, 1788–1800.* New York: Oxford University Press, 1993.

Elliott, Jack D., Jr. "City and Empire: The Spanish Origins of Natchez." *Journal of Mississippi History* 59 (Winter 1997): 271–321.

Elliott, J. H. *Empires of the Atlantic World: Britain and Spain in America, 1492–1830.* New Haven, Conn.: Yale University Press, 2006.

———. *Spain, Europe and the Wider World, 1500–1800.* New Haven, Conn.: Yale University Press, 2009.

Ermus, Cindy. "Reduced to Ashes: The Good Friday Fire of 1788 in Spanish Colonial New Orleans." *Louisiana History* 54 (Spring 2013): 292–331.

Fabel, Robin F. A. *Bombast and Broadsides: The Lives of George Johnstone.* Tuscaloosa: University of Alabama Press, 1987.

———. *Colonial Challenges: Britons, Native Americans, and Caribs, 1759–1775.* Gainesville: University Press of Florida, 2000.

———. *The Economy of British West Florida, 1763–1783.* University, Ala.: University of Alabama Press, 1988.

———. "An Eighteenth Colony: Dreams for the Mississippi on the Eve of the Revolution." *Journal of Southern History* 59 (November 1993): 647–72.

———. "Encounters Up the Mississippi, Yazoo, and Big Black Rivers: The Explorers of the Company of Military Adventurers." *Gulf Coast Historical Review* 8 (Fall 1992): 95–103.

———. "George Johnstone and the 'Thoughts Concerning Florida'—A Case of Lobbying?" *Alabama Review* 29 (July 1976): 164–76.

———. "The Letters of R: The Lower Mississippi in the Early 1770s." *Louisiana History* 24 (Fall 1983): 402–27.

———. "Ordeal by Siege: James Bruce in Pensacola, 1780–1781." *Florida Historical Quarterly* 66 (January 1988): 280–97.

———. "Reflections on Mobile's Loyalism in the American Revolution." *Gulf South Historical Review* 19 (2003): 31–45.

Faber, Eberhard L. "The Passion of the Prefect: Pierre Clément de Laussat, 1803 New Orleans, and the Bonapartist Louisiana That Never Was." *Louisiana History* 54 (Spring 2013): 261–91.

Faragher, John Mack. *Daniel Boone: The Life and Legend of an American Pioneer.* New York: Henry Holt, 1992.

———. *A Great and Noble Scheme: The Tragic Story of the Expulsion of the French Acadians from Their American Homeland*. New York: Norton, 2005.

Foley, William E. *The Genesis of Missouri: From Wilderness Outpost to Statehood*. Columbia: University of Missouri Press, 1989.

Frank, Andrew K. *Creeks and Southerners: Biculturalism on the Early American Frontier*. Lincoln: University of Nebraska Press, 2005.

Gallay, Allan. *The Indian Slave Trade: The Rise of the English Empire in the American South, 1670–1717*. New Haven, Conn.: Yale University Press, 2002.

Gayarré, Charles. *History of Louisiana*. 3rd ed. 4 vols. New Orleans: A. Hawkins, 1885.

Gibson, Arrell M. *The Chickasaws*. Norman: University of Oklahoma Press, 1971.

Gipson, Lawrence Henry. *The British Empire before the American Revolution*, vol. 8, *The Great War for the Empire: The Culmination, 1760–1763*. New York: Knopf, 1954.

Girard, Philippe R. "*Rêves d'Empire*: French Revolutionary Doctrine and Military Interventions in the Southern United States and the Caribbean, 1789–1809." *Louisiana History* 48 (Fall 2007): 389–412.

Gitlin, Jay. *Bourgeois Frontier: French Towns, French Traders, and American Expansion*. New Haven: Yale University Press, 2010.

Gold, Robert L. *Borderland Empires in Transition: The Triple-Nation Transfer of Florida*. Carbondale: Southern Illinois University Press, 1969.

Gould, Eliga H. *Among the Powers of the Earth: The American Revolution and the Making of a New World Empire*. Cambridge, Mass.: Harvard University Press, 2012.

———. "Entangled Histories, Entangled Worlds: The English-Speaking Atlantic as a Spanish Periphery." *American Historical Review* 122 (June 2007): 764–86.

———. *The Persistence of Empire: British Political Culture in the Age of the American Revolution*. Chapel Hill: University of North Carolina Press, 2000.

Gracy, David B., II. *Moses Austin: His Life*. San Antonio: Trinity University Press, 1987.

Graffagnino, J. Kevin. "'Twenty Thousand Muskets!!!': Ira Allen and the *Olive Branch* Affair, 1796–1800," *William and Mary Quarterly*, 3rd ser., 48 (July 1991): 409–31.

Grant, Ethan A. "Anthony Hutchins: A Pioneer of the Old Southwest," *Florida Historical Quarterly* 74 (Spring 1996): 405–22.

Green, Michael. "The Creek Confederacy in the American Revolution: Cautious Participants." In *Anglo-Spanish Confrontation on the Gulf Coast during the American Revolution*, edited by William S. Coker and Robert R. Rea, 54–75. Pensacola: Gulf Coast History and Humanities Conference, 1982.

Greene, Jack P. "Empire and Identity from the Glorious Revolution to the American Revolution." In *The Oxford History of the British Empire: The Eighteenth Century*, edited by P. J. Marshall, 208–30. New York: Oxford University Press, 1998.

———. *Imperatives, Behaviors, and Identities: Essays in Early American Cultural History*. Charlottesville: University Press of Virginia, 1992.

Hahn, Steven C. *The Invention of the Creek Nation, 1670–1763*. Lincoln: University of Nebraska Press, 2004.

Hall, Gwendolyn Midlo. *Africans in Colonial Louisiana: The Development of Afro-Creole Culture in the Eighteenth Century*. Baton Rouge: Louisiana State University Press, 1992.

Hämäläinen, Pekka, and Samuel Truett. "On Borderlands." *Journal of American History* 98 (September 2011): 338–61.

Hancock, David. *Citizens of the World: London Merchants and the Integration of the British Atlantic Community, 1735–1785.* Cambridge: Cambridge University Press, 1995.

Hardin, J. Fair. "Juan Filhiol and the Founding of Fort Miró, the Modern Monroe, Louisiana," *Louisiana Historical Quarterly* 20 (April 1937): 463–85.

Harper, John Lamberton. *American Machiavelli: Alexander Hamilton and the Origins of U.S. Foreign Policy.* Cambridge: Cambridge University Press, 2004.

Harrison, Lowell H. *Kentucky's Road to Statehood.* Lexington: University Press of Kentucky, 1992.

Haskins, Charles Homer. *The Yazoo Land Companies.* New York: Knickerbocker Press, 1891.

Haynes, Robert V. *The Mississippi Territory and the Southwest Frontier, 1795–1817.* Lexington: University Press of Kentucky, 2010.

———. *The Natchez District and the American Revolution.* Jackson: University Press of Mississippi, 1976.

Henderson, Archibald. "The Spanish Conspiracy in Tennessee." *Tennessee Historical Magazine* 3 (December 1917): 229–43.

Hilton, Sylvia L. "Movilidad y expansión en la construcción política de los Estados Unidos: 'Estos errantes colonos' en las fronteras españolas del Misisipí (1776–1803)." *Revista Complutense de Historia de América* 28 (2002): 63–96.

Hoffman, Paul E. *Florida's Frontiers.* Bloomington: Indiana University Press, 2002.

———. *A New Andalucia and a Way to the Orient: The American Southeast during the Sixteenth Century.* Baton Rouge: Louisiana State University Press, 1990.

Hoffman, Ronald, Thad W. Tate, and Peter J. Albert, eds. *An Uncivil War: The Southern Backcountry during the American Revolution.* Charlottesville: University Press of Virginia, 1985.

Holmes, Jack D. L. "Alabama's Bloodiest Day of the American Revolution: Counterattack at the Village, January 7, 1781." *Alabama Review* 29 (July 1976): 208–35.

———. "The Calcasieu Promoter: Joseph Piernas and His 1799 Proposal," *Louisiana History* 9 (Spring 1968): 163–67.

———. *Gayoso: The Life of a Spanish Governor in the Mississippi Valley, 1789–1799.* Baton Rouge: Louisiana State University Press, 1965.

———. "Indigo in Colonial Louisiana and the Floridas." *Louisiana History* 8 (Fall 1967): 329–49.

———. "Joseph Piernas and a Proposed Settlement on the Calcasieu River, 1795." *McNeese Review* 13 (1962): 59–80.

———. "Joseph Piernas and the Nascent Cattle Industry of Southwest Louisiana," 17 *McNeese Review* (1966): 13–26.

———. "Juan de la Villebeuvre: Spain's Commandant of Natchez during the American Revolution." *Journal of Mississippi History* 37 (February 1975): 97–129.

———. "Some Economic Problems of Spanish Governors of Louisiana." *Hispanic American Historical Review* 42 (November 1962): 521–43.

———. "The Southern Boundary Commission, the Chattahoochee River, and the Florida Seminoles, 1799." *Florida Historical Quarterly* 44 (April 1966): 312–41.

———. "The Value of the Arpent in Spanish Louisiana and West Florida." *Louisiana History* 24 (Summer 1983): 314–20.

Holmes, Jack D. L., and J. Leitch Wright Jr. "Luis Bertucat and William Augustus Bowles: West Florida Adversaries in 1791." *Florida Historical Quarterly* 49 (July 1970): 49–62.

Hook, Jonathan B. *The Alabama-Coushatta Indians*. College Station: Texas A&M University Press, 1997.

Howard, Clinton N. *The British Development of West Florida, 1763–1769*. Berkeley: University of California Press, 1947.

Hudson, Angela Pulley. *Creek Paths and Federal Roads: Indians, Settlers, and Slaves and the Making of the American South*. Chapel Hill: University of North Carolina Press, 2010.

Hurt, R. Douglas. *The Ohio Frontier: Crucible of the Old Northwest, 1720–1830*. Bloomington: Indiana University Press, 1996.

Hutson, James H. "Benjamin Franklin and the West." *Western Historical Quarterly* 4 (October 1973): 425–34.

Hyde, Samuel C., ed. *A Fierce and Fractious Frontier: The Curious Development of Louisiana's Florida Parishes, 1699–2000*. Baton Rouge: Louisiana State University Press, 2004.

Ingersoll, Thomas N. "The Slave Trade and the Ethnic Diversity of Louisiana's Slave Community." *Louisiana History* 37 (Spring 1996): 133–61.

Jacobs, James Ripley. *Tarnished Warrior: Major-General James Wilkinson*. New York: Macmillan, 1938.

James, D. Clayton. *Antebellum Natchez*. Baton Rouge: Louisiana State University Press, 1968.

James, James Alton. *Oliver Pollock: The Life and Times of an Unknown Patriot*. New York: D. Appleton-Century Co., 1937.

Jasanoff, Maya. *Liberty's Exiles: American Loyalists in the Revolutionary World*. New York: Knopf, 2011.

John, Elizabeth A. H. *Storms Brewed in Other Men's Worlds: The Confrontation of Indians, Spanish, and French in the Southwest, 1540–1795*. 2nd ed. Norman: University of Oklahoma Press, 1996.

Johnson, Cecil. *British West Florida, 1763–1783*. 1942. Reprint, n.p.: Archon Books, 1971.

Johnson, Sherry. "The Spanish St. Augustine Community, 1784–1795: A Reevaluation." *Florida Historical Quarterly* 68 (July 1989): 27–54.

Jones, Howard Mumford. "The Colonial Impulse: An Analysis of the 'Promotion' Literature of Colonization." *Proceedings of the American Philosophical Society* 90 (May 1946): 131–61.

Kamen, Henry. *Empire: How Spain Became a World Power, 1492–1763*. New York: HarperCollins, 2003.

Kastor, Peter J. *The Nation's Crucible: The Louisiana Purchase and the Creation of America*. New Haven: Yale University Press, 2004.

Kastor, Peter J., and François Weil, eds. *Empires of the Imagination: Transatlantic Histories of the Louisiana Purchase*. Charlottesville: University of Virginia Press, 2009.

Kennedy, Roger G. *Mr. Jefferson's Lost Cause: Land, Farmers, Slavery, and the Louisiana Purchase*. New York: Oxford University Press, 2003.

Kinnaird, Lawrence. "The Significance of William Augustus Bowles' Seizure of

Panton's Apalachee Store in 1792." *Florida Historical Quarterly* 9 (January 1931): 156–92.

Kinnaird, Lawrence and Lucia B. "Choctaws West of the Mississippi, 1766–1800." *Southwestern Historical Quarterly* 83 (April 1980): 349–70.

Klein, Rachel N. *Unification of a Slave State: The Rise of the Planter Class in the South Carolina Backcountry, 1760–1808*. Chapel Hill: University of North Carolina Press, 1990.

Korn, Bertram Wallace. *The Early Jews of New Orleans*. Waltham, Mass.: American Jewish Historical Society, 1969.

Kuethe, Allan J. *Cuba, 1753–1815: Crown, Military, and Society*. Knoxville: University of Tennessee Press, 1986.

Kukla, Jon. *A Wilderness So Immense: The Louisiana Purchase and the Destiny of America*. New York: Knopf, 2003.

Kyte, George W. "A Spy of the Western Waters: The Military Intelligence Mission of General Collot in 1796." *Mississippi Valley Historical Review* 34 (December 1947): 427–42.

Landers, Jane G. *Atlantic Creoles in the Age of Revolutions*. Cambridge, Mass.: Harvard University Press, 2010.

———. *Black Society in Spanish Florida*. Urbana: University of Illinois Press, 1999.

———, ed. *Colonial Plantations and Economy in Florida*. Gainesville: University Press of Florida, 2000.

Langley, Linda. "The Tribal Identity of Alexander McGillivray: A Review of the Historic and Ethnographic Data." *Louisiana History* 46 (Spring 2005): 231–39.

La Vere, David. "Between Kinship and Capitalism: French and Spanish Rivalry in the Colonial Louisiana-Texas Indian Trade." *Journal of Southern History* 64 (May 1998): 197–218.

Leglaunec, Jean-Pierre. "Slave Migrations in Spanish and Early American Louisiana: New Sources and New Estimates." *Louisiana History* 46 (Spring 2005): 185–209.

Lemmon, Alfred E., John T. Magill, and Jason R. Wiese, eds. *Charting Louisiana: Five Hundred Years of Maps*. Chicago: University of Chicago Press, 2003.

Lewis, James A. "Anglo-American Entrepreneurs in Havana: The Background and Significance of the Expulsion of 1784–1785." In *The North American Role in the Spanish Imperial Economy, 1760–1819*, edited by Jacques A. Barbier and Allan J. Kuethe, 112–26. Manchester: Manchester University Press, 1984.

Lewis, James E. "A Tornado on the Horizon: The Jefferson Administration, the Retrocession Crisis, and the Louisiana Purchase." In *Empires of the Imagination: Transatlantic Histories of the Louisiana Purchase*, edited by Peter J. Kastor and François Weil, 117–40. Charlottesville: University of Virginia Press, 2009.

Liljegren, Ernest R. "Jacobinism in Spanish Louisiana, 1792–1797." *Louisiana Historical Quarterly* 22 (January 1939): 47–97.

Link, Eugene Perry. *Democratic-Republican Societies, 1790–1800*. 1942. Reprint, New York: Octagon Books, 1973.

Linklater, Andro. *An Artist in Treason: The Extraordinary Double Life of General James Wilkinson*. New York: Walker, 2009.

Liss, Peggy K. *Atlantic Empires: The Network of Trade and Revolution, 1713–1826.* Baltimore: Johns Hopkins University Press, 1983.

Loomis, Noel M., and Abraham P. Nasatir. *Pedro Vial and the Roads to Santa Fe.* Norman: University of Oklahoma Press, 1967.

López-Chicheri, Eduardo Garrigues, coordinador. *Norteamérica a finales del siglo XVIII: España y los Estados Unidos.* Madrid: Marcial Pons, 2008.

Lycan, Gilbert L. *Alexander Hamilton and American Foreign Policy: A Design for Greatness.* Norman: University of Oklahoma Press, 1970.

Lynch, John. *Bourbon Spain, 1700–1808.* Oxford: Basil Blackwell, 1989.

Lyon, E. Wilson. *Louisiana in French Diplomacy, 1759–1804.* Norman: University of Oklahoma Press, 1934.

Mackesy, Piers. *The War for America, 1775–1783.* 1964. Reprint, Lincoln: University of Nebraska Press, 1992.

Maier, Charles. *Among Empires: American Ascendancy and Its Predecessors.* Cambridge, Mass.: Harvard University Press, 2006.

Mapp, Paul E. *The Elusive West and the Contest for Empire, 1713–1763.* Chapel Hill: University of North Carolina Press, 2011.

Márquez, Graciela. "Commercial Monopolies and External Trade." In *The Cambridge Economic History of Latin America, Volume I: The Colonial Era and the Short Nineteenth Century*, edited by Victor Bulmer-Thomas, John H. Coatsworth, and Roberto Cortés Conde, 395–422. Cambridge: Cambridge University Press, 2006.

Marshall, P. J. *The Impeachment of Warren Hastings.* London: Oxford University Press, 1965.

———. *Remaking the British Atlantic: The United States and the British Empire after American Independence.* New York: Oxford University Press, 2012.

Martin, Lloydine Della. "George Victor Collot in the Mississippi Valley, 1796." M.A. thesis, San Diego State Teachers College, 1934.

Masterson, William H. *William Blount.* Baton Rouge: Louisiana State University Press, 1954.

May, Robert E. *Manifest Destiny's Underworld: Filibustering in Antebellum America.* Chapel Hill: University of North Carolina Press, 2002.

———. "The United States as a Rogue State: Gunboat Persuasion, Citizen Marauders, and the Limits of Antebellum American Imperialism." In *America, War and Power: Defining the State, 1775–2005*, edited by Lawrence Sondhaus and A. James Fuller, 29–63. London: Routledge, 2007.

McAlister, Lyle N. "William Augustus Bowles and the State of Muskogee." *Florida Historical Quarterly* 40 (April 1962): 317–28.

McCadden, Helen Matzke. "Juan de Miralles and the American Revolution." *Americas* 29 (January 1973): 359–75.

McCormick, Richard P. *Experiment in Independence: New Jersey in the Critical Period, 1781–1789.* New Brunswick: Rutgers University Press, 1950.

McGrath, C. Peter. *Yazoo: Law and Politics in the Early Republic. The Case of Fletcher v. Peck.* Providence: Brown University Press, 1966.

McGroarty, William Buckner. "Major Andrew Ellicott and His Historic Border Lines." *Virginia Magazine of History and Biography* 58 (January 1950): 98–111.

McMichael, Andrew. *Atlantic Loyalties: Americans in Spanish West Florida, 1785–1810.* Athens: University of Georgia Press, 2008.

Medina Rojas, F. de Borja. *José de Ezpeleta: Gobernador de la Mobila, 1780–1781.* Seville: Escuela de Estudios Hispano-Americanos, 1980.

Meinig, D. W. *The Shaping of America: A Geographical Perspective on 500 Years of History, Volume 1, Atlantic America, 1492–1800.* New Haven, Conn.: Yale University Press, 1986.

Melton, Buckner F., Jr. *The First Impeachment: The Constitution's Framers and the Case of Senator William Blount.* Macon, Ga.: Mercer University Press, 1998.

Mitchell, Jennie O'Kelly, and Robert Dabney Calhoun. "The Marquis de Maison Rouge, the Baron de Bastrop, and Colonel Abraham Morhouse: Three Ouachita Valley Soldiers of Fortune. The Maison Rouge and Bastrop Spanish Land 'Grants.'" *Louisiana Historical Quarterly* 20 (April 1937): 289–462.

Miller, Janice Borton. *Juan Nepomuceno de Quesada: Governor of Spanish East Florida, 1790–1795.* Washington, D.C.: University Press of America, 1981.

———. "Rebellion in East Florida in 1795." *Florida Historical Quarterly* 57 (October 1978): 173–86.

———. "The Struggle for Free Trade in East Florida and the Cédula of 1793." *Florida Historical Review* 55 (July 1976): 48–59.

Moore, John Preston. *Revolt in Louisiana: The Spanish Occupation, 1766–1770.* Baton Rouge: Louisiana State University Press, 1976.

Moore, R. Woods. "The Role of the Baron de Bastrop in the Anglo-American Settlement of the Spanish Southwest." *Louisiana Historical Quarterly* 31 (July 1948): 606–81.

Morgan, Edmund S. *American Slavery, American Freedom: The Ordeal of Colonial Virginia.* New York: Norton, 1975.

Morison, Samuel Eliot. *John Paul Jones: A Sailor's Biography.* Boston: Little, Brown, 1959.

Morris, Christopher. *Becoming Southern: The Evolution of a Way of Life, Warren County and Vicksburg, Mississippi, 1770–1860.* New York: Oxford University Press, 1995.

———. *The Big Muddy: An Environmental History of the Mississippi and Its Peoples from Hernando de Soto to Hurricane Katrina.* New York: Oxford University Press, 2012.

Mouhot, Jean-François. "The Emigration of the Acadians from France to Louisiana: A New Perspective." *Louisiana History* 53 (Spring 2012): 133–67.

Mowat, Charles Loch. *East Florida as a British Province, 1763–1764.* 1943. Reprint, Gainesville: University of Florida Press, 1964.

Murdoch, Richard K. "Citizen Mangourit and the Projected Attack on East Florida in 1794." *Journal of Southern History* 14 (November 1948): 522–40.

———. "Elijah Clarke and Anglo-American Designs on East Florida, 1797–1798." *Georgia Historical Quarterly* 35 (September 1951): 173–90.

———. *The Georgia-Florida Frontier, 1793–1796: Spanish Reaction to French Intrigue and American Designs.* Berkeley: University of California Press, 1951.

———. "Governor Céspedes and the Religion Problem in East Florida, 1786–1787." *Florida Historical Quarterly* 26 (April 1948): 325–44.

Myers, Robert A. "Cherokee Pioneers in Arkansas: The St. Francis Years." *Arkansas Historical Quarterly* 56 (Summer 1997): 127–57.

Narrett, David E. "Geopolitics and Intrigue: James Wilkinson, the Spanish Borderlands, and Mexican Independence." *William and Mary Quarterly*, 3rd ser., 69 (January 2012): 101–46.

———. "José Bernardo Gutiérrez de Lara: *Caudillo* of the Mexican Republic in Texas." *Southwestern Historical Quarterly* 106 (October 2002): 195–228.

———. "Liberation and Conquest: John Hamilton Robinson and U.S. Adventurism Toward Mexico, 1806–1819." *Western Historical Quarterly* 40 (Spring 2009): 23–50.

Nasatir, Abraham P. *Spanish War Vessels on the Mississippi, 1792–1796*. New Haven, Conn.: Yale University Press, 1968.

Náter, Laura. "Fiscalidad imperial y desarrollo regional en el siglo XVIII: El monopolio del tabaco como instrumento de fomento en la Luisiana." *Historia Mexicana* 54 (July–September 2004): 59–91.

Nichols, David A. "Land, Republicanism, and Indians: Power and Policy in Early National Georgia, 1780–1825." *Georgia Historical Quarterly* 85 (Summer 2001): 199–226.

O'Brien, Greg. *Choctaws in a Revolutionary Age, 1750–1830*. Lincoln: University of Nebraska Press, 2002.

O'Donnell, James H. III. *Southern Indians in the American Revolution*. Knoxville: University of Tennessee Press, 1973.

Oltra, Joaquín, and María Ángeles Pérez Samper. *El conde de Aranda y los Estados Unidos*. Barcelona: PPU, 1987.

Onuf, Peter S. "'Empire for Liberty': Centers and Peripheries in Postcolonial America." In *Negotiated Empires: Centers and Peripheries in the Americas, 1500–1820*, edited by Christine Daniels and Michael V. Kennedy, 301–17. New York: Routledge, 2002.

Owsley, Frank Lawrence, Jr., and Gene A. Smith. *Filibusters and Expansionists: Jeffersonian Manifest Destiny, 1800–1821*. Tuscaloosa: University of Alabama Press, 1997.

Pagden, Anthony. *Lords of All the World: Ideologies of Empire in Spain, Britain, and France, c. 1500–c. 1800*. New Haven, Conn.: Yale University Press, 1995.

Pares, Richard. *War and Trade in the West Indies, 1739–1763*. 1936. Reprint, London: Frank Cass and Co., 1963.

Parish, John Carl. "The Intrigues of Doctor James O'Fallon." *Mississippi Valley Historical Review* 17 (September 1930): 230–63.

Pearce, Adrian J. *British Trade with Spanish America, 1763–1808*. Liverpool: Liverpool University Press, 2007.

Pease, Theodore C. "The Mississippi Boundary of 1763: A Reappraisal of Responsibility." *American Historical Review* 40 (January 1935): 278–86.

Parcero Torre, Celia. "Comercio y contrabando en Cuba (1760–1766)." In *El sistema atlántico español (siglos XVII–XIX)*, edited by Carlos Martínez Shaw and José María Oliva Melgar, 255–70. Madrid: Marcial Pons Historia, 2005.

Piker, Joshua A. "'White & Clean' & Contested: Creek Towns and Trading Paths in the Aftermath of the Seven Years' War." *Ethnohistory* 50 (Spring 2003): 315–47.

Powell, Lawrence N. *The Accidental City: Improvising New Orleans*. Cambridge, Mass.: Harvard University Press, 2012.

Powell, Philip Wayne. *Tree of Hate: Propaganda and Prejudices Affecting United States Relations with the Hispanic World.* New York: Basic Books, 1971. Reprint, Albuquerque: University of New Mexico Press, 2008.

Quattrocchi, Anna Margaret. "Thomas Hutchins, 1730–1789." Ph.D. diss., University of Pittsburgh, 1944.

Provine, W. A. "Lardner Clark: Nashville's First Merchant and Foremost Citizen." *Tennessee Historical Magazine* 3 (March 1917): 28–50; 3 (June 1917): 115–33.

Ramos, Raúl A. *Beyond the Alamo: Forging Mexican Ethnicity in San Antonio, 1821–1861.* Chapel Hill: University of North Carolina Press, 2008.

Rea, Robert R. "Brigadier Frederick Haldimand: The Florida Years." *Florida Historical Quarterly* 54 (April 1976): 512–31.

———. "'Graveyard for Britons,' West Florida, 1763–1781." *Florida Historical Quarterly* 47 (April 1969): 345–64.

———. "Lieutenant Colonel James Robertson's Mission to the Floridas, 1763." *Florida Historical Quarterly* 53 (January 1974): 33–48.

———. *Major Robert Farmar of Mobile.* Tuscaloosa: University of Alabama Press, 1990.

———. "Military Deserters from British West Florida." *Louisiana History* 9 (Spring 1968): 123–37.

———. "Redcoats and Redskins on the Lower Mississippi, 1773–1776: The Career of Lt. John Thomas." *Louisiana History* 2 (Winter 1970): 5–35.

Reeves, Carolyn Keller, ed. *The Choctaw before Removal.* Jackson: University Press of Mississippi, 1985.

Reséndez, Andrés. *Changing National Identities at the Frontier: Texas and New Mexico, 1800–1850.* Cambridge: Cambridge University Press, 2005.

Rice, Geoffrey W. "Great Britain, the Manila Ransom, and the First Falklands Dispute with Spain, 1766." *International History Review* 2 (July 1980): 386–409.

Rice, Howard C. *Barthélemi Tardiveau: A French Trader in the West.* Baltimore: Johns Hopkins University Press, 1938.

Riordan, Patrick. "Finding Freedom in Florida: Native Peoples, African Americans, and Colonists, 1670–1816." *Florida Historical Quarterly* 75 (Summer 1996): 24–43.

Robertson, James Alexander. "A Projected Settlement of English-speaking Catholics from Maryland to Spanish Louisiana, 1767, 1768." *American Historical Review* 16 (January 1911): 319–27.

Rodriguez, Mario. *La revolución americana de 1776 y el mundo hispánico: Ensayos y documentos.* Madrid: Editorial Tecnos, 1976.

Rodríguez Casado, Vicente. *Primeros años de dominación española en la Luisiana.* Madrid: Consejo Superior de Investigaciones Científicas, 1942.

Rothman, Adam. *Slave Country: American Expansion and the Origins of the Deep South.* Cambridge, Mass.: Harvard University Press, 2005.

Ruigómez de Hernández, María Pilar. *El gobierno español del despotismo ilustrado ante la independencia de los Estados Unidos de América: Una nueva estructura de la política internacional (1773–1783).* Madrid: Ministerio de Asuntos Exteriores, 1978.

Sánchez-Fabrés Mirat, Elena. *Situación histórica de las Floridas en la segunda mitad del siglo XVIII (1783–1819).* Madrid: Ministerio de Asuntos Exteriores, 1977.

Sarson, Steven. *British America, 1500–1800: Creating Colonies, Imagining an Empire.* London: Hodder Arnold, 2005.

Saunt, Claudio. *A New Order of Things: Property, Power, and the Transformation of the Creek Indians, 1733–1816.* Cambridge: Cambridge University Press, 1999.

Savelle, Max. *George Morgan: Colony Builder.* 1932. Reprint, New York: AMS Press, 1967.

Schafer, Daniel L. "'A Swamp of an Investment'? Richard Oswald's British East Florida Plantation Experiment." In *Colonial Plantations and Economy in Florida*, edited by Jane G. Landers, 11–38. Gainesville: University Press of Florida, 2000.

Searcy, Martha Condray. *The Georgia-Florida Contest in the American Revolution, 1776–1778.* University, Ala.: University of Alabama Press, 1985.

Serrano y Sanz, Manuel. *El Brigadier Jaime Wilkinson y sus tratos con España para la independencia del Kentucky (años 1787 á 1797).* Madrid: Revista de Archivos, Biblioteca y Museos, 1915.

Shepherd, William R. "The Cession of Louisiana to Spain." *Political Science Quarterly* 19 (September 1904): 439–58.

Siebert, Wilbur H. "The Loyalists in West Florida and the Natchez District." *Mississippi Valley Historical Review* 2 (March 1916): 465–83.

———. "The Port of St. Augustine during the British Regime." *Florida Historical Quarterly* 24 (April 1946): 247–65; 25 (July 1946): 76–93.

Skemp, Sheila L. *William Franklin: Son of a Patriot, Servant of a King.* New York: Oxford University Press, 1990.

Smith, F. Todd. *The Caddo Indians: Tribes at the Convergence of Empires, 1542–1854.* College Station: Texas A&M University Press, 1995.

Smith, Gene Allen. *The Slaves' Gamble: Choosing Sides in the War of 1812.* New York: Palgrave Macmillan, 2013.

Smith, Gene Allen, and Sylvia L. Hilton, eds. *Nexus of Empire: Negotiating Loyalty and Identity in the Revolutionary Borderlands, 1760s–1820s.* Gainesville: University Press of Florida, 2010.

Snapp, J. Russell. *John Stuart and the Struggle for Empire on the Southern Frontier.* Baton Rouge: Louisiana State University Press, 1996.

Snyder, Christina. *Slavery in Indian Country: The Changing Face of Captivity in Early America.* Cambridge, Mass.: Harvard University Press, 2010.

Solano Costa, Fernando. "La colonización irlandesa de la Luisiana española: dos proyectos de inmigración." *Estudios 1980–1981*, 201–8. Zaragoza, 1981.

———. "La emigración acadiana a la Luisiana española (1783–1785)." *Cuadernos de Historia "Jerónimo Zurita."* 85–125. Zaragoza: C.S.I.C., 1951.

Sosin, Jack M. *Whitehall and the Wilderness: The Middle West in British Colonial Policy, 1760–1775.* Lincoln: University of Nebraska Press, 1961.

Stagg, J. C. A. *Borderlines in Borderlands: James Madison and the Spanish-American Frontier, 1776–1821.* New Haven, Conn.: Yale University Press, 2009.

Starr, J. Barton. "Campbell Town: French Huguenots in British West Florida." *Florida Historical Quarterly* 54 (April 1976): 532–47.

———. *Tories, Dons, and Rebels: The American Revolution in British West Florida.* Gainesville: University Presses of Florida, 1976.

Stein, Stanley J., and Barbara H. Stein. *Apogee of Empire: Spain and New Spain in the Age of Charles III, 1759-1789*. Baltimore: Johns Hopkins University Press, 2003.
———. *Silver, Trade, and War: Spain and America in the Making of Early Modern Europe*. Baltimore: Johns Hopkins University Press, 2000.
Sturtevant, William C. "The Cherokee Frontiers, the French Revolution, and William Bowles." In *The Cherokee Indian Nation: A Troubled History*, edited by Duane H. King, 61–91. Knoxville: University of Tennessee Press, 1979.
Surrey, N. M. Miller. *The Commerce of Louisiana during the French Régime, 1699-1763*. New York: Columbia University Press, 1916.
Tanner, Helen Hornbeck. *Zéspedes in East Florida, 1784-1790*. 1963. Reprint, Jacksonville: University of North Florida Press, 1989.
———. "Zéspedes and the Southern Conspiracies." *Florida Historical Quarterly* 38 (July 1959): 15–28.
Taylor, Alan. *The Divided Ground: Indians, Settlers, and the Northern Borderland of the American Revolution*. New York: Knopf, 2006.
TePaske, John J., "Spanish America." *International History Review* 6 (November 1984): 511–18.
Thonhoff, Robert H. *The Texas Connection with the American Revolution*. Austin: Eakin Press, 2000.
Treagle, Joseph G., Jr. "British Spy along the Mississippi: Thomas Hutchins and the Defenses of New Orleans, 1773." *Louisiana History* 8 (Fall 1967): 313–27.
Troxler, Carole Watterson. "Loyalist Refugees and the British Evacuation of East Florida, 1783–1785." *Florida Historical Quarterly* 60 (July 1981): 1–28.
Usner, Daniel H., Jr. *Indians, Settlers, and Slaves in a Frontier Exchange Economy: The Lower Mississippi Valley before 1783*. Chapel Hill: University of North Carolina Press, 1992.
Villiers du Terrage, Marc de. *Les dernières années de la Louisiane française*. Paris: E. Guilmoto, 1903.
Watlington, Patricia. "John Brown and the Spanish Conspiracy." *Virginia Magazine of History and Biography* 75 (January 1967): 52–68.
Watson, Thomas D. "Continuity in Commerce: Development of the Panton, Leslie and Company Trade Monopoly in West Florida." *Florida Historical Quarterly* 54 (April 1976): 548–64.
Weber, David J. *Bárbaros: Spaniards and Their Savages in the Age of Enlightenment*. New Haven, Conn.: Yale University Press, 2005.
———. *The Spanish Frontier in North America*. New Haven, Conn.: Yale University Press, 1992.
Weddle, Robert S. *Changing Tides: Twilight and Dawn in the Spanish Sea, 1763-1803*. College Station: Texas A&M University Press, 1995.
———. *The French Thorn: Rival Explorers in the Spanish Sea, 1682-1762*. College Station: Texas A&M University Press, 1991.
———. *Spanish Sea: The Gulf of Mexico in North American Discovery, 1500-1685*. College Station: Texas A&M University Press, 1985.
Weeks, Charles A. *Paths to a Middle Ground: The Diplomacy of Natchez, Boukfouka, Nogales, and San Fernando de las Barrancas, 1791-1795*. Tuscaloosa: University of Alabama Press, 2005.

Whitaker, Arthur Preston. "The Commerce of Louisiana and the Floridas at the End of the Eighteenth Century." *Hispanic American Historical Review* 8 (May 1928): 190–203.

———. "Harry Innes and the Spanish Intrigue, 1794–1795." *Mississippi Valley Historical Review* 15 (September 1928): 236–48.

———. "James Wilkinson's First Descent to New Orleans in 1787." *Hispanic American Historical Review* 8 (February 1928): 82–97.

———. *The Mississippi Question, 1795–1803: A Study in Trade, Politics, and Diplomacy.* 1934. Reprint, Gloucester, Mass.: Peter Smith, 1962.

———. "The Muscle Shoals Speculation, 1783–1789." *Mississippi Valley Historical Review* 13 (December 1926): 365–86.

———. "Reed and Forde, Merchant Adventurers of Philadelphia: Their Trade with Spanish New Orleans." *Pennsylvania Magazine of History and Biography* 61 (July 1937): 237–62.

———. "The South Carolina Yazoo Company." *Mississippi Valley Historical Review* 16 (December 1929): 383–94.

———. *The Spanish-American Frontier: 1783–1795: The Westward Movement and the Spanish Retreat in the Mississippi Valley.* 1927. Reprint, Gloucester, Mass.: Peter Smith, 1962.

———. "Spanish Intrigue in the Old Southwest: An Episode, 1788–1789." *Mississippi Valley Historical Review* 12 (September 1925): 155–76.

White, Richard. "The Louisiana Purchase and the Fictions of Empire." In *Empires of the Imagination: Transatlantic Histories of the Louisiana Purchase*, ed. Peter J. Kastor and François Weil. Charlottesville: University of Virginia Press, 2009.

———. *The Middle Ground: Indians, Empires, and Republics in the Great Lakes Region, 1650–1815.* Cambridge: Cambridge University Press, 1991.

———. *The Roots of Dependency: Subsistence, Environment, and Social Change among the Choctaws, Pawnees, and Navajos.* Lincoln: University of Nebraska Press, 1983.

Woodward, Ralph Lee, Jr. "Spanish Commercial Policy in Louisiana, 1763–1803." *Louisiana History* 44 (Spring 2003): 133–64.

Wright, Esmond. *Franklin of Philadelphia.* Cambridge, Mass.: Harvard University Press, 1986.

Wright, J. Leitch, Jr. *Anglo-Spanish Rivalry in North America.* Athens: University of Georgia Press, 1971.

———. *Britain and the American Frontier, 1783–1815.* Athens: University of Georgia Press, 1975.

———. *Creeks and Seminoles: The Destruction and Regeneration of the Muscogulge People.* Lincoln: University of Nebraska Press, 1986.

———. *Florida in the American Revolution.* Gainesville: University Presses of Florida, 1975.

———. *William Augustus Bowles, Director General of the Creek Nation.* Athens: University of Georgia Press, 1967.

INDEX

Abbadie, Jean-Jacques Blaise d', 15, 33–35
Acadians: and migration to Louisiana, 49, 145–46, 155–56; support for revolt of 1768, 51, 56, 279 (n. 50), 303 (n. 18)
Adventurism: defined as historical phenomenon, 3–6
African Americans, 27, 56, 62, 81–83, 151–53, 157–58; and population, 32–33, 46–47, 99, 122; as soldiers and combatants, 56, 92, 107, 109, 261, 265; as refugees and runaways, 99, 115–16, 232; and Bowles's incursions, 221, 224, 261. *See also* Slavery
Alabama River, 61, 167, 231, 252
Alcudia, duque de. *See* Manuel de Godoy
Alibamons, 12, 15, 33–34, 39, 119, 244, 254–55, 275 (n. 61), 327 (n. 81), 333 (n. 87)
Amherst, Gen. Jeffrey, 11–12, 33
Apalachicola Bay and River, 25, 46, 90, 219–20, 254, 258–60, 296 (n. 87)
Aranda, Pedro Pablo Abarca de Bolea, conde de, 54, 69, 110–11, 113, 126, 143, 231, 296 (n. 86), 297 (n. 90), 300 (n. 46)
Arkansas: and Arkansas Indian nation (Quapaws), 29, 254; as frontier outpost, 86, 95, 106–7, 290 (n. 92); and Arkansas River, 235
Arnold, Benedict, 77
Aubry, Charles-Philippe, 47–48, 277 (n. 8), 278 (n. 29)

Bahama Channel (Florida Straits), 13, 24
Bahama Islands, 8, 15, 90, 103, 116–19, 211–13, 215, 218, 223, 226, 254, 260, 321 (n. 8), 322 (n. 17), 323 (n. 33), 326 (n. 67), 334 (nn. 6, 8)

Balize: as locale at Mississippi River's mouth, 19, 48, 93, 164
Barbé-Marbois, François, 126–27
Bastrop, Felipe Enrique Neri, baron de, 160–61
Baton Rouge, 44, 83, 91–93, 95, 100, 106–7, 123, 150, 156, 264, 291 (n. 9), 293 (n. 45), 299 (n. 35)
Bayou Manchac. *See* Iberville River
Bayou Pierre, 66–67, 194, 245, 306 (n. 57)
Bellin, Jacques-Nicolas: and cartography of Louisiana, 15–16, 18, 271 (n. 21)
Black Legend: in historiography, 6; and anti-Spanish prejudice, 40, 53, 124, 269 (n. 13)
Blacks. *See* African Americans; Slavery
Blommart, John: as leader of Natchez revolt, 101, 104–6, 293 (n. 46), 294 (nn. 48, 56, 58), 295 (nn. 60, 62, 68)
Blount, William, 203, 227–29, 238–41, 249–50, 258, 263, 330 (n. 32)
Board of Trade: and British imperial policy, 21, 24–26, 37, 65
Bonaparte, Napoleon, 234, 263
Boone, Daniel, 163
Borderlands: definition of, 2–3, 139–40
Bouligny, Francisco, 81, 121–23, 299 (n. 25), 303 (n. 15), 308 (n. 80)
Boundaries: changing imperial bounds, 1–2, 16, 24–26, 34–35, 110–11, 159; and Indian perceptions of, 15–16, 35, 40, 214, 225; and indefinite national boundaries, 198, 214, 263–65
Bourbon County scheme. *See* Georgia
Bourbon Family Compact, 11, 48, 54, 195
Bowles, William Augustus: as archetypal adventurer, 6, 139, 253, 259–60; and

Florida adventures, 211–13, 215–28, 254–55, 259–61, 263

Brion de la Tour, Louis: as cartographer, 113

Brown, John: and Kentucky politics, 165–66, 182

Browne, Montfort, 49–57, 67, 83, 108, 277 (n. 18), 279 (n. 47), 280 (n. 55)

Bruin, Peter Bryan, 155, 194, 245, 306 (n. 57)

Bute, John Stuart, earl of, 12, 23, 36

Caddos, 65, 254

Cameron, Alexander: as British Indian agent, 96, 292 (n. 31)

Caminade, François, 51–52

Campbell, Gen. John, 92, 96–105, 108, 293 (n. 31)

Campbell, John (author), 5, 21

Campo, Bernardo del, 172, 217, 223

Canada, 13, 16, 24, 108, 110, 172, 194, 196, 215, 217–18, 224, 235, 237, 241, 263

Canary Islanders: as Louisiana immigrants, 93, 158

Carlos III (king of Spain), 11, 13, 15, 45, 54–55, 74, 79, 85, 102–4, 115, 141

"Carolana" colonial scheme, 28–31, 273 (n. 29)

Carondelet, Francisco Luis Hector, barón de: and immigration policy, 155–63; and James Wilkinson and Kentucky, 173–76, 203, 242, 244; and French Revolution and freebooting threat, 199–201, 236–37; and William Augustus Bowles, 220, 222–23; and Indian policy, 227–31; and U.S. treaty's execution, 233–34, 242, 245

Charleston (Charles Town) (South Carolina), 42, 89, 103, 108–9, 187–92, 196–98, 203, 209, 290 (n. 98)

Chattahoochee River, 25–26, 111, 120, 128, 211–12, 225, 231, 254, 262, 296 (n. 87), 333 (n. 92)

Cherokees, 15, 32, 43, 61, 72–73, 133, 167, 176–77, 184, 188, 210, 213, 215, 217, 224, 230, 226–27, 230–31, 239–40, 262, 281 (n. 69), 313 (n. 74), 321 (n. 9), 322 (nn. 17, 25), 325 (n. 62), 327 (n. 81), 329 (n. 28)

Chester, Peter, 60, 62–63, 66–68, 72, 79, 81, 83–84, 100, 283 (n. 90), 281–82 (n. 74), 288 (n. 60), 293 (n. 44)

Chickasaw Bluffs, 188, 203, 228, 232, 331 (n. 50)

Chickasaws, 2, 31–32, 39–43, 61, 72–73, 88, 91, 96–97, 104, 106–7, 120–21, 184, 188, 190, 210, 213, 226–32, 235, 262, 275 (n. 65), 276 (n. 74), 295 (n. 71), 326 (n. 73), 327 (n. 82)

Chisholm, John, 237–41, 329 (nn. 28, 29)

Choctaws, 2, 12, 15, 31–35, 39–43, 51, 53, 60–62, 66, 72–73, 87–88, 91, 95–98, 100, 121, 188, 190–91, 193, 210, 226–30, 232, 243, 254, 262, 276 (n. 75), 290 (nn. 27, 28, 31), 293 (n. 46)

Choiseul, Étienne-François, comte de Stainville, duc de, 12–13, 16, 18–19, 54–55, 270 (n. 19), 271 (n. 27)

Clark, Daniel (the elder), 173–74, 183

Clark, Daniel (the younger), 174–75, 242, 247–50, 253

Clark, George Rogers, 88, 130–33, 139, 191–93, 197–98, 201–2

Clark, Lardner, 185–86

Clarke, Elijah, 206, 208

Colbert, James (the elder): as Scots-Chickasaw headman, 106–8

Colbert, James (the younger), 229

Colbert, William, 232

Collot, Georges-Henri-Victor, 234–37, 330 (n. 36)

Colonialism, as differentiated from imperialism, 1–2

Company of Military Adventurers, 45, 65–67, 100

Connolly, John, 172

Contraband trade and smuggling, 7, 15, 21–22, 52, 54, 60, 63–65, 78, 108, 139, 146–48, 151, 157, 166, 171–72, 257–58, 291 (n. 13), 307 (n. 76)

Cox, Zachariah, 251–52, 332 (n. 78)
Coxe, Dr. Daniel: and claim to "Carolana," 28–31, 273 (nn. 29, 33)
Creek Indians (Muscogulge), 2, 6, 16, 28, 31–32, 34, 40–44, 60–62, 72–74, 91, 97–99, 117, 120, 130, 133, 139, 176–77, 184, 189–90, 197, 203–15, 217–32, 240, 254–55, 259–62, 276 (nn. 75, 80), 292 (n. 31), 320 (nn. 92, 93), 321 (n. 3), 322 (nn. 17, 23, 25, 29), 323 (n. 38), 326 (nn. 68, 69, 77), 327 (nn. 81, 82), 334 (n. 9)
Cruden, John, 118, 298 (nn. 11, 14)
Cuba, 11, 13, 19–21, 37, 45, 55, 61, 63, 65, 71, 89, 103, 148–49, 161, 167, 208, 222, 242, 250
Cumberland (frontier region), 129–30, 169–70, 176–77, 184, 202, 227, 258, 301 (n. 61), 310 (n. 26), 326 (n. 73)
Cunningham, William (British agent to the Creeks), 221, 223–24, 324 (n. 42)
Cunningham, William (Tory refugee), 118–19

Dartmouth, William Legge, earl of, 66–67
Deerskin and fur trade, 30, 35, 41–42, 52–53, 55–56, 60–61, 64, 67, 74, 77, 81, 85, 98, 106, 108, 117, 119, 123, 187, 197, 204, 210, 224–26, 262
Delassus, Carlos Dehault, 233
Delassus de Luzières, Pierre Charles Dehault, 162
Delaware Indians, 154, 184, 229
Descoudreaux, Charles, 60
Dickson, Alexander, 92–93, 100
Dunbar, William, 81, 243, 288 (nn. 64, 65)
Dunmore, John Murray, earl of: plan of Loyalist interior colony, 108–9, 296 (nn. 78, 82); and support of Bowles and Lower Creeks, 212, 223–24, 226, 322 (n. 24), 334 (n. 8)
Dunn, Isaac, 170, 174, 182
Durnford, Elias, 34, 46, 58–59, 67, 94, 280 (nn. 59, 60), 283 (n. 93)

East Florida: as British colony, 1, 23–27, 62–63; and Spanish policy, 27, 90, 116–18, 155, 189, 210, 297 (n. 5), 313 (n. 62), 321 (n. 4); and Revolutionary War, 77, 90, 99, 107, 109, 111, 271; influx of British Loyalists and enslaved blacks, 111, 115–19; freebooting projects aimed at, 187–88, 197, 204–7, 212
Ellicott, Andrew: as U.S. boundary commissioner, 242–55, 332 (n. 65)
Emisteseguo (Creek headman), 61–62, 73–74, 98, 281 (n. 68), 285 (n. 20)
Empire, conceptions of, 1–2, 5–6, 25, 28, 45, 56, 65, 75, 95, 109, 111, 139–41, 159, 188, 191, 196, 202, 234, 238, 247, 253, 258
Escochabey (Lower Creek headman), 61
Evia, Josef (José de Evia), 222, 310 (n. 28)
Ezpeleta, José de, 167, 218

Falkland Islands (Islas Malvinas), 2, 57–58, 63
Farmar, Robert, 27–28, 33–35, 40–41, 273 (n. 28)
Favrot, Pedro (Pierre-Joseph), 92, 107, 119, 123, 201, 263
Fergusson, John: as British naval captain, 83–85
Filhiol, Juan (Jean-Baptiste), 160
Fitzpatrick, John: as merchant of Manchac, 84, 279 (n. 48), 282 (n. 79), 283 (n. 92)
Floridablanca, José Moñino y Redondo, conde de, 111, 113, 128–29, 131, 142–43, 155, 165, 181, 218, 222, 284 (n. 3), 301 (nn. 55, 56), 302 (n. 8)
Forbes, John, 228, 261–62
Forts: at Pensacola, 28, 97–98, 101; at Mobile, 28; Fort Bute, 36, 39, 48, 53, 92–93; at Natchez, 50, 53, 63, 101, 104, 120–21, 236, 243–44; Fort Pitt, 70, 75, 80, 184; at Baton Rouge, 91–93; at Nogales (Walnut Hills), 191, 230, 237; San Marcos de Apalache, 222, 224, 254–55, 260; Fort Confederation (on the Tombigbee), 230–31; at Chickasaw Bluffs, 231–32

France: and Louisiana's transfer to Spain, 1–2, 13–19, 35–36; and New Orleans revolt of 1768, 51–55; and alliance with Spain (1779), 58, 69, 91–92, 95; and war against Spain (1793–95), 139, 157, 159, 174, 195–99, 231, 241; and Louisiana's renewed value to France, 234–36, 240, 250–51, 262–64

Franchimastabé, as Choctaw headman, 40, 87, 230

Franco, as slave informer, 224, 325 (n. 55)

Franklin, Benjamin: as colonial promoter, 5, 30–31, 296 (n. 84); as U.S. diplomat, 109–10

Franklin (State of), 132–33, 165–70, 258, 302 (n. 71), 309 (n. 10), 310 (n. 26)

Freebooting plots and attacks, 105, 125, 129–33, 139, 149, 172, 187–88, 191–93, 195–208, 214, 237–41, 249, 258–60, 264–65, 315 (n. 6), 319 (n. 70)

Gage, Gen. Thomas: and West Florida policy, 44, 53, 56, 63, 67; and plan of attacking Louisiana, 57–58

Galliard, Tacitus, 122, 125

Gálvez, Bernardo de: as governor, 72, 76, 78–79, 89, 108, 286 (nn. 30, 40, 44), 288 (nn. 60, 62, 65, 71), 289 (n. 74), 290 (n. 88); and James Willing's raid, 79–88; and Spain's war with Britain, 91–105, 110, 113, 124, 200–201, 226, 294 (nn. 51, 55, 58), 296 (n. 77); and the postwar era, 118, 122–23, 141–42, 149, 193, 316 (n. 30)

Gálvez, José de, 71–72, 90, 141–42, 145, 147, 286 (n. 38), 288 (n. 71), 304 (n. 25)

Gardoqui y Arriquibar, Diego María de, 77, 89; as envoy to the United States, 127–29, 130–32, 144, 149–50, 152, 155, 165–67, 178–186, 189, 301 (nn. 55, 56, 66), 313 (nn. 59, 62), 316 (n. 30)

Gayoso de Lemos, Manuel Luis: as governor of Natchez, 152–53, 167–68, 173–75, 201–3, 318 (n. 65), 331 (n. 45); as Louisiana's governor-general, 162–63, 247–48, 251–52, 254; and western separatism, 176, 194, 239, 242, 311–12 (nn. 46, 47), 330 (n. 41); and Indian relations, 230–32; and U.S. treaty's execution, 241–48

Genet, Edmond Charles: and freebooting schemes, 196–203

Georgia: as colony, 13, 26–27, 42–43, 61; and Revolutionary War, 73, 77, 90, 98–99, 104–5, 108, 111, 113–14, 116–17, 119; and state's plan of annexing Natchez, 115, 120–30, 149; and trans-Appalachian politics, 167, 176, 187; and Yazoo land companies, 182, 243; and warfare with Creeks, 197, 206–8, 210–14, 231; and freebooting, 198–99, 203–7; and U.S.–Georgia compact of 1802, 261–62

Germain, George, 72, 81, 92, 96, 101

German immigration, 49, 51, 56, 119, 143, 145, 156, 158–59, 303 (n. 8), 307 (n. 70)

Gibraltar, 27, 125

Gibson, George: and mission to New Orleans, 70–71, 74, 284 (n. 8), 285 (n. 24)

Grant, James: as governor of British East Florida, 23, 25–26

Great Britain: and acquisition of the Floridas, 13, 24–26; and imperial policy in the Floridas, 34–39, 44, 57–58, 63–64, 66–68, 72–73, 81, 92, 96; and loss of the Floridas, 99–101, 108–114; and Nootka Sound crisis, 194–95; and William Augustus Bowles, 211–13, 215–18, 225–26, 254–56; and Blount conspiracy, 237–41; and Alexander Hamilton's plan of conquest, 249–50

Green, Thomas: and Bourbon County scheme, 121–22, 126–27; freebooting plan with George Rogers Clark, 130–31, 139; and return to Natchez, 177, 301 (n. 66), 302 (n. 3)

Godoy, Manuel de (duque de Alcudia), 173, 231, 233–34, 241, 243, 247

Grimaldi, Pablo Jerónimo, marqués de, 13, 76

Guion, Isaac, 233, 254

Haldimand, Brig.-Gen. Frederick, 48, 63; and New Orleans revolt, 51–53, 277 (n. 12), 278 (nn. 29, 32)

Hamilton, Alexander: and idea of attacking Louisiana and the Floridas, 249–51; and Wilkinson's command, 249, 252, 255, 333 (n. 79)

Hammond, Abner: and freebooting plot, 203–4, 319 (nn. 75, 78)

Hammond, Samuel: and freebooting, 203–5, 207, 319 (n. 75)

Havana, 11–13, 20–21, 23, 27, 31–31, 45, 51, 56, 61–64, 71, 77, 86, 89, 101–3, 113, 146, 148, 150, 161, 167–69, 193, 199, 201, 204, 209, 222–24, 242, 250, 261

Henry, Patrick, 70, 89, 284 (n. 9), 290 (n. 90)

Hume, David: and adventurism as historic phenomenon, 19, 269 (n. 9)

Hutchins, Anthony: as Natchez settler and schemer, 123–25, 152–53, 179, 300 (nn. 38, 42); and Natchez crisis of 1797, 244–45, 252

Hutchins, Thomas: as military engineer and spy, 58, 272 (n. 21), 280 (nn. 53, 59); as colonial promoter and lobbyist, 67, 92; as geographer and ally of George Morgan, 179–80, 183–84, 236, 312 (nn. 56, 57, 58), 313 (n. 59)

Iberville River (Bayou Manchac), as boundary, 16, 18, 48, 79, 313 (n. 28); as site of fort, 36, 39, 48, 53, 84, 86; as zone for canal construction and settlement, 36–39, 44, 55, 58–60, 68, 84, 158, 280 (n. 60)

Illinois, 2, 13, 33–34, 40–41, 47, 54, 65, 75, 86, 88, 105, 107, 109, 131–32, 154, 178–80, 184, 195, 235–36, 251, 263, 285 (n. 25), 312 (nn. 55, 58)

Illinois Company, 75, 178–79

Immigration, 3, 19, 46–47, 49; Indian migration to Louisiana, 34, 154, 253–54, 327 (n. 74); and Catholic immigration, 49, 57, 142, 145, 162, 172, 189, 298 (n. 10); and French Louisiana migration to West Florida, 50–51, 54–56, 280 (n. 54); and British migration to Spanish Louisiana, 64, 81–85, 257; and U.S. immigration to Spanish territories, 141–42, 151–55, 169, 177–86, 197, 204; European immigration proposals, 156–61

Imperialism: in relation to private adventurism, 2–5, 7–8, 23, 26–27, 30, 46, 54, 57, 62, 64–68, 109, 137–42, 145, 150, 155, 159, 176, 184, 193, 197, 201, 217, 228, 234, 240–41, 255, 257, 262–65

Indian peoples: and control of commerce, 3, 19, 41–43, 64–65, 73–74, 96–97, 106, 117, 210–12, 217–20, 223–27, 231, 260–61; and competition for Indian alliance, 4, 24–25, 30–34, 39–40, 45–46, 50, 53–54, 58–61, 72–73, 88, 95–98, 129, 184, 191, 207–8, 213–14, 228, 230–32, 241, 253; and imperial treaties, 15–16, 115, 209, 231–32, 254–255; and resistance to colonialism, 34–35, 43, 57, 62, 87, 107, 119, 133, 176–77, 190, 197, 207, 254; and conflicts between native peoples, 42–43, 61–62, 229; and slave raiding, 46, 99, 261. *See also* Mestizos; *headings under particular native groups*

Indiana Company, 75

Innes, Harry, 176, 311 (n. 46), 319 (n. 70), 331 (n. 50)

Intrigue: and its place within frontier history, 2–3, 7–8, 24, 35, 40, 45, 53, 56, 61, 69, 72, 76, 86, 94, 101, 109–10, 115, 120, 133, 139, 151, 161, 163–66, 169, 172–76, 179, 187, 197, 201, 203, 209–10, 212, 214, 218, 223–24, 234, 239, 244, 246–53, 257, 259, 263, 265, 275 (n. 64), 309 (nn. 3, 10), 312 (n. 47), 314 (n. 79), 325 (n. 17), 334 (n. 88)

Irish immigration: projects for Louisiana and the Floridas, 49, 67, 123, 143, 145, 155–56, 159, 172, 181, 194

Jáudenes, Josef (José) de, 156, 185, 314 (n. 71), 318 (n. 61)

Jay, John, 108, 132, 149; and Paris peace negotiations, 109–10; and proposed Spanish treaty, 127–30, 165; and Jay Treaty, 234, 242, 296 (n. 83), 300 (nn. 48, 51), 301 (n. 66)

Jefferson, Thomas: and appeal for Spanish aid, 103; and Nootka Sound crisis, 194; and Genet's scheme, 198, 205; and James O'Fallon, 192; and U.S. colonization of East Florida, 204; and U.S.–Georgia compact, 261–62; and Louisiana Purchase, 263–65

Jews: as settlers and traders, 60, 63, 152, 273 (n. 27), 296 (n. 77)

Johnstone, George, 21–23, 26–27, 34–44, 46–49, 94, 111, 193, 258, 272 (n. 9), 273–74 (n. 41), 275 (nn. 57, 64), 276 (nn. 77, 80, 81)

Jones, John Paul: and prospective Mississippi expedition, 80, 287 (n. 50)

Kentucky, 129, 217, 263; and freebooting schemes, 130–31, 189–94, 196–203, 205, 241, 249, 317 (n. 53), 319 (n. 70); and disaffection from the Union, 133, 137, 149, 169–70, 182; and maneuvers for Louisiana colonization and trade, 139, 142–44, 147, 150, 153–56, 161–66, 169–78, 182, 185, 189, 239, 242, 244, 257–58, 301 (n. 59), 310 (nn. 21, 25, 30), 311 (nn. 43, 44)

Kinache (Seminole headman), 260

Kinnaird, John (Jack), 208, 220–21, 320 (n. 96), 323 (nn. 39, 40)

Knox, Henry, 132, 202, 206, 213–15, 226, 229, 319 (n. 73), 326–27 (n. 77)

Lacassagne, Michel: as Spanish agent, 251, 319 (n. 67)

Lachaise, Auguste: and militant republicanism, 200, 202

Lafrénière, Nicolas Chauvin de: and revolt of 1768, 52, 57, 279 (n. 49), 279–80 (n. 52)

Lake Pontchartrain, 16–18, 25, 28, 39, 48, 50, 58, 78, 93, 108, 291 (nn. 15, 16)

Las Casas, Luis de, 193, 222–23, 323 (n. 32)

Laurens, Henry, and opposition to Mississippi invasion, 77; and distrust of Spain, 90, 290 (n. 97); and Florida plan, 290 (n. 98)

Laussat, Pierre-Clément de, 263, 335 (nn. 19, 20)

Lee, Arthur, 76

Lee, Gen. Charles, 71, 73

Leslie, John, 117–18, 211–14, 257

Leslie, Robert, 224, 226, 323 (n. 39), 325 (n. 55)

Linder, John, Jr., 119, 321 (n. 12)

Linder, John, Sr., 119, 298 (n. 17)

Liston, Robert: and Blount conspiracy, 237–40, 249, 263

Livingston, Robert R., 110

Lloyd, Thomas, 78,

Loftus, Maj. Arthur, 34–35, 251

Louisiana: as a Spanish barrier province for Mexico, 4, 19–20, 54–55, 69, 95, 140, 156, 243; French geographic conceptions of, 13, 16; and population of, 46–47, 146–47

Louisiana Purchase, 262–64

Lower Louisiana: and geographic definition of, 47, 299 (n. 28)

Lyman, Gen. Phineas: and Company of Military Adventurers, 31, 63–67, 282 (n. 87)

Lyman Thaddeus, 66, 100, 293 (n. 44)

Madison, James, 127–28, 184–85, 193, 264–65, 300 (nn. 48, 54), 313–14 (n. 76)

Maison Rouge, marquis de, 160, 308 (n. 81)

Manchac: as border and settlement zone, 60, 62, 70, 81, 83–87, 89, 91–95, 122, 155, 174, 179, 288 (n. 62), 289 (n. 76). *See also* Iberville River

Mangourit, Michel-Ange-Bernard, 196, 198, 203, 205, 317 (n. 46), 319 (n. 76)

Masan, Balthasar: and revolt of 1768, 51–51, 278 (n. 27)

McGillivray, Alexander, 97, 117, 119–20, 177, 184, 189–90, 209–29, 257, 261,

315 (n. 14), 321 (nn. 7, 8, 11, 14), 322 (nn. 19, 21), 323–24 (n. 41), 325 (n. 64), 326 (n. 74)
Meinig, D. W.: on geographic interconnections, 8
Mestizos: as Indian leaders and traders, 2, 107, 209, 211, 213, 215, 220, 225, 229, 254, 321 (n. 13), 323 (n. 33)
Mexico (New Spain), 19, 37, 48, 53–56, 64, 69, 71, 95–96, 102, 121–22, 140, 156, 161, 168, 217, 243, 247, 250, 264–65, 282 (nn. 77, 84)
Miccosukee: as Seminole town, 221, 260–61
Minor, Esteban (Stephen), 152, 201, 244, 254, 331 (n. 52)
Miralles, Juan de, 89–90, 290 (nn. 93, 95, 99)
Miró, Esteban Rodríguez, 107, 120–26, 133, 137, 141–42, 144, 147, 149–53, 155–56, 158, 164, 167–79, 181–84, 189–94, 200, 210–11, 222, 227–28, 246, 299 (n. 36), 301 (n. 66), 304 (nn. 26, 27), 306 (n. 47), 307 (nn. 61, 68), 309 (n. 1), 310 (nn. 15, 30), 311 (n. 40), 312 (n. 57), 313 (n. 68)
Mississippi River: and navigation rights on, 3, 16–19, 48, 74–75, 78, 82, 88–90, 94, 108–13, 115, 123, 126–33, 141, 143, 147–48, 159, 165–67, 170–71, 176–77, 181–82, 185–86, 189–90, 193–94, 202, 248; and navigability of, 36–39, 58–59, 65, 79
Mobile, 2–3, 13, 25, 27–29, 31–34, 37, 39, 41–42, 46, 50–51, 53–54, 70, 72–73, 75–77, 90–91, 94–99, 103, 106, 110, 113, 118–19, 123, 167, 179, 210, 228–29, 252, 264, 285 (n. 17), 292 (n. 28), 294 (n. 54)
Mobile Bay, 13, 20, 26, 28–29, 34, 97, 119, 264, 272 (n. 26)
Montault de Monberaut, chevalier, 39–40
Montgomery, John, 120, 202
Morales, Juan Ventura, 161, 231
Morandière, Étienne Robert de la, 104

Morgan, George, 70, 225; and plans for attacking British West Florida, 74–77, 80, 285 (n. 25), 286 (n. 26), 287 (n. 51); and scheme for New Madrid, 178–86, 312 (n. 58), 313 (nn. 59, 60, 68, 74), 314 (nn. 76, 78)
Morris, Robert: and Mississippi investments, 63, 86; and Revolutionary War, 70, 72, 74, 77, 79–80, 82, 94, 146, 285 (n. 24), 286 (n. 35), 287 (n. 50); and trade with Cuba, 89, 302 (n. 69)
Moultrie, Alexander, 189, 192–93, 315 (n. 10)
Moultrie, William, 197–98, 204
Mountflorence, James Cole, 185, 195, 314 (n. 79)
Muscle Shoals (on Tennessee River), 167, 203, 210
Muscogulge. See Creek Indians
Muskogee (State of), 218, 255, 259–60, 323 (n. 34), 334 (nn. 3, 4, 5)

Natchez: as native people, 15, 51; as French outpost, 27; as district in West Florida, 31, 44, 46, 49–53, 62–63, 65–67, 258; and Revolutionary War, 70, 80–81, 86–87, 89; and Anglo-Spanish war, 91, 93–94, 100–101, 103–8, 110–11; and Bourbon County crisis, 120–27; and freebooting threat, 129–32, 139, 187–88, 190–94, 201, 203; and settlement and trade under Spanish rule, 142–45, 147–49, 151–56, 162, 167–69, 171–74, 177, 179, 183; and Spanish Indian policy, 230; and crisis of 1797, 241–47; and Wilkinson's military command, 251–52, 255
Natchitoches, 50, 64–65, 147
Native Americans. See Indians; *listings of particular nations and groups*
Navarro, Martín (intendant of Louisiana), 133, 137, 141–42, 144–47, 149, 151, 153, 158, 169, 171, 211, 299 (n. 36), 303 (nn. 14, 15, 16, 21), 302–3 (nn. 22, 25)
New Madrid, 182–86, 203, 232–33

INDEX 371

New Mexico, 16, 270 (n. 20); as area of imagined wealth, 30, 108, 197, 239, 249

New Orleans, 2–3, 7–8, 12–20, 24, 27, 30, 33–39, 41–42, 58, 60–65, 67, 121–24, 130, 132, 137–38, 155–58, 162, 165, 178, 227–29, 233, 236, 238–40, 242, 245–48, 250, 252–54, 256–58, 261–63; and revolt of 1768, 45–49, 51–57; and Revolutionary War, 70–79, 81–88; and Anglo-Spanish warfare, 91–99, 104–8, 113; and fire of 1788, 149–50; and trans-Appalachian west, 129, 133, 142–51, 154, 159, 166–67, 169–77, 182–85, 188–90, 192–93, 225; and French Revolution, 196, 199–1, 203; and William Augustus Bowles, 217, 221–23, 225; and Louisiana Purchase, 261–63

New Spain. *See* Mexico

New York City, 11, 20, 30, 33, 43–44, 53, 57, 64–65, 71, 77, 101, 103, 109, 126, 144, 150, 152, 157, 165–66, 178, 186, 200–201, 213–15, 238–39, 282 (n. 81), 294 (n. 52)

Nogales. *See* Walnut Hills

Nolan, Philip, 246–48, 331 (n. 58)

Nootka Sound: and Anglo-Spanish crisis, 2, 194–95

Noyan, Jean-Baptiste de, chevalier, 51–52, 57, 279 (n. 49)

Ochlockonee River, 219–20, 225–26, 260

O'Fallon, James: as freebooting conspirator, 189–94, 197, 201–2, 217, 329 (n. 11)

O'Reilly, Gen. Alejandro, 45, 55–57, 62–63, 65, 104, 145, 149, 279 (nn. 48, 50), 281 (n. 66)

Oswald, Richard, 109, 310 (n. 85)

Ouachita River: and colonization, 160–61, 308 (nn. 83, 85)

Paine, Thomas, 197

Panis, Jacinto, 85, 105

Panton, William, 117–18, 184, 210–14, 219–21, 224–29, 255, 260, 298 (n. 10), 321 (n. 4), 323 (n. 40), 324 (n. 42), 326 (n. 76)

Panton, Leslie, and Company, 117–18, 203, 210–14, 219–20, 224–26, 257, 298 (n. 10), 321 (n. 7), 323 (n. 40), 324 (n. 42), 326 (nn. 67, 70)

Payne (Seminole headman), 207–8, 311 (n. 13), 320 (n. 93)

Pensacola, and British rule, 2–3, 17, 20, 23–26, 31–32, 34–35, 37, 39–46, 48–53, 56, 58, 61–62, 64–68, 173, 179; and Revolutionary War, 70–78, 80, 82, 84–86, 90; and British-Spanish warfare, 91–92, 94–95, 97–108, 110, 113–14; and postwar politics and Indian trade, 115, 117, 122, 200, 209–12, 225–27, 229, 239–40, 257, 264

Pensacola Bay, 21, 28, 46, 101, 116, 271 (n. 1), 272 (n. 26)

Perryman (Lower Creek headman): as friend of Bowles, 211, 213, 220, 225, 322 (n. 17)

Perryman, Tom, 220–21, 323 (nn. 39, 40)

Philadelphia, 89, 93, 103, 105, 126, 131–32, 156, 158, 163, 165, 179–80, 185, 198, 201–2, 205, 207, 214, 234–39, 246, 253; and New Orleans trade, 44, 63, 70, 74–77, 80, 113, 148–52, 174–75, 311 (n. 43)

Philatouche (Lower Creek headman), 225–26, 325 (n. 64), 326 (n. 67)

Pickering, Timothy, 175, 239, 247, 249, 251, 253, 333 (n. 83)

Pickles, William: as privateer, 108, 291 (nn. 12, 16)

Piomingo (Chickasaw headman), 228–30, 232, 326 (nn. 73, 75), 327 (n. 82)

Pisgignoux, Jean-Pierre, 200–201, 318 (n. 65)

Pittman, Philip, 18, 37–39

Pointe Coupée, 47, 55, 82–83, 88, 160

Pollock, Oliver: as colonial merchant and U.S. agent, 63, 70, 72, 74–76, 78, 80–82, 85–86, 88–89, 93, 282 (n. 78), 285 (n. 24), 286 (nn. 39, 40), 288 (n. 70), 289 (nn. 74, 86), 290 (n. 88), 291 (nn. 13, 15); and postwar era, 124, 132, 148–50, 174–75, 178, 300 (n. 41), 302

(n. 69), 304 (nn. 30, 31, 33), 304 (nn. 35, 36, 37), 311 (nn. 38, 43)
Pope, Lt. Percy, 243–45
Population: of Louisiana, 47, 146; of West Florida 25, 32, 47, 99, 146; of East Florida, 115–16; of Southern Indian nations, 32; of trans-Appalachian frontier zones, 129; and policy issues concerning, 32, 46, 53, 68, 141, 144, 147, 162, 181–86, 199
Powell, Philip Wayne: and historiography, 7, 269 (n. 15)
Powell, Thomas: and freebooting scheme, 187, 314 (n. 1)
Proyectistas, 143–45, 160, 317 (n. 10)

Quesada, Juan Nepomuceno de, 204–8, 323 (n. 32)

Randolph, Edmund, 199, 205
Robertson, James, 176–77, 203, 229
Romayne, Nicholas, 238–40
Ross, Robert, 64, 108–9, 296 (nn. 77, 78), 299 (n. 27)
Rousseau, Pedro, 200, 223, 270 (n. 16)

Saint-Domingue (Haiti), 19, 88, 139, 157, 171, 199–201, 203, 258, 261–62, 287 (n. 44), 294 (n. 58), 308 (n. 81)
San Marcos de Apalache (St. Marks), 90, 210, 212, 219, 222–25, 254–55, 257, 260, 321 (n. 5), 325 (n. 55), 334 (n. 6)
Savannah (Georgia), 90, 97, 205
Seagrove, James, 214, 220, 226–27, 322 (n. 23), 326 (n. 69)
Sebastian, Benjamin, 172, 176, 239, 311 (n. 46), 312 (n. 52), 329 (n. 23)
Seminoles, 31, 99, 207–8, 218–21, 223–25, 232, 254, 259–61, 265, 321 (n. 13), 324 (n. 43)
Sevier, John, 166–67, 169, 323 (n. 10), 310 (n. 12)
Shawnees, 61, 154, 184, 226–27, 229, 281 (n. 69), 313 (n. 74), 326 (n. 69)
Shelburne, William Petty, 2nd earl of, 44, 276 (n. 80)

Shelby, Isaac, 205, 317 (n. 53), 320 (n. 84)
Shouloushamastabé ("Red Shoes"): as Choctaw headman, 42; Alibamon headman, 254, 327 (n. 81)
Slavery, 2, 19, 25, 36, 43, 46–47, 50, 56, 62, 65–67, 81, 85–86, 90, 92–93, 99–100, 105–6, 109, 115–16, 118–19,121–23, 146–47, 151–55, 158, 161, 174, 193, 208–9, 212, 221, 238–39, 262–63; and slave trade, 21, 51, 63–64, 79, 82, 146, 157, 160, 192, 258, 262; and Indian slaves, 32, 47, 65; and slave revolt, 83, 107, 139, 142, 146, 160, 200, 203; and slave runaways, 84, 99, 261. *See also* African Americans
Small Indian Nations, 35, 50, 60, 281 (n. 66)
Smith, Daniel, 176
Smuggling. *See* Contraband trade and smuggling
Solano, José: as Spanish admiral, 101, 113
South Carolina Yazoo Company, 188–94, 197–98, 315 (nn. 15, 22), 316 (n. 32), 323 (n. 37)
Spain, and imperial policy for Louisiana and the Floridas, 1, 13, 16, 19–20, 27, 45, 48, 52–56, 62, 64–65, 69, 71–72, 85–86, 89–91, 94–95, 103, 109–14, 122–23, 127–29, 138–48, 153–59, 165–66, 170–72, 185–86, 193, 209–11, 217–18, 222–23, 231–34, 247, 250, 258, 262–64. *See also* France; Great Britain; United States
St. Augustine, 4, 11, 13, 23, 27–28, 31, 53, 73, 77, 90, 98, 107, 115–16, 118, 187, 204, 207–8, 210, 214, 225, 257, 261, 290 (nn. 95, 98), 320 (n. 86), 323 (n. 33)
Ste. Genevieve, 47, 105, 180, 314 (n. 82)
St. Johns River, 26, 116–19, 197, 204, 207, 210, 212
St. Louis, 47, 107–8, 235
St. Marys River, 26, 90, 111, 116, 118, 197–98, 205–7
Stuart, Charles: as British Indian agent, 41–42, 60, 73, 281 (n. 66)
Stuart, John: as superintendent of Indian affairs, 32, 39–42, 61–62, 73, 99, 281 (n. 63)

Sullivan, John: and freebooting scheme, 131–32, 149, 301 (n. 66)
Swayze, Rev. Samuel, 66, 283 (n. 92)

Tangipahoa: as settlement of Lake Pontchartrain, 50, 94, 277 (n. 19), 282 (n. 78), 291 (nn. 13, 16)
Tardiveau, Barthélemi, 156–57, 179, 201, 307 (nn. 63, 65), 312 (n. 55)
Tardiveau, Pierre, 201, 318 (n. 67)
Tate, William: and freebooting plot, 196, 198, 205
Tensaw River, 28–29; and colonization, 119–20, 123, 273 (n. 28)
Texas, 48, 64–65, 95, 126, 159, 161, 246, 264–65
Thomas, Lt. John: as British Indian agent, 45, 60, 281 (n. 64)
Tobacco: as staple crop, 35, 40, 47, 50, 52, 56, 64, 174; and Spanish royal purchase of, 93, 100, 122, 144, 147, 150, 152–53, 155–56, 170, 173, 194
Tomatly Mingo (Choctaw headman), 40, 42
Tombigbee River, 32, 34, 40, 167, 188, 228, 231, 244, 252, 264, 273 (n. 39), 331 (n. 50)
Treaties: Fontainebleau, 13; Treaty of Paris (1763), 12–16, 18–19, 24–27, 48, 78–79; Treaty of Paris (1783), 103, 109–13, 116, 120, 127; Treaty of San Lorenzo (Pinckney's Treaty), 159, 162–63, 175, 232, 241–43, 247–48, 255; Treaty of New York, 213–15, 219–20, 232–34; Treaty of Nogales, 230–31; Jay Treaty, 234, 242; Louisiana's retrocession to France, 234; Louisiana Purchase, 262–64
Trudeau, Zenon, 106, 162
Tunicas, 34–35, 50, 60, 251

Ugulayacabé (Chickasaw headman), 232
Ulloa, Antonio de, 45, 48–49, 51–53, 104, 145, 277 (nn. 8, 14, 15), 278 (nn. 27, 29)
United States: and control of frontiers, 3, 110, 126, 130–33, 139, 181–82, 184–87, 198–99, 204–7, 213–15, 217, 226–27, 232, 238–41, 247, 252–54; and government relations with Spain, 4, 69–71, 74–77, 89–91, 93–94, 103–4, 109–13, 127–29, 159, 162–63, 165–66, 179, 194, 213, 231, 242–47, 249–51, 263–65. *See also* France; Great Britain; Spain
Unzaga y Amezaga, Luis de, 58, 63, 67, 70–72, 148, 280 (n. 58)
Upper Louisiana, 107, 144, 154, 156, 158, 162–63, 178–79, 182, 235, 237, 241–42, 306 (n. 55), 318 (n. 66), 328 (n. 16)

Valdés, Antonio, 142
Viar, Josef (José) de, 156, 185, 314 (n. 71), 318 (n. 61)
Villebeuvre, Juan de la: as frontier commandant, 85, 87–88, 101, 281 (n. 67)
Villiers, Balthazar de, 88, 95
Virginia, 5, 62, 66, 70–71, 73–75, 77, 87–89, 105, 121, 128, 130, 150, 155, 165–66, 180, 182, 185, 188, 192, 245, 283 (n. 95), 284 (n. 8), 286 (n. 26), 287 (n. 51)

Walnut Hills (Nogales, and site of modern Vicksburg, Mississippi), 87, 190–91, 201, 230–31, 236–37, 243, 247, 315 (n. 20), 332 (n. 66)
Washington, George: and interest in West Florida, 71; and Gálvez's military success, 103, 113, 294 (n. 54); and Georgia's Natchez project, 126–27; and George Morgan's project, 185–86; and opposition to freebooting, 192, 194, 198–200, 202, 204, 206; and treaty with Creek Indians, 213, 229; and war scare with France, 239, 250–51
Washington (Walsh), Thomas: and Yazoo scheme, 192, 315 (n. 15), 316 (n. 27)
Watts, John (Cherokee leader), 227
Watts, Steven: and Baton Rouge plantation, 93, 291 (n. 9)
Wayne, Gen. Anthony, 202, 242, 330 (n. 41)
West Florida: origins as British province, 1, 23–27

White, Dr. James, 167, 169, 202, 310 (n. 12)
Wilkes, John, 23–24
Wilkinson, James: and opposition to filibusters, 130–31, 133, 139, 191–92, 301 (n. 63); and declaration of Spanish allegiance, 137–38; and Kentucky–New Orleans trade, 144, 147–48, 151, 169–75, 304 (n. 26), 310 (n. 25); and Louisiana colonization, 152, 163, 177–78; as informant for Spain, 164–65, 172–73, 176, 181–83, 189–92, 200, 217, 229, 242–45, 249, 252, 258, 309 (n. 1), 310 (nn. 20, 30), 311 (nn. 36, 44), 318 (n. 62), 327 (n. 78), 330 (n. 41); as U.S. general, 173, 246, 251–56; and his death in Mexico City, 265
Willing, James: as revolutionary marauder, 70, 79–89, 93–94, 100, 105–6, 124, 128, 289 (nn. 74, 76, 86), 290 (nn. 88, 92), 296 (n. 77), 300 (n. 52)
Winfree, Jacob, 105–6
Wouves d'Argès, Pierre Rezard: as colonial promoter, 142–44, 148, 302–3 (n. 8)

Yazoo land companies, 188–94, 228, 243, 315 (nn. 7, 14), 316 (n. 27), 323 (n. 37), 331 (n. 45)
Yazoo River, 26, 32, 66, 110, 120, 128–29, 133, 178, 228, 244, 283 (n. 91), 316 (n. 30)
Yrujo (Irujo), Carlos Martínez de, 163, 237

Zéspedes, Vicente Manuel de, 116–19, 187, 189, 210, 214, 218, 297 (n. 5), 314 (nn. 1, 3), 321 (n. 4), 322 (n. 17), 325 (n. 57)

www.ingramcontent.com/pod-product-compliance
Lightning Source LLC
Chambersburg PA
CBHW020634230426
43665CB00008B/169